# Human Relations in Organizations

*Third Edition*

# Human Relations in Organizations

*Third Edition*

**Dan L. Costley**
*New Mexico State University*

**Ralph Todd**
*American River College*

*West Publishing Company*
*St. Paul    New York    Los Angeles    San Francisco*

*Copy Editor:* Joan Torkildson
*Artwork:* Rolin Graphics
*Cover Design: Paul Konsterlie, Designteam*

**Library of Congress Cataloging-in-Publication Data**

Costley, Dan L.
    Human relations in organizations.

    Includes index.
    1. Organizational behavior. 2. Personnel management.
3. Psychology, Industrial. I. Todd, Ralph. II. Title.
HD58.7.C65  1987        658.3        86–18910
ISBN 0–314–27035–3

# Contents

## Chapter 2 *Organizations: People and Structure* 28

## Chapter 3 *Management and Organizations* 54

# Part 2   Communication   77

# Part 3   Motivation and Performance   163

## Chapter 7   Motivation Concepts   164

# Part 4 Working Together— Leaders and Groups 259

# Part 5   Beliefs and Realities  349

# Part 6   Values and Responsibilities   433

## Chapter 16   Change: Stimulation, Guidance, and Control   434

# *Preface*

The productivity of organizations depends on people. This book focuses on the behavior of individuals in organizations. The subject of this book is sometimes called human relations at work, behavior in organizations, or human resources management.

A developmental approach is used in combining theory, research, and applications for improving interpersonal effectiveness in organizations. Anyone who works in an organization should find the material in this book helpful in dealing with the day-to-day problems associated with interpersonal relations and productivity. Much of the material in this book grew out of the authors' management experience and extensive consulting with a variety of organizations.

The emphasis of this book is on the knowledge and skills needed for individuals to perform effectively in organizations, including the ability to communicate, to cope with conflict and frustration, to motivate others, to use authority, and to increase group productivity. We have tried to provide an opportunity for anyone interested in human behavior in organizations to read and learn from material that is understandable, interesting, accurate, and enjoyable.

## *Organization of the Third Edition*

The overall organization of the second edition has been retained in the third edition. Theory, practice, practical examples, and application guidelines have been incorporated within each chapter. Topics are covered in sufficient depth and breadth for the student to gain a solid background in the fundamentals of human relations as they occur in organizations. The first three chapters provide a framework for human relations in organizations by presenting a discussion of the essential elements in the relationships between the individual, management, and the organization. Concrete examples are used frequently throughout the book to increase the value and relevance of the concepts for the student.

The reader is given a variety of viewpoints and approaches in dealing with problems of managing people. This book is designed to present accepted areas of knowledge and to avoid extremes of controversial and argumentative theories of organizational behavior.

## *Features Retained from the Second Edition*

The feedback we received from students, instructors, and reviewers indicated many strengths in the second edition. The following key features have been retained and improved.

*Writing Style*   We have made a special effort to make the material readable, engaging, and clear without compromising the validity or quality of the content. We have minimized the use of theoretical terms and complex language structure. We have tried to write in a straightforward, specific, and interesting style. We have illustrated concepts with real world examples from organizations that the students will recognize and identify with. Our objective has been to appeal to the student's interests without sacrificing rigor or substance.

*Accurate, Balanced, and Current Information*   We have retained the widely accepted concepts and theories presented in the second edition and have added material from recent research and reports of the most contemporary practices. There is a balanced coverage of theories, practices, and points of view on human relations in organizations. Throughout the book we present and illustrate different approaches to analyzing and understanding human behavior in organizations. There are real world examples from a wide variety of organizations, e.g. large and and small, public and private, and manufacturing and service organizations. Specific practices and techniques are described as they are used in organizations to improve human performance and productivity. Basic concepts necessary for effective human relations are presented in early chapters to provide the student with the basic knowledge necessary for developing effective human relations. This includes coverage of the essential areas of perception, communications, motivation, leadership, and group behavior.

*Applied with Real World Examples*   In each chapter there are applications of the theory, research, and concepts presented. Specific examples are provided to show how methods and techniques can be put into practice. Applications of concepts are approached from several points of view to show how they are applicable at individual, managerial, and organizational levels. Topics that are contemporary and of high interest are focussed on throughout the text, such as stress management, employee motivation, the impact of expectations on performance, and the role of goal setting in individual and organizational productivity. Examples are presented in a way that leads the reader to think seriously about how he or she would behave in the situation and could apply the concepts. Applications are presented so students can use the methods and techniques regardless of the position they may have in an organization.

## *Learning Approaches Used in the Book (Pedagogy)*

The following features combine to attract and hold reader interest by offering a pleasant, challenging, and relevant reading experience.

- Learning Objectives

Clearly stated learning objectives are presented at the beginning of each chapter. These objectives enable the reader to evaluate understanding of the chapter material and can serve as an aid in studying for examinations.

- Chapter Topics and Preview

Each chapter begins with a list of the major topics to be covered in the chapter so the reader has a brief overview of the coverage. This is followed by a short preview that introduces the chapter by highlighting some of the key issues in a realistic and meaningful way.

- Self-Assessment

To involve the reader in human relations issues presented in the chapter there is a self-assessment before the body of each chapter. The self-assessment presents statements and questions with a range of possible responses. Some items are designed to measure knowledge of research and practices, and some items are designed for assessment of attitudes and beliefs where there are no "correct" answers. The self-evaluation allows the readers to relate their "life experiences" to the material covered in the chapter. There is a discussion of each question based on research by behavioral scientists at the end of the chapter.

- Key Terms

Each time a new important term is introduced it is presented in boldface. A list of key terms appears at the end of each chapter. A glossary is provided at the end of the book with definitions for the important terms and concepts that are used.

- Figures and Tables

Important concepts and relationships are illustrated with figures, diagrams, charts, and tables. There is frequent use of graphic summaries of key concepts.

- Real World Examples

Boxed examples are presented in each chapter that describe the ways concepts are put into practice in organizations that are familiar to the reader. Examples are from a wide variety of types of organizations such as General Foods, Texas Instruments, Digital Equipment, Sony, Blue Shield and Blue Cross, and IBM.

- Quick Review

At the end of each chapter there is a quick review of key concepts. The review is presented in outline form and can be used to study for examinations and obtain an overview of the material in the chapter.

- Discussion and Review Questions

At the end of each chapter there are discussion questions that can serve as reinforcers of the material. Readers can monitor their comprehension of material by answering these questions. The questions can also be used effectively to stimulate class discussions.

- Action Exercises

There is an "action exercise" at the end of each chapter that allows the reader to assume the position of a decision maker in an organizational situation. The exercise is structured to provide the setting for the reader to decide courses of action that should be taken and which courses of action should be taken first. Each exercise provides the reader with ten to twelve alternative courses of action that are typical and realistic in terms of decisions that have been made in organizations.

- Implications and Guidelines for Managers

Throughout the text material is summarized and applied through the use of sections detailing the implications for managers. These implications sections provide the reader with specific approaches to developing effective human relations and increasing performance. Action oriented guidelines are presented to assist the reader in applying material in the text by providing concise and specific suggestions for applying concepts to improve both individual and managerial performance.

- Two Points of View Cases

There is a case at the end of each chapter which views a situation as seen by a manager and as seen by an employee. These cases provide the reader with the opportunity to evaluate a realistic situation from two points of view. The reader can respond both in terms of what the manager should do and what the employee should do. All the two points of view cases were developed from the authors' experiences in actual situations.

- Case Incidents

At the conclusion of each of the six parts of the book there are four or five case incidents. These cases give the reader the opportunity to apply and integrate the material that has been presented in this part of the book. All these case incidents are drawn from real world situations.

- References

Each chapter ends with a set of end notes which provides the essential references that could be used for further study of the areas covered in the chapter.

- Indexes

Comprehensive author and subject indexes can assist the reader in locating information in the text.

- Appendix

This Organizational Evaluation Questionnaire can be used to identify the characteristics of an organization that contribute to effective interpersonal relations and increasing productivity.

# *Acknowledgments*

Many managers, professors, and students have contributed to the development of the material in this book. Even though they are not all mentioned by name, they have our thanks, especially our students. Special recognition and appreciation is deserved by Faye A. Moore for invaluable assistance in preparation of the third edition.

We are grateful to the administrators and faculty of New Mexico State University and American River College for creating and supporting an environment that made the writing of this book possible.

For excellent support and assistance, we thank the people at West Publishing Company. We appreciate the assistance of our editors, Richard T. Fenton, Esther W. Craig, Nancy M. Roth, and Joan M. Torkildson.

The following individuals provided many good ideas and suggestions in their roles as reviewers of the second edition: Stephen C. Branz, Triton College; Samuel C. Gant, Nashville State Technical Institute; Leo Kiesewetter, Illinois Central College; Michael E. Kolivosky, Hillsdale College; Mark A. Mallinger, Pepperdine University; Jim Lee Morgan, West Los Angeles College; Albert A. Seretney, Waterbury State Technical College; Michael Wubnig, New York Institute of Technology.

We are grateful for the unqualified support of our families while we worked on this manuscript. It is to our families that this book is dedicated.

# Human Relations in Organizations

*Third Edition*

# Part 1

# Organizations

# Understanding People in Organizations

## Learning Objectives

After reading this chapter, you should be able to do the following:

1. Understand the importance of human relations, both in work organizations and in other aspects of life
2. Discuss some of the primary reasons for people behaving as they do
3. Describe the major skills needed to develop effective human relations
4. Understand the effect of environmental forces, especially those of the work place, on human behavior
5. Develop a basis for personal philosophy of effective human relations

# Chapter Topics

- Human relations, management, and the work place
- Why people do what they do
- Organizational trends
- The influence of organizations
- Environment of work and organizational culture
- Linking the individual and the organization
- Motivation and performance
- Working together—leaders and groups
- Beliefs and realities
- Change and the future

# Preview

Few, if any, aspects of life and work are as difficult, frustrating, important, and rewarding as the relationships that people develop with each other. In work organizations, managers often find that employees have priorities, areas of interest, and feelings different from their own. Those same managers may also find their assumptions about human behavior different from those of other managers. Employees further complicate the work environment by being individuals with unique values, beliefs, and attitudes. Just as relationships between people are complex and frequently not well understood in nonwork situations, they are equally misunderstood and complicated in the work place.

To accomplish organizational goals, managers must work with and through the efforts of other people. Their ability to channel employees' skills, knowledge, and energy is the primary way they are measured as either successful or unsuccessful. In a real sense, managers and the organizations for which they work are dependent on the efforts of employees who perform required tasks. Unlike machines, however, employees do not turn on and off at management's command. They are influenced not only by their immediate managers but also by other employees, by the type of work that they are assigned, by the organizations to which they belong, and by their personal perceptions of themselves. An understanding of the forces that affect human behavior and the ability to utilize that understanding to create conditions in which employees can meet both organizational and personal goals are essential management skills.

This first chapter introduces some of the many areas of concern that may help in understanding human behavior, especially in organizations that provide the services and goods that society depends upon.

## SELF–ASSESSMENT ▬▬▬▬▬▬▬▬▬▬▬▬▬▬▬▬▬▬▬▬▬▬

To help you measure personal understanding of human relations issues, complete this self-assessment. The self-assessment is different from the familiar multiple-choice or true-false formats. Each statement or question has a range of possible responses. A scale of 1 to 6 between two words with different meanings allows you to mark either the word that is considered correct or a place between the two words that represents some agreement and some disagreement. Selection of a high number such as 5 or 6 may be either correct or incorrect, just as selection of lower numbers may be correct or incorrect. Some responses may be partly correct and partly incorrect.

Answers based on research by behavioral scientists, with a short explanation of why the response was considered correct, may be found on page 21. Some items are designed for personal assessment and do not have a correct answer, but will help in defining beliefs, attitudes, and values.

**1.** Awareness of the moods and feelings of others is evident in very young children as well as in adults. This type of sensitivity is:

instinctive  1...2...3...4...5...6  learned

**2.** Some people believe that a happy worker will be a productive worker. Competent managers know that such a belief is:

incorrect  1...2...3...4...5...6  correct

**3.** Experience has shown that under competent management, the workers most likely to produce high quality are:

american  1...2...3...4...5...6  japanese

**4.** Perception is the interpretation of what is experienced through our senses, both from the world around us as well as from within ourselves. Studies show that perception is largely:

instinctive  1...2...3...4...5...6  learned

**5.** In most organizations people work:

as part of a group  1...2...3...4...5...6  as individuals

**6.** When it comes to letting managers know where problems are, most employees are:

reluctant to  1...2...3...4...5...6  eager to
communicate                        communicate

7. Which of the following two organizational groups are likely to see things from a personal frame of reference?

> managers  1...2...3...4...5...6  employees

8. Change in work organizations is:

> preventable by  1...2...3...4...5...6  inevitable
> competent
> managers

9. Accomplishment of social goals such as a clean environment, equal employment, and effective use of resources are primarily problems of:

> organizations  1...2...3...4...5...6  government

10. Most managers believe that individual job success is dependent to a large degree on:

> motivation  1...2...3...4...5...6  analysis, interpretation,
> and ideation

## HUMAN RELATIONS, MANAGEMENT, AND THE WORK PLACE

Since the earliest recorded times, people have attempted to explain human behavior. After thousands of years, the guessing, experimentation, and observation continue. Few areas of knowledge are as important or contain such a complex mixture of fact and fiction. In work organizations, as most managers realize, success or failure may be directly related to the way people are treated. Managers also know that solving technical, procedural, or systems difficulties is usually easier than dealing with people. To a large extent, the same can be said of all human relations, whether at work, in a family group, in social groups, or in incidental day-to-day encounters.

**Human relations**, as a field of study, is concerned with understanding the forces that help shape human behavior. Its ultimate goal is to predict and influence conditions that affect performance of people. Applications of some of the findings of human relations studies have gained special importance to managers of work organizations who are responsible for both work effectiveness and efficiency. **Effectiveness** means accomplishing a task correctly; **efficiency** focuses on getting work done with the least amount of effort, time, cost, and resources feasible. Together they are the primary contributors to productivity, quality, and profits. Both effectiveness and efficiency in the work force are directly related to management's skill in building sound relationships with employees, both as individuals and in groups.

*Search for Keys to Productivity*   From the pioneering work of industrial engineers and organizational analysts in the early part of this century to the contributions of contemporary behavioral scientists, the quest for keys to unlock the productive capacities of people has been a major area of concern. But the sad fact remains that managers and nonmanagement employees have not succeeded in finding those keys. In recent years, productivity in the United States has not risen nearly as rapidly as it has in many other countries; yet we have been leaders in behavioral research regarding people at work. Admittedly, many disagreements exist among different investigators of behavior in work organizations. The relationship between job satisfaction and productivity is a good example of many issues still being debated (see Figure 1.1).

Some organizational behavior specialists believe that job satisfaction leads to improved productivity. They cite studies showing that productivity declines when employees become dissatisfied. Other studies show that as employees become more productive, satisfaction with work improves. Yet, because work conditions such as the speed of machines, the amount of assistance available, and the requirements of specific tasks vary greatly from one organization to another, factors leading to either satisfaction or productivity are neither clearly known nor well understood.

Under some conditions, especially those in which employees can control their work pace to some extent, increased job satisfaction may lead to increased productivity. But equally possible is that when people are rewarded for their performance, increased productivity may lead to job satisfaction and feelings of competence. Finally, in jobs such as automated manufacturing or processing, there may be little relationship between satisfaction and productivity.

Productivity is only one of many people problems that managers face at work. Managers are also concerned with issues such as stability of the work force—especially absenteeism and turnover—communication effectiveness, interpersonal conflicts, and day-to-day relationships with employees and other managers who may have conflicting attitudes, values, and beliefs. A primary reason that studying behavior in organizations is important is that it enables us to learn to observe, predict, and influence behavior at work. To do this requires a grasp of what people are doing, why they are doing it, and methods for implementing desired changes. When we speculate or guess why people do the things they do, we enter the age-old realm of defining causes of human behavior.

---

Which of the following statements is true?

1. Increased job satisfaction leads to higher productivity.
2. Higher productivity leads to increased job satisfaction.
3. Satisfaction and productivity have little or no direct relationship at work.
4. Statements 1, 2, and 3 are true.
5. Statements 1, 2, and 3 are false.

Figure 1.1   An example of a difficult organizational behavior problem.

## WHY PEOPLE DO WHAT THEY DO

Some thinkers believed that people were naturally aggressive, hostile, and greedy and accepted control only to protect themselves from others. A few believed that people were born without knowledge and had to learn all their behavior. But attempts to study and understand behavior scientifically began only about one hundred years ago. Since then, such experimental studies have steadily increased in scope and complexity.

A lasting explanation of human behavior was proposed by Edward Thorn-dike over seventy years ago.[1] Thorndike stated that we tend to repeat actions that are followed closely by satisfaction or reward and avoid actions followed by discomfort or punishment. Thorndike called his theory "the empirical law of effect." Since Thorndike's early studies, many newer, more comprehensive theories of human behavior have been developed. From a practical point of view, however, Thorndike's observations still seem valid. Most people tend to seek rewards and avoid punishments in most of their activities.

But Thorndike's empirical law of effect did not adequately explain much more than casually observed behavior. Newer and more elaborate methods were needed to understand how and why people act as they do.

A major problem encountered in dealing with the actions of people at work is related to the way our understanding of behavior is learned. From infancy, we develop concepts, beliefs, and values concerning our own behavior and that of others. Very young children are sensitive to the moods and feelings of their parents and quickly learn what kind of behavior is rewarded, punished, or ignored. As children grow older, they learn about the behavior of other people as well.

Day-to-day experiences also teach us sets of attitudes, beliefs, and values that affect the way we relate to others. Our own behavior influences to some extent the behavior of the other people we encounter in day-to-day activities. When these relationships are not understood, the potential for people problems increases.

### *Learned Actions*

Much of our early learning is a mixture of skills that require body movement and control. Such **psychomotor** skills, as psychologists call them, include walking, tying shoelaces, riding bicycles, and any activity that requires coordinated body movement. As we grow older, psychomotor skills become more complex and include writing with a pencil, typing, playing musical instruments, and performing complex mechanical tasks. Often psychomotor skills also require knowledge of *what* to do as well as *how* to do it. Some skills require understanding, knowledge of principles, and a basis for making reasonable decisions. These **cognitive** skills, as behavioral scientists identify them, are learned in many ways. Most classroom learning involves improving cognitive skills. However, from a human relations point of view, values, beliefs, and attitudes, or **affective** skills, may be most important.

## Values, Beliefs, and Attitudes

As growth and development take place throughout a person's life, some concepts become more important or worthwhile than others. These are our **values.** Values include a wide range of feelings, such as the importance of honesty, fairness, and helping others. Other values may involve religion, education, ethics, morality, or power, status, and recognition. Values are those concepts that help shape what a person is attracted toward or repelled from. Once formed, values rarely change, although new values may have greater strength than some older ones.

**Beliefs** are based on knowledge that may be either accurate or inaccurate. People will defend an incorrect belief as readily as a correct one. For example, prejudice, the belief that a person may be inferior because they are somehow different, is not easily changed by information. Some people believe that women are not as capable as men and therefore cannot do certain tasks as well as men. Statistical evidence indicating little difference in job performance related to sex (except in certain mechanical tasks that women seem to perform better than most men) has little effect in changing the prejudice. This can be said of almost any issue that involves learning. Beliefs are altered primarily by experience, learning over a long period of time, and confidence in the authority of someone considered more knowledgeable.

Based on experience, beliefs, and values, people develop **attitudes**. Although difficult to define, attitudes are the way people feel and act toward other people, groups, or situations. If people have grown to believe that managers have little real interest in employees other than as labor, they may easily develop negative feelings and actions toward managers as a class of people. Some attitudes may be directed toward a specific situation, such as a particular subject in school, a type of employment or lifestyle, an individual sport, or a certain restaurant. Other attitudes are more general and involve a person's outlook on life, other people, politics, or government, as well as almost any class of individuals, institutions, or conditions. Attitudes are usually described as being either positive or negative and, once formed, tend to be long lasting.

Although the precise way in which values, beliefs, and attitudes are learned is not clearly understood, they have a profound effect on the way people relate to each other in any given set of circumstances. A challenging organizational task is developing positive employee attitudes toward work, management, and support of the organization.

## Where Are We Now?

Human behavior can be explained by a number of theories, each with its own merits and deficiencies. Yet, managers of work organizations need a framework to help them not only interpret the behavior of people but also accomplish three essential tasks:

1. Accurately describe what people are doing in specific situations
2. Predict behavior, based on objective descriptions

---

## Attitude Development in the Work Place ▬▬▬▬▬▬▬▬

Over ten years ago, the Gaines Dog Food Division of General Foods Corporation received a great deal of attention when it installed a radically different type of organizational system. Employees worked in teams without supervisors, were involved in doing a variety of tasks, and were even given, as a group, the authority to hire and fire other employees. Although a relatively small plant, it set an example for other companies of what innovative managers can do to build positive employee attitudes. Employees responded favorably to less control. Other companies, including Texas Instruments in Dallas, the probable pioneers of increased employee control and responsibility over their own work, have moved toward building positive employee attitudes toward their jobs and their organizations. The result has been improved productivity, better quality, and lower employee turnover.

At its Enfield, Connecticut, plant the Digital Equipment Corporation has launched an experiment that takes worker control one step further. Employees plan their own schedules, check their own work, and take team responsibility for building the computer circuit board modules used in other plants. There are no time clocks and no security guards, and every employee has a key to the building. Digital's management emphasizes individuality, both personal and work team responsibility, and flexibility. Each employee is expected to be able to do any of the steps required to make a circuit board module.[2]

These methods may not be appropriate for all work situations or for employees who prefer management to make job decisions, especially in a unionized environment, but they do forecast a trend. To a large extent, job attitudes are shaped by the way employees are treated. If management demonstrates confidence, high expectations, and respect for employee integrity, work attitudes tend to be positive and supportive of the organization's goals.

---

3. Influence behavior by creating situations that will in turn lead to desired, predictable behavior

For instance, a manager notices that some employees respond favorably each time they are given increased responsibility. As a result, the manager can use added responsibility as a predictable factor in getting positive results from these employees in specific situations.

Although not ignoring the value and contributions of other theories, we believe it is most useful to view employees in an organizational setting as interacting with each other, with what is going on within themselves, with their work, and with their boss.

---

### Japanese (Management) Spoken at Sony, U.S.A. ━━━━

If American employers are wondering whether Japanese-style management works with American employees, Masayoshi (Mike) Morimoto,
plant manager at Sony Electronic Company in San Diego, can answer,
"Yes."

The approximately eighteen hundred employees of Sony often out-
produce their counterparts in Japan in meeting productivity goals and
quality standards. Mike Morimoto believes that American workers, like
the Japanese, respond well when they are involved in company decisions, when there is less social distance between themselves and management, and when management loyalty to workers is emphasized as
strongly as worker loyalty to management.

Hallmarks of the Japanese approach are evident in many ways.
Before major decisions are made or implemented, the plant manager
meets with all Sony employees, usually in groups of about one hundred
workers at a time. Also, the executive dining room is conspicuously
absent. Mike Morimoto eats in the cafeteria with other employees and
makes a point of sitting with a different group each day. The only private
parking space is reserved for the company nurse in event of an emer-
gency. And even when consumer demand for new televisions has
dropped, no layoffs have occurred.

With all of these factors, it's not difficult to see why the Japanese
management style gets results. Through an understanding of employee
needs and the ability to predict results, Sony management has been
able to influence employee behavior effectively and consistently.[3]

---

By *interaction*, we mean that people are continually influencing and being
influenced by several major factors. At work, major factors are other employees,
the job (situation), and management (see Figure 1.2, page 12). Employees
influence and are influenced by their managers and their jobs, most often
simultaneously. Managers must begin to understand the principles of achievement-oriented human relations along with the techniques that change theory
into practice. Among many vital management skills, understanding people and
creating conditions to help maximize employee performance may be the most
difficult to master.

## ORGANIZATIONAL TRENDS

Several major trends have emerged that promise to continue to influence the
way organizations will function throughout the remainder of this century. One
significant trend is called **quality of work life (QWL)**. In all Western European countries and the United States, management, behavior scientists, and industry experts are analyzing the many factors that contribute to employee produc-

---

### Out of the Office and Back to the Home? ━━━━━━━━━━

Modern work trends may be taking us full circle from cottage industries in the home to the modern factory and office, right back to the home again—courtesy of the computer and telecommunications. At Blue Shield and Blue Cross in Columbia, South Carolina, a few women "cottage keyers" process 70 percent of Blue Shield claims on their home computers. They communicate with their supervisors by telephone and never have to visit the company's office. Control Data Corporation of Minneapolis and a number of other companies have similar programs.

People who are employed by traditional companies, yet control their own hours and choose their own work place, may be the wave of the future. With access to a telephone and electrical outlets, workers can do computer-assisted jobs from any location in the country. Workers simply feed information into the main office and receive assignments in return.

Jack Niles of the University of Southern California estimates that by 1990, 15 to 20 percent of the American work force will work in the home and from other locations—vacation spots, business travel sites, and so on. They won't ever need to report physically to a main office or other company facility.

---

tivity and to conditions that foster personally satisfying work experiences—all important to the quality of work life. At this time, QWL is a philosophy of improving conditions of work but not a specific technique. In addition, electronic technology has dramatically changed and will continue to change the nature of work itself, both in the office and in factories. Robots are replacing workers on the assembly line, and offices increasingly rely on computer-linked word-processing equipment rather than on traditional clerical support. Virtually every facet of organizational life is affected by changes in technology and in the ways people are seen at work. Organizations, with their complex people relationships, promise to be vastly different in the future from those we have known in the past.

## THE INFLUENCE OF ORGANIZATIONS

We begin our study of the ways people relate to each other by examining the influence of organizations on people's lives. During what is usually considered a normal working career, many people will change jobs several times, become part of and leave several organizations, and have their attitudes, beliefs, and values at least partially shaped by their work environment.

Organizations influence human relations in many important ways. By *human relations*, we mean the kinds of relationships that occur in work organizations. Effective human relations are management actions and decisions that lead to productivity by all members of an organization.

The formal structure of an organization, though highly important, has less influence on the long-term actions of people at work than do the attitudes, beliefs, and values of managers. Every day, managers must communicate with and set examples for nonmanagement employees, other managers, and at times, people outside their immediate organizational unit (section, department, division, and so on). In addition, the skill level, training, and attitudes of individual employees influence the manager's behavior, as well as the behavior of other employees. Finally, the behavior of people at work is influenced by the jobs to which they are assigned. Some jobs require creative application of specialized training, some are paced by machines, some are highly routine and repetitive, and some have a broad range of activities and responsibilities. These three major forces—the manager's attitudes and actions, the characteristics of the employee, and the type of work—all interact with each other to influence what happens in the work situation.

Figure 1.2 shows this relationship among job, employee, and manager. Each is constantly influencing the other two. The precise effect of the three-way relationship on performance depends on many complex factors. A bright, ambitious employee who sees his or her job assignment as dull may translate resentment against the job to resentment against the manager. That same employee's manager, who sees the assigned job as necessary, valuable, and simple, may interpret the employee's attitude as being typical of those "damn know-it-alls."

## ENVIRONMENT OF WORK AND ORGANIZATIONAL CULTURE

For over sixty years, management researchers, as well as managers themselves, have recognized that people work for more than money. Although money and benefits are important, factors such as geographical location, the type of work,

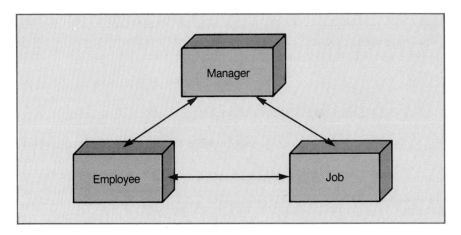

**Figure 1.2**  The basic organizational relationship. Each factor constantly influences and is influenced by the other two.[4]

relationships with other employees, the way managers are seen, the reputation of the organization, opportunities for development of skills, advancement possibilities, and many other similar factors influence the reasons people choose and continue to work for a given organization. People work for money, but they also work for more than money. Most employees want to be proud of their organizations, to have good relationships with other employees and managers, and to believe they have worthwhile jobs.

Many factors influence both individuals and groups in organizations, but not all are usually considered when trying to understand the behavior of people at work. Among those most frequently overlooked are the **environment** and **culture** of the organizations with which individuals are associated. Environment means more than **working conditions**. It includes, as Arthur Bedeian stated,[5] factors such as the way the local community sees the organization, governmental requirements at the federal, state, and local levels, customers, suppliers, competitors, and in some cases, absentee owners such as stockholders. Like individuals, organizations are influenced by their surroundings, and the people who make up and operate organizations are equally affected.

Organizational environment includes all of the legal, economic, and social factors that affect the way organizations are managed as well as the way their employees react to decisions and actions that impact their lives. If sales decline as a result of an economic slump and jobs are threatened by potential layoffs, employees may react in somewhat unpredictable ways. Some will blame the organization for not foreseeing potential difficulties, others will be fearful of losing their jobs and become defensive, and still others will resign themselves to what seems the inevitable. In all cases, employees will react as a total organization to environmental factors in much the same way as individuals do to similar factors in their lives away from work. Governmental edicts, customer demands, supplier delays, changing technologies, and shifts in societal goals all impact people at work.

Recently some students of management have realized that organizations develop their own culture. As John Schermerhorn, Jr., has noted, culture may be defined as the predominant values of the organization. For many years, IBM has been noted for the development of **IBM people** who are dedicated to the organization both on and off the job. Service to customers is instilled as a primary value. During the period of time when it operated defense plants for the government, the Remington-Rand Corporation (later to become Sperry-Rand) prided itself on never missing delivery schedules. Its culture was one of dedication to schedules. Some high-technology organizations such as Hewlett-Packard and Varian Associates have made innovation and employee excellence hallmarks of their organization's culture. There is little doubt that the culture of organizations permeates the feelings, attitudes, and behavior of all of its members, including managers, professional, and nonmanagerial, nonprofessional employees.

## LINKING THE INDIVIDUAL AND THE ORGANIZATION

Within any organizational structure, people are constantly acting and reacting to each other and to their jobs. Their behavior is also affected by a wide variety of personal factors not directly job related. People are also guided by less easily identified influences, ranging from the state of the economy to the weather.

## Perception

A highly important aspect of human behavior in any situation is the array of experiences and sensations called perception. **Perception**, as it is used here, refers to the ways we interpret our experiences. It includes those things we have learned to identify through taste, smell, touch, sight, and hearing. Also, feelings, hunches, and anything we are aware of are the result of perceptual responses to either external or internal stimulation. The thought of a movie seen last evening, a growling stomach, a feeling of anxiety, or a peak experience are all internal perceptions.

For the most part, our perceptions are learned. We are taught what the color red is, what a smile means, and that a hot stove will burn, either through personal experience or through instructions from others, from books, television, or simple observation. What we learn creates a set of conditions inside our bodies that leads to highly personalized reactions. A person who, as a child, fell from a tall tree may perceive heights as frightening, while another who does not share the same experience will have a different perception. Likewise, what one employee perceives as an attractive and challenging assignment may be dull and ordinary to another.

Perception is also selective. Often we perceive only what is meaningful or significant to us in our world. We tend to ignore those things that have little positive *or* negative value. When we find ourselves part of a group, we are usually aware of only those people or events that stand out in appearance, speech, or location. We are incapable of perceiving all of the thousands of factors in our environment that constantly compete for attention. Temperature, humidity, background noise, light, personal dress, and so forth, are noticed only in the extreme.

The way employee perceptions are selected and interpreted profoundly influences behavior at work. Skilled managers are concerned with developing personal behavior that their employees will perceive as encouraging openness, confidence, and trust. They also try to minimize decisions or actions that employees may perceive as threatening or nonrewarding.

## Communication

Another important factor linking the individual and the organization is skill in understanding and being understood—the process of communication. Communication is the act of understanding and being understood. It involves sending, receiving, and interpreting messages. All too often, what is said or written, or even shown in pictures or graphic symbols, is not understood. **Communication**, however, is not limited to what is spoken or written. Tone of voice, loudness, and emphasis on certain phrases frequently transmit more real meaning than the words themselves. The ways people stand, sit, dress, and speak, as well as their facial expressions, movements, and mannerisms, all communicate.

An additional stumbling block in effective communication lies in the words themselves. If the simple statement "Sally is fast" is made, it is difficult to know whether Sally is a speedy runner, a true friend, is stuck in one place, completes her work quickly, or has too many men friends. Our language is complicated by common words that can have several meanings.

Although communication is a complex human activity, an understanding of some of its basic processes, difficulties, and techniques is a necessary ingredient of effective organizational life. People at work are constantly relating to each other. With adequate knowledge and skill, managers may direct many of these relationships toward the achievement of organizational goals such as improvement in schedules, costs, quality, and productivity—the basic ingredients of nearly all organizations. Realistic managers know that performance is judged by results.

## MOTIVATION AND PERFORMANCE

Few topics have been given as much attention by behavioral scientists as motivation. Many managers believe that employee motivation is a key to organizational success. **Motivation** is a word used to describe all of the many causes of human behavior. Three questions are frequently voiced by managers concerning motivation: Can employees be understood? Can their actions be predicted? Is it possible to control or direct employee behavior? Although these questions are often hard to answer, workable approaches to increase motivation can be learned.

In many ways, motivation can be considered the core of human behavior studies. If human behavior is to be accurately predicted and directed toward achievement of organizational goals, its causes must be understood.

But understanding behavior is not easy. Some physiologists believe that behavior is largely determined by complex chemical and electrical changes throughout the body, especially in the central nervous system. Anthropologists and sociologists have demonstrated the influence of culture and environment on the ways people behave. Psychologists have emphasized the influence of learning and perception on motivational patterns. Although all of these behavioral research efforts are interesting and valuable, managers want practical, applicable concepts that will help them to get work accomplished. The most valuable theories for managers are those that can easily be translated into meaningful action.

Several useful approaches to motivational problems are available to managers. First, they must understand the needs of employees. All too often, increases in pay, improvement in benefits, and a cleaner, more attractive working environment are seen as the primary tools of motivation. These are important and necessary, but employees have other needs as well.

Yet, understanding needs is not the only route to effective motivational program development. Another important factor is the conditions that affect personal adjustment. Frustration and conflict, for example, are unavoidable in most work situations, and they often reduce a worker's effectiveness. The intensity and causes of frustration and conflict are directly related to how well employees, including managers, can adjust to the complexities of day-to-day work situations. Stress, burnout, and boredom are major management concerns.

## WORKING TOGETHER—LEADERS AND GROUPS

People do not work alone in most organizations. They are usually part of formal and informal groups. Leaders, both formal and informal, and other group members strongly influence what individual employees, including managers, do or do not do.

Most people can recognize leaders, but how do we define leadership? We can say that leaders are people who get others to do things, who show support for causes, or who actively demonstrate beliefs in principles supported by others. But there are many different kinds of leaders. Some are charismatic, dependent primarily on their dynamic personalities for their leadership strength; others are recognized experts that people rely on for information and direction; still others may be quietly competent decision makers, autocratic but effective dictators, deeply philosophical geniuses, or less romantic but invaluable achievement-oriented managers. Although leadership is difficult to characterize, a great deal of data is available concerning leadership effectiveness. Leaders are necessary. If not formally designated, they will be chosen by people who believe that a particular leader can best help them achieve their personal and group goals. In a sense, leadership springs from followers and not necessarily from the qualities or characteristics of a person designated as leader.

Leaders do not operate in a vacuum. They are leaders of groups. Groups may be either formal or informal and may have both formal and informal leaders. Effective leaders and managers with leadership qualities recognize that much of what is done or not done springs from group feelings. The strong adherence by many employees to group norms (what most group members believe and expect) is a major factor in an organization's effectiveness in achieving necessary goals.

Groups are major forces in the lives of work organizations. People are joined together for many reasons. For the most part, groups at work are formed of people with similar interests, jobs, values, or likes and dislikes. Friendships and alliances with others serve several purposes that an individual alone may find difficult to achieve. As a member of a group, the individual employee is able to enjoy a certain degree of security. The employee can rely on others for support when job difficulties are encountered. However, groups protect members in more subtle ways than friendship and support. Over a period of time, work groups frequently develop internal standards or norms. A group that has a high degree of agreement and support among its members may frequently control output far more than its formal managers do. A closely knit group can actually countermand a manager's order or production quotas and set its own informal ones.

A key part of this text is concerned with groups and their influence on organizational goals. Managers who understand not only the dynamics of

---

### The Brown Streaks

A famous soap maker allegedly discovered an unidentified brown impurity in some of its soap. When questioned, employees seemed unable to identify its origin or identity. In desperation, the company hired a consultant who walked through the processing line and quickly learned that a new and eager safety inspector had removed cans from the initial work station as a matter of health and sanitation. The cans were used by tobacco-chewing employees. As a matter of both revenge and convenience, they were getting rid of their tobacco juice directly into the soap mix. Although the mystery was solved, several case lots of soap had to be destroyed.

---

groups (the way they work) but also individual group member characteristics are most effective in helping to create high rather than low norms within the group.

## BELIEFS AND REALITIES

Other major factors in the growing body of knowledge concerning human behavior at work are the effect that management beliefs have on their interactions with employees, the kinds of power and status relationships in an organization, and the managerial skills of those who are in positions of authority.

What managers believe and what actually occurs are sometimes different. A common behavioral problem is that employees are reluctant to let their supervisors know where real problems actually lie.

The late Douglas McGregor, while a professor at the graduate school of management at the Massachusetts Institute of Technology, repeatedly emphasized that employee performance is directly related to managers' assumptions. Managers with low expectations generally get low performance. An employee who is not expected to tell managers where problems exist will avoid volunteering information. One whose management does not expect more than minimum performance, gives minimum performance. McGregor's powerful message is that high-achieving managers are those who have high expectations for themselves and their employees, who lead rather than push their workers, and who include employees in decision making.

### *Power*

Power is the degree to which one person or group influences another person or group. In an organization, power relationships exist among differing levels of management, between managers and employees, and among various levels of employees. Some people obtain a degree of influence or power through politics. They become acquainted with those who have legitimate power, they enlist others in their own personal causes, or they become experts and dispense their knowledge to carefully selected people. Legitimate power is usually proportionate to a person's job or position. The higher an individual is on the organizational ladder, the more power the individual is assigned or expected to have.

In real-life situations, managerial effectiveness is dependent to some degree on the recognition of power, politics, and human behavior on the job. As we shall discuss later, power is not the sole property of management in work organizations; it is shared by many.

## CHANGE AND THE FUTURE

In a special April 1986 supplement, the *Wall Street Journal* highlighted a significant social and organizational change of the twentieth century: the impact of women in the work force and especially in management. The changing status of women in U.S. society is among the most profound social movements of any country. It represents, however, only one of the changes that have affected the way we live and work and our probable futures.

Titled "The Glass Ceiling," the *Wall Street Journal* article points out that although substantial progress has been made, women still find it difficult to enter higher levels of management. Regardless of their competence, an invisible psychological and social barrier seems to block women's moving to upper levels of management in many companies. Glass ceilings and walls exist not only for women but also for all employees. With change a constant fact of life, the future is rarely as bright as optimists predict or as gloomy as pessimists predict. All kinds of glass walls, created by special interests and political and personal beliefs, slow some types of change that have potential benefit. Fortunately, glass walls can be broken or sometimes climbed.

Equally important to the future is the increasing awareness that we live in a world community rather than in discrete countries as in the past. Economically, socially, and technically, as well as in the development of resources, developed and emerging countries are becoming increasingly interdependent. This seems true even when the countries have differing political systems and are diplomatically unfriendly. Trade continued with Iran and Libya during the worst of their relations with the United States. Official boycotts were simply ineffective. Russia, with its visibly opposing economic and political systems, has many Americans working within its borders while an equal number of Russians are in this country. In the United States, recognition of the world as a pluralistic, multiethnic, culturally mixed society is becoming widely accepted.

### Change, Values, and Responsibilities

We live in a world of rapid change. In some cases, to adjust we must find different ways of doing things, reassess our moral values, and evaluate our social and work responsibilities.

Change is an inevitable consequence of existence. Most changes are difficult to predict and control. In organizations, however, change is frequently planned

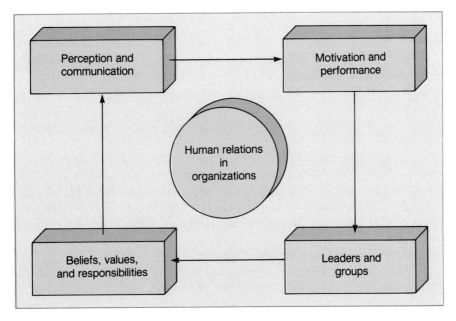

Figure 1.3   Factors affecting human relations in organizations.

and results from a known cause. A number of techniques have been developed to encourage orderly and productive change. Some psychological techniques, such as transactional analysis, have gained wider acceptance by management consultants and trainers than by professional behavioral scientists. A few organizations have used behavior modification techniques, popularized by B. F. Skinner, while others have installed long-range organizational development programs. These and many other techniques are used to bring about change that will improve organizational effectiveness. Some changes cannot be accurately predicted or controlled. When confronted with the unanticipated, managers need even greater skills in change management.

Another organizational concern is the ever-present question of moral values and policy requirements. A company may espouse fairness to customers but have highly selective credit policies, limited warranties, and few consumer policies. Managers, aware of new market developments, may take advantage of inside information to enhance their stock holdings or investments. Surplus company materials may be purchased and resold. What is "right" remains an ever-present problem.

Closely related to rightness are the social policies of an organization. How much an organization can afford to pay for the welfare of society as a whole is a pressing problem for many managers. The degree to which companies have responsibilities extending beyond profit, services, and product production is still somewhat unanswered. Do companies need to be concerned with social goals that extend beyond the bounds of the work place? If the answer is yes, then the question of to what degree becomes critically important.

## Human Relations—A Primary Concern

What, then, can realistically be done to improve managerial effectiveness in its human relations policies and activities? Both theory and practice provide a basis for making rational decisions concerning human behavior in work organizations. As used here, *human relations* is a much broader term than the simple slogan "Do unto others before they do unto you." It is a term describing management actions and decisions that lead to effective performance by all members of a work organization.

In a real sense, human relations has been an almost universal concern of humanity from antiquity. Not only places of work but also whole societies are structured to encourage cooperative, mutually beneficial relationships based on exchange of goods, services, and respect. With few exceptions, most societies recognize that survival is dependent on cooperative effort to achieve common social goals.

Work organizations are dependent on similar conditions. Like societies, they are dependent on employees cooperatively directing efforts toward achieving organizational goals of producing products or services. Management is charged with the difficult responsibility of creating conditions that stimulate effective individual and group performance.

It is difficult to overemphasize the necessity for managers to understand the impact of their behavior on others and the way behavior of all people is linked together. The Adinkra tribe of Ghana lives by the slogan "We are linked in both life and death." Although the origins of the slogan are lost in antiquity, its meaning is as important to us today as it was to older societies. The Adinkra symbol for human relations is shown in Figure 1.4.

The way employees are linked to each other, their jobs, and their managers involves many complex and frequently misunderstood types of behavior. Managers, with the primary responsibilities for planning, coordinating, organizing,

**Figure 1.4**   The Adrinkra human relations symbol: "We are linked in both life and death."

evaluating, and correcting the activities of others, as well as defining the goals that must be attained, frequently have an entirely different point of view than employees. Their concerns encompass more than the immediate job to be accomplished and individual employee problems. Managers tend to be more involved with organizational needs than personal needs. Nonmanagement employees, because of the limits of their authority and responsibility, see their jobs from a much more personal frame of reference. Satisfaction of individual human needs is their primary area of interest.

## SELF–ASSESSMENT DISCUSSION

**1.** (6) No evidence indicates that unlearned behavior, called instinct, actually exists in human beings. Possible exceptions are the sucking response in feeding and certain emotional responses, all of which may be learned.

**2.** (3) Some happy workers are productive and some aren't. Many employees may be perfectly content doing poor work, visiting, and drinking coffee. Others may be happy while being highly productive.

**3.** (3) To date, no one has verified any ethnic or national group as being the most productive. Evidence indicates that American workers are equally productive as any others in the world when working in well-managed organizations.

**4.** (6) Selection of what is perceived, as well as the ways experience is interpreted and organized, is learned.

**5.** (4, 5, 6) Nearly all employees are part of some type of group. Although some people seem to work alone, their efforts are usually part of the function of a larger organization of which they are a part. Only a relatively few employees are totally independent of some sort of work group.

**6.** (1, 2) Most employees do not like to bring bad news to their managers. Frequently, employees will try to solve problems or minimize their importance rather than tell managers where real problems exist.

**7.** (5, 6) Managers, like employees themselves, have personal concerns. In most cases, however, managers see work from an organizational frame of reference, such as productivity, quality, costs, and schedules. Employees tend to focus on personal, individual concerns, such as pay, work rules, advancement possibilities, and individual work assignments.

**8.** (6) Like it or not, change occurs constantly. Managers can affect the frequency of some types of change, the impact of change on employees, and some types of change. They cannot stop change, however.

**9.** (1, 2, 3, 4, 5, 6) Social goals such as a clean environment and equal employment are concerns of both private and governmental organizations. Government is concerned with assuring compliance with legal mandates requiring social responsibility, while private organizations make the laws either work or not work.

**10.** (1, 2, 3, 4, 5, 6) Most managers know that being successful takes motivation as well as job skills. Both know-how and willingness to work hard to achieve goals are necessary.

## QUICK REVIEW

I. Human Relations, Management and the Work Place
   A. In work organizations, success or failure may be directly related to the way people are treated.
   B. Human relations is concerned with understanding the forces that help shape human behavior.
   C. Effectiveness means accomplishing a task correctly.
   D. Efficiency means getting work done with the least amount of resources feasible.

II. Why People Do What They Do
   A. The empirical law of effect states that people tend to repeat behavior that is rewarding and avoid behavior that has no rewards.
   B. We learn psychomotor, cognitive, and affective skills.
   C. Values involve feelings of what is right or wrong and what is important in our lives.
   D. Beliefs are based on information that may be either correct or incorrect.
   E. Attitudes are characteristic ways of acting toward people, groups, or situations.
   F. Managers must describe, predict, and influence behavior.

III. Organizational Trends
   A. Some organizations are developing quality of work life (QWL) programs.
   B. Technology is changing the basic nature of the work place.

IV. Environment of Work and Organizational Culture
   A. Work environment includes all of the legal, economic, and social forces that affect the way organizations operate.
   B. Organizational culture is based on the fundamental values of the organization. It is the type of emphasis the organization places on aspects of its operations and consequently on its employees.

V. Linking the Individual and the Organization
   A. Perception can be defined as the way we interpret our experiences.
   B. For the most part, perceptions are learned.
   C. Perception is selective.
   D. Communication helps link the individual to the organization.

VI. Motivation and Performance
   A. Managers believe that employee motivation is a key to organizational success.

   B. Motivation can be considered the core of human behavior studies.

   C. Frustration and conflict are unavoidable in most work situations.

VII. Working Together—Leaders and Groups

   A. Individual employees are part of both formal and informal groups.

   B. Most people can recognize leaders.

   C. In a sense, leadership springs from followers.

   D. Both formal and informal groups are major organizational forces.

   E. Managers who understand groups are more effective than those who don't.

VIII. Beliefs and Realities

   A. Employee performance is often directly related to managerial assumptions.

   B. Power is the degree to which a person influences others.

   C. Power and politics are realities of organizational life.

IX. Change and the Future

   A. We are a pluralistic, multiethnic, internationally interdependent society.

   B. Change is an inevitable consequence of existence.

   C. Organizations need managers who can effectively manage change.

   D. Ethical and moral values are major management concerns.

   E. Organizations must be concerned with social goals that extend beyond the work place.

## KEY TERMS

| | | |
|---|---|---|
| Human relations | Attitudes | Motivation |
| The empirical law of effect | Environment of work | Leaders |
| | Organizational culture | Groups |
| Learned actions | Perception | Power |
| Values | Communication | Change |
| Beliefs | | |

## DISCUSSION QUESTIONS

1. Explain why people with similar backgrounds often understand human behavior differently.
2. How does organizational culture affect both management and employees?
3. Why is it important for managers to realize that we live in a pluralistic world that is linked socially and economically?
4. Based on your own experience, give some examples of how change affects people in work organizations.

5. What are some of the causes of recent interest in organizational ethics and social responsibility?

_____ **EXERCISE** _____

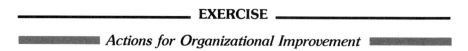 *Actions for Organizational Improvement*

You are to recommend to your boss strategies for improving the company's productivity. The company is experiencing increasing pressure from foreign competition. If the current trends of increased costs and lower sales continue, the company will start losing money within a year.

*Evaluate the following list of suggested actions to improve the company.* Which actions should be taken? Which should be taken first?

1. Hire younger workers who can be trained easily and quickly.

2. Get rid of older employees and "deadwood" immediately.

3. Have managers spend part of each day talking with employees to get suggestions for improvement.

4. Redesign jobs so that they are more interesting and provide a greater challenge for employees.

5. Have training programs for supervisors on how to improve performance and productivity.

6. Have social and recreational activities to increase the morale of employees.

7. Delegate more authority and responsibility to employees for decision making and problem solving.

8. Review policies and procedures to ensure that employees are treated fairly and without favoritism.

9. Order an immediate 10 percent personnel cut in all departments.

10. Eliminate all fringe benefits to make quick cost savings.

11. Have an 800 toll-free number stamped on all products. Have employees and managers listen to customer comments and complaints that have been recorded with their permission.

_____ **TWO POINTS OF VIEW** _____

*"The Friendly Supervisor"*

*What would you do if you were the manager?*

You manage the customer relations department of a public utility company. The department is responsible for replying to customer requests for information and to customer complaints. Seven typists in the department handle the staff-dictated correspondence to customers.

You recently promoted Barbara Thompson to office supervisor. Barbara had been a typist in the department for ten years. She is the fastest and most accurate typist who has ever worked for you. Barbara has the best attendance record and is the most dependable employee in the department. She is well liked by the other employees, and they consider her a good friend.

As a supervisor, Barbara does a good job of handing out work assignments, but she does little else to supervise the typists. She does not like to criticize the typists and does not enforce office rules. No matter what a typist does, Barbara will not take any disciplinary action. She makes no attempt to check the work of the typists for compliance with quality standards or to see that work is completed on time. She spends most of her time typing to reduce the work load of the other typists.

You have been receiving an increasing number of complaints from the department staff about the poor quality of typing and the slow turnaround time for work. You have also received complaints about the typists taking excessively long coffee breaks and spending time on personal phone calls.

The typists have told you that Barbara frequently invites them to her house for dinner or to play bridge. The typists apparently like Barbara as a friend, but they are becoming concerned about her lack of supervision. When you told Barbara that she should focus her effort on supervising to improve the work of the typists, she said, "These women are my friends, and I don't feel right about cracking down on them."

*What would you do if you were Barbara Thompson?*

You were promoted to the position of office supervisor after being a typist in the customer relations department for ten years. You had always enjoyed your job because you knew you were the fastest and most accurate typist in the department. You believe the company deserves your best effort and have always tried to be a dependable employee. You have never had any trouble working with other people. In the past, the other employees were always your best friends.

As a supervisor, you believe that people will do their best work if they get along well together and are friends with their supervisor. To better understand how the typists feel about their work and to establish good personal relations, you have them over to your house for dinner or bridge twice a month. You don't often criticize the typists because they know their job and recognize when they need to improve the quality of their work or are not getting enough work done. You believe that if you are always "on their case," it will make things worse rather than better. You always did your best work when the supervisor left you alone and saw that you were not interrupted.

The part of the supervisor's job that you like most is that you can avoid enforcing the unnecessary office rules that you always believed just interfered with getting the work done. You especially did not like the rule that coffee breaks were to be from 10:00 to 10:15 in the morning and from 3:00 to 3:15 in the afternoon. You have told the typists to take breaks when they need a break so they can work more effectively. You have also told the typists to disregard the rule prohibiting personal phone calls if they need to get personal matters taken care of so they can concentrate on their work.

Recently the work load has increased because the company's new billing system has generated a lot of customer complaints that must receive replies. Because the typists are trying to get more work out, the errors have increased. You believe that if you help them by doing more typing, this temporary problem with quality and turnaround time will be corrected.

You know that your boss is under considerable pressure from the staff who dictate the correspondence because he has asked you to crack down on the typists and see that they improve their quality and quantity of work. Your boss has hinted that you may need supervisory training by asking you if you would like to attend a seminar offered by the local college, called "Improving Productivity through Effective Supervision."

### ENDNOTES

1. Edward L. Thorndike, *Animal Intelligence* (New York: Macmillan, 1911).
2. Wendy Fox, *Boston Globe*, 14 October 1984.
3. Adapted from a syndicated news release written by Steve Sonsky of the Knight-Ridder Newspapers, January 1982.
4. John R. Schermerhorn, Jr., *Management Per Productivity*, 2d ed. (New York: Wiley, 1986), p. 137ff.
5. Arthur Bedeian, *Management* (New York: Dryden Press, 1986), chap. 3.

# Organizations: People and Structure

## Learning Objectives

Some of the things that you will be able to understand after reading this chapter include the following:

1. Ways that people become interdependent in organizations
2. Major forces that influence behavior in organizations
3. How organizational size influences employees
4. Organizational climate and its influences on both employees and managers
5. Psychological contracts, responsibility, and authority
6. How different types of organizations affect people
7. Management styles: do they make a difference?

# Chapter Topics

- People and organizations
- Types of organizations
- Influences of organizational structure
- Influences of organizational size
- Organizational climate
- Responsibility, authority, and psychological contracts
- Situational influences

# Preview

Undoubtedly, people influence organizations, and organizations influence people. When a large organization such as General Motors adds someone to their payroll, the life of the person joining the company is changed. The work schedule, type of supervision, attitudes of fellow employees, training, and job assignments affect the employee's on-the-job behavior. People who become members of smaller organizations experience much the same forces, to a somewhat lesser degree.

As the organizations to which they belong change, people change. Because organizations both influence behavior and are influenced by their employees, individuals and their organizations are interdependent. The success or failure of each is influenced by the other. Interdependence is a primary organizational characteristic. Every segment and every person in an organization in some way supports the efforts of others.

A feature of all effective organizations is promotion of the ideal that personal goals and organizational goals are, in reality, the same. Individual success is tied directly to the success of the organization. It is important to be aware that in today's complex world of technological, economic, and social change, individuals working in organizations create the goods and services on which society depends. Organizations are only as successful as their individual members.

## SELF-ASSESSMENT ▬▬▬▬▬▬▬▬▬▬▬▬▬▬▬▬▬▬

Each statement or question has a range of possible responses. A scale of 1 to 6 between two words with different meanings allows you to mark either the word that is considered correct or a place between the two words that represents some agreement and some disagreement. Selection of a high number such as 5 or 6 may be either correct or incorrect, just as selection of lower numbers may be correct or incorrect. Some responses may be partly correct and partly incorrect.

Answers based on research by behavioral scientists, with a short explanation of why the response was considered correct, may be found on page 47.

The self-assessment for this chapter allows for a variety of responses. Simply mark your response on the scale. Remember that the numbers 1 through 6 are for convenience only. Six is not necessarily a higher score than 1. Place a mark closest to the answer you agree with most.

1. In today's organizations, most employees work in an environment of:

isolation  1...2...3...4...5...6  interdependence

2. Compared with small organizations, most jobs in large organizations are:

specialized  1...2...3...4...5...6  nonspecialized

3. The part of an organization that contributes most directly to the end product or service is called:

staff  1...2...3...4...5...6  line

4. A felt obligation to perform the duties of an assigned task or to support the goals of the organization is called:

authority  1...2...3...4...5...6  responsibility

5. The right to decide, direct, approve or disapprove, and perform needed tasks is called:

authority  1...2...3...4...5...6  responsibility

6. Which of the following best describes the unwritten agreement between employees and managers, based on mutual expectations?

psychological  1...2...3...4...5...6  organizational
contract                                climate

7. Compared with large organizations, small organizations tend to be more:

flexible  1...2...3...4...5...6  rigid

**8.** Compared with larger organizations, most small organizations offer:

greater opportunities  $1\ldots2\ldots3\ldots4\ldots5\ldots6$  fewer opportunities

**9.** Research shows that low-skilled, low-demand jobs, when compared with higher-skilled, higher-demand jobs, tend to be:

more satisfying  $1\ldots2\ldots3\ldots4\ldots5\ldots6$  less satisfying

**10.** Recognition that most people are in many ways dependent on others' efforts is:

an ancient concept  $1\ldots2\ldots3\ldots4\ldots5\ldots6$  a relatively new concept

## PEOPLE AND ORGANIZATIONS

Anthropologists tell us that even primitive human beings banded together to achieve common goals such as mutual security, gathering and distributing food, companionship, and preservation of traditional lifestyles. Early in human history, individuals began to develop specialized skills in making tools, weapons, and pottery, and in healing and storytelling. People learned that survival of the species and, most important, an improved and more comfortable life depended not only on their own abilities but also on those of others. Although the early tribal and extended family organizations were not the same as organizations in which people work today, they have a notable common element: people joining together to accomplish personal and group goals.

If we look carefully at organizations, we find that few, if any, people are totally independent of others. Instead, we are interdependent; each person must to some extent rely on others. Most of what we know and what we have is the result of all the knowledge and effort of generations before us. Since organizations seem to be a natural and universal human development, it is helpful to understand some of the characteristics of organizations and their significance to the people within them.

## TYPES OF ORGANIZATIONS

When we walk into a library, we automatically lower our voices, talk less, and disapprove of anyone who speaks or laughs loudly. From childhood we have learned that most libraries have rules designed to minimize reader disturbance. We expect people who work in libraries to be quiet, helpful, and by their very actions, to disapprove of noise. Libraries aren't the only organizations that affect behavior in clearly observable ways. People in banks, construction companies, factories, mines, newspaper companies, retail stores, hospitals, or any other of the hundreds of types of organizations, act, dress, and behave differently to some extent. Many factors affect the ways employees act at work. The characteristics of the organization in which they are employed, however, are among the most important influences on their behavior.

To understand their influence, one must examine some of the basic characteristics of work organizations. An **organization** can be defined as a group of people working together in a coordinated effort to accomplish known goals. As used here, the term **coordination** refers to people doing the right things at the right time. **Cooperation** involves the degree to which people help each other achieve the organization's goals. People may be either voluntarily cooperative or cooperative because of rules and direction.

*Purposes of Organizations*    In addition to varying degrees of cooperation and coordination, or their absence, organizations have different primary purposes:

1. Product organizations, such as lumber companies, basic chemical producers, toy manufacturers, automobile manufacturers, food processors, and carton manufacturers, are concerned chiefly with converting raw materials into usable forms.

2. Service organizations, typified by stock brokerages, airline companies, and beauty salons, are concerned with assisting, helping, and providing means for more enjoyable or secure living.

3. Some companies provide both products and services through the production of items that they sell, maintain, and train people to use. Prominent examples are IBM and Xerox.

Another way to look at organizations and some of their complexities is to examine the way an organization actually develops.

## INFLUENCES OF ORGANIZATIONAL STRUCTURE

After graduating from college with a degree in real estate and passing her state broker's license examinations, Marla Adams decided to go into business for herself rather than seek employment with an established firm. Marla had worked during her college career for two different real estate firms in both sales and office administration. She believed she knew at least the basics of the business. With the help from one part-time employee, Ed James, an accounting major at a local college, Marla had the beginnings of an organizational structure. **Organizational structure**, in this sense, means the arrangement of work in such a way that the objectives of the organization can be effectively accomplished. Structure defines who reports to whom, as well as the major areas of responsibility. Later we will see that organizational structure has other purposes as well. A chart of Marla's beginning organizational structure is shown in Figure 2.1.

As the figure shows, even at this early stage, several important features of organizational structure are identifiable:

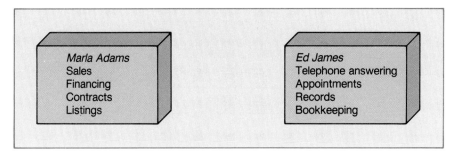

Figure 2.1   Marla Adams' organization: How she and Ed James divide their tasks.

1. Work has been divided in such a way that both people know their primary duties and the duties of the other person in the organization.

2. Both people know what kinds of decisions they are primarily concerned with.

3. A reporting relationship has been established. Each person knows what kind of information the other person in the organization must have to function effectively.

4. From a psychological point of view, Marla and Ed realize that the organization cannot function smoothly unless they both do their jobs well.

Since Marla and Ed were an effective team, soon evident was that if more people were in the organization, the company could increase sales, earn greater profits, and provide broader services to customers. The Adams Realty Company now had three different kinds of objectives, although they were not formally composed or recorded:

1. Operational, defined by the intent to increase sales

2. Profit, defined by the desire to increase revenue from sales

3. Service, defined by the desire to provide greater services to customers

The objectives of Adams Realty, like those of any other organization, have a major influence on the type of structure the organization develops. The life-blood of the real estate business is sales. Its organizational structure must support sales activities. The second stage in the development of Adams Realty resulted in the structure shown in Figure 2.2.

After graduating, Ed James accepted full-time employment with another firm. Fortunately, Marla was able to convince Carlene Veglia, a trained office management specialist, to join her staff. With the addition of Carlene and new sales personnel, Adams Realty had developed a new structure. Again, we see that work has been divided in two ways: by sales area, to preclude the salespeople from trying to serve the same accounts, and by function. The functions, or activities, performed by the salespeople are distinctly different from those of Carlene or Marla.

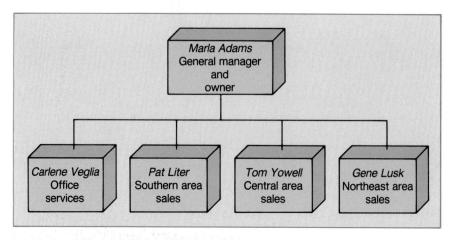

Figure 2.2   Adams Realty: Organizational structure in the second stage.

When an organizational structure is represented by charts, boxes on the chart (containing names and job titles) define areas of responsibility. Lines connecting the boxes represent flow of authority.

*Influences of Type of Work*   Organizations, whether small like Adams Realty or highly complex like IBM, affect the people within them in a number of ways. Research has indicated that the type of organization and skills required to perform a task have strong effects on behavior. Low-skilled jobs where workers are closely supervised and perform repetitive work tend to be less satisfying and

## The Great Coupon Shuffle

Grocery cooperatives, formed to provide various services for small grocery chains and independent markets, must handle thousands of discount coupons collected from customers by their member stores. Before the coupons can be sent to the issuing manufacturer or processor to be redeemed, they must be sorted according to product and price.

In one major western cooperative, 120 women have the task of sorting these countless coupons into their proper categories. After only six to twelve weeks on the job, most employees quit. People who have worked longer than a year are called ''lifers'' by other employees.

Management has tried to compensate for the tedious work by raising pay, increasing rest periods, and improving the work stations. These steps have helped slow the rapid turnover, but a worker who has been on the job more than a year is still known as a ''lifer.''

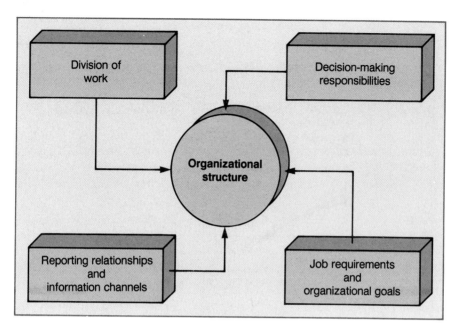

Figure 2.3   Factors affecting the structure of organizations.

may result in high employee turnover. Likewise, many other types of jobs offer little opportunity for personal development of transferable skills and knowledge. In such cases, economic incentives and association with co-workers may be the only attractions of the job. The work itself has little meaning.

In contrast, jobs that require substantial training, developed skills, and a large degree of control over assigned work are usually more satisfying. Employees can be strongly attached to their work even if they do not like the organization that employs them. Workers in this category often include computer programmers, nurses, statisticians, law enforcement officers, machinists, accountants, electronic technicians, and other professionals. In all of these fields, the work is controlled to a large extent by the person performing the task rather than by external direction (supervision) or by machines.

## INFLUENCES OF ORGANIZATIONAL SIZE

In addition to the type of assigned work, organizational size is another important factor affecting people on the job. If we examine the growth of Adams Realty, we can readily see that Marla's relationship to the people reporting to her changes as the organization grows. Small organizations usually differ from large companies in several ways:

1.  Everyone knows everyone else in the organization.

2.  Usually, work assignments are highly flexible. Tasks are not greatly specialized.

**3.** Relationships between managers and employees are more informal.

**4.** Managers often perform the same types of activities as employees.

**5.** Although there is greater diversity, there is also less opportunity for promotion or the development of highly specialized skills.

**6.** Small organizations frequently pay less and have fewer employee benefits than do large organizations.

After seven years of operation, the Adams Realty organization shown in Figure 2.4 has 139 full-time employees (number of workers is in parentheses under each major organizational unit). By usual standards, Adams Realty is still

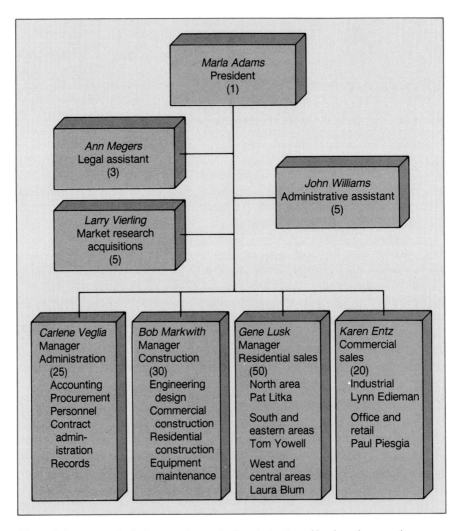

**Figure 2.4**   Adams Realty's current organizational structure: Numbers in parentheses represent full-time employees only.

a relatively small organization. Because of its increase in size, however, it has developed some characteristics of a larger company:

1. Increased specialization has occurred.
2. Reporting relationships are more rigidly defined.
3. Marla Adams no longer knows everyone in the organization as well as she could in the beginning.
4. Several of the functions in the organization are ones in which Marla has no expertise.
5. Employees have no need to know and have little interest in functions performed by people outside their immediate work group.
6. Each employee is relatively anonymous outside his or her assigned department or section.

There are, however, some positive aspects to larger organizations:

7. There is greater opportunity for promotion by virtue of increased organizational subdivisions.
8. Specialization can lead to increased efficiency within the specialized area as long as employees believe their full potential is being used. Too much specialization leads to dissatisfaction and inefficiency.
9. Employees usually have more complete resources for accomplishing their tasks.

As Figure 2.4 shows, the types of activities performed by members of an organization change as the organization grows. When an organization is small, there tends to be greater flexibility in what an individual person does and much less formality than in large organizations. Satisfactions are derived from knowing everyone in the total work group on a first-name basis, and from understanding the functions of other people. If we examine the Adams Realty structure in Figure 2.4, we can see that Marla's tasks have changed dramatically. Even though she may still sell on occasion, she is no longer Marla Adams, real estate salesperson. She is, instead, Marla Adams, president, concerned primarily with assisting Ann, John, and Larry in accomplishing their goals and with resolving unusual problems, approving transactions, planning future activities, evaluating and correcting where necessary the performance of her organization as a whole, and projecting her company's image through personal contacts.

***Line and Staff Functions***  Before leaving the structural and size components of Adams Realty, let's take a brief look at the organization from Marla's point of view. As her organization grows, Marla's interpersonal relations with her employees tend to decrease. Any individual employee is only $1/139$ of the total organization. Her primary interactions are with her division managers, external contacts (large accounts, community organization, professional associations, other realtors, and so on), and staff specialists John Williams and Ann Megers. Organizational units or functions that contribute directly to the primary purpose of the company are called **line** organizations. Those that provide specialized information, advice, or services not directly associated with the end product or service are considered to be **staff**. Although staff people generally have more daily contacts with the manager, line people have the primary responsibility for achieving the organization's objectives.

From the individual employee's point of view, the organization is the employee's immediate work unit, including the unit supervisor plus, in some cases, the supervisor's immediate manager. One way to examine this limited employee viewpoint is by the way Ann Stewart, newly employed in residential sales, is affected (Figure 2.5).

As Figure 2.5 shows, Ann is 1 of 6 people to her immediate supervisor, but to Marla Adams, she is 1 of 139. In any organization of more than 20 people, a certain amount of anonymity exists. Ann may have seen or perhaps been introduced to Marla Adams, but she does not know a great deal about Marla or other departments of Adams Realty.

A number of inferences can be drawn from the Marla Adams example that are applicable, to some extent, to all organizations:

1. All work organizations have purposes. The purposes, originally defined by the owner or top management, are broadened, interpreted, and developed by others in the organization.

2. Visibility of the total organization is difficult for people at the top and is usually impossible for nonmanagement employees. The organization is, for the most part, the perceptions an employee has of his or her depart-

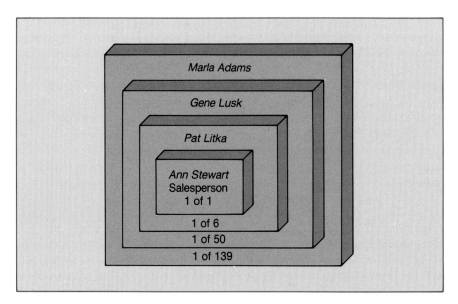

**Figure 2.5**   Ann Stewart is only 1/139 of Marla Adam's staff, 1/50 Gene Lusk's, 1/6 Pat Litka's. Each organization level increases her anonymity in the total organization.

ment. Except at **points of interface**, little is known of other segments of the organization.

3. *Points of interface* are those people or functions in other sections or departments that serve as sources of necessary information, material, or approval. If Ann needs information on property appraisal, she calls someone in the property appraisal department for help. The person with whom she communicates her needs (face-to-face, by telephone, by written memorandum, or indirectly through her immediate supervisor) is a point of interface. Ann's knowledge of the total organization outside her immediate work unit is limited largely to her understanding of the points of interface she uses.

***Organizational Centrism***   A major difficulty in most large organizations is that employees and many lower-level managers have difficulty understanding the functions of other areas. Employees, like Ann Stewart in sales, may have little knowledge of the contribution that employees in procurement, market research, or construction make to the organization's success or failure. They may develop a type of **organizational centrism**—that is, the belief that their part of an organization is the most important one. Maintenance mechanics and their maintenance supervisor may believe that their department is the most essential one in the total organization. No one could work if the maintenance crew failed to replace burned-out lights or let wastepaper accumulate. Salespeople, technicians, and accountants may all believe the same about their areas. Each thinks his or her department is the glue that holds the entire organization together. In truth, it is held together by all of them.

## ORGANIZATIONAL CLIMATE

Most work places develop a distinct personality, or climate.[1] Climate may be thought of as the fundamental internal character of an organization that sets the pattern for how things get done. It is the rules of the company game that evolve over the years. Work climate is determined largely by the expectations and attitudes of managers and the reactions of employees to those expectations and attitudes, as the following example shows.

Don Nelson and Alan Yelverton worked part-time for a local brick manufacturer as pallet makers. (Pallets are wooden frames on which bricks are stacked for easier loading on and off trucks.) Bill Boswell, the pallet area foreman, constantly criticized Don and Alan for not holding their hammers correctly, parking lift trucks too close to their work, and paying too much attention to "them damn college books" during their lunch breaks. Not once did Bill acknowledge that Don and Alan were the best pallet construction team the company had ever employed or that both of them had been just as effective on other assignments in the plant. When pallet lumber arrived one morning, Don and Alan both determined it was three inches shorter than specifications. "O.K., geniuses," said Bill in a loud voice when he saw them discussing the problem, "you guys hop-to." By two o'clock in the afternoon, forty undersized pallets had

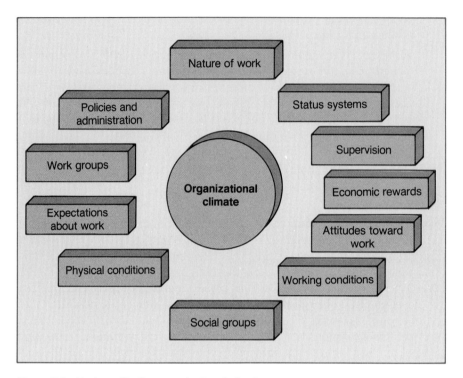

**Figure 2.6**   Factors affecting organizational climate.

been constructed. When Bill angrily confronted Don and Alan, they both shrugged and commented, "We were only doing what you told us to do."

If most employees in any part of an organization, whether a section, department, division, or total organization, have similar beliefs about the way in which the organization responds to employee needs, we then have a measurement of its organizational climate. Organizational climate encompasses more than individual or group morale, although the two concepts are closely related. Morale is generally considered the extent to which an employee or group of employees believe the goals of the organization are important and the extent to which they are willing to cooperate voluntarily in achieving the organization's goals. Climate concerns the emotional core of an organization. Some places of work are cold, formal, and impersonal; some are warm, friendly, and supportive; others are stormy, going from one crisis to another; and still others seem to create a climate of stagnation with no rewards and little punishment. The possible varieties of climate within a work place are almost endless.

However, the major factor in an organization's climate is still management's attitudes and expectations and employee reactions to them. In his early studies of management, Rensis Likert described organizational systems varying from those with little support, employee participation, and trust to those whose basic position involves high degrees of trust, participation, and support.[2] To positive concepts such as trust, participation, and support we must also add clarity of objectives and managerial expectations. If, as Douglas McGregor pointed out, managerial expectations and assumptions tend to guide employee feelings about organizations,[3] we can predict critical climate factors by examining the way managerial assumptions and expectations affect employee attitudes and performance.

Managers who have high expectations of employees, based on the assumption that most people are capable, responsible human beings, tend to demonstrate strong support for their employees' ability to achieve. With this type of leadership, employees tend to respond to the positive achievement-oriented climate with both high performance and personal satisfaction.

Decreases in managerial expectations can result in employees lowering their personal standards; a decrease in trust, supportive supervision, or openness can result in suspicion and hostility. By the same token, the lack of objectives will result in crisis or firefighting organizational climates.

Climate, although important, does not necessarily determine the effectiveness of an organization. External conditions such as the state of the economy, changes in technology, market demands, or relevance of product or service also influence the organization and the effectiveness of its employees. When California's Public Utilities Commission changed its rate structure formula, most customers, especially in rural areas, found their utility bills increasing as much as 300 percent. Within two weeks, Pacific Gas and Electric became the most hated and feared organization in the state. As citizen attacks against the rate hikes increased, employees reacted by becoming defensive. One maintenance mechanic reported, "Yes, we are aware of public opinion. Some of us just don't let anyone know where we work. It's tough to be hated." [4]

Under some conditions, a mixed climate is relatively common. Part of an organization may be optimistic, voluntarily cooperative, with an overall "can-do" attitude. Another section or department can be apathetic, with little creativity or innovation, yet be able to meet normal job requirements. In a third part of the same organization, we may find general hostility toward work, between managers and employees, and between different functions.

Usually, however, an organization will develop an overall climate generally characteristic of all its parts. A major factor affecting organizational climate is the way employees evaluate the status of their assignments. Also, the degree to which employees are trained and competent can influence organizational effectiveness. Nevertheless, our contention is that the primary organizational lifestyle or climate, although influenced by many factors, is determined primarily by the perceptions employees have of managerial expectations and attitudes, and by their knowledge of the organization's objectives.

## RESPONSIBILITY, AUTHORITY, AND PSYCHOLOGICAL CONTRACTS

If we accept an assignment and perform the required tasks, we have acted responsibly. **Responsibility** is a broad term encompassing any act, set of actions, or belief about what we should or should not do. The degree to which

## Power and Status at the Keyboard

At the independent Data Computing Corporation, computer programmers clearly enjoy the highest status. Their training, skills, and work assignments often mean they make key decisions that directly affect customers and other employees. Programmers collaborate with top management and frequently work side by side with customers to solve problems. In general, programmers are highly motivated and show strong support for management goals.

At the other extreme, key data entry operators, who type endless reams of statistical data and other material, describe their jobs as tedious and boring, and consider themselves in the lowest echelon of the organization.

The most complaints, however, come from computer operators. They continually feed data, monitor production, change tapes and disks, and complete jobs that come to them from programmers. They feel under continual pressure to meet deadlines set by others and claim they are held responsible for errors usually not their fault. Their morale is correspondingly low, and they have little motivation to support company goals.

The climate of each work area within the company is distinctly different. It is interesting to speculate on the influence of the organization's general manager, who was once a programmer.[5]

we hold ourselves accountable for our actions is one measure of responsibility. In a work organization, responsibilities are defined to a large extent by what we believe the legitimate duties of our job encompass. When we take actions outside either the formally or informally defined areas of our regular assignment, we are assuming responsibilities that may be necessary but which we are not authorized to perform. Some organizations restrict the areas of all employees' responsibilities, while others encourage expansion of responsibilities. To be effective, however, we must also have the authority that is necessary to carry out the responsibilities.

Responsibility is tied directly to our own personal value system and the obligations we have accepted. We are limited in exercising our responsibilities unless we also have the authority to obtain necessary resources or assistance. **Authority** can be viewed several ways. In one sense, it is the legitimate right to assign work and expect it to be accomplished. Authority can also be viewed as the right to requisition tools and supplies, to sign documents committing the organization's funds, or to delegate actions to others. Often, authority refers to the degree of expertise a person has in a given skill or field of knowledge. There are many definitions of authority, but the common element in all of them is that authority implies influencing the actions or thinking of others. When authority is not recognized or is ignored, there is no influence and consequently no authority. As Chester Barnard pointed out several years ago, authority, although seeming to flow downward through an organization, also flows upward.[6] It embodies the ancient concept that one can govern only with the consent of the governed.

*Reactions to Authority*   In our society, groups and individuals react to authority in many ways. The traditional Protestant ethic stressed, along with hard work, frugality, and individualism, the respect for authority. Even today, large segments of our society stress respect for authority and, in many cases, fear of authority. In ancient traditions, the only time a person was involved with higher authority was when punishment or, on rare occasions, reward was administered. Some managers create the same feelings in employees today, giving rise to fear, suspicion, even hatred of authority. As a reaction to the way authority is often used to subjugate or demean, many employees, especially younger ones, reject and rebel against almost any display of authority. More and more managers are realizing that power and authority, although related, are not necessarily the same. Appropriate use of legitimate authority involves building respect, recognizing organizational functions, and often, developing new concepts of managerial roles. Accepting individual differences, recognizing needs, and realizing different employee perceptions all enhance the effective use of authority. Power is derived from the perceived ability to punish, to give rewards, or to influence status, pay, promotion, or longevity.

## Psychological Contracts

Both employees and employers have certain expectations of each other in the work environment. When an employee knows what the manager expects and the manager knows that the employee understands what is expected, then a psychological contract exists. A **psychological contract** is the unspoken set of implied agreements that relates to a manager's feeling that "if you do your job, you'll be treated as you want to be treated" and an employee's "if you treat me as I want to be treated, I'll do my job." [7]

*Employee Expectations*   Work relationships are built on sets of expectations and the degree to which those expectations are fulfilled.[8] In an organization, employees have many expectations:

1. An assignment that demands ability and aptitude
2. Fair treatment
3. Acceptance as a person by the immediate supervisor as well as peers
4. Recognition for accomplishment
5. Belief in ability to learn, understand, and accept responsibility
6. High expectations of what can be accomplished given the right assignment, training, and direction

7. An opportunity to influence decisions through participation or consultation

Admittedly, not all employees want the same things or have the same expectations. Strong evidence, however, indicates needs in a work situation that are closely related to acceptance, self-worth, and personal development, in addition to the desire for material gain.

**Management Expectations of Employees**   Managers also have expectations of employees:

1. Willingness to perform, to the best of ability, assigned tasks
2. Voluntary cooperation in identifying and solving problems
3. Acceptance of personal responsibility
4. Recognition of legitimate authority
5. Obedience to established rules and procedures
6. Ability and willingness to learn
7. Positive feelings toward the organization and its managers

Managers, as well as employees, may have other expectations than those just listed. Our concern, however, is that any actions that frustrate either an employee's or manager's expectations will weaken the psychological contract. When expectations of either (or both) parties go unfulfilled, the psychological contract ceases to exist. Absence of the psychological contract results in ineffective work and in feelings of distrust and suspicion on the part of both employee and manager.

As can readily be seen, psychological contracts are closely related to the concept of trust. The degree of trust and confidence employees and managers may have in each other depends on whether each believes that the other is supporting the psychological contract. If employees seem unwilling to follow established rules and procedures, accept responsibility, or perform as well as the manager knows they can, the contract is broken, and the manager may no longer trust the employee to complete an assigned task. Managers who are seen as unfair, insincere, incompetent, or unwilling to listen and respond also break the contract and are not trusted by employees. Without mutual trust and confidence, the primary conditions of an effective psychological contract performance deteriorate. Eventually, the organization not only suffers losses in productivity, quality, schedules, and cost but also sees the development of strong adversarial relationships between managers and employees.

Some experiments are being made to put psychological contracts into written employee-manager agreements and then require that the two sides meet periodically to see if the contract is working. At this time, such practices are rare. Whether they will become commonplace depends on many changes in the way managers and employees relate to each other. In some organizations, psychological contracts are discussed but not put in writing. It is a move in the right direction.

## SITUATIONAL INFLUENCES

Experience has taught us that the type of technology used, the type of product or service produced, the kinds of people employed, and the attitudes of management all influence the organizational structure and its functions. When viewed this way, organizations are composed of sets of psychological assumptions about the way work should be divided and performed, as well as an analysis of what is necessary to accomplish the organization's tasks. To help managers with their organizational problems, principles have been evolved over the years that apply to most organizations. At one time, the belief was that the principles could be used as universal rules. We now know that the type of work and level of employee knowledge and skill, as well as management attitudes and ability, all affect the way the basic principles are used. Some of the more important organizational principles are as follows:

1. **Span of control** refers to the number of people that report to a single manager. The size of a department or section is determined by management's concept of the ideal number of people (or in some cases, functions) one manager can effectively direct. Early management theorists believed that spans of control should be relatively small, in most cases no more than seven to ten employees for each supervisor.

   During the past few years, two separate views of span of control have developed. One view advocates a broad span of control, or a relatively large number of subordinates reporting to each manager at all levels of

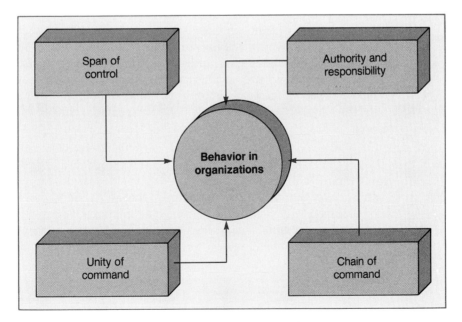

**Figure 2.7**  Situational influences on behavior in organizations.

an organization. With a broad span of control, individual subordinates are forced to rely to a greater extent on their own decisions and abilities rather than on direction from their immediate superior. Managers with broad spans of control (ten or more subordinates) are forced to rely more on the assumption of responsibility, appropriate exercise of authority, and decisions of individual employees. When spans of control are narrow, managers can interact more directly with their employees and exercise greater control. In either case, the important determinants of span of control remain the nature of the tasks to be performed, the skill and knowledge of employees, and the attitudes of management.

2. **Authority and responsibility** every person in an organization needs to know to whom he or she reports and what that person's scope of authority encompasses as well as the area of responsibility. As organizations increase in size, the number of divisions of work and the number of organizational layers tend to increase. When work is divided into specialized areas, as in Marla Adams's case, and similar functions such as products, services, programs, or processes are grouped together in a logical manner, we see the organizational principle of *departmentation*. If departments are grouped together into divisions, we then have another layer of management. Each layer represents a step in a hierarchy or *scalar chain*.

   The position a person holds in the scalar chain represents his or her authority, status, power, and area of responsibility.

3. **Unity of command** refers to the principle that no employee should be required to report to more than one superior for instructions and evaluation of performance. In modern organizations, employees in many types of assignments find that although there is a person to whom they administratively report, there are many people whom they must please, take direction from, and respond to in order to accomplish their assigned tasks. Although somewhat altered in its application, the principle of unity of command is still a necessary component of organizations. It provides the stability of knowing where the buck stops as far as individual work is concerned.

4. Among the many other principles defined by early management students are **chain of command**, or lines of reporting and accountability; **delegation** to the lowest level capable of making the correct decision or taking the correct action; and **organization balance**, the concept that each organizational segment should have equal influence if not equal size with other organizational units. Perhaps most important, however, is the concept that the organization must have clearly defined and well-known objectives.

   Current management thinking does not invalidate any of the early or classical principles but applies them with selective emphasis dependent on the type of work, objectives, skill, and knowledge of employees, and beliefs of the organization's managers. As conditions change, so do organizational formats and their influence on the organization's core of existence, its employees.

## A FINAL THOUGHT

Dr. Austin Gerber, dean of the School of Business at Sacramento State University, has pointed out that organizations ultimately develop an *executive* or *associative style*.[9] Executive organizations are those that stress control, precision, and direction from the top. Associative companies, on the other hand, tend toward participation, individual responsibility, and reliance on informal systems. Both systems work. The effectiveness and conditions under which each operate are the subject of later discussions. We believe that modern management, however, is constantly torn between the philosophy of each system. As organizations grow in size and complexity, philosophical decisions about which systems help employees become more effective are increasingly difficult to make.

We have seen that organizations vary in size, purpose, complexity, and design. Yet it is through organizations that most meaningful work is accomplished. Through the common efforts of people working together, the world is supplied with its needs and is changed. Whether we, as individuals, like or dislike the organizations with which we are associated is immaterial. The fact remains that these directed group efforts enable us to survive.

In an era that is witnessing the growth of new technologies—such as the automated office, increasingly sophisticated communication technology, and robotics in nearly all phases of routine work—combined with massive social and economic change, work organizations require employees to be more adaptable, creative, and innovative than ever before. We live in an exciting and challenging historical period of organizational life.

## SELF–ASSESSMENT DISCUSSION

**1.** (6) Few people are totally independent of others. Food, clothing, books, everything in life for nearly all of us, is produced or supplied by others. In work organizations, we are dependent on the efforts of others to provide the supplies, equipment, training, or other components of our jobs.

**2.** (1) As organizations grow, they become more specialized. In small organizations, employees may perform many different jobs. Employees in large organizations are usually members of highly specialized departments that frequently find themselves with highly specialized assignments.

**3.** (6) The part of an organization that is concerned directly with the end product or service is called the line organization. Staff functions provide services to other organizational components but are not directly involved in the production or delivery of services or products.

**4.** (6) Responsibility is the self-imposed obligation to do what we believe is right. In work situations, it is to perform assigned duties and to assist the organization in achieving its goals. Responsibility is not a right; it is what most people know as duty.

**5.** (1) Unlike responsibility, authority is the right to carry out responsibilities. Authority is delegated from higher levels of management to lower levels and to employees in work organizations. It is a necessary part of most jobs, as is responsibility.

**6.** (1) Psychological contracts are the unwritten agreements between managers and employees and are based on the expectations each has of the other. Psychological contracts provide the basis for trust in the work environment. If either party believes the other is not meeting reasonable expectations, trust declines and the contract is either broken or weakened.

**7.** (1) Small organizations are usually highly flexible and are far more responsive to change than their larger counterparts. Flexibility means the ability to respond quickly to changing demands and situations.

**8.** (6) Because of their size, larger organizations usually offer greater numbers of opportunities, more varied possibilities, and often, greater rewards. Small organizations, especially stable ones, are rarely able to offer either variation or advancement to most of their employees.

**9.** (10) Low-skilled jobs are nearly always boring, repetitive, and lack the challenges that most people need to stay interested and motivated. Jobs that require training and experience and have high demands tend to be more satisfying for most people.

**10.** (1) From the earliest times, people have recognized their dependence on others. People have formed groups to assist each other in all types of activities from assuring survival needs to formation of social groups. Interdependence, the mutual dependence of individuals on others, is a universal human condition.

## *QUICK REVIEW*

   I. Types of Organizations

      A. The way people act at work is influenced by the type of organization to which they belong.

         1. Societal expectations, job demands, public image, and peer acceptance help shape behavior in organizations.

         2. Type, size, structure, methods of control, authority relationships, and climate are all important organizational characteristics.

      B. Major types of organizations include those that produce products, those that provide services, and those that provide both products and services.

  II. Influences of Organizational Structure

      A. Organizational structure is defined as the way work can be arranged to accomplish the objectives of the organization.

      B. Some of the important structural considerations include:

         1. Division of work

         2. Decision-making level

3. Reporting relationships

4. Everyone knowing his or her job and reporting relationship

C. Organizational objectives include those that are operational, profit oriented, and service oriented.

D. On an organizational chart, boxes represent areas of responsibility; lines represent the way authority is delegated.

E. Organizations can be structured according to geographic area, type of product, customer, process, or programs.

F. Variations of organization are almost endless.

III. Influences of Organizational Size

A. As organizations grow larger, they change in several ways.

B. *Staff* refers to advisory, informational, or specialized services to management. *Line* refers to the segments of the organization that actually produce products or services.

C. All organizations have purposes.

D. Employees have visibility and recognize points of interface.

IV. Organizational Climate

A. Organizational climate includes more than morale.

B. Organizational climate includes managerial expectations, trust, support and openness, and clarity of objectives.

V. Responsibility, Authority, and Psychological Contracts

A. Responsibility involves acceptance of an obligation to perform.

B. Authority involves the right to act, decide, or delegate without prior approval.

C. Psychological contracts involve the expectations of the employee interacting with the expectations of management.

D. Both managers and employees have expectations. Unfulfilled expectations can weaken or nullify the psychological contract.

VI. Situational Influences

A. Classical principles include span of control, departmentation, scalar chain, chain of command, organizational balance, and development of clear objectives.

B. No two organizations apply organizational principles in precisely the same manner.

VII. Final Thought

A. Organizations evolve into primarily executive or associative patterns. Both work.

B. Meaningful work and, indeed, human survival is dependent upon organizations.

## KEY TERMS

| | | |
|---|---|---|
| Organization | Line and staff functions | Psychological contracts |
| Coordination | Organizational centrism | Departmentation |
| Organizational structure | Organizational climate | Scalar chain |
| Objectives | Responsibility | Executive and associative |
| Points of interface | Authority | styles |

## DISCUSSION QUESTIONS

1. Describe some major differences between two organizations with which you are familiar.
2. Why are organizations different in their style and structure?
3. What influence does the chief executive of an organization have on the organization's climate?
4. Explain the difference between authority and responsibility in work organizations.
5. How will increased use of computers affect employees in small businesses?

---

### EXERCISE

### Actions to Improve Organizational Climate

You have been selected as the new president of a state university. Upon assuming the presidency, you characterize the organizational climate as being cold, formal, and impersonal. Faculty and staff believe that there is little real participation in decision making and that the administration acts with suspicion and hostility toward employees. You want to develop a positive achievement-oriented climate with both high performance and personal satisfaction. You would like the organizational climate to be characterized by a high degree of interpersonal trust, friendliness, participation, and supportive management.

*Evaluate the following list of suggested actions to improve the climate.* Which actions would you take? Which would you take first?

1. Establish a system for merit pay increases.

2. Have each department develop a statement of objectives and high-priority activities using the input from all employees.

3. Encourage competition among academic departments by having students evaluate the departments.

4. Make training available to all employees so they can improve their job performance.

5. Establish a policy of everyone going by first name and eliminate the use of academic titles.

6. Do more direct decision making rather than refer issues to committees for analysis and reports.

7. Provide all employees with specific information on financial conditions, including funding, budgets, and expenses.

8. Clearly communicate university objectives, policies, and procedures.

9. Require employee input in the determination of work schedules and assignments.

10. Establish committees of faculty, staff, and students to evaluate the strengths and weaknesses of all departments.

## TWO POINTS OF VIEW

### *"Overdependent"*

*What would you do if you were the supervisor?*

You supervise six tellers in a savings and loan company. The tellers handle opening accounts, deposits, withdrawals, and loan payments. The tellers are in constant contact with customers and can have a major effect on customer satisfaction.

Few complaints have been made about the behavior of the tellers, with the exception of Don Holt. When a customer asks Don a question, he comes to you to check on the answer. If you are busy, Don keeps the customer waiting until he can check with you or someone else. It seem to you that he checks with you on every minor detail related to his job. Don's dependence on you has been increasing, and he wants approval for decisions that the other tellers routinely make on their own. He is consuming a great deal of your time by checking and double checking to see that everything is done exactly the way you want it done.

Don appears to have a strong desire to do a good job. He is always at work on time, is polite, dresses exceptionally well, and tries to cooperate with the other employees.

Your gut feeling is that you are sick and tired of answering Don's questions and listening to the customer complaints about having to wait for Don to complete routine transactions.

*What would you do if you were Don Holt?*

You are a teller in a savings and loan. Your job involves working directly with customers in opening accounts, making deposits and withdrawals, and handling loan payments. You try hard to always make a favorable impression and to avoid making any errors in handling customer transactions.

You want to make a career with the savings and loan and would like to be promoted into a management position someday. You have never missed a day of work and have always been to work on time. You know that some employees take sick leave when they are not sick and some are in the habit of getting to work a few minutes late each day. It appears to you that these bad work habits are ignored by management, but you believe that not always putting in a full day's work would be cheating your employer. You have tried to dress appropriately for the job. You know that making a bad first impression on customers can create a poor image for the savings and loan. You know that dress is important because the managers frequently comment on whether or not an employee is dressed appropriately. You like the other employees and always try to be helpful and cooperate with them.

Your supervisor has repeatedly emphasized the importance of accurate transactions. A small error can destroy the confidence of customers in the savings and loan. To ensure that you don't make any mistakes, you always check with your supervisor if you have any doubt about how to handle a transaction. You believe that your supervisor is sometimes irritated by your checking with him. Other employees have told you that you are getting a reputation for not being able to make routine decisions and that your keeping customers waiting results in complaints to management.

### *ENDNOTES*

1. Wendell L. French, Fremont E. Kast, and James E. Rosenzweig, *Understanding Human Behavior in Organizations* (New York: Harper & Row, 1985), pp. 521–45.
2. Rensis Likert, *The Human Organization* (New York: McGraw-Hill, 1977).
3. Douglas McGregor, *The Professional Manager* (New York: McGraw-Hill, 1967).
4. *Time*, 22 March 1982, p. 58.
5. Based on an interview with a manager of Independent Data Computing Company (fictitious name; facts are correct), February 1982.
6. Chester Barnard, *The Function of the Executive* (Cambridge: Harvard University Press, 1938).
7. Herbert G. Baker, "The Unwritten Contract: Job Perceptions," *Personnel Journal* (July 1985): 37–41.
8. Phillip L. Hunsaker and Curtis W. Cook, *Managing Organizational Behavior* (Reading, Mass.: Addison-Wesley, 1986), pp. 689–94.
9. Based on a speech delivered to the California Business Educators Association, Lake Tahoe, 14 April 1980.

# Management and Organizations

————— *Learning Objectives* —————

After reading this chapter, you should be able to do the following:

1. Describe how organizations influence the lives of individuals
2. Discuss changing attitudes toward work and resulting problems for organizations
3. List the characteristics of bureaucratic organizations
4. Describe the advantages and disadvantages of bureaucratic organizations
5. Identify challenges that organizations face and the type of actions required to meet the challenges
6. Discuss the responsibilities of management

# Chapter Topics

- The influence of organizations
- People problems in organizations
- The bureaucratic model
- Challenges facing organizations
- Management responsibility

# Preview

Louis Salazar had been a supervisor in the computer center of a large state university for five years. The university's rigid procedures and regulations became so frustrating that he decided to look for a position in private business. With his outstanding experience and educational background, he obtained a job supervising the data processing for a bank. After a month on the new job, he stopped by the university to see a management professor that he had frequently complained to about the bureaucratic operation of the university. Louis said, "I left the university to escape restrictive rules and unreasonable procedures, but my new job is even worse. The bank's operating procedures are an end in themselves rather than a means to achieve objectives. I spend all my time fighting red tape while trying to develop an effective data processing system. I thought it would be different in private business."

Louis's complaint is one commonly heard from employees who believe they must fight the organization to do an effective job. To understand the factors that influence Louis's attitude toward organizations, we must examine the managerial approaches and organizational policies that shape the work environment. This chapter reviews some of the influences and problems that employees and managers encounter.

## SELF–ASSESSMENT

As in the first two chapters, for the following items choose the response closest to your own knowledge by marking the appropriate number. Remember that each statement or question has a range of possible responses. Base your response on your personal experience and what has been learned in other classes. A scale of 1 to 6 between two words with different meanings allows you to mark either the word that is considered correct or a place between the two words that represents some agreement and some disagreement. Selection of a high number such as 5 or 6 may be either correct or incorrect, just as selection of lower numbers may be correct or incorrect. Some responses may be partly correct and partly incorrect.

Answers based on research by behavioral scientists, with a short explanation of why the response was considered correct, may be found on page 68.

**1.** In their relationships with organizations, people are becoming:

more dependent on   1...2...3...4...5...6   less dependent on
organizations                                    organizations

**2.** In many organizations, the number of nothing jobs—jobs seen as having little real value—is:

increasing   1...2...3...4...5...6   decreasing

**3.** Emphasis on satisfying psychological needs of employees in work organizations is:

increasing   1...2...3...4...5...6   decreasing

**4.** In most work organizations, which of the following is most important?

facilities and   1...2...3...4...5...6   competent,
equipment                                  dedicated employees

**5.** Maximizing the use of individual abilities is a measure of:

efficiency   1...2...3...4...5...6   effectiveness

**6.** Bureaucratic organizations tend to lack:

adaptability   1...2...3...4...5...6   functional
specialization

**7.** Bureaucratic organizations tend to be which of the following in dealing with people?

personal   1...2...3...4...5...6   impersonal

**8.** A narrow view of management responsibility is one that centers on:

creating opportunities   1...2...3...4...5...6   responding to crises

**9.** The potential for more effective management is usually:

limited  1...2...3...4...5...6  unlimited

**10.** To motivate individuals in organizations, communication must be:

controlled  1...2...3...4...5...6  open

## THE INFLUENCE OF ORGANIZATIONS

It is one of the central features of an industrial society that most of its productive work is carried out in organizations. There is a real discontinuity in our complex society between the places where we work for a living, and the places where we find our recreation, social activities, and family life. Our productive labor is, almost without exception, carried out in some kind of organization as owner, manager, or employee.[1]

Everyone's life is continually influenced by organizations. Each day, individuals have contacts with numerous organizations with varied purposes and functions. The organizations that make up our society are large and small, formal and informal, and those with widely varied objectives, such as religious, economic, educational, governmental, social, military, and political organizations.

Organizations have made possible many of the major advances in civilization. Through organized effort, we have achieved better health care and extended the human life span. Organizations make it possible to provide an ever-expanding range of goods and services, from automobiles and professional sports to fire and police protection. We work and play in an environment that is dominated and continually influenced by organizations. People are, at least partially, products of the organizations that influence them. Organizations affect the way people dress, what they eat, where they travel, their attitudes and values, and their individual aspirations. The effectiveness of the management in organizations has a direct impact on our quality of life.

An organization's greatest asset can be its people. One of the primary responsibilities of management is to create conditions that will maximize the productivity of people. In business, government, and nonprofit organizations, human resources are often not used effectively. Many organizational problems can be traced to people and people problems.

Organizations are pervasive, forming the fabric of society. Much of what is done in society is accomplished in or through organizations. Organizations, however, do not run themselves—individuals run them.[2]

## PEOPLE PROBLEMS IN ORGANIZATIONS

Skill in human relations has increasingly become an essential ingredient for effective management. The emphasis on satisfying the psychological needs of employees will probably become stronger in the future. The desire of employees to be involved in decisions about working conditions has been continually increasing.

Many approaches can be taken in managing people in the work environment. No known management approach or system will work with everyone or in every type of situation. As has been pointed out,

> you should be wary of "getting religion" or adopting one managerial approach and rejecting the rest. If you find yourself doing this, it will be because you are paying more attention to your own experiences (or problems) than you are to the study of various alternatives for a particular organization with which you must deal in the future. There is not now, nor probably ever will be, any one technique of management which is best over periods of time and for diverse organizations.[3]

***Are Organizations Becoming Our Masters?***   More people than ever before seem to believe that organizations are becoming their masters. Many people resent the power and influence of organizations, believing they threaten individual freedom and dignity. Problems of the effective use of human resources will always be a concern of managers.

Robert Townsend, former president of Avis Rent-A-Car Company, provided the following comment on the problem of the use of people in organizations:

> In the average company the [folks] in the mailroom, the president, the vice-presidents, and .  .  . the steno pool have three things in common: they are docile, they are bored, and they are dull. Trapped in the pigeonholes of organization charts, they've been made slaves to the rules of private and public hierarchies that run mindlessly on and on because nobody can change them.[4]

Even with all the problems that face organizations today, we are using organizations to satisfy more of our needs, and we are becoming more dependent on complex organizational structures. "It has been demonstrated throughout human history that most individuals can achieve more of their goals or achieve them faster, easier, more completely, or more efficiently through organizations." [5]

John D. Rockefeller concisely stated the importance of skill in human relations when he said, "I will pay more for the ability to deal with people than any other ability under the sun." [6]

To be effective, managers must understand human behavior in organizations and must be aware of approaches that will maximize the productivity of people. Although the effective use of human resources does not constitute the entire area of management, it is a vitally important aspect of any manager's job.

### Employee Attitudes

A critical problem that many organizations face is the changing attitude toward work. This change in attitude is demonstrated by the experience of a personnel manager in a large manufacturing company. While interviewing a recent high school graduate who had expressed an interest in going to work, he asked the graduate what type of work he wanted. The graduate replied, "What's available in management?" The interviewer indicated that there were no positions open in management, but that there were openings for production workers. The individual expressed his rejection of the possibility of working in production by replying, "No thanks, man. Those are nothing jobs." Managers are finding that

---

**Efficiency or Effectiveness?** ━━━━━━━━━━━━━━━━━━━━━━━

A well-known story tells of Henry Ford's experience with an efficiency expert he hired to evaluate Ford Motor Company.

After analyzing the company operations, the efficiency expert made a favorable report to Henry Ford with the exception of the activity of one individual. The expert reported, "There's a man down the hall who's wasting your money. Every time I've gone by his office, he's just sitting with his feet on the desk."

Henry Ford's reply to the expert was: "That man once had an idea that saved us millions of dollars. At that time his feet were right where they are now."

---

an increasing number of individuals refuse to accept what *they* define as "nothing jobs."

*Unsatisfied Needs*    Many managers face the problem of developing methods to motivate employees *they* have classified as stubborn, apathetic, and unproductive. Although some problems in productivity result from younger workers questioning traditional work values, productivity problems can also be attributed to organizational practices, as is pointed out by Steers:

> "It appears that younger workers have not lowered the value they place on hard work. Instead, they generally want to contribute to organizations in meaningful ways and get frustrated by what they perceive as bureaucratic or needless hurdles to their effective job performance." [7]

"Problem employees" are trying to tell management something, but often they believe that management is not listening. When management does listen, employees may believe that management is not willing to take any action. These employees are usually *not* asking to "do their thing without contributing to the organization"; they are *not* asking for a "nice and polite supervisor." Their major unsatisfied needs will not be met by more fringe benefits. Many employees are saying, "Let me be involved in achieving meaningful and challenging goals," "Use my time and ability well," and "Let me do responsible and meaningful work."

The number of "nothing jobs" appears to be increasing in many organizations. These jobs may have been designed to develop more efficient production in industries making use of rapidly expanding technology. Under pressure to reduce costs, the efficiency experts may break jobs down into smaller and smaller units, creating the "nothing job." The **nothing job** exists where the individual has no planning or controlling functions. Often, these functions are stripped away from the job under the assumption that this will lead to more efficiency. In many cases, however, there is an increase in efficiency without an increase in the overall effectiveness of the organization.

Likewise, the assumption is often made that efficiency is the key to achieving organizational objectives and making higher "profits." Managers are trained to plan and control the performance of workers. Although efficiency is an element in productivity, it may be achieved at the expense of employee motivation and pride in work done. Ineffective use of human resources may result in increased turnover, a lower quality of workmanship, a lower output, and increased downtime. The effective organization maximizes the use of individual abilities (effectiveness) rather than simply attempting to make individuals more efficient.

> Generally, the work force of the future probably will be more seriously interested in the overall quality of work life than any other work force that has preceded it. Quality of work life can be defined as the opportunity of workers to make decisions that influence their work situation.[8]

## THE BUREAUCRATIC MODEL

The concept of the **bureaucratic model** was formed during the Industrial Revolution. Early in the revolution, "management" was criticized for nepotism, cruelty, and whimsical and subjective judgments. Thus, the need for order in the organizations and the workers' demands for impartial treatment shaped the bureaucratic model. The purpose of the bureaucratic model is to provide a framework for organizing and directing various business activities. The bureaucratic model stresses the following features: [9]

1. A rigorous chain of command, usually structured as a pyramid
2. Extreme specialization and division of labor in all tasks
3. A set of procedures and rules specifying actions for all situations related to work activities
4. Selection and promotion of employees based on technical competence
5. General impersonality in regard to human relations

This model leads to the development of well-defined functional specialization with control exercised through the formal hierarchy of authority. The bureaucratic organization tends to have rigid structures developed to provide better control and to promote efficiency. The characteristics of the bureaucratic organization can lead to the following negative results:

- limiting the organization's ability to meet changing conditions because it lacks flexibility and adaptability
- reducing innovation and creativity
- developing functional specialists who may become isolated without making effective contributions to the achievement of organizational goals
- increasing downtime because the formal control by the hierarchy forces employees to wait for a decision to be passed down from the top

The hierarchy of the bureaucratic model has certain well-accepted advantages, as shown in Figure 3.1. Discipline is usually good, and routine procedures are well controlled. If the top manager is exceedingly strong, he or she can make the whole organization respond quickly. The hierarchy takes time to develop, but once established, is exceedingly effective for controlling large numbers of people.

Figure 3.1 also lists bureaucratic weaknesses. In *Management and Machiavelli*, Anthony Jay cites "grave disadvantages" of the hierarchy. One disadvantage is "its depressing effect on the human spirit":

> A man strives for promotion and reward and success up to a certain point, but, earlier or later, almost all realize that whatever they do they are not going to get much further. They then change from aiming at the maximum possible to the minimum excusable; their ingenuity and energy are converted from the task of getting more power and money to that of giving less time and effort.[10]

A second disadvantage that Jay cites is that the hierarchical system grows rigid with time:

> The hierarchic system enshrines and sanctifies the qualities that brought that success in the past, and continues to search for and promote men with those qualities even when circumstances have changed and different qualities are needed.[11]

Such a system has a tendency to inhibit and discourage flexibility, adaptability, and change. This environment may produce the "problem" employee.

*Motivation Problems*   As problems of motivating employees arise in a bureaucratic organization, often the response is to develop fixed systems of rights, duties, and procedures. These fixed systems limit the individual's freedom on the job and in many cases reduce commitment to the job and to the

Figure 3.1   Potential advantages and disadvantages of bureaucratic organizations.

organization. Under the fixed system, individuals "go by the book" and have no incentive to improve methods for reaching organizational goals.

## The Conflict Between Individuals and Organizations

One approach taken to deal with the problems of individual versus organization in the bureaucratic model is to develop an impersonal approach to human relations. Managers become impersonal in their dealings with employees and attempt to ignore individual differences and focus on the task accomplishments. This leads to individual dissatisfaction, because the employees believe that the organization is impersonal and is using them like a machine. Under these conditions, obtaining cooperation and coordination among individuals and groups within the organization is almost impossible.

Creating more bureaucratic organizations does not seem to be a fruitful approach in using and challenging the potential of human beings. New approaches and different models are needed if organizations are going to become more effective. More productive organizations must be based on more productive individuals. Some people are realizing that organizations have not used them well. They are refusing to accept the role of a machine-like object to be used as a factor of production. In a changing social and psychological environment, organizations are faced with individuals who are demanding that their importance as human beings be recognized. Individuals are examining their roles in society and in organizations. They are questioning whether they are using their potential for creativity, productivity, and achievement. In the absence of opportunities to use their potential, employees may engage in unproductive behaviors.

Finding examples of undesirable behavior in organizations is not difficult. Where there is a lack of respect for employees, energy may be devoted to "playing games" rather than achieving objectives and solving problems. Individuals become status seekers, and the status seekers become status symbol seekers. Politicking turns into a game of destructive competition that prevents effective achievement.

Many difficulties in motivating individuals in organizations can be traced to management assumptions that people are inherently bad. When organizations develop tight controls to limit, push, check upon, inhibit, and punish individuals, these controls are usually based on the assumption that people are evil, lazy, destructive, and irresponsible. Employees will recognize these assumptions and may behave much in the way the manager assumed they would. As a result, employee behavior may arise partially from management expectations and partially from resentment.

To help prevent lazy, destructive, and irresponsible behavior, managers must change their assumptions about the nature of their employees and the manner in which the organization influences on-the-job behavior.

## CHALLENGES FACING ORGANIZATIONS

The conflict between the changing values toward work and adherence to the bureaucratic model points to the need for change in management practices.

This conflict, coupled with the rapid state of technological growth, is forcing most organizations to change their structures, management practices, and work procedures.[12]

The problems for organizations using outdated machines and production processes are heightened by more intense competition. Competition is increasing both for the customer's dollar and for skilled workers.[13] Also, the cost of labor has been rapidly accelerating, which places additional pressure on organizations to use their human resources effectively.

These **social-psychological** changes are now having a greater impact on many organizations than mechanical and technical changes. Organizations are becoming more involved in the total environment in which they operate. Pollution, housing, education, civil rights, and other problems of the quality of life are becoming major concerns. These challenges will become increasingly important in the future. Organizations must deal effectively with the emerging challenges if they are to remain viable in a rapidly changing society. The challenges facing organizations are illustrated in Figure 3.2.

### The Effective Organization's Reaction to Challenges

To meet the challenges of the future, organizations will need to use creative planning approaches. To meet the demands of rapid change, managers must effectively use both short- and long-range planning. Managers need to approach all plans with the attitude that critical analysis must be made from time to time. Clearly, fixed plans for a five- or ten-year period may not be valid without continuous revisions.

Figure 3.2  Challenges facing organizations.

Systems of organization must be developed that foster cooperation with organizations. To obtain cooperation and commitment within the organization, managers need to develop methods that will involve employees in more planning and organizing activities. Management must ask itself, Is the organization related to individual employees in such a way to produce meaningful goals and objectives that can lead to long-term commitments by the individuals in the organization?

Successful motivation of individuals in organizations requires the establishment of continual and open communication among individuals and between groups. To achieve organizational goals, individuals need to be able to communicate across organizational lines without being blocked by rigid structures and status barriers.

Most organizations are extremely complex systems that deal with complex problems. Instead of looking for quick-fix solutions to problems, managers must identify and solve their underlying causes. Dealing with real causes is better than trying to simplify management processes to a set of "management rules." Searching for absolute principles of management that will work in every situation does not lead to more effective management. Effective management requires that knowledge about organizations be adapted to specific situations to meet the requirements of complexity and change (see Figure 3.3).

> More effective organizations are made about interested and able people; in small, freely communicating, face-to-face groups; under articulated and dedicated leadership; deeply committed to a clear and challenging objective and thoroughly involved in solving the problems which stand in the way of achieving the objectives.[14]

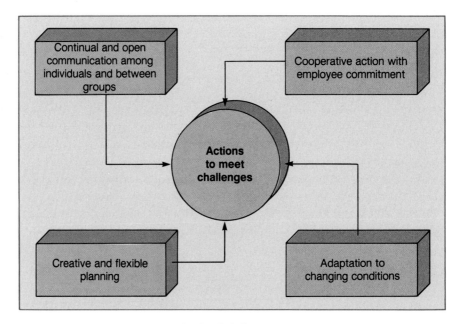

**Figure 3.3**  Actions to meet organizational challenges.

## MANAGEMENT RESPONSIBILITY

Some hope that the area of management responsibility will someday stabilize into a set of well-defined activities. This goal might be desirable if the manager's role and responsibilities were simple to understand and easy to communicate. Presently, the hope for such universally agreed upon definitions appears to be an unrealistic dream.

> Our society is changing rapidly in many ways. This means that products and services, technology, production, organizational design, and management practices all must undergo change if they are to remain viable as we move toward the twenty-first century.[15]

As long as changes are taking place in the environment within which organizations operate, there will be corresponding changes in responsibility that management must assume. Social and legal changes taking place in society force the modification of management's responsibilities both inside and outside the organization.

A narrow view of responsibility sees management performing specific activities, such as solving day-to-day problems or completing weekly production reports. The broader view of responsibility sees management creating opportunities and anticipating future problems.

### Responding to Needs—A Narrow View of Responsibility

A "respond to needs" approach assumes that management's responsibility is limited to regulating and controlling the activities that take place within the organization. The purpose of regulation is to promote efficiency in the accomplishment of tasks. This implies a sound decision-making approach to recurring problems. When problems arise in the organization, management responds by defining and implementing corrective measures. This reactive approach concentrates on eliminating activities that violate organizational policies and procedures. In short, management's primary responsibility is to make employees more productive by eliminating problems as quickly a they present themselves.

Management views its role *as the result of* economic development and financial conditions. A narrow view of responsibility encourages management to be primarily or exclusively concerned with the economic activities involved in making a profit or meeting budget requirements. Management must meet the economic and financial responsibilities that the organization requires, but the manager who is concerned only with financial activity has defined management narrowly.

The range of activities that a manager is responsible for varies in different organizations and in different positions within an organization. A manager's responsibility may range from directing the accomplishment of known and well-defined tasks to the broadest possible responsibilities of creativity and innovation.

## *Creating Opportunities—A Broad View of Responsibility*

Management's responsibility may be broadly defined to include the achievement of organizational objectives relating to internal operation and the external effects the organization has on society. A broad definition of management's role includes responsibility for the quality of life in the organization. Improving the quality of life in an organization includes responsibility for adapting the organization's structure to the needs, aspirations, and potential of individuals.

Management can be viewed as a subculture with its own systems of values and beliefs. If the management subculture's values are broad in scope, the focus is on innovation and creativity, such as the discovery and application of new knowledge to increase productivity.

Rather than merely responding to situations as they occur, management concentrates on creating opportunities in the environment in which the organization functions. Economic and social development in our society is the result of the management of the organizations that we depend on for goods and services. Table 3.1 summarizes both broad and narrow approaches to defining management responsibilities.

## EASIER SAID THAN DONE

Practices and techniques of management are relatively easy to write about, but effective implementation is difficult and time-consuming. Philosophies and theories of management are more highly developed than are the procedures and

---

**Table 3.1**
Management Responsibilities

| Narrowly Defined (Responds to Needs) | Broadly Defined (Creates Opportunities) |
| --- | --- |
| Responsible for economic and financial activity | Responsible for the quality of life in an organization |
| Responsible for responding to changes in economic and social conditions | Responsible for the economic and social impact of the organization |
| Responsible for directing employee activity to provide goods and services | Responsible for discovering and applying new knowledge to increase the quality and quantity of output |
| Responsible for solving problems that occur in the organization | Responsible for designing creative and innovative systems that prevent problems from occurring |
| Responsible for adapting and training individuals to serve organizational needs | Responsible for development of the organization to utilize the potential of individuals |

## Employee Relations Philosophy at Nucor Corporation  ▬▬▬▬

Employee relations, general management methods, and productivity bonuses at Nucor Corporation have sparked the company's spectacular growth. From 1974 to 1980, sales have increased by 600 percent while profits have risen a whopping 1,500 percent. A multimillion dollar steel manufacturing firm, Nucor has developed a philosophy of employee relations based on four primary components:

1. First and foremost, management must provide employees with the opportunity to earn according to their productivity.

2. The company must be managed so that employees will believe that if they are doing their jobs properly, they will have a job tomorrow.

3. Employees must believe that they are being treated fairly.

4. Employees must have an avenue of appeal if they are being treated unfairly.

Nucor's philosophy is reflected in many ways through its management policies. For example, all employees from the president down have the same benefit plan in areas of insurance, vacations, and holidays. The success of Nucor's employee relations has been attributed to the high degree of mutual respect and confidence between employees and managers. As recognition of Nucor's success, the corporation was selected by NBC to be included in a 1980 documentary on productivity entitled "If Japan Can, Why Can't We?"

The experience of Nucor is a demonstration of the willingness of American employees to work and the effects of a progressive human relations management policy.[16]

methods for their implementation in organizations. For the effective operation of any management system, the organizational environment must be supportive of management systems and practices. A difficult problem in management is to develop practices and policies within an organization that are consistent with each other. With economic, political, and social changes requiring rapid changes in organizational policies, inconsistencies can easily occur. Effective management requires that practices be flexible enough to be adapted according to the changing requirements of the organization.

The potential for more effective management is unlimited. Most organizations find that they must continually adapt and modify their management practices to meet the challenges of an ever-changing environment. The future effectiveness of organizations will depend on the application of a broad spectrum of management concepts and practices.

## SELF-ASSESSMENT DISCUSSION

**1.** (1) Nearly all of people's needs, from food to entertainment, are dependent to a large extent on organizations that develop, produce, distribute, and supply both essential and nonessential products and services. Even those who try to do many things for themselves depend on organizations for tools, supplies, and the requirements for both physical survival and psychological development.

**2.** (1) As people become better educated and more knowledgeable and have values that are centered on self-worth, an increasing number of types of employment are seen as nothing jobs. People want jobs that offer opportunity for social and psychological need satisfaction as well as for money and security.

**3.** (1) An increasing number of organizations are making attempts to design both jobs and management systems to provide greater personal need satisfaction for employees. More control over work, greater participation in organizational decisions, and challenging and interesting tasks are all part of the effort.

**4.** (5, 6) With little doubt, facilities and equipment are important in organizations. But competent, dedicated employees who are committed to an organization's goals are far more important.

**5.** (4, 5, 6) Efficiency is the performance of work with minimum effort, time, and costs. It is usually dependent on equipment, methods, work simplification, and training. Like effectiveness, efficiency is necessary in successful organizations. Effectiveness of people goes beyond efficiency. Effectiveness includes innovation, creativity, personal responsibility, and commitment to organizational goals. It is far more dependent on people than on efficiency.

**6.** (1) Bureaucracies tend to have highly specialized work assignments in major functional areas, strong procedures, impersonal application of rules, and a marked lack of flexibility and adaptability to change and new requirements.

**7.** (6) One of the foundations of modern bureaucracy as defined by Max Weber, who defined advantages of bureaucratic organizations, is impersonal treatment of employees. Everyone is to be treated alike without consideration for individual differences or circumstances.

**8.** (6) Some managers see themselves as problem solvers rather than as problem preventers. Reactive managers move from one crisis to another. This is a narrow view of management. A much broader view is to create opportunities for development of new approaches to services and products provided by the organization and to help employees optimize their capabilities.

**9.** (5, 6) Only lack of imagination and creative intelligence limit the potential for more effective management. In a world of constant change, management can always do better. What was effective yesterday may not be effective today.

**10.** (6) Closed communication that limits what a manager discusses with employees may be a means of dominating employees, but it usually demotivates rather than motivates employees. Open communication that builds trust and confidence between managers and employees is an effective motivational tool.

## QUICK REVIEW

I. The Influence of Organizations

   A. Organizations continually influence everyone. They have many pur-
      poses and are formal as well as informal, large as well as small.

   B. Organizations have made possible much of human progress. They affect
      most aspects of our lives.

   C. People are a major asset, expense, and source of problems for manag-
      ers of organizations.

II. People Problems in Organizations

   A. No known management style or system works equally well for all people
      in every type of situation.

   B. Organizations are becoming more complex, and people are increasingly
      dependent on organizations to satisfy their needs.

   C. Effective human relations is a vital part of successful management.

   D. Employees want meaningful work with more responsibility and more
      challenge.

III. The Bureaucratic Model

   A. The model stresses rigorous chain of command, specialization, proce-
      dures and rules, technical competence, and impersonality.

   B. Potential advantages are effective discipline, control, and quick response
      with strong management.

   C. Potential disadvantages are lack of flexibility, reduced creativity, isolated
      specialists, and complex procedures.

IV. Challenges Facing Organizations

   A. Social-psychological as well as technical and competitive changes pro-
      vide important challenges to managers.

   B. New and creative management approaches are necessary for effective
      adaptation to organizational changes.

   C. No set of rules or principles will help management as much as open-
      minded examination of everyday realities and adaptation to complexi-
      ty and change.

V. Management Responsibility

   A. The narrow view of management responsibility is largely reactive. It
      views management as responding to day-to-day needs and activities.

   B. A broad view of management responsibilities focuses on innovation and
      creativity—prevention as well as cure.

   C. Although writing about management problems is easy, the realities of
      the work environment are complex. A broad spectrum of concepts
      and practices is necessary for effective management.

## KEY TERMS

Nothing jobs
Efficiency
Bureaucratic organization
    model

Bureaucratic hierarchy
Management attitudes
Social-psychological
    changes

Management
    responsibility

## DISCUSSION QUESTIONS

1. What are the most direct influences of organizations on your life?
2. Give an example of a way effective or ineffective management has directly affected you.
3. Are organizations "becoming our masters"?
4. What are the most important problems of change and uncertainty currently facing managers of organizations?
5. What do you believe are the major demands that employees will make on management in the next five years?
6. What are the advantages and disadvantages of the bureaucratic model of management?
7. What do you consider to be the characteristics of an ideal job?
8. What are the characteristics of effective organizations?

## ─── EXERCISE ───

### ▰▰▰ Actions to Increase Creativity ▰▰▰

You have accepted the position as manager for the product development department of a company that produces small home appliances. The company is highly bureaucratic in its structure and procedures. Your department has lacked the creativity necessary to develop competitive new products. You were told that if the department does not begin producing new product designs that are innovative, you won't have the job for long. You believe that the bureaucratic nature of the organization is the major factor inhibiting innovation and creativity.

*Evaluate the following list of proposed actions to obtain creativity and reduce the stifling effects of the bureaucracy.*
Which actions would you take? Which would you take first?

1. Take all employees on a retreat. Present information on the lack of creativity and make it clear that you expect immediate improvement.

2. Tell employees that the bureaucratic nature of the company has caused the low creativity and they can ignore all bureaucratic policies and procedures.

3. Go to your boss and request that your department be exempted from all bureaucratic rules, policies, and procedures.

4. Hire a consultant in creativity and product development.

5. Tell the employees you will manage the department any way they want, but if they don't produce competitive product designs, you will start firing people.

6. Privately discuss the need for increased creativity with each employee. Be specific with each employee about ways to improve creativity.

7. Develop employee communication with customers and professional groups outside the company.

8. Provide each employee with a written report on the creativity problem and request written feedback on solutions.

9. Request to higher management that your department be moved to a location that is remote from other company facilities.

10. Set an example by developing an innovative product yourself.

---

## TWO POINTS OF VIEW

### *"The Conflict Situation"*

*What would you do if you were the supervisor?*

You have accepted your first supervisory job after graduating in the top 5 percent of your college class with a degree in management. Your new position is as supervisor of the purchasing department for a federal government agency. By working hard in the agency's training program and spending considerable time studying on your own, you have gained an in-depth understanding of the agency's policies on how jobs are to be done. From your first day on the job, you have carefully explained to employees how the agency's policies and procedures are to be followed in accomplishing all work. Even with repeated explanations, some employees insist that they be allowed to do their jobs their "own way," which you believe is not according to agency policies.

You told Ed Andrews, one of the employees who continually refuses to cooperate, "You are going to have to do the job according to agency procedures."

Ed replied, "No, sometimes you have to be practical and get around the agency's bureaucratic procedures. The way I do the job is the most effective way."

You responded, "I am not going to be a party to getting around agency policies and procedures. You either do it the way I told you, or I'll recommend you be replaced."

Ed retaliated with, "If you knew anything about management, you'd realize that you should support employees. We can do the best job when we do it our own way."

You are beginning to wonder if there is any way to get through to Ed Andrews that things must be done according to agency policies and procedures.

You know that he thinks that because he is a civil service employee, you cannot fire him or take severe disciplinary action.

*What would you do if you were Ed Andrews?*

You are a purchasing processor for a government agency. You are a civil service employee who has worked for the federal government for seventeen years. You have always gotten along well with your supervisors, and your performance evaluations have always been above average. Your current supervisor is a new college graduate that is "still wet behind the ears." He is pleasant but has a lot to learn about managing in the government bureaucracy. You like him and would like to help him do well as a supervisor.

When you try to help him understand that you can't do everything "by the book," he just reacts by repeating policy statements he has memorized. No one goes exactly by the written policies and procedures of the agency if they expect to get anything done. The bottom line is that some of the agency's procedures work and others don't. You know that you can't directly disobey your supervisor's orders, or he will have grounds for recommending your termination. If you don't establish good working relations with your supervisor, you could get low performance evaluations or be transferred to an undesirable location.

You could do as your supervisor wants and go strictly by agency policy and procedures, which would mean that the job would not be done effectively and your supervisor would encounter difficulties in the long run.

## ENDNOTES

1. Robert Dubin, *Human Relations in Administration* (Englewood Cliffs, N.J.: Prentice-Hall, 1974), p. 31.
2. Michael A. Hitt, R. Dennis Middlemist, and Robert L. Mathis, *Management: Concept and Effective Practices*, 2d ed. (St. Paul: West, 1986), p. 8.
3. David Hampton, Charles E. Summer, and Ross A. Weber, *Organizational Behavior and the Practice of Management* (Glenview, Ill.: Scott, Foresman, 1973), p. xviii.
4. Robert Townsend, *Further up the Organization* (New York: Knopf, 1984), p. xi.
5. Herbert G. Hicks, *The Management of Organizations: A System and Human Resources Approach* (New York: McGraw-Hill, 1967), p. 16.
6. John D. Rockefeller as quoted in Garret L. Berten and William V. Hangley, *Organizational Relations and Management Action* (New York: McGraw-Hill, 1966), p. 3.
7. Richard M. Steers, *Introduction to Organizational Behavior* (Glenview, Ill.: Scott, Foresman, 1981), p. 9.
8. Samuel C. Certo, *Principles of Management*, 3d ed. (Dubuque, Iowa: Brown, 1986), p. 547.
9. Don Hellriegel and John W. Slocum, Jr., *Management*, 4th ed. (Reading, Mass.: Addison-Wesley, 1986), pp. 41–46.
10. Anthony Jay, *Management and Machiavelli* (New York: Holt, Rinehart & Winston, 1967), p. 70.
11. Ibid.
12. F. Warren McFarlan, "Information Technology Changes the Way You Compete," *Harvard Business Review* (May–June 1984): 98.

**13.** M. Magnet, "It's Shape Up or Shake Out in a Shook-Up World," *Fortune*, 10 June 1985, pp. 166–172.

**14.** J. P. Jones, "People: The Independent Variable," in *Organization Theory in Industrial Practice*, ed. I. M. Hairs (New York: Wiley, 1962), p. 550.

**15.** Phillip L. Hunsaker and Curtis W. Cook, *Managing Organizational Behavior* (Reading, Mass.: Addison-Wesley, 1986), p. 60.

**16.** John Savage, "Incentive Programs at Nucor Corporation Boost Productivity," *Personnel Administrator* (August 1981): 33–36, 49, and S. Scredon and B. Iverson Nussbaum, "Smashing the Corporate Pyramid," *Business Week*, 21 January 1985, p. 71.

---
### ▬▬▬▬▬ CASE INCIDENTS FOR PART 1 ▬▬▬▬▬
---

## The "No-Match" Rule

The Top-Line Paint Company had two serious fires and put into effect the following regulation: "No matches, lighters, or other fire-producing devices are permitted inside the plant. Violation of this rule will mean automatic and permanent dismissal for any employee." The new rule was posted on the bulletin board at each entrance to the plant.

Previously, many employees had brought matches and cigarette lighters into the plant. The old "no-smoking" rule had been respected, and there was no evidence that any fires had been caused by employees' smoking in the plant.

Tom Neal had worked for Top-Line for twenty years and was considered one of the best processing inspectors in the plant. Two weeks after the no-match rule went into effect, Tom was climbing up to inspect a mixing vat when a book of matches fell from his pocket. They landed at the feet of Mr. Christy, Tom's supervisor.

Mr. Christy picked up the matches and told Tom, "I'm going to have to report these matches, and it'll mean your job."

Tom climbed down from the vat without saying a word. He looked at Mr. Christy and said: "I did nothing that created any safety hazard. If you try to fire me, I'll sue you for every penny you have."

1. If you were Mr. Christy, what would you do? Why?
2. Was there anything wrong with how the rule was worded?
3. Did the company effectively communicate the new rule?
4. How could this situation have been handled more effectively?

## The Right Ingredients for Success

Nancy Ribody and John Crago had become acquainted during an evening management class at a local college. They were both experienced in bakery operations and, after some discussion, pooled their resources to open a small store specializing in French, Belgian, and Swiss pastries. John cooked, waited on walk-in customers, and with part-time help ran the bakery while Nancy concentrated on sales to restaurants and hotel dining establishments.

As their outside and in-house sales increased, they realized they could easily double their business by hiring more permanent employees, opening new locations, and perhaps expanding into other cities. Since their first venture was successful, obtaining additional money was not a problem.

Their primary concern was to maintain the quality that had built their company's reputation and established long-lasting relations with their customers. To achieve their goal, they were required to do some careful planning.

1. What are Nancy and John's first planning steps?

2. How can they ensure that their quality standards will be met in new stores?

3. What types of problems will they probably encounter?

## The Branch Manager's Replacement

Dorothy Curtis is a branch manager for the city credit union, with two assistant managers working for her. She is to be promoted to a position in the main office as soon as she can find a person to fill her position. Dorothy's boss has told her that she should select one of her assistant managers. In her opinion, neither of her assistants has shown any leadership ability or desire to manage on his own. When she talks to her assistants, each indicates that he is not interested in assuming the responsibility for decisions that the branch manager's job requires. They enjoy their current positions and do not have any desire for promotion.

1. Why would an employee not want to be promoted?

2. Would it be desirable for Ms. Curtis to try to convince one of the managers to take the job, even though she thinks he is not qualified, so that she may be promoted?

3. Why would her boss want her to select one of her employees?

4. Should she try to convince her boss that her employees are not capable and do not want the position? If so, how?

5. Other than promoting her subordinates, what alternatives could she suggest to her boss for filling the position?

## Paid to Do Their Jobs

Al Woodward handed a thick folder to Beverly Dunn and breathed a sigh of relief. "Well, it's done and it looks good," he said. "Personally, I think it's the best analysis of market trends we've ever done—*and* it's a day ahead of schedule." "Thanks, Al," Beverly said, smiling. "You did a great job. Tell the crew not only do I appreciate their knocking themselves out over this report, but pizza and drinks will be on the house after work. Wait until Tony Davis sees this!"

"So, you finally got it done?" was Tony Davis's first comment when Beverly laid the report on his desk. As marketing director, he relied heavily on Beverly's research section for future sales and advertising planning as well as new product development. "Look, Tony, our crew really went to bat over this one, worked overtime, beat the schedule, and did a first-class job," Beverly responded. "Maybe some thanks or appreciation from you is in order." "Now, Bev," said Tony, "why baby them? They're paid to do their job, and they did it. I don't see anything special about people doing what they're assigned."

That afternoon Beverly called Al Woodward into her office. "I just told Tony to take this job and fly with it, Al. He didn't give us one word of recognition or appreciation for the future trends report, just like always. It's plain stupidity! In any case, I've recommended you for the job, and I imagine you'll get it." "Don't quit, Bev," Al urged. "We need you." Privately, he made up his mind that if she really left, he'd start looking for another job as well. With his skill, it wouldn't be hard to relocate.

1. Contrast Tony's point of view with Beverly's and Al's. Who is right?
2. Does Tony realize the effect of his attitude on his employees?
3. How do you think Beverly's resignation will affect other employees in the market research department?

# Part 2

# Communication

# *Perception*

## _____ *Learning Objectives* _____

After reading this chapter, you should be able to do the following:

1. Describe the perceptual process and its effect on behavior
2. Explain how people selectively perceive information
3. Discuss how people's expectations affect the way they interpret information
4. Identify the ways individuals organize perceptions
5. Describe how an individual's frame of reference influences the selection, organization, and interpretation of information
6. List the effects of individual needs on perception
7. Identify how the perceptions of managers and employees differ
8. Explain how managers can apply knowledge of perception to improve employee performance

# Chapter Topics

- Perceptual process
- Selective perception
- Perceptual organization
- Frame of reference
- Interpretation of perceptions
- Stereotypes
- We perceive what we need
- Differing perceptions of managers and employees

# Preview

A cafeteria manager told this true story: "One of my biggest problems is the way people taste things. One customer will complain that the soup is too highly seasoned. Another will protest just as loudly that the soup is not seasoned enough. The cook says it's just right. No two people seem to taste the soup or anything else alike."

Nor do any two people see, hear, feel, understand, or interpret the world around them in the same way. Perception, the way we interpret our experiences, is a fascinating and troublesome facet of human behavior. Its importance to employees and managers is far greater than most people realize. When managers and employees have differing perceptions regarding quality, quantity, schedules, and the importance of a given task, accomplishing meaningful objectives is nearly impossible. In this chapter, perception is discussed from several vantage points. "Perception is the way stimuli are selected and grouped by a person so that they can be meaningfully interpreted. It is *a person's view of reality*." [1]

> If one's concern as a supervisor . . . is to try to effect some change in the behavior of other people, . . . then it is critical that one seek to understand their perceptions if one is to understand the circumstances under which their behavior might change.[2]

The effective manager realizes that views of work, the world, and jobs are not necessarily shared and agreed upon. As numerous studies of perception show, however, many people assume that others see the world in the same way they do. These same studies show that the best supervisor is the one who can accurately estimate employee perceptions. Since there are no formulas to help managers understand what is on another's mind, managers are left to their own inventiveness and sensitivity.

## SELF–ASSESSMENT ▬▬▬▬▬▬▬▬▬▬▬▬▬▬▬▬▬▬▬▬▬▬▬▬

Perception deals with the interpretation of what is seen, heard, smelled, tasted, and felt. For the following items, mark the responses that are most nearly correct based on your personal experience, other classes, or readings. Each statement or question has a range of possible responses. A scale of 1 to 6 between two words with different meanings allows you to mark either the word that is considered correct or a place between the two words that represents some agreement and some disagreement. Selection of a high number such as 5 or 6 may be either correct or incorrect, just as selection of lower numbers may be correct or incorrect. Some responses may be partly correct and partly incorrect.

   Answers based on research by behavorial scientists, with a short explanation of why the response was considered correct, may be found on page 96.

1. Which of the following is most likely to underestimate the importance of psychological and social needs of employees?

   managers  1...2...3...4...5...6  union leaders

2. All people tend to perceive the world around them in much the same way.

   agree  1...2...3...4...5...6  disagree

3. Human beings make which of the following part of their conscious experience?

   experiences that  1...2...3...4...5...6  everything in their
   are selected                                immediate environment

4. Which of the following is a stereotype?

   absentminded  1...2...3...4...5...6  tall Watusi warriors
   professors

5. Which of the following is usually ranked as most important by employees who have worked for an organization for relatively long periods of time?

   pay  1...2...3...4...5...6  appreciation of work
                                accomplished

6. When compared with those who live in southern latitudes, people who live in northern latitudes are:

   more likely to be  1...2...3...4...5...6  less likely to be aware
   aware of cold                              of cold

7. Part of our time in human relationships is spent estimating another person's mood or feelings.

   true in most cases  1...2...3...4...5...6  rarely true

**8.** The way anything is perceived is usually dependent on:

its surroundings  1...2...3...4...5...6  the needs of the person
or context in                                            who perceives
which it appears

**9.** Whether or not $10,000 is considered a large sum of money depends on:

degree of  1...2...3...4...5...6  knowledge of
economic need                                   monetary values

**10.** Which of the following usually has the greatest influence on perception of
magnitude (how big, loud, bright, and so on)?

intensity  1...2...3...4...5...6  adaptation level

## PERCEPTUAL PROCESS

Perception is the process through which we actively select, organize, and interpret information brought to us by our senses in order to understand the complex world around us.[3]

Figure 4.1 illustrates the perceptual process in a somewhat simplified form.
Perception, therefore, is the starting point for all behavior. It is the process by
which one begins to understand what is going on in the surrounding world.
There can be no behavior without individual perceptions, because it is not the

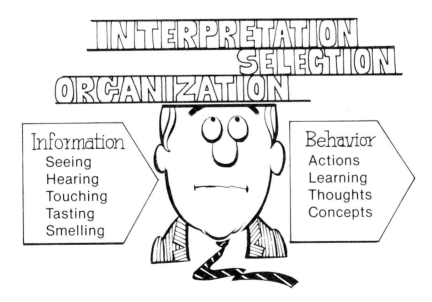

**Figure 4.1**   The perceptual process.

physical stimulation of the senses that completes the perceptual process but the interpretation of those sensations by the receiver.

However, if behavioral situations are viewed only in terms of stimulus and response, the key factors involved in individual perception are omitted from the resulting interpretations. When an individual is confronted with information, at least three perceptual processes take place: selection, organization, and interpretation (Figure 4.1).

Most people assume that everyone perceives things in the same way. After all, we do live in the same world, see the same sun, and drive the same highways. But do we see things in the same way? The best evidence suggests that perception is a creative process by which individuals construct a unique and relatively private view of the world. Individuals begin creating their images of the world early in life and continue to form them until death.

Each employee brings to the organization a unique storehouse of perceptions. It is important for managers to understand the employee's pattern of perceptions that affect how the individual views the job, the supervisor, fellow workers, and the organization. An employee's perceptions influence job performance, attitude, and interpersonal relationships.

## SELECTIVE PERCEPTION

Much of the information that is available to an individual is not perceived and made a part of that person's conscious experience. **Selective exposure** involves deciding to pay attention to some things and to ignore or avoid others. The employee who decides to listen to the union representative and to avoid talking with the supervisor is involved in selective exposure.

The selective nature of perception also involves **selective awareness**, in which people are able to filter out information they do not want to be consciously aware of. Students are able to ignore noise made by others in a class when they are concentrating on what the instructor is saying. Employees are able to tune out the constant noise of machinery on the production line. While reading a book, an individual may be unaware of smells, noises, and pressures on the skin.

Much of the information available in the environment does not become a part of conscious experience because of the selective nature of perception. Your nose provides an example of selection that is with you all of the time. Close your left eye and you see your nose with the right eye; close your right eye and you see your nose with your left eye; open both eyes and your nose disappears.

Perceptual selection is affected by an individual's needs, expectations, interests, and the characteristics of the information.

### *Intensity*

If messages are loud or bright, there is a greater chance that people will select them. As the volume of the radio is increased, there is a greater likelihood that individuals will "hear" it. This does not mean the desired interpretation of the message will be created, but merely that there is a greater chance that the

---

### How Many *F*'s? ━━━━━━━━━━━━━━━━━━━━━━━━━━━━━━━━━━━━

Read the following sentence and see how good you are at counting the *F*'s in the sentence.

- - - - - - - - - - - - - - - - - - - - - - - - - - - - - - - - - - - - - - - - - - - - - -

FOULED UP FILES ARE THE RESULT OF FOOLISH NEGLECT AND FINISHED FILES ARE THE RESULT OF SCIENTIFIC STUDY COUPLED WITH THE EXPERIENCE OF MANY YEARS.

- - - - - - - - - - - - - - - - - - - - - - - - - - - - - - - - - - - - - - - - - - - - - -

How many *F*'s did you count? If you did not find *nine* *F*'s, try again. Why did you miss some of the *F*'s?

It is easy not to perceive the *F* in the word *of*. Most people select out a third of the *F*'s and count six *F*'s. Perception is often influenced by what we think is important. If you did not think *of* was important, you probably did not count all the *F*'s.

---

individual will attend to the information. *Intensity* functions to increase chances of selection. Common examples of intensity are the volume of the speaker, the size of a billboard, or the brightness of a color. Attempts to achieve desired responses from individuals through intensity alone will probably be disappointing. Intensity does not increase the accuracy of perception; it only increases the probability that the information will be selected.

### Frequency

The more often information is presented, the greater the chance of selection by the individual. Sometimes effectiveness is attributed to the amount of information alone. There is no guarantee of achieving desired results by just repeating information. Repeatedly telling employees to work harder is not likely to result in increased individual effort.

Confusing information repeated frequently is still confusing information. *Frequency*, in and of itself, does increase the probability of selection by receivers, but it does *not* increase the chance that the receiver will accurately interpret and organize the information.

Frequency can inhibit desired behavior when the information is transmitted so often that the receivers become bored or irritated. An increase in frequency may result in a feeling of being "talked down" to, and the receiver may respond negatively.

## *Expectations*

Read the phrases printed within the triangles below.

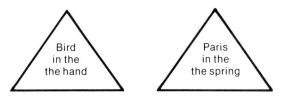

Did you see what was really in the triangles? Or did you see what you expected to see?

Most people will report what they expected to see. In the case of "Bird in *the the* hand," they report seeing "Bird in *the* hand," omitting one of the words in the phrase (there are two *the*'s). We never expect to find two *the*'s next to each other. As we perceive, we select, organize, and interpret the information to conform with our expectations. When reality differs from our expectations, changing our perceptions of reality is often easier than grappling with the difference between our expectations and the information.

The context in which information appears affects our *expectations* and structures the interpretation of the message by receivers. Let's take the simple sentence "I went to the bank and wrote a chack." When most people hear this sentence, they repeat it back by saying, "I went to the bank and wrote a *check*." We develop a set of expectations by setting the scene in a bank, where under normal circumstances one would expect a check to be written. But in this case we have introduced *chack* in an incongruent context, which the individual automatically reinterprets to fit the context or surrounding.

We could use the term *chack* in another sentence and get a different interpretation: "I went out to a chicken farm to show my children the baby chacks." When people interpret this sentence, they convert *chack* to *chick*.

Evaluating information is not a question of what the information says but what the individual *expects* the information to say. Much of the dissatisfaction within organizations occurs because managers do not hear what employees say

How do your expectations affect your perception? Do you think you can follow directions? Take the three-minute test that follows and see how you rate.

## READ EVERYTHING BEFORE DOING ANYTHING
### *How to Follow Instructions*

1. Put your name in the upper right-hand corner, last name first.
2. Circle the word *name* in sentence one.
3. Underline the words *upper right-hand* in sentence one.
4. Now draw a circle around the word *how* in the title.
5. Sign your name under the title.
6. In sentence three, draw a circle around the word *underline*.
7. Draw an *x* in the lower left-hand corner.
8. Draw a circle around the *x* you just drew.
9. If you think you have followed instructions to this point, write *I have*.
10. Close your eyes and raise your left hand over your head.
11. Write the name of your occupation:
12. *Count out loud* in your normal speaking voice backward from ten to one.
13. Now that you have read the instructions carefully, do only what sentence three asks you to do. Ignore all other directions.

but what they *expect* them to say. The same is true of message transmission from managers to employees; the employee does not hear what the manager says but what is *expected*.

> It's impossible to communicate clearly with everyone. Sometimes even the simplest message is misunderstood because employees hear what they want to hear rather than what was intended.[4]

*Sandwich Technique*   Often attempts are made to change behavior by criticism. A frequently used method of criticism is referred to as the sandwich technique: First tell the individual something nice, something desirable, or something good. Then criticize the individual. Follow with something positive at the end of the conversation. The effectiveness of this technique is questionable because it develops a set of positive expectations: "We're talking about nice things, and everything is going fine." Suddenly the context is changed, and the individual is expected to immediately switch expectations to deal with criticism. Often the individual does not change expectations to deal with criticism, the criticism is ignored, and no change results.

## PERCEPTUAL ORGANIZATION

Each individual has to try to organize a sensible and coherent world out of an environment that may not make sense in itself. This tendency is often referred to as *perceptual organization*. A never tells B everything when they talk. B fills in the gaps. A common result is that B's response to the message may be quite different from A's expectation. Behavior depends on the image.

Try the following problem:

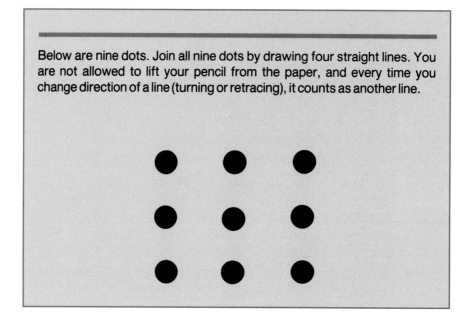

Below are nine dots. Join all nine dots by drawing four straight lines. You are not allowed to lift your pencil from the paper, and every time you change direction of a line (turning or retracing), it counts as another line.

Most people try to solve the problem by staying inside a square defined by the dots. Many people even perceive the instructions as saying that they must stay in a square. But there is no square! The dots provide an environmental stimulus that may be organized into a square by the perceiver—and this blocks successful task performance. (Solution on next page.)

How would you describe the following?

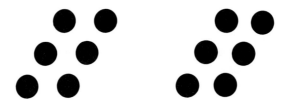

## Grouping

Most people say there are two sets of six dots; practically no one will respond by saying there are twelve dots. To summarize the data by saying you see two sets of six dots is a harmless and trivial selection from the basic description of the information that appears. The phenomenon occurring is one of organization and grouping of the data on the basis of nearness. This factor is almost always involved in perception and interpretation. Things that are close are perceived as alike.

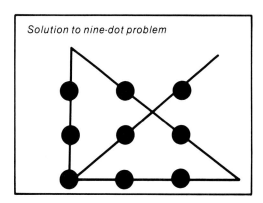

Solution to nine-dot problem

## Association

In many cases, grouping results in a phenomenon referred to as *association*. Let's assume we have an employee who is classed as "lazy," who "doesn't work hard," and who "puts out very little effort." We now hire a new employee who eats lunch with the lazy employee, rides with him to work, and frequently associates with him on the job. It would not be hard to draw the conclusion that both employees are lazy. Association or reality?

How would you describe the following to someone?

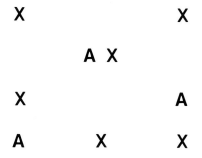

Most people say there are six *X*'s and three *A*'s. Why? Why not nine letters?

### Closure

When we perceive information, we tend to organize it into whole and continuous patterns. If the pattern is incomplete, we tend to fill in the missing elements. The incomplete "circle" must be completed. The perceptual process involved in completing figures is referred to as *closure*. "Thus, a person may perceive more than the information seems to indicate. We add to the information input whatever seems appropriate, in order to close the system and make it meaningful and supportive." [5]

The need for closure may apply to many activities. For example, it may apply to the tension that accompanies the interruption of a task and the satisfaction and relief that come from its completion. Task completion is in essence the attainment of the whole figure.

Now let's consider another characteristic of perception that is not as directly tied to social perceptions.

Reproduce the following figures:

Did you introduce any systematic distortions or change? Most people do. These figures are usually changed, in the process of being reproduced, as follows:

The perception of things as belonging to common groups is achieved by the use of grouping according to similarity and proximity and by attaining closure. We structure information by putting similar concepts together and attempting to provide a "complete story."

A generalizable proposition about behavior is that *people respond neither to individual elements one at a time nor to the sum total of individual elements; they respond to the relationship among the elements.*

When we *think* we have the complete picture or the whole story, we stop looking and listening.

*Ambiguous Information*     How do you react to ambiguous information? People were shown a series of simple ambiguous drawings and were asked to reproduce a labeled figure. Each picture was preceded by a word indicating what was to be drawn. The redrawn pictures were distorted from the original stimulus according to the label attached. The labels attached were systematically varied so that the same word did not always precede the drawing. Examples of some of the results are shown in Figure 4.2.

## FRAME OF REFERENCE

External *and* internal influences interact to shape the processes of selection, organization, and interpretation of information. We develop a personal *frame of*

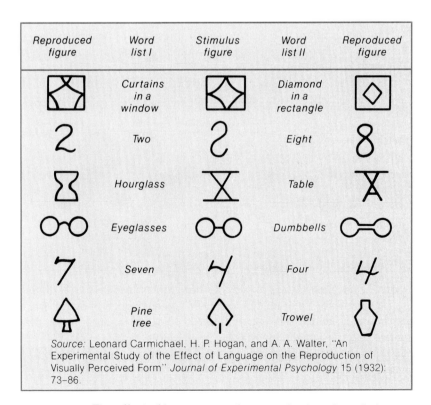

| Reproduced figure | Word list I | Stimulus figure | Word list II | Reproduced figure |
|---|---|---|---|---|
| | Curtains in a window | | Diamond in a rectangle | |
| | Two | | Eight | |
| | Hourglass | | Table | |
| | Eyeglasses | | Dumbbells | |
| | Seven | | Four | |
| | Pine tree | | Trowel | |

*Source:* Leonard Carmichael, H. P. Hogan, and A. A. Walter, "An Experimental Study of the Effect of Language on the Reproduction of Visually Perceived Form" *Journal of Experimental Psychology* 15 (1932): 73–86.

**Figure 4.2    The effect of language on the reproduction of symbols.**

*reference* that includes all the internal and external factors that affect behavior at a given time.

Any accurate analysis of behavior must examine an event in the appropriate frame of reference. This does not imply that all influences operating at a given time have equal effects on our behavior. Within any situation are major reference points that weigh more heavily in shaping the outcome of an event. Major reference points may be in external situations or internal influences, depending on the interrelationships of factors at the time.

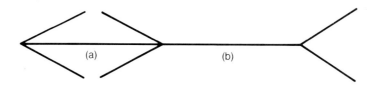

(a)                              (b)

Which of the horizontal lines is longer? Did you measure them?

Take any two lines of *equal* length. Add inward-pointing arrows to one line and outward-pointing arrows to the other. The lines no longer look equal. In our experience they are *not the same lines* because the frame of reference is different. Each line and its arrows are part of a perceptual unit. Architects have long utilized this type of phenomenon to create impressions of height, spaciousness, and curves in the form of buildings. Why does the moon look so much larger while ascending—when seen just over the top of horizon trees?

Are the center circles the same size or different? Which of the two center circles in the illustration below looks the largest?

***Perception Involves Relationships***    Even simple objects like these two circles are experienced in a relational way. In the complex and dynamic area of human relations, where individuals interact with one another, the relational effects become even more important.

Although the center circles are the same size, most people don't see them as equal because of the circles around them—their frame of reference. To perceive the size of the circle accurately, we can change the frame of reference by removing the surrounding circles.

In some situations, the accuracy of perception can be increased by changing the frame of reference. In most cases, communication must succeed within the existing frames of reference even though they are constantly changing.

What is wrong with the question, Which one is larger? Often, all you can tell is which one *looks* larger. We don't ask an individual what *appears* to be the best; we ask it as if it is an absolute. In this sense, the better question would be, Which circle *appears* to be the larger?

Which of the three men is tallest?

## INTERPRETATION OF PERCEPTIONS

The key to understanding perception is to recognize that it is a unique *interpretation* of the situation, not an exact recording of it.[6]

The way anything is interpreted depends on its surroundings or the context in which it appears. What happened with the dots occurs with all perception.

The context in which information appears affects what you think you see or hear.

Suppose the same message is given to the employees by the company president and by the union president. Ask the employees to interpret it, and you will get two different interpretations. *The context always affects interpretation.*

The simplest judgment of physical objects to the most complex social judgments involves making comparisons. To judge or interpret, some basis for comparison must exist. Time and space judgments require comparison within a frame of reference. If no objects are available for a point of reference, we cannot determine the location in space or whether something is moving or standing still.

### Adaptation Level

What is normal? Small? Large? What feels heavy? What feels light? What appears to be effective or ineffective depends on a series of comparisons and who is viewing an object or event. Human perceptual judgment occurs within the particular background an individual brings to a situation. *Adaptation level* refers to the perceptual changes that occur as an individual makes a series of comparisons. No absolute relationship exists between the perceived magnitude and the actual physical magnitude. People develop adaptation levels with regard to any given evaluation of magnitude (e.g., temperature, light intensity, size, and so on). Evaluations are based on a series of perceived comparisons. An orange tastes sweet after eating a lemon, but sour after eating candy.

The important implication of the adaptation phenomenon is that judgments are not simply intellectual evaluations; they are the result of perceptual comparisons. Whether objects feel heavy or light and whether individuals appear intelligent or stupid depends on a series of comparisons. Individual responses will vary depending on the individual's background and the context in which the judgment occurs.

When a manager is evaluating employee productivity, the manager's judgments are based on an evaluation scale that has been developed through experience. As a result of observing a number of people involved in accomplishing tasks, the manager has acquired a personal scale for rating employee productivity.

### STEREOTYPES

Stereotypes are attitudes that serve as shorthand guides to characterizing groups of people. The term *stereotype* was originally used in printing to refer to a plate that printed the same image over and over again. Stereotypes exist for religious groups, racial groups, occupational groups, and nationality groups. People select characteristics to identify groups of people and attribute those characteristics to each person in the group.

> Careful inquiry would show that very few if any members of a given group possess the characteristics they are said to have. Yet stereotyping is a common and wide-

---

**An Exercise in Stereotyping** ━━━━━━━━━━━━━━━━━━━━━

*Identify a group described by each of the following sets of characteristics.*

Absentminded, unrealistic, impractical _____

Artistic, impulsive, passionate _____

Emotional, weak, gentle _____

Witty, quick-tempered, quarrelsome _____

Strong, logical, aggressive _____

Lazy, clannish, superstitious _____

Hardworking, dependable, honest _____

Mercenary, shrewd, industrious _____

Quiet, careful, patient _____

Compare your answers with someone else's.

---

spread phenomenon. Stereotypes persist because they are useful and they help us organize the world around us.[7]

What characteristics come to mind when you think about lawyers, Protestants, blacks, truck drivers, professors, or football players? Each of these terms probably calls to mind a mental picture containing characteristics that stereotype the group. The stereotype one has of a group will usually strongly affect the way one perceives an individual who is seen as a member of the group.

The use of stereotypes makes it possible to describe people within simple and well-organized categories. Stereotypes save the time and effort required to find out what a person is really like. The implication is that all the people belonging to a group are alike: "When you've seen one, you've seen them all."

> Your stereotyped perception can give people an advantage they don't deserve or a disadvantage that's decidedly unfair.[8]

Stereotypes limit the ability to perceive other people accurately. They can result in individuals being seen only as a part of a group. Stereotyping can prevent people from finding out how a person is unique and different apart from the group.

## WE PERCEIVE WHAT WE NEED

Although communication is possible because of similar interpretation of experiences, neither individual experiences nor interpretations of them are identical. Even when two people look at the same thing (object, person, movie, and so on) from nearly the same spot, their interpretations differ. Our needs, desires, wishes, dislikes—our frame of reference—are the boundaries surrounding our perceptions.

A family visits a department store and browses together. As they leave, they discuss what they saw. The father noticed lawn mowers and power tools; the mother, fur coats and dishwashers. The daughter noticed bathing suits and cosmetics; the son, a candy counter.

Did they visit the same store? Although the physical reality was the same, the information perceived by the individuals was not. Because they had different needs and wants, from a perceptual point of view they visited different stores. "In general, people perceive things that promise to help satisfy their needs and that they have found rewarding in the past." [9]

Examine what people report they've heard after listening to a political speech. Their needs directly affect their perceptions. For example, the farmer heard about farm-price supports, the teacher heard about support for education, and the construction executive heard about plans for a new highway.

Our needs alter our perceptions. In one experiment, people looked at cards through a screen that blurred the pictures. People who had not eaten for nine hours before looking at the pictures described more of them as food items than did people who had recently eaten.

In another experiment, children were asked to estimate the size of coins. Poor children tended to estimate all coins to be physically larger than did children from higher income brackets.

In our daily search for order and certainty, we interpret according to our expectations and work from these to predict future responses. How can we know enough about human nature or an individual's experiences to infer how he or she might react? We develop expectations as we come to know an individual and we empathize. We project our thoughts to other people. Part of our time is spent in estimating the other person's feelings and thoughts and tempering our remarks to provide the most effective stimulus or response.

Man prefers to believe what he prefers to be true.

Francis Bacon

Those oblivious to external cues about others' internal experiences are not taking full advantage of the feedback possibilities that contribute to more effective communication. Through our ability to "feel out" people, we learn to adjust to new situations and environments and increase our ability to communicate.


## DIFFERING PERCEPTIONS OF MANAGERS AND EMPLOYEES

Accurate perception of the needs of employees is an important aspect of a manager's job. If managers do not accurately perceive the relative strength of employee motivation, their efforts to improve productivity through motivation will be ineffective. Managers may be appealing to needs that are already satisfied or are unimportant to employees.

R. L. Kahn's study of management perceptions of employee needs revealed that management greatly overestimated the importance employees attached to high wages.[10] In the study, only 28 percent of the employees ranked wages as most important, while 61 percent of the managers perceived that wages were

---

## How Position in an Organization Influences Perceptions ▬▬

The effect on perception of a person's position in an organization was demonstrated in a classic study of managers by Dearborn and Simon.

A group of twenty-three executives of a large manufacturing company were asked to read a factual case often used in college business administration courses. The case described the problems of a medium-sized manufacturing company that produced seamless steel tubes. Each executive was asked to identify the most important problem facing a new president in that company. Which problem should be addressed first?

Six of the executives were sales managers, five were production managers, four were accounting managers, and eight managed staff functions such as legal, public relations, industrial relations, and medical. The researchers wanted to find out if the executives would perceive the key problem in terms of their own positions and the activities of their department.

The results of the study indicated that, indeed, the managers' positions did influence their perception of the most important problem facing the new president. Sales executives saw sales as the most important problem. Production executives identified production problems as most urgent. Public relations and industrial relations executives saw human relations as the company's biggest problem.[11]

---

the most important for employees. The study showed that management underestimated the importance of the social and psychological needs of their employees.

The problem of accuracy of management perception of what employees want from their jobs is also apparent in research reported by Paul Hersey and Kenneth Blanchard.[12] The research involved supervisors who were asked to put themselves in the position of their employees and to rank the importance of a series of items describing what they wanted from their jobs. Supervisors ranked good wages, job security, and promotion as most wanted by employees. The workers themselves ranked the most important items as full appreciation of work done, to be "in" on things, and sympathetic understanding of personal problems. The results of this study indicate the inaccuracy of management perceptions.

The results of these and similar studies are especially important for management, because both managers and employees act on the basis of their perceptions. If management perceptions can be brought closer to the reality of employee perceptions, managers may be able to increase their effectiveness in working with individuals.

Two researchers compared managers' and labor leaders' perceptions of employee needs with the employees' report of their needs.[13] They found that both union leaders and managers held inaccurate perceptions of employees' wants. They overemphasized the importance of material rewards and working conditions and underestimated the importance employees placed on getting along with supervisors and co-workers. An interesting point is that in this study, managers considerably overestimated the employees' evaluation of the union's importance.

Because the process of motivation always takes place within the framework of employee perceptions of the situation, employees act in ways that make sense to them based on what they perceive to be important. An important implication for management is that the employee's perception of the relationship with the boss is critical. As Rensis Likert pointed out: "An individual's reaction to any situation is always a function not of the absolute character of the intervention, but of his perception of it. It is how he sees things that counts, not objective reality.[14]

## SELF–ASSESSMENT DISCUSSION

**1.** (1, 6) Studies show that both managers and union leaders underestimate the importance of psychological and social factors at work for employees who are union members.

**2.** (5, 6) Although some commonality may exist in the way a situation is perceived by different people, there is always a great deal of individual variation. Psychologists say that no two people ever experience the same thing in the same manner.

**3.** (1) A number of experiments indicate that perception is highly selective. We perceive only that part of our environment which is important or which we have learned to perceive.

**4.** (1) Many professors are not absentminded, but it is a popular stereotype of college faculty. All Watusi warriors are tall people. Their tallness is a fact, not a stereotype.

**5.** (6) Although pay is important, people who are receiving a regular wage with periodic increases usually rank appreciation for their efforts, interesting work, and being "in" on things as most important.

**6.** (6) People tend to adapt to their surroundings. Baffin Island Eskimo live in one of the coldest inhabited environments and have been known to complain about the heat when the temperature rises to 33 or 34 degrees Fahrenheit (just above zero degrees Celsius).

**7.** (6) Most people perceive others' moods, feelings, and attitudes. In most cases, communication is shaped to fit the perception.

**8.** (1, 2, 3, 4, 5, 6) Environment, context, and personal needs all help shape perceptions.

**9.** (1) In a famous study, children of poor parents perceived money as being physically larger than it actually was. Economic need, like other needs, helps determine perceptual values.

**10.** (6) As in the case of the Baffin Island Eskimo (item 6), adaptation level determines degree of magnitude perceived in most instances. Six inches of snow may be a lot to someone who lives where snow rarely falls. To people who live in a high-snowfall area, six inches of snow may be considered a small amount.

## QUICK REVIEW

I. Perceptual Process
- A. Effective managers realize that all individuals have differing perceptions.
- B. The tendency is for people to assume that others perceive as they themselves do.
- C. No formulas are available for piecing together what is in another person's mind.
- D. Perception involves the process by which a person selects, organizes, and interprets sensory stimulations.
- E. Perception is the starting point of all behavior.
- F. Employee perception influences performance, attitude, and interpersonal relations.

II. Selective Perception
- A. Perception tends to be selective. Much of the information around us is not perceived.
- B. Selective exposure involves paying attention to some things and ignoring others.
- C. Selective awareness refers to filtering out information we do not want to be consciously aware of.
- D. Perceptual selection is affected by several characteristics of the stimulus.
    1. Intensity is the strength of the stimulus, such as loudness, brightness, size, movement, and so on.
    2. Frequency refers to repetition of the same stimulus.
    3. Expectations involve the tendency to react to things as we expect them to be rather than as they are.

III. Perceptual Organization
- A. We tend to organize things in such a way that they make sense to us.
- B. One way of organizing is by grouping similar stimuli.
- C. Closure, the tendency to perceptually complete the incomplete, is another method of organizing perceptions.
- D. People respond to the relationship between elements of a stimulus rather than to the individual elements.

E. Three perceptual processes involve selection, organization, and interpretation.

IV. Frame of Reference

A. External and internal influences of perception constitute a person's frame of reference.

B. Major reference points influence behavior and perception more heavily.

C. Communication must succeed within constantly changing frames of reference.

V. Interpretation of Perceptions

A. Adaptation level refers to perceptions based on comparison with other similar but different stimuli. (A baseball player will swing two bats so the one actually used feels lighter.)

B. Stereotyping involves the assignment of characteristics to a whole group based on beliefs about that group.

VI. We Perceive What We Need

A. Individual needs alter the way we perceive information and events.

B. We interpret data according to our expectations and use this information to predict future responses.

C. Such feedback can help us develop more effective communication.

VII. Differing Perceptions of Managers and Employees

A. Incorrect managerial perceptions lead to ineffectiveness.

B. Studies indicate that managers and union leaders tend to perceive employee needs incorrectly.

C. Motivation always takes place within the framework of what employees perceive as important.

## KEY TERMS

| | | |
|---|---|---|
| Perception | Expectations | Closure |
| Perceptual process | Frequency | Frame of reference |
| Selective exposure | Perceptual organization | Adaptation level |
| Selective awareness | Association | Stereotypes |
| Intensity | | |

## DISCUSSION QUESTIONS

1. How do employees usually want to be perceived their first day at work?
2. Describe a personal experience involving incorrect perceptions. What caused the errors?
3. Jumping to conclusions is a form of perception based on inadequate information. Why do people jump to conclusions?

4. How do our perceptions help and hinder problem solving?
5. Based on personal experiences, describe ways in which frames of reference can differ. Give real-life examples.
6. List some conditions to which most people become perceptually adapted (e.g., normal background noises at work or in restaurants or schools).
7. How can stereotypes be changed?
8. Explain why, once formed, perceptions of people or events are difficult to change.

---

## EXERCISE

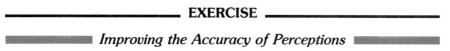 *Improving the Accuracy of Perceptions*

Your management is committed to the position that "if managers do not accurately perceive the relative strength of employee needs, efforts to improve employee productivity will be ineffective." A study done by company executives indicated that managers greatly overestimated the importance that employees attach to some needs and greatly underestimated others. Managers have been directed to bring their perceptions closer to the reality of employee perceptions to develop the basis for increasing managerial effectiveness. As a manager, you are to develop courses of action to improve the accuracy of your perception of your employees' needs.

*Evaluate the following list of proposed actions to improve the accuracy of your perception of employee needs.*
Which actions would you take? Which would you take first?

1. Have your employees fill out a survey of their needs every two months and discuss the results with the employees.

2. Hire a consultant to determine what needs are most important to your employees and report the findings to you.

3. Have a group meeting with your employees once a week to discuss your perceptions of the importance of their needs.

4. Take a course in psychology.

5. Meet with each employee privately once a month to discuss needs.

6. Have your secretary tell you what employees are talking about.

7. One day a month, do the job of one of your employees.

8. Promote two-way communication with employees on a day-to-day basis in the process of helping employees improve their job performance.

9. Put up a suggestion box for employees to inform you of their needs and desires related to their jobs.

10. Select an employee to keep you informed of the strength of employee needs so you can improve the accuracy of your perception of their needs.

―――――――――――――― **TWO POINTS OF VIEW** ――――――――――――――

▬▬▬▬▬▬▬▬▬▬▬▬ *"Performance"* ▬▬▬▬▬▬▬▬▬▬▬▬

*What would you do if you were the supervisor?*

You supervise the purchasing department on a military installation. The five employees you supervise are all college graduates with degrees in scientific fields. They are experts in evaluating purchases of scientific and technical equipment and services.

Ann Cord is a specialist in the purchase of electronic equipment and has worked for you for three years. She has a bachelor's degree in electrical engineering and actively continued her education by taking graduate courses and attending professional training programs. Her work is outstanding, and she is highly respected by everyone who works with her. She is cooperative and always willing to work extra hours when it is necessary to meet deadlines in equipment evaluation.

You rated Ann outstanding on the annual performance evaluation and justified the high evaluation by citing specific accomplishments where she had been exceptionally productive. When the manager of support services reviewed Ann's evaluation, he called you in and said it was definitely too high. He believed that Ann could not be considered outstanding because she did not participate in the "official" social activities. She had not attended the reception held by the installation commander for employees, she did not come to the employee picnic, and she had avoided other social activities.

The manager of support services made it clear that you have the right to refuse to change the evaluation but that he would consider it a major error in judgment if you did not lower the evaluation.

*What would you do if you were the manager of support services?*

You have been the manager of support services for a military installation for over ten years. You report directly to the installation commander and are responsible for all civilian employees who support the military units. The support services has gained the respect and cooperation of the military commanders, and you are proud of the people who work for you.

A difficult situation that has arisen lately involves the performance evaluation of Ann Cord, an engineer who is a specialist in the purchase of electronic equipment. Ann's supervisor has rated her outstanding on the annual performance evaluation. You know that the installation commander will strongly oppose the high evaluation because Ann does not participate in the social activities for civilian employees. Based on Ann's job performance, the outstanding evaluation is justified and you would like to support it. The reality is, the commander believes that if employees do not participate in social activities, it has a negative impact on morale. The commander believes that high morale is absolutely necessary for there to be high performance in support of the military mission of the installation.

You believe that Ann's supervisor does an excellent job of getting high performance from the people in the purchasing department. You wish he were better able to perceive the realities that exist in the organization. You have considered having a meeting with both Ann and her supervisor to explain the situation, but you know that they might not understand the problem and might conclude that you don't appreciate their work performance. You have also considered taking a "hard line" with the installation commander in support of an outstanding evaluation for Ann, but this position might negatively affect the working relations with the military commanders.

## ENDNOTES

1. Steve Altman, Enzo R. Valenzi, and Richard M. Hodgetts, *Organizational Behavior: Theory and Process* (New York: Academic Press, 1985), p. 85.
2. Harold J. Leavitt, *Managerial Psychology*, 2d ed. (Chicago: University of Chicago Press, 1964), p. 35.
3. Robert A. Baron, *Behavior in Organizations: Understanding and Managing the Human Side of Work*, 2d ed. (Boston: Allyn & Bacon, 1986), p. 106.
4. Joseph A. Banik, "The Marketing Approach to Communicating with Employees," *Personnel Journal* (October 1985): 67.
5. Wendell L. French, Fremont E. Kast, and James E. Rosenzweig, *Understanding Human Behavior in Organizations* (New York: Harper & Row, 1985), p. 148.
6. Fred Luthans, *Organizational Behavior*, 4th ed. (New York: McGraw-Hill, 1985), p. 155.
7. Henry L. Tosi, John R. Rizzo, and Stephen J. Carroll, *Managing Organizational Behavior* (Marshfield, Mass.: Pitman, 1986), p. 149.
8. Phillip L. Hunsaker and Curtis W. Cook, *Managing Organizational Behavior* (Reading, Mass.: Addison-Wesley, 1986), p. 81.
9. Don Hellriegel, John W. Slocum, and Richard W. Woodman, *Organizational Behavior*, 4th ed. (St. Paul: West, 1986), p. 89.
10. R. L. Kahn, "Human Reactions on the Shop Floor," in *Human Relations and Modern Management*, ed. E. M. Hugh-Jones (Chicago: Quadrangle Books, 1959).
11. D. C. Dearborn and H. A. Simon, "Selective Perception: A Note on Departmental Identification of Executives," *Sociometry* 21 (1958): 142.
12. Paul Hersey and Kenneth H. Blanchard, *Management of Organizational Behavior*, 2d ed. (Englewood Cliffs, N.J.: Prentice-Hall, 1972), pp. 38–40.
13. Ury M. Gluskinos and Bruce J. Kestlemen, "Management and Labor Leaders' Perception of Worker Needs as Compared with Self-Reported Needs," *Personnel Psychology* (Summer 1971): 239–46.
14. Rensis Likert, "A Motivational Approach to the Modified Theory of Organization and Management," in *Modern Organization Theory*, ed. Mason Haire (New York: Wiley, 1959), p. 161. For additional examples of perceptual differences, see John Senger, "Seeing Eye to Eye: Practical Problems of Perception," *Personnel Journal* (October 1974): 744–51.

# The Process of Communication

_____ *Learning Objectives* _____

After reading this chapter, you should be able to do the following:

1. Discuss the importance of communication in human relations
2. Describe basic models of communication
3. Explain how language usage can determine the effectiveness of communication
4. Identify barriers to effective communication
5. Describe what an individual can do to be a more effective listener
6. Explain how nonverbal communication affects human relations in organizations
7. List the major nonverbal dimensions of communication

# Chapter Topics

- The importance of communication
- Models of communication
- Language and meaning
- Barriers to effective communication
- Effective listening
- Guides for listening improvement
- Nonverbal communication

# Preview

Human beings interact with each other through the process of communication. Although understanding and being understood are basic activities, the complexities of communication are still not fully understood. In management-employee relations, no single behavior is as important as the process of communication. In this chapter, we examine some of the more important aspects of communication in the work place.

A manager must communicate effectively to achieve personal success in an organization. Managers are judged by their ability to communicate with superiors, subordinates, and others at their own level in the organization. Promotions and job assignments are affected by management's evaluation of individual abilities to communicate. Much of the needed satisfaction that individuals achieve in organizations is through communicating with others. Do not be deceived. Communicating, a seemingly simple task, is one of the most difficult things we do. Yet we spend 85 percent of our day doing it.[1]

The greatest enemy of communication is the illusion of it.

W. H. Whyte, Jr.

## SELF–ASSESSMENT

Like other areas of human relations, many misconceptions surround communications in organizations. For the following statements concerning communications, choose the response that best fits your communications beliefs, based on
your experience and knowledge. Each statement or question has a range of
possible responses.  A scale of 1 to 6 between two words with different meanings allows you to mark either the word that is considered correct or a place
between the two words that represents some agreement and some disagreement. Selection of a high number such as 5 or 6 may be either correct or
incorrect, just as selection of lower numbers may be correct or incorrect. Some
responses may be partly correct and partly incorrect.

   Answers based on research by behavorial scientists, with a short explanation
of why the response was considered correct, may be found on page 128.

1. What percentage of all business communications fail to achieve their intended purpose?

   20...30...40...50...60...70

2. Which of the following best describes transmitted communication?

   meanings 1...2...3...4...5...6 messages

3. When communication conflicts with personal beliefs, people tend to:

   seek more information 1...2...3...4...5...6 avoid conflicting<br>information

4. What percentage (or less) of what they see and hear do most people retain?

   15...20...25...30...55...75

5. Interpretation of the meaning of a message is ultimately determined by the:

   sender 1...2...3...4...5...6 receiver

6. Messages are usually transmitted by:

   many channels 1...2...3...4...5...6 a single channel

7. In communications, we must keep in mind that meanings are in:

   words 1...2...3...4...5...6 people

8. Good listening habits are something that people:

   are endowed with at 1...2...3...4...5...6 must learn<br>birth

**9.** Nonverbal behavior is usually learned by:

imitation $1\ldots2\ldots3\ldots4\ldots5\ldots6$ instinctive reactions

**10.** Studies indicate that body language is:

probably the same for $1\ldots2\ldots3\ldots4\ldots5\ldots6$ affected by
all people                                          individual
                                                    differences

## THE IMPORTANCE OF COMMUNICATION

Management must communicate to gain understanding, to motivate, and to obtain cooperation from employees. Every aspect of management is related in some way to the process of communication. **Communication** is the vehicle through which human abilities and physical resources are combined to produce outputs and attain objectives. A large part of a manager's time is spent in some form of communication. Research studies indicate that managers spend from 57 to 89 percent of their time just communicating orally.[2]

Although we can send messages around the world and to astronauts on the moon, management and labor often have difficulty communicating with each other across a table. Our technical ability to transmit messages is highly developed, but person-to-person communication is often ineffective.

### The Difference One Word Made

Achievements often depend on the use of symbols. What difference can words make? What difference can one word make?

An interpretation of the Japanese word *mokusatsu* destroyed thousands of lives and changed millions more. The word has two commonly used meanings: (1) to ignore and (2) to refrain from comment. In July 1945, the Japanese emperor was ready to end the war and had the power to do so. The members of the Japanese cabinet were prepared to concede to the Allies' ultimatum but wanted more time to discuss the terms. A press release was issued announcing a policy of *mokusatsu*, with the no-comment implication. But, through a choice in translation, it was transmitted on the foreign wires with the "ignore" implication. To recall the release would have resulted in an apparently unthinkable loss of face. Had the meaning the Japanese government intended been interpreted correctly, the cabinet might have backed the emperor's decision to surrender. What difference did it make? There probably would have been no atomic bombs dropped on Hiroshima and Nagasaki, no Russian armies in Manchuria, and maybe no Korean War to follow. One word . . . and tens of thousands of lives.[3]

We are all surrounded by more messages than we can possibly pay attention to, much less interpret. The first obstacle any message must overcome is to be selected from all the messages competing for the receiver's attention. Once selected for interpretation, the message content may be accepted or rejected. Acceptance depends on the receiver's interpretation and how the message fits with his or her values and beliefs. Part of the process of acceptance may be rational; part, emotional; and part, below the level of conscious thought.

Opinion Research Corporation surveyed approximately 250,000 employees in 2,000 different companies and found that communication is one of the biggest problems in corporations.[4]

> The most important thing I learned in school was how to communicate.
>
> Lee Iacocca, *Iacocca* (New York: Bantam Books, 1985), p. 15

## MODELS OF COMMUNICATION

No single model of human communication takes into account all the elements that may be involved in a specific situation. Communication models are not as complex as the communication situations they attempt to predict. All models of communication include at least three basic elements: a **source**, a **message**, and a **receiver**. The source may be an individual or a group. The message may be in the form of ink on paper, sound waves, a gesture, or any other signal capable of being interpreted. The receiver or destination may be an individual or group.

The complex process of communication can be reduced to a fairly simple model. The model in Figure 5.1 presents the major elements in the communication process.

*Message Transmission*   The individual desiring to send information starts with some concept or idea that is in his or her mind. The individual decides to share the information with someone else. The information must be *encoded*, or put in a form that makes transmission possible. This can involve words, symbols, sounds, or expressions that can be transmitted. Transmission may involve face-to-face conversations, written messages, drawings, the telephone, or

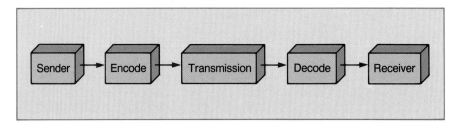

**Figure 5.1   Basic communication model.**

other methods of getting information to a receiver. The message is received (through the senses of hearing, sight, and so on), and the receiver *decodes* the message. The receiver interprets the decoded message and assigns meaning to its symbols. Figure 5.2 shows a difference in sender and receiver interpretation of a message.

For communication to be effective, both the source *and* the receiver must understand the code system being used. The source can encode and the receiver can decode only according to the experience each has had. The source and the receiver must have had similar experiences for communication to be effective. By using information about the receiver's past experience, the source can encode the message so it relates to that experience.

Shared knowledge of the code does not necessarily mean that messages will produce the desired responses. The message is more than the code system. When a painter applies oils to canvas according to rules of perspective, we "see" a clear lake nestled among the mountains. The lake is in neither the oil paints nor the rules governing their application to the canvas. The effect results from the combination of the message elements.

*We can draw some conclusions from this basic approach to communication:*

1. If the source doesn't have adequate or accurate information, the message generated has little chance of producing desired responses.

2. The receiver, not the source, determines whether the message is encoded fully, accurately, and effectively.

3. The attitudes, experiences, and motivations of the receiver determine whether the message is decoded in a way that corresponds to the source's intent.

**Figure 5.2**   Both sender and receiver must share the same code.

*Encoding and Decoding*    Each person in a communication situation both encodes and decodes. **Encoding** is the process by which an individual's ideas are converted into symbols that make up a message. To put ideas into words is encoding. **Decoding** is the process of interpreting symbols contained in a message by determining what the symbols refer to.

Individuals can receive and transmit information simultaneously. Either the sender or the receiver in a human communication system can be represented in the way shown in Figure 5.3.

We are constantly decoding information from our environment, interpreting this information, and encoding information. As information passes *through* us, it is changed by our interpretations, and it changes us. The inputs always affect the outputs in some way.

In a conversation between two people, there is constant communication. The process involves feedback indicating how our messages are being interpreted. This process is shown in Figure 5.4.

*Communication Channels*    An important element in the communication process is the **channel**. In face-to-face communication, many people consider only the voice transmission channel. But other channels, such as facial expressions, posture, gestures, and intonation patterns, are often more important. These channels gain importance as a result of two things: (1) increased experience with a particular person and (2) increased sensitivity to nonverbal communication.

Messages are seldom transmitted by means of a single channel. In a speech communication situation, sound may be the primary channel. Others are the expressions on the speaker's face, his or her gestures, the lighting in the room, the feel of the seats, and the information communicated by the nature of the audience.

When we communicate, we are trying to satisfy our felt needs (Figure 5.5). Communication is one of the tools available to us to affect behavior and achieve

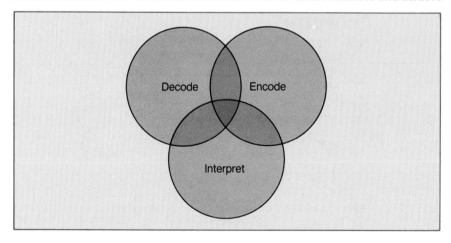

**Figure 5.3**  Encoding, decoding, interpreting process.

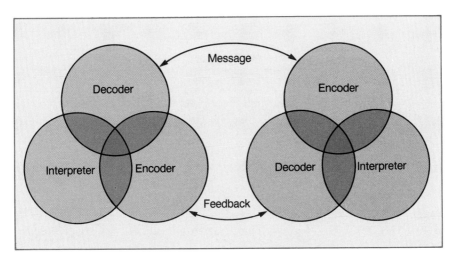

**Figure 5.4**   The message/feedback process in communication.

objectives. We use communication to inform, to interpret, and to motivate. Regardless of the specific form of behavior we want from a receiver, we are basically trying to obtain a behavioral response that will satisfy our felt needs. Communication is most effective when the receiver knows what we mean and reacts in the way we desire.

## LANGUAGE AND MEANING

*Assumption:* Meanings are in words.

   *Reality:* Meanings are in people (see Figure 5.6). Without people, there are no meanings.

**Figure 5.5**   Communication is a way of satisfying needs.

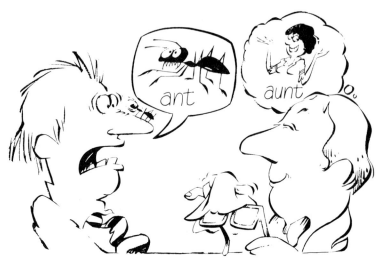

**Figure 5.6**   Only people have meanings.

*Assumption:* Because there is a word, the thing the word represents must exist.

*Reality:* There can be words that do not represent reality. This assumption leads to confusing words with things. It can also result in the creation of verbal monsters. The bogeyman created by a child or the nonexistent irate customer can become verbal monsters. The imagined threat of losing one's job can become a verbal monster.

*Assumption:* Communication consists of the transmission of meanings.

*Reality:* We cannot transmit meanings—only messages. Meanings are in the mind of the message receiver.

These assumptions give us a starting place in dealing with symbolic processes.

### Is the Word the Thing?

Physical things have both a functional value and a **symbolic value.** Often, the symbolic value is what leads us to accept or reject a specific object. Food has functional value, for example, and how and with whom we dine can be symbolic. Special foods may symbolize festivals and special occasions. Clothes are selected not only for functional values but also for symbolic values reflecting taste, wealth, or social position. When buying a house, your choice is not based totally on functional value, or an "economic good buy." You also take into account the symbolic value of a "good address."

Language is a highly developed and complex system. Most of the desirable and undesirable qualities of language result from that characteristic. No necessary connection exists between the language symbol and what it symbolizes. We can say that something is beautiful when we have actually judged it ugly. Our feelings are expressed through language, and in turn, feelings are generated by the language we use. We often begin to feel about the word as we have felt about the object the word represents. When we do this, we treat the symbol as if it were the thing symbolized.

Is it more important to have the symbol than the thing it stands for? For some students and teachers, the symbol of learning (the grade) is more important than learning itself.

Managers function in a verbal and symbolic environment. They are bombarded with communications from employees, other managers, salespeople, customers, and so forth. Through the use of words and other symbolic arrays, managers create the symbolic world they live in.

## Fact, Fiction, or Inference?

Can *all* statements be judged true or false? Can *any* statement be judged true or false? Are there some statements that we know are false by the nature of the statements? Language is a powerful tool for analyzing many dimensions of reality. Though words won't keep you dry in a rainstorm, and wordless beavers build dams, a modern jet aircraft could not have been conceived or manufactured without the use of symbols and language.

"Reasoning" from observation is called *inference making*, and we are continually making inferences. Most of the statements we make are not reports of observations, but **inferences**. To make no inferences is impossible, yet we often treat our statements as if they were observations of absolute accuracy. We may observe an individual *doing* something—throwing a book, pounding on a desk, or kicking a chair. But we may not observe that the individual is angry. An individual's state of mind can only be inferred.

We make inferences quickly and automatically. A: "Look at that drunk." B: "Did you see a drunk?" A: "Well, I saw a man in messy clothes weaving down the street." B: "Well, he looked (I inferred) drunk."

The question is not whether we make inferences, but whether we are aware of the nature of the inferences we make. All situations contain a degree of uncertainty about the nature of what we experience or observe. Often we cannot predict with complete accuracy what will happen next.

Managers responsible for policy decisions and program implementation do not always have all the factual evidence they would like to have to make decisions. They must often deal with inferences selectively passed along to them. Not surprisingly, the inferences are sometimes treated as factual evidence. This practice may be a highly effective technique for gaining power, because making organizational decisions in the face of uncertainty demands assurance.

*Observations*    Observational statements are referred to as "denotative." This implies that we think what we have said is highly representative of some event or thing. When we use language to describe reality, we are dealing with a symbol-to-object *relationship*. Problems occur when we forget that meaning is a relationship between an individual and reality. Meaning is not a characteristic of

Let's take a look at a series of statements:

*To use words properly, you must know their meanings.* Right or wrong? Wrong, of course. To use words properly, you must be able to estimate the approximate meaning that will be elicited in the receiver. The accuracy of communication is the degree of similarity between what the source wants the receiver to think and what the receiver thinks.

*The purpose of writing is to transmit meaning.* Right or wrong? Wrong. The purpose of writing is to transmit symbols and messages that we hope will elicit or evoke meaning.

*I hear a noise that sounds like thunder; that means rain soon.* That means nothing soon. The receiver implies and creates meaning from the sounds reaching him or her. Interpretation of messages provides additional inputs for an individual. Communication is not an action/reaction system, but a feedback system in which we can adapt and change meanings according to the situation.

an object. We use words that have clear references for us but not necessarily for our receivers.

How can we clarify reports? How can we be "accurate"? Point to the object, or if you can't point, approximate pointing by using models or pictures of objects. We often overlook this simple approach to clarifying meaning. Remember that completely denotative definitions require the presence of the symbol *and* the object.

When we fail to recognize that we have made an inference, we take an uncalculated risk. We behave, however, as if we were not taking a risk at all. All inference situations involve some uncertainty. When we fail to recognize this uncertainty, we do not bother to evaluate the probabilities of the outcome. This means we can be caught off guard when unexpected consequences occur.

Communication involves the transmission of symbols and messages from source to receiver. Meanings are attached to the symbols by the receiver. We do not transfer meaning as we would transfer milk from a pitcher to a glass (see Figure 5.7).

> A sender cannot really transfer meanings; rather, the mind of the receiver *creates* meanings. The sender's task is to use symbols that trigger responses that accurately create meanings similar to the senders.[5]

## BARRIERS TO EFFECTIVE COMMUNICATION

We do not react to a message in isolation; we react to the relationship created by the situation, the message symbol, and the individual. Focus on the sender's

**Figure 5.7**   We do not transfer meaning—only messages.

meaning for the word, not on the word itself. Our meaning for an object does not include all the characteristics of the object but only selected characteristics. In developing and changing meaning, we consider features of the situation: our expectations and previous experiences, our motives and desires.

## *Process of Abstracting*

Experiences cannot be communicated directly. A headache or an emotion, whether joy or sorrow, cannot be directly transferred to a receiver. We use language to represent experiences and feelings.

Communication involves the process of **abstracting**. When we report on an observed event, we abstract by reporting only the characteristics that seem valuable to us. These are often more a product of inference than of observation. We observe only partially. As we attempt to convert observations into language, we further abstract by using general rather than specific terms.

Using language involves leaving out details. We cannot communicate *every* detail of any given event. We are forced by the limitations of observation to leave out those details we cannot observe. If we tried to *completely* describe a simple object, such as a table, we would fill volumes and still not succeed. Seeing the limitations of language is easy. We may become frustrated when we attempt to describe in detail a complicated process because of our inability to complete the description.

In language, a movement from lower to higher levels of abstraction occurs. A simple example of choosing a level of abstraction would be moving from a term such as *transportation* to the more specific term *motorcar* to an even more specific term, *automobile*, and continuing to *four-door sedan* and a description of make, color, year, accessories, and so on. As we move from the abstract to the more specific, we increase the probability of obtaining the desired response from the receiver.

Proceeding from lower to higher levels of abstraction and back again can occur continuously. Varying levels of abstraction are most effective when the variation is adjusted to the needs of the receiver. We attempt to increase our effectiveness by determining what level of abstraction has the highest probability of obtaining the desired response.

Abstracting may result in generalizations with weak connections to reality. We may become lazy in our usage and depend heavily on highly abstract and general terms, stereotypes, labels, and pigeonholing. When operating at a high level of abstraction, we may use terms that lump dissimilar characteristics into one highly abstract group. We must generalize, but we should not be surprised when a generalization does not produce the desired response from the receiver.

### Confusing Symbols with Realities

A communication barrier involves confusing **symbols** with things or processes. The inability to distinguish between the word and the thing it stands for makes it difficult to compare the communication of an individual with the realities of the physical world. An example of this tendency is the social taboo attached to the use of some obscene and sacred words. The words are regarded as the objects for which they stand. It is easy to overlook that a word is but a symbol, not the thing for which it stands.

Words may be considered as pointers, indicators, or forms of representation intended to correspond to anything whatsoever that may exist or be experienced. To oversimplify, we can say there is a world of words and a world of not-words. The universe of discourse is not the universe of direct experience. A word is not a complete representation—if it were, it would not be a word but a nonverbal fact. Words can be manipulated independently of any nonverbal event or fact. No *inner* necessity governs the use of words in their relationship to things, feelings, and circumstances. We can use language to distort, lie, write fiction, or tell fables. Words can be used according to the whim of the user. Language cannot force a user to adhere to actual facts. Every receiver of messages should attempt to determine whether the verbal statements correspond to realities.

Awareness of the different characteristics of symbols and what they stand for should lead to the understanding that messages should be neither blindly rejected nor blindly accepted. We should be conscious of the possibility of structural dissimilarity between words and things.

### Experience and Expectations

The way in which people live influences their manner of thinking, feeling, and acting. People have experiences that result in a set of expectations concerning

After a tour of a company's newly acquired department store, three corporate managers sat down to discuss needed improvements. Their discussion quickly became an argument over each manager's perception of the "real" problems in the store. The marketing manager saw major problems in the display of merchandise and the way salespeople were serving customers. The finance manager saw major problems in the way sales slips were completed and the use of the cash register. The maintenance manager saw major problems in the operation of the escalator and the fire protection system. It seemed as if they were talking about different department stores. The communication problem in this situation resulted from the selected perception of the managers.[6]

communication situations. These experiences and expectations give meaning to our language. One basis for effective communication is the similar experiences and expectations people attach to similar language symbols. The farmer whose experiences and expectations differ from those of the factory worker, the doctor, or the banker finds it as hard to understand them as they do to understand the farmer.

Our expectations in a specific situation affect our interpretations of messages. For example, when individuals are exposed to ambiguous messages or words (e.g., *chack*) they respond according to their expectations. When expecting the name of an animal, the interpretation is *chick*. When expecting a term related to money and banking, the interpretation is *check*.

### Attitudes and Values

People tend to interpret messages so they are consistent with their attitudes and values. When forced to deal with individuals and events beyond individual experience, people tend to fill in the gaps according to their attitudes. Thus, from a limited knowledge of Germans, a person can build a complete description of them.

The process of interpreting information so that it is consistent with existing attitudes and values often characterizes our thinking. In the absence of *any* relevant experiences, our attitudes and values may be the basis for our judgments. Attitudes and values may have an emotional basis, which makes them resistant to fact and logic. Emotionally loaded attitudes often result in stereotypes that are extremely difficult to change.

Many studies have shown that attitudes are not necessarily abstractions from personal experience. They are often learned from others.

Attitudes and values serve personal needs. In some cases the content of the attitude is wish fulfillment. Studies have shown that anti-Semitic attitudes are strongest among people dissatisfied with their own achievements. These studies argue against the notion that all attitudes are rationally founded. Attitudes are seldom revised under the impact of new factual evidence if they are providing need satisfaction for the individual. The attitude will not be modified until the individual finds another way of satisfying the need.

## Individual Differences

Overcoming psychological barriers to communication would be easier if there were no individual differences—if we all had common abilities, experiences, and environments. Because we are different in so many ways, however, we distort the intended meaning of messages according to our predispositions. Individual psychological differences are great barriers to communication (see Figure 5.8). Our communication is affected by our needs and interests.

## EFFECTIVE LISTENING

Since we spend such a large percentage of our time listening, we should be concerned about improving our listening ability. Successful communication

**Figure 5.8**  When people have different experiences, they develop different meanings.

depends as much on the ability to receive messages as it does on the ability to send messages. When a person speaks and no one listens, obviously no communication takes place.

## How Well Do We Listen?

Most people do not listen very well. Research indicates that an average individual retains about 50 percent of the main content of a ten-minute speech immediately after listening to it. After forty-eight hours, the retention drops to about 25 percent of the original content.[7] A number of other studies have found basically the same results. A conservative estimate is that most people retain 25 percent or less of what they hear. Everyone has observed situations in which a communication failure occurred because of poor listening.

As individuals go about their daily activities, they are often preoccupied with their own problems, which makes it difficult to listen effectively. Better listening means paying attention to what is said. A total focus on one's own concerns results in psychological deafness.

The lack of good listening is a major communication problem in organizations. If individuals would listen attentively, misunderstandings and conflicts could be drastically reduced.

No communication skill has been more neglected in the education system than listening behavior. Most individuals are continually taught the skills of reading, writing, and speaking throughout the educational process. Rarely are individuals taught how to listen effectively. Listening that results in accurate comprehension requires concentration and hard work. There are no easy approaches or shortcuts to improving listening.

## Barriers to Effective Listening

Individuals are not born with good listening habits. Like all other communication skills, effective listening must be learned. Bad habits must be eliminated, and more effective listening behaviors must be developed. The following bad habits form barriers to effective listening.

*Daydreaming or Creative Distractions*   Poor listeners often lose the speaker's words by concentrating on their own train of thought. Daydreaming may involve thinking about pleasant past experiences or anticipating some desirable future event. A student may replay last night's party rather than listen to a lecture in class. An employee may visualize a forthcoming fishing trip rather than listen during a meeting on safety procedures. Individuals can also create distractions by worrying about problems. A student may fail to listen to the 8:00 class because he or she is worrying about a test in the 10:00 class. An employee may worry about overdue bills rather than listen to the manager's instructions.

*Mentally Arguing with the Speaker*   Instead of listening to what someone is saying, the poor listener often begins to disagree mentally and starts planning

> ## Sperry Corporation Promotes the Importance of Listening Skills
>
> The following quote from a Sperry Corporation advertisement in *Business Week* illustrates the importance that businesses place on effective listening:
>
> "A listener loose in a world of talkers has one unbeatable edge: the flow of new ideas through his ears to his mind never stops.
>
> It has been said there's at least one thing to learn from everyone one meets. Provided one bothers to listen.
>
> Unfortunately for most people, no one ever bothered to teach us how.
>
> Which is why listening is available to Sperry employees, worldwide.
>
> Helping our people become better listeners helps make us a better corporation.
>
> For one thing, it eliminates the enormous costs of simple listening errors.
>
> But more than that, it's making our employees better thinkers. Better problem solvers. And ultimately more open to the original and unexpected." [8]

a rebuttal. Mentally arguing with the speaker often involves making assumptions about what is going to be said. Developing arguments before comprehending the total message usually leads to misunderstanding and conflict. Individuals may develop arguments because their emotions have reduced their objectivity. Conclusions reached before a speaker is finished are often inaccurate.

If a speaker uses emotionally loaded terms, the poor listener may mentally argue with the use of the terms. The poor listener may attempt to censor the message rather than try to understand it. The listener may try to rebut or discredit the speaker who uses loaded terms such as *pig* for police officer or *broad* for woman. Effective listening takes place when the speaker is allowed to finish before evaluations and judgments are made.

***Desire to Talk***    Frequently, individuals are poor listeners because they are preoccupied with talking. They may use "listening time" to rehearse what they are going to say when it is their turn to talk and fail to hear what the speaker is saying. Many individuals feel more active, more useful, and more important when talking. They must have a strong desire to listen if they are to resist the need to talk.

***Indifference and Lack of Interest in Message Content***    Those who assume that a message is going to be dull and boring will be poor listeners. Once a listener becomes indifferent to the message, a speaker can do little to recapture attention. When viewed objectively, identifying a subject that is totally uninteresting is difficult. If the listener concentrates on the message, there is usually information that is meaningful and useful. A good listener will look for useful information in any message. Good listeners expose themselves to messages that broaden their interests and develop their abilities. Deciding that a message is going to be of no value means that listening stops before it begins.

*Negative Reactions to the Speaker's Appearance or Delivery*    You cannot listen effectively if you are mentally responding to the speaker's dress, voice qualities, or mannerisms. Listeners may fail to comprehend important and useful information if they react negatively to the characteristics of the speaker. It is often easy to focus on a mannerism to the point that the message content is secondary to the style of delivery. To the effective listener, the message content is much more important than characteristics of the speaker.

## GUIDES FOR LISTENING IMPROVEMENT

To improve listening requires a commitment to communication. The following are practical guides for more effective listening. They do not provide an easy way to better listening—you will have to work at improving your skills.

1. Stop talking. You can't listen while you are talking.
2. Empathize with the speaker. Try to put yourself in the speaker's place. Try to determine how the speaker feels about the message. Try to understand the speaker's point of view, taking into account his or her attitudes, values, and background.
3. Ask questions. This shows that you are interested, and it encourages the speaker. Ask questions to further your understanding, not to embarrass or show up the speaker.
4. Concentrate on what the speaker is saying. Actively focus your attention on concepts, ideas, attitudes, and feelings related to the message.
5. Show the speaker that you want to listen. Look and act interested. Listen to understand rather than to argue. Try to put the speaker at ease. Don't be antagonistic; the speaker may then conceal his or her true ideas, attitudes, and feelings. Try to evaluate the effect you are having on the speaker.
6. Control your emotions and your temper. Anger usually leads to distortion and misinterpretation. Try to put worries, fears, and problems aside; they interfere with good listening. Try not to get emotional about what is said.
7. Get rid of distractions. Put down papers, pencils, and other objects that may distract you. If you are in an office, shut the door. Eliminate as many outside distractions as you can.
8. Look for areas of agreement. Mentally developing arguments sets up a barrier to understanding. Listen for areas of common interest and

---

## Open-Door Policy at COBE Laboratories, Inc.  ━━━━━━━

COBE Laboratories, a Colorado manufacturer of medical therapeutic systems, has found a way to encourage greater employee participation and involve more workers and managers in the decision-making process.

COBE's open-door policy promotes the discussion of problems, criticisms, and suggestions as they arise. If an employee feels dissatisfied with a supervisor's response in a particular case, the employee has a direct line to the next higher level of management. The open-door policy makes it possible to bypass the normal chain of command; if necessary, employees can even take their concerns directly to the president of the company.

Generally, COBE encourages employees to solve problems with their immediate supervisors. Yet going to a higher level of management does not necessarily mean that the immediate supervisor cannot handle the problem. The problem or suggestion may simply require the knowledge and experience of more people. For those supervisors threatened by the open-door policy, management counsels them to listen to and ask for employees' opinions more often. All supervisors meet with top-level management every two months to discuss concerns in their areas.

COBE has found that its open-door policy has improved the quality of input on company problems and facilitated better decision making.[9]

---

agreement. A speaker may be "turned off" if he or she perceives disagreement.

9. Avoid jumping to conclusions and making evaluations. Try to listen nonevaluatively, without making judgments about what is being said at the time. Making evaluations and drawing conclusions usually results in getting ahead of the speaker and "hearing" things that are not said. Understanding what the speaker is saying is difficult if you concentrate on what you think is going to be said. Listen to understand the conclusions and evaluations that the speaker is making.

10. Listen for the main points. Concentrate on the speaker's main ideas and the material used to support them. Sometimes we hear only the illustrative material, the examples, stories, and statistics. It is easy to miss the main points if we listen for minor details. Don't allow your reactions to distract you from the key concepts.

To become better listeners, individuals must be genuinely interested in what others have to say and less preoccupied with themselves.

## NONVERBAL COMMUNICATION

One of the most important keys to understanding communication is to realize that much of it is never put into words. A nonverbal message can be transmitted by a nod of the head, a frown, an enthusiastic tone of voice, leaving one's office door open or closed, or arriving late for an appointment.[10]

Much of the communication that affects people is never verbalized. People communicate by the way they look at another person or by the gestures they make. A **nonverbal message** can be transmitted by a handshake, a pat on the back, a smile, a frown, or any observable behavior. The most important expressions of emotional states are usually communicated on the nonverbal level.

Managers who tell employees that they are interested in their suggestions but ignore their ideas and information are communicating a lack of interest. The statement "Actions speak louder than words" is especially true for communication in organizations, as shown in Figure 5.9. Employees are influenced more by managers' actions than by their words. "There are essentially two dimensions to interpersonal communication—the verbal and the nonverbal—and they can sometimes contradict. . . . When a contradiction occurs, other people will almost always believe the nonverbal message." [11]

Individuals often spend a great deal of time and thought preparing verbal messages. Usually assumed is that writing or speaking effectively requires conscious thought and real work, learning how to spell, to write sentences, to read, and to make speeches. Nonverbal communication behaviors, on the other hand, are usually learned by imitation. As a result, people tend to be less aware of the nonverbal messages they transmit and receive. This lack of awareness can lead to problems in communication. Silence is an example of a type of nonverbal communication that is often not consciously considered. Employees may believe that their efforts are unappreciated if managers fail to compliment them on outstanding work.

Five major nonverbal dimensions that directly affect communication are (1) kinesics, or body language; (2) proxemics, or spatial relations; (3) chronemics, or the use of time; (4) paralanguage, or the use of the voice; and (5) artifacts, or object language.

### *Body Language (Kinesics)*

**Kinesics** is the study of body movements and the visual aspects of behavior. Included in the study of kinesics are the effects of posture, facial expressions, movement, and gestures. Body language can support and supplement verbal communication. Body language can also be used to attempt to hide attitudes and feelings. You have probably told someone that you liked his new clothes when you really didn't like them. To support your verbal statement of "liking," you may have attempted to look pleased by smiling and nodding with approval.

Body language also contradicts verbal statements when an individual says, "I am interested in what you have to say" while looking out the window, tapping her fingers on the desk, and continually glancing at the clock. The more the

**Figure 5.9**    Actions speak louder than words.

individual fidgets, the stronger the nonverbal message, "I am not interested and want to leave."

Because of individual differences, it is easy to misinterpret body language. An individual who is yawning could be anxious, fatigued, or bored. Judgments about the meaning of body movements must be made carefully. Although facial expressions provide information about emotional states, distinguishing between emotions such as anger, grief, and despair is difficult.

The study of kinesics has not been extensive enough to determine direct relationships between specific body movements and meaning. The following are some of the preliminary conclusions that may help increase awareness of body language:

* Orienting the body or crossing the legs toward another person may indicate a desire to include the other in communication.

* Leaning forward and facing a person may indicate a favorable attitude toward the individual.

* Turning the shoulders and legs away from a person may indicate dislike.

* As the intensity of an emotional state increases, the individual tends to increase body movements.

* Positioning of the shoulders and legs toward one person and away from another may indicate, "I am with you and against the other person."

* Raising the head and shoulders may indicate assumption of a superior role position or higher status. Lowering the head and shoulders may indicate assumption of an inferior role position or lower status.

* Direct eye contact may indicate attraction and interest. Avoiding eye contact may indicate a rejection or lack of interest.

No single body movement, however, should be considered as an absolute indication of individual's attitudes, feelings, or emotions.

### Spatial Relations (Proxemics)

**Proxemics** is the study of how individuals structure and use space. Important spatial relations include the distances maintained between people during communication and the use of space in houses, offices, cities, and buildings. Individuals learn what is considered to be the appropriate distance to maintain in communication situations. The appropriate distance for communicating with friends may not be the same as the appropriate distance for talking with the boss.

Giving an employee a private office conveys a nonverbal message of that individual's importance to the company. Most employees are concerned about the space in which they work. The amount and type of space in an office, the office location, and the way it is furnished can represent authority, status, position, and protection. Although the amount of space is not an absolute indication of status, it is usually a sign of importance. The location of an office may also function as an indication of importance. Executive offices are usually located on the top floors of a building.

Most people will move physically closer when communicating with individuals they like and will maintain more distance from those they dislike. If someone gets too close (according to the individual's distance standards), the individual will become uncomfortable and probably move away. If the receiver moves too far away, the communicator tends to move toward the receiver to reestablish the desired spatial relationship.

A study of office layout found that most people feel more comfortable in offices where the desks face the wall (referred to as an open arrangement).

People feel uncomfortable when furniture forms a barrier between them and the office occupant.[12]

Individuals usually maintain a greater distance from people with high status. For example, an employee may stand in the doorway of the manager's office to talk, while the manager's boss will walk up to the edge of the desk.

The higher the status of individuals, the more right they usually feel to invade the space of those with lower status. The president of the company can invade the space of managers by barging into their office at any time, but barging into the president's office is not acceptable behavior for the managers. A teacher can invade the space of students by looking over their shoulders as they write an exam. Students cannot return the invasion by looking over the teacher's shoulder while the exams are being graded.

The use of space is a significant aspect of any communication situation.

## Use of Time (Chronemics)

An important but often overlooked element of nonverbal communication is the use of time, or **chronemics**. Time is often viewed as a commodity that can be spent, saved, earned, or wasted. American society is very time conscious, as reflected in our dependence on clocks and time schedules. In business one frequently hears that time is money. Attitudes toward time are communicated by the ways individuals deal with it.

The importance of time in organizational communication can be seen everywhere. We set completion dates for projects, use time clocks, establish specific pay periods, schedule meetings, and negotiate working hours. Specific times are often established for coffee breaks and lunch periods. Completing a project within a specific time period may be a major consideration in an employee's performance evaluation. The employee who is frequently late to work will most likely be communicating disorganization, disinterest, and unreliability to management.

Much of the communication of the use of time involves arrival times. When an individual arrives ahead of time for a meeting, it may communicate interest and respect for the person holding the meeting. To arrive late for a meeting may communicate disinterest and disrespect for the person holding the meeting.

Whether an arrival at a meeting or appointment or party is considered early, on time, or late depends on beliefs about acceptable arrival times. When invited to a cocktail party at 7:00 P.M., the expected arrival time may be 7:30 P.M. or later. An appointment with the boss at 9:00 A.M. may involve an expectation that the employee arrive ten minutes early in case the boss is "running ahead of time." Usually expected is that employees will never arrive late for an appointment with the boss. However, usually acceptable is for the boss to arrive late for an appointment with an employee or to keep an employee waiting. Most organizations develop definite standards to be observed in the use of time. The standards may vary as a result of job function, status in the organization, and the nature of the situation; but failure to observe the standards communicates nonverbal messages that can reduce the individual's chances for success in the organization.

## Use of the Voice (Paralanguage)

**Paralanguage** is concerned with how something is said rather than what is said. The meaning of a sentence can differ significantly depending on which words are stressed. Consider the following variations:

- *How* did he do the job?
- How *did* he do the job?
- How did *he* do the job?
- How did he *do* the job?

By shifting the emphasis, the sentence can convey different meanings. The way the voice is used is an important element in understanding messages. Individuals can "read between the lines" of written messages, and they can "hear between the words" of spoken messages.

Paralanguage can be broken down into the following four major elements: (1) *voice qualities*, which include tone, rhythm, resonance, and tempo; (2) *vocal characteristics*, which include crying, laughing, whispering, sighing, yelling, yawning, and so forth; (3) *vocal irregularities*, which include nonfluencies (em, uh-hum, er, and so on) and silent pauses; and (4) *vocal qualifiers* of intensity (how loud or soft), rate (how fast or slow), and pitch (how high or low). The combination of these elements results in each individual having unique speech patterns.

Most people are quick to make judgments about another's personality based on a combination of paralinguistic characteristics. In some cases the judgments turn out to be accurate; in some cases, inaccurate. The number of times these judgments are accurate or inaccurate does not seem to affect the frequency with which the judgments are made. Some common personality stereotypes based on voice characteristics are as follows:

- Individuals with nasal voices are nagging, whiny, and unpleasant.
- Men with deep, throaty voices are mature, sophisticated, and well adjusted, but women with deep and throaty voices are boring, dull, and ugly.
- Women with high-pitched and breathy voices are feminine, pretty, shallow, and petite. Men with high-pitched and breathy voices are artistic, unrealistic, and unmanly.
- Individuals who speak in a monotone are cold and withdrawn and have little interest in life.

These judgments about personality made from voice characteristics are not generally supported by research evidence. A variety of studies have found mixed results on the accuracy of using voice characteristics to predict personality traits.[13]

Studies of paralanguage have demonstrated that individuals vary in their ability to determine the emotions of a speaker from vocal cues and that individuals also vary in their ability to express their emotions through the use of the voice.[14] Some emotions are much easier to distinguish than others. For example, it may be easy to distinguish between sympathy and hate but difficult to distinguish between anxiety and fear.

The rate or speed with which individuals speak may be an indication of their emotional state. Studies have found that faster rates, short comments, and frequent pauses indicate anger, stress, or fear; slower rates, longer comments, and less frequent pauses indicate grief or depression.[15]

### Object Language (Artifacts)

Object language, or **artifacts**, refers to the communication that results from the display of material things. Some of the objects that frequently influence communication are clothes, furniture, methods of transportation, and architectural arrangements. Individuals attempt to enhance their personal object language by purchasing items such as clothes, lipstick, eyeglasses, hairpieces, and false eyelashes. A person's office furnishings and their arrangement also convey messages about the individual. The arrangement of furniture in a conference room can affect the communication patterns that occur in a meeting. A work

**Figure 5.10**   Actions need to be consistent with words.

environment's architectural style, furnishings, equipment, color, and attractiveness are all important elements in organizational communication.

Physical settings convey information about the kind of activities that are to take place and the kind of behaviors that are acceptable. The restaurant that wants quick turnover has bright lighting, less comfortable chairs, and tables placed closely together. If the desire is to encourage customers to stay longer, the lighting is dim, the colors are subdued, and the furniture is comfortable. The benches in shopping malls are usually hard, encouraging people to circulate among the shops rather than sit. The manager who has hard plastic chairs for visitors may be trying to discourage them from staying too long.

The furnishings in an office can be used to communicate the status of the occupant. A large wooden desk and an executive swivel chair indicate more status than a small metal desk and a straight chair. Carpeting may indicate a status level, and awards and pictures placed on office walls may convey status or prestige. Each object in an office delivers its message about the occupant.

The way furniture is arranged in an office can affect the communication that takes place there. A desk placed between a manager and an employee may be a psychological barrier as well as a physical barrier because it represents authority and power.

The nonverbal communication of a manager's clothing, personal mannerisms, and office all affect the total message that employees receive.

Objects in the environment both communicate and affect other communication processes. The way an individual uses objects tells others a great deal about the user.

The importance of nonverbal communication is stated very specifically by Nancy K. Austin: "If excellence is what you're after, words are not enough. Be prepared to put your money (and time and attention) where your motto is. In other words, you have to *walk the talk*." [16]

## CONCLUSIONS

Our perceptions and interpretations of messages are shaped by our individual needs and desires. The message is not only what you want to say and how you say it; it is also what the other person wants to hear.

It is difficult to communicate with people who do not already agree with the position expressed by a message. We tend to avoid information that conflicts with our own attitudes and beliefs; consequently, people who are not already in favor of the content of a message are difficult to reach. The people who may "need" the message most may be those least likely to hear it.

Knowledge about communication will always be important to anyone who wants to function more effectively in an organization. Communication is the vital link between people that makes it possible for an organization to function. Developing effective communication is never easy, and no cure-alls are available for communication problems. Effective communication requires more than knowing techniques or mastering skills. It must be based on cooperation, trust, and confidence among people.

In recognition of the difficulties involved in gaining understanding, a manager placed the following sign on his desk:

> I know you believe you understood what you think I said, but I am not sure you realize that what you heard is not what I meant.

## SELF-ASSESSMENT DISCUSSION

**1.** (70) Research by Max Ways, a researcher in participative management, indicates that approximately 70 percent of organizational communications fail to achieve their intended effects.

**2.** (6) Messages are transmitted. Their interpretation and meaning are in people.

**3.** (6) Information that challenges beliefs is often rejected and goes unheeded. Most people find changing beliefs, especially those that have been held for a period of time, threatening and emotionally disturbing.

**4.** (25) Research in communication indicates that most people retain no more than 25 percent of messages that are transmitted.

**5.** (6) Ultimately, the receiver determines the meaning of a message. It may be different than that intended by the sender. Meanings, however, are in people, not in words.

**6.** (1) Many channels—from facial expressions, tone of voice, posture, gestures, emphasis on certain points, and eye movements—are used in communication transmittal. Even written material that is typed or handwritten, on formal or informal stationery, personally or impersonally addressed, transmits messages through varied channels.

**7.** (6) Meanings are in people. Words mean only what people translate them to mean. The word *fly*, for instance, like most other words, has several different possible meanings. Depending on the context in which it is used and the person receiving the message, meaning is assigned.

**8.** (6) Effective listening is a skill that must be learned and practiced to perfect. We are not born with good listening skills.

**9.** (1) Most human behavior is probably learned through imitation of others. This includes body language, speech patterns, and other nonverbal communication.

**10.** (6) Studies indicate a great many individual differences in the use of body language. Often, incorrect interpretations of body language are made because of assumptions that fail to consider individual differences.

## *QUICK REVIEW*

    I. The Importance of Communication

        A. All aspects of a manager's job are accomplished through communication.

    B. Our ability to understand others has lagged far behind our technical accomplishments in communication transmission.

    C. The first obstacle in any communication is the process of selection.

II. Models of Communication

    A. Although no communication model is complete, all communications involve a source, a message, and a receiver.

    B. Once coded and sent, a message is beyond control of the sender.

    C. For communication to occur, both the source and the receiver must understand the same code systems.

III. Language and Meaning

    A. Words link together all human activities.

    B. Words are symbols. We tend to confuse symbols with things.

        1. Meanings are in people, not in words.

        2. Because there are words does not mean there are things.

        3. We cannot transmit meanings—only messages.

    C. Physical things have both symbolic and functional values.

    D. Denotative statements are those based on actual observation.

    E. Because we often confuse our observations with inferences and treat inferences as if they were observations, we are led to incorrect conclusions.

IV. Barriers to Effective Communication

    A. We do not react to a message in isolation but to the relationships of situation, message, symbol, and individual.

    B. To encode observations, we abstract parts of them and transmit only our abstractions and inferences.

    C. We must be aware of abstraction and inferences in order to develop effective communication.

    D. Change is always taking place. We have a tendency to freeze our abstractions as if a dynamic, ongoing event is frozen in time.

    E. We must keep in mind that

        1. The word is not the object.

        2. The word does not represent all of the object.

    F. Experiences and expectations often cause us to interpret the world around us in widely differing ways.

    G. People tend to interpret messages in a way consistent with their values and attitudes.

    H. Our tendency to select what we see, hear, and understand is based on our individual psychological differences.

V. Effective Listening
   A. The lack of good listening is a major communication problem in organizations.
   B. Barriers to effective listening include
      1. Daydreaming or creative distractions.
      2. Mentally arguing with the speaker.
      3. Preferring to talk rather than listen.
      4. Indifference or lack of interest in message content.
      5. Negative reactions to the speaker's appearance or delivery.

VI. Guides for Listening Improvement
   A. Stop talking.
   B. Empathize with the speaker.
   C. Ask questions.
   D. Concentrate on what the speaker is saying.
   E. Show the speaker you want to listen.
   F. Control your emotions and your temper.
   G. Get rid of distractions.
   H. Look for areas of agreement.
    I. Avoid jumping to conclusions and making evaluations.
   J. Listen for the main points.

VII. Nonverbal Communication
   A. The most important expressions of emotional states are usually communicated on the nonverbal level.
   B. The lack of awareness of nonverbal messages can result in ineffective communication.
   C. Five major dimensions of nonverbal communication are
      1. Kinesics, or body language.
      2. Proxemics, or spatial relations.
      3. Chronemics, or the use of time.
      4. Paralanguage, or the use of the voice.
      5. Artifacts, or object language.

## KEY TERMS

| | | |
|---|---|---|
| Communication | Communication channels | Kinesics |
| Source | Symbolic value | Proxemics |
| Encoding | Inferences | Chronemics |
| Receiver | Levels of abstraction | Paralanguage |
| Decoding | Symbols | Artifacts |
| Message | Nonverbal messages | |

## DISCUSSION QUESTIONS

1. How can communication models be used to improve the effectiveness of communication?
2. How is an individual's position in a social system important in communication?
3. Discuss the effect of group pressure on communication.
4. Comment on the following assumptions about language and meaning:
   a. Meanings are in words.
   b. Because there is a word for it, a thing must exist.
   c. Communication consists of the transmission of meaning.
   d. All statements are either true or false.
5. What are the characteristics of an inference?
6. Does communication require identical meaning in both sender and receiver?
7. How do people learn meanings?
8. Give an example of a low-level abstraction and a high-level abstraction.
9. Discuss the following barriers to effective communication:
   a. Confusing symbols and facts
   b. The influence of expectations
   c. Selective perception
10. Discuss the major barriers to effective listening.
11. What advice would you give an individual who wants improved listening ability?
12. Why is nonverbal communication important to a manager?
13. Describe a situation in which an individual's motivational state was communicated nonverbally.

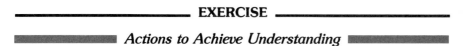

## EXERCISE

### Actions to Achieve Understanding

You manage a fast-food restaurant. The employees are high school and college students who work part-time. The only employee you have difficulty communicating with is Tom Davis. He seems to want to do a good job and is always pleasant. Tom has worked for you for six months and is making the same mistakes in food handling over and over again. Several times you have explained the proper way to handle food to comply with health regulations. His improper food handling has resulted in two warnings from the health department inspector. You must get through to Tom, or you will have major problems with the health inspector.

*Evaluate the following list of actions to achieve effective communication.*
Which actions would you take? Which would you take first?

1. Have Tom watch the other employees to observe the proper way to handle food to meet health regulations.

2. Send Tom to a course on listening.

3. Fire Tom and hire an employee you can communicate with.

4. Have Tom perform the food handling while you watch and correct him when he makes mistakes.

5. Have one of the other employees explain proper food handling to Tom.

6. Communicate the importance of proper food handling by telling Tom the health inspector could close the restaurant.

7. Get advice from Tom's parents on how to communicate with Tom.

8. Give Tom a written copy of the food handling instructions and have him take a written test on them.

9. Have the health department inspector talk with Tom.

10. Have a meeting with all employees to explain proper food handling and discuss food handling problems.

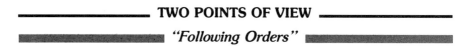

## TWO POINTS OF VIEW

### "Following Orders"

*What would you do if you were the supervisor?*

You are the supervisor of the employee benefits section in the personnel department of a large company. The benefits section handles employee health insurance, life insurance, retirement benefits, educational benefits, and worker compensation claims.

The six employees who work for you have become a close-knit group, and a high degree of cooperation exists among them. The benefits section has established an excellent reputation within the company, and few complaints are made about how benefits are handled.

Sharon Hill has been in the section longer than any of the other employees and is looked to for assistance and advice. She has recently started spending a great deal of her time advising employees on how to do their jobs. Sometimes you must correct inaccurate advice she gives the employees. During a training session on new procedures for processing health insurance claims, Sharon interrupted the meeting and told the employees that you did not understand the new procedures. You told the employees that Sharon was mistaken and finished your explanation of the new procedures, which were "cut and dried." Later, Sharon had the employees to her house for dinner and advised them not to follow your instructions because your information was incorrect. The employees agreed with Sharon and ignored the new procedure you had described.

The day after Sharon had the meeting at her house, one of your employees went to the personnel manager and complained that you could not communicate effectively with the employees in the section. The employee told the personnel manager that your explanations were difficult to understand and that you avoided answering employee questions about new procedures. The employees should have easily understood the new procedures because you presented them in a simple and straightforward manner. It seems to you that the problem may be that Sharon is just trying to gain power because you had to correct some of her inaccurate advice.

Tomorrow you must meet with the personnel manager (your boss) to discuss, as he put it, "your communication problems with employees."

*What would you do if you were Sharon Hill?*

You have worked in the benefits section of the personnel department for the last thirteen years. The company has sent you to numerous training seminars on the administration of benefit programs. Because of your formal education and considerable time spent at professional meetings, you consider yourself an expert on administration of benefit programs.

You know how important your work is to the company employees who need the benefit programs. You try to be cooperative in all your work relations but believe your first loyalty is to the company and the employees who use the benefit programs. When the benefit program is poorly administered, the employees suffer.

In the meeting your supervisor had to explain new procedures for processing health insurance claims, he so confused the employees that you had to interrupt the training session to correct his inaccuracies. Since your supervisor did not accept your corrections, you had a meeting of the employees at your home to explain how the claims should be processed. Fortunately for the company employees, you straightened things out and the claims will be properly processed.

One of the employees that was at the meeting at your home was so disgusted with your supervisor that he went to the personnel manager to complain about the ineffective communication. He told you that he also suggested to the personnel manager that you should be made supervisor of the benefits section.

You wish he had not gone to the personnel manager, but you recognize that this may produce an opportunity for you to get the recognition you deserve.

## ENDNOTES

1. Kathleen A. Bishop, "The Silent Signals," *Training and Development Journal* (June 1985): 36.
2. Leon C. Megginson, Donald C. Mosley, and Paul H. Pietri, Jr., *Management: Concepts and Applications*, 2d ed. (New York: Harper & Row, 1986), p. 328.
3. For a more detailed account, see W. J. Coughlin, "The Great Mokusatsu Mistake: Was This the Deadliest Error of Our Time?" *Harper's*, March 1953, p. 31.
4. "Communicate or Get Ready for High Turnover," *Infosystems* 30 (1984): 20.
5. Paul R. Timm, *Managerial Communication: A Finger on the Pulse*, 2d ed. (Englewood Cliffs, N.J.: Prentice-Hall, 1986), p. 29.
6. Mason Haire, *Psychology in Management* (New York: McGraw-Hill, 1964).
7. Jane Whitney Gibson and Richard M. Hodgetts, *Organizational Communication: A Managerial Perspective* (Orlando, Fla.: Academic Press, 1986), p. 67.

   **8.** *Business Week*, 18 January 1982, p. 50.

   **9.** *Management Review* (November 1979): 48.

   **10.** Dalmar Fisher, *Communications in Organizations* (St. Paul: West, 1981), p. 118.

   **11.** I. Thomas Sheppard, "Silent Signals," *Supervisory Management* (March 1986): 31.

   **12.** Tim R. V. Davis, "The Influence of the Physical Environment in Offices," *Academy of Management Review* (April 1984): 271–83.

   **13.** R. Buck, *Nonverbal Behavior and the Communication of Affect* (New York: Guilford Press, 1984).

   **14.** Joseph A. DeVito, *The Interpersonal Communication Book* (New York: Harper & Row, 1976), p. 362.

   **15.** D. C. Barnlund, ed., *Interpersonal Communication: Survey and Studies* (Boston: Houghton Mifflin, 1968), p. 529.

   **16.** Nancy K. Austin, "Eight Toughest Lessons from a Passion for Excellence," *Success*, April 1986, p. 50.

# Chapter 6

# Communication Effectiveness in Organizations

———————— *Learning Objectives* ————————

After reading this chapter, you should be able to do the following:

1. Identify recent changes in management practices and their impact on communication
2. Describe the characteristics of power-oriented and achievement-oriented approaches to communication
3. State the causes for ineffective communication in organizations
4. List practices to improve communication in organizations
5. State how managers can increase productivity by effective communication practices

# Chapter Topics

■ Changing management concepts in communication
■ Managerial approaches to communication
■ Practices to improve communication
■ Simple and direct language
■ Positive motivational appeals
■ Provide complete information
■ Obtain feedback
■ Develop source credibility
■ Reinforce verbal communication with action

# Preview

Successful communication in organizations depends on more than a knowledge of principles and pitfalls. Before the most effective communication technique can be selected, it is necessary to develop sensitivity to people, change in organizational environment, and forces external to the work organization. Of all human activities, communication is one of the most used and, in many ways, least understood. What is effective in one set of circumstances may be entirely ineffective in another. This chapter explores the applications of communication principles to behavior in work organizations.

A great many factors affect employee and managerial performance. Among the most important are verbal and nonverbal communication. Anything one person does or is believed to do can communicate to others and can affect their performance.

Managers are faced with increasingly difficult problems in achieving effective communication with employees. Communication problems have resulted from such factors as changes in technology, social values, and in individual expectations of work.

Most managers have no problem talking *to* employees, but many find it difficult to talk *with* them.[1]

**SELF–ASSESSMENT** ▬▬▬▬▬▬▬▬▬▬▬▬▬▬▬▬▬▬▬▬▬

This chapter continues the discussion of communication, with emphasis on applications in organizations. For the following items, choose the response that is most appropriate. Each statement or question has a range of possible responses. A scale of 1 to 6 between two words with different meanings allows you to mark either the word that is considered correct or a place between the two words that represents some agreement and some disagreement. Selection of a high number such as 5 or 6 may be either correct or incorrect, just as selection of lower numbers may be correct or incorrect. Some responses may be partly correct and partly incorrect.

   Answers based on research by behavorial scientists, with a short explanation of why the response was considered correct, may be found on page 154. Use your personal experiences and knowledge from other classes to help in your responses.

1. Long-term effectiveness in employees is best obtained by communication that emphasizes:

   managerial power  1...2...3...4...5...6  achievement

2. Effective management communication requires:

   control  1...2...3...4...5...6  feedback

3. Clear, concise communication:

   guarantees  1...2...3...4...5...6  does not guarantee
   understanding                          understanding

4. Which of the two types of communication is most effective in work organizations?

   written  1...2...3...4...5...6  face-to-face

5. In organizations, the most important communication characteristic is:

   credibility of the  1...2...3...4...5...6  content of the message
   sender

6. Effective communicators know that sensitivity to the feelings, emotions, and beliefs of others requires:

   sympathy  1...2...3...4...5...6  empathy

7. Traditional management communication is and has been:

   power oriented  1...2...3...4...5...6  achievement oriented

8. Management actions are a form of communication that is important. A type of management action that tends to get results is:

power-oriented  1...2...3...4...5...6  changing job structure
communication                          to add responsibility
                                       and meaning

9. In dealing with rumors, it is better to be:

direct and specific  1...2...3...4...5...6  indirect and general

10. An increasing number of managers are:

attempting to  1...2...3...4...5...6  attempting to keep
involve                                employees from
employees in job                       becoming involved in
decisions                              job decisions

## CHANGING MANAGEMENT CONCEPTS IN COMMUNICATION

Effective communication requires more than improving the form and style of communication. It requires more than good speech presentation, clear writing, and well-organized meetings. Clarity and organization of communication are important factors, but they do not ensure effectiveness. Many of the difficulties in communication involve organizational practices and procedures and the nature of management's relationships with employees. A supervisor may communicate in an organized, clear, and concise manner yet still be seen as incompetent or unfair by employees. As long as the supervisor is perceived as either incompetent or unfair, communication with employees will be generally unsuccessful.

> The complexity of modern organizations and the competing demands for time make effective communication essential.[2]

Management practices and procedures designed to improve interpersonal relations can have long-range positive effects. In other words, effective communication depends upon good interpersonal relations between management and employees. Although it is difficult to predict the final outcome of recent changes in management practices and their impact on communication, here are some types of activities being used to improve the quality of organizational communication:

1. *Interaction with Employees.* An increasing number of managers are attempting to involve employees in solving problems on their jobs. In changing their approach, management attempts to interact with employees to achieve better planning and a higher quality of job performance rather than focus on selling employees on practices and procedures. Examples of this approach were reported by Alfred S. Warren, Jr., director of personnel development for General Motors.[3] In one General Motors plant, glass breakage rose to 46 percent of the glass handled. Management tried all the traditional methods of persuading, selling, and

threatening to convince employees to be more careful, but nothing worked. The problem of determining the causes of breakage was then turned over to the employees. The glass installers began talking with employees doing other body work about problems that resulted in glass breakage and ways of correcting them. As a result of the improved interaction, glass breakage in the plant almost ceased.

2. *Employee Participation.* Managers have traditionally concentrated on developing clear and concise ways of communicating information and instructions to employees. This emphasis on the downward flow of information is changing to an approach that involves developing two-way communication between management and employees directed toward achieving organizational objectives. Such management practices emphasize employee participation and interaction. M. Scott Myers cites the following example of employee participation with management to achieve company objectives. Assemblers were given the opportunity to help their company solve a problem: the company was losing money on the production of radar units. Management shared information with the assemblers concerning costs, delivery schedules, and production requirements. Management also worked with the employees to develop methods of reducing costs and creating more efficient assembly. In a year, using the employees' ideas, the number of hours of labor required to assemble a radar unit was reduced from 138 to 41.[4] This example illustrates the potential for increased productivity by employee participation and interaction.

3. *The Job Communicates.* Verbal communication has always been important in organizations, but management actions are also an extremely important form of communication with employees. To increase the effectiveness of human interaction, managers are attempting to structure jobs so that the work is seen as more meaningful. When employees' jobs are controlled by the speed of an assembly line, workers may receive the message that management sees individuals as less important than equipment. If employees can make decisions independent of machine actions, management may be seen as having trust and confidence in the workers' abilities.

4. *Attitudes and Feelings.* Managers are increasingly recognizing that communication is strongly affected by employee attitudes and feelings about management practices. In addition to the factual and logical content of communication, emphasis must be placed on the ways communication affects employees' attitudes and feelings.

## MANAGERIAL APPROACHES TO COMMUNICATION

With the coming of large organizations, talk was no longer trivial. It became essential for such organizations to cultivate the art of communication.[5]

Some of the newer and more successful management practices involve using different approaches to communication. These changes can be characterized as moving from a power-oriented approach toward an achievement-oriented approach to communication.

## Power-Oriented Approach to Communication

A **power-oriented approach** assumes that management alone regulates and controls the flow of information in an organization. Regulating information is seen as an efficient method of controlling performance. When poor work occurs, power-oriented management attempts to direct the flow of information toward corrective actions. With a power-oriented approach, communication problems are frequently major causes of poor performance.

The power-oriented manager relies on persuasion and force to improve morale and establish stable communication. Telling people what to do becomes a method of coping with problems. Verbal messages are sent where they are believed to do the most good. Communication with employees focuses on remedial approaches and concentrates on stopping violations of organizational policies and procedures. Management communication with employees often focuses on persuading employees to believe they are getting a good deal from management. Information often becomes distorted in management's attempt to sell people on the organization. This approach may involve "propaganda" attempts, which result in employee suspicion and distrust.

## Achievement-Oriented Approach to Communication

An **achievement-oriented approach** assumes that effective communication is a necessary part of productive work. Communication difficulties are seen as symptoms or indications of organizational and managerial problems. Communication is not seen as an independent function of the organization, but as a tool that is used in all aspects of management.

The achievement-oriented approach does not require "special communication programs," because information is communicated to employees through the job and involvement with management. Individuals at all levels in the organization communicate in planning and controlling functions related to their jobs. The management practices in an achievement-oriented approach attempt to develop communication among individuals as a part of the job.

The assumption underlying achievement orientation is that effective communication results from people having meaningful jobs and doing challenging work.

Davidson found that "employees that are kept informed of organizational and departmental objectives will ultimately become more productive." [6]

Improvement in the quality of communication can be achieved by rearranging work groups, changing organizational patterns, reorganizing jobs, and creating different person-job relationships. To help employees achieve goals, the manager changes behavior rather than verbal communication.

Most managers realize that no matter how well they listen, how effectively they speak, how clearly they write, or how often they hold meetings, in the end the most powerful effect on communication in an organization is the language of the job. Improvements in communication often require changes in the nature of jobs, management styles, or organizational policies.[7]

A desirable approach is to create conditions in which the focus of communication is on achievement through problem solving, obtaining information, and expressing feelings. If communication follows the demands of the work situation, it will help to create trust. Managers who rely on actions as well as words to communicate are frequently more effective. When something goes wrong, however, effective managers concentrate on obtaining as much information as they can—they stop telling and start listening. Table 6.1 summarizes the characteristics of power-oriented and achievement-oriented approaches to communication.

## PRACTICES TO IMPROVE COMMUNICATION

Many valuable methods are used to improve communication in organizations. Although communication is emphasized, the practices of broad-based management approaches attempt to maximize the use of human resources.

More effective communication can be developed by trying to identify the problem before attempting to find the answers. We must be able to identify why communication is not effective before looking for additional information to transmit.

> Even a relatively small effort to improve organizational communication can put a company at a competitive advantage.[8]

### *The Sender Must Accept Responsibility*

One problem in communication is the **"I told you so" fallacy**. The statements "The employee didn't pay attention" and "I told them, but they didn't listen" are frequently heard in organizations.

**Table 6.1**
Communication Orientations

|  | Power-Oriented Approach | Achievement-Oriented Approach |
|---|---|---|
| Purpose | Persuasion to control employee behavior | Problem solving to achieve organizational objectives |
| Focus | Control flow of information to employees | Development of trust and openness with employees |
| Content | Concentration on verbal communication | Management action to create productive environment |
| Direction | Downward, one-way communication by management | Interaction among management and employees |
| Effects desired | Knowledge of procedures and logical carrying out of instructions | Positive attitudes and feelings and achievement of objectives |

One company changed its inspection procedures to require inspection of every unit produced. The chief inspector told his group, "I want you to inspect every unit." He had transmitted the message; however, what the inspectors heard was, "We will still sample and inspect every other unit as we have done for the last five years." When the chief inspector found a defective unit that had not been inspected, he blamed the inspectors for not listening. The problem, however, was the chief's assumption that to tell is all that is necessary. He did not find out if the inspectors understood what action to take.

The effectiveness of communication can be increased if the person transmitting information accepts responsibility for understanding. When this responsibility is not accepted, the "I told you so" fallacy frequently results.

The sender's accepting responsibility does not reduce the responsibility of the receiver in the communication process. Effective communication requires a mutual acceptance of responsibility by sender *and* receiver.

### Use Simple and Direct Language

We have all been in situations in which we were unable to understand what people were saying because of their use of technical terms or **jargon**. Lawyers, for example, use terminology that is different from that of farmers or dentists. Some writers have labeled this jargon "gobbledygook." Technical jargon can often be found in government agencies, courts of law, universities, and hospitals. "Too much of what is being communicated today is being distributed in peer group or 'privileged class' language." [9]

An example of jargon is the phrase Herman Kahn used in describing a war policy as "a policy which emphasized the threat that we could hit the Soviet Union with a counterforce-countervalue 'spasm' attack." *Counterforce* refers to an attempt to degrade or destroy the enemy's offensive capability. *Countervalue* refers to an attempt to damage things that the enemy values. *Spasm* is meant to imply that the first attack is total and a reflex reaction.

Problems associated with jargon can be reduced *by using abbreviated phraseology distinguished for its lucidity*; that is, using simple and direct language (see Figure 6.1). Using "big words" such as those italicized in the preceding sentence may prove you have a large vocabulary, but it does not necessarily increase understanding.

Effective communication depends on language adapted to the vocabulary of the receiver. The purpose of communication is not to test the receiver's vocabulary; it is to develop mutual understanding.[10]

### Use Positive Motivational Appeals

Most of us have attempted to change the behavior of others by using threats of punishment. In most cases, it is not the most effective method of changing behavior.

A prime example is a pack of cigarettes bearing the message: "SURGEON GENERAL'S WARNING: Cigarette Smoke Contains Carbon Monoxide." The same message is seen often in newspapers along with information linking smoking to lung cancer and heart disease. Because of the threatening nature of this information, many people quit reading, listening, and watching the ads. A more effective approach in motivating people to change their behavior involves concentrating on rewards rather than threats, fear, and punishment.

A major problem in using threats is that people may want to avoid the sources of the threats and the places in which the threats occur. Threats usually tell people what not to do. They seldom lead to positive, goal-oriented actions. Communication is more effective if it focuses on positive and rewarding courses of action.

**Figure 6.1**   Use simple and direct language.

Examples of using positive motivation to correct problems usually dealt with by threats and punishment have been summarized by Harry Wiard.[11] One of the more interesting examples was a steel plant that gave trading stamps to the families of employees who had uninterrupted periods of attendance. Absentee rates were considerably reduced. The traditional approach of reducing absenteeism involves some form of punishment for "unexplained" absences. In another example cited by Wiard, employees were provided with an extra break whenever they could increase production. If they completed a specified number of units in a given hour, the rest of the hour could be used as they wanted. Production, as hoped, improved.

### *The Receiver Must See Benefits*

Individuals are most affected by messages providing chances to satisfy needs. They are attentive to messages that are potentially rewarding and tend to disregard those having no reward value. The receiver rather than the sender defines whether the message contains possible rewards. Effective managers are "receiver oriented" and have developed the ability to analyze whether messages provide incentives for the receiver to listen, understand, and act to achieve organizational goals.

### *Provide the Receiver with Complete Information*

Often messages are transmitted without all the information required for a complete message. Incomplete messages leave room for the receiver to fill in missing information and distort the intended meaning. When rumors transmitted through organizational grapevines are analyzed, one of their main characteristics is that they started as incomplete messages. Messages become rumors when information is added or deleted as the message is transmitted from one person to another.

One way to help combat distortions is to ensure that *who, what, when, where, why*, and *how* are included in every message transmitted. Communication will usually not be 100 percent accurate, because some changes will be made to the information as it is transmitted from person to person. However, one company saved thousands of dollars simply by printing the words *who, what, when, where, why*, and *how* on all scratch pads, phone message pads, and memo pads. Messages were far more complete than they would have been otherwise.

Messages transmitted to employees should explain how the information will affect them and their jobs. If all essential elements of a message are included, the chance of distortion is reduced.

### *Obtain Feedback*

A problem in organizations is that communication is often one way—without feedback. **Feedback** involves checking responses to communication to determine if messages are understood. The basis of advanced electronic communications systems is feedback. In most advanced technological systems, two-thirds of

## Management Guidelines for Dealing with Rumors

1. Define the rumor.
   a. What is the specific content of the rumor?
   b. Why was the rumor started?
   c. Rumors result from uncertainties. Identify these uncertainties.
2. Evaluate the rumor.
   a. Is it important enough for management to deal with?
   b. Has the impact of the rumor affected productivity?
   c. Does the rumor have the potential to affect productivity in the future?
3. When providing information or answers, be sure information is factual and is supported with specific details.
4. Evaluate the available methods to inform employees.
   a. Consider whether the grapevine and informal channels should be used.
   b. Use official methods of communication such as memos, meetings, and letters.
   c. Suit the method of communication to the situation.
   d. Use face-to-face communication whenever possible.
5. Be sure to use a credible source of information—sources that employees will believe.
6. Be sure to answer questions directly and specifically whenever possible. When impossible, admit uncertainty and explain the causes of uncertainty.
7. Management should try to involve employees in the problem-solving process or when changes are being considered.

the system is used to check reliabilities, to feed back information on system operation, and to check and double-check the accuracy of the transmission of information.

Unfortunately, human beings often ignore the basic principles of feedback. To avoid misunderstandings, the sender must obtain, by observing the reactions of the receiver or by asking appropriate questions, the receiver's interpretation of the message. To ensure action-oriented communications, it is necessary to have feedback.

In some cases management has a *closed-door policy*, although the stated policy is that of an open door. When an employee walks in, the closed-door manager starts looking at the clock or tapping on the table. The manager asks the employee to hurry up, keep it important, keep it relevant, and make it quick.

The message is that the manager's time is important. Feedback received by the employee in such cases is largely negative.

Managers need feedback to evaluate whether information is being effectively received, as Figure 6.2 illustrates. An essential ingredient of effective human interaction is two-way communication.[12]

To obtain feedback, Baron suggests that "it is usually better for an executive who genuinely seeks increased feedback to use the open door as an invitation to walk *out* and visit employees." [13] The use of the open door to go to see employees where they work can communicate that the manager is really interested in their views and encourages increased feedback.

### Eliminate Noise through Message Isolation

Another problem that occurs in organizations is lack of **message isolation**. Frequently, employees are bombarded with so many messages that telling what is important is difficult (see Figure 6.3). Consequently, they tend to ignore much of the information. Managers buried with reports and memoranda often spend time shuffling papers from one side of the desk to the other, moving from the in basket to the out basket, from the out basket to the file. Information and reports are often not read but merely moved around or filed.[14]

**Psychological noise**, or *interference*, involves not accurately receiving a message because of preoccupation with other things. After an emotional or traumatic experience, an individual is especially susceptible to psychological interference. An employee walked into the supervisor's office and said, "I've got

Figure 6.2    Without feedback there is a loss of information.

to tell you about this problem I have at home." The supervisor replied, "Just a minute, wait until I explain a new safety procedure." In this case, the employee pointed out the psychological interference that needed the manager's attention before safety procedures could be discussed. Supervisors are more effective in such situations when they deal with psychological interferences before talking about procedures or other work-related matters.

If an employee's problems are of such magnitude that he or she can't pay attention to the job, effective management may consider allowing the employee to take care of the problem the same way sick leave is provided. Employees with pressing personal problems are often susceptible to injury and may cause injury to those around them. They also have difficulty concentrating on their assigned tasks and are generally ineffective.

An important factor in eliminating psychological noise is the careful timing of messages. Many organizations hold important meetings just prior to lunch or quitting time. These are two of the worst times to try to communicate. Employees may be worried about missing a ride home, running an errand, or other pressing personal needs. In addition, lower energy levels during these times of day often result in inattention and irritability.

### *Use Multiple Channels*

To transmit messages effectively, one can us **multiple communication channels** to stimulate more than one sense in a receiver. When more sensory perceptions are used, such as sight, smell, or touch, the brain receives more stimulation; and the possibility of understanding and retaining messages is greater. "Since most communication is subject to at least some distortion, the

**Figure 6.3**    **Lack of message isolation creates communication problems.**

---

### "Open-Line" Programs to Improve Communication ━━━━━

Many organizations claim to be concerned about two-way communication between employees and management, but some companies like Sun Oil, IBM, and Bank of America are actually doing something about it. These firms have established what are known as "open-line" communication programs. The technique is characterized by confidentiality and candor.

Basically, the program establishes a confidential channel between employees and management. The channel can be used by any employee who wants to submit a problem, complaint, opinion, or suggestion to management. To ensure confidentiality, communications are directed to a coordinator, who is the only one aware of the writer's identity. The program guarantees that a confidential, written reply from management will be sent to the employee's home.

The open-line program can help an organization compensate for managers who lack strong communication skills or who do not encourage two-way communication with their employees. One of the major advantages of these programs is that concrete suggestions to improve company operations can be channeled directly to top management.

The open-line program conveys the nonverbal message to employees that management believes communication is a two-way street and is working to make it clear and direct.

---

chances of a message being received as intended increases when two or more channels are used." [15]

The use of multiple channels provides a variety of reinforcing messages and helps eliminate interference. If the individual sees the message as well as hears it, there will be less interference from seeing other information. If other senses are also involved, interference will be further reduced.

### *Use Face-to-Face Communication*

One advantage of **face-to-face communication** is that immediate feedback from the receiver is possible. Face-to-face communication uses multiple channels of communication with ease and efficiency and makes it possible to obtain message isolation. Involvement and participation can be developed in face-to-face interaction much more readily than through any other media such as telephone calls, correspondence, reports, or charts.

Face-to-face communication is sometimes avoided because it takes more time than other methods or because the situation can be uncomfortable. The immediate feedback of interpersonal interaction can reveal misunderstanding, ineffective communication, and feelings that neither the sender nor receiver wishes to expose. A useful technique is to approach all face-to-face interactions

```
┌─────────────────────────────────────────────────────────────┐
│  Advisory Panels to Improve Communication  ──────────────    │
│                                                               │
│  The Equitable Society has increased communication between    │
│  top man-agement and employees by the use of a series of      │
│  rotating advisory panels. Each panel is composed of twelve   │
│  people who meet with the president and other executives at    │
│  least four times a year. Panel members are selected by the   │
│  personnel department and management in each area of the      │
│  company. The panels represent a wide range of employees,     │
│  including minorities, women, and management.                 │
│     A facilitator works with the panel to organize the agenda │
│  for each meeting. Panel members are periodically changed to  │
│  obtain a variety of viewpoints.[16]                          │
└─────────────────────────────────────────────────────────────┘
```

with three goals: (1) to obtain information, (2) to give information, and (3) to establish a relationship of trust and confidence.

### Develop Empathy

Effective human interaction requires a sensitivity to the world of the receiver— the receiver's attitudes, emotions, and feelings. Developing **empathy** with an individual involves putting yourself in the other person's shoes. Messages can then be more effectively constructed, and you can determine the best approach to ensure understanding. Part of the process of developing empathy is to understand how others see us. We can gain this knowledge by encouraging others to give us direct and meaningful feedback about our behavior and our communication. This requires a climate of trust and confidence. No technique, however, can substitute for careful observation and sensitivity to the way others react to our verbal and nonverbal messages.[17]

### Develop Credibility as a Source of Information

Communication studies have shown that the **credibility** of the source of information often overrides a message's real value. If receivers believe the source of the information is credible, they are likely to pay attention to the message and to be affected by the content. Messages from sources lacking credibility are frequently ignored, even though the content may be perfectly valid.[18]

Evaluation of the source's credibility depends on the perceived competence and trustworthiness of the source. These factors are not the "property" of the source but are determined by receivers. Credibility is in the eye of the beholder.

The perceived credibility to perform a task and make task-related decisions depends on the source's qualifications, expertise, or competence. Individuals perceived as having high credibility are usually seen as possessing some desirable combination of experience, training, education, skill, ability, information, and intelligence.

Trustworthiness tends to be a general credibility factor covering the total range of an individual's behavior. Trust of a person is not limited to a job or an area of influence. Trust involves being perceived as having characteristics such as honesty, fairness, justice, ethics, and dependability. Trustworthiness has an influence in all communication situations.

*Fortune* magazine described an interesting experiment on source credibility. A cartoon chart of "the Four Goals of Labor" was clipped from a union newspaper and photostated. A new source of the goals was attached at the bottom: "From June 3, National Association of Manufacturers Newsletter" (a management publication). Twenty union members were then shown the ad and asked if they thought it was a fair presentation of labor's goals. Four grudgingly said it was, and two couldn't make up their minds. The responses of the remaining fourteen included "patronizing," "loaded," "paternalistic," and "makes me want to spit." [19]

### Reduce Status Awareness and Social Distance

Status can be a barrier to effective communication in three ways: "(1) it is often used to insulate a manager from things he or she does not want to hear; (2) it influences the amount and kind of information that subordinates channel upward; and (3) it encourages status seekers to misuse information in their drive to reach the top." [20]

One of the barriers to effective communication is the social distance among people that arises when there are status differences. Although status differences will probably always be with us, communication can be made more effective by reducing or eliminating the status symbols that heighten existing social differences. Some of the status symbols that reduce communication are titles, forms of dress, reserved parking spaces, special privileges, office furniture and fixtures, the executive dining room, and so on. Most people possess **status awareness** when they realize that these symbols communicate a variety of nonverbal messages about power, prestige, and position. Although status symbols are difficult to avoid, many organizations have dramatically reduced the most objectionable ones and have improved interpersonal relations.

### Use Direct Communication Whenever Possible

Communication in an organization is often characterized by messages passing through a number of people and organizational layers before reaching their destinations. In other words, the communication process frequently has too many links. The more individuals the message goes through, the greater the chance of systematic distortion. Whenever possible, a highly desirable approach is to communicate directly with the individuals who must take the action.

### Reinforce Verbal Communication with Action

Much of the communication that directly affects our behavior is nonverbal— that is, actions interpreted by other people. A simple example of this phenomenon in operation was a supervisor who tried to influence employees to stop taking company-owned items out of the plant. The supervisor gave a thirty-minute speech and successfully made his point. Then, he went back to his office, picked up two boxes of the company's drawing pencils and walked out of the plant, passing by the same employees to whom he had just lectured. At this point, some of the employees were asked, "What did you think of the speech; will it have any effect on your behavior?" They said it would not affect what they did at all, since the supervisor was still stealing pencils. In such cases, nonverbal behavior overrides any verbal communication. Many times, the things that irritate individuals and block effective communication are the nonverbal elements. Often said is that 65 percent of our face-to-face communication is nonverbal. As shown in Figure 6.4, people react more to our actions, our tone of voice, and our manner of delivery than to our message.

Figure 6.4   Actions are the message.

## CONCLUSIONS

Concepts and techniques of communication are relatively easy to write about, but their effective implementation is difficult and time-consuming (see Figure 6.5). Philosophies and theories of communication are much more highly developed than are the procedures and methods for their implementation in organizations.

The effective implementation of any system or procedure to improve communication requires organizational support, particularly from top management. Effective implementation always requires flexibility so procedures can be adapted to meet requirements of the organization.

**Figure 6.5**    Steps in effective communication.

The potential rewards of more effective communication are unlimited. For most organizations, the traditional and conventional concepts and practices are no longer sufficient to meet current challenges. The future of the richly varied and complex processes of organizational communication will require application of a broad spectrum of new concepts and practices.

> Consistent, constructive communications are the "lubricants" of a well-run organization.[21]

## SELF–ASSESSMENT DISCUSSION

**1.** (6) Emphasis on achievement is far more important than power and control in achieving long-term effectiveness. Power-oriented communication is demotivating, while achievement-oriented communication is motivating.

**2.** (6) Feedback is an essential ingredient to effective communication. A major reason for management communication failure is that it is one-way without feedback.

**3.** (6) Although we would like it to, clear, concise communication does not guarantee either understanding or effectiveness. Although clearness and conciseness are valuable, lack of interest, lack of credibility of the sender, and lack of understanding of the message content can all keep understanding from occurring.

**4.** (6) Face-to-face communication is nearly always more effective than written messages. Face-to-face communication provides opportunity for multiple channel communication, explanation, feedback, and all of the ingredients of truly effective communication.

**5.** (1, 2, 3) Content is important, but credibility is most important. Without credibility, the sender's messages will be largely ignored, regardless of content.

**6.** (6) Sympathy is virtually useless as a communication tool. Empathy is the sensitivity to the feelings, emotions, attitudes, and beliefs of others. It is an essential ingredient of effective communication.

**7.** (1) Management is and has been largely power oriented in its communications even though achievement-oriented communication has been demonstrated to be more effective.

**8.** (6) Actions such as adding responsibility to jobs, involving employees in planning and decisions that affect their work, and seeking information from employees on ways of job improvement all demonstrate trust and confidence in communication.

**9.** (1) It is better to be direct and specific in most communication. Evasion tends to confirm rumors. If a manager doesn't know the facts, admission of lack of information is far better than evasion.

**10.** (1) Managers in many organizations are beginning to realize that employee involvement with management problems is an effective motivational and communication tool. It helps increase the employee's identity and support of the same organizational goals that are important to management.

## QUICK REVIEW

I. Changing Management Concepts in Communication

   A. Changes in technology, social systems, values, and individuals entering the work force all affect communication in organizations.

   B. Some general directions of managerial changes toward communication include

      1. Changing from emphasis on management's use of threats and persuasion to emphasis on motivating employees to participate in analyzing and solving their own job problems.

      2. Changing from emphasis on control of flow of communication to emphasis on establishing employee participation and interaction with management.

      3. Changing from emphasis on merely getting employees to do their jobs to emphasis on structuring the job so it is more meaningful to them.

      4. Increasing emphasis on the way communication affects employees' attitudes and feelings.

II. Managerial Approaches to Communication

   A. In power-oriented approaches, managers assume the responsibility of regulation and control of information. They focus on remedial concerns and propaganda.

   B. In achievement-oriented approaches, managers assume that effective human interaction is an intrinsic component of productive work. Communication problems are seen as symptoms of managerial inadequacy.

   C. Problems in communication are basically organizational problems.

III. Practices to Improve Communication

   A. The sender must accept responsibility for the effectiveness of the communication.

   B. Simple, direct language is most effective.

   C. Positive motivational appeals are stronger than those based on fear.

   D. The receiver must see benefits in the communication.

   E. The receiver must be provided with understanding, including the *who, what, where, when, why,* and *how* of the subject being discussed.

   F. Feedback, or two-way involvement, is necessary for understanding.

   G. Through message isolation, "noise" or extraneous messages can be minimized.

   H. Multiple channels of communication should be used when possible.

   I. Face-to-face communication is superior to letters, memoranda, or telephone communication.

J. Empathy is a necessary component of all successful communication.

K. Development of credibility is mandatory for successful communication.

L. Status awareness and social distance are barriers to communication and should be reduced.

M. Direct communication is more effective than communication passed through several layers of organization.

N. Actions reinforce verbal communication.

IV. Conclusions

A. Effective implementation of organizational communication is difficult and time-consuming but rewarding.

B. Communication practices, to be effective, must have the support of all levels in the organization.

C. Traditional concepts and practices no longer meet the challenges of creating effective organizational communication.

## KEY TERMS

Power-oriented communication
Achievement-oriented communication
"I told you so" fallacy
Jargon

Message isolation
Feedback
Empathy
Credibility
Face-to-face communication

Psychological noise
Status awareness
Multiple communication channels

## DISCUSSION QUESTIONS

1. What do you believe will be the most critical issues involving organizational communication in the future?
2. What are the major differences between a power-oriented approach and an achievement-oriented approach to communication?
3. Comment on the statement "Communication problems are basically problems resulting from the environment created by the organization."
4. How can the "I told you so" fallacy be avoided?
5. How can you determine what information will be important to an individual?
6. What elements are necessary for a message to be complete and to reduce the chance for message distortion?
7. What are possible advantages and disadvantages of an "open-door policy"?
8. What action can a manager take to reduce "psychological noise"?
9. How would you determine your credibility as a source of information?
10. Discuss a specific situation in which the verbal communication of an individual was not consistent with the individual's actions.

11. Why is the effective implementation of new communication concepts and techniques difficult?

-------------------------- **EXERCISE** --------------------------

*Actions to Obtain Feedback*

While talking with employees at the company picnic, your boss became convinced that there was a lack of communication between employees and managers. Employees told your boss that they had suggestions and complaints that were not being communicated to managers. They mentioned suggestions for cutting costs and increasing quality that impressed your boss. They also told him of grievances that he believed had the potential for producing major problems in management relations with employees. As a manager, you have been told to take courses of action to obtain employee feedback on possible improvements and complaints. Your boss has make it clear that he does not think you know what is going on in the department you manage.

*Evaluate the following list of actions to obtain feedback from employees.* Which actions would you take? Which would you take first?

1. Take a confidential survey of employees to obtain suggestions for improvement and complaints.

2. Offer an award for the best suggestion to cut costs or improve quality that is submitted each month.

3. Provide employees with additional information on customers, quality control standards, costs, and how individual jobs contribute to the final product.

4. Have a counselor from the personnel department meet with each employee to determine complaints and grievances.

5. Become better friends with employees by participating with them in off-the-job activities.

6. Have employees elect a representative group to evaluate suggestions and complaints and make recommendations to you.

7. Establish a suggestion program so employees can confidentially communicate suggestions and complaints to you by using a suggestion box.

8. Have all employees attend a communication training program.

9. Have an open-door policy and encourage employees to bring you suggestions and complaints.

10. Listen in on employee conversations whenever possible.

————————— **TWO POINTS OF VIEW** —————————

█████████████████ *"Delayed Shipments"* ████████████████

*What would you do if you were the shipping clerk?*

You work in the mail-order department of a large department store. As a shipping clerk, your job is to see that customer orders are accurately and promptly filled. You do not have the authority to make substitutions for items not in stock or to adjust for errors in advertised prices. For these decisions, you must go to your department supervisor.

When you ask your department supervisor for a decision on filling an order, you are usually told that the decision will need to be checked with the store manager, who has final authority. Often, weeks pass before you can ship the order. In an effort to get decisions faster, you started reminding your supervisor each day of the decisions that were pending. After two weeks of your reminders, the department supervisor told you, "You mind the shipping, and I'll take care of the decisions. I don't need any more of your reminders."

You now have to wait for decisions, and shipments are delayed. When customers complain to the store manager, he blames you for the delayed shipment and lets you know in no uncertain terms that getting orders out promptly is your responsibility.

When you try to explain your problem of getting decisions from the department supervisor to the store manager, he cuts your explanation short with, "Don't give me any excuses; your job is to get the orders out."

*What would you do if you were the department supervisor?*

You supervise the mail-order department for a large department store. You have been continually having problems with the shipping clerk. He does not get all the orders out promptly.

Some of the delays are understandable because he must get your approval when items are not in stock or an error has been made in the advertised price. For these items, he must get your approval and you must check with the store manager. The shipping clerk can't seem to understand that it takes time for you to check with the store manager because he is a very busy man. Instead of doing his job, the shipping clerk even started a campaign of reminding you every day of the decisions that were pending. All this did was waste your valuable time. The store manager got back to you as soon as he could on substitutions for items not in stock and adjustments for advertising errors.

In addition to shipping, you have responsibility for all the other aspects of the mail-order department. If you spend all your time "baby-sitting" the shipping clerk, the whole department will suffer.

The shipping clerk is now creating additional problems by going directly to the store manager with his excuses for not getting orders out promptly. The store manager has told you that if you can't handle your employees, he may need to look for someone who can.

## ENDNOTES

1. Walter D. St. John, "Plain Speaking," *Personnel Journal* (June 1985): 83.
2. Charles M. Kelly, "Effective Communications—Beyond the Glitter and Flash," *Sloan Management Review*, (Spring 1985): 74.
3. Max Ways, "The American Kind of Worker Participation," *Fortune*, October 1976, p. 176. See also "Workers: Eager for Responsibility," *Nation's Business*, November 1980, p. 38.
4. M. Scott Myers, *Every Employee a Manager* (New York: McGraw-Hill, 1970), p. 49.
5. Roger D'Aprix, *Communicating for Productivity* (New York: Harper & Row, 1982), p. 37.
6. Jeff Davidson, "Informing Employees Can Boost Productivity," *Data Management* (February 1984): 46.
7. For a detailed example, see Jeremy Main, "How to Battle Your Own Bureaucracy," *Fortune*, June 29, 1981, pp. 54–58.
8. Jane Whitney and Richard M. Hodgetts, *Organizational Communication: A Managerial Perspective* (Orlando, Fla.: Academic Press, 1986), p. 395.
9. Joseph A. Banik, "The Marketing Approach to Communicating with Employees," *Personnel Journal* (October 1985): 62.
10. For analysis of how people improve communication skills, see Gary T. Hunt, *Communicative Skills in the Organization* (Englewood Cliffs, N.J.: Prentice-Hall, 1980).
11. Harry Wiard, "Why Manage Behavior? A Case for Positive Reinforcement," *Human Resources Management* (Summer 1972): 15–20.
12. Lyle Sussman and Paul D. Krivonos, *Communication for Supervisors and Managers* (Sherman Oaks, Calif.: Alfred, 1979).
13. Robert A. Baron, *Understanding Human Relations: A Practical Guide to People at Work* (Boston: Allyn & Bacon, 1985), p. 80.
14. More is not always better is illustrated in Charles A. O'Reilly III, "Individuals and Information Overload in Organizations: Is More Necessarily Better?" *Academy of Management Journal* (December 1980): 684–96.
15. Andrew J. DuBrin, *Effective Business Psychology* (Reston, Va.: Reston, 1985), p. 359.
16. *Personnel Administrator* (January 1980): 19.
17. See Otis W. Baskin and Craig E. Aronoff, *Interpersonal Communication in Organizations* (Santa Monica, Calif.: Goodyear, 1980).
18. John M. Ivancevich, James Donnelly, Jr., and James L. Gibson, *Managing for Performance*, 3d ed. (Plano, Tex.: Business Publications, 1986), p. 283.
19. "Is Anybody Listening?" *Fortune*, September 1950, p. 82. See also J. L. Di Gaetani, "The Business of Listening," *Business Horizons* (October 1980): 40–46.
20. Don Hellriegel and John W. Slocum, Jr., *Management*, 4th ed. (Reading, Mass.: Addison-Wesley, 1986), p. 206.
21. Marjorie A. Shumaker, " 'Human' is Our Vital Resource," *Personnel Administrator* (February 1986): 14.

---
### ▰▰▰▰▰ CASE INCIDENTS FOR PART 2 ▰▰▰▰▰
---

—————————— **What Did I Say?** ——————————

Roger Peck, salesman for an aircraft manufacturer, reported the results of his trip to the sales manager, Mr. Fest: "Well, I got the order for five twin-engine model 243C's from the Vito Corporation. They sure gave me a bad time. I had to make one demonstration after another. I must have answered a million questions for half of the company officers. They didn't give me a minute's rest for the whole week. It seemed like I was there a month. They even had a meeting scheduled for me every night. I sure don't like these pressure sales situations with customers that are impossible to please. I hope I never see another sales job like that. It was ridiculous."

Mr. Fest turned to Roger and said, "Great, now let's go to work on how you can wrap up the International Company order."

1. What was Roger trying to say?
2. How did Mr. Fest perceive Roger's message?
3. What reaction do you think Roger had to Mr. Fest's reply?
4. If you were Mr. Fest, how would you have replied?
5. What basic problems in perception are illustrated by this situation, and what can be done to prevent them in the future?

—————————— **The Rumor** ——————————

A municipal hospital was experiencing a severe financial squeeze. Occupancy was lower than had been forecast, and collections were slow. Equipment costs were running higher than expected, and the cost of supplies was rising.

As the year ended, there was increased discussion among the hospital's two hundred employees about the effect of the current financial situation on salaries for the next year. A rumor began to circulate that there would be no salary raises and that personnel reductions were possible. Employees were shocked by the extent of the financial problems indicated by the rumor.

They began to ask their supervisors, "Does top-level administration agree with this rumor or not?"

The administrators made no comment, refusing to confirm or deny the rumor. The information in "official" communication from administration was that "the matter was under study." While employees waited for word on pay increases and wondered if they might be laid off, their morale dropped lower and lower. Most employees began to believe there would be no pay increases.

The administration finally announced that no employees would be laid off and that pay raises would average 4 percent. The employees were delighted when they received the announcement.

The administration was pleased with the employee reaction, since six months before there had been demands for 10 percent pay increases and a reduction of work loads.

1. Was the acceptance of work loads and the lower pay raise better than it would have been if the rumor had not started?
2. Should the administration have taken any action when the rumor was circulated?
3. What are possible long-term effects of this type of situation?
4. What guidelines should management use in dealing with rumors?

_____ **For Me or Against Me?** _____

Mr. Cook, production manager, began his weekly meeting with supervisors by stating, "The new production control system will eliminate our current problems of excessive cost due to rejects that do not meet quality standards. I want every supervisor to make this system work."

Before he could continue, James Belt, a senior supervisor who had been with the company fifteen years, spoke up. "Mr. Cook, I've met with the other supervisors, and we have a list of twelve changes that have to be made in the new system before it can operate effectively."

"Now Jim," replied Mr. Cook, "on implementing this new system, either you control costs or you don't. I am not going to argue about the system. The industrial engineering staff has assured me that it will work, because it's worked at other plants."

"But Mr. Cook," Belt persisted, "I think we need to work out a few problems before we try to implement the system."

At this, Mr. Cook became angry. "Belt, you're obviously against my system and my attempts to cut excessive costs. I don't want any more discussion on this!"

He then turned to the entire group of supervisors and asked, "Are there any questions?"

Not surprisingly, there were no questions, and the meeting was adjourned.

1. What communication problems are illustrated by this situation?
2. How do you think James Belt and the other supervisors felt after the meeting? Did the meeting help develop a commitment on the part of the supervisors to help make the new system work?
3. Could the communication have been handled more effectively by Mr. Cook? If so, how?

_____ **Too Much Paperwork?** _____

Mary Richards is the laboratory supervisor in a 1,500 bed, city-owned hospital. She has complete responsibility for personnel, supplies, equipment, scheduling work, and providing reports of laboratory tests to the doctors. The hospital personnel who use the laboratory believe it is efficiently managed and upholds high professional standards. The only complaints are from patients who must sometimes wait thirty to forty-five minutes to have tests run.

The hospital administrator seldom visits the lab and does not discuss problems or performance with Mary face-to-face. When a patient complains about having to wait for lab tests, the administrator writes Mary a memo and requires her to make a written response. Also, the administrator has been requiring weekly reports on use of supplies and materials; these reports previously were made only once a month.

Lately Mary has become so bogged down with the required paperwork that she cannot adequately supervise her laboratory. She has reached the point of considering looking for another job if the "put it in writing" policy of the administrator continues.

1. Does the administrator's policy of depending on written memos and reports promote effective communication?

2. What would you advise the hospital administrator to do to improve communication with Mary Richards?

3. If you were in Mary Richards's position, what could you do to improve communication with the administrator and reduce the time spent on paperwork?

4. Excessive paperwork is a common complaint by people in organizations. What approaches can be used to reduce or more effectively handle paperwork?

# Part 3

# Motivation and Performance

# Motivation Concepts

_____ *Learning Objectives* _____

After reading this chapter, you should be able to do the following:

1. Discuss the importance of motivation in organizations
2. Explain the process of motivation and the basic characteristics of human motives
3. Describe the need hierarchy theory and its implications for management
4. Identify the characteristics of individuals with high achievement motivation
5. Describe how managers can promote achievement motivation
6. Explain how affiliation motivation can be satisfied
7. Describe the types of power motivation and how they affect management styles
8. Explain expectancy theory of motivation and how it can be applied to improve performance

## Chapter Topics

- Motivation and management
- Definition of motivation
- Characteristics of motivation
- The process of motivation
- Maslow's needs hierarchy
- Achievement motivation
- Affiliation motivation
- Power motivation
- Expectancy theory of motivation

## Preview

Three areas of human behavior—perception, learning, and motivation—have been studied more than all others. Although all three are important, none is more central to organizational effectiveness than motivation. Motivation deals with the fundamental question, Why do people act as they do? Perhaps more important to managers is the question, What can be done to help employees become more productive in their jobs? There are many theories of motivation, ranging from purely mechanistic behavioral approaches to those that are almost mystical in their view of human activity. In this chapter, we take a pragmatic, understandable view that has been useful to many people in developing insights into behavior. Nearly everyone has a personal theory of human motivation.

People usually do things for an organization because the organization does things for them. When management asks employees to provide something for the organization, the employees expect to receive rewards for their efforts.

When an organization is managed so that employees can satisfy their individual needs by achieving organizational objectives, they exert full effort on the job. If employees perceive management as hindering their need satisfaction, they reduce their efforts or, in extreme cases, even fight the organization.

## SELF–ASSESSMENT ▮▮▮▮▮▮▮▮▮▮▮▮▮▮▮▮▮▮▮▮▮▮▮▮

Motivation is a complex topic that involves many considerations. Nearly everyone has their own theories of why people do what they do. For the following items, mark the response that agrees with your own experience and knowledge. Each statement or question has a range of possible responses. A scale of 1 to 6 between two words with different meanings allows you to mark either the word that is considered correct or a place between the two words that represents some agreement and some disagreement. Selection of a high number such as 5 or 6 may be either correct or incorrect, just as selection of lower numbers may be correct or incorrect. Some responses may be partly correct and partly incorrect.

Answers based on research by behavorial scientists, with a short explanation of why the response was considered correct, may be found on page 187.

1. Motivation deals with:

observable, external  1...2...3...4...5...6  unobservable,
conditions                                        internal
                                                  conditions

2. Human behavior is, to a large extent:

random  1...2...3...4...5...6  not random

3. Psychologists have learned that motives for a particular behavior:

can easily be  1...2...3...4...5...6  can be difficult to
determined                             determine clearly

4. It has been shown that:

goals do not control  1...2...3...4...5...6  goals control
behavior                                      behavior

5. Expectations of success or failure in achieving desired goals have been shown to:

have little effect on  1...2...3...4...5...6  have a strong
motivational strength                         influence on
                                              motivational
                                              strength

6. A single goal will usually satisfy:

a single need  1...2...3...4...5...6  many different
                                      needs

**7.** A number of different goals may contribute to the satisfaction of:

a single need  $1\ldots2\ldots3\ldots4\ldots5\ldots6$  many different
needs

**8.** When compared with lower-level needs such as food and safety, higher-level needs such as self-esteem and recognition can be satisfied:

in a greater variety of  $1\ldots2\ldots3\ldots4\ldots5\ldots6$  in fewer ways
ways

**9.** Most motivational studies indicate that satisfied needs are:

strong motivators  $1\ldots2\ldots3\ldots4\ldots5\ldots6$  not motivators

**10.** For a goal to be strongly motivational, achievement of the goal must be:

expected  $1\ldots2\ldots3\ldots4\ldots5\ldots6$  attractive or seen
as valuable

## MOTIVATION AND MANAGEMENT

The most productive organizations are those in which people can satisfy personal needs while contributing to the achievement of organizational objectives. The most effective managers make sure that employees have an opportunity to satisfy their needs on the job.

Because people are unique, their behavior in complex organizations is not easily understood. Enough similarity exists in the basic needs of individuals, however, to make it possible for organizations to provide satisfaction. Understanding motivation in organizations is difficult, since individual behavior is affected by various interactions that take place between people in an organization.[1]

Individual motivational patterns affect productivity in work organizations. But problems of employee motivation do not necessarily stem from lack of personal motivation. Motivational problems exist when behavior is focused on other goals than organizational ones or at a level far below an employee's capability.

## DEFINITION OF MOTIVATION

The term **motivation** has a variety of meanings. Numerous, lengthy definitions of motivation go into great detail regarding internal systems and discuss the interaction of factors such as needs, drives, and motives. These detailed psychological analyses are not dealt with here. Instead, we will summarize and abstract material on motivation that will be helpful in understanding behavior in organizations.

As a beginning toward understanding work behavior, we will use the definition of motivation provided by Bernard Berelson and Gary Steiner: "A motive is an inner state that energizes, activates, or moves [hence "motivation"], and that directs or channels behavior toward goals." [2] From this definition, several factors should be kept in mind.

*First, motivation deals with internal conditions that are not actually observed and cannot be isolated for physical analysis.* Motives such as hunger, security, sex, and recognition cannot be seen. What we do observe are the behaviors that result from the internal motives. Eating, drinking, talking, operating a machine, or making a sale can be observed; but the motives that lead to these behaviors can only be inferred. In other words, we attempt to make educated guesses as to why specific actions occur. Our primary purpose for studying motivation is to increase the accuracy of our inferences concerning people in work situations.

*Second, many of the discussions of motivation involve the construction of models and terms describing processes that have not been observed.* Most of our analysis of motivation depends on observing a set of conditions confronting an individual, observing the resulting behavior, and hypothesizing why the behavior occurred.

*Third, the result of motivation is always activity.* People respond to internal motives by activities directed toward goals they believe will produce satisfaction. When the internal motivation is hunger, for example, a person responds by actively seeking food.

*Fourth, motivation and behavior are not the same.* Motivation is an important factor in determining behavior, but there are also other influences, such as biological, social, cultural, and organizational factors, perception, and so forth.

In some cases a specific motive behind the observable behavior of an individual cannot be inferred. The differences in eating behavior illustrate that the motive for selecting food and a place of eating is not always simple hunger. Eating behavior may also be connected with satisfying the need for status or prestige. The rising executive who "must" eat lunch at the country club may be motivated more by status needs than by hunger. A single behavioral act may involve several complex underlying motives (see Figure 7.1).

## CHARACTERISTICS OF MOTIVATION

*Human behavior is not random.* All behavior is the result of some internal motivation. This does not mean that all human behavior is predictable, but that there is some cause for it, known or unknown. In observing a busy street, we note all the people going their diverse ways. As observers, we do not know where they are going or what prompts their movements, but surely there are reasons. The observed movements are in some way, perhaps only indirectly, the result of people fulfilling unsatisfied needs.

*Individuals do not always understand their own motivations.* They may not understand the reasons for their actions or the needs they are trying to fulfill. Suppose a person, apparently without reason, decides to hop in her car and take a ride. She has no destination in mind, and the drive may appear pointless. Just by driving around, however, the individual can be fulfilling a number of needs. In a rather low-key way, she may be fulfilling social needs by interacting

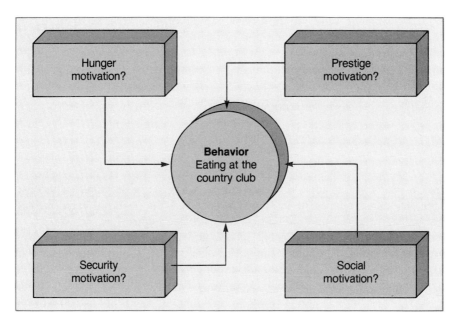

**Figure 7.1**   A behavior may involve several different motives.

with people on the roads. Esteem needs may be partially fulfilled by the very act of driving; the driver may be manifesting competence and knowledge of driving. Another possible motive may be a demonstration of affluence or daring by the model of car being driven. Any, all, or none of these reasons could have prompted the drive. But the driver was motivated in some way, even though she did not recognize the specific motives involved.

*Human behavior is directed toward obtaining goals.* The assumption is that personal needs will be satisfied when the goals are reached. "The goals that an employee seeks to reach are viewed as forces that attract the individual." [3] An employee with strong social needs may believe that the way to obtain friends in the office is to become a supervisor. This develops into a dominant goal, and the employee's behavior is directed toward achieving a promotion.

*Goals do not control behavior.* Goals *influence* behavior and give an individual direction in the attempt to satisfy needs. The attractiveness of the goal is related to the amount of frustration produced by unsatisfied needs. Running five miles a day, for example, may not sound attractive; but as an individual goal, it may be very satisfying. It can satisfy a safety need for a police officer who wants to be in good condition. It can satisfy an esteem need for an individual who perceives the ability to run five miles a day a challenge. Whatever the goal, it derives its attractiveness from the needs it fulfills.

*As soon as one need is satisfied, another appears.* People are in a never-ending chain of need fulfillment, always striving to improve and perfect their existence.

A satisfied need is not a motivator. After a need has been satisfied, we have no motivation to direct behavior toward goals related to it. Air is a basic physiological need. When an individual's supply of air is threatened or cut off, the need for oxygen becomes a prime motivator. Normally, we are not motivated by the need for air; we take it for granted. If you went to an employer for a job and he offered as salary all the air you could breathe, you would probably think he was crazy. It is a commodity we already have; why should we work for it? When a need is satisfied, it does not motivate.

## THE PROCESS OF MOTIVATION

The process of motivation begins with the internal need creating a state of tension, which results in an individual selecting a goal and striving to achieve it. If the actions are successful and the goal achieved, the need has been satisfied (or partially satisfied) and the tension reduced (see Figure 7.2).

The relationship among needs, goals, and behaviors to achieve goals is extremely complex. At any one time, an individual has a number of needs that exist at different levels of intensity. We experience simultaneous needs for food, friendship, achievement, rest and security, and so forth. The intensity of the needs we experience is in a constant state of change as a result of some needs being satisfied and other needs increasing in intensity.

The goals that individuals select to satisfy needs depend upon the individual's perception of the expected satisfaction to be obtained from a specific goal, the availability of goals in the environment, and the individual's estimate of ability to achieve the goal. An individual will attempt to select goals that can be achieved and that will provide the greatest need satisfaction. Almost any goal that is chosen will satisfy some needs while at the same time prevent the satisfaction of others. In developing behavior patterns, individuals tend to choose goals that they have found to be rewarding in the past. They will tend to avoid goals that they have not been able to achieve or that they found to be unrewarding once achieved. Goal selection is also influenced by the social norms, values, and codes of behavior that are believed to be acceptable.

Figure 7.2  Motivation process.

## Difficulties in Need Satisfaction

In the process of need satisfaction, difficulties can be encountered in any of the following areas:

1. The individual may not be able to indentify a goal that is seen as being related to the need.
2. The individual may not be able to identify a form of behavior (method) to achieve a goal.
3. The individual may identify a behavior but not be able to success- fully perform the behavior to accomplish the goal.
4. The individual may achieve the goal but find that it doesn't satisfy the need.

After a goal has been selected, a number of forms of behavior are usually available to achieve it. The particular pattern of behavior selected is affected by the individual's evaluation of abilities and an estimate of the most effective form of behavior in achieving the goal. When choosing behavioral patterns, individuals tend to repeat those patterns that have been most successful in the past.

The simplest behavioral model of motivation involves the process of people selecting goals they believe will satisfy needs and then selecting behaviors they believe will lead to successful attainment of the goals. Although the model of the motivation process illustrated in Figure 7.2 is simple and straightforward, the relationships involved are extremely complex. As shown in Figures 7.3, 7.4, and 7.5, goal-directed behavior involves the following factors:

1. A single goal may satisfy many different needs.

**Figure 7.3**   A single goal may satisfy several needs.

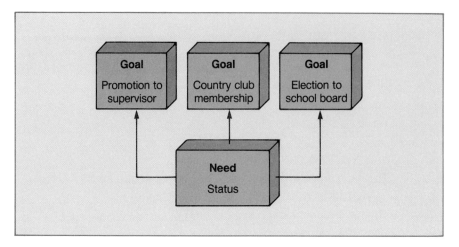

**Figure 7.4**   Several goals may satisfy the same need.

2. A number of different goals may contribute to satisfaction of the same need.

3. A number of different behaviors can lead to the achievement of a goal.

Keep in mind that what we observe is an individual's behavior. We cannot observe the internal motivation that leads to the behavior. In many cases, we must infer the "real" goal that the individual is trying to achieve, since it may not be directly observable.

## Classification of Needs

Many systems and methods have been developed for categorizing human needs. Any of the systems that have been developed may have value for a given

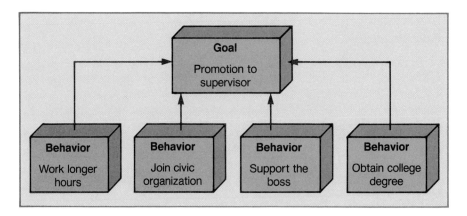

**Figure 7.5**   Several behaviors may be used to achieve a goal.

individual or for dealing with specific problems. But each system of classifying needs has the problem of individual differences. No descriptive system could be completely accurate or applicable to every individual or every situation. The classification systems that have been developed stem mostly from the areas of psychology, social psychology, and sociology. Most of these systems are similar. The primary differences are usually the degree of detail and number of categories used. There are, however, differences of opinion concerning types of needs and the importance of various need categories. The basic classification of needs discussed here is based upon observable goals and behavior. Needs are grouped on the basis of similarity of goals rather than on the similarity of inferred needs. This is the most widely applied approach to motivation, and it appears to be the most useful for managers.

Since behavior is directed toward goals that will satisfy felt needs, the manager has two basic choices in attempting to increase productivity by "motivating" employees. First, the manager can attempt to "create" felt needs within the employees. Second, the manager can offer the possibility of satisfying needs already felt by the employees. With either approach, the use of a system of categorizing needs is necessary.

## MASLOW'S NEEDS HIERARCHY

A. H. Maslow developed the concept of a hierarchy of needs.[4] It has been extensively applied to managerial situations. Before discussing the specific categories involved in Maslow's needs hierarchy, the basic underlying assumptions of his system should be understood:

1. Motives are highly complex, and no single motive affects behavior in isolation. A number of motives are always in operation at the same time.

2. There exists in each individual a hierarchy of needs that requires, in general, that lower-level needs must be partially satisfied before higher-level needs affect behavior.

3. A satisfied need is not a motivator. When a need is satisfied, another need emerges, so that the individual always remains in a motivated state.

4. Higher-level needs can be satisfied in a greater variety of ways than can lower-level needs.

As shown in Figure 7.6, needs may be classified into five major groups.

### *Physical or Physiological Needs*

The lowest and most basic level on the needs hierarchy is composed of universal physiological needs. People generally concentrate on meeting physiological needs before concerning themselves with higher-level needs. **Physiological needs** include the need for food, water, oxygen, temperature control, reproduction, and shelter.

In our society, the satisfaction of physiological needs is usually associated with money. In this sense, individuals use money to satisfy basic motivations. It

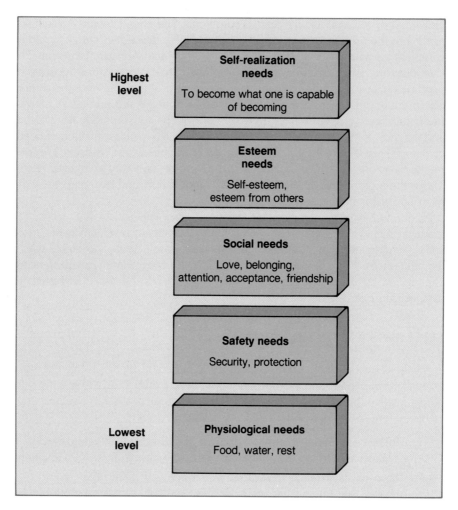

Figure 7.6   Maslow's needs hierarchy.

is not money itself, however, but what money can buy that satisfies physiological needs. Money can play an important role in obtaining need satisfaction at all levels of the hierarchy.

For individuals who are starving, higher-level needs are relatively unimportant; their behavior is directed toward the satisfaction of hunger needs. However, once physiological needs are relatively well satisfied, other needs become more dominant.

## Safety or Security Needs

The second level consists of needs for safety and security. **Safety needs** relate to protection from physical harm. Individual motivation involves developing protection from a wide variety of threatening events including accidents, injuries, sicknesses, and a multitude of unknowns. Safety and security needs in the work place involve worker safety and job security factors. Safety needs do not result in the necessity for absolute security, but in the knowledge that reasonable precautions are being taken to minimize risk. Safety programs, job security guarantees, and fair disciplinary procedures are examples of management attempts to satisfy safety needs. To provide additional protection and security, many organizations have some form of job tenure and provide various types of health and accident insurance for employees.

Some writers have suggested that many organizations tend to overemphasize the satisfactions of safety and security needs by providing unnecessarily elaborate programs of fringe benefits in the areas of health and accident insurance and retirement plans. When management places extreme emphasis on satisfying security needs, it may affect employee behavior by reducing initiative as employees follow management's lead and focus on their concern for security. In cases where security needs are negatively influenced by fears of being fired, laid off, or demoted, employees may become extremely cautious and defensive.

## Social or Belonging Needs

**Social needs** can be satisfied only by contacts between individuals or individuals and groups. Such needs include affection, affiliation, companionship, and belonging. Most people are concerned about their social relationships and want to belong and be accepted by others. Relationships, both on and off the job, satisfy social needs. The satisfaction of social needs begins with the family and expands to include social and work groups. Managers must expect that employees will want to satisfy the need for social relationships on the job. If the satisfaction of social needs is hindered, individuals may become antagonistic, uncooperative, and even aggressive toward the organization.

Belonging to a group helps satisfy social needs. Individuals seek affiliation because they desire to have their values and beliefs reinforced by group members. In the process of satisfying social needs, individuals tend to seek out groups that support their strongly held beliefs. If they are deprived of social needs, people will seek them as intensely as a hungry person seeks food.

## Esteem or Ego Needs

**Esteem needs** relate to individuals achieving the confidence and respect they desire in themselves and want to be accorded by others. Most individuals want to have a high level of self-esteem. Esteem needs can be satisfied by gaining knowledge, developing abilities, and successfully accomplishing tasks. When physiological, safety, and social needs are met, individuals usually channel their behavior toward developing higher levels of self-esteem. When esteem needs are satisfied, feelings of independence and confidence usually result. Satisfaction of esteem needs involves the internal factor of individuals' self-perception and the external factor of acceptance and recognition by others. On-the-job esteem needs are expressed in the desire for promotion, achievement, accomplishment, prestige, and status. Failure to satisfy these needs can lead to feelings of inferiority and helplessness, which may lead to passive and apathetic behavior.

Many jobs offer little opportunity for the satisfaction of esteem needs. Most of these jobs are found in the lower levels of organizations in which work has been highly specialized. Such jobs involve the repetition of simple tasks and allow only minimal use of ability. Individuals holding these jobs are often frustrated because they cannot use their abilities to satisfy ego or self-esteem needs.

## Self-Actualization or Self-Realization Needs

The highest level of needs in Maslow's hierarchy involves the development of full potential. Little is known about the effect of **self-actualization needs** on an individual's behavior. People satisfy needs at this level in many different ways. In addition, self-actualization is often difficult to identify and analyze. Two specific areas linked with self-actualization needs are competence and achievement.[5]

Functioning at this highest need level requires a psychologically healthy state. Many individuals never become self-actualized because they are unable to adequately satisfy needs at lower levels. People who do operate at this level have an accurate perception of reality, are able to accept themselves and others, are creative in their endeavors, and are continually involved in self-development. Self-actualized people want to use their capabilities to the fullest and continue to grow.

## Implications of Maslow's Needs Hierarchy for Management

Maslow's theory of human motivation includes two basic premises that have important implications for any manager. First, human needs are arranged in a hierarchy of importance. Higher-level needs do not become important in motivating behavior until lower-level needs are relatively well satisfied. This means that people are continually attempting to satisfy needs. When needs in one level have been satisfied, people move to the next higher order of needs. If lower-level needs are not satisfied, the individual may never be motivated by higher needs. For example, if a person's security needs are not being satisfied, the individual will not be motivated by the higher-level needs of esteem and self-actualization. Security needs will continue to dominate the individual's behavior. If management appeals to employees' higher-level needs when lower-level needs have not been satisfied, workers will not be motivated to increase their efforts.

Second, satisfied needs are not motivators. An important point for management to keep in mind is that employees are motivated by needs that are *not* satisfied. In other words, it is what people are seeking that is motivational, not what they already have. As lower-level needs are satisfied, they retain less motivational value in an individual's behavior. A need doesn't have to be completely satisfied, however, before the next level of needs emerges. An individual may move from security needs to social and esteem needs when the security

---

### Is No News Good News? ━━━━━━━━━━━━━━━━━━━━━━━━━━━

When Marie Lee stormed into Mike Smith's office, he was both startled and concerned. Before he could react, Marie burst out, "You've got to get me away from that no-good foreman." As personnel representative for the Comptop Data Equipment Company, Mike has rarely encountered such strong emotions. "Why don't you sit down," he said, "and tell me the problem." "Well," Marie blurted in a somewhat more controlled voice, "George Wright, my foreman, never talks to me, never tells me what to do or what not to do—he just barely says hello." Her voice rose again, "It makes me furious—he just never talks to me no matter how hard I work. He just totally ignores me. I can't stand it."

Later that day, Mike called George Wright, assembly foreman, into his office. "George, Marie Lee is one of your crew. What kind of worker is she?" asked Mike. "Excellent," George responded. "She comes in on time, does her job, and goes home. I never have to say a word to her. She just does her job."

---

need is "80 percent satisfied." One difficulty in analyzing motivation and using the needs hierarchy concept is the individual variability in the amount of satisfaction required before moving from one category to another. Managers must determine which needs are relatively unsatisfied in order to influence the behavior of employees.[6]

## ACHIEVEMENT MOTIVATION

Everyone has observed that some individuals seem to have a great desire to achieve. We observe individuals in every field who seem to have more drive and more commitment to reach the top than others.

The process of **achievement motivation** has been extensively studied by David C. McClelland.[7] For over twenty years, McClelland and his associates have studied achievement motivation in both laboratory settings and organizational environments. Their studies have led to the identification of achievement motivation as a distinct human need that varies in intensity among people. An extremely important contribution in this area of study has been the ability to measure the amount of achievement motivation possessed by individuals and its effect in specific situations.

A significant aspect of the behavior of individuals with high achievement motivation is that they choose goals that are both challenging and attainable. This behavior was illustrated by McClelland in an experiment in which individuals were asked to throw rings over a peg at any distance they chose. Most individuals varied the distance, throwing some rings from very close and some from very far away. Those with high achievement motivation chose distances that they thought would make success both challenging and attainable—not too close to make the task extremely easy and not too far away to make it extremely difficult or impossible. We observe this form of behavior frequently when employees on a job begin to establish higher but realistically attainable goals. The individual in sales who continually increases sales objectives so that it is necessary to "stretch" to reach them may be exhibiting high achievement motivation.

McClelland's research has indicated that individuals with high achievement motivation are *not gamblers*. They prefer work situations in which they can directly affect the outcome. Whenever possible, they choose to work on problems where chance has a minimal effect on the outcome. People without high achievement motivation may tend to be extreme in their approach to risk situations, either favoring highly risky gambles or attempting to minimize any chances of loss.

People who favor a "gamble" tend to choose high-risk situations where the outcome doesn't depend on individual ability or effort. The individual is provided an easy out to avoid personal responsibility for objectives that are not achieved.

Those who avoid risk taking are able to make small achievements that are almost certain. High satisfaction of security needs is provided, and the probability of anything going wrong for which the individual could be blamed is avoided.

### Aggressive Realism

Individuals with high achievement motivation are, in essence, taking a middle ground position that involves a degree of risk and a high probability of obtaining goals. Such a position can provide high levels of satisfaction because success is heavily influenced by the individual's ability and effort. This characteristic of individuals with high achievement motivation has been referred to as *aggressive realism*.

Another characteristic of individuals with high achievement motivation is that they are more concerned with the achievement itself than with any rewards that result from their success.[8] Rewards that may result from achieving goals are not seen as essential to the motivation for accomplishment. They do not refuse to accept rewards, but they obtain greater satisfaction from solving a problem than from receiving monetary rewards or praise. The value of money for people with high achievement motivation is in its representation of a measure of accomplishment. Usually, people with high achievement motivation do not modify their behavior to directly seek additional status, recognition from superiors, or pay raises.

Since those with high achievement motivation are primarily concerned with individual accomplishment, they tend to have a desire for specific feedback on how successful they are in reaching objectives. Achievement-motivated individuals with a strong desire for job-related feedback are often salespeople or operators of their own businesses. They are concerned not only with the amount of feedback received but also with the nature of the feedback. They respond most favorably to information concerning their productivity on the job. They usually consider feedback irrelevant if it deals with how cooperative they are, how helpful they are, their physical appearance, their personality, or any of a wide range of social attitudes. Figure 7.7 illustrates the conditions that promote high achievement motivation.

Individuals with high achievement motivation spend more time thinking about performing high-level accomplishments than do individuals with low achievement motivation. McClelland's research has found that when people begin thinking about achievement, their levels of achievement increase. High achievement motivation results in the individual's concentrating on higher levels of accomplishment and focusing behavior on reaching objectives.[9]

## Development of Achievement Motivation

The level of an individual's achievement motivation can be affected by the expectations of individuals he or she associates with. Levels of expectation that parents have for their children affect the levels of achievement motivation the child develops. In the same way, the level of employee achievement motivation can be affected by the expectations of management. If managers expect their employees to show initiative on the job and solve work-related problems, the employees tend to develop higher levels of achievement motivation. In this respect, managers often tend to make two types of errors.

First, the manager may expect too much too soon from employees, leading to their withdrawal from problem solving and decision making on the job. Expecting too much too fast tends to develop employee behavior patterns that are characterized by a defeatist attitude as well as by passive and indifferent behavior. In many cases, this behavior results when employees fail to achieve the objectives that managers set for them.

**Figure 7.7**   Conditions that promote high achievement motivation.

Second, management may assume that employees cannot function independently or cannot solve any problems without management's direct supervision. This extreme produces an environment of overprotection and restricts employee behavior. In an overprotective environment, there is little chance to develop challenging objectives, and employees become excessively dependent on management.

Current research indicates that achievement motivation can be developed and increased in individuals.[10] Many training programs have been successful in increasing the achievement motivation of both managers and employees. An organizational environment that offers opportunities for individuals to set and pursue challenging and attainable objectives, and offers supportive management behavior, is important in developing achievement motivation.

## AFFILIATION MOTIVATION

The need for affiliation—for human companionship and reassurance—produces a desire to interact with people. All indications are that everyone has affiliation needs; they experience some desire to give and receive attention. The intensity of **affiliation motivation** varies among individuals. Some people have high affiliation motivation, while others have relatively low levels.

### *Satisfaction of Affiliation Motivation*

The ability to satisfy affiliation needs is affected by the environment and the individual's interpersonal skills. The means available to an individual for satisfying affiliation needs are influenced by social and cultural factors. In organizations, individuals often concentrate on satisfying affiliation needs by interaction with other employees. Individuals expect to provide friendly support to other employees and to receive support when needed. These needs are satisfied when there is acceptance from other employees, and there is dissatisfaction when rejection occurs. Some jobs provide greater opportunities for satisfaction of affiliation needs than others.

For individuals with high affiliation motivation, social relationships will usually take precedence over task accomplishment. Trying hard to get along with others and enjoying the company of others are indications of high affiliation motivation.

Behaviors that result from affiliation motivation are friendliness, high levels of interaction, participation in group activities, coordination of people's efforts, and sensitivity to the feelings of others. Individuals with high affiliation motivation will tend to organize and participate in group activities such as meetings, parties, bull sessions, and reunions. In their interactions with others, they are often involved in helping solve personal problems, coaching, consoling, and sympathizing. They are concerned about the well-being and happiness of others.

Individuals can satisfy their affiliation needs in organizations by (1) receiving approval and reassurance from employees and managers, (2) conforming to the desires of work groups and management, (3) helping and supporting others in the organization, and (4) having frequent interpersonal contacts and good interpersonal relations (see Figure 7.8). Individuals with strong affiliation motivation tend to take jobs characterized by a high level of interpersonal interactions, such as public relations, personnel, sales, and teaching.

> When supervisors can create a cooperative, supportive work environment in which positive feedback is tied to task performance, employees with a high need for affiliation are more productive.[11]

There are individual differences in the desire for contact with others. A desirable approach is for organizations to provide individuals with opportunities to satisfy their affiliation needs but not to force employees into social situations. Managers should try to create a reassuring and cooperative work environment. Individuals should receive positive feedback when they achieve organizational objectives so that higher productivity results in satisfaction of affiliation needs.

## POWER MOTIVATION

The need for power produces a desire to influence others and control one's environment.[12] **Power motivation** is specifically related to an individual's relationships with other people. Everyone has some concern for the impact they have on others and would like to have a degree of control in interpersonal relations. In the simplest terms, the goal of power motivation is to feel powerful.

Obtaining power may help an individual satisfy other needs and achieve personal objectives. People also seek power as a primary objective in order to

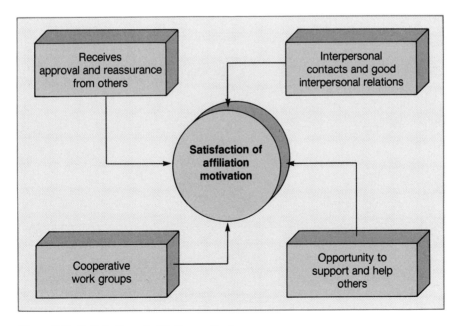

Figure 7.8   Satisfaction of affiliation motivation.

be dominant and forceful. Power is an important factor in the operation of any organization. An organization cannot function without people who have the motivation to obtain power and to influence the behavior of others. A manager's job involves getting things done through the effort of others, and he or she must be motivated to influence other people. Leadership and power appear to be two closely related concepts.

## Satisfaction of Power Motivation

The need for power can be satisfied in a variety of ways involving the control of resources, the control of information, and the control of people. As shown in Figure 7.9, power motivation may result in individuals trying to own prestige items, such as expensive cars, clothes, houses, or collections of rare objects. Satisfaction of the need for power may result in destructive or constructive behavior. In an organization, destructive results of power motivation could be attacks on others, destruction of property, promoting conflict, or theft. In its most positive form, power motivation can result in accepting responsibility, promoting effective team efforts, and developing productive organizations. Power motivation is neither "good" nor "bad." The way in which needs for power are satisfied by individuals in an organization can be a major factor affecting the quality of human relations.

Power motivation may be expressed in interpersonal relations in a number of forms ranging from making suggestions and stating opinions to using persuasion techniques to win an argument. Individuals may try to influence others by providing information, trying to teach others, attempting to inspire, giving com-

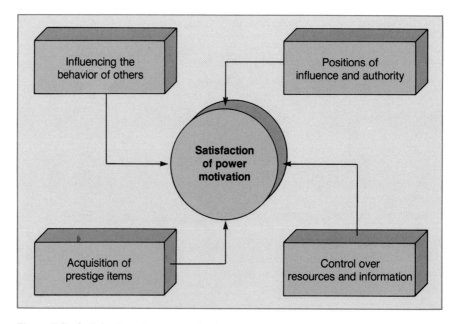

Figure 7.9  Satisfaction of power motivation.

mands, or demanding. Power motivation can result in a desire to be in a superior position and may lead to behaviors such as telling someone off. Individuals with high power motivation may appear to be pushy and domineering or strong leaders with a high sense of responsibility.

### Power and Management Styles

Research by David C. McClelland indicates that power motivation of managers can result in two very different management styles identified as **personal power** and **institutional power**. [13] Personal power can be thought of as "power over" and institutional power as "power with" others.

*Personal Power Style*   Managers with a personal power style try to be dominant. They can be inspirational and gain strong personal loyalty from employees. The personal power style can result in managers being overbearing and interfering with the work of others because of their own need to dominate. They may reject organizational responsibility and focus on their desire to be in a superior position. Personal power has been associated with being aggressive, acquiring prestige symbols, and developing dominance-submission relationships. Managers with a personal power style want employees to be loyal and responsible to them personally, not to the organization.

*Institutional Power Style*   The institutional power manager is concerned with organizational problems and actions that will result in attaining organizational objectives. Managers with this style concentrate their efforts on influencing others to make commitments to effective task performance. They do not try to obtain personal submission or to dominate individuals. The manager with institutional power style wants loyalty to the organization and is concerned with group goals. Helping people to identify and achieve group goals, and providing support for individual effort, are characteristics of the institutional power style.

According to McClelland, individuals with a high institutional power orientation have the following characteristics: (1) they feel responsible for developing an effective organization; (2) they like work and doing things in an orderly way; (3) they are willing to sacrifice some of their self-interest for the welfare of the organization; (4) they believe people should receive just rewards for their efforts; and (5) they are more mature and willing to get advice from others.

Organizations have one of their greatest challenges in providing constructive means for individuals to satisfy power needs. Problems can arise from variances in individual desires for power and differences in the way individuals choose to satisfy power needs. Not everyone wants a great deal of power, and some who want power do not use it effectively. In providing employees with opportunities to satisfy power needs, managers should determine the employees' actual need for power and their ability to use it well. Both formal and informal authority can satisfy power needs.

## EXPECTANCY THEORY OF MOTIVATION

Several **expectancy theories** of motivation have been developed, all founded on the assumption that people choose behaviors based on their expectations about the outcomes.[14]

In other words, the effort a person puts into his or her performance is a function of the value placed on the possible rewards *and* the perceived probability that the effort will be successful (see Figure 7.10). The basic concept of all expectancy theories is that the individual's motivation depends on what the individual expects to receive for his or her efforts.

### Valence

According to expectancy theory, motivation begins with the individual's desire for something (e.g., a pay raise, promotion, more responsibility, recognition). The strength of a person's preference for a particular outcome such as a goal or reward is referred to as the **valence**. The valence can be positive (desired) or negative (not desired) and can vary from $-1.00$ to $+1.00$. For example, the valence for a promotion would depend on the strength and direction of the individual's preference for the promotion. If the individual had a strong positive desire for advancement, the valence would approach $+1.0$.

The valence is a result of the individual's internal desires, which are affected by past experiences. The valences for specific goals (or rewards) will vary greatly from person to person.[15]

### Expectancy

The individual's probability estimate that a behavior will result in a specific outcome is referred to as *expectancy*. This is the perceived relationship between effort and rewards. Since expectancy is a probability, it can range from 0 to $+1.0$. Regardless of the accuracy of the individual's perception, expectancy influences whether a person will increase the level of effort.

For example, how certain are you that working harder will result in a promotion? If you believe that harder work would almost certainly result in a promotion, your expectancy would approach $+1.0$. If you believed that no matter how hard you worked, it would probably not result in a promotion, the expectancy would approach 0.

**Figure 7.10**   Basic expectancy formula.

Expectancy and valence are multiplied to determine the amount of motivation. If expectancy *or* valence is zero, motivation will be zero. If the individual has a high desire (high valence) for promotion but does not believe that better performance would result in promotion (low expectancy), there would be no motivation for better performance.

An individual may take several expectations into account when deciding how much effort to expend and how to behave (see Figure 7.11). For example, for an individual to be motivated by the possibility of a promotion, he or she must have at least the following three expectations:

1. The individual must expect that he or she has the capability to improve performance.[16] This may include expectations about individual ability, opportunity to improve, and resources needed to perform.

2. The individual must expect that improved performance will actually result in promotion. Because a reward is said to be available does not mean an individual believes the reward will actually be received.

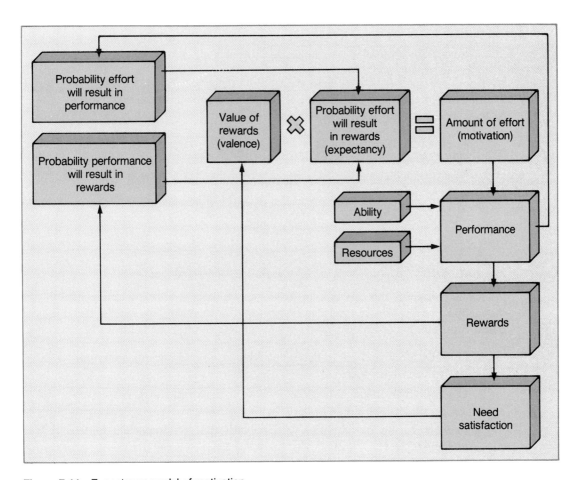

**Figure 7.11**   Expectancy model of motivation.

---

### What Must an Individual Believe Before Changing Behavior or Increasing Effort?

1. There is a high probability the behavior (or effort) will lead to the desired performance.
2. There is a high probability that as a result of the performance, a desired goal (or reward) will be obtained.
3. There is a high probability the goal (or reward) will satisfy important needs.
4. The goal (or reward) has high enough value to be worth the effort required.
5. If the probability of getting the goal (or reward) is low, the value of the goal (or reward) must be very high.

---

3. The promotion must be desired by the individual. The individual must expect the promotion will satisfy felt needs such as recognition, status, achievement, and so on.

If managers want to affect employee behavior by applying expectancy theory, they should ask three basic questions:

1. Are the potential rewards for the behavior highly valued by the individual?
2. Will the individual believe that the rewards are worth the effort required?
3. Does the individual believe that the reward will be received if he or she behaves as desired?

## Managerial Implications of Expectancy Theory

Managers can apply the concepts of expectancy theory to improve employee motivation to achieve organizational objectives. The following are specific suggestions on the use of expectancy theory to influence employee behavior:

1. Observe, listen, and ask to determine what goals and rewards are important to each employee.
2. Communicate management's objectives and expectations. Employees should understand the behaviors that are desired.
3. Reward desired performance with rewards that are important to the employee.
4. Increase expectations that desired performance will be rewarded. Tie rewards to desired performance and make reward visible to employees.

**5.** Provide adequate training and resources to increase the probability that individuals can achieve desired performance. Managers can use guidance and coaching to ensure that efforts will result in desired performance.

## SELF–ASSESSMENT DISCUSSION

**1.** (6) Motivation is an internal process. It stems from within an individual and cannot be directly observed. Only its results can be seen.

**2.** (6) Human behavior is purposeful, not random. Every action is directed toward some purpose and is the result of some internal motivation.

**3.** (6) Even under the most favorable circumstances, specific motives are difficult to recognize and define. Results of internal motives are observable, but the motives themselves must be inferred.

**4.** (1) Goals influence behavior but do not control behavior. A person who has the goal of gaining great wealth, as an example, may never work seriously to achieve the goal because of other overriding interests and demands.

**5.** (6) Expectations of achievement as well as the value or attractiveness of a goal are believed by many motivational specialists to be the primary determiners of the effort a person will expend in any given activity.

**6.** (6) Single goals will usually satisfy more than a single need. Ownership of an automobile can satisfy the need for transportation as well as needs for independence and self-esteem.

**7.** (1) Just as single goals will help satisfy many different needs, multiple goals may contribute to the satisfaction of a single need. The need for transportation to work may be satisfied by car pools, public transportation, or automobile ownership.

**8.** (1) Higher-level needs such as those for recognition, friendship, responsibility, satisfying work, and achievement may be satisfied in a wider variety of ways when compared with lower-level needs such as food and safety.

**9.** (6) Satisfied needs are not motivators. Some satisfied needs will return after initial satisfaction, and some needs are never fully satisfied. When a need is fully satisfied, it is no longer a motivator.

**10.** (1, 6) For motivation to occur, a reasonable achievement of a goal must be expected, and the goal must also be attractive or have some value.

## *QUICK REVIEW*

I. Motivation and Management

   A. People usually do things for an organization because the organization is doing things for them.

   B. The most productive organizations are composed of people who are satisfying personal needs while contributing to the achievement of organizational objectives.

II. Definition of Motivation

   A. A motive is an inner state that energizes, activates, or moves a person and that directs or channels behavior toward goals.

      1. Motivation deals with internal conditions not actually observed.

      2. The result of motivation is always some type of activity.

      3. Motivation and behavior are not the same.

III. Characteristics of Motivation

   A. Human behavior is not random.

   B. Individuals do not always understand their own behavior.

   C. Behavior is goal directed.

   D. Goals do not control behavior.

   E. As soon as one need is satisfied, another appears.

   F. A satisfied need is not a motivator.

IV. The Process of Motivation

   A. Motivation begins with an internal need creating a state of tension.

   B. Difficulties in the need satisfaction process arise because

      1. The individual may not be able to identify a goal as being related to the need.

      2. The individual may not be able to identify a form of behavior to achieve the need.

      3. The individual may not be successful in accomplishing the goal.

      4. The goal, once attained, may not satisfy the need.

   C. Individuals tend to select goals that are both achievable and satisfying.

   D. Goal-directed behavior involves the following:

      1. A single goal may satisfy different needs.

      2. A number of goals may satisfy the same need.

      3. A number of behaviors may achieve a desired goal.

V. Maslow's Needs Hierarchy

   A. Four basic assumptions underlie Maslow's system:

      1. Motives are highly complex; no single motive affects behavior in isolation.

      2. Lower-level needs must be at least partially satisfied before higher-level needs affect behavior.

      3. A satisfied need is not a motivator.

      4. Higher-level needs can be satisfied in a greater variety of ways than lower-level needs.

B. The levels in the hierarchy, beginning with the lowest-level needs, are: (1) physiological needs, (2) safety needs, (3) social needs, (4) esteem needs, and (5) self-realization needs.

C. Maslow's needs hierarchy has several implications for management:

    1. Human needs are arranged in a hierarchy of importance.

    2. A satisfied need is not a motivator.

    3. Managers must concentrate on unsatisfied needs to influence employee behavior.

## VI. Achievement Motivation

A. People's achievement needs vary in intensity.

B. High-achievement people choose goals that are both challenging and achievable.

C. High achievers are not gamblers. They want to affect the outcome of their efforts.

D. High-achievement people are more interested in achieving a goal than receiving external rewards for their efforts.

E. Managerial behavior can depress achievement motivation:

    1. Managers may expect too much too soon.

    2. Managers may assume that employees cannot function without direct, close supervision.

F. Managers should set challenging yet attainable goals for themselves and their employees.

## VII. Affiliation Motivation

A. The need for affiliation produces a desire to interact with others.

B. The means available to an individual to satisfy affiliation needs are influenced by social and cultural factors.

C. Social relationships will usually take precedence over task accomplishment for individuals with high affiliation motivation.

D. Affiliation needs can be satisfied in organizations by

    1. Obtaining approval and reassurance from employees and managers.

    2. Conforming to the desire of work groups and managers.

    3. Helping and supporting others in the organizations.

    4. Having frequent interpersonal contacts and good interpersonal relations.

## VIII. Power Motivation

A. The need for power produces a desire to influence others and control one's environment.

B. Power motivation can be satisfied in a variety of ways involving the control of resources, information, and people.

C. Two very different types of management can result from power motivation:

   1. Personal power managers, who try to be dominant

   2. Institutional power managers, who are concerned with organizational problems and objectives

IX. Expectancy Theory of Motivation

   A. The basic concept of all expectancy theories is that people choose behaviors based on their expectations about the outcomes.

   B. Motivation (effort) is a function of the value placed on possible rewards (valence) *and* the perceived probability that effort will lead to the reward (expectancy).

   C. Some of the key expectations affecting motivation and effort are:

      1. The individual has the capacity to achieve a goal.

      2. There is a strong probability that increased effort will result in the desired reward.

      3. The reward will satisfy a felt need.

## KEY TERMS

| | | |
|---|---|---|
| Motivation | Esteem needs | Personal power motivation |
| Need satisfaction | Self-actualization needs | Institutional power motivation |
| Needs hierarchy | Achievement motivation | |
| Physical needs | Affiliation motivation | Expectancy theory |
| Safety needs | Power motivation | Valence |
| Social needs | | |

## DISCUSSION QUESTIONS

1. Explain the meaning of the statement "There is *no* random behavior."
2. Discuss the relationship among needs, goals, and behavior to achieve goals.
3. What are the implications of Maslow's needs hierarchy for a supervisor?
4. Explain how a manager could use Maslow's needs hierarchy to increase the productivity of employees.
5. Give an example of a situation in which individuals were able to satisfy their needs and at the same time achieve organizational objectives.
6. How could an organization provide the opportunity for individuals to satisfy self-realization needs?
7. Discuss the characteristics of individuals with high achievement motivation.
8. How can management's expectations affect employees' levels of achievement motivation?
9. How can affiliation motivation be satisfied in an organization to improve the achievement of organizational objectives?

10. Describe how power motivation can result in constructive *and* destructive behavior.

11. How do expectancies affect the motivation of employees?

12. What can a manager do to improve performance by increasing expectations?

---

**EXERCISE**

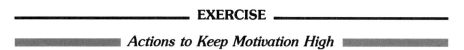 *Actions to Keep Motivation High*

As office manager you supervise fourteen young, enthusiastic, and highly motivated employees who do secretarial and clerical work for executives. The quality and quantity of their work is outstanding. Several of the executives have mentioned to you that after a time, the employees in the office will begin to lose interest in their work and their motivation will drop. Your boss has asked you for a plan of action to keep the motivation of the office employees at a high level.

*Evaluate the following list of possible actions to keep motivation high.*
Which actions would you recommend taking? Which should be taken first?

1. Create a relaxed atmosphere in the office to prevent employee burnout from the job pressures.

2. Have employees each develop challenging and attainable job objectives so they will concentrate on high levels of performance.

3. Develop work schedules and assignments so there will be motivation to produce from the assignments rather than from direct supervision.

4. Provide specific performance feedback to each individual and communicate your expectations for increased performance.

5. Place employees in a competitive situation by posting a chart showing each individual's output in quantity and quality.

6. Develop highly supportive relations with employees by frequently communicating your approval and reassurance to them.

7. Encourage cooperation among employees by having an office party once a month.

8. When an individual's motivation appears to be getting low, have him or her take some vacation time.

9. Frequently change job assignments to keep a high level of interest and spur motivation.

10. Develop training programs for employees so they will continue to increase their skills and abilities.

---

## TWO POINTS OF VIEW

### *"The Office Slob"*

*What would you do if you were the manager?*

You have recently been promoted to manager of financial planning for a public utility. You had been in the accounting department for six years, having taken the job with the company when you graduated from college with a degree in finance. Eighteen people work in the financial planning office, including statisticians, accountants, engineers, secretaries, and a computer programmer.

From your first day on the job, people in the office have been making comments about the appearance of Tom Gibson. Tom has been with the company for over fifteen years and has a reputation for being a highly qualified systems analyst and computer programmer. You had been told by the previous manager of financial planning that you could always count on Tom to provide the needed computer programs and data analysis using the planning data bank. In reviewing the work of all the employees in the department, you found that Tom's past work was outstanding. His data bank was invaluable, and his programs produced essential analysis. He has never been given the time to completely document the computer programs or the use of the computerized data bank, so replacing him would be almost impossible. If you were to fire Tom, a new programmer would have to spend considerable time to understand the current systems or develop totally new programs.

The employees are making jokes about his appearance and starting to avoid contact with him. You have noticed that his clothes are often soiled and wrinkled. His hair is often not combed, he occasionally comes to work without shaving, and his clothes are frequently mismatched. In the past few weeks, his office has become messy and the work he has given to the secretaries was, as they put it, "a disaster area." He apparently no longer cares about his personal appearance or the appearance of his work. The other employees are beginning to refer to Tom as "the office slob." You believe that if this recent trend of sloppiness continues, you may have major problems.

*What would you do if you were Tom Gibson?*

You are the systems analyst and computer programmer for the financial planning department of a public utility. You have been with the company for over fifteen years and are highly respected for your computer programming ability. You have always received high performance evaluations and have twice been recognized by the company as Employee of the Year. Management relies on you to write the computer programs for financial analysis and maintain a data bank that is the basis for all financial analysis. Since you have never been given the time to completely document the computer programs, there is no one who could do your job without having to start from scratch. You know that they could not afford to fire you, because no one could come in and use the computer systems without documentation. Programmers for this type of system are extremely difficult to find.

You always try to do the best possible job on any assignment. In the past you enjoyed doing the assigned work, but recently the job has become "a drag." You believe that the assignments you are being given don't make effective use of your systems analysis abilities and experience in financial analysis.

The other employees are much younger than you, and you don't have much in common with them. They seem to be more interested in how people dress than in how they do their job. You could care less what they think about your appearance. You have recently started to dress in ways that call attention to your lack of interest in appearance. Sometimes you don't even bother to comb your hair or shave. You get a lot of attention when you wear wrinkled suits or when your coat and pants are mismatched. The other employees have become so interested in your appearance that you have heard them refer to you as "the office slob."

You are not sure if they are ever going to get the message that what people do is important, not their appearance. You do enjoy your newfound attention from the employees, which often takes the form of their actively avoiding you. But you are becoming concerned about what the new department manager thinks about your work. Your new boss has never said anything to you specifically about your work. You have always believed that management's responsibility is to let people know if the work is not going the way they want.

### ENDNOTES

1. C. Pinder, *Work Motivation* (Glenview, Ill.: Scott, Foresman, 1984).
2. Bernard Berelson and Gary A. Steiner, *Human Behavior* (New York: Harcourt, Brace & World, 1964), p. 240.
3. Don Hellriegel, John W. Slocum, and Richard W. Woodman, *Organizational Behavior*, 4th ed. (St. Paul: West, 1986), p. 173.
4. A. H. Maslow, *Motivation and Personality* (New York: Harper & Row, 1954), p. 13.
5. Ellen L. Betz, "Two Tests of Maslow's Theory of Need Fulfillment," *Journal of Vocational Behavior* (April 1984): 204–20.
6. For detailed review of motivation theories, see Kae H. Chung, *Motivational Theories and Practices* (Columbus, Ohio: Grid, 1977) and Terence R. Mitchell, "Motivation: New Directions for Theory, Research, and Practice," *Academy of Management Review* (January 1982): 80–88.
7. David C. McClelland, J. W. Atkinson, R. A. Clark, and E. L. Lowell, *The Achievement Motive* (New York: Appleton-Century-Crofts, 1953) and *The Achieving Society* (Princeton, N.J.: Van Nostrand Reinhold, 1961); David C. McClelland, "Business Drives and National Achievement," *Harvard Business Review* (July–August 1962): 99–112.
8. John G. Nicholls, "Achievement Motivation: Conceptions of Ability, Subjective Experience, Task Choice, and Performance," *Psychological Review* (July 1984): 328–46.
9. A. Cox, *The Making of the Achiever* (New York: Dodd, Mead, 1985).
10. Heinz Heckhausen, Heinz-Dieter Schmalt, and Klaus Schneider, *Achievement Motivation in Perspective* (Orlando, Fla.: Academic Press, 1985).
11. Richard L. Daft and Richard M. Steers, *Organizations: A Micro/Macro Approach* (Glenview, Ill.: Scott, Foresman, 1986), p. 46.

**12.** John R. Schermerhorn, Jr., James G. Hunt, and Richard N. Osborn, *Managing Organizational Behavior*, 2d ed. (New York: Wiley, 1985), p. 138.

**13.** David C. McClelland, "Power Is the Great Motivator," *Harvard Business Review* 54(2) (1976): 100–10.

**14.** For reviews of expectancy theory, see D. P. Schwab, J. D. Olian-Gottlieb, and H. G. Heneman III, "Between Subjects Expectancy Theory Research: A Statistical Review of Studies Predicting Effort and Performance," *Psychological Bulletin* 86 (1979): 139–47 and Terence R. Mitchell, "Expectancy-Value Models in Organizational Psychology," in *Expectancy, Incentive, and Action*, ed. N. Feather (New York: Erlbaum, 1980).

**15.** James A. F. Stoner and Charles Wankel, *Management*, 3d ed. (Englewood Cliffs, N.J.: Prentice-Hall, 1986), p. 434.

**16.** H. Garland, "Relations of Effort-Performance Expectancy to Performance in Goal-setting Experiments," *Journal of Applied Psychology* 69 (1984): 79–84.

# Chapter 8

# Increasing Performance Effectiveness

———— *Learning Objectives* ————

After reading this chapter, you should be able to do the following:

1. Describe the process of relating employee needs to the achievement of organizational objectives
2. Discuss the motivation-maintenance theory of motivation and its applications in organizations
3. Identify the principles of work redesign and job enrichment
4. Describe how organizations use job enrichment and work redesign to improve motivation and productivity
5. State why motivational programs fail to improve productivity
6. Discuss effective approaches to motivation that will improve productivity

# Chapter Topics

- Motivation and productivity
- Motivation-maintenance theory
- Effect of maintenance and motivation factors
- Job enrichment
- Work redesign
- Reasons why motivational programs do not work
- Workable approaches to motivation

# Preview

Both managers and organizations want employees that are motivated to achieve organizational objectives. This chapter discusses applications of motivation theory to increase productivity in organizations. Although there are no simple "how-to" approaches, on-the-job research has begun to provide meaningful guidelines for motivating people to higher levels of productivity. Current research illustrates approaches that make it possible for employees to satisfy their needs by contributing to the achievement of organizational objectives. Ways in which managers have successfully applied motivation theories are reviewed in this chapter.

Motivation is an essential element in achieving productivity in any organization. The essence of managing people is to develop conditions that result in employees being motivated to achieve organizational objectives. Successful management depends on developing and maintaining conditions in the organization that integrate employee efforts with the physical and financial resources necessary for success of the organization. The efforts of people determine whether the use of physical and financial resources will result in organizational achievement.

## SELF–ASSESSMENT

This chapter deals with the application of motivational theory to performance improvement at work. Respond to the following items by marking the response that best matches your personal experiences and beliefs. Each statement or question has a range of possible responses. A scale of 1 to 6 between two words with different meanings allows you to mark either the word that is considered correct or a place between the two words that represents some agreement and some disagreement. Selection of a high number such as 5 or 6 may be either correct or incorrect, just as selection of lower numbers may be correct or incorrect. Some responses may be partly correct and partly incorrect.

Answers based on research by behavioral scientists, with a short explanation of why the response was considered correct, may be found on page 215.

1. Every relationship a manager has with employees affects their:

    motivation  1...2...3...4...5...6  job effectiveness

2. Which of the following factors is most likely to improve productivity on the job?

    a 10 percent pay  1...2...3...4...5...6  additional
        increase                              responsibility

3. Which of the following factors is most likely to fail to improve productivity on the job?

    guaranteed job security  1...2...3...4...5...6  recognition for
                                                     work well done

4. People are always motivated by something.

    strongly agree  1...2...3...4...5...6  strongly disagree

5. For motivational effect, compliments should be:

    in private  1...2...3...4...5...6  in front of others

6. Employee needs should be related to:

    organizational goals  1...2...3...4...5...6  external goals
                                                  outside of the
                                                  organization

7. When people are satisfied with recognition, responsibility, and achievement opportunities, concern for pay, organizational policies, and working conditions:

    increases  1...2...3...4...5...6  decreases

**8.** Which of the following has a greater impact on employee performance?

management behavior  1...2...3...4...5...6  messages urging
greater
performance

**9.** Effective managers:

solve employee work  1...2...3...4...5...6  involve employees
problems in solving work
problems

**10.** Most people consider their greatest asset to be their:

occupation  1...2...3...4...5...6  individuality

## MOTIVATION AND PRODUCTIVITY

People are motivated by a variety of personal needs, not by some external technique. The best results come from knowing what these needs are and giving subordinates room to satisfy them while achieving company goals.[1]

Regardless of the size of the organization or its activities, managers are concerned about the level of motivation in the organization. *Every relationship a manager has with employees affects their motivation.* Management's behavior must be analyzed according to the direction and degree of motivation. Motivating employees to achieve organizational objectives is a continual management responsibility.

Employee motivation depends on the perceived degree of need satisfaction. When workers perceive that performance will be personally rewarding, they are usually motivated to achieve high levels of productivity.

Recent research emphasizes the necessity to understand employee motivation, to carefully plan courses of action, and to be consistent and patient in carrying out plans.[2] Motivating others requires hard work and self-control.

### *Relating Employee Needs and Organizational Objectives*

The process of relating employee need satisfaction to the achievement of organizational objectives is shown in Figure 8.1. It involves the following steps:

1. *Make an evaluation of the needs that employees are trying to satisfy.* Managers must determine employees' strongest needs. Since needs are internal and cannot be directly observed, managers must infer the strength of needs from behaviors. Determining these needs accurately is often difficult.

2. *Determine the goals and activities that employees believe will satisfy their needs.* Different employees have different needs and will develop desires for different goals. The goals of individuals change over time. Some

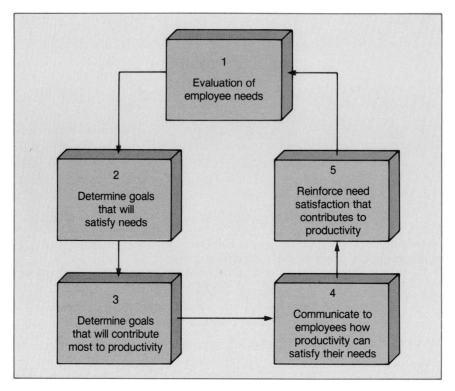

**Figure 8.1**   Process of relating employee needs to productivity.

employees will simply tell their goals to managers when asked. Other employees may not be able to specify goals or may not be willing to tell management. By observing the enthusiasm with which employees engage in activities, a manager should be able to distinguish the rewarding from the unrewarding activities.

3. *Determine the employee needs that can be satisfied in the process of achieving organizational objectives.* The ability of an organization to provide need satisfaction for employees is never unlimited. The means available for employee need satisfaction should be evaluated through their contribution to achieving organizational objectives. For most organizations, the purpose of satisfying employee needs is to achieve productivity.

4. *Inform employees of the opportunities available for need satisfaction.* Managers often "overlook" informing employees of opportunities that are available within an organization. In some cases, informing employees may involve making them aware of the possible rewards for desired behaviors. To integrate organizational and individual needs, managers must communicate to employees how achievement of organizational objectives can result in satisfaction of their own needs.

---

## No One Asked Me

At a prominent southeastern Iowa dairy, the manager called his staff together to tell them, "We're getting complaints from everyone. The milk's spoiling faster than it should. Consumers, store owners, and restaurant managers are all yelling." After an exhaustive study by qualified experts, the problem remained unsolved. One day, in complete exasperation, the manager walked through the processing section vainly searching for a clue. He stopped momentarily by a pasteurizing unit being repaired by a somewhat shy but industrious older mechanic. "If I only knew where to look for the trouble," the manager murmured. The mechanic looked up and said, "Your experts didn't check the old vent we sealed off when we installed the new processing unit. Maybe it's leaking a little and bacteria are finding their way in." The manager immediately called the chief of maintenance and asked if the vent had been checked. "No, sir," he replied, "there's no old vent on the plans." "Well, check it anyway," snorted the plant manager. A few days later, after the old unrecorded leaky vent was repaired and the early spoilage problem solved, the manager called the maintenance worker to his office. "Why," he queried, "didn't you tell anyone about this sooner?" The answer came promptly. "No one asked me, and if I told them, they probably wouldn't believe me."

---

5. *Reinforce employee satisfaction of needs that contribute to organizational productivity.* The reinforcement of desired employee behavior can result in additional needs being satisfied and increase the chances of the behaviors being continued. At the most basic level, this involves giving people credit for doing a good job. One of the strongest reinforcements for an employee is recognition for contributions to the organization.

## MOTIVATION–MAINTENANCE THEORY

A widely used approach for analyzing the organizational factors that affect employee motivation is **motivation-maintenance theory**. Frederick Herzberg conducted the original research that led to the formulation of the theory.[3] It is often referred to as the two-factor theory of motivation because it describes two sets of factors that are independent but not opposite each other.

**Maintenance factors** are those factors that make people unhappy or dissatisfied with their jobs. **Motivation factors** are those that make people happy or satisfied and lead to motivation on the job. The basis of the theory is that maintenance and motivation factors are essentially independent of each other and affect behavior in different ways. The opposite of job satisfaction is not dissatisfaction but *no* job satisfaction. The opposite of job dissatisfaction is not satisfaction but *no* dissatisfaction.

> Alleviating potential dissatisfaction can be thought of as administering preventive medicine.[4]

One study found that when maintenance factors were not present on the job, employees became dissatisfied. When maintenance factors were present, however, employees were not motivated to high levels of performance.

Motivational factors were found that produce high levels of job satisfaction and motivation. But if they are not present, they do not produce dissatisfaction.

Maintenance needs are generally equivalent to Maslow's lower-order needs in the physical, safety, and social categories. Motivation factors generally relate to Maslow's higher-order needs for esteem and self-realization (see Table 8.1).

## Maintenance Factors

In interviews with employees, Herzberg found that when people felt dissatisfied about their jobs, they were concerned with the conditions that surrounded the jobs. These maintenance factors involved the environment and conditions in which work was accomplished. Maintenance factors do not involve the nature of the work itself and are not an intrinsic part of a job. Maintenance factors include physical working conditions, job security, company policies and administration, social and interpersonal relations, and pay and economic benefits.

If any of these factors are not present to the liking of employees, the result is dissatisfaction, which may be expressed in ways that hinder the achievement of organizational goals. Providing for maintenance factors does not produce in-

**Table 8.1**

**Comparison of Maslow's Needs Hierarchy and Herzberg's Motivation-Maintenance Theory**

| Maslow | Herzberg |
|---|---|
| Self-realization needs | **Motivation factors** |
| Esteem needs | Achievement |
| | Recognition |
| | Work itself |
| | Responsibility |
| | Advancement |
| Social needs | **Maintenance factors** |
| | Interpersonal relations |
| Safety needs | Company policy and administration |
| Physiological needs | Salary |
| | Working conditions |
| | Supervision |
| | Job security |

creases in employee output but prevents losses due to reduced worker performance. Herzberg found that poor working conditions were often a factor in
negative job feeling, while good working conditions were seldom a reason for
positive feelings about the job. M. Scott Myers summarized the effect of maintenance factors by stating that "maintenance factors are characterized by the fact
that they inspire little positive sentiment when added, but incite strong negative
reactions when removed." [5] The following are specific maintenance factors that
are usually important considerations in an organization.

*Physical Working Conditions*   Physical working conditions involve the
quality of the physical environment in which the individual performs the job.
The lighting, temperature control, ventilation, and noise levels are physical
factors that directly affect the work environment. Working conditions are also
affected by the availability of employee facilities such as parking, rest rooms,
and cafeterias. When physical working conditions are undesirable, employees
tend to focus their attention on these problems and productivity suffers. What is
expected by employees as desirable working conditions varies depending on the
nature of the job.

The secretary who gets a new electric typewriter will probably respond
favorably and appear to be motivated. Within a few weeks, however, what
appeared to be motivation will level off to a condition better described as the
absence of dissatisfaction. If a typewriter does not function properly, the result is
dissatisfaction and lower productivity. When the broken typewriter is repaired,
the complaints will stop and the dissatisfaction will go away.

*Security*   When individuals feel certain about their continuation in a job,
security needs are usually being met. In a work situation, feelings of security are
affected by whether individuals believe they are protected by a fair and just
system. For most employees, security needs are most affected by how workers
perceive the behavior of their immediate supervisor. A supervisor who is
reassuring, supportive, consistent in decisions, and easy to talk with strongly
reinforces employees' feelings of security. The importance of security is reflected
in employee concern for seniority rights, disciplinary action, review processes,
and complaint procedures.

*Organization Policies and Administration*   For many employees,
dissatisfaction frequently centers on the policies and administrative procedures
of the organization. A common complaint involves the red tape and excessive
paperwork in an organization. An organization's goals, policies, procedures,
practices, and rules can be dissatisfiers when they are perceived by employees to
be inadequate or unfair. For example, promotional policies are often a source of
dissatisfaction when they seem to place artificial barriers in the employee's way.

Other policies, and their administration, cover a wide range of activities, such as vacations, overtime work, safety rules, and dress requirements.

***Social and Interpersonal Relationships***   An important part of the work environment is the social interaction that takes place among employees. Social needs are satisfied in organizations through both formal and informal group interaction. However, interpersonal relations can cause conflict and dissatisfaction when workers clash over job-related factors such as work load, pay, and advancement. Conflict and dissatisfaction can also result from disagreement about issues not related to the job, such as religion, politics, and other personal matters. Factors affecting social maintenance needs include coffee-break groups, professional groups, committees, lunch groups, parties, car pools, and recreational activities.

***Pay and Other Economic Factors***   Any direct or indirect compensation for performing a task can function as an economic maintenance factor. These include wages, salaries, and increases in benefits that are received automatically as a result of being in a position. The benefits that go with the job, such as social security, sick leave, unemployment compensation, retirement benefits, paid vacations, health insurance, paid holidays, and educational benefits, are maintenance factors. Maintenance factors do not include compensation or benefits that are received as a result of outstanding performance.

Figure 8.2 summarizes factors that can result in job dissatisfaction.

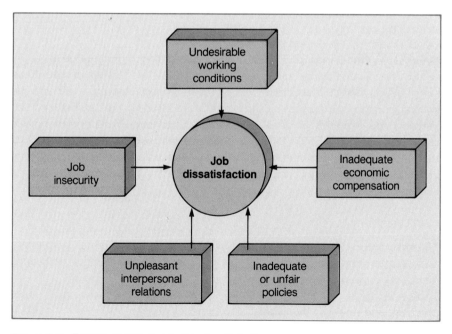

**Figure 8.2**   Factors contributing to job dissatisfaction.

## Motivation Factors

When employees feel good about their jobs, it is primarily because of the nature of the work itself. Factors that lead to positive feelings and motivation include achievement, recognition for accomplishment, responsibility, and personal growth. The presence of these factors leads to job satisfaction and employee commitment to higher levels of performance.

Motivation factors lead to high levels of satisfaction and increased productivity when they are present, but their absence does not lead to significant dissatisfaction. For example, responsibility leads to feelings of satisfaction about a job, but the lack of responsibility seldom causes dissatisfaction and "bad" feelings.

When motivation factors are present, they serve not only to increase productivity but also to develop greater employee effectiveness.

*Achievement*   As a motivational factor, achievement is present when employees have feelings of personal accomplishment or the need to accomplish. For achievement motivation to be present, the job must be challenging. Two factors are important in analyzing on-the-job achievement motivation: (1) the level of achievement motivation and (2) the ability to perform a specific job.

Since individuals differ in their needs for achievement, jobs that offer opportunities to achieve tend to attract people with high achievement motivation. Jobs with few such opportunities tend to attract people with low achievement motivation who are looking for satisfaction of maintenance needs such as security, desirable working conditions, and a favorable social environment.

For achievement to occur on the job, the individual must be able to succeed, which requires the ability to solve job-related problems and perform effectively. If a person is to be successful in writing a book, he or she must know how to write. For achievement to be a motivator, a person must have opportunity, ability, and desire.

Factors that can increase the opportunity for on-the-job achievement include delegation of authority and responsibility, involvement in planning and goal setting, availability of information concerning performance, and individual control of the quality of job performance.

*Recognition*   To function as a motivator, recognition must be the result of accomplishment. Recognition can come from the organization, managers, fellow employees, customers, or the public. For many employees, their jobs form only a small part of an organization's total activity, and recognition is the only way they can evaluate their achievement and contribution to organizational objectives. Research studies have found that praising job performance increases workers' motivation to improve job performance.[6]

Recognition may take many forms, from verbal or written recognition to pay increases and bonuses. Regardless of the form, the motivational value of recognition does not last very long. Frequent reinforcement is necessary for it to be of continuing motivational value.

Recognition not related to accomplishment is not a motivational factor but may satisfy status, security, and social needs. This type of recognition often takes the form of friendliness from others or conversations and discussions that involve the employee's personal interests. Unearned recognition may serve to satisfy maintenance needs by making the environment more pleasant, but it is not a substitute for recognition of accomplishment.

***Responsibility***   When individuals accept responsibility for decisions affecting their work, they develop a commitment to the job. If responsibility is to be a motivational factor, individuals must have the opportunity to accept responsibility. As responsibility is accepted, external control can be reduced. Individuals who work under close supervision seldom develop the desire to accept responsibility. In other words, increased job freedom and responsibility go hand in hand. When some jobs are closely examined, the discovery is made that the individual is responsible only for following instructions. Put more strongly, some jobs have been structured in such a way that employees' sole responsibility is to act like robots.

A study by M. Scott Myers of Texas Instruments revealed that a sense of responsibility is a function of level and supervisory style in the organization.[7] People in top-management positions had a higher sense of responsibility than did employees at lower levels. An even stronger relationship existed between accepting responsibility and the style of supervision. The employees' sense of responsibility was higher when their supervisor helped them develop by providing information, delegating responsibility, and encouraging risk taking.

***Growth***   Individual growth takes place through development of new skills and abilities and acquisition of additional knowledge. Growth is motivational for employees and advantageous for the organization, since it increases the effectiveness of its human resources. Opportunities for individual growth can involve formal or on-the-job training made available by an organization. The involvement of employees in problem solving and decision making is a highly effective way of providing opportunities for growth and, at the same time, increasing the effective use of human resources.

For growth to take place on the job, employees must receive timely, accurate, and specific feedback on the quality of their performances. Managers can promote growth by helping employees learn how to evaluate personal performance and determine areas in which additional skills or knowledge are needed. By encouraging self-evaluation and performance improvement, management can create the conditions for continual individual growth. The most visible opportunities for growth are through promotion, transfers, and job rotation.

Figure 8.3 presents a summary of maintenance and motivation factors.

## EFFECT OF MAINTENANCE AND MOTIVATION FACTORS

Research on motivation-maintenance theory has extended to every level of an organization, from hourly employees to top-level executives. Myers concluded

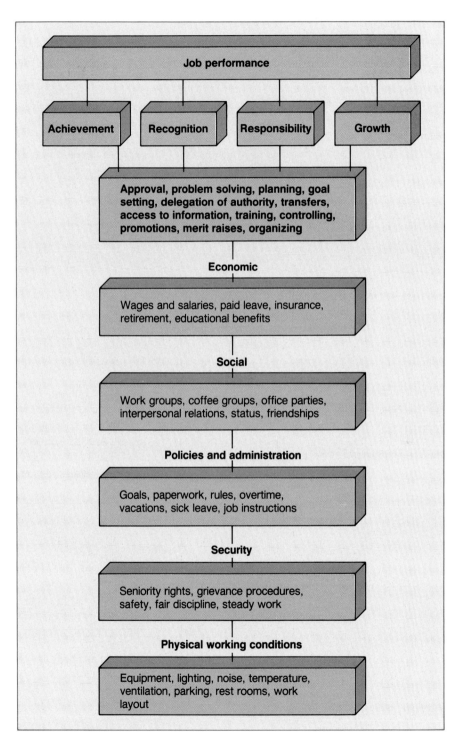

**Figure 8.3**   Maintenance and motivation factors that affect job performance.

from his studies that the motivation-maintenance theory "is easily translatable to supervisory action at all levels of responsibility." [8]

Research on the motivation-maintenance theory indicates that when people do not have motivational opportunities, they become preoccupied with maintenance factors. When employees are not able to obtain need satisfaction in the performance of their job, they tend to become "maintenance seekers" and try to reach a point where all dissatisfiers are absent. If employees focus on elimination of dissatisfiers, they tend to look for and find undesirable elements in their environment.

In situations in which employees are satisfying motivational needs, there is usually a reduced concern for maintenance factors. When they are involved in meaningful achievement, their behavior may be little influenced by dissatisfactions arising from the lack of maintenance factors. Some of the effects of maintenance and motivation factors are shown in Table 8.2.

## Some Implications for Managers

The most basic implication of the motivation-maintenance theory is that to maximize human productivity, one must satisfy employees' maintenance needs and provide the opportunity to satisfy their motivation needs. To develop high levels of motivation, managers must design jobs that provide employees with challenging work in which they can assume responsibility for achieving objectives. In many situations, jobs can be structured to provide increased opportunities for achievement, responsibility, growth, and recognition.

The manager's skill in organizing and planning can be a major influence on the employee's ability to perform effectively on a job. If management has not organized and planned, confusion and lack of coordination can occur, resulting in wasted time and effort. The effectiveness of day-to-day supervision of job-related activities can have a major impact on the employee's ability to accomplish tasks. If materials are not available for the individual who is assembling a product, the job cannot be performed.

The role of the manager in providing conditions for motivation includes developing an atmosphere of support and approval, communicating all neces-

**Table 8.2**
**Effects of Maintenance and Motivation Factors**

|  | Satisfaction on the job | No satisfaction of the job |
| --- | --- | --- |
| Maintenance needs | No job dissatisfaction; losses due to employees restricting productivity are prevented | Job dissatisfaction; activities that hinder achievement of organizational goals may occur |
| Motivation needs | Job satisfaction and motivation for higher levels of performance | No job satisfaction and no incentive to increase the quantity or quality of performance |

sary job-related information, encouraging individual goal setting, and providing recognition for achievement.

## JOB ENRICHMENT

The degree of job dissatisfaction and its impact on many industries has been carefully studied and documented.[9] Classic cases of dull, boring, and demotivating job situations have been highly publicized by the press. Job dissatisfaction is a major problem facing management today. "Although a number of different approaches to job enrichment can be used, a common theme is that job enrichment enables workers to meet more of their higher level needs." [10]

To solve many of the problems of motivation and productivity, managers must recognize that the nature of the job has a powerful effect on employee motivation. One approach to increase motivation and productivity is to make basic changes in the nature of jobs. One of the most prevalent approaches being taken to improve motivation on the job is the application of **job enrichment** techniques.[11]

To apply job enrichment, jobs must be created that are characterized by increased responsibility, personal advancement, recognition, and individual growth. An enriched job involves providing meaningful feedback and allowing employees to participate in decision making, problem solving, and goal setting. Job enrichment does not mean just assigning additional duties to an employee.

The following principles of job enrichment are useful in restructuring jobs (see also Figure 8.4).[12]

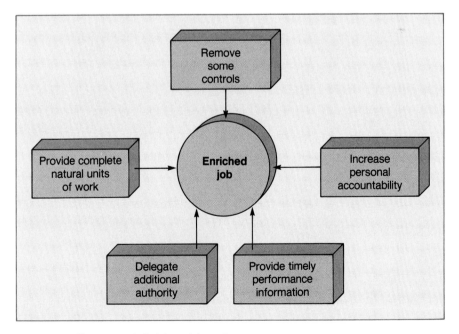

**Figure 8.4**  Key concepts in job enrichment.

### *Principles of Job Enrichment*

1. *Remove some controls.* Restructure jobs by removing some of the day-to-day control over the individual, with accountability being retained. For example, one company restructured jobs by allowing employees to decide how their jobs should be done instead of having job methods dictated to them.

2. *Increase personal accountability.* Restructure jobs to increase the accountability of individuals for their own work. As an example, the job of employees assembling electrometers at Corning Glass Works was restructured so they also inspected the meters and were personally accountable for quality.

3. *Provide complete natural units of work.* **Natural units of work** are jobs complete enough so that workers feel a sense of worthwhile achievement. This usually involves combining before and after operations into complete jobs. For example, Indiana Bell Telephone company allowed employees to compile the thinner telephone books personally and completely, with their own verification. This made one book "owned" by one employee and combined fourteen steps of work into one unit.

4. *Delegate additional authority to employees.* Restructure jobs so employees are provided with more freedom of action in their jobs. For example, Precision Castaparts allows employees to decide what information they need to do the job and to seek out the information for themselves without having to go through all the formal channels.

5. *Provide employees with direct and timely performance information.* Restructure communication to provide information directly to the employees instead of having them go through the normal, formal channels of their supervisor. Donnelly Mirrors reports company information on sales, production, inventories, and profits directly to employees.

At a basic level, job enrichment changes the structure of the job so that individuals are planning and controlling as well as performing their work. The great advantage of job enrichment seems to be that it changes the message communicated to employees by the nature of their job. Employees believe they are important and vital assets of the organization. Job enrichment involves employees in decision-making processes and relies on felt needs for responsibility, achievement, and recognition. Many nonenriched jobs seem to communicate that management believes employees are irresponsible, unmotivated, and incapable of learning or growth on the job. The nonverbal communication resulting from the nature of the job can easily override verbal messages transmitted by management in attempting to motivate employees.

*Examples of Job Enrichment* Some examples of successful job enrichment programs may help in developing an understanding of the processes involved.[13] Many of the typists at the Banker's Trust Company of New York had repetitive jobs recording stock transfers. The quality of work was poor, production was low, employee attitudes were negative, and absenteeism and turnover were high. To help change the organizational climate, the typists were involved in altering their work tasks to enrich their jobs. The following changes were made: (1) the typists made their own corrections on computer output tapes rather than having "specialists" make the changes, (2) each typist was responsible for a specific group of customers, (3) the typists checked their own work and eliminated the need for a checker, and (4) the typists scheduled their own work. These changes resulted in an annual savings of $360,000, improved attitudes, and greater employee satisfaction.

Motorola restructured an assembly operation so that each employee would assemble a combination of eighty different components. With the previous assembly methods, an employee worked on one or two components of the total product. The employee's name was put on the units he or she assembled and each employee became personally responsible for the quality of the units assembled. Any units that did not meet testing requirements were repaired by the employee who assembled them.

Additional training was required to enable the employees to assemble complete units. The total assembly operation also required 25 percent more employees. But these increased costs were offset by higher productivity, the need for fewer inspectors, reduced repair costs, improved quality, and less turnover.[14]

A Kaiser Aluminum plant was faced with a problem of low productivity of maintenance employees. Morale was low, and walkouts and slowdowns had occurred. To improve productivity, the following changes were introduced: (1) time clocks were removed and employees kept their own time records, (2) direct supervision was virtually eliminated, and (3) the employees decided what maintenance jobs were to be done and in what order. As a result, morale improved, and employees did better work and took pride in it. Maintenance costs were reduced by 5.5 percent.

Employees may resist management's efforts to enrich jobs. Effective job enrichment requires employee training and care not to threaten existing social systems. The two major reasons for resistance are that enrichment programs "are (1) not understood well by some workers and by some managers and (2) such programs may have implications for the redistribution of power."[15]

## WORK REDESIGN

**Redesign of work** can go well beyond the basic concepts of job enrichment. The redesign of work has provided some promising results in productivity and motivation. Although extensive work redesign is still in an experimental stage, some systems in operation have resulted in increased employee satisfaction and, at the same time, reduced costs.

Most of the efforts in work redesign have been confined to small work groups. Work redesign in a large setting was implemented in the General Foods manufacturing plant in Topeka, Kansas. The existing plant had had high product waste, expensive recycling, and acts of sabotage; and employees worked effectively only a few hours each day. A new plant was designed to provide a high quality of work life, develop strong employee involvement, and achieve high productivity.

Management, with the advice of employees and consultants, developed the following approach to plant operation: [16]

1. *Self-managed work teams.* Work teams of eight to twelve members were formed and given collective responsibility for segments of the production process. The team members decided who would perform the tasks, and most members learned all tasks in the team. Group meetings were held for decision making and coordination.

2. *Support functions included as a part of each team's responsibilities.* The teams were responsible for quality testing and maintaining quality standards. The team was responsible for functions typically performed by maintenance, quality control, custodial, industrial engineering, and personnel.

3. *Challenging job assignments.* Dull or routine jobs were eliminated wherever possible. Every set of tasks was designed to require responsibility and to challenge employees. The nonchallenging tasks that could not be eliminated were divided among the employees. For example, custodial activities were included in every assignment to avoid having anyone who did nothing but cleaning.

4. *Rewards for learning.* The objective was to have each set of tasks require unique skills that were equally challenging. Pay increases were given for mastering an increasing number of jobs. Individuals were rewarded for learning more aspects of the total manufacturing system. No limit was placed on the number of jobs employees could receive pay increases for mastering.

5. *Facilitative team leadership.* No supervisors planned, controlled, and directed the work of team members. A team leader position was created to facilitate decision making and team development.

6. *Managerial decision information provided to operators.* Production decisions that would normally be made by management were made at the operator level. The operators were provided with the necessary economic information and the managerial decision rules.

7. *The plant democratically governed.* Rules affecting employees were developed from collective experience rather than specified in advance by management.

8. *Physical and social settings developed to encourage interactions among employees.* Differentiating status symbols were minimized. There was one parking lot for all employees. Everyone used the single entrance to the plant and office area. A common decorating scheme was used in all areas, from offices to the locker rooms. The plant facilities were designed to promote informal communication among employees during working hours. The informal communication provided an opportunity to coordinate work and inform employees about each other's jobs.

The results of the work redesign at the General Foods plant were impressive. Standard methods of industrial engineering had indicated that 110 employees would be needed to operate the plant. With the application of the team concept, it took fewer than 70 employees. Quality rejects were 92 percent below the industry norm, and the absenteeism rate was 9 percent below. Reductions in variable manufacturing costs resulted in annual savings of $600,000.

## REASONS WHY MOTIVATIONAL PROGRAMS DO NOT WORK

1. Clear and measurable objectives for improvements in productivity may be lacking. Time and effort is spent on removing the symptoms of employee dissatisfaction. The basic reasons for employee needs not being satisfied are not dealt with.

2. "Canned" approaches to motivate employees are often ineffective, because they are not adapted to meet employee needs or the characteristics of the organization. Canned approaches often ignore the highly personal nature of motivation and the specific conditions that exist in the organization.

3. People are always motivated by something. Problems in productivity result from the motivation not being directed toward achieving organizational objectives. When "motivation programs" attempt to convince employees that they "lack motivation," they resent the implication of deficiency and react in a defensive manner.

4. The motivational impact of the organizational climate is not adequately considered. Often, too much emphasis is placed on gimmicks or procedures to "quickly" motivate employees to increase productivity.

## WORKABLE APPROACHES TO MOTIVATION

1. Most employees want to be productive. Yet barriers in the work environment often keep employees from being as productive as they could be. For improvement to occur, either the nature of the job must be changed or the employee must modify behaviors to adapt to the work environment more effectively. In most situations, a more effective approach is to increase productivity by changing the work environment to fit the individual rather than by trying to change the individual.

2. Programs to improve productivity need to focus on the emotions and needs of employees as well as the "logical" and mechanical aspects of productivity.

3. Management's behavior tends to have more effect on employee motivation than messages urging more productivity. Managers must pay careful attention to the way employees perceive management behavior.

## Guidelines for Human Relations to Improve Productivity ▬▬

*Treat People as Individuals*

- Most people consider their greatest asset to be their individuality.
- Most people consider their abilities, skills, and personality as unique.

*Make the Best Use of Each Person's Abilities*

- Look for abilities that may not be in use.
- Attempt to develop unused abilities.
- Reward people who are using their abilities effectively.

*Tell People How They Are Getting Along*

- Let people know what you expect of them.
- Encourage people on their strong points.
- Train people to overcome weak points.

*Give Credit When Due*

- Show appreciation when an individual does an outstanding job.
- Compliment individuals in front of others.
- Compliment individuals while the incident is still fresh in their minds.

*Tell People in Advance about Changes That Will Affect Them*

- Give people as much background about the change as you can. Explain why the change is being made.
- Explain the advantages of the change.
- Get the information about changes to people in the organization first.

*Be Sure to Keep Your Promises*

- Don't promise anything you cannot deliver.
- Keep promises to a minimum.

*Use Authority with Sound Judgment*

- Don't substitute your authority for reason.
- Lead, don't drive.

4. Increased productivity in an organization does not start somewhere "down the line." The most effective efforts to improve motivation and productivity start with top-level management.

5. Organizational policies, procedures, and techniques to improve motivation must be adapted to meet the needs of individuals and situations. An

effective approach is to involve individuals closest to problems in developing solutions that can be implemented in the situation.

6. Trying to force people to increase their motivation is not effective. The best approach is to support employees by making it possible for them to work through problems, develop alternative solutions, and evaluate the results of their actions.

## SELF–ASSESSMENT DISCUSSION

1. (1, 6) Both motivation and job effectiveness are affected by relationships between managers and employees. Positive, supportive relationships lead to greater effort and improved performance. Negative relationships depress both motivation and performance.

2. (6) Although people like pay increases and never seem to tire of receiving more money, little evidence indicates that money, in itself, improves performance. Added responsibility communicates confidence by management in an employee's ability and nearly always has positive motivational value.

3. (1) Like money, security is a desirable job characteristic. Improving security, however, does not improve motivation. Recognition for good work is a powerful motivational tool that reinforces high levels of performance.

4. (1) People are always motivated by something. Needs are always present, and actions are taken to satisfy those needs.

5. (6) Public compliments have greater importance for most people than those made in private.

6. (1) Employee needs, such as those for belonging, self-esteem, and meaningful achievement, can be satisfied within the organization. Managers who help employees satisfy needs through identification with organizational goals are builders of effective work forces.

7. (6) Concern for lower-level maintenance needs decreases as higher-level motivational needs are increasingly satisfied in the work environment.

8. (1) Management action by job restructure, job assignment, and other confidence-building techniques is much more effective than messages urging increased performance.

9. (6) Effective managers involve employees in solving work problems rather than provide the solutions. Good managers know that independence and responsibilities are valuable employee assets. Solving problems for others may be appreciated but it also increases dependency on the problem solver.

10. (4, 5, 6) With little doubt, a person's occupation is important. More important, however, is the personal recognition of uniqueness and individuality that all people possess.

*QUICK REVIEW*

I. Motivation and Productivity
   A. The essence of management is the development of conditions that help motivate employees to achieve organizational objectives.
   B. Every relationship a manager has with employees affects their motivation.
   C. Employee needs can be related to organizational objectives by
      1. Making an evaluation of the needs employees are trying to satisfy.
      2. Determining the goals and activities employees believe will satisfy their needs.
      3. Determining employee needs that can be satisfied in the process of achieving organizational objectives.
      4. Informing employees of opportunities available for need satisfaction.
      5. Reinforcing employee satisfaction of needs that contribute to organizational productivity.

II. Motivation-Maintenance Theory
   A. Herzberg's two-factor theory describes motivation and maintenance as two sets of conditions that are not opposites of each other.
   B. The absence of maintenance factors leads to dissatisfaction.
   C. The presence of motivational factors leads to satisfaction.
   D. Maintenance factors include physical working conditions, security, organization policies and administration, social and interpersonal relationships, and pay.
   E. Motivational factors include the nature of the work itself, achievements, recognition, responsibility, and personal growth.

III. Effect of Maintenance and Motivation Factors
   A. Achievement is reduced by dissatisfaction with maintenance factors.
   B. When employees are satisfying motivational needs, there is reduced concern for maintenance needs.
   C. Job design, organization, and planning all influence employee effectiveness.

IV. Job Enrichment
   A. To apply job enrichment, conditions must be created that are characterized by increased responsibility, personal advancement, recognition, and individual growth.
   B. Job enrichment principles include
      1. Removing some controls.

   2. Increasing personal accountability.

   3. Providing complete natural units of work.

   4. Delegating additional authority to employees.

   5. Providing employees with direct and timely performance information.

V. Work Redesign

   A. Work redesign involves redesign of not only the task but also the total system in which work is accomplished.

   B. Experiments in work redesign seek to provide high quality of work life, employee involvement, and high levels of productivity.

VI. Reasons Why Motivational Programs Do Not Work

   A. Lack of clear, measurable objectives.

   B. "Canned" appproaches not characteristic of the organization.

   C. Lack of consideration of organizational climate.

   D. Lack of direction toward organizational objectives.

VII. Workable Approaches to Motivation

   A. Removing of barriers in the work environment.

   B. Focusing on emotions and needs as well as on mechanical aspects of productivity.

   C. Emphasizing employees' perceptions of management behavior.

   D. Starting motivational programs at top echelons of the organizations.

   E. Designing policies, procedures, and techniques to meet individual needs.

   F. Supporting employees, developing alternative approaches, and helping them evaluate the results of their actions.

## KEY TERMS

| | | |
|---|---|---|
| Motivation-maintenance theory | Motivation factors | Natural units of work |
| Maintenance factors | Job enrichment | Work redesign |

## DISCUSSION QUESTIONS

1. Describe the process of relating employee need satisfaction to the achievement of organizational objectives.

2. How would you determine the activities that individuals believe will satisfy their needs?

3. What methods are available to a supervisor to reinforce employee need satisfaction?

4. What are the basic differences between maintenance factors and motivation factors?

5. Why do you think motivation-maintenance theory has become popular with managers?

6. What are examples of organizational policies that are sources of dissatisfaction?

7. How would you increase the opportunities to satisfy motivation needs on a job with which you are familiar?

8. Comment on the statement "When individuals are not able to satisfy motivation needs, they tend to become maintenance seekers."

9. Describe the characteristics of an "enriched" job.

10. What are the potential advantages of job enrichment?

11. Describe how the following jobs might be enriched: (a) service station attendant, (b) city garbage collector, (c) high school teacher, and (d) secretary.

12. Can a program of work redesign increase productivity in one organization and decrease productivity in a different organization? Why?

---
## EXERCISE
---

### Actions to Improve Productivity

Your department's productivity has dropped more than 20 percent in the last two months. Your boss has informed you that unless you get the productivity level up, you may be replaced.

*Evaluate the following list of actions to improve productivity.*
Which actions would you take? Which would you take first?

1. Call a department meeting. Release the productivity information and make it clear that you expect immediate improvement.

2. Discuss the decreased productivity with each employee privately. Be specific with each employee about ways to improve productivity.

3. Say nothing to employees about the productivity problem. Put on pressure for more productivity by your actions. Be strict in discipline.

4. Immediately start correcting all unacceptable behavior through private conferences with employees. Be pleasant but firm.

5. Avoid contact with employees until they feel sorry for you and, as a result, start to solve the problems.

6. Begin involving employees in solving problems that you previously handled yourself.

7. Have a party for employees and develop off-the-job relations with them.

8. Go to other supervisors and ask for help in solving the problem.

**9.** Provide each employee with a written report on the problem and request written feedback on solutions.

**10.** Go to higher-level managers and ask for help in solving the problem.

---
### TWO POINTS OF VIEW
#### *"Super Efficient"*
---

*What would you do if you were the supervisor?*

You supervise the shipping department for an electronics manufacturing company. Seven packers put calculators in individual boxes and place them in cartons for shipment. Each packer works individually to complete his or her share of the calculators to be boxed each day. Betty Rogers finishes her work in about half the time required by the other packers. Because she finishes her work faster, Betty takes longer breaks and more time for lunch than the other packers. On breaks and after she has completed her work for the day, Betty usually works on the assignments for courses she is taking at the local college. Betty does not seem to have much in common with the other packers and spends little time talking with them.

All the packers receive the same pay, and no extra pay is given for greater output. The company policy is that the pay for jobs that are primarily manual labor is to be on an hourly basis, with all employees doing the same job receiving the same hourly pay rate.

You are becoming concerned about Betty's interpersonal relations with the packers, because the other packers are frequently complaining about her longer breaks and her studying for classes. You encouraged Betty to work toward a college degree and had approved her studying during breaks as long as she did her share of the packing. You are now questioning whether you should continue to let Betty take the longer breaks and do her studying on the job. Even though the other packers agree that Betty gets her share of the work done, they have requested that you have her slow down or that you assign her more work. You know that if you don't take some action, conflict will continue between Betty and the other packers.

*What would you do if you were Betty Rogers?*

You are a packer in the shipping department for an electronics manufacturing firm. You pack calculators in individual boxes and place them in cartons for shipment. You work independent of the other six packers, and each packer has his or her share of calculators to box each day. You are able to finish your work in about half the time it takes the other packers because you don't spend any time in conversations. The other packers seem to have a lot to talk about with each other. You would rather get your work done so you can study for the courses you are taking at the college. You know that the other packers don't like your working faster than they do. They have suggested that you should "slow down and be more friendly." You know that if you don't do some studying on your breaks and at lunch, you will not be able to do well in your college courses.

The most important thing in your life at present is your education. You want to have a career as an engineer, which requires that you obtain a college degree. You have thought that if it was absolutely necessary, you could look for another job where it would be easier for you to get your class assignments done. Your supervisor had encouraged you to work toward your degree and had even approved your studying on the job as long as you did your share of the work.

No one is complaining that you don't do your share of the work, but you know that the other packers have complained to the supervisor about your longer breaks and studying at work. The other packers seem to be bound and determined that you will work at their pace and be their friend. Since you have little in common with them, you don't want to be friends. You just want to do your job and study for your courses. You are concerned that this may not be possible, because the others have started trying to talk with you when you try to study during your breaks.

## ENDNOTES

1. Hensleigh Wedgewood, "Meatballs and Motivation," *Supervisory Management* (May 1970): 2.
2. Benjamin Schneider, "Organizational Behavior," in *Annual Review of Psychology*, eds. Mark R. Rosenzweig and Lyman W. Porter (Palo Alto, Calif.: Annual Reviews, 1985), pp. 573–611.
3. Frederick H. Herzberg, "One More Time: How Do You Motivate Employees?" *Harvard Business Review* (January–February 1968): 53–62.
4. Phillip L. Hunsaker and Curtis W. Cook, *Managing Organizational Behavior* (Reading, Mass.: Addison-Wesley, 1986), p. 163.
5. M. Scott Myers, *Every Employee a Manager* (New York: McGraw-Hill, 1970), p. 72.
6. Louis P. Cusella, "The Effects of Feedback Source, Message, and Receiver Characteristics on Intrinsic Motivation," *Communication Quarterly* (Spring 1984): 211–21.
7. M. Scott Myers, "Conditions for Manager Motivation," *Harvard Business Review* (January–February 1966): 58–71.
8. M. Scott Myers, "Who Are Your Motivated Workers?" *Harvard Business Review* (January–February 1964): 73–88.
9. *Work in America: Report of a Special Task Force to the Secretary of Health, Education, and Welfare* (Cambridge, Mass.: M.I.T. Press, 1973); H. L. Sheppard and Neal Q. Herrick, *Where Have All the Robots Gone?* (New York: Free Press, 1972).
10. Don Hellriegel and John W. Slocum, Jr., *Management*, 4th ed. (Reading, Mass.: Addison-Wesley, 1986), p. 419.
11. Robert A. Baron, *Understanding Human Relations: A Practical Guide to People at Work* (Boston: Allyn & Bacon, 1985), p. 127.
12. For detailed discussion of job enrichment, see Richard M. Steers and Lyman W. Porter, eds., *Motivation and Work Behavior*, 3d ed. (New York: McGraw-Hill, 1983), pp. 483–516; G. R. Ferris and D. C. Gilmore, "The Moderating Role of Work Context in Job Design Research: A Test of Competing Models," *Academy of Management Journal* (December 1984): 885–92; and R. E. Walton, "From Control to Commitment in the Work Place," *Harvard Business Review* (March–April 1985): 76–84.

13. These examples were drawn from an appendix to *Work in America*, which summarizes thirty-four cases studied involving job enrichment.

14. For a more detailed description, see Walter B. Scott, "Participative Management at Motorola—the Result," *Management Review* (July 1981): 26–28.

15. Henry L. Tosi, John R. Rizzo, and Stephen J. Carroll, *Managing Organizational Behavior* (Marshfield, Mass.: Pitman, 1986), p. 232.

16. Richard W. Walton, "How to Counter Alienation in the Plant," *Harvard Business Review* (November–December 1972): 70–81; D. A. Whitsett and L. Yorks, "Looking Back at Topeka: General Foods and the Quality-of-Work-Life Experiment," *California Management Review* (Summer 1983): 93–109.

# Chapter 9

# Conflict, Frustration, and Stress

―――――― *Learning Objectives* ――――――

After reading this chapter, you should be able to do the following:

1. Describe the types of motivational conflict experienced by individuals
2. Discuss the nature of frustration and how it affects people
3. Identify the constructive and disruptive effects of frustration
4. Describe the nature of defense mechanisms and the types of defense mechanisms
5. Discuss the implications of defense mechanisms for effective human relations
6. Describe the causes and consequences of stress
7. Identify individual courses of action to reduce stress
8. List courses of action an organization can take to control job stress

## Chapter Topics

- Motivational conflict
- Frustration
- Constructive results of frustration
- Disruptive effects of frustration
- Defense mechanisms
- Stress management
- Causes of stress
- Consequences of stress
- Individual actions to reduce stress
- Sources of job stress
- Controlling job stress
- Minimizing stress in organizations

## Preview

William James, the father of American psychology, observed that it is not work that tires people but the burdens of unmade decisions. The longer we take to decide on a course of action, the more likely we are to experience anxiety, tension, and physical symptoms of stress such as headaches, digestive disturbances, and emotional upsets. Philosophers have said that if a mule is placed precisely between two equal bales of hay, it will starve to death rather than make a choice. Conflict, the inability to choose between two or more alternatives, is an integral part of the human condition. Inability to resolve conflict or to achieve a goal once a course of action has been determined leads to frustration, along with aggression, withdrawal, and stress. In this chapter, we review the problems of conflict, frustration, and stress management and offer suggestions to alleviate these problems on the job.

The complexity of human behavior is reflected by the many motives that simultaneously affect an individual's behavior. People must continually make choices when attempting to satisfy needs. When a person works to achieve a goal, a number of different motives are usually involved.

## SELF–ASSESSMENT

Frustration, stress, and conflict can have many causes. This chapter explores some important sources of these problems and suggests ways of handling them. Each statement or question has a range of possible responses. A scale of 1 to 6 between two words with different meanings allows you to mark either the word that is considered correct or a place between the two words that represents some agreement and some disagreement. Selection of a high number such as 5 or 6 may be either correct or incorrect, just as selection of lower numbers may be correct or incorrect. Some responses may be partly correct and partly incorrect.

Answers based on research by behavioral scientists, with a short explanation of why the response was considered correct, may be found on page 247.

1. Choosing between goals is more difficult when the goals are seen as having:

equal value  1...2...3...4...5...6  different value

2. Causes of frustration are often:

external conditions  1...2...3...4...5...6  internal conditions

3. The results of frustration can be:

constructive  1...2...3...4...5...6  destructive

4. Intense frustration will often result in:

aggression  1...2...3...4...5...6  withdrawal

5. Defense mechanisms, such as rationalization, provide solutions to causes of frustration.

agree  1...2...3...4...5...6  disagree

6. For most people, dealing with high levels of frustration and conflict leads to:

stress  1...2...3...4...5...6  goal satisfaction

7. Stress is a:

specific response  1...2...3...4...5...6  nonspecific response

8. Stress responses are usually:

physical  1...2...3...4...5...6  psychological

**9.** A highly effective stress reliever is:

   an alcoholic beverage  1...2...3...4...5...6  exercise
            or drink

**10.** Moderate levels of stress most frequently:

   increase performance  1...2...3...4...5...6  depress performance


## MOTIVATIONAL CONFLICT

When goals cannot be obtained, an individual may be forced to choose between satisfactions. The motives themselves are not in conflict; the goals or the methods to obtain goals are incompatible. Conflict then develops.

   In the simplest situation for analysis, two conflicting desires will result in three basic types of conflict situations. Psychologists usually call them approach-approach, approach-avoidance, and avoidance-avoidance.


### *Approach-Approach Conflict*

The **approach-approach conflict** forces the individual to choose between two different courses of action, each leading to satisfaction. Two different goals or objects are involved, but the individual can obtain only one (see Figure 9.1).

   In the approach-approach conflict situation, the individual must choose one course of action and reject another. The choice is often forced because of limited resources such as time or money. The individual may want both a new car and a new boat, but cannot afford them.

   Choosing between two rewarding (positive) goals becomes more difficult and takes longer when they are seen as having equal value. But in most cases of approach-approach conflict, the decision is relatively easy because both alternatives are rewarding. Approach-approach conflicts usually do not result in high levels of tension and frustration. An example of such conflict is having two good job offers and finding them both attractive. A choice must be made between them.

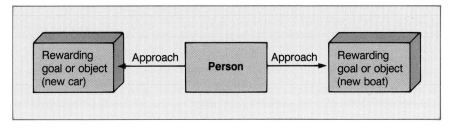

Figure 9.1   Approach-approach conflict.

## *Approach-Avoidance Conflict*

In the **approach-avoidance conflict**, an individual is attracted to an object or activity and, at the same time, wants to avoid it. The conflict occurs because the goal has both positive and negative features. Approach-avoidance conflict occurs in the case of the offer of a job that pays well but involves living in an undesirable location. The approach-avoidance conflict is diagrammed in Figure 9.2.

Approach-avoidance conflict often occurs when an individual makes a purchase. The object purchased may have attractive characteristics, but its cost is often a negative factor. The decision to approach or avoid involves evaluating the gain versus the losses. Most decisions involve an element of approach-avoidance conflict; few objects, activities, or goals are without some negative aspects.

Approach-avoidance conflict may occur when the goal is positive but the behavior required to achieve the goal has negative characteristics. Receiving additional pay may be a positive goal for an individual, but working overtime to obtain the pay is a nonrewarding activity.

In some situations, the positive goal is obtained, but undesirable consequences follow. For example, missing work to go fishing means a loss in pay and, possibly, disciplinary action from the boss.

## *Avoidance-Avoidance Conflict*

**Avoidance-avoidance conflict** occurs when an individual is forced to choose between two undesirable alternatives. The individual would like to avoid both alternatives (see Figure 9.3).

For example, a student may want to avoid both studying and making a low grade. An individual may be required to choose between transferring to an undesirable city and resigning from the company. Many sayings reflect the existence of the avoidance-avoidance conflict: "between a rock and a hard

**Figure 9.2**   Approach-avoidance conflict.

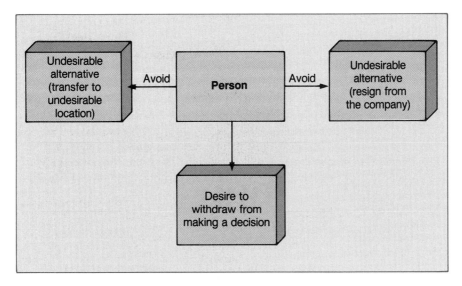

**Figure 9.3**  Avoidance-avoidance conflict.

place," "from the frying pan into the fire," "between the devil and the deep blue sea," "the lesser of two evils," and so on.

Because two undesirable alternatives are present in the avoidance-avoidance conflict situation, it is unlike the approach-approach situation and the approach-avoidance situation, which contain possibilities for need satisfaction. *In the avoidance-avoidance situation, there is typically a desire to escape, either physically or psychologically.* If the alternatives are extremely negative and the individual can't escape, he or she may turn to aggression and attack.

When a person tries to induce others to do something disagreeable or threatening by imposing punishment as an alternative, the procedure can be only as effective as the perceived strength of the punishment. If people operate on avoidance-avoidance conflict for a prolonged period of time, they may become psychologically ill.

## FRUSTRATION

When an individual is unable to attain a goal because of a perceived barrier, frustration results. **Frustration** takes place when efforts to satisfy a need are blocked before the desired goal is reached. The barrier may be in the situation or environment (external to the individual), such as the typewriter that breaks in the middle of typing a term paper. The barrier may be personal to the individual (internal barriers), such as a tendency to procrastinate when faced with a difficult deadline. Frustration is an individual condition based on individual perception and not a characteristic of the external environment.

There are many possible reactions to frustration. When individuals are unable to attain desired goals, they may engage in constructive efforts such as working harder to achieve their goals or redefining their objectives. Other behaviors can be disruptive, such as aggressive behavior directed at a real or imagined barrier.

Frustration is always accompanied by tension. Tension develops when needs are not being satisfied. At one time or another, all individuals involved in human organizations will experience feelings of personal frustration. As individuals work toward achieving personal goals, they often find that barriers exist that make it difficult or impossible for them to reach a desired goal. Individual barriers can result from an inaccurate estimate of physical or mental abilities. A young man who has career goals that require a college education but lacks the mental aptitude for college work has overestimated his abilities.

A woman who wants a promotion to a job she is capable of but who lacks the confidence to try for it has erected an individual barrier by underestimating her ability. Employees commonly attempt to reach goals and quit in the process because they underestimate their abilities to succeed. If an employee *perceives* a goal to be beyond his or her abilities, then the barrier is real to the individual.

The work environment can produce barriers that result in frustration. An employee may desire to achieve high production but is blocked by the machine breaking down frequently. A manager who wants to make a good impression on top management by getting a report in ahead of time may be frustrated by a typist who makes so many errors that the report is late. On-the-job barriers may involve the quantity or quality of physical, financial, and human resources.

Most on-the-job frustration appears to result from conflicts between individual wants and the restraints imposed by the organization. In any human organization, there are attempts to balance individual needs and organizational needs. As individuals become part of an organization and accept its methods and procedures, the area of conflict shifts from outside to within them.

## CONSTRUCTIVE RESULTS OF FRUSTRATION

Frustration is often regarded as undesirable because of its destructive effects. These effects frequently occupy our attention, and we tend to overlook those situations in which frustration results in positive outcomes. Frustration can cause individuals to become more effective in attaining personal and organizational goals. Figure 9.4 illustrates some constructive effects of frustration.

### *Increasing Efforts*

As tension increases in the individual, the tendency is to focus on goal attainment and to eliminate irrelevant and distracting behaviors. In some cases, frustration is part of the challenge of attempting to attain a goal.

One constructive effect of frustration may be an increase in the effort required to reach a goal. If this type of behavior is to take place, the goal must be seen as attainable, and there must be a perceived method to overcome the barrier. Most individuals can tolerate the mild levels of frustration that result from goals being challenging and attainable. However, if the barrier cannot be

**Figure 9.4    Constructive results of frustration.**

overcome by the individual, behavior will usually be redirected to another method or goal.

### Trying Other Methods

A frequent redirection of behavior is to choose another method of reaching an existing goal. As tension increases because underlying needs are not satisfied, the individual may notice previously ignored elements in the situation. For example, if an employee wants a promotion and does not achieve it by putting in extra hours of effort, he or she may try another method, such as doing personal favors for the boss.

### Choosing Another Goal

Another commonly observed reaction to frustration is a search for alternative goals that are more easily achieved. As tension increases because a barrier cannot be eliminated, alternative goals usually begin to appear more attractive.

In the most extreme cases, the individual may attempt to change environments, which may mean a change in jobs. When the situation is perceived as producing the frustration, most individuals consider the problem to be in the situation and look for another environment.

A person's view of the environment may change when comparing it with other situations. For example, an employee may investigate other job openings and decide that the current job "isn't so bad after all." This redefining of situations may cause a person to lower the level of aspiration and find ways to satisfy needs in the present job.

## DISRUPTIVE EFFECTS OF FRUSTRATION

If constructive efforts to reach goals and satisfy needs are not effective, tension will continue to increase. The tension can reach levels where its effects disrupt goal-directed activity.

When the tension level becomes high, the individual may concentrate so completely on the unsuccessful attempt to reach the goal or on the goal itself that other methods and goals are not considered. The individual may become extremely emotional and panicky and lose the ability to deal constructively with the situation.

The amount of tension that is experienced as a result of frustration depends on the individual and the nature of the situation. Some individuals can handle more tension than others. The ability of an individual to deal with frustration partially depends on previous experience with similar situations and on the anticipated outcome of the issue. A person may be able to tolerate a high degree of frustration for a long time without losing control. Some individuals are able to perform well under pressure and can make realistic and rational choices in situations in which most people would panic and lose control. Since most management jobs involve more pressure and frustration than nonmanagerial positions, managers must have the ability to tolerate frustration.

When the individual's tolerance level is exceeded, major disruptive effects may occur. Two frequent responses to prolonged frustration are aggression and withdrawal (see Figure 9.5).

### Aggression

**Aggression** in its simplest form involves a direct attack upon the perceived barrier to achieving the goal. If possible, the individual will direct aggression

AGGRESSION                                              WITHDRAWAL

**Figure 9.5**   **Disruptive effects of frustration.**

against the person or object that is perceived as the cause of the frustration. Direct aggression may involve physical or symbolic attack, or both. The employee who "cusses" out his supervisor for not approving a transfer is exhibiting a direct symbolic attack. A frustrated employee who thinks that a manager is the "barrier" preventing goal attainment may verbally or physically attack the person or may attempt, by rumors or other means, to "get revenge." Aggression can take many forms, including antagonistic behavior, theft, disobedience, sabotage, absenteeism, and interference with the work of others.

Aggression may be displaced toward an object or a person who is not directly involved in the situation. For example, an employee whose supervisor will not recommend a pay raise may displace an aggressive response toward his or her family. There are numerous forms of displacement, from slamming a door to kicking a dog. Usually, the target of displaced aggression is something or somebody not able to return the aggression.

When an individual cannot clearly identify a barrier, generalized aggression toward objects and people may result. As frustration increases and its sources become more difficult to identify, the generalized aggressive behavior may increase. In extreme cases, the individual may begin to attack everyone and everything within reach.

Many reasons may explain why an individual cannot direct aggression toward the source of the frustration. For example, if an employee were to direct aggression toward the boss, the worker could get fired.

### Withdrawal

A general behavioral reaction to intense frustration of one's efforts is **withdrawal** from the frustrating situation. An employee who cannot decide which of two transfers to take may withdraw from making a decision by staying on the current job.

Withdrawal may reduce tension, but it is usually not functional since the goal cannot be attained. This type of withdrawal is not the same as the escape reaction that results when individuals are in dangerous situations. The individual may withdraw from a situation by physically leaving, as is the case when an employee quits a highly frustrating job. The physical withdrawal may be temporary, as in the case of putting off writing a term paper until the last minute.

The employee who has been turned down for promotion several times may ask not to be considered for future promotions, thus physically withdrawing from a frustrating situation. Other ways in which employees may physically withdraw include absenteeism, taking sick leave when not sick, increasing the length of coffee breaks, and coming to work late and leaving early.

Withdrawal may also be psychological, as in situations where the individual develops an "I don't care" attitude. For example, a student originally wanted to get an A in a course. After making D's on the first two tests, however, the student decides that simply passing the course will be good enough. Employees who daydream on the job may be withdrawing psychologically from a frustrating work environment. Since the work situation seems to be beyond the employee's control, he or she will do the least amount of work necessary to keep the job, not caring if it is done correctly.

## DEFENSE MECHANISMS

When someone continually uses forms of withdrawal to deal with frustration, withdrawal becomes a part of their personality. It is no longer a simple withdrawal from a frustrating situation but a **defense mechanism**. The use of defense mechanisms makes it possible for a person to temporarily reduce his or her tension level and its accompanying feelings of anxiety. All defense mechanisms involve a degree of distortion of true relationships between the individual and external reality. Although defense mechanisms provide some relief from tension and anxiety, they do not satisfy underlying needs. Individuals learn defense mechanisms at an early age and continue to use those mechanisms that have worked for them in the past.

Defense mechanisms affect the way individuals relate to each other in organizations and the way they understand and adapt to their environments. Since problems of conflict and frustration are everyday occurrences, the use of defense mechanisms is also common. Everyone uses them to help cope with the barriers that arise in trying to achieve goals. Individual behavior patterns are partially determined by the types of defense mechanisms used and the extent of their use.

### Rationalization — "Everybody Does It!"

**Rationalization** involves a process of justifying behaviors and feelings that are undesirable or inconsistent by providing explanations that make them acceptable. The employee who takes company property for personal use may rationalize the theft by saying "everybody does it."

Rationalization involves developing a "good" reason rather than dealing with the real reason for behavior. In developing rationalizations, individuals usually distort the effects of emotions and motivational factors to maintain their self-esteem and avoid frustration. The individual who says, "I don't quit smoking because I would gain weight if I did, and that would be worse for my health" is rationalizing when the real reason for not quitting is that the individual can't break the habit.

Rationalization can take many forms. When people experience personal failure or violate moral principles, they can be creative in developing "good reasons" for their behavior. "I failed the exam because the questions were unfair." "I did not get the report done because the library was too noisy." "I did not make an A in the course because I'd rather get an education than make grades."

***Sour-Grapes***    Two common forms of rationalization are popularly referred to as "sour grapes" and "sweet lemons." Sour grapes involves convincing oneself that something is not worth having when one finds it cannot be obtained. When you discover you can't afford a Cadillac, you decide they aren't any good because they have a lot of maintenance problems (or any other reason you choose). The employee who did not get a promotion may say, "I really didn't want it because it would require more travel and longer hours." A student may drop a course he or she is failing and tell others, "The material wasn't worth knowing."

*Sweet-Lemons*   Sweet lemons involves convincing oneself that something one is forced to accept is really desirable. The sales manager who did not meet sales goals says, "It's just as well that sales were low, because they'll listen to my requests for more advertising money and give me more sales help." Another form of sweet lemons occurs when employees identify their jobs by more prestigious titles, as in the case of elevator operators who are referred to as "transportation specialists."

Rationalization can involve a complex set of reasons used to explain a behavior. With a number of reasons available, the individual has defenses in depth, so that if one rationalization does not work, others are still available. The employee accused of damaging a machine may say, "Someone else was the last to use the machine," or "The machine had not been working properly for some time," or "The machine has never been repaired properly by maintenance, and besides, this type of machine is not a quality product anyway."

Limited use of rationalization can be beneficial in reducing frustration and helping individuals in tension-producing situations to function effectively. However, if rationalization is used to extreme, an individual can become so entangled in unreal justifications that any realistic problem solving is avoided.

### Repression—"Motivated Forgetting"

**Repression** involves "forgetting" painful and frustrating information by unconsciously putting it out of one's memory.[1] As a result, the individual is not able to recall the original incident. Repression is a type of motivated forgetting, but at an unconscious level.

The deliberate suppression of painful or unpleasant information is a frequent form of behavior, but it is not repression. Repression is not a deliberate act; it occurs as a defense reaction to threatening information. An employee who "forgets" a responsibility that, when assigned, triggered fears of failure *may* have repressed the assignment. Feelings and experiences that produce a sense of guilt may result in repression. For example, an employee may "forget" to tell the boss about an embarrassing argument with a customer.

### Reaction-Formation—"Methinks the Lady Doth Protest Too Much"

**Reaction-formation** occurs when the individual reacts to a desire or behavior by exhibiting opposite attitudes and behaviors. The repression of strong tension-producing desires can be accompanied by behavior that is the opposite of the repressed desire.

The manager who represses the desire to have an affair with his secretary may go on a crusade against such type of "sinful" activity by employees. The real desire has been repressed and his behavior changed by denouncing his own feelings as perceived in others. Another example of reaction-formation is the mother of an "unwanted" child who becomes overprotective to prove to herself and others that she has no negative feelings toward the child.

An employee's extreme obedience to the boss could be a reaction of hate for the boss. In this situation, reaction-formation may create tension and frustration that could eventually cost the employee a job.

Just because we have a little knowledge of reaction-formation, we should not develop a skeptical attitude toward people's motives. Reaction-formation does illustrate that behaviors can sometimes reflect the opposite motivation of what the behavior seems to be. In specific cases, determining the "real" motivations of an individual may be difficult. You will need to know a great deal about the person and the particular circumstances before you can accurately interpret an intense attitude or behavior such as reaction-formation.

## Projection—"It's All Your Fault"

Through the use of **projection**, individuals protect themselves from awareness of their own undesirable characteristics and feelings by attributing them to others.[2] Projection allows an individual to hide feelings by projecting them onto another person. The employee who feels hostility toward the supervisor might use projection to hide the feeling by attributing hate to the supervisor. The individual may say, "The supervisor is out to get me, but I'll get something on the supervisor first." Individuals who have been unsuccessful in obtaining promotions may project their feelings and believe that others are out to get them, or they may attempt to block the promotion of others in the organization.

Individual security or insecurity on the job may have an effect on the use of projection. As pointed out by Sick, insecure employees tend to project their inadequacies onto others. "Those who are well adjusted and secure perceive positive traits in others, while those who are insecure and unable to recognize and accept their shortcomings tend to perceive others as having the same characteristics." [3]

The supervisor who has a production crisis because equipment is breaking down and tells employees, "Don't panic, don't panic, don't panic!" may be using projection. The supervisor has redefined the situation by projecting the undesirable feelings of panic onto employees. Individuals are using projection when they attempt to avoid dealing with unacceptable feelings or unsuccessful behaviors by blaming others or attributing their own characteristics to others.

## Identification—"Hero Worship"

Individuals are using **identification** when they pattern their behavior after others. Identification can involve assuming the values, attitudes, and behaviors of someone else. By identifying with someone, one can "share" the success of another individual. The achievements of a successful person can become satisfactions for the individual frustrated by failure.

An employee may adopt the values and behaviors of a respected and admired manager. This may be carried to the point where the employee adopts the mannerisms, speech, dress, hobbies, and eating habits of the admired person.

An employee may make no attempt to develop abilities through education, training, or experience but obtain satisfaction by identifying with people who are famous, rich, and successful. Identification with heroes can become the most important aspect of an individual's life.

Failures as well as successes are shared in identification. An individual may feel real pain and disappointment when a hero is injured or fails. Conflict can occur when an administrative assistant identifies with the boss to the extent of assuming not only some mannerisms but also the authority and responsibility of the boss. Secretaries are frequently observed identifying so closely with their bosses that they make the boss's decisions and assume that authority of the boss's position.

### Regression — "Disneyland, Here I Come"

**Regression** involves responding to frustration by reverting to earlier and less mature forms of behavior. The individual may revert to childish behavior or attempt to go back to an earlier and more comfortable time.

Regression may take the form of participation in activities that are usually reserved for children. An individual may escape a frustrating situation through regression by going to an amusement park and becoming a child again. Many activities can reduce tension, including building model airplanes, flying kites, playing with model railroads, and other such activities. Forms of play may allow individuals to escape the realities of responsibility and accompanying frustration.

Regression may also take the form of less mature and possibly destructive behavior. Temper tantrums as a response to frustration can be a form of regression. When frustrated on the job, regression may be reflected in pounding the desk, hitting a machine, horsing around, throwing a report on the floor, storming out of a meeting, or crumpling up a letter of complaint. The manager who cannot get approval for an additional secretary might begin typing, filing, and doing other activities more appropriate for subordinates.

The individual exhibiting regressive behavior may want the manager to assume the role of a parent in dealing with the situation. Regression is seldom helpful in achieving goals and solving problems because it does not focus on the present. It is based on the past and a return to earlier and less responsible behaviors.

### Implications for Human Relations

This review of defense mechanisms has not covered all of those that could be identified or described. It has focused on the more prevalent mechanisms. *All defense mechanisms lead to a degree of distortion in order to preserve one's self-image and reduce tension.*

Because direct satisfaction of needs is not always possible, defense mechanisms are used by everyone. Our human relationships are characterized by a complex interaction among underlying motives, individual goals, and behaviors. The conscious or apparent reasons for any behavior may not be the real reasons. Behaviors, attitudes, and feelings are not always what they appear to be. Our interpretations of observed behavior may also be inaccurate when we try to draw conclusions about the underlying motivation. The use of defense mechanisms serves to illustrate that individuals do not always understand their own behavior or the relationship between their behavior and the underlying motivation.

Even though a relationship always exists between underlying motivation and behavior, it is not one that is simple or easy to determine. The expressed feelings and attitudes toward another person may in fact be the real ones. But also possible is that the expressed feelings and attitudes do not reflect the internalized motivation.

Since we develop and use defense mechanisms to protect ourselves, they are a consideration in any human relationship. Because the development and use of defense mechanisms is neither recognized nor understood by the individuals using them, they are often difficult for individual comprehension. In other words, for a defense mechanism to be effective, it must "fool" the person who is using it. It is not important that other people may also be fooled.

The defense mechanisms that an individual uses are those that have been effective in the past in protecting the individual's self-image. People do not always use the same defense mechanisms over and over. An individual may vary the frequency with which any specific defense mechanism is used. The methods individuals develop for protecting their self-image produce distinctive patterns of behavior that seem to persist over long periods of time. Those defense mechanisms that are used in on-the-job situations are usually ones that have been developed early in the individual's life.

All people need defense mechanisms to cope with the frustrating situations that arise in any organization. Most people face many situations in which they can develop no realistic defense, and without the use of defense mechanisms, the tension level can become incapacitating. The continual use of them, however, is undesirable.

Everyone can think of situations in which individuals are observed using defense mechanisms as a reaction to frustration. Any individual operating in an organization should find it useful to understand these mechanisms, because they help us understand our own behavior and the behavior of others. The manager should view the use of defense mechanisms by employees as a symptom of possible work-related problems rather than as behavior to be somehow stamped out. In many situations, the use of defense mechanisms may be the result of an incompatibility between the nature of the job and an individual's personality. The employee who frequently comes to work late may be exhibiting avoidance reactions toward a job that is dull, boring, and unchallenging. In situations such as this, the most desirable managerial action is to eliminate the cause of the frustration rather than to discipline the employee harshly.

By evaluating the frequency with which employees use defense mechanisms, managers may gain insight into the degree to which employees are fulfilling their needs. Management can then help reduce frustration resulting from job-related barriers and help employees accomplish their goals.

## STRESS MANAGEMENT

**Stress management** has recently become a subject of intense interest. Although research on the cause and effect of stress has increased dramatically, there is still much that is not known.[4] For most people, dealing with conflict and overcoming frustration produce high levels of stress. Everyone experiences stress or pressure as they cope with day-to-day problems. Employees must deal with stress that results from the demands of their job and their managers.

Job-related stress can result in undesirable effects for both organizations and individuals. Mild forms of stress may produce discomfort, indigestion, fatigue, and headaches. High levels of stress can contribute to severe conditions, such as ulcers, strokes, heart attacks, and high blood pressure. However, avoiding all stress is undesirable, if not impossible. Moderate amounts of stress tend to increase performance and result in higher levels of achievement. Stress that is effectively managed by an individual is a positive force. Otherwise it can result in undesirable or unproductive behavior. The amount and type of stress that is most desirable depends on the individual's ability to handle pressure situations. As a result, the goal of stress management is to use stress as a natural and productive force.

### What Is Stress?

**Stress** is the nonspecific response of the body to any demand made on it that results in the individual preparing to take action. In everyday terms, people know the feelings that result from stress—racing heart, damp hands, dry mouth, and tension. Conflict and frustration produce stress as the individual attempts to adapt to pressures. Stress is the normal reaction of the individual to adapt to the demands of the environment. It is a necessary part of life; without it there are no challenges, no learning, and no achievements.

If you learn that you are being fired or that you are receiving a promotion, your *physical* stress response is the same even though you would evaluate these situations differently. Either situation will produce feelings of pressure, stimulating the nervous system. As a result, the body reacts by increasing the pulse, the lungs take in more oxygen, muscle tension increases, blood pressure goes up, pupils of the eyes dilate, and perspiration increases. In short, the body prepares to meet the challenge. These physiological reactions of the body occur to some degree every time a stressful situation occurs.

Keep in mind that situations producing undesirable levels of stress for one individual may be the source of major satisfaction for another.

## CAUSES OF STRESS

Stress can result anytime individuals face a situation that requires a change in behavior or higher level of activity. *Anything that occurs that puts an individual off balance or increases the need to do something can produce stress.* Although different factors result in stress in different people, the following are typical causes of stress: [5]

- *Physical factors* such as excessive heat, cold, noise, vibrations, air pollution, and light.
- *Interpersonal relations* with demanding or distressed individuals such as a dissatisfied customer, the employee who is angry about disciplinary action, the individual who demands that something be done faster, or individuals who want others to solve their problems.
- *Organizational and job requirements* such as risk of physical injury, dull jobs, deadlines, extreme responsibility, making high-risk decisions, fear of losing a job, performance failure, and time pressures. Physical and interpersonal factors can also produce stress in organizations.

Some individuals may experience pressure because they are too conscientious and work too hard. Individuals who are willing to impose demanding deadlines on themselves may experience the negative effects of stress. Situations that involve significant changes can create stressful conditions. Social, technological, and economic changes can produce high levels of stress for many people. When change or novelty leaves people uncertain and confused about what is going on, their stress increases.

***Emotionally Induced Stress***   Stress can result from the way individuals emotionally respond to situations. In **emotionally induced stress**, the individual develops expectations that something undesirable (or even terrible) will happen. Although emotionally induced stress can be classified in a number of ways, the following types are most common:

1. Emotional responses to *time pressures*. Individuals experience the pressure of deadlines. They may believe that "I must do something right now," be obsessed with "using" time, or try to make every minute count.
2. Emotional responses to *future events*. The individual experiences anxiety about what will happen in the future, anticipates the worst possible outcome of future events, and is fearful or worried about the future.
3. Emotional responses to *threatening situations*. When situations are perceived to be beyond one's control and there is the possibility of undesirable outcomes, stress can result. Threatening situations can involve past events that an individual feels guilty about.
4. Emotional responses in *interpersonal relations*. Dealing with unpleasant people can produce high levels of anxiety. Also, simply too much contact

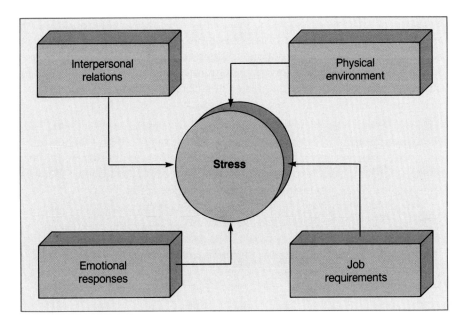

**Figure 9.6**  Factors contributing to stress.

with other people can result in interaction overload. Figure 9.6 summarizes the factors contributing to stress.

## CONSEQUENCES OF STRESS

Stress has been reported to be a primary or contributing factor in numerous physical and psychological disorders.[6] Although individuals vary widely in their responses to stress, the following four effects are representative of consequences often associated with stressful conditions. Keep in mind that causes other than stress can contribute to these conditions.

*Physiological Effects of Stress*   The possible physical responses to stress include increased heart rate, high blood pressure, hot and cold spells, numbness, headaches, indigestion, skin disorders, physical fatigue, ulcers, strokes, and heart attacks.

*Psychological Effects of Stress*   The psychological responses to stress can be a wide range of *feelings* that include anxiety, depression, aggression, fatigue, guilt, boredom, low self-esteem, alienation, loss of concentration, and feelings of inadequacy. The individual may become upset, nervous, jittery, highstrung, or overly excited. As a result of stress, individuals may make extensive use of defense mechanisms.

***Behavioral Effects of Stress***   Included in the possible behaviors that may result from stress are the use of drugs and alcohol, overeating or undereating, nervous gesturing, pacing, emotional outbursts, restlessness, difficulty sleeping or too much sleep, aggression, and poor interpersonal relations. In extreme situations, stress can be a strong factor in suicide attempts.

***Organizational Effects of Stress***   As a result of the behaviors of individuals experiencing high stress, organizations can be affected in a number of ways. These include absenteeism, lower productivity, interpersonal conflict, accidents, turnover, job dissatisfaction, and antagonism at work.

Individuals attempt to adjust and cope with stress through a wide variety of behaviors. Individuals should develop reactions to stress that allow them to be productive and avoid the undesirable consequences of stress.

Figure 9.7 provides a graphic summary of the effects of severe stress on individuals and organizations.

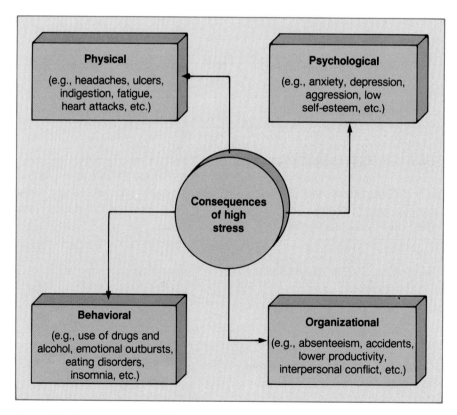

**Figure 9.7**  Consequences of high stress.

## INDIVIDUAL ACTIONS TO REDUCE STRESS

An individual can take a number of approaches to control stress. There is no one most effective approach. What works for one individual may not be effective for another. *A basic principle in any action to reduce stress is that individuals must obtain and maintain control of their behavior.*

The following are three approaches that can form the basis for an effective strategy to control stress. They are summarized in Figure 9.8.

1. *Avoid high-pressure situations that produce unacceptable levels of stress.* For example, don't accept unnecessary additional responsibility. Don't volunteer to serve on committees. Don't go to the shopping mall when it is crowded. Don't make unnecessary trips in bad weather.

2. *Manage situations to control the amount of stress and pressure.* Delegate some of the responsibility to someone else. Get deadlines extended. Obtain additional resources. Plan alternative courses of action in case the situation changes.

3. *React less intensely to situations.* Although it is easier said than done, a more relaxed response to pressure situations can produce significant reductions in stress. A technique that has been found useful is to ask yourself, "What is the worst thing that could happen?" and "Is this important enough to get upset about?" One manager put the following sign on his desk to help put situations in a realistic perspective:

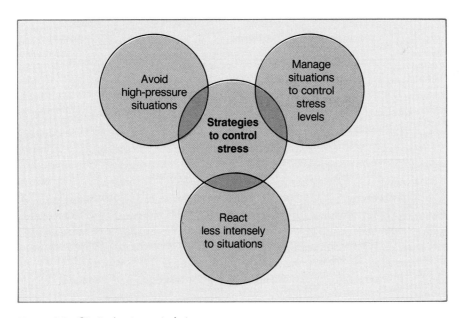

Figure 9.8   Strategies to control stress.

> I am not responsible for all the
> problems of the world.

*Stress Self-Analysis*   A desirable approach is for individuals to identify what is a reasonable level of stress and what is too much stress for them. In analyzing and controlling stress, answering the following questions may be useful:

- How much stress can I handle?
- What kinds of stress do I have difficulty handling?
- What kinds of stress can I avoid by removing myself from situations?
- What kinds of stress can I control by managing the situation?
- What situations should I respond to with less intensity?
- How can I maintain reasonable levels of stress while achieving my personal goals?

For controlled-stress living, individuals need to continually evaluate stress levels and control the total stress in their life by adapting to situations and maintaining a balance in their activities.

**Adaption** means taking events in stride. Change those things you can, but accept the things you can't change. Make time to relax and get away from pressure situations. Adapt to situations by reducing the emotional intensity of responses.

In a **balanced life**, needs are satisfied in a variety of different ways. To use an old saying, "Variety is the spice of life." A balanced approach to life includes work and leisure, challenge and relaxation, solitude and socializing, exercise and rest.

> Probably the most important way to reduce the negative effects of stress is to develop the habit of viewing problems optimistically and acting decisively toward them—experiencing commitment, control, and challenge rather than alienation, powerlessness, and threat.[7]

## SOURCES OF JOB STRESS

Although there are a variety of conditions that affect the overall stress level experienced by individuals, job pressures are a major source of the stress in day-to-day living.[8] Since individuals may react differently to the same situation, *any job situation can produce stress*. A change in work methods can reduce stress for one employee and increase stress for another employee.

The following are job conditions that tend to produce stress in most people:

1. *Quantitative job overload.* Although an individual can do the work, there is too much to do in the time available. Pressures can result from unrealistic deadlines. When the work load is too heavy, there is overstimulation. The engineer who has the ability to design a new model but can't finish

---

**Controlled-stress living** means achieving goals and satisfying needs while enjoying life. Individuals who are living a controlled-stress life tend to exhibit the following behaviors:

- They express their emotions, desires, and feelings without giving explanations or apologies.
- They exert positive control over pressure situations and can say no without feeling guilty.
- They defend their personal rights and don't allow others to force unreasonable responsibilities on them. They protect their personal right to privacy.
- They have a sense of humor and participate in activities just for fun.
- They have escape routes and are able to get away from problem situations and distressed people.

---

the design by the deadline is subject to stress from quantitative **job overload**.

2. *Qualitative job overload.* The individual lacks the ability to perform the required tasks. The job is "too challenging." Performance standards may be the source of job pressure when the individual cannot meet management's expectations. The engineer who lacks the specific training and ability to design a new model is subject to qualitative job overload.

3. *Underutilization of abilities.* The job is dull and boring, or the nature of the work does not require individuals to use their abilities. The engineer who must spend the majority of time doing routine office work and filling out forms may have stress from underutilization.

4. *Role ambiguity.* Lack of clear job objectives; the scope of responsibility is not understood. When individuals do not know what specific job performance is expected, they begin to experience stress. **Role ambiguity** can also result from not understanding what part a job plays in meeting organizational objectives. When individuals say, "I don't know what I'm supposed to be doing," they are indicating pressure from role ambiguity.

5. *Role conflict.* In this situation, stress is the result of conflicting job demands, expectations, and goals.[9] To do a job both faster and better may not be possible. For example, the production supervisor may want units produced faster, while the quality control manager wants better units. Individuals caught between these two managers will experience the stress of role conflict. Who should they listen to? **Role conflict** can also involve conflicting expectations of an individual's family and the organi-

zation. The job demands more traveling, but the family wants the employee to spend more time at home.

6. *Undesirable physical working conditions.* Stress results from physical conditions such as noise, heat, cold, crowding, safety hazards, air pollution, vibration, motion, and uncomfortable spatial arrangements.

7. *Extreme responsibility.* Stress occurs when individuals have responsibilities that cannot be effectively managed. The stress may be heightened when individuals do not have adequate authority to carry out responsibilities.

8. *Destructive competition.* When the competition among individuals results in destructive actions, stress is increased. Some individuals may believe that if they can't get promoted, they will make sure no one else does either. Job-related pressures intensify when people try to look good by making others look bad.

9. *Changes.* A major source of stress involves frequent or significant changes that have a direct impact on an individual's job. The process of adjusting to the new elements of a job also produces pressure. Most changes have an element of uncertainty and risk that contributes to stress. Change can be especially stressful if the person is afraid of losing a job.

10. *Contacts with distressed people.* The angry boss, the dissatisfied customer, or the obnoxious fellow worker can increase on-the-job stress. People's stress level is influenced by contact with individuals who are highly anxious, demanding, indecisive, depressed, or angry. These individuals have been referred to as **stress carriers**.

The major job conditions that often produce stress are summarized in Figure 9.9.

## CONTROLLING JOB STRESS

As part of a three-year study on managing job stress, Howard, Rechnitzer, and Cunningham identified techniques that were used to cope with stress.[10] Although there were individual differences in the use of these techniques, some interesting patterns of effective and ineffective methods were found, as outlined in the box on page 246.

Howard, Rechnitzer, and Cunningham concluded that "successful and unsuccessful coping with job tension seems to be characterized by the difference between working smarter and working harder." Individuals who effectively controlled stress were action oriented, took a preventive approach to stress, were aware of their capacities, and had a problem-solving orientation to factors causing stress.

## MINIMIZING STRESS IN ORGANIZATIONS

Managers can do a number of things to help minimize stress in organizations.[11] The effectiveness of any specific action will depend on the employees involved and the nature of the situation.

**Figure 9.9    Sources of job stress.**

Managers can begin by helping employees analyze the sources of stress on their jobs. Understanding the factors that contribute to job tension is a necessary starting point to control the stress levels in organizations.

Organizations can provide employees with information on stress management. Managers can work with individuals in developing approaches that they can use to control the sources of stress on their jobs. Some organizations have found it desirable to make stress management training available to their employees.[12]

Managers can make sure they are available to *listen* to employees. When individuals experience high job stress, they often need a manager who will listen and understand. Managers should avoid trying to tell the employee what to do right away. Often the temptation is to get the problem out of the way. Approaches need to be developed and adapted to the needs of the individual. Managers should not try to practice psychotherapy or psychiatry. They should deal only in areas where they are competent, which is usually work-oriented problem solving.

*The five best techniques for coping with job tensions and stress were:*

1. Build resistance by regular sleep, exercise, and good health habits.
2. Separate work and nonwork life.
3. Engage in physical exercise.
4. Talk through problems with peers on the job.
5. Withdraw physically from high-stress situations.

*The five worst techniques for coping with job tension and stress were:*

1. Change to a different work activity.
2. Change the strategy of attack on work.
3. Work harder.
4. Talk through job problems with spouse.
5. Change to a nonwork activity.

When confronted with employees who have severe psychological problems, usually the best approach is for the manager to try to help the individual obtain professional help.

Managers can analyze the conditions that exist in the organization to identify those that tend to produce job stress.

Actions to reduce stress must always be adapted to the organization and the individuals involved. The following are action-oriented questions a manager can ask to begin developing approaches to reduce major sources of stress:

1. *Quantitative job overload.* Can more resources be made available to reduce the load? Can better work methods be utilized? Can some of the work be done by someone else? Can more time be provided to accomplish the tasks?

2. *Qualitative job overload.* Can training be provided? Can some of the jobs be assigned to other individuals? Can the job be restructured so individuals will have the ability to perform effectively?

3. *Underutilization of abilities.* Can the nature of the job be expanded? Can individual assignments be changed to make better use of abilities? Could techniques of job enrichment be used?

4. *Role ambiguity.* Can clear job objectives be developed? Can specific performance criteria be developed? Can the scope of responsibility and authority be better defined?

5. *Role conflict.* Can a compatible set of job objectives be developed? Can methods be developed to resolve conflicts in demands and expectations from manager and employees? Can management structure jobs to minimize conflicts with off the job roles?

6. *Undesirable physical working conditions.* Can the physical sources of stress be reduced? Can employees be better protected from physical sources of stress? Can the spatial arrangements be modified to reduce stress?

7. *Extreme responsibility.* Can individuals be provided with resources that will help them carry out responsibilities? Do individuals need more or different types of authority? Can the level or type of responsibility be reduced?

8. *Destructive competition.* Can management redirect competition so it is productive? Can objectives and evaluation be reoriented to reduce destructive competition? Can rewards be implemented for constructive competition?

9. *Changes.* Can people be informed before changes occur to reduce the impact? Can training help people adapt to changes? Can the uncertainty about the outcome of changes be reduced?

10. *Contacts with distressed people.* Can employees be trained to deal effectively with distressed people? Can the frequency of contact with distressed people be reduced? Are there distressed people who should be removed from the organizational environment?

Management can be more effective in reducing job tension by being aware of the causes and consequences of stress. Effective stress management can produce a more satisfying work environment and can increase productivity.[13]

## SELF–ASSESSMENT DISCUSSION

**1.** (1) When goals are of equal value, choices are more difficult to make and levels of conflict increase.

**2.** (1, 2, 3, 4, 5, 6) Causes of conflict may be either internal, external, or a combination of both.

**3.** (1, 2, 3, 4, 5, 6) Frustration may lead to problem solving, creativity, and innovation, or to destructive behavior such as anger, aggression, or withdrawal.

**4.** (1, 6) Either withdrawal or aggression may result from intense frustration.

**5.** (6) Defense mechanisms may provide temporary relief from frustration but do not solve its causes.

**6.** (1) Dealing with high levels of frustration is a leading cause of stress in most people.

**7.** (6) Stress is a nonspecific response that manifests itself in many ways. Most notable are changes in characteristic behavior, physical symptoms, psychological problems such as anxiety and uncertainty, or feelings of complete exhaustion.

**8.** (1, 2, 3, 4, 5, 6) Stress responses can be either physical, psychological, or a combination of both.

**9.** (6) A highly effective stress reliever is physical exercise. Alcohol is among the most destructive and least effective.

**10.** (1) Moderate levels of stress most often increase performance.

*QUICK REVIEW*

  I. Motivational Conflict

    A. Many motives simultaneously affect an individual's behavior.

    B. An individual may not be aware of the motives leading to a specific behavior.

    C. When people have to choose between differing alternatives, conflict often occurs.

    D. The three basic types of conflict are

      1. Approach-approach conflict.

      2. Approach-avoidance conflict.

      3. Avoidance-avoidance conflict.

  II. Frustration

    A. Frustration is the result of the inability to attain a goal because of a perceived barrier.

    B. Frustration is an individual condition and not a characteristic of the external environment.

    C. Frustration can arise from either real or imagined barriers.

    D. Frustration is always accompanied by tension.

  III. Constructive Results of Frustration

    A. Increased effort can result from the focus on goal attainment to eliminate the cause of frustration.

    B. Creative approaches to problems can result from frustration through more thorough exploration of alternatives.

  IV. Disruptive Effects of Frustration

    A. Frustration tension can lead to emotional reactions.

    B. A wide range of frustration tolerance exists among people.

    C. Aggression is a common reaction to frustration and may be directed toward either objects or people.

    D. Withdrawal is another common form of frustration reaction.

  V. Defense Mechanisms

    A. Defense mechanisms are psychological reactions to frustration that allow temporary relief from frustrating conditions.

    B. Some common defense mechanisms include

      1. Rationalization—making excuses.

      2. Repression—motivated forgetting.

      3. Reaction-formation—denial of desires.

      4. Projection—it's someone else's fault or problem.

      5. Identification—hero worship.

      6. Regression—childhood revisited.

   C. Defense mechanisms are used at one time or another by nearly all people.

   D. Managers should view people exhibiting defensive behavior as needing help.

VI. Stress Management

   A. Everyone experiences stress as they cope with day-to-day problems.

   B. Avoiding all stress is undesirable because moderate levels of stress increase performance.

   C. When individuals don't effectively manage stress, undesirable or unproductive behavior occurs.

VII. Causes of Stress

   A. Any situation requiring a change in behavior or a higher level of activity can produce stress.

   B. Sources of stress include

      1. Physical factors.

      2. Interpersonal relations.

      3. Organizational and job requirements.

      4. Emotional responses to situations.

VIII. Consequences of Stress

   A. Stress can be a primary or contributing factor in numerous physical and psychological conditions.

   B. Stress consequences can be grouped into four basic categories:

      1. Physiological.

      2. Psychological.

      3. Behavioral.

      4. Organizational.

IX. Individual Actions to Reduce Stress

   A. Three approaches can form the basis for controlling stress:

      1. Avoid high-pressure situations that produce high stress.

      2. Manage situations to control the level of stress.

      3. React less intensely to situations.

   B. Controlled-stress living requires adaptation and balance in activities.

X. Sources of Job Stress

   A. Any job situation can produce stress.

   B. Job conditions that reduce stress for one individual may increase stress for another.

    C. Conditions that tend to produce job stress include job overload, underutilization of abilities, role ambiguity, role conflicts, undesirable physical conditions, excessive responsibility, destructive competition, changes, and contacts with distressed people.

XI. Controlling Job Stress

    A. Techniques that individuals have found to be effective include the following:

      1. Build resistance by regular sleep, exercise, and good health habits.

      2. Separate work and nonwork life.

      3. Engage in physical exercise.

      4. Talk through problems with peers on the job.

      5. Withdraw physically from high-stress situations.

XII. Minimizing Stress in Organizations

    A. Managers can help employees manage stress by

      1. Helping workers analyze the sources of job stress.

      2. Providing information and training on how to control stress.

      3. Being available to listen to employees and helping them deal with work-oriented problems.

      4. Taking action to reduce and control the major sources of organizational and job stress.

## KEY TERMS

| | | |
|---|---|---|
| Motivational conflict | Withdrawal | Emotionally induced stress |
| Approach-approach conflict | Repression | Controlled-stress living |
| Approach-avoidance conflict | Defense mechanisms | Adaptation |
| Avoidance-avoidance conflict | Reaction-formation | Balanced life |
| Frustration | Projection | Job overload |
| Aggression | Identification | Role ambiguity |
| Rationalization | Regression | Role conflict |
| | Stress management | Stress carriers |
| | Stress | |

## DISCUSSION QUESTIONS

1. Give an example of approach-approach, approach-avoidance, and avoidance-avoidance conflict situations.
2. Can frustration be an aid to a manager? If so, how?
3. What constructive results can frustration have on an individual?
4. Describe an example of rationalization that you have observed individuals using.

5. Comment on the statement "Behaviors can sometimes reflect the opposite motivation of what the behavior seems to be."

6. How could an employee who feels hostility toward the supervisor hide these feelings by using a defense mechanism?

7. Why do individuals use defense mechanisms?

8. What should a manager do when an employee becomes heavily dependent on the use of defense mechanisms to deal with frustration?

9. Describe the characteristics of a job that would tend to produce high levels of stress.

10. Develop an approach to control stress for a specific situation by using the strategies of avoiding pressure, managing the situation to control tension, and reacting less intensely.

11. Describe how you would apply the principles of adaptation and balance for controlled-stress living.

12. Using a job you have had or would like to have, identify possible sources of job stress and the actions you would take to control stress.

## EXERCISE

### Actions to Reduce Job Stress

You manage a research and development department for a large company that develops computerized control systems for aircraft. The company has recently lost several lawsuits by employees for illness resulting from the effects of job-related stress. The courts awarded large payments to the employees in compensation for their stress-related illnesses. The company has directed all managers to take action to reduce job stress.

*Evaluate the following list of actions to reduce job stress.*
Which actions would you take? Which would you take first?

1. Identify employees with symptoms of high stress and arrange for them to get medical help.

2. Make stress management training available for all employees.

3. Have a consultant in stress management work with each employee to determine their stress level and assist them in controlling stress.

4. Set up an exercise and physical fitness program for employees.

5. Have a program to teach relaxation techniques, and have a time each day for employees to relax and meditate.

6. Reduce the work load of any employee who shows signs of high stress.

7. Counsel employees who are having family problems that cause stress.

8. Help employees analyze the sources of stress on their jobs.

9. Work with each employee to establish specific job objectives and performance criteria.

10. Remove distressed employees from the department if they are causing
stress for others.

11. Provide job training for employees who have stress because they lack the
skill or ability to effectively perform their jobs.

## TWO POINTS OF VIEW

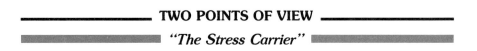

### *"The Stress Carrier"*

*What would you do if you were the manager?*

You manage the research and development department of a toy manufacturing
company. The most productive and creative designer in the department is Bill
Dixon. Bill is very demanding and inconsiderate of other employees. He expects
his work to be done immediately, even if it means that other people's work must
wait. Bill frequently demands that people work overtime on his projects. He will
often watch the people doing drafting and specification writing on his designs
while they try to complete his work. If they are not working as fast as Bill thinks
they should, he suggests they work over their lunch hour or during their break
time. Everyone in the department recognizes that Bill is extremely productive
and creative, but they resent his high-handed manner. Because Bill puts so
much pressure on employees, they refer to him as "the stress carrier."

Employees who do drafting and technical writing for Bill have approached
you with an ultimatum. They stated, "Bill Dixon's work is no longer going to
receive special treatment without your specific approval. We have had enough
of Bill's pressure. We want Bill's work to go through you first, and he is not to
set foot in our work areas."

You know that Bill puts a lot of pressure on the employees, but he gets the
work out. Bill's designs have resulted in the most successful toys manufactured
by the company for the last two years. You could not likely find another
designer as productive as Bill.

*What would you do if you were a drafter doing work for Bill?*

You are a drafter who works for the designers in a toy manufacturing firm. For
the most part, the designers are considerate and reasonable in their demands.
Your work is both interesting and challenging.

The only undesirable part of your job is doing work for Bill Dixon. Bill is the
most creative designer in the department, but he is also pushy and inconsiderate. He demands that his work always receive first priority. When you are
working on one of his designs, he will stand over you and give unwanted advice.
If you are not completing his work as fast as he wants, he suggests that you
work over your lunch hour or overtime. Sometimes you put in extra time

without pay just to get Bill off your back. He seems to thrive on pressuring other people and has justly earned his nickname of "the stress carrier."

You and some of the other drafters and technical writers met with the manager of your department and told him, "We do not want to continue to do Bill Dixon's work ahead of the other designers' work without your specific approval. We want Bill's work to come to us through you." You have also requested that management not allow Bill in the drafting work area. Realistically, you don't think anything will come of the meeting with the department manager because he has done nothing to control the high-handed methods Bill uses in dealing with employees. You believe that management does not attempt to control Bill's behavior because they are afraid he might quit and go to work for a competitor.

## ENDNOTES

1. Jane Whitney Gibson and Richard M. Hodgetts, *Organizational Communication: A Managerial Perspective* (Orlando, Fla.: Academic Press, 1986), p. 78.

2. Steve Altman, Enzo Valenzi, and Richard M. Hodgetts, *Organizational Behavior: Theory and Practice* (Orlando, Fla.: Academic Press, 1985), p. 148.

3. Henry L. Sick, *Management and Organization*, 2d ed. (Cincinnati: South-Western, 1973), p. 461.

4. For detailed reports of research on causes and effects of stress, see Michael T. Matteson and John M. Ivancevich, *Job Stress and Health* (New York: Free Press, 1982); John M. Ivancevich and Michael T. Matteson, *Stress and Work: A Managerial Perspective* (Glenview, Ill.: Scott, Foresman, 1980); and James C. Quick and Jonathan D. Quick, *Organizational Stress and Preventive Management* (New York: McGraw-Hill, 1984).

5. W. H. Hendrix, N. K. Ovalle, and R. G. Troxler, "Behavioral and Physiological Consequences of Stress and Its Antecedent Factors," *Journal of Applied Psychology* 70 (1985): 188–201.

6. Phillip L. Hunsaker and Curtis W. Cook, *Managing Organizational Behavior* (Reading, Mass.: Addison-Wesley, 1986), pp. 238–39.

7. James A. F. Stoner and Charles Wankel, *Management*, 3d ed. (Englewood Cliffs, N.J.: Prentice-Hall, 1986), p. 537.

8. Saroj Parasuraman and Joseph A. Alutto, "Sources and Outcomes of Stress in Organizational Settings: Toward the Development of a Structural Model," *Academy of Management Journal* (June 1984): 330–50.

9. R. L. Kahn, D. M. Wolf, D. M. Quinn, R. P. Snoek, and R. A. Rosenthal, *Organizational Stress: Studies in Role Conflict and Ambiguity* (New York: Wiley, 1984).

10. John H. Howard, Peter A. Rechnitzer, and D. A. Cunningham, "Coping with Job Tension—Effective and Ineffective Methods," *Public Personnel Management* (September–October 1975): 317–26.

11. For additional approaches to deal with job stress, see Rosalind Forbes, *Corporate Stress: How to Manage on the Job and Make It Work for You* (New York: Doubleday, 1979); Alan A. McLean, *Work Stress* (Reading, Mass.: Addison-Wesley, 1979); Arthur P. Brief, Randall S. Schuler, and Mary Van Sell, *Managing Job Stress* (Boston: Little, Brown, 1981); S. W. Hartman and J. Cozzetto, "Wellness in the Workplace," *Personnel Administrator* (August 1984): 108–17; and Katy Koontz, "Beating Burnout," *Success!* May 1986, pp. 28–33.

**12.** Robin L. Rose and John F. Veiga, "Assessing the Sustained Effects of a Stress Management Intervention on Anxiety and Locus of Control," *Academy of Management Journal* (March 1984): 190–98; and Dennis W. Organ and Thomas Bateman, *Organizational Behavior*, 3d ed., (Plano, Tex.: Business Publications, 1986), pp. 368–400.

**13.** Lawrence R. Murphy, "Occupational Stress Management: A Review and Appraisal," *Journal of Occupational Psychology* 57, (1984) pp. 1–15.

---

**CASE INCIDENTS FOR PART 3**

---

## The Inspection Department

The inspection department of a food processing company has three shifts of inspectors, with ten inspectors and a shift supervisor for each shift. The supervisor reports to a chief plant inspector. All of the supervisors have been promoted from line inspectors primarily on the basis of seniority.

Although the inspectors know that they can advance to management positions, most of them are dissatisfied with their present jobs. Most of the inspectors hired try to transfer to another department after only six months in inspection. Much of the dissatisfaction seems to stem from the supervisors' treatment of the inspectors. The major complaint is that supervisors are too restrictive and do not treat inspectors fairly.

For example, the supervisors in the inspection department always take disciplinary action when an employee is absent or tardy without an exceptionally good reason. The chief inspector continually stresses perfect attendance. If inspectors are late, every minute of tardy time is recorded on their records, which decreases their chances of receiving approval for a transfer.

Also, supervisors continually push for error-free inspection. They consider it unsatisfactory if one defective item out of a thousand gets past an inspector. In addition, inspectors believe that although their supervisors may listen to suggestions, they never act on them. The inspectors have continually suggested modifying work procedures to increase effectiveness, but in the past two years, the supervisors have never replied to their recommendations.

On the other hand, the supervisors repeatedly complain to the chief inspector and to personnel that their employees lack proper motivation and interest to do an effective job.

1. What is the motivation for individuals to request a transfer from the inspection department?

2. Is the supervisors' complaint about their employees justified?

3. How would you evaluate the current attempts to motivate the inspectors?

4. What other approaches might the supervisors take to motivate the inspectors?

## The Problem of the Temporary Employee

The southwest regional warehouse of Allen Variety Stores provides the merchandise for the company's retail stores in ten states. As the orders for Christmas stock began to come in, Tom Reid, the warehouse manager, requested temporary help from the Regional Administration Center.

This year the regional manager selected Vic Johnson to be temporarily assigned to the warehouse. Before Vic reported to work, Mr. Reid was informed by one of his shipping clerks that Vic Johnson was considered a problem employee because he was "lazy." Mr. Reid decided that he should take action to prevent problems when Vic began working in the warehouse.

The day Vic reported to work, Mr. Reid gave him the orders that he was to fill and the amount of time it would take to fill each one. At 2:00 on the first day, Vic told Mr. Reid that he would not be able to get the orders out on time. When Mr. Reid asked why, Vic explained that the method used to cross-check the accuracy of the orders was slowing him down. Mr. Reid thought he had heard enough. He told Vic, "I want you to realize I will not tolerate any more delays or excuses—now get to work."

Vic replied, "I was not trying to make excuses. I wanted to suggest a faster way of cross-checking."

"Vic, if there were a faster method of cross-checking, we would be using it. Your job is to cooperate with the other employees and get the orders out."

During the next week, work assigned to Vic went slowly. The other employees began to complain that Vic was not doing his share. In response to the complaints, Mr. Reid took Vic off filling orders and assigned him to cleanup duties. This only created another problem, since there was not enough cleanup to keep Vic busy. The employees now complained that Vic was disrupting their work by trying to carry on conversations while they filled and checked orders.

1. Was the action taken by Mr. Reid the day Vic reported to work the best way to attempt to motivate Vic?

2. How would you have replied to Vic's reason for not being able to get the orders out within the specified time and his desire to suggest a faster method for cross-checking?

3. Do you think that Mr. Reid was taking an appropriate course of action by assigning Vic to cleanup?

4. What course of action would you take if Vic were now assigned to the warehouse permanently?

## The Continuing Argument

Pat Walker is the supervisor of the claims department for a life insurance company. During the past two months, two of the claims processors in the department have been continually interfering with each other's work. They do not provide each other with the information they need to complete claims reports and continually argue. Lately they have been sabotaging each other's work. Another employee reported to Pat Walker that one of the individuals knocked some completed forms off the other's desk, then wadded up the forms and said, "Oh, I'm so sorry. I'm sure it won't take you long to redo that work."

Pat Walker has been aware of the conflict between the two workers but has been hoping that by ignoring the problem, it will go away.

1. Should Pat Walker continue to ignore the conflict in hopes that the individuals involved will solve the problem?

2. What alternative courses of action should Pat Walker consider to solve the problem of reduced effectiveness?

3. Can a course of action be developed that would lead to the employees involved accepting the responsibility for resolving the conflict?

————————————— **"Sick Leave"** —————————————

Ralph Scott supervises a group of eight social workers in a county social services department. The social workers, all highly trained professionals, are assigned welfare cases and are expected to work with little direct supervision. A social worker may be confronted with a wide range of difficult problems, including clients' family conflicts and their problems with relatives, landlords, businesses, and government agencies. In addition, workers may not be able to obtain enough funds for the people who need money. Client demands on social workers are heavy.

Jane Prentice is a capable social worker but has fallen behind in her case load reports because of her absences. She takes one or two days' sick leave each month, usually on Friday or Monday. The social service departmental policy states that a physician's statement is required after an absence of three working days, but Jane is never off that long. When Mr. Scott asks for an explanation of an absence, Jane always says that the stress of the job is the cause of the illness.

1. Should Mr. Scott accept Jane's explanation for the absences?

2. What should Mr. Scott do to deal with Jane's reported job stress?

3. What could Jane do to control the stress and get her reports completed?

# Part 4

# Working Together— Leaders and Groups

# Leadership

## ——— Learning Objectives ———

After reading this chapter, you should be able to do the following:

1. Discuss the importance of effective leadership for organizations
2. Describe the major approaches used to analyze and explain leadership
3. Explain the advantages and disadvantages of permissive, autocratic, and participative leadership styles
4. Describe the five basic leadership styles used to analyze leadership with the managerial grid
5. Discuss the contingency model of leadership effectiveness
6. Identify the dimensions of Fiedler's contingency theory
7. Describe the path-goal theory of leadership
8. Identify the basic elements in effective leadership

# Chapter Topics

- Definition of leadership
- Theories of leadership
- Styles of leadership behavior
- The managerial grid
- Fiedler's contingency approach
- Path-goal theory
- Leadership effectiveness

# Preview

Leadership has been a subject of great interest for thousands of years. There have been many approaches to the study of leadership, ranging from the scrutiny of individual leaders to attempts to determine the traits that leaders have in common. The lives of outstanding leaders have been the subjects of countless papers and biographies. Scientists and nonscientists have attempted to identify the skills and abilities that have enabled outstanding leaders to produce significant effects on society.

The behavior of leaders seems to contain elements of magic and glamour. People are fascinated by the impact great leaders have had on society and how things might have been different if another person had been in the leadership role. The impact of effective leadership has been demonstrated in the history of every country and organization. Napoleon, Robert E. Lee, and George Patton are referred to in terms of their effects on military campaigns. The history of a country is often identified by the periods individuals served as leaders. It would be difficult to separate the history of any country or organization from the influence of its leaders. The business leadership of men such as Henry Ford and Andrew Carnegie is legendary. The general agreement is that an organization without effective leadership is in trouble.

In this chapter we explore the meaning of leadership, its styles, and applications of leadership.

## SELF-ASSESSMENT

Leadership is one of the more difficult concepts to deal with in management studies. It is easily recognized but difficult to define. Based on your experience and knowledge, respond to the following questions and statements by choosing the answer that most closely agrees with your own beliefs. Each statement or question has a range of possible responses. A scale of 1 to 6 between two words with different meanings allows you to mark either the word that is considered correct or a place between the two words that represents some agreement and some disagreement. Selection of a high number such as 5 or 6 may be either correct or incorrect, just as selection of lower numbers may be correct or incorrect. Some responses may be partly correct and partly incorrect.

Answers based on research by behavioral scientists, with a short explanation of why the response was considered correct, may be found on page 283.

1. Research evidence indicates that leadership is, for the most part:

    learned  1...2...3...4...5...6  inherited

2. Leadership is concerned primarily with:

    influence  1...2...3...4...5...6  intelligence

3. Which style of leadership is most flexible and adaptable?

    autocratic  1...2...3...4...5...6  permissive

4. Situations can develop where responsibilities are not clear-cut when which of the following leadership styles is adopted?

    autocratic  1...2...3...4...5...6  participative

5. High levels of motivation are most likely to occur when which of the following styles are used?

    participative  1...2...3...4...5...6  permissive

6. Leadership requires:

    full-time continuous  1...2...3...4...5...6  part-time carefully
    effort                                      timed, sporadic
                                                effort

7. Directive leadership is more effective for which of the following?

    highly structured tasks  1...2...3...4...5...6  unstructured tasks

8. Stressful tasks require:

    supportive leadership  1...2...3...4...5...6  directive leadership

**9.** Current management theories agree that the most significant factor determining appropriate leadership style is the:

situation  $1\ldots2\ldots3\ldots4\ldots5\ldots6$  leader's educational
background

**10.** There is no universally agreed-upon definition of leadership.

agree  $1\ldots2\ldots3\ldots4\ldots5\ldots6$  disagree

## DEFINITION OF LEADERSHIP

When **leader** and **leadership** are used in everyday language, there is a great
deal of difference in what is meant by the terms. There is no universally agreed-
upon definition of what leadership is, and even less agreement on what it
should be. The definitions of leadership range from short, general statements to
long, detailed theories.

*Leaders* can be defined as those individuals who have the loyalty of others
who are willing to follow them. No matter how leadership is defined, the
essential ingredient in leadership is followers. The ability to obtain followers is
what makes a person a leader. Individuals who are perceived as providing
methods to achieve objectives and satisfy personal needs tend to attract followers. Leadership and motivation of followers are interrelated. Leaders who do
not facilitate satisfaction of the needs of followers are usually not leaders for
long.

A common element in most definitions of leadership is *influence*. The
process of leadership involves influencing individuals to work toward achieving
organizational goals.[1] Leadership is a relationship between people in which
influence is unevenly distributed. The leader's influence may be the result of a
legal agreement, consent of group members, delegation of authority by management, or possession and use of information.

In his definition of leadership, Ralph Stogdill states that *leadership is "a
process of influencing the activities of an organized group in its tasks of goal
setting and goal achievement."* [2] This definition can serve as a starting point for
the analysis of leadership.

The concept of influence recognizes that individuals differ in the degree to
which they are able to affect activities of a group. It requires interaction between
leaders and followers to affect the behavior of group members and the group's
activities.

## THEORIES OF LEADERSHIP

A number of theories of leadership have been developed in an attempt to
explain why individuals become leaders and why some leaders are more effective than others. The first attempts concentrated on the individual characteristics
of leaders. The basic approaches of studying leadership generally fall into three

categories: (1) the "great person" theories, (2) the traits and abilities theories, and (3) behavioral interaction theories.

### The "Great Person" Theory—"Leaders Are Born"

The earliest studies of leadership focused on the hereditary backgrounds of great men in an attempt to explain leadership on the basis of inherited characteristics. Some of these studies advanced conclusions that leadership, power, and influence were the result of inherited abilities. One writer even advocated that an adequate supply of superior leaders depends on a high birthrate among the biologically superior classes.[3]

Those who believe the **"great person" theory** assume that inherited characteristics determine whether a person will be a leader. This theory is the simplest of all the approaches to leadership, and it is probably believed by more people in the world than any other leadership theory. For those who are not in positions of leadership, a satisfying belief may be that they are not leaders because they were not born with leadership ability. The individual who is in a position of leadership may find the "great person" theory convenient, because any failures or lack of effectiveness can be attributed to abilities that were not inherited.

An organization following the "great person" theory of leadership would concentrate on the selection of managers through the "great person" process. It would be concerned primarily with whether or not relatives of the potential managers had been successful leaders. The selection process might be heavily influenced by the assumption "Like parent, like child." When there is an assumption of inherited leadership ability, usually little effort is directed toward developing management programs or structuring management positions to fit individuals.

Most social scientists reject the "great person" approach to leadership because it is an oversimplification and because research evidence does not support the position that leadership abilities are inherited.

### The Traits and Abilities Approach to Leadership

Extensive research efforts have been devoted to discovering specific personal characteristics that distinguish leaders from nonleaders. Those who use the trait approach attempt to find out why leaders are successful by analyzing the personal characteristics of leaders.

The number of traits considered in leadership studies ranges from fewer than ten to more than twenty-five. With this wide difference in the number of traits investigated, comparing studies of leadership traits is difficult. Another difficulty results from the different methods used to measure the traits and the variety of definitions that are found for a given trait.

An example of the problem of definition is illustrated by a study conducted by Perrin Stryker and reported in *Fortune*.[4] Seventy-five executives were asked to give definitions of various qualities of executives. The concept of "dependability" was defined by 147 different descriptive statements. From the 147 statements, a list of 25 different definitions for the trait was compiled. The definitions given for dependability included: behaves predictably, uses initiative, considers others, learns from mistakes, inspires confidence, and has good personal habits. This study points out that there is a great deal of difference in the way any given trait can be defined.

The general agreement among those currently involved in research on leadership is that the study of leadership traits has not been a very useful approach.[5] One of the problems with application of the trait approach is that most of the traits that are associated with leadership are indications of patterns of behavior that are expected from an individual in such a position. A critical analysis of the trait approach was made by Eugene Jennings, who stated, "Research has produced such a varied list of traits presumably to describe leadership that for all practical purposes, it describes nothing. Fifty years of study have failed to produce one personality trait or set of qualities that can be used to discriminate between leaders and nonleaders." [6] Many nonleaders possess most or all of the traits that have been studied, and most leaders do not have all of them. Traits are hard to define and identify, and the trait approach does not enable one to determine how much of a trait is needed to become an effective leader.

The failure of the trait approach to explain leadership may be primarily due to the complex interaction between the leader's behavior and the situation in which the leadership takes place. As Charles R. Milton pointed out, "The trait approach failed because it is the leadership situation—nature of the subordinates and the task—that determines what leader traits are essential for effective leadership. Such traits differ somewhat from situation to situation." [7]

*Five Groups of Leadership Traits*  Nevertheless, even with the limitations of trait studies in mind, five groups of traits have been found to be associated with leadership effectiveness. In an analysis of over three thousand books and articles in the field, Stogdill found a relationship between leadership and the traits he labeled capacity, achievement, responsibility, participation, and status.[8] Stogdill's conclusions were supported by fifteen or more studies he reviewed in which the person in the leadership position possessed more of the trait than did the average member in the group. Each trait as defined by Stogdill involves a number of factors:

- *Capacity* was defined in terms of intelligence, mental alertness, verbal ability, originality, and judgment.
- *Achievement* referred to having made better grades, knowing how to get things done in a group, being able to present constructive ideas, and being successful in athletics.
- *Responsibility* was evaluated in terms of dependability, willingness to assume responsibility, initiative, persistence, self-confidence, and the desire to excel.
- *Participation* reflected a high activity level, sociability, cooperation, and adaptability.
- *Status* referred to social and economic position and popularity.

These leadership traits should not be surprising, since individuals obtain leadership positions through participating in group activities and by demonstrating the ability to help the group achieve goals. To maintain a position of leadership requires participation and acceptance of responsibility for directing the activities of a group. The traits associated with leadership all involve relationships with the activities, characteristics, and objectives of the followers.

## The Behavioral Approach to Leadership

Behavioral approaches to the analysis of leadership recognize the importance of the relationship among the leader, the followers, and the situation. With this approach, the most effective leadership style depends on the nature of the situation, the characteristics of the individuals in the group, and the leader's abilities.

Behavioral approaches include contingency theories and other situational approaches to leadership. Contingency theory is often referred to as the "it depends" approach to effective leadership. It assumes that there is no one best approach to leadership and stresses the influence of the total set of conditions in which the leader must function. Since the most effective leadership behavior varies with the situation, the leader must adapt personal behavior to the situation or be able to modify the characteristics of the situation to be compatible with his or her leadership style.

The multidimensional approach to leadership is supported by studies conducted at Ohio State University by Stogdill and his associates.[9] Their study of 470 navy officers who had forty-five different positions indicated that the effectiveness of their leadership was heavily influenced by situational factors such as the nature of the job, the organizational environment, and the characteristics of subordinates.

Additional studies have supported the position that the effectiveness of leadership depends on (1) the leader's personality, needs, skills, abilities, attitudes, and values; (2) the subordinate's personality, needs, skills, abilities, attitudes, and values; and (3) situational factors, which include the characteristics of the group and the task, organizational policies and objectives, the physical environment, and external events that affect the situation.[10]

A person who is an effective leader in one situation may not be an effective leader in another. A person who can lead one group effectively may fail to lead another group with different characteristics and goals. An individual who is an effective company president might be unable to lead a church youth group or coach a little league baseball team effectively.

The most realistic approach to leadership takes into account the effect of the leader, the subordinates, and the situation. Figure 10.1 shows how these three factors are interrelated.

## STYLES OF LEADERSHIP BEHAVIOR

Three frequently discussed leadership styles are identified as permissive, autocratic, and participative. These three styles are seldom found in their pure form,

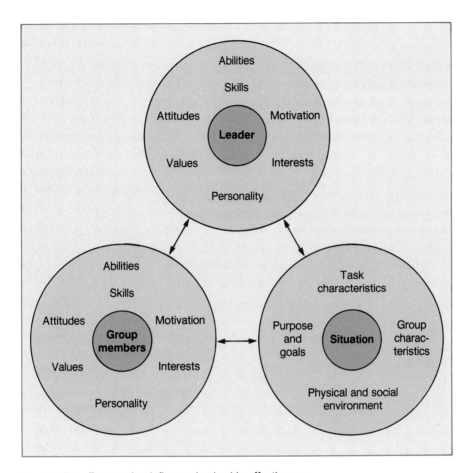

Figure 10.1   Factors that influence leadership effectiveness.

because leaders vary in their behavior and the types can be considered as extremes. These leadership styles or behaviors focus on the approach the leader takes in attempting to influence the behaviors of individuals.

An individual in a leadership position does not have to choose to use the pure form of one of these three styles. These styles represent a range of behaviors that can be combined or used in differing degrees. Each of these styles of exerting influence has benefits and limitations. A leader may use variations of all three styles over a period of time. But most leaders tend to depend primarily on one style as their "normal" way of operating.

## Permissive: Hands-Off Leadership

A "pure" permissive leader would not often attempt to influence the members of the group. "Followers" would be encouraged to accomplish the group tasks by using the methods they believe most desirable. Individuals would be allowed to devote their efforts to accomplishing individual objectives. Totally permissive leaders are rarely found, because in this style, little leadership is exerted. When a person with a permissive style holds a formal leadership position, the actual leader may be an assistant or someone who is an informal leader in the group.

**Permissive leadership** depends on the group to establish its own objectives and solve problems as they arise. This approach can work effectively if group members are highly motivated to achieve group objectives and will assume responsibility for leadership functions. The leader's primary function may be making outside contacts for the group and obtaining information for group members. Since the leader does not provide direction and coordination, groups within an organization may perform in ways that are detrimental to the achievement of organizational objectives. The widespread use of permissive leadership in an organization can lead to confusion or even chaos. Organizations have few leadership situations in which the manager can leave decisions entirely to a group of employees. Table 10.1 presents a summary of permissive leadership.

## Autocratic: Power-Oriented Behavior

The autocratic leader allows group members little or no voice in decisions. Subordinates are expected to follow instructions without any arguments. The effectiveness of employees is measured to a large degree by their compliance

---

**Table 10.1**
Summary of Permissive Leadership

---

STYLE CHARACTERISTICS
- Group members can make decisions independent of the leader.
- Leader does not attempt to control actions of group members.
- Group effectiveness depends on individual responsibility.
- The major influence on goals and procedures is desire of group members.
- Leader's role is to help individuals achieve personal goals.

POTENTIAL BENEFITS
- Working independently can be motivational for some people.
- May encourage suggestions, creativity, and innovations.
- Group is usually flexible and can adapt quickly to change.
- Open and direct communication with opportunity for self-expression.
- May increase the quality of life for some group members.

POTENTIAL DISADVANTAGES
- Can be a lack of coordination of group activities.
- Group objectives may be ignored, and individual objectives may dominate activities.
- Disruptive behavior may occur because of a lack of control.
- Individuals may go their own ways, resulting in confusion.
- Little cooperation may exist within group.

with the wishes of the leader. **Autocratic leadership** depends on the formal power of the leader's position and the ability to administer rewards and punishment. The leader makes the decisions and sets the goals for the group. Participation by group members in decision making is usually discouraged.

As with other management styles, there are few pure autocrats. Even the most autocratic leader is usually influenced somewhat by the attitudes and values of group members.

Autocratic leaders frequently use fear as a power base. They tend to (1) distrust the people being led, (2) filter information given to the followers, (3) attempt to control and manipulate the motivations of the followers, and (4) attempt to control individual behavior. Most autocratic leaders have varying degrees of uncertainty about their own adequacy. Often, leaders attempt to camouflage the underlying fears that support the strategies of manipulation and control.

Major benefits of autocratic leadership can be orderly operations, fast decisions, and consistency in goals. When a major problem or crisis occurs, the leader can take direct control. Recent research indicates that the potential benefits of autocratic leadership can be enhanced and the disadvantages minimized if the leader is warm and friendly toward group members.[11]

The autocratic leader may be continually challenged to create new rewards and gimmicks as old ones become ineffective. The punishment system may foster resistance, rebellion, resentment, cynicism, and a variety of other negative feelings. People who work under autocratic leaders learn to compete for rewards from the leader. Extrinsic rewards do not satisfy needs for self-satisfaction and self-respect, which are gained by achieving personal goals as unique individuals. If the relationship between a manager and a subordinate is basically one of distrust, almost any action on either's part is perceived by the other as untrustworthy. Table 10.2 presents a summary of autocratic leadership.

## Participative Leadership

In **participative leadership**, the leader shares authority and responsibility with members of the group. Leadership responsibilities are shared by involving group members in planning and decision making. This type of leadership allows group members to influence the decision-making process and the leader's behavior. Group members are treated with respect, and their opinions are valuable inputs in decision making.

Participative leaders do not reject the responsibilities of leadership and attempt to be "just another member of the group." They are active leaders in making decisions, using the input of group members. They focus the activities of the group on achieving objectives and direct the flow of communication to provide group members with adequate information.

The participative leader assumes that individuals learn to evaluate their own abilities and can develop their basic potential. Subordinates are provided every opportunity to maximize self-evaluation and self-development. Individuals are allowed to assume responsibility for achieving objectives.

---

**Table 10.2**
Summary of Autocratic Leadership

---

STYLE CHARACTERISTICS

- Leader makes most decisions without consulting with group members.
- Leader controls group members by using rewards and discipline.
- Leader permits little individual freedom of action.
- Leader tries to develop obedient and predictable behavior from group members.
- Group members are dependent on the leader to establish goals and plan activities.

POTENTIAL BENEFITS

- Can provide consistency in goals and procedures by leader making decisions.
- Decisions can be made rapidly.
- Control can be centralized for orderly operations.
- Well-developed leadership skills can be applied directly to group activities.
- The leader can take direct control when a major problem or crisis occurs.

POTENTIAL DISADVANTAGES

- May result in low motivation. Developing motivation is difficult when the leader makes all decisions.
- Tends to reduce creativity.
- Group members may avoid responsibility for their performance.
- Misunderstandings may result from the one-way communication.
- Adapting to change may be difficult.

---

The participative leader tries to create a climate in which there is no need to impose external controls. Individuals who have participated in setting group objectives and have clearly stated their own goals tend to work to achieve those objectives without the leader having to exert control. Table 10.3 presents a summary of participative leadership.

Any leadership style has advantages and disadvantages, depending on the results desired by the leader. The permissive style may stimulate individual initiative and creativity but may also result in confusion and a lack of coordination. The autocratic style may produce order and obedience but produce few suggestions for improvement by group members. The participative style may result in coordination of activities and high motivation of group members, but the process of participation may result in compromise decisions that are not the most effective.

A leader must be a good diagnostician and match the situation with an appropriate style: sometimes relatively autocratic and sometimes quite participative.[12]

## THE MANAGERIAL GRID

The **managerial grid** approach to analyzing leadership identifies five styles of leaders, based on their concern for people and production. The grid approach

---

**Table 10.3**
**Summary of Participative Leadership**

---

STYLE CHARACTERISTICS
- Leader involves individuals in decision making and goal setting.
- Authority and responsibility are delegated to group members.
- To achieve group goals, the leader coordinates involvement of group members.
- The leader uses two-way communication.
- Attitudes and feelings of group members are considered by the leader in making decisions.

POTENTIAL BENEFITS
- Participation can result in high motivation of group members.
- The knowledge and experience of group members can be used in decision making.
- Members may feel more committed to group goals.
- Individual abilities can be developed through participation.
- Group members may be better informed as a result of two-way communication.

POTENTIAL DISADVANTAGES
- Individuals may dominate the participation or make disruptive contributions.
- This approach can be time-consuming for the leader.
- Compromises can result in actions that are not the most effective.
- Conflict may be resolved by making the least offensive decision rather than the most effective.
- Situations can develop where responsibilities are not clear-cut.

---

has been widely used in identifying leadership styles since its development by Robert Blake and Jane Mouton.[13] The grid is usually presented as a graph or chart indicating the manager's degree of concern or interest for people and production. The basic elements of grid representation are presented in Figure 10.2.

As the grid indicates, a leader can have both high concern for people and high concern for production. The five styles identified on the grid involve combinations of varying degrees of concern for people and production. The five basic styles are summarized in the following descriptions.

*Impoverished Leadership*   The impoverished leadership style is similar to the laissez-faire leader. The leader has low concern for people and low concern for production. Decisions of group members are accepted without question. The leader avoids taking sides and tries to avoid disagreeing with the opinions, attitudes, and ideas of others. This style involves trying to stay out of conflicts or remaining neutral when involved in conflicts. The leader tries to avoid responsibility and decision making by remaining neutral and not raising any controversial issues. Mistakes in task performance are ignored. The leader does just enough to get by.

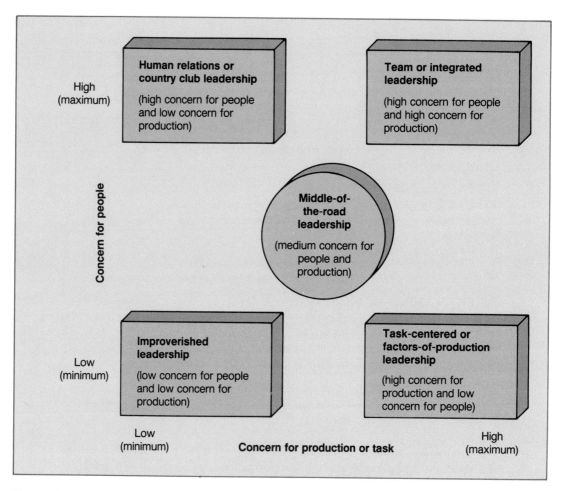

**Figure 10.2**   Managerial grid leadership styles.

*Human Relations or Country Club Leadership*   The human relations leader has high concern for people and low concern for production. There is high value for maintaining good interpersonal relations. The leader prefers to accept the opinions, attitudes, and ideas of group members and does not push for acceptance of personal positions. Every effort is made to avoid generating conflict. If conflict does occur, the leader attempts to soothe feelings and keep people together. The human relations leader is usually a warm and friendly person. Interpersonal relations are considered all-important, and task accomplishment is of minor interest. Task-related mistakes are glossed over with an attitude of "you'll do better next time." One of the leader's main objectives is for group members to be happy.

*Task-centered or Factors-of-Production Leadership*   The task-centered leader has high concern for task accomplishment and low concern for people. The main concern is efficiency of operations and output. Human relations problems are viewed as interferences in getting jobs done. The leader places high value on making decisions that stick and wants group members to follow orders without raising questions. People are viewed solely according to their contribution to achieving task-related objectives. Tight controls of job behavior are usually developed, and punishment systems are used to keep people in line. Creativity and suggestion are suppressed. The leader concentrates on direct control of group members to get tasks accomplished as effecientty as possible.

*Middle-of-the-Road Leadership*   The middle-of-the-road leader has medium concern for people and medium concern for production. An attempt is made to balance the necessity for task accomplishment and the morale of group members. In balancing the concern for people and production, the leader is not highly energetic or overenthusiastic about individual satisfaction or job accomplishment. The leader looks for decisions that are workable, rather than trying for "perfection." The leader's behavior is characterized by taking middle-of-the-road positions when there are competing demands for getting the job done and satisfying the individuals. When conflict arises, the leader attempts to be fair but firm and to obtain a compromise solution. The desire is to maintain a good, steady job pace without creating conflict or dissatisfied individuals.

*Team or Integrated Leadership*   The team leadership style is the ideal. It involves high concern for people and high concern for production. The team leader concentrates on motivating and developing individuals while achieving the highest possible level of task accomplishment. High value is placed on obtaining sound creative decisions that result in understanding and agreement among group members. The leader has strong personal convictions but seeks out different ideas and opinions from group members. This style is characterized by a willingness to change as a result of objective analyses of problems and situations. When conflicts arise, the leader looks for the reasons and tries to eliminate underlying causes. There is a commitment to quality performance and effective interpersonal relations. When mistakes occur, the leader's approach is to help people learn from them. In relations with group members, the leader focuses on developing acceptance of responsibility and self-control.

The managerial grid approach to analyzing leadership styles has been found to be a useful method for identifying and classifying the extent of concern leaders have for people and production. The five primary styles that have been described are extremes or "pure types"; rarely do leaders consistently behave according to one style. Most leaders vary their behavior in response to the nature of the situation. If the leader faces major problems in interpersonal relations in a group, he or she is likely to develop increased concern for people and move toward the human relations style. If the group is not accomplishing the tasks to maintain required levels of productivity, the leader will usually move toward the task style of leadership.

Although the grid provides a system of classifying styles, it does not provide an explanation of why a leader uses a particular style. Determining the way a leader adopts a specific style requires analysis of the total situation, including the leader's characteristics, the characteristics of the group members, the environment in which the group operates, the nature of the tasks, and other situational factors affecting the relationships between group and leader.

According to the theory behind the managerial grid, the style that should get the "best" results is the team style, with its high concern for both people and production. But the concept of one best style for all situations is not supported by research in leadership effectiveness. After reviewing the leadership studies, Lawrence Steinmetz and H. Ralph Todd concluded that "some leaders were very effective when they had low concern for people, yet others were very effective when they had low concern for production. Furthermore, still others were effective when they had low concern for both people and production." [14]

## FIEDLER'S CONTINGENCY APPROACH

Extensive research by Fred Fiedler has resulted in the development of the "contingency model of leadership effectiveness." [15] In Fiedler's model, effective leadership requires that the leader's style match the demands of the situation. Leader effectiveness is defined in terms of group performance and how well the group accomplishes assigned functions. The effectiveness of the group depends on the relationship between the leadership style and the group situation.

Fiedler defines two basic styles of leadership. One style is "*task oriented*," in which the leader's major satisfaction comes from effective task performance. The other style is "*relationship oriented*" and focuses on having good interpersonal relations and achieving a position of personal acceptance.

*Three Dimensions of Situations Affect Leader*   Fiedler studied a wide variety of groups, including military units, boards of directors, manufacturing companies, church groups, student groups, and basketball teams. In these studies he found that three dimensions of the situation had a critical effect on the leader's effectiveness.

1. **Leader-member relations.** This dimension refers to the degree of liking and trust between the leader and the group members. The most favorable condition for the leader exists when the group members are willing to follow him or her; the use of superior rank is not required to get the task accomplished. Fiedler regards this dimension as the most important from the leader's point of view, since the leader may not be able to control the "official" rank and power associated with his or her position.

2. **Task structure.** The task can be specifically defined so that it can be performed according to a standardized set of procedures, or it can be left unstructured and vague. When the task is specifically defined by a set of operating procedures, it is difficult for an employee to question the

leader's right to give instructions. Also, it is easier to control the quality of performance, and group members can be held responsible for performance according to the task definitions.

3. **Position power.** The amount of formal power the leader has because of the position is position power. It can be measured by the leader's authority to reward and punish group members. High position power is indicated by having the authority to promote and demote, to decide pay rates, to hire and fire, and to determine work schedules. Most managers in business and industry have high position power. Leaders of voluntary groups usually have low position power.

These three dimensions are outlined in Table 10.4.

*Leadership Effectiveness*    Fiedler's research supports the position that neither the task-oriented style nor the relationship-oriented style can be considered effective in itself. The effectiveness of the leadership style depends on the three situational factors described earlier; that is, when the leader has good relations with the members, the task is highly structured and the position power is high. The situation is unfavorable when the leader has little support

**Table 10.4**
**Situation Favorableness for the Leader**

|  | High Influence | Low Influence |
|---|---|---|
| Leader-member relations | Leader is trusted and liked by group members. Pleasant relations among members and with leader. Cheerful and cooperative environment in the group. | Leader is not trusted and is disliked by group members. Tense and antagonistic relations among members and with leader. Gloomy and uncooperative environment in the group. |
| Task structure | Job requirements clearly stated. Problems encountered can be solved by only one method. Only one correct solution to problem. Correctness of decisions can be objectively demonstrated. | Job is unstructured and requirements are vague. There may several correct solutions to a problem. Correctness of decisions is a matter of opinion. Job can be accomplished by a variety of procedures. |
| Position power | Leader controls rewards and punishments of group members. Leader establishes work rules and work schedules. Leader has authority to hire, fire, and raise salaries. | Group members control discipline and rewards. Individuals work independently of the leader. Leader's evaluation of performance has no impact on group members. |

from the group, the task is vague and unstructured, and there is little position power. Using Fiedler's definition, the favorableness of the situation depends on the degree to which a given situation enables the leader to exert influence over a group.

Studies of the effectiveness of leadership styles indicate that the style most effective in one type of situation may be the least effective in another. The task-oriented leadership style was the most effective in situations in which the leader had either very little or a great deal of influence. The leader who devoted time to interpersonal relations in the group was most effective in moderately favorable situations. In situations that were very favorable or very difficult, the task-oriented leader was the most effective.

An analysis of 178 studies that tested various aspects of Fiedler's contingency theory concluded that taken together, the 178 studies show strong support for Fiedler's model.[16]

## Implications of the Contingency Approach

Organizations should not limit the criteria for selecting leaders to individual traits or abilities. Specific traits and technical ability may be necessary, but they are only two of the factors that contribute to effective leadership. The effectiveness of a leader depends on a broad range of factors involving relations with group members and the nature of the situation.

The selection of leaders should focus on matching the attitudes, values, abilities, skills, and personality of the leader with the characteristics of the group members and the demands of the situation. If a change is necessary to improve leadership effectiveness, changing factors in the situation or moving the leader is usually more desirable than trying to change his or her leadership styles.

Most leadership training programs attempt to develop or change patterns of behavior in the individual. This often means that the individual must make basic changes in leadership style and personality. Although the personality can be modified, the cost is high and the rate of success is low. Getting an individual to make basic changes in leadership style and personality to match a situation and the group members is not practical in many situations. Since there is no one best style of leadership, there is no one most effective approach to leadership training. Flexibility in behavior and ability in analyzing situations should be emphasized in leadership training. Leadership styles in an organization should vary with the requirements of the situations. Organizations should not attempt to require the same leadership style from all managers.

Improving leader effectiveness depends upon a match of (1) the leader's behaviors, (2) the group members, and (3) the situational factors. The interaction of the factors involved in the situation is what controls the leader's effectiveness in working with a group to accomplish objectives.

## PATH–GOAL THEORY

The **path-goal theory** is a situational or contingency approach to leadership developed from the work of Martin G. Evans and Robert J. House.[17] The theory is termed *path-goal* because it concentrates on the leader's influence on (1) perceptions of work goals, (2) personal goals, and (3) paths (means) to attain goals.

According to the path-goal theory, leadership performance depends on how well the leader clarifies the path to desired rewards and makes rewards dependent on effective performance. Leader effectiveness depends on the ability to recognize strong unmet needs and help individuals satisfy these needs. To achieve organizational goals, the leader must develop paths for individuals so that both personal needs and work goals are fulfilled.

Path-goal theory suggests that a leader should behave differently with different individuals and in different situations. With this approach, the leader must adapt his or her behavior to the characteristics of subordinates and the nature of the task situation.

Path-goal theory has resulted in the development of two important propositions: [18]

1. Leader behavior is acceptable and satisfying when subordinates perceive the behavior as an immediate source of satisfaction or as a way to obtain future satisfaction.

2. Leader behavior will be motivational when it makes satisfaction of subordinates' needs contingent on effective performance, and when it provides guidance, clarity of direction, and rewards necessary for effective performance.

Path-goal theory advises leaders to increase the number and kinds of rewards available to subordinates and to clarify the ways these rewards can be obtained. It is based on the expectancy theory of motivation which was discussed in Chapter 7. According to expectancy theory, the strength of motivation to perform work is a function of expectancies that effort will lead to desirable rewards. Path-goal theory deals with how leaders can affect motivation by increasing the availability and attractiveness of rewards and by strengthening expectations that these rewards can be earned. Individuals must be able to see the relationship between their efforts and the rewards for effective performance.

## Leadership Styles

Path-goal theory differs from the contingency models that characterize leadership styles. The theory involves a higher degree of task orientation and relationship orientation, and a more complete set of leader behaviors. Four types of leader behavior studied are directive, supportive, participative, and achievement oriented.

1. **Directive leadership**—lets subordinates know what is expected of them, provides guidelines, sets performance standards and controls behavior to obtain compliance.

2. **Supportive leadership**—shows concern for the welfare and personal need satisfaction of subordinates, concentrates on developing good interpersonal relations and cooperation.

3. **Participative leadership**—shares information and consults with subordinates, uses their ideas in making decisions, and is employee oriented.

4. **Achievement-oriented leadership**—sets challenging goals for subordinates, emphasizes excellence in performance, shows confidence that subordinates will assume responsibility and obtain challenging goals.

The leaders should use the style that will have the greatest positive effect on performance and achievement of organizational objectives.

## Situational Factors

Two sets of situational factors are important in deciding on the most effective leadership style: (1) the personal characteristics of subordinates and (2) characteristics of the work environment. All the possible effects of situational factors on the effectiveness of leader behavior have not yet been researched. The following are some examples of the interaction of situational factors and leader behavior.

### Personal Characteristics of Subordinates

1. Supportive leadership is more effective with individuals who have a *high* need for affiliation.
2. Directive leadership is more effective with individuals who have a *high* need for security.
3. Participative leadership is more effective with individuals who have a *high* degree of self-confidence (who believe outcomes are a function of their own behavior).
4. Directive leadership is more effective with individuals who have a *low* degree of self-confidence (who believe outcomes are a function of chance or luck).
5. Supportive leadership is more effective with individuals with *high* social needs.
6. Directive leadership is more effective with individuals who have a *low* perceived ability to do the work.
7. Supportive leadership is more effective with individuals who have a *high* perceived ability to do the work.
8. Achievement-oriented leadership is more effective with individuals who have a *high* need for achievement.

### Characteristics of the Work Environment

1. Directive leadership is more effective for unstructured or ambiguous tasks.
2. Supportive leadership is more effective for boring tasks or simple tasks.

3. Supportive leadership is more effective when jobs involve stressful or frustrating tasks.

4. Participative and achievement-oriented leadership are more effective when jobs involve complex tasks.

The essence of path-goal theory is that leaders should select from among the four leadership styles ways of behaving that complement the characteristics of followers and the demands of their tasks.[19]

It is easy to draw conclusions that oversimplify the complex relationships between leader behavior and situational factors. Managers should be careful to adapt the path-goal theory to the complexities of their situation. Because the theory has been introduced recently, supporting research is lacking in many areas. However, the path-goal approach is expected to make major contributions to the understanding of leadership effectiveness. Figure 10.3 summarizes the major elements in the theory.

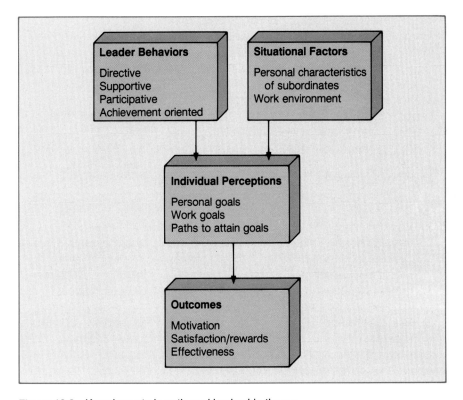

**Figure 10.3**   Key elements in path-goal leadership theory.

## A New Thrust: Substitutes For Leadership ▬▬▬▬▬▬

In many situations, a leader is not effective in influencing behavior and may even have no influence at all on the group. An example might be when a new, young supervisor tries to tell experienced and highly trained employees how they should do their jobs. The employees will likely tolerate the new supervisor until he or she learns the way "things are done around here." In cases like this, factors exist in the work situation that prevent the leader from having a direct effect on employees. These factors provide the employees the necessary guidance, information, and motivation to get the job done without direct influence of the leader.

Consider what often happens in an experienced work group when the leader is absent. Do things automatically fall apart because the leader is not there? In many cases, no leader—formal or informal—is needed. This is true if the group is composed of highly skilled people who have worked well together for a long period of time. They will simply continue working in a cooperative manner.

What occurs in these situations is being addressed by relatively new research on what is called "substitutes for leadership." [20] These leadership substitutes may be characteristics of individuals, characteristics of the task, or characteristics of the organization that may prevent the leader from influencing individuals. These leadership substitutes may replace the leader's influence by helping to guide, direct, and motivate people in the process of accomplishing tasks.

In the first situation described earlier, the ability, experience, and training of the workers provided the guidance needed for them to do their jobs effectively. Their experience also made them realize that the new supervisor was just trying to get established in the position. They continued doing their jobs the way they knew best and "tolerated" the new supervisor.

In the second situation, the workers made up a closely knit group with positive interaction patterns that had been worked out over a long period of successful performance. They knew what was expected of them, and they helped each other by providing guidance and coaching to get tasks accomplished.

Path-goal theory of leadership suggests that the leader's role is a supplementary one in that the leader provides guidance, coaching, and support not otherwise available in the situation, but which individuals need for successful task accomplishment or for the satisfaction of important needs. Path-goal theory recognizes the existence of conditions that may provide the needed information to accomplish tasks and thus make direct action by the leader unnecessary.

Individual ability, experience, training, knowledge, and the existence of a closely knit group have been found to be substitutes for directive leadership in some situations. The existence of an intrinsically satisfying task may substitute for supportive leadership, and the existence of a large number of rules and regulations may substitute for the guidance provided by a directive leader. Professional orientation of employees may be a substitute for either supportive or directive leadership. Professional workers usually develop close working relationships with each other and place more value in feedback from peers than from people in formal leadership positions. The direct feedback from the performance of tasks can substitute for directive leadership by making directive leadership unnecessary.

Several implications for managers have emerged from the research on substitutes for leadership. First, if substitutes are ignored, they may interfere with the leader's attempts to influence behavior or organizational attempts to improve performance. Second, awareness and identification of leadership substitutes can allow formal leadership to be used only where it is needed to improve employee satisfaction or performance. Third, leadership substitutes can benefit organizations by improving the consistency of managerial leadership across different organizational units. This is particularly important in organizations where leaders are frequently transferred, such as the military. Fourth, substitutes may allow managers to supervise larger numbers of individuals and thus increase their span of control, reducing managerial costs. Fifth, individual substitutes may help employees adjust to or counteract poor management.

---

Jon P. Howell, New Mexico State University

## LEADERSHIP EFFECTIVENESS

As the research evidence indicates, attempts to explain leadership by analyzing only the traits and abilities of the leader or the style of leadership oversimplify the determinants of effective leadership. No trait or ability has consistently been related to improved group performance, regardless of the situation. Studies of leadership effectiveness provide no support for the conclusion that there is one style of leadership. Successful leadership involves the interaction of the leader, the group, and the situation. To be effective, the leader's behavior must meet the needs of the group and the demands of the particular situation (see Figure 10.4). There are always some similarities among groups and among situations, but there are also unique aspects that the leader must take into account.

The way in which the leader's skills and abilities are applied must be adapted to the particular situation. Since the leader is trying to influence individuals, decisions must be made from analysis of individual characteristics of group members and not from research findings about other groups. The personal characteristics and personality of the leader are not as important as the ability to determine the leadership style that will fit the needs of a specific group.

---

## Ten Guidelines for Managerial Leadership to Improve Productivity

1. *LEAD*

   Managers must be leaders who make judgments and take action.

2. *OBJECTIVES*

   Develop clear and measurable objectives that are challenging and attainable.

3. *PRIORITIES*

   Establish priorities and allocate resources according to these priorities.

4. *STANDARDS*

   Have specific and challenging performance standards with individual accountability.

5. *COMMUNICATE*

   Develop understanding and agreement; provide necessary, relevant, and accurate information.

6. *FEEDBACK*

   Provide frequent and specific feedback on performance.

7. *CONTROL*

   Take corrective action when standards are not met, priorities are not observed, or objectives are not achieved.

8. *TRAIN*

   Provide training to develop individual abilities and effectively utilize human resources.

9. *ADAPT*

   Take a problem-solving approach and adapt to changing situations.

10. *REWARD PRODUCTIVITY*

    Provide meaningful rewards for high levels of performance.

---

Leadership requires continuous effort; it is a full-time job. The effective leader does not wait to respond to problems or crisis situations. Leaders are effective because group members allow them to influence their behavior. The most effective leaders are able to generate cooperative and willing effort by group members in obtaining group goals.[21]

Nothing leads as well as example.

Andrew S. Grove President Intel Corporation [22]

Figure 10.4   Basic elements in effective leadership.

## SELF–ASSESSMENT DISCUSSION

**1.** (1, 2, 3) In some cultures, national leadership is inherited through titles such as king, queen, sovereign, and so on. Most true leadership, however, is learned or is in response to situational demands.

**2.** (1) Influence is the essential element of leadership. Intelligence is an important attribute, but many followers of leaders may have greater intelligence than the leader but little influence.

**3.** (6) Permissive leadership is far more flexible than autocratic leadership. Permissive leaders depend on followers to make decisions and, as a consequence, are not dependent on set systems as are autocratic leaders.

**4.** (6) Since participative leadership encourages every member of the work unit to be involved in decisions, specific responsibility may be difficult to define.

**5.** (1, 2, 3, 4) High levels of motivation are usually present in both participative and permissive management styles. It is usually evident in members of participatively managed groups to a greater extent than permissively managed work teams.

**6.** (1) Effective leadership of any kind requires full-time, continuous effort. It cannot be administered effectively on a part-time, sporadic basis.

**7.** (6) When work conditions involve lack of clear definition of requirements, lack of training, or lack of structure, directive leadership is always preferable to participative or permissive styles.

**8.** (1) Stressful tasks require supportive leadership styles. Directive leadership tends to add stress unless there is a crisis situation or a lack of structure.

**9.** (1) Many leadership theorists believe that the greatest determinant of appropriate leadership style is the situation. Some situations require directive, autocratic leadership, and others more permissive, participative styles. The leader's educational level is not an important consideration.

**10.** (1) For many years, attempts have been made to define leadership. To date, no one definition is universally accepted. In general, most people agree that the word *leadership* is like *love*. Its definition depends on how it is used.

## QUICK REVIEW

I. Definition of Leadership
  A. The essential ingredient of leadership is that the leader have followers.
  B. An effective leader is one who attracts followers and can influence them toward the achievement of organizational goals.
  C. Stogdill defined leadership as "a process of influencing the activities of an organized group in its tasks of goal setting and goal achievement."

II. Theories of Leadership
  A. The "great person" theory assumes that leaders are born, not made. Heredity makes the leaders.
    1. Most social scientists reject the "great person" approach to leadership.
  B. The "traits and abilities" approach attempts to identify physical and psychological factors associated with leadership.
    1. The trait approach has not been very useful in explaining leadership behavior.
    2. Trait approaches fail to consider the entire leadership environment.
  C. Behavioral interaction approaches consider the interaction of the leader, the followers, and the situation.

III. Styles of Leadership Behavior
  A. Permissive leadership does not try to influence the behavior of members of the group. The permissive leader depends on the group to establish its own objectives.
  B. Autocratic leadership allows group members little or no voice in decisions.
  C. Participative leadership involves the sharing of authority and responsibility with group members.
  D. All leadership styles have both advantages and disadvantages.

IV. The Managerial Grid

    A. The grid measures the leader's orientation toward both people and productivity.

    B. The managerial grid identifies five types of leader behavior:

        1. Improverished leadership

        2. Human relations or country club leadership

        3. Task-centered or factors-of-production leadership

        4. Middle-of-the-road leadership

        5. Team or integrated leadership

V. Fiedler's Contingency Approach

    A. Fiedler's contingency model of leadership identifies three dimensions:

        1. Leader-member relations

        2. Task structure

        3. Position power

    B. According to Fiedler, the effectiveness of a given leadership style depends on the degree of favorableness of the situation for the leader. In moderately favorable conditions, Fiedler found that relationship-oriented styles worked best. In highly favorable and highly unfavorable conditions, task-oriented styles were more effective.

    C. Leadership selection should focus on matching the attitudes, values, abilities, and skills of the leader with those of group members and the demands of the situation.

VI. Path-Goal Theory

    A. Path-goal theory is a contingency approach that concentrates on the leader's influence on:

        1. Perceptions of work goals.

        2. Personal goals.

        3. Paths (means) to attain goals.

    B. Two important propositions of path-goal theory are:

        1. Leader behavior is acceptable and satisfying when it is seen as a source of satisfaction.

        2. Leader behavior is motivational when it makes need satisfaction dependent on effective performance.

VII. Leadership Effectiveness

    A. Leadership effectiveness depends on the interrelationships involved in a specific situation with a specific group.

    B. The basic elements in effective leadership are:

        1. To adapt to the needs and characteristics of individuals.

2. To take a preventive approach to task and human relations problems.

3. To adapt to the needs of the situation.

4. To devote continuous effort toward achieving objectives through the abilities of individuals.

## KEY TERMS

| | | |
|---|---|---|
| Leader | Autocratic leadership | Situation favorableness |
| Leadership | Participative leadership | Path-goal theory |
| "Great person" theory | Managerial grid | Directive leadership |
| Traits and abilities approach | Fiedler's contingency model | Supportive leadership |
| Situational approach to leadership | Leader-member relations | Participative leadership |
| Permissive leadership | Task structure | Achievement-oriented leadership |
| | Position power | |

## DISCUSSION QUESTIONS

1. Why do some people choose to be leaders and others choose to be followers?
2. Do some people have unique abilities for leadership?
3. Describe how group characteristics can be determinants of leadership effectiveness.
4. Describe the potential benefits and potential disadvantages of permissive, autocratic, and participative leadership.
5. How should leadership styles vary as the characteristics of situations differ?
6. Why would a task-oriented leader tend to perform more effectively in some situations?
7. Using the managerial grid styles, could there be situations in which any one of the five styles would be the most effective?
8. What would be the most effective leadership style in each of the following situations?
   a. The intensive-care unit of a hospital
   b. A "great books" discussion group
   c. An automotive production assembly line
   d. The English department in a university
   e. A group of design engineers in an aircraft manufacturing company
   f. A group of salesclerks in a discount department store
   g. A road maintenance crew for a city government

## EXERCISE

### *How to Implement Participative Leadership*

You are a production supervisor for an electronics manufacturing company. Your company's management has directed that all supervisors are to practice participative leadership to help the company "catch up with the Japanese." Management has indicated that they will survey employees for feedback on the implementation of participative leadership.

*Evaluate the following list of actions to implement participative leadership.* Which actions would you take? Which would you take first?

1. Hold a meeting with all employees once a week to discuss job-related problems and get suggestions from employees.

2. Tell all employees you have an open-door policy, and encourage them to come in and discuss ideas and suggestions for improving quality and cutting costs.

3. Get to know employees better by having each employee and his or her family come to your house for dinner.

4. Be lenient in enforcing work rules and company policies. Overlook minor infractions of rules.

5. Determine training needs for individual employees and see that they get the needed training.

6. Have employees set their own performance standards.

7. Involve employees in the selection decisions for new employees.

8. Have a private meeting with individual employees once a week to discuss their attitudes and feelings toward their job.

9. When job problems arise, have the employees vote on the course of action to be taken.

10. Delegate more authority and responsibility to employees for improving quality and reducing costs.

11. Let your employees know that everyone's life will be much better if there is "very positive" feedback about your implementation of participative leadership.

--------------------- **TWO POINTS OF VIEW** ---------------------

*"The Real Leader?"*

*What would you do if you were the supervisor?*

You are the supervisor of the parts department for an automobile dealership. The employees are beginning to depend heavily on Tom Vale, who was recently transferred to your department by the owner of the dealership. Tom has been with the dealership longer than any of the other employees and is respected because he is a local war hero. The other employees you supervise look to him for advice on how to do their jobs, and they ask him what rules they should and should not be concerned about. They talk with him every day during lunch and at coffee breaks to obtain information about what is happening in the warehouse in relation to work rules, raises, layoffs, and job changes.

The employees have told you that "everything will run effectively without your doing anything" because Tom can help them when any problems or questions arise about what should be done. Since the owner occasionally comes to the warehouse to talk with Tom, the employees believe he has a lot of "pull" with the owner and is in a position to give them inside information.

Obvious to you is that Tom is the "informal leader," but now he is apparently becoming the "real leader." You believe you are losing the ability to supervise the department, because the employees are becoming more and more dependent on Tom.

*What would you do if you were Tom Vale?*

You have been working for the same automobile dealership for the past fifteen years. You have worked in most departments of the dealership since you started as a mechanic's helper. You know the total operation of the dealership and are good friends with most of the employees. You are the only employee still with the dealership who was there when the current owner bought it thirteen years ago. The owner has learned he can depend on you to help out in any area that he believes needs to be improved. The owner has offered you management positions several times, but you don't want to be a manager. You enjoy your work and especially like helping new employees.

The owner recently transferred you to the parts department because there has been a high turnover of employees. He thought the new employees could benefit from your knowledge of how the dealership was managed. You had no trouble establishing good relations with the employees in the parts department. Their eagerness to do a good job and learn more about the automobile business even surprised you a little. Since helping them learn the business was enjoyable, you started having lunch with them and talking with them during coffee breaks. The owner occasionally comes by the parts department and seems pleased with the way the employees are doing their jobs.

The only difficulty you have had in the parts department is getting along with your supervisor. Every time you help another employee, he wants to know why you were talking to the employee. He has mentioned several times that "you are hired to do your job and not to do other employees' jobs." Most of the time, your supervisor apparently goes out of his way to avoid you.

## ENDNOTES

1. Don Hellreigel, John W. Slocum, and Richard W. Woodman, *Organizational Behavior*, 4th ed. (St. Paul: West, 1986), p. 329.
2. Ralph M. Stogdill, "Leadership, Membership, and Organizations," *Psychological Bulletin* (January 1950): 4.
3. A. E. Wiggam, "The Biology of Leadership," in *Business Leadership*, ed. H. C. Metcalf (New York: Ditman, 1931).
4. Perrin Stryker, "On the Meaning of Executive Qualities," *Fortune*, June 1958, p. 189.
5. James A. F. Stoner and Charles Wankel, *Management*, 3d ed. (Englewood Cliffs, N.J.: Prentice-Hall, 1986), p. 465.
6. Eugene E. Jennings, "The Anatomy of Leadership," *Management of Personnel Quarterly* (Autumn 1961): 2.
7. Charles R. Milton, *Human Behavior in Organizations: Three Levels of Behavior* (Englewood Cliffs, N.J.: Prentice-Hall, 1981), p. 296.
8. Ralph M. Stogdill, *Handbook of Leadership* (New York: Free Press, 1974), pp. 63–64.
9. Ralph M. Stogdill, C. L. Shartle, and associates, *Patterns of Administrative Performance*, Bureau of Business Research, Ohio State University (Columbus, Ohio, 1956), sec. IU.
10. James L. Gibson, John M. Ivancevich, and James H. Donnelly, Jr., *Organizations*, 4th ed. (Plano, Tex.: Business Publications, 1982), pp. 252–82.
11. D. Tjosvold, "Effects of Leader Warmth and Directiveness on Subordinate Performance on a Subsequent Task," *Journal of Applied Psychology* 69 (1984): 422–27.
12. Wendell L. French, Fremont E. Kast, and James E. Rosenzweig, *Understanding Human Behavior in Organizations* (New York: Harper & Row, 1985), p. 211.
13. Robert R. Blake and Jane S. Mouton, *The Managerial Grid* (Houston: Gulf Publishing, 1964); Robert R. Blake and Jane S. Mouton, *The New Managerial Grid* (Houston: Gulf Publishing, 1978); Robert R. Blake and Jane S. Mouton, *The Managerial Grid III*, (Houston: Gulf Publishing, 1984).
14. Lawrence L. Steinmetz and H. Ralph Todd, *First-Line Management: Approaching Supervision Effectively*, 4th ed. (Plano, Tex.: Business Publications, 1986), p. 141.
15. Fred H. Fiedler, *A Theory of Leadership Effectiveness* (New York: McGraw-Hill, 1967); Fred E. Fiedler and Martin M. Chemers, *Leadership and Effective Management* (Glenview, Ill.: Scott, Foresman, 1974). For interpretations of contingency models, see "Leadership Symposium," *Organizational Dynamics* (Winter 1976): 2–43; L. H. Peters, D. D. Hartke, and J. T. Pohlman, "Fiedler's Contingency Theory of Leadership: An Application of the Meta-Analysis Procedures of Schmidt and Hunter," *Psychological Bulletin* 97 (1985): 274–85.
16. M. J. Strube and J. E. Garcia, "A Meta-Analytic Investigation of Fiedler's Contingency Model of Leadership Effectiveness," *Psychological Bulletin* 90 (1981): 307–21.
17. M. G. Evans, "The Effects of Supervisory Behavior on the Path-Goal Relationship," *Organizational Behavior and Human Performance* (May 1970): 278–98; R. J. House, "A Path-Goal Theory of Leader Effectiveness," *Administrative Science Quarterly* (September 1971): 321–32. Research support for path-goal theory is reported in Charles N. Green, "Questions of Causation in the Path-Goal Theory of Leadership," *Academy of Management Journal* (March 1979): 21–41; Chester A.

Schriesheim and Angelo DeNisi, "Task Dimensions as Moderators of the Effects of Instrumental Behavior: A Path-Goal Approach," *Academy of Management Proceedings* (1979): 103–6.

**18.** Robert J. House and Terrence Mitchell, "Path-Goal Theory of Leadership," *Journal of Contemporary Business* (Autumn 1975): 84.

**19.** John R. Schermerhorn, Jr., *Management for Productivity*, 2d ed. (New York: Wiley, 1986), p. 292.

**20.** Jon P. Howell, Peter W. Dorfman, and Steven Kerr, "Moderator Variables in Leadership Research," *Academy of Management Review* (January 1986): 88–102.

**21.** For a detailed report of leadership research, see Gary A. Yuki, *Leadership in Organizations* (Englewood Cliffs, N.J.: Prentice-Hall, 1981); Bernard M. Bass, *Stogdills' Handbook of Leadership: A Survey of Theory and Research*, rev. ed. (New York: Free Press, 1981); Bernard M. Bass, *Leadership and Performance Beyond Expectations* (New York: Free Press, 1985); Barbara Kellerman, ed., *Leadership: Multidisciplinary Perspective* (Englewood Cliffs, N.J.: Prentice-Hall, 1985).

**22.** Andrew S. Grove, "Manager's Journal," *Wall Street Journal*, 12 September 1983,

# Chapter 11

# Group Behavior

## Learning Objectives

After reading this chapter, you should be able to do the following:

1. Discuss the importance of group behavior in organizations
2. Describe the properties of groups
3. Explain how group norms influence behavior in groups
4. State how role relationships affect behavior of individuals in groups
5. Discuss how status develops and affects group processes
6. Identify conditions that increase and decrease group cohesiveness
7. Explain how groups apply pressure to members to obtain conformity with norms
8. Discuss how individuals respond to and are affected by group pressure
9. List guides for working effectively with groups

- Groups
- Definition of a group
- Group norms
- Roles
- Status
- Group cohesiveness
- Group pressure
- Responses to group pressure
- Implications for managers

---
## Preview
---

History is crowded with instances of individual achievement. Most meaningful work, however, is not accomplished by individuals working alone but by people working together to achieve common goals. In work organizations, people may be placed in formal, structured relationships with specific areas of authority and responsibility. There are also the ever-present informal relationships derived from friendship, physical proximity, common interest, common assignments, or similar values. All organizations include both formal and informal groups. Sometimes strong, informal ties weld the formal organization into a cohesive force. Other times, groups within larger groups, frequently known as cliques, can be divisive and counterproductive. Groups, with their own internal norms, role conflicts, and status relationships, are the subject of this chapter.

An understanding of group processes is important in dealing with human behavior in an organization. Since we are all involved in groups, understanding group processes is also important in functioning effectively as individuals. All organizations involve interrelationships among groups within the organization and with groups in other organizations.

## SELF-ASSESSMENT ▰▰▰▰▰▰▰▰▰▰▰▰▰▰▰▰

Group behavior is an important organizational reality that managers deal with on a daily basis. In the following statements about groups, mark the response that is most correct. Each statement or question has a range of possible responses. A scale of 1 to 6 between two words with different meanings allows you to mark either the word that is considered correct or a place between the two words that represents some agreement and some disagreement. Selection of a high number such as 5 or 6 may be either correct or incorrect, just as selection of lower numbers may be correct or incorrect. Some responses may be partly correct and partly incorrect.

Answers based on research by behavioral scientists, with a short explanation of why the response was considered correct, may be found on page 313.

1. Recent studies indicate that all people are:

    involved in groups  1...2...3...4...5...6  not involved in groups

2. Most people belong to:

    a single group  1...2...3...4...5...6  several different groups

3. Group situations exist when individuals participate as members of a:

    group structure  1...2...3...4...5...6  togetherness situation

4. The values that group members hold concerning acceptable behavior in specific situations are called:

    situational determinants  1...2...3...4...5...6  norms

5. Groups usually provide guides for what members should not do, should do, and:

    may do  1...2...3...4...5...6  must do

6. For a group to function effectively, it must maintain the:

    commitment of its  1...2...3...4...5...6  nonconformity of
    members                                      its members

7. Behavior expected of those in particular positions in a group are called:

    norms  1...2...3...4...5...6  roles

8. An individual's relative position or rank in a group is referred to as:

    roles  1...2...3...4...5...6  status

**9.** Cohesiveness is higher when group members are in:

cooperative  1...2...3...4...5...6  internal
relationships                                competition

**10.** Group pressure is directed toward an individual member to encourage:

conformity  1...2...3...4...5...6  independence


## GROUPS

Individuals seldom, if ever, behave without being influenced by the groups they belong to. Most people spend the majority of their lives involved with family groups, social groups, professional groups, recreational groups, civic groups, and work groups, among others. For most people, individual success depends on the ability to function effectively within groups.

> While many managers wish fervently for more time alone, group activities are an almost inescapable fact of managerial careers. Up to 80 percent of a manager's time, for better or for worse, is wrapped up in group interactions.[1]

Most people belong to several groups. Groups have a major effect on individual behavior while the individual is interacting in the group. This effect carries over when the individual is outside the group. But individuals may behave differently when they are involved in group activities than when they are functioning on their own. To increase the complexity of the relationship between individual behavior and groups, it has been observed that the same individual may change behavior patterns when involved in different groups. Most people probably underestimate the degree to which their behavior is affected by the groups they belong to.[2]

The chance for individuals to assume leadership roles is much greater in small-group situations. Few individuals will ever have the chance to be top-level managers or executives of large organizations. But most people will assume a variety of leadership positions in different types of small groups during their lives. Even those individuals who become executives of large organizations find that their critical leadership roles depend on their ability to work in small groups. An organization involves a number of small groups that are linked together to achieve organizational objectives.


## DEFINITION OF A GROUP

A **group** can be defined as two or more individuals working together to achieve a common goal. Any definition of a group process necessarily involves face-to-face interaction and communication among individuals as a basic component. As individuals interact to achieve goals, status relationships inevitably develop—a necessary element in any group situation.

Possibly the most discussed characteristic of groups are their norms and values. Every group develops sets of values and norms that regulate the behavior of individual members in areas important to the group process.

## Distinction between Togetherness Situations and Group Processes

**Togetherness situations** are temporary associations in which individuals interact. There are no prolonged, stable status and role relationships among the individuals. No sets of values or norms extend beyond the particular situation. In togetherness situations, the nature of the immediate task or problem is the only effect on the behavior of the individuals involved.

**Group situations** exist when individuals participate as members of a group structure. Specific status relationships indicate each member's authority and responsibility within the group. Role relationships define the areas of activity that are appropriate for each member of the group. A set of shared norms defines the acceptable behaviors in the process of achieving objectives that involve the group.

Togetherness situations can result in the development of a group. For this to occur, the individuals must interact over a period of time and develop shared objectives. Obvious degrees of relationship exist among individuals, ranging from the casual meeting of strangers to the highly structured interaction of close-knit groups.

Groups do not suddenly exist with a set of well-defined relationships among members. Groups develop well-defined sets of relationships as their members communicate and achieve objectives (see Figure 11.1). The most important relationships center on the development of status, roles, and norms. These relationships develop and stabilize as a group defines its objectives and develops methods of rewarding and punishing group members for their behaviors.

## GROUP NORMS

**Group norms** are the values that group members hold concerning acceptable behaviors in specific situations. The group norms are the "ideal" behaviors expected of group members. The norms specify what individuals should do, not necessarily how they actually behave. Norms apply only to those situations that are most important to the group; they do not cover all possible behaviors in every situation.

Norms are a significant product of the interaction among individuals working together to achieve common objectives. As norms develop, they specify the expected behavior in performing the tasks the group is involved in and the expected behavior in interpersonal relations. They cover people, physical objects, and situations. Norms also include the value judgments of the group, what is "good and bad" and "right and wrong." [3]

One example of an employee group norm is the belief that "we should not help new employees learn their jobs because that is management's responsibili-

—Reward Systems—    —Status—    —Structures—    —Norms—

—Roles—    —Tasks—    —Values—    —Objectives—

**Figure 11.1**    **Properties of groups.**

ty." Another group norm might be to take *every* production problem to the boss, but to settle interpersonal problems within the group. The norms form guidelines, and the individuals decide on the specific behavior that falls within the guidelines. Norms can have positive or negative influences on the effectiveness of individuals and groups.[4]

The norms of a group usually provide guides for three general types of behavior: the things you *should not do*, the things you *should do*, and the things you *may do*.

Examples of "should not" norms include: You should not swear in the group. You should not criticize group members outside the group. You should not have long hair. You should not wear a tie.

Examples of "should" norms include: You should take your coffee break with the other group members. You should tell group members about any proposed changes in work rules. You should lend tools to group members.

Examples of "may do" norms include: You may help group members when they have personal problems, but you are not expected to. You may make suggestions to management on how to improve production, but you are not expected to.

*Norms Direct Behavior*    Most groups will develop sets of norms that they find useful in directing the behavior of individuals toward achieving the objectives of the group. These norms may become powerful in standardizing the behavior of group members. Individuals who do not behave in accordance with the norms are usually subjected to group pressure to force their behavior within the acceptable range of the norm.

Group norms seldom specify just one way of behaving. They usually designate a range of acceptable (or at least tolerable) behaviors, which may vary a great deal from group to group. The "permissiveness" of the group usually depends on the importance of the situation and the position of the individual in the group's hierarchy. Norms that do not involve important group issues usually allow for wide variations in behavior. Matters that are of critical concern may involve norms where the acceptable range of behavior is narrow. The most critical norms of behavior usually involve the identity and reputation of the group, the achievement of major group goals, and the continued existence of the group.

The development of group norms is influenced by three basic factors: (1) the nature of the environment in which the group functions, (2) the characteristics of the individuals in the group, and (3) the group goals and tasks required to achieve the goals (see Figure 11.2).

***Conformity to Norms***   Obtaining conformity to group norms is important if the group is to function effectively and maintain the commitment of its members. A group establishes itself and develops its identity by members conforming to group norms. Groups are often referred to by the characteristics reflected by their norms. A university department may be characterized by a high level of faculty publication and research, effective teaching and concern for students, or faculty service to the community.

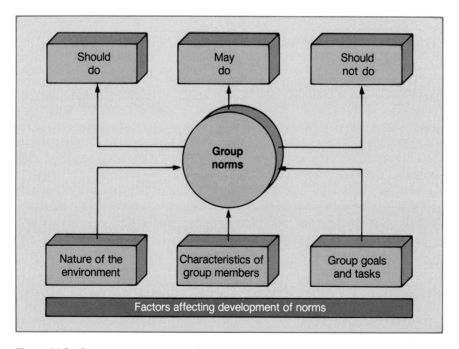

**Figure 11.2**   Group norms are established by the group and affect the behavior in the group.

---

## The Comfortable Pace ━━━━━━━━━━━━━━━━━━━━━━━━━━━

At Zadandma Clothing Company, a major women's sportswear manu-facturing firm in Fair Oaks, California, workers are paid by both piece and hourly rates. No worker earns less than $3.50 per hour. Standards for different sewing tasks allow operators to earn much more if they produce more than the established standard. Nearly all Zadandma workers earn $4.63 per hour. Workers who, because of higher produc-tion than that of most other employees, earn more, are often totally ostracized by the rest of the group. One worker, whose average earn-ings are $7.38 per hour, said when asked, "I don't have a damn friend here. They hate me and harass me because of my pay. I just work harder than those lazy bums." Newcomers to Zadandma are warned by fellow employees not to work too hard. Slower workers are frequent-ly helped to "keep up." Few workers achieve their full capacity. The norm is a comfortable pace slightly above standard.

---

By enforcing norms, groups protect themselves from outside threats and maintain the commitment of their members to group goals. The attitudes and behaviors of individuals are modified by the norms of the groups they belong to, and separating individual goals from those of the group is often difficult. A student who joins a group that emphasizes campus activities will probably achieve prominence in extracurricular activities. If the group places a high value on academic achievement, its members will usually make higher grades than they would have otherwise.

*Norms Affect Productivity*   The norms of work groups can have a powerful effect on productivity. Individual levels of work are almost always affected by group norms and the pressures to conform to them. Those who work above the norm in industry are usually referred to as rate-busters and are often subjected to severe group pressure to reduce output. In some situations, union members were charged by fellow workers with "working too hard." Cases have occurred in which individuals were fined or suspended from a union for working at speeds above a normal standard provided in a contract with an employer.[5] Norms may be established by a work group as a means of achieving job security goals, avoiding extra work, and obtaining better working conditions or other benefits.

> One way to encourage group norms that support high output is to minimize employ-ee-management antagonism deliberately, perhaps by involving employees more in the decision-making process.[6]

## ROLES

**Roles** are the behaviors expected of those in particular positions in a group. In formal organizations, job or position descriptions usually define behavioral expectations. In most group situations, role expectations are developed by the group members. In many situations, the most important role expectations are never written. They develop as a result of experience on the job.

All members of a group develop a definition of the role they believe they are expected to assume and the roles that other members of the group should assume. The development of these role expectations involves the perceptions, attitudes, and feelings of the individuals toward other group members and toward the objectives of the group. Much of an individual's learning involves determining the "appropriate" or "accepted" role behavior in different group situations. In a family role, expectations affect the behavior patterns of the wife, husband, and children. Although role definitions vary from family to family, common elements often exist in the role expectations of a wife or husband. The role of the husband may involve responsibility for maintenance of family cars, mowing the grass, driving on family trips, painting the house, and so forth, while the wife may be responsible for child care, fixing meals, washing clothes, cleaning the house, and so forth. As with any role definition, these roles imply the existence of related positions. The position of the husband implies the position of the wife. The relationship between husband and wife is a role relationship from which other roles may arise. The wife may be a daughter-in-law, a mother, and the family purchasing agent. Multiple roles are shown in Figure 11.3.

The structure of a group involves the pattern of role relationships within the group. In a business, complex role relationships may be present among managers, technicians, staff advisers, secretaries, and a variety of specialists. In an organization, individuals are influenced by sets of role expectations that are part of the formal organizational requirements. These expectations also affect their role relations with superiors, subordinates, fellow employees, and individuals in a wide variety of positions.[7]

Individuals in organizations are involved in carrying out a number of roles in meeting organizational responsibilities. The individual's formal role responsibilities include relating to others in the organization's chain of command, the authority associated with a position, the specific functions required by a position, the formal status in the organization, and the decision-making responsibility.

The structure of roles in a formal group is designed to help accomplish group responsibilities. These responsibilities are translated into role responsibilities for group members. The roles may be initially structured without any consideration for specific individuals. The assumption is that those who have the ability and desire to perform according to the role definition will fill the position. As any group functions, the roles change as a result of the abilities and desires of the individuals in the positions. The role expectations of individuals are usually modified when the manager of the group is changed. A new manager may expect different role behaviors and may use different methods to reach

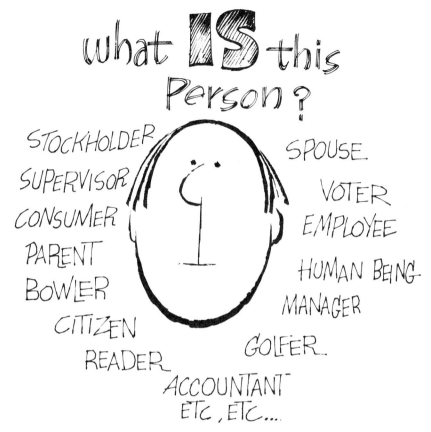

**Figure 11.3   Multiple roles.**

group objectives. When role expectations change, the individuals involved must adjust their behavior if the group is to function effectively.[8]

### Role Conflict

**Role conflict** occurs when an individual is faced with role expectations that are incompatible. For example, if a role expectation of the family is that a parent should spend time with the children in the evening, and a company role expectation is for salespeople to spend evenings entertaining clients, a role conflict could result. Conflicts between family and career roles can take a number of forms, as shown in Figure 11.4.

To obtain acceptance as a member of an informal group of employees, an individual may be required to violate the role expectations of the formal organization. For example, workers may have to engage in a work slowdown to place

# ROLE CONFLICT

**Figure 11.4    Role conflict.**

pressure on the organization to meet employee demands for pay increases or other changes. Conflicts between union and management are obvious examples of situations that can produce role conflict for employees.

Role conflict can have its origin in any of the forces that influence role expectations: the formal organization's role expectations, the informal or work group role expectations, and the individual's role expectations. Role conflict will occur more frequently in situations in which inconsistent role expectations are rigidly enforced by the groups involved. The effect of a role conflict on an individual depends on his or her ability to ignore some of the conflicting role expectations or to "play" the expected role while interacting with a group.

The plant manager's expectation for the production supervisor may be to increase output by reducing quality, while the informal work group expects to produce the highest-quality product, reflecting their professional pride. In this situation there is a conflict in role expectations involving the formal organization and the informal work group.

The production supervisor could face conflicting role expectations from individuals in different positions within the formal organization. Quality-control managers may expect the quality of the final product to improve by closer inspection and reworking items that do not meet high-quality standards. The accounting department may expect the production costs to be reduced by not enforcing the quality standards.

An employee may face a conflict between management's job expectations and individual value systems. For example, a secretary is expected to "fake" expenses so the bosses can receive payment for expenditures that, according to policies of the organization, are not supposed to be paid. If the secretary's role expectation is to be totally honest, then a role conflict can result.

A role conflict may also result when the individual's definition of appropriate job responsibilities differs from the manager's. A manager assumes that the role of the secretary includes cleaning the conference room after meetings, and the secretary assumes that cleaning is part of the janitor's role. A role conflict occurs because of the confusion over who's supposed to do what.

The specific behavior of an individual in a role conflict situation will depend on the individual's values and the perceived rewards and punishments associated with the expected role behaviors. If an individual is forced to make a choice between conflicting role behaviors, the choice will usually be made on the basis of maximizing rewards and minimizing the chance for punishment. If informal work group membership is valued, and the reward system of the formal organization is seen as weak or more remote than the reward system of the work group, the individual will usually behave in ways to meet the role expectation of the work group.[9]

## STATUS

**Status** refers to an individual's relative position or rank in a group. Basic to the concept of status is the comparison of group members according to their value to the group. The evaluation of a person's rank is usually based on the extent to which the individual is able to influence the achievement of group objectives and meet the needs of group members.

Status is often classified as either formal or informal. **Formal status** is the "official" rank of an individual, as designated by an organization. The position of vice-president indicates a formal status designation by the organization. **Informal status** refers to the social position or rank of an individual as a result of the evaluation of others in a group. A group of employees may look for advice and leadership from an individual who has no formal management position but has been accorded informal status by the group.

Both formal and informal status have an impact on the behavior of individuals in an organization. The actions of individuals and groups are affected by the desire for status. In many cases, status considerations are significant factors in attracting individuals to join groups and organizations. Individuals tend to be attracted to groups perceived as having high status and to avoid groups with low status. An individual may accept a job with lower pay in an organization that has high status. Some individuals are much more concerned with achieving status than with the amount of pay they receive.

Status is important in many groups because it defines the rights and privileges that an individual has. The effect of status is reflected in the frequently heard statement "Rank has its privileges." Usually, the privileges of status are a result of the position occupied by the individual in a social structure. The privileges cannot be obtained through more or harder work.

## GROUP COHESIVENESS

**Cohesiveness** refers to the amount of unity in the group and the degree to which members are pulling in the same direction. The cohesiveness of a group results from the attraction of the group for its members. Attraction depends on the need satisfaction that results from membership. Individuals join groups to satisfy needs; if the group's ability to satisfy individual needs decreases, the attractiveness of the group will decrease.

Group cohesiveness is reflected in the attitudes and actions of the members. The following factors are often used as cohesiveness indicators: loyalty to the group, defense of the group, responsibility for group activities, identification with the group, acceptance of group decisions, conformity to group norms, and agreement with group goals (see Figure 11.5).

To contribute to group activities and conform to group norms, the individual may be required to change personal objectives or methods of satisfying needs. As a result, members frequently develop goals that are consistent with essential group activities.

Changes occur in society that affect the role of groups in satisfying individual needs. During times of high unemployment, individuals may join groups that they believe will help maintain employment. For example, an employee might join a union. An individual who has lost status in the community may be attracted to a group because of its prestige. Employees may desire to belong to a group that includes managers because they believe that it would give them higher status.

Association with the members of the group may be a major factor in group attraction. An individual may join the group to satisfy social needs for belonging and friendship. If the individuals in the group are primarily satisfying social needs, the other goals and activities of the group may be unimportant. The cohesiveness of some groups can be attributed to the desire of group members to be with each other.

Groups may be attractive because they help in attaining goals that are outside the group itself. In this type of situation, the individual's needs are not satisfied by the achievement of the group's goals. For example, a manager may join the country club because the prestige of membership may help in obtaining a promotion. The manager's promotion is not a goal of the country club, but the

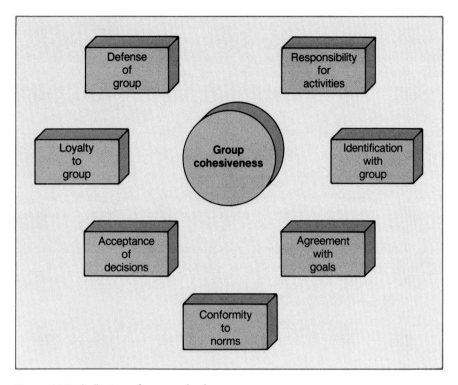

**Figure 11.5**  Indicators of group cohesiveness.

manager sees value in membership because it helps meet needs outside the group.

***Satisfying Member Needs***   The cohesiveness of a group is a function of the contribution the group makes in satisfying the needs of its members. The nature of a group's activities varies, depending on the sources of attraction for the group members. When the primary attraction is satisfaction of social needs, the activities will focus on interpersonal relations. The attractiveness of a professional group may depend on satisfaction of needs for achievement and recognition, and its activities will be oriented toward the professional development of members. The attractiveness of a work group may be more strongly affected by the employee's ability to perform and the recognition for achievement than by the number of friends made.

Different ways in which cohesiveness is produced result in different patterns of influence and communication. When cohesiveness is based on personal attraction, the group members may focus on influencing each other through long discussions and conversations. When cohesiveness is based on effective task performance, discussions may be short and directly related to completing the task quickly and effectively, with influence based on achieving effective performance. When attraction is based on the prestige or status resulting from belonging to the group, the group members may concentrate on their own actions and be cautious about trying to influence each other so as not to risk their status. Under conditions of minimum cohesiveness, the group members may behave independently of each other and with little consideration for others in the group.

## Conditions Increasing Group Cohesiveness

Although there is no absolute formula for increasing the cohesiveness of a group, the following conditions usually result in the attractiveness of the group increasing:

1. The group becomes more attractive for individuals who gain prestige or status within the group.

2. Cohesiveness is higher when group members are in cooperative relationships than when there is internal competition.

3. When group members can fulfill more needs through participating in the group, the attraction of the group increases.

4. An increase in the prestige or status of the group in an organization or in the community usually results in increased attraction for group members.

5. When the group is attacked from the outside, the cohesiveness usually increases as the members deal with the external threat. When the group shares a common fate as a result of external attack, the reaction is usually to focus the group's resources on protecting the group. The response to an outside threat is reflected in the statement "United we stand, divided we fall."

To increase the attractiveness of a group, the group must be made to better serve the needs of the group members. A group will be more attractive the more it satisfies the needs for recognition and achievement, the more cooperative the relationships, the freer the communication, and the greater the security provided for members.

## Conditions Decreasing Group Cohesiveness

Although the behavior of groups is complex and difficult to predict accurately, the following conditions usually result in the cohesiveness of the group decreasing:

1. When interpersonal conflict results from members' disagreements over ways to achieve group goals or solve group problems, the attractiveness of the group will decrease. The greater the interpersonal conflict, the greater the decrease. Members of highly cohesive groups may often have disagreements, but they try to settle them quickly.

2. If participation in the group results in unpleasant experiences for an individual, the attractiveness of the group will decrease. When group

activities result in embarrassment for an individual, the individual's attraction to the group is usually reduced.

3. If membership places limits on the individuals' participation in other activities or groups outside the group, cohesiveness may be lowered.

4. If conditions exist in the group that prevent or restrict effective communication, cohesiveness will decrease. Reduced communication may result if some members are too dominating or if some members are unpleasant or obnoxious in their communication behavior.

5. The cohesiveness may be reduced if group members believe the activities involve too great a personal risk. The risks could be physical danger or psychological threats. Risk could involve the group engaging in activities that individuals believe may be illegal or immoral. Risk could also involve group actions in an organization that the individual believes might result in getting disciplined or fired.

6. If the evaluation of the group by outsiders who are respected becomes negative, this can result in the group becoming unattractive to its members.

In general, the attractiveness of the group will decrease if the needs it has been satisfying for the individual can be better satisfied by other means or if the needs that led to the individual's involvement in the group have been reduced. The suitability of a particular group in satisfying an individual's needs may change drastically over time.

## Results of Cohesiveness

*Commitment to Group Goals*   Members who are highly attracted to a group tend to assume more responsibility for the achievement of objectives. In highly cohesive groups, members tend to have a high level of participation, remain in the group longer, and work longer and harder to achieve group goals.[10]

*Interpersonal Influence*   Highly cohesive groups are able to more effectively influence the behavior of group members. Members are more willing to attempt to influence others in the group, and individuals are more willing to listen to others in the group. In highly cohesive groups, there is usually greater acceptance of the opinions of others and more willingness to change attitudes to be consistent with other group members. Highly cohesive groups have less tension, misunderstandings, and hostility than groups with little cohesion.[11]

*Similarity of Values and Standards*   Where there is strong member attraction to the group, there is usually close agreement on group standards. Members work to protect the group's standards by exerting pressure on individuals who do not conform. In highly cohesive groups, members who do not adopt the group's values and standards are usually "expelled" from the group. The greater the cohesiveness of the group, the more the group will expect and enforce compliance with group standards.

*Group Productivity*   Highly cohesive groups usually have specific expectations of how much each member should contribute to group productivity. The more cohesive a group, the more it will try to ensure conformity with group norms for production. A cohesive group will make every effort to have members increase output if it is lower than expected, and pressure will be applied to members who are seen as producing "too much." Highly cohesive groups outperform groups with little cohesion.[12]

   A highly cohesive group will regulate productivity so it conforms to group norms. As a result, the greater the group cohesiveness, the higher the achievement of organizational objectives if the group supports the organization, and the lower the achievement if the group objects to organizational goals. Within an organization, a highly cohesive group that opposes management can be very effective in reducing output and preventing the achievement of organizational objectives. Figure 11.6 illustrates the results of strong group cohesiveness.

## GROUP PRESSURE

To obtain conformity with norms, groups exert pressure on members. At the most basic level, they reward members who behave in accordance with group

**Figure 11.6**   Results of high group cohesiveness.

## Group Pressure: Rate-Busters and Chiselers ━━━━━━━

One of the best-known studies of the effect of group norms on productivity was conducted in the early 1930s at Western Electric's Hawthorne plant near Chicago.[13] The study was conducted under the assumption that with an incentive pay system, employees would try to maximize their pay, even though group pressure would be exerted on individuals to conform to an "acceptable" level of output. The pay system was set up so the individual's hourly pay rate was revised every six months based on individual productivity levels. There was also the possibility of a bonus based on the output of the department. Under the system, employees' total pay was affected by changes in individual output and changes in the output of the total group. A group could increase the total earnings of individuals by increasing the total output of the group. The assumption was that employees' economic interests would result in motivation to maximize output.

The study found that there were group norms concerning an appropriate day's output. An employee's wiring two units a day was considered an acceptable output. Usually, most of the work was done in the morning, and work slowed down when employees were sure they could finish two units.

*Results of group pressure.* The group norms resulted in individuals who produced "too much" being referred to as rate-busters. Individuals who produced "too little" were called chiselers. Anyone who said anything negative about a fellow employee to management was called a squealer.

As in all groups, the work group developed methods for the enforcement of norms. The assumption had been that the incentive system would result in group pressure being exerted on the slower employees, but the strongest pressure was actually exerted on the highest producers. Pressure applied to the individuals producing more than the norm included calling them names such as Speed King and Slave, and "binging" them, which involved a blow to the upper arm.

norms and work to achieve group objectives. When members fail to conform to norms and do not contribute to achieving objectives, the group provides some form of punishment. In most organizations, individuals become members of work groups composed of individuals who work on the same project, in the same department, or in the same area.

Most work groups have specific norms relating to work behavior, including norms regulating the quantity and quality of productivity expected from individuals. When individual output is above or below that expected by the group, pressure is usually applied by the group to "bring the individual into line."

Norms generally are enforced only for behaviors that are viewed as important by most group members. Groups do not have the time or energy to regulate each and every action of individual members.[14]

***Steps in Applying Group Pressure***   When members of a group do not conform to its norms, the first step in applying group pressure is usually to describe the expected behavior.[15] This description is usually accompanied by the reasons the behavior is necessary for group members. If the individual does not begin behaving within the group norms, members usually try forceful persuasion, which may include threats of some form of punishment. If the individual can withstand the group persuasion long enough, the group will usually isolate the individual from interaction with the group. If isolation fails, the group may harass the individual with verbal statements or use some form of physical violence. At this point, the individual may withdraw from the group to avoid pressure or may be forced out of the group. The individual is then no longer a part of the group, and the group members may act as if the individual did not exist. Figure 11.7 presents the steps in applying group pressure.

## RESPONSES TO GROUP PRESSURE

When subjected to group pressure, some individuals resist conforming to the norms. The extent of the resistance will usually depend on the value the individual places on membership and the amount of pressure exerted by the group. An initial resistance to group pressure may take the form of attempting to get the group to change the norm or to have the group make an exception to the norm. Unless the individual has abilities or resources that are highly valuable to the group, an exception will not likely be made. If a group is playing baseball and the owner of the only bat wants to get four strikes, the group might allow it in order to be able to continue using the bat. But the next time they play, more than one person will probably bring a bat. Fraternities commonly allow individuals who are star athletes or campus leaders to deviate from the group norms.

If the individual is unsuccessful in obtaining an exception to the norm, he or she usually conforms. When behavior required by the norm is objectionable, the individual may remain in the group and continue to endure the pressure.

When enduring the pressure is no longer "worth it," the individual will withdraw from the group by physically leaving or by psychologically isolating him- or herself from the group. In a work group situation, physically leaving may not be possible without quitting. Individuals commonly try to transfer in an organization or look for another job to avoid the pressure of conforming to work group norms.

When an individual becomes isolated from groups within the organization, the manager should be concerned about the reasons that led to the isolation. The manager should know whether the individual was isolated by the group or if the individual withdrew from it. The manager should also be aware of the group pressures being exerted on group members. The manager may need to

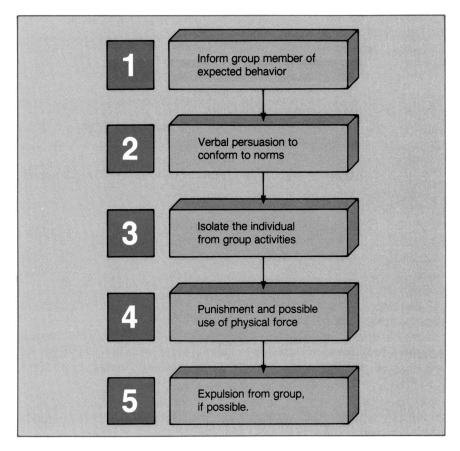

1  Inform group member of expected behavior

2  Verbal persuasion to conform to norms

3  Isolate the individual from group activities

4  Punishment and possible use of physical force

5  Expulsion from group, if possible.

**Figure 11.7**  Steps in applying group pressure to obtain conformity with norms.

take action if the pressures are excessive, become detrimental to the welfare of individuals, or prevent the achievement of organizational objectives.[16]

## IMPLICATIONS FOR MANAGERS

Effective managers must develop productive working relationships with groups. Achievement of organizational objectives requires effective coordination of group efforts. Unless groups within an organization integrate group goals with organizational goals, conflict will result. Management must continually work to develop harmony among and within groups in the organization. The integration of group and organizational goals is often a difficult task.

To develop effective working relations with groups, the manager must consider the motivational impact of the group on its members, the involvement of individuals in group decision-making processes, and methods of maintaining effective communication with the group.

---

## Guides for Working with Groups

1. Participation in groups is a basic source of social need satisfaction for employees.

2. Informal groups try to protect their members and provide security. They will try to protect members from perceived threats from management.

3. Groups develop communication systems to provide information that members want. If management does not provide the information employees want, the informal group will try to obtain it.

4. Both formal and informal groups obtain status and prestige within an organization. Groups may use their status and prestige as a power base to influence others in the organization.

5. Groups develop and enforce norms for the behavior of members. The group norms may be supportive of management or may work against management objectives.

6. The more cohesive a group is, the more control it has over the behavior of its members. The highly cohesive group can produce high achievement of organizational goals. However, it can work just as effectively against organizational objectives when the group opposes management.

7. Both formal and informal groups within an organization establish roles that affect the activities and responsibilities of members. Accepting role responsibilities in an informal group may require that an individual violate the role expectations of management.

---

If the actions of the manager threaten satisfaction of individual needs, the result may be defensive action by the group. If the group develops a defensive position, the manager's actions may unwittingly encourage the development of group norms and goals that conflict with organizational goals.

If group norms and goals support productivity for the organization, the manager should encourage strong group loyalties. When the group is supportive of organizational objectives, the manager should help the group increase cohesiveness. This can be done by rewarding the group, providing status to individuals because of their group membership, providing resources for the group, or delegating responsibility to the group.

*Informal Group Leaders*   The manager should develop effective working relationships with the informal group leaders. Managers often consider informal leaders as troublemakers. But because these leaders usually represent the group's norms and goals, the manager should communicate with them and respect their positions. Effective managers obtain advice and assistance from informal leaders in achieving organizational goals.

Managers should use *every* opportunity to illustrate how groups fit into the organization and how they contribute to the success of the organization. They should recognize the contributions that groups make to the organization. They should reinforce individual pride in group membership and group achievement. Managers should support group efforts to increase their effectiveness in contributing to organizational goals and member need satisfaction.

Since much of the behavior of individuals is influenced by the groups they belong to, effective management requires continuous attention to group processes.

## SELF–ASSESSMENT DISCUSSION

1. (1) Group membership is a part of being human. Work groups, family groups, social groups, religious groups, and professional groups are just a few of those in our daily lives.

2. (6) Most people are involved in several—often many—groups, both formal and informal.

3. (1) Structure is a feature that differentiates groups from togetherness situations. In a structure, members have specific things they do to support the group's purpose.

4. (6) Norms are among the most important group characteristics. They represent the values and expected behavior of group members.

5. (1) Group norms determine what its members may do as well as what they should or should not do. "May do" actions are those that are not required but are permissible.

6. (1) Commitment is a requirement for group effectiveness. Strong, cohesive groups have members with strong commitment to the group.

7. (6) Behavior that is shaped by expectations of others, including those in groups, is called roles. Roles, like norms, are an important group characteristic.

8. (6) Rank in a society, organization, or group is known as status. Status is essentially the perceived worth of an individual to the society, organization, or group.

9. (1) Cooperative relationships are necessary for groups to function well. Internal competition destroys group effectiveness.

10. (1) To assure that norms are established and maintained, group pressure is directed toward assuring conformity. Individual members who deviate from the norms are pressured to conform or leave the group.

## QUICK REVIEW

I. Groups

   A. An understanding of group processes is important in dealing with human behavior in organizations.

   B. The chance for leadership is greater in small groups.

   C. People underestimate the degree to which their behavior is affected by the groups they belong to.

II. Definition of a Group

   A. A group can be defined as two or more people working together to achieve a common goal.

   B. An important element in group situations is the relationships individuals have with each other, including status relationships.

   C. There is a clear distinction between togetherness situations and group processes.

      1. In togetherness situations, there are no stabilized status and role relationships that continue for prolonged periods of time.

      2. Togetherness situations can result in the development of a group.

III. Group Norms

   A. Group norms are the values that group members hold concerning the way members should behave in specific situations.

   B. Norms establish the expected behavior regarding people, physical objects, and situations.

   C. Norms include judgments of things members should, should not, or may do.

   D. Group norm development is influenced by:

      1. The nature of the group's environment.

      2. The characteristics of the individuals in the group.

      3. The group goals and the tasks required to achieve the goals.

IV. Roles

   A. Roles refer to the behavior expected of a particular position in a group.

      1. All members of the group develop roles and assume expected role behavior.

      2. Role relationships are affected by group structure.

   B. Role conflict occurs when role expectations are incompatible.

V. Status

   A. Status is either the formal or informal position of the person in a group.

   B. Status defines individual rights and privileges.

VI. Group Cohesiveness

    A. Cohesiveness refers to the degree of group unity that exists.

        1. Cohesiveness is a function of the contributions the group makes to satisfy the needs of its members.

        2. Conditions increasing cohesiveness include:

            a. Increase of prestige or status.

            b. Cooperative relationships.

            c. Participation.

            d. Community or organizational recognition.

            e. A threat from outside forces.

        3. Conditions decreasing cohesiveness include:

            a. Interpersonal conflict.

            b. Unpleasant personal experiences in the group.

            c. Limitation of individual participation.

            d. Restriction of effective communication.

            e. High personal risk resulting from group membership.

            f. Negative evaluation by outsiders.

    B. Cohesiveness can result in both positive and negative organizational behavior.

VII. Group Pressure

    A. Groups exert direct and indirect social pressure to ensure conformity.

    B. Group pressure to conform to group norms may depress as well as enhance individual performance.

VIII. Implications for Managers

    A. Managers must develop productive working relationships with groups.

    B. Managers should keep the following factors in mind:

        1. Participation in groups is a basic source of social need satisfaction.

        2. Informal groups provide security from threats.

        3. Groups develop communication systems.

        4. Both formal and informal groups obtain status and prestige.

        5. Groups develop and enforce norms.

        6. Highly cohesive groups exert strong controls over members.

        7. Formal and informal groups establish role behavior.

## KEY TERMS

| | | |
|---|---|---|
| Groups | Norms | Roles |
| Togetherness situations | Conformity | Role expectations |

| Role relationships | Formal status | Cohesiveness |
| Role conflict | Informal status | Group pressure |
| Status | | |

## DISCUSSION QUESTIONS

1. How do groups affect the behavior of individuals?
2. Why do groups that are not a part of the formal organizational structure develop within organizations?
3. What kinds of effects can group norms have on productivity in an organization?
4. How do the role expectations of an individual affect his or her behavior?
5. What are examples of role conflict that a student may face?
6. Why would individuals want to have high status in an informal group?
7. What conditions would tend to increase the cohesiveness of a group?
8. How do highly cohesive groups differ from groups with little cohesion?
9. How do groups apply pressure to group members to conform to norms?
10. What can an individual do to resist group pressure?

## ——————— EXERCISE ———————

### ▬▬▬▬ *Actions to Change An Undesirable Group Norm* ▬▬▬▬

You are the manager of a discount department store. A group norm has developed among the employees that "it is all right for employees to steal 'a little' merchandise to meet family needs." They do not condone stealing the merchandise to sell for money. The employees are a close group, and they protect each other when they steal merchandise for their families.

*Evaluate the following list of proposed actions to reduce employee theft.* Which actions would you take? Which would you take first?

1. Inform all employees in writing that an aggressive program will be initiated to apprehend and prosecute those involved in theft.

2. Do nothing until corporate management exerts pressure.

3. Ask employees to submit suggestions to you for courses of action to eliminate the theft.

4. Hire a private detective to catch an employee stealing and make an example of the employee who is caught.

5. Discuss the problem of theft with employees individually and request their assistance in stopping the employee theft.

6. Offer a reward for employees who turn in other employees who are stealing.

7. Tell employees you know they are stealing and you will not take any action as long as the theft does not exceed 2 percent of the stores sales.

8. Hire a new employee to "get in" with the other employees and provide you with evidence on the employees who are stealing.

9. Set up a program to provide merchandise to employees at cost so they will not need to steal.

10. Have a meeting with all employees to discuss the theft problem and possible courses of action.

<hr>

## TWO POINTS OF VIEW

### "The New Secretary"

*What would you do if you were the new secretary?*

You are a secretary who works in a secretarial pool that provides typing and clerical support for company managers. You are the newest and, according to your supervisor, "the best-trained secretary."

The pressure from the other secretaries is starting to get to you. When your supervisor and his boss were gone last Friday, the other secretaries in the office decided to call it a day and stopped work at 3:30. Because work needed to be done, you continued to work. When another secretary noticed you were working, she told you, "You make everyone look bad if you keep working when the bosses are gone."

The other secretaries have told you that you should not work so hard or you will suffer job burnout. There have been several indications that you don't fit in with the office group. You are excluded from most of the conversations in the office. The others manage to avoid you at lunch, so you don't eat with the group anymore.

You don't have much in common with the other secretaries and couldn't care less what they think. They all sit around at lunch and crochet or knit while they talk about whoever happens to be absent that day. You know that your goals are not the same as the others. You are trying to complete your college education so you can obtain a management job, while their goals seem to be babies and afghans. You don't think they want to improve their minds beyond reading *Woman's Day*.

You explained your opinion about the office group to one of the secretaries, and it immediately got back to them, so they actively avoid you now. You don't know how long you can put up with the pressure from the office group without losing your temper and telling them off. Your supervisor has mentioned to you several times that you need to try harder to get along with the other secretaries, because the office staff should be "one happy family."

*What would you do if you were the supervisor?*

You supervise the secretarial pool that provides typing and clerical support for company managers. You have always prided yourself on having a cooperative group of employees who work well together. Your boss has mentioned to you that he likes the friendly atmosphere in your office and hopes you can maintain a "happy work family."

Ever since you hired the new secretary, the office atmosphere has started becoming tense. The new secretary cannot get along with the other employees. She is the best-trained secretary you have ever hired, but she seems to have little in common with the other secretaries. The situation has reached the point where the new secretary is actively avoided by the others. You see the possibility for open conflict between the new secretary and the other secretaries.

One of the secretaries told you that the new secretary is "a fire-breathing dragon who is stomping around and stirring up trouble." A supervisor in another section told you that the grapevine was full of rumors about how the new secretary was out to make the others look bad and was trying to get them fired.

You have told the new secretary that she needs to cooperate and make friends with the other secretaries. But she does not seem to think cooperation and friendship are important on the job because she replied, "As far as I am concerned, the lunch bunch can sit and mold."

## ENDNOTES

1. Dennis W. Organ and Thomas Bateman, *Organizational Behavior*, 3d ed. (Plano, Tex.: Business Publications, 1986), p. 459.

2. Rodney W. Napier and Matti K. Gershenfeld, *Groups: Theory and Experience* (Boston: Houghton Mifflin, 1985), pp. 73–92.

3. For additional discussion of group norms, see Richard M. Steers, *Introduction to Organizational Behavior* (Santa Monica, Calif.: Goodyear, 1981); Marvin E. Shaw, *Group Dynamics: The Psychology of Small Group Behavior*, 2d ed. (New York: McGraw-Hill, 1976).

4. J. L. Pearce and R. H. Peters, "A Contradictory Norms View of Employer-Employee Exchange," *Journal of Management* 11 (1985): 19–30.

5. *Wall Street Journal*, 10 November 1961, p. 2.

6. James A. F. Stoner and Charles Wankel, *Management*, 3d ed. (Englewood Cliffs, N.J.: Prentice-Hall, 1986), p. 478.

7. For relevant studies, see J. Jackson, *Norms and Roles Studies in Systematic Psychology* (New York: Holt, Rinehart & Winston, 1976); R. S. Schuler, "Role Perceptions, Satisfaction, and Performance: A Partial Reconciliation," *Journal of Applied Psychology* (December 1975): 683–87; C. E. Schneier and P. W. Beatty, "The Influence of Role Prescriptions on the Performance Appraisal Process," *Academy of Management Journal* (March 1978): 129–34.

8. For an excellent discussion of roles, see L. Roos and F. Starke, "Roles in Organizations," in *Handbook of Organizational Design*, eds. W. Starbuck and P. Nystrom (Oxford, England: Oxford University Press, 1980).

9. Phillip L. Hunsaker and Curtis W. Cook, *Managing Organizational Behavior* (Reading, Mass.: Addison-Wesley, 1986), pp. 424–31.

10. For additional research, see P. Cartwright and A. Zander, *Group Dynamics: Research and Theory* (New York: Harper & Row, 1968); K. L. Dion, "Cohesiveness as

a Determinant of Ingroup-Outgroup Bias," *Journal of Personality and Social Psychology* 28 (1973): 163–71; Steve Penrod, *Social Psychology*, 2d ed. (Englewood Cliffs, N.J.: Prentice-Hall, 1986).

**11.** David O. Sears, Jonathan L. Freeman, and Letitia A. Peplau, *Social Psychology*, 2d ed. (Englewood Cliffs, N.J.: Prentice-Hall, 1985), pp. 367–68.

**12.** Peter W. Dorfman and Walter G. Stephan, "The Effects of Group Performance on Cognitions, Satisfaction, and Behavior: A Process Model," *Journal of Management* 10 (1984): 173–92.

**13.** Committee on Work in Industry, National Research Council, *Fatigue of Workers: Its Relation to Industrial Production* (New York: Van Nostrand Reinhold, 1941), pp. 77–86. See also Henry A. Landsberger, *Hawthorne Revisited* (Ithaca: Cornell University, NY State School of Labor Relations, 1968), and "Hawthorne Revisited: The Legend and the Legacy," *Organizational Dynamics* (Winter 1975): 66–80.

**14.** David C. Feldman, "The Development and Enforcement of Group Norms," *Academy of Management Review* 6 (January 1984): 47–53.

**15.** Serge Moscovici, "Social Influence and Conformity," in *Handbook of Social Psychology*, vol. 2, 3d ed., eds. Gardner Lindzey and Elliot Aronson (New York: Random House, 1985), chap. 7.

**16.** Relation of personal goals to group goals is discussed in Alvin Zander, Thomas Natsoulas, and Edwin J. Thomas, "Personal Goals and the Group's Goals for the Member," in *Group Development*, ed. Leland P. Bradford (La Jolla, Calif.: University Associates, 1978).

# Group Performance and Productivity

After reading this chapter, you should be able to do the following:

1. Discuss the conditions that make groups potentially more productive than individuals working alone
2. State the factors that contribute to the productivity of a group
3. Explain how task factors affect group productivity
4. Describe how interpersonal relations effect the achievement of group objectives
5. Identify sources of interpersonal conflict and approaches to reduce conflict
6. Describe the characteristics of highly productive groups
7. Discuss how effective group leaders behave

# Chapter Topics

- No magic in groups
- Groups and individual productivity
- Group productivity
- Task factors affecting productivity
- Interpersonal relations and productivity
- Effective group leadership

# Preview

People are the basic ingredient of any organization. By the very nature of organizations, tasks are accomplished through the coordinated efforts of people working together in job-related groups. Groups either may be formally designated or may develop spontaneously on an informal basis. A primary characteristic of groups is the dependency of members on one another to accomplish group goals. Cooperative, coordinated groups are powerful tools available to management. They can, and often do, accomplish more than the most highly motivated individual working independently of others. Unfortunately, the tendency is to forget that groups are made of individuals with differing values, needs, attitudes, and abilities. True organizational effectiveness depends on the manager's understanding of both groups and individuals in groups.

In this chapter, groups and forces affecting individuals in groups are discussed. Factors that encourage productivity as well as those that decrease productivity are examined.

Two heads are better than one
but,
too many cooks spoil the broth.


In unity there is strength
but,
a chain is no stronger than its weakest link.

**SELF–ASSESSMENT** ▰▰▰▰▰▰▰▰▰▰▰▰▰▰▰▰▰▰▰▰▰▰▰▰

Group performance and productivity are primary management concerns. Employees are often influenced more by the informal groups with which they identify than by management directives. In the following statements, mark the answer that you believe is most appropriate. Each statement or question has a range of possible responses. A scale of 1 to 6 between two words with different meanings allows you to mark either the word that is considered correct or a place between the two words that represents some agreement and some disagreement. Selection of a high number such as 5 or 6 may be either correct or incorrect, just as selection of lower numbers may be correct or incorrect. Some responses may be partly correct and partly incorrect.

Answers based on research by behavioral scientists, with a short explanation of why the response was considered correct, may be found on page 340.

**1.** The statement has been made that groups:

lack the variation of  1...2...3...4...5...6  are widely varied,
individuals                                    like individuals

**2.** From a realistic point of view, groups have:

potentially greater  1...2...3...4...5...6  potentially fewer
resources than                              resources than
individuals                                 individuals

**3.** Performance in groups is strongly influenced by:

self-actualization  1...2...3...4...5...6  social motives
motives

**4.** The prerequisite to motivating employees is that they have:

established group  1...2...3...4...5...6  ability
membership

**5.** In any group, the efforts of individuals must be:

coordinated  1...2...3...4...5...6  normalized

**6.** Interpersonal relationships of group members are affected most by:

ability  1...2...3...4...5...6  status

**7.** A common reason for interpersonal problems is that managers avoid dealing with:

conflicts  1...2...3...4...5...6  group roles

8. The primary form of communication between group leaders and group members are the leader's:

directives  1...2...3...4...5...6 actions

9. Predictions of group effectiveness are made uncertain by:

individual differences  1...2...3...4...5...6 group norms

10. Ability of groups to achieve organizational objectives is strongly influenced by:

effectiveness of  1...2...3...4...5...6 freedom from
support personnel                              support personnel

## NO MAGIC IN GROUPS

Much of the success of any organization depends on how effectively individuals work in groups. The basis of productivity is often the collective, cooperative effort of groups. If managed effectively, groups can reach levels of productivity that exceed what individuals can accomplish working by themselves.

Although groups are often highly productive, they are not automatically effective because people are together. Forming a group will not necessarily solve problems or increase output, although some people seem to attribute superior virtues to togetherness. In some organizations, the response to problems is "Let's form a group."

The **"do-it-in-a-group" disease** plagues many companies. Every organization is a potential victim, and the destruction of individual effort can result. "Do-it-in-a-group" is not a new disease. Organizations in all fields and of all sizes are constantly forming new groups. Anyone who refuses to affiliate with all the appropriate groups can become an object of curiosity, if not suspicion.

*Groups Have Psychological Value*   What is the basic cause of "do-it-in-a-group"? Can it be stamped out or controlled? It should not be destroyed, because in some cases the pool of intelligence—or ignorance, as the case may be—aids in the solution of problems and contributes to the understanding of the people involved. The group also has certain psychological values for the participants and especially for the leader, who can reaffirm a status position in the group. Some may need the psychological security provided by groups. Some may also need to let people know where they stand on a variety of group-supported issues.

A group can serve a useful function only when it is well organized and concerned with a problem that can best be solved on the level of group interaction. A group should not deal with problems that could be better solved on an individual level. Groups cannot and should not take the place of individual initiative.

*Analyzing Group Productivity*   Organizations that are group conscious and suffer from "do-it-in-a-group" should ask the following questions:

1. Are the groups composed of people who are willing to do nothing individually, but as a group can meet and decide that nothing can be done?

2. Are the groups popular because the individuals are afraid to go out on a limb?

3. Do the groups engage in transferring problems from one graveyard to another?

4. Are the groups a storehouse of knowledge because the individuals bring so much knowledge in and take so little out?

5. Are the groups considered useful in proportion to the time they consume rather than their capacity for productivity?

## GROUPS AND INDIVIDUAL PRODUCTIVITY

Our discussion of groups has emphasized the great differences among groups as well as among individuals in groups. The **productivity** of a given group is often hard to predict because of these differences. Under certain conditions, one group may be successful while another may fail. Making accurate generalizations about group productivity is difficult.

Groups have the potential to destroy individual responsibility and creativity, and at the same time increase individual initiative and productivity. Many researchers have compared the productivity of individuals working alone with the productivity of individuals working together in a group. When research on group versus individual productivity is analyzed, one cannot conclude that groups are superior to individuals working alone. The productivity of a group is only *potentially* greater than the productivity of individuals working alone. To achieve its potential, a group must use its resources effectively and motivate members to achieve group goals.[1] Furthermore, the influence of members on each other in decision making should result in "better" decisions.

1. *Groups have potentially greater resources.*[2] A group is not necessarily more productive than individuals working alone. There are no group characteristics that, in and of themselves, make the group productive. Group situations can result in low levels of productivity. A group has potentially greater resources than individuals operating alone for two basic reasons:

   a. In groups, division of labor is possible. Effective **division of labor** involves individuals doing jobs they are best prepared to do. Individuals can specialize, each performing the job for which he or she has the highest aptitude and training.

   b. In group situations, **duplication of effort** is also possible. If part of the group is not meeting required schedules, employees can help each other. If a production line slows down, one way to speed it up is to move additional people from another production line. The basic concept of duplication of effort is that when something "catches fire," everybody goes to put out the fire. In a group, people can be shifted to the area where they are the most needed. However, duplication of effort can become an excuse for not solving basic problems in an organization. It is possible to keep shifting people rather than deal with the basic problems. Duplication of effort often turns into wasted effort when too many people are assigned to a job.

2. *Social motives in groups influence individual performance.* Motivational effects occur as a result of **social motives** evoked in a group. Primary social motives include esteem, affection, and recognition. Social motives can act as an incentive for increased production, or they can satisfy social needs without contact with other people. Satisfaction of affection or friendship needs requires interaction with others. In a close-knit or cohesive work group, an individual may also obtain both status and recognition from the group.

   A group can be productive from the individual's point of view and be unproductive in achieving organizational objectives. Members of a work group may get together and say "We're tired of busting a gut, and we're all going to slow down!" The individual who doesn't slow down is "going to get it from the group." The group may withhold status, affection, or recognition from those who refuse to restrict productivity. Cohesive groups can be highly effective in achieving their own objectives when they slow down or, conversely, choose to increase productivity.

   Management's problem is to make group objectives consistent with the objectives of the organization. This task is often difficult. The objectives do not have to be identical but must lead to the same end result.

3. *Decisions in groups can be better because of social influences.* A potential advantage of groups is social influence for better decisions.[3] Groups involved in decision making usually demand supporting evidence. If a procedure is to be changed, individuals in the group will want evidence to support the desirability of the change. A group can perform an **error-correcting function** by insisting that decisions are consistent with the objectives of the organizations. A group may also use the experience of members to prevent the repetition of mistakes. If group members are committed to the achievement of organizational objectives, it usually exerts a positive influence on decision making. Figure 12.1 illustrates the potential for group productivity.[4]

## GROUP PRODUCTIVITY

The productivity of a group depends on the resources available to it and its ability to use those resources to achieve group objectives. By effectively using the available resources, the group's productivity may exceed that of the individuals working alone. The way group members relate to one another and to the

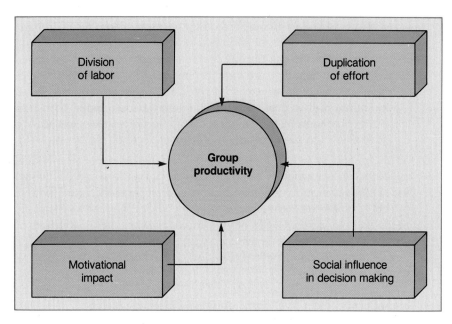

Figure 12.1   Potential for group productivity.

task can result either in effective coordination to achieve objectives or in wasted effort.

Two major factors that contribute to the productivitiy of a group are (1) individual effectiveness in accomplishing tasks and (2) interpersonal relations of group members.

*Group Bonus Effect*   Contributions that are made to the total group productivity by individuals working alone vary with the nature of the task and the organization of the group. Many of the outputs of groups can be produced by individuals working alone. Also possible is for groups to produce outputs that are better than those the best group member can produce alone and which are not the result of a simple addition of individual member productivity. A **group bonus effect** occurs when the group is able to achieve objectives that could not have been achieved by an individual working alone or by a combination of individual efforts. Group bonus effect is achieved through cooperation, interdependent effort, division of labor, and the motivational influences of the group.

As illustrated in Figure 12.2, the productivity of a group depends on individual task performance and the effectiveness of group members working together. A group has tasks to be accomplished in order to achieve group objectives. The employees in the group must be able to develop interpersonal relationships that facilitate productivity.

## "Groupthink"

High group cohesiveness can work to a group's disadvantage. Agreement can be overemphasized to maintain the group's attractiveness. When the group avoids disagreements, it can result in poor decisions because no critical evaluation of ideas and actions is done.

Irving Janis studied this tendency of highly cohesive groups to lose the capacity for critical evaluation and called it "groupthink." [5]

### Symptoms of Groupthink

Eight characteristics of a group's behavior indicate that "groupthink" may be occurring:

1. The group believes it is beyond criticism or invulnerable.
2. The group refuses to accept unpleasant or contradictory data.
3. The group believes it is above criticism from outsiders.
4. The group sees opposition as weak, evil, or stupid.
5. The group refuses to tolerate members who suggest it may be wrong.
6. The group members do not express their concerns about group actions.
7. The group assumes that consensus exists without checking with members.
8. The group protects itself from disturbing ideas from outside.

### Actions to Avoid Groupthink

Groupthink can result in poor decisions because of inaccurate information, failure to consider alternatives, and failure to examine risks. To avoid the negative consequences of groupthink, group members should be encouraged to critically evaluate ideas and courses of action. The following actions can be used by a group to improve decisions and avoid groupthink:

- Discuss issues and courses of action with outsiders.
- Have a group member play devil's advocate at each meeting.
- Get the reaction of outside experts to group decisions.
- Use subgroups to work on the same problem to get different views.
- To get input, the leader should avoid taking a position during discussion.
- After agreement is reached, have a meeting to test consensus on issues.

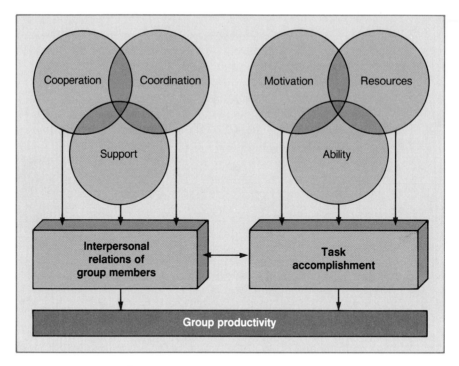

**Figure 12.2**  Factors affecting group productivity.

## TASK FACTORS AFFECTING PRODUCTIVITY

Individual responses to task accomplishment depend on the *motivation* to do the task, the *ability* to perform the task, and the *support* received. Obstacles or problems that create difficulties for individuals in trying to accomplish tasks can be grouped into three areas: (1) lack of task structure, including vague objectives; (2) lack of adequate resources (either physical or human) to support task accomplishment; and (3) lack of skill or training to accomplish the task.[6]

### *Structure and Objectives*

Although having unstructured groups with virtually unlimited freedom in performing tasks may appear desirable, the resulting productivity is usually low. Without specific objectives, group members have only a vague idea of what accomplishments are expected. As the old saying goes, "If you don't know where you are going, there is no way to get there."

Some people may be initially attracted to an unstructured group atmosphere, but they become dissatisfied when they realize that there are no goals to be reached. The lack of specific goals usually results in confused and frustrated group members.

An example of an unstructured situation can occur in a college course. How would students react if the instructor announced to a class, "We will just play it by ear in this course and decide as we go along what will be covered and how it will be covered. At the end of the course, a grading procedure will be determined. The course will be unstructured, with no course outline and no specified testing procedures."

The same situation can occur in an organization. If work groups do not have specific goals, people are uncertain about the way in which they are going to be evaluated.[7] They question whether their jobs are going to exist over a period of time. Groups are more productive when there are specific and measurable objectives that are understood by group members. The objectives are most meaningful to people when they are tied to individual evaluations and reward systems.

When the structure of a task is clear and specific, productivity is higher. To determine if tasks are specific, individuals have been asked what they are expected to do to contribute to group productivity. Responses such as "I am supposed to do a good job" or "I am supposed to work hard" may indicate ambiguous tasks. When people are uncertain of roles in performing group tasks, productivity usually suffers.

Two factors are needed for effective structure: (1) specific and measurable group objectives and (2) a definition of specific tasks that are necessary to accomplish objectives.

## Support Resources

A group must use physical and human resources to achieve objectives. Physical resources include space, equipment, and supplies. Human resources include the people directly involved in performing the tasks to achieve objectives and the support personnel.

When the level of support is reduced, one effect may be to reduce the level of individual motivation. Where the quality of **support resources** is low, the message communicated to group members may be that the task performance expectation is for low-quality work. As an employee of a machine shop put it, "When you give me junky equipment to work on, you're telling me you want a junky job done." The way resources are allocated is a key element in the nonverbal communication on any job.

An interesting experiment was performed with highly trained machinists. New machinery was rigged so that half of the machinery would periodically break down. (This was done by electronically rigging the equipment to stop operating on a random basis.) The machinists that worked on the equipment that broke down periodically were provided with a recreation room equipped with all kinds of facilities. When the equipment broke down, they were allowed to go to the recreation room and still receive full pay. The equipment was down one-fourth of each day. Half of the machinists worked on equipment that was well maintained and operated approximately eight hours each day. Which group had the highest productivity per hour when the machines were operating?

## Goal Setting at Tenneco

Setting goals for any company is no easy matter. The problems are compounded when that company is a multi-industry firm employing approximately 82,000 people and operating eight major industries. One such firm, Tenneco, based in Houston, Texas, has developed a unique approach to the problem of goal setting.

The system emphasizes that personal development goals should receive equal weight with quantitative, organizational goals. Measurements used to evaluate progress should look at both development and organizational objectives.

The program was designed by a task force comprising representatives from all of Tenneco's companies. The task force stressed that the program would depend on continual communication between managers and employees to develop good measures of performance, taking into account the unique characteristics of each job and each worker. The hope was that the program would help prepare more employees for promotion, since workers set their own achievement goals.

The task force also emphasized the following four conditions to help the program succeed: (1) management support at all levels, (2) minimum of procedure and paperwork, (3) training for managers in how to implement the program, and (4) continual communication and feedback among participants.

When the companies began to implement the program, Tenneco took five key steps to make sure the goal-setting technique got off to the best possible start:

1. Management determined if the employees and the organization were suited for this particular program.
2. They prepared employees for goal setting through training, communication, and action plans.
3. They emphasized the characteristics of goals that should be understood.
4. They conducted reviews to modify the goals.
5. They performed final reviews to check on goals, modifications, and accomplishments.[8]

The machinists that worked the full eight hours a day on the machines that were well maintained had the highest productivity per hour. The group that had approximately two hours off each day to go play in the recreation room had the lowest productivity per hour. The eight-hour-a-day people had the highest productivity in both quality and quantity. When people are provided with low-quality support facilities and equipment, the quality and quantity of task accomplishment will be below their ability to achieve.

*Support Personnel*   In most groups, the ability to achieve objectives in a group situation is dependent to a large extent on support personnel. An engineer may need the support of technical writers, drafters, and test personnel. When cost reductions are necessary, the drafter rather than the engineer is cut from the work force first. Why the drafter? The decision is usually based on the assumption that people with the lowest qualifications are the easiest to replace. When the lowest-qualified support personnel are cut, highly qualified technical and professional people must do support jobs.

Some organizations try to save money by not hiring adequate numbers of support personnel. Such organizations often become overstaffed with highly trained and highly paid technical and professional workers. When they lack support personnel, the technical and professional employees spend valuable time doing support tasks. They are often inefficient and dissatisfied in performing support jobs. They become frustrated, and motivation effectiveness drops.

Organizations have been criticized for not using enough support personnel, even in medicine. Doctors may be doing tasks that could be done by nurses. Nurses may be doing tasks that could be done by orderlies. Doctors may also be doing tasks that could be done by accounting support personnel. Nurses may find themselves doing tasks that could be done by administrative assistants.

Organizations need both professional staff and support staff to develop effective work groups. Resources must be appropriately allocated to ensure that the concept of division of labor is used effectively.

## Skill and Training

The prerequisite for motivating employees is that they have the ability to accomplish an assigned task. If a letter is to be typed, the employee assigned the task of typing must know how to type before he or she can be motivated. If an employee lacks the skill and training to perform an assignment adequately, he or she cannot be motivated.

Individuals are often placed in jobs without adequate evaluation of their ability to perform the required tasks. The usual assumption—often incorrect—is that they will be trained once they get on the job. Individuals are also promoted without adequate training to positions that differ significantly from the jobs they previously held. A skilled machinist who does an outstanding job may be promoted to a supervisory position without training or analysis of his or her skills or readiness for supervision. Often, promotions take place on the assumption that the individual will learn on the job. This usually results in low effectiveness from first-line supervisors who are promoted from line positions without being given adequate management training.

An evaluation of an individual's ability to perform the tasks required in a position should always be made. The best salesperson in an organization may not have the abilities needed to be an effective sales manager. The tasks involved in sales and the tasks involved in sales management are not the same. An individual would not be expected to be able to play the piano just because he or she is a good basketball player. By the same reasoning, the assumption should not be made that just because a person is skilled in the technical aspect of a job, he or she is able to manage effectively. Task factors promoting group productivity are presented in Figure 12.3.

## INTERPERSONAL RELATIONS AND PRODUCTIVITY

The achievement of group objectives depends not only on individual task performance but also on how well group members can work together. In any group, the effort of individuals must be coordinated.

Developing interpersonal relations that produce cooperative effort is difficult in any group. Members must devote time that could be spent on accomplishing tasks to interacting with others. The coordination and cooperation resulting from interpersonal relations must balance the time consumed in developing and maintaining them. An employee working alone can direct his or her efforts solely to accomplishing a task. When working with others, however, the employee must deal with interpersonal relations.

Group members usually understand *task problems* much better than **interpersonal conflict**. Yet, dealing effectively with interpersonal problems can contribute to productivity as much as solving task problems. In many groups, interpersonal conflicts are the major obstacles to achieving group objectives.

These conflicts arise from a wide range of factors, including conflicts in attitudes, **individualistic motivation**, and status differences.[9]

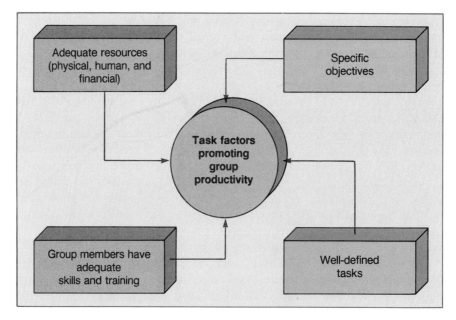

**Figure 12.3**  Task factors that facilitate group productivity.

### Differences in Attitudes and Values

People in groups nearly always have differences in attitudes and values. These differences provide the potential for interpersonal conflicts. When conflicts arise and individuals spend time arguing with each other, it detracts from efforts to achieve group objectives.

One approach that can minimize attitude conflicts is to control group membership. A group can be composed of members with similar backgrounds and attitudes. When people agree with each other, the possibility of conflicts is usually lessened. If groups are composed of similar individuals, however, they lack the variety of inputs necessary for creative problem solving.

When attitude conflicts arise, management can handle the problem by requiring that both parties assume responsibility for developing methods to resolve their conflicts and work together cooperatively. To do this, management must first develop a climate in which each individual feels responsible for supporting efforts leading to cooperative work relations.

A manager must be concerned about the effect of interpersonal conflict on group productivity but should not try to get people to agree for agreement's sake. Group members must be able to have attitude differences and still work effectively with each other. At the most basic level, each group member's responsibility should be not to interfere with anyone else's work.

Off-the-job conflicts often influence job performance. A conflict arose between two engineers when they coached opposing little league football teams. One of the engineers accused the other of coaching his team to play rough and dirty. As a result of the outside conflict, they began interfering with each other's work. They did not provide each other with information needed to complete engineering designs and continually argued about how to coach a little league football team. The situation reached a point where they sabotaged each other's effectiveness by withholding test data or providing inaccurate test results.

At first the manager ignored the conflict, hoping it would go away. But when the conflict was clearly not subsiding, he decided to place the responsibility for solving the problem on the engineers. The manager met with them and made it clear that whatever their personal differences, the reduction in productivity must be stopped. He gave the engineers a room to meet in and assigned them responsibility for determining how they were going to eliminate the conflict. He pointed out that if they could not solve the problem, he would have to take action, which could include termination.

The manager was amazed at how quickly the engineers developed a plan to cooperate. The manager did not have to get in the middle of an employee conflict. Managers can deal with conflict by placing responsibility with employees.[10]

### Individualistic Motivation

When rewards are based on individual productivity and working with others in a group is not rewarded, there is usually high **individualistic motivation**. Situations that promote individualistic motivation are characterized by people not being rewarded for cooperation or coordination. As a result, cooperation is reduced, and people concentrate only on their own productivity. When cooperation is necessary to achieve group objectives, the conditions do not exist that are necessary to obtain the desired cooperation.

If rewards are provided that promote high individualistic motivation, having people working independently is more productive than having them working interdependently. To achieve group productivity, individuals must be rewarded for cooperating with and supporting the efforts of other group members.

*Rewards for Group Achievement*    Benefits can be structured so that individuals are rewarded for their total contribution to group productivity. Some organizations provide rewards to groups for achievement of group objectives. A technique that some organizations use is to allocate bonuses to work groups for high group productivity. In some cases, the work group is given the opportunity to divide the bonus among members in any way it wants, as long as members unanimously agree on the allocations. For group allocation of rewards to work effectively, provision needs to be made that if the group cannot come to a unanimous agreement, management will decide on the allocations to group members. When the choice is whether the group will agree on how to allocate the bonus or have management decide, group members almost always agree to a group-developed allocation method.

To reduce individualistic motivation, efforts that support group productivity must be rewarded. Benefits that are usually available include pay raises, promotions, recognition, and job assignments.

## Status and Status Symbols

Status affects the interpersonal relations of every member of a group. The privileges often associated with status are used to provide extra rewards. A leader may use status to achieve control over group members. Since all groups have members with differing degrees of status, it is a factor that must be dealt with if group objectives are to be achieved.

When people's awareness of status positions is heightened by status symbols, the effect is to increase social distance and reduce interaction. As interaction is reduced, the ability to coordinate is reduced.

High-status individuals in a group have increased power, prestige, and ability to influence group members. High-status differentials often undermine the competition for respect among the group members. Instead of competing for respect with other group members, individuals compete for respect from the high-status individual. Where there are very strong status positions, cooperation among group members is reduced, and individuals compete for the rewards that the leader has the power to provide. When individuals look to high-status members to provide rewards, they usually do not help each other correct errors or improve performance.

Problems resulting from status cannot be completely eliminated, but they can be reduced. In the following situation, the people in the tool shop were

## Status and the Ten Thousand Parts

The effect of status and status symbols became dramatically clear in one manufacturing firm. Parts designs were sent from the engineering department to the tool shop, which made the tools required to produce the parts. The company had specified that the engineers would certify the drawings by placing their approval stamp on them. The use of this stamp, which was the engineers' status symbol, made the people in the tool shop more aware of the engineers' status. Before this procedure was required, workers in the tool shop would notify engineering of any suspected errors in a drawing. After awareness of the engineers' status was heightened, the people in the tool shop decided they were supposed to say nothing if they thought there was an error. In one instance, they were to make couplings to connect parts for which they had previously made the tools. Even though the workers determined that the couplings were the wrong size, they made the tools and sent them to production. Ten thousand parts were made that did not fit and had to be scrapped. Such incidents can happen when errors are known but not corrected because of a heightened emphasis on status.

irritated by the emphasis on status symbols. Status symbols that create social distance include a bigger name on the door, a key to the executive washroom, the ability to eat in the executive dining room, and a reserved parking space. What do status symbols motivate people to do? They motivate people to work for more status symbols. A system that places a high value on status symbols will motivate people to seek status symbols rather than to be more productive.

### *Avoiding Interpersonal Relations Problems*

A common reason for interpersonal relations problems is that managers avoid dealing with conflicts. When employees do not get along with each other, a manager may ignore the problem and hope it will go away. Interpersonal relations problems usually adversely affect productivity, and they seldom work themselves out. Employees involved usually find the situation uncomfortable, and the manager who avoids the problem is not accepting the responsibilities of managing.

One reason managers avoid dealing with interpersonal conflict is that they find the situation uncomfortable. If managers are uncertain about their ability to handle interpersonal relations, they will probably be reluctant to deal with the problems employees have with one another.

Figure 12.4 presents a summary of interpersonal conflicts and methods of dealing with them. Most managers can identify interpersonal relations problems and determine approaches to solve them. However, in most areas of human activity, people do not practice what they know. Students usually know how to

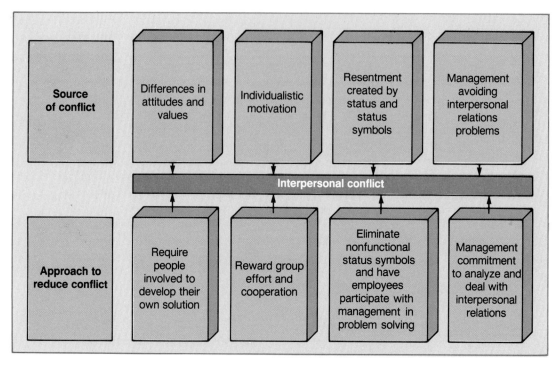

**Figure 12.4**  Sources of interpersonal conflict and approaches to reduce conflict.

make better grades in a course but often fail to do it. Although most managers know how to manage more effectively, they often avoid dealing with interpersonal relations problems.[11]

An honest answer to the question, "Why don't you manage as effectively as you know how?" came from the manager who replied, "Because I don't want to." When asked why he didn't want to, the manager answered, "I would rather spend my time and effort doing more enjoyable things."

> The management challenge is to try to create a climate in which goals sought by groups are congruent with organizational goals, and in which groups can experience group success.[12]

A difficulty is determining methods to bridge the gap between knowing how to manage and putting that knowledge into practice.

Important interpersonal relations factors that promote group productivity are presented in Figure 12.5.

## EFFECTIVE GROUP LEADERSHIP

The research on **group leadership** has produced a variety of findings that contribute to our understanding of leadership effectiveness in groups. Hundreds of research projects have been conducted to identify the behaviors of

**Figure 12.5**   Interpersonal relations factors that promote group productivity.

effective group leaders.[13] The research strongly supports the necessity for group leaders to adapt their behavior to the specific situation and the group members. With the caution to adapt leadership behavior, the following are generalizations from the research studies on group leadership that can be applied in most situations:

- There are *no* universal traits of leaders, but some leadership behaviors do contribute to group effectiveness in most situations.

    For example: Unlike ineffective leaders, effective leaders let group members know what is expected of them, inform group members of changes, explain reasons for decisions, and get members' reactions before going ahead with changes.

- Leadership effectiveness depends on group members perceiving the leader as competent and fair.

    These perceived qualities are not independent but affect each other. It is not a question of whether the leader is genuinely competent and fair but whether group members *believe* the leader is competent and fair. A leader's competence is judged in large part by whether the leader can distinguish between effective and ineffective performance. The leader's fairness is usually evaluated on the basis of how the leader distributes rewards and punishments in relation to individual needs and the performance of group members.

- For a leader to be effective, group members must perceive the leader's behavior as consistent and predictable.

---

### Characteristics Frequently Observed in Productive Groups [14]

- Group members accept leadership responsibilities.
- Relationships among group members are relaxed and cooperative.
- Members express loyalty to the group and support group activities.
- There is mutual confidence in the ability of group members.
- Group members trust each other.
- There is understanding of and agreement with group goals.
- A supportive atmosphere exists where group members help each other to succeed.
- Members communicate openly and directly with each other.
- Group members understand and accept the norms and values of the group.
- Members of the group help each other to develop their full potential.
- The group sets challenging goals.
- There is a strong team spirit.

---

If the leader's behavior is predictable and consistent, the group can generally function without unnecessary disturbances. There is more certainty in the group, and ongoing activities will be smoother.

- The leader's *actions* are the primary form of communication to indicate the behaviors desired of group members.

By actions, the leader indicates priorities and the activities that are most important. Effective leaders communicate through their *behaviors* as a way of securing commitment to joint action and achievement of group goals. Leaders who can translate information into action are more effective than leaders who depend on talking and writing to communicate with group members.

- In some situations, group leadership is most effectively exercised by "keeping hands off."

Effective leadership requires giving group members the opportunity to develop and grow. Restraint is one of the hardest things for most leaders to practice. Often present is a strong temptation to overload—to "do something" as an exercise of authority and leadership.

- Autocratic leadership is necessary and effective in some situations.

Although participative leadership can be effective with most groups, it is not effective in all situations. In a crisis situation, an autocratic style is

## Suggestions for Developing Effective Group Leadership ▬▬

The following guidelines indicate leader behaviors that usually have a positive effect on group productivity. Although these behaviors are not equally applicable in all group situations, they are frequently exhibited by effective group leaders.

- Make a genuine effort to understand group members as individuals.
- Try to match individuals to the group activities for which they are best suited.
- Involve group members in decisions that affect them.
- Develop high standards and high expectations for performance.
- Encourage and support individual efforts to improve performance.
- Listen to suggestions, answer questions, and discuss problems.
- Provide individuals with frequent feedback on performance.
- Recognize and give credit for outstanding performance.
- Make a special effort to help individuals who have low performance.
- Maintain two-way communication and accept feedback from group members.
- Avoid trying to impose personal attitudes and values on group members.
- Make decisions as fast as possible.
- Develop priorities and time limits for group activities.
- Anticipate problems whenever possible and take preventive action.
- Accept responsibility for your decisions and their consequences.
- Avoid putting individuals down.
- Explain reasons for decisions.
- Get the facts before criticizing.
- Show respect for individuals and for their ideas and feelings.

usually effective. Crisis creates conditions that call for prompt and decisive action. An autocratic style may be more effective in cases when the group leader has the information and ability to make high-quality decisions and group members are willing to accept the leader's judgment.

- Effective group leaders develop a "sense of what might occur" and plan for possible future events.

Leadership effectiveness requires that plans are developed for contingencies. These plans may not be needed, but developing alternatives contributes to effectiveness by providing options for the group and identifying possible pitfalls.

- Effectiveness as a group leader depends on having the ability to exert social influence.

  Skills in social influence include developing peer relationships, carrying out negotiations, motivating group members, resolving conflicts, and disseminating information. Without the ability to influence the behavior of group members, a leader has no hope of being effective.

## SELF-ASSESSMENT DISCUSSION

**1.** (6) The statement has been made that there are as many types of groups as there are individuals in groups. Although this may not be literally true, groups vary to a great extent.

**2.** (1) A real value of groups is that their resources of ideas, knowledge, and creativity are potentially greater than those of individuals.

**3.** (6) With little doubt, social motives are the primary determinants of behavior in groups of all sizes. The extent of individual conformity to group norms is a measure of social need.

**4.** (6) Motivation is useless unless employees have the ability to perform.

**5.** (1) Without coordination of efforts through direction of activities of group members, group effectiveness is impossible.

**6.** (6) Perceived status is a highly important factor affecting relationships in groups.

**7.** (1) Failure to deal with conflicts is a major cause of continued and increasingly destructive interpersonal problems, both between individuals and in groups.

**8.** (6) "Actions speak louder than words" may sound somewhat banal, but it is true. Leadership actions are always more powerful forms of communication than words.

**9.** (1) Individual differences are the strongest influence on group behavior.

**10.** (1) Effective support is necessary for work groups in organizations to achieve organizational goals. Without necessary support, goal attainment may be impossible.

## *QUICK REVIEW*

I. No Magic in Groups

   A. The basis for productivity in most organizations is the collective, cooperative effort that takes place in groups.

   B. To test whether a group will be effective, the following questions should be asked:

      1. Is the group made up of nondeciders who believe that nothing can be done?

2. Does the group provide a security blanket?

3. Does the group transfer problems from one place to another?

4. Do the group members fail to use pooled knowledge?

5. Is the group judged by time in meetings rather than by productivity?

II. Groups and Individual Productivity

    A. Individual differences make prediction of group effectiveness uncertain.

    B. Groups can both destroy and increase individual initiative.

    C. The productivity of a group is potentially greater than the productivity of individuals.

       1. Groups have potentially greater resources. Both division of labor and duplication of effort are possible.

       2. Social motives in groups influence individual performance.

       3. Decision in groups can be better because of social influences.

III. Group Productivity

    A. The productivity of a group depends on the availability of resources and the ability of the group to use those resources.

    B. A group bonus effect occurs when groups achieve more than an equivalent number of individuals can achieve working alone.

IV. Task Factors Affecting Productivity

    A. Task factors affecting productivity include:

       1. Task structure and objectives.

       2. Adequate resources.

       3. Skill and training.

    B. Structured groups with clear objectives are more effective than unstructured groups with vague objectives.

    C. An organization must have support resources that allow groups and individual specialists to concentrate fully on their primary tasks.

    D. Skill and training is mandatory for both group and individual effectiveness.

V. Interpersonal Relations and Productivity

    A. The basic organizational unit is the individual, whether working in a group (interdependent) or functioning independently.

    B. Interpersonal relations have a direct effect on cooperation, coordination, and productivity.

       1. Conflict in groups may arise because of differences in attitudes and values. One solution to conflict is to require that the people involved develop their own solutions.

       2. Individualistic motivation destroys group effectiveness. Rewards should support group rather than individual activity.

3. Status and status symbols often create psychological distance and resentment.

4. The poorest course of action for managers to take is to avoid interpersonal relations problems.

VI. Effective Group Leadership

A. No universal leadership traits have been identified, but some leader behaviors are effective in most situations.

B. Where group members perceive the leader as competent and fair, the leader is more effective.

C. Consistent and predictable behavior by the group leader contributes to effectiveness.

D. Leaders indicate desired behaviors by their actions.

E. Effective leadership requires giving group members the opportunity to develop and grow.

F. In some situations, autocratic leadership is necessary and effective.

G. Effective leaders develop contingency plans.

H. To be effective, a group leader must be able to exert social influence.

## KEY TERMS

| | | |
|---|---|---|
| "Do-it-in-a-group" disease | Social motives | Support resources |
| Group productivity | Error-correcting function | Interpersonal conflict |
| Division of labor | Group bonus effect | Individualistic motivation |
| Duplication of effort | Group objectives | Group leadership |

## DISCUSSION QUESTIONS

1. What are some examples of using groups to do tasks or solve problems that could be better dealt with by individual effort?

2. Why is the productivity of a group *potentially* greater than the productivity of individuals working alone?

3. Describe a specific example of the use of division of labor.

4. How can the motivational impact of a work group adversely affect the achievement of organizational objectives?

5. Describe a situation in which the output of a group could be better than the best group member could have produced alone and which could not have resulted from simply adding the productivity of individual members.

6. How can task structure affect group productivity?

7. What effect can the lack of support resources have on the motivation of members of a group?

8. Why would a manager avoid dealing with interpersonal conflict?

9. List all the methods you can think of for reducing conflicts that could result from differences in attitudes and values.

10. What action can management take to reduce individualistic motivation?
11. Give an example of a conflict in a group that resulted from status differences.
12. What can be done to bridge the gap between knowing management concepts and putting them into practice?

—————————— **EXERCISE** ——————————

▬▬▬▬▬▬▬▬▬ *Actions to Develop Cooperation* ▬▬▬▬▬▬▬▬▬

You supervise a group of nine employees who fill and ship orders from a warehouse for a large department store. The employees are constantly arguing among themselves. The don't cooperate in doing their jobs. Because they interfere with each other's work, errors are made in the shipments and often the shipments do not go out on time. Some of the shipments that do not contain the ordered items are the result of employees providing each other with inaccurate information. Your boss has told you that either you develop cooperative effort among the employees or you may be out of a job.

*Evaluate the following list of actions to develop cooperation.*
Which actions would you take? Which would you take first?

1. Single out an individual who is not cooperating and discipline him or her to set an example for the other employees.

2. Delegate authority, responsibility, and accountability for filling the orders to the group of employees.

3. Have the employees participate with you in problem solving and decision making.

4. Set up a program by which you will recognize "the most cooperative employee of the week."

5. Require the nine employees to develop methods to promote cooperation. Advise them that if they don't solve the problem, you will take action that could include termination of one or more employees.

6. Have social activities for the employees and their families so they will get to know each other better.

7. Set up rewards for group effort and cooperation that eliminate errors in filling orders and get the orders out on time.

8. Identify the employees who are the least cooperative and have them transferred or recommend they be terminated.

9. Do nothing because the employees will eventually settle their disagreements and start cooperating.

10. Have a training program in group performance and productivity for the employees.

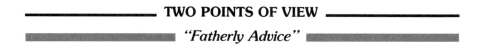

## TWO POINTS OF VIEW

### *"Fatherly Advice"*

*What would you do if you were the manager?*

You manage the loan department for a bank located in a large southwestern city. As a result of a suggestion from the bank president, you hired George Casper as a loan officer. George had previously been vice-president of a bank in a small northern town and moved to the Southwest for his health.

From his first day on the job, George Casper began giving unrequested and unwanted advice to the other employees. He would look through the work on the desks of the other employees and provide advice on its disposition. When his advice is rejected, he usually comments, "People just don't want to learn from those with more experience."

George does not limit his advice to "how to do the job" but also attempts to be a personal adviser to employees. He makes suggestions on the clothing people should wear, where they should go out to eat, who their friends should be, and almost every aspect of their personal life. Employees try to avoid George whenever they can and alert others of his approach with, "Look out, here comes Father George."

Obvious to you is that George has been interfering with other people's work. The situation has now reached the point where employees are mentioning to you that if they get one more piece of fatherly advice from George, they might "hit him in the mouth."

*What would you do if you were George Casper?*

You have recently taken a position as a loan officer in a bank located in a large southwestern city. You have over twenty-five years' experience in banking, and your previous position was vice-president of a bank in a small northern town. You decided to move primarily for health reasons. Your doctor advised you to move to a mild and dry climate.

From your first day on the job, you have tried to help other employees to be more effective in performing their jobs. Most of the employees you work with are considerably younger than you, and they have little banking experience. You try to notice the work on the other employees' desks so you can provide them with the benefit of your experience and help them make the best possible decisions. You know that it takes only a few mistakes to end someone's career in banking.

You personally like all the employees you work with and want to help them be successful in banking. Since customer relations and public image are critical in banking, you have tried to advise the other employees on how to put their best foot forward. Even though they seem to resent it, you have given them the benefit of your experience on how they should dress and the people it would be desirable to associate with to enhance their career.

The more you try to help the other employees, the more they seem to try to avoid you. The other day as you were coming into the office, you overheard an employee say, "Look out, here comes Father George." Today the manager of the loan department mentioned to you that you should keep your opinions to yourself and not bother the other employees.

## ENDNOTES

1. For analysis of group productivity, see Dennis W. Organ and W. Clay Hammer, *Organizational Behavior: An Applied Psychological Approach*, rev. ed. (Plano, Tex.: Business Publications, 1982), chap. 13; James H. Davis, *Group Performance* (Reading, Mass.: Addison-Wesley, 1969).

2. John R. Schermerhorn, Jr., *Management for Productivity*, 2d ed. (New York: Wiley, 1986), p. 364.

3. Frederick C. Miner, "Group Versus Individual Decision Making: An Investigation of Performance Measures, Decision Strategies, and Process Losses/Gains," *Organizational Behavior and Human Performance* (February 1984): 112–24; W. C. Swap and Associates, eds., *Group Decision Making* (Beverly Hills, Calif.: Sage, 1984).

4. Techniques for group decision making are presented in Don F. Seaman, *Working Effectively with Task-Oriented Groups* (New York: McGraw-Hill, 1981).

5. Irving L. Janis, *Groupthink*, 2d ed. (Boston: Houghton Mifflin, 1982); C. R. Leana, "A Partial Test of Janis's Groupthink Model: Effects of Group Cohesiveness and Leader Behavior on Defective Decision Making," *Journal of Management* 11 (1985): 5–17.

6. For research studies, see Alvin Zander, *Groups at Work* (San Francisco: Jossey-Bass, 1979); Rensis Likert, "The Nature of Highly Effective Groups," in *Readings in Organizational Behavior*, eds. Jerry L. Gray and Frederick A. Starke (Columbus, Ohio: Merrill, 1977).

7. R. S. Spich and R. S. Keleman, "Explicit Norm Structuring Process: A Strategy for Increasing Task-Group Effectiveness," *Groups and Organizational Studies* 10 (1985): 37–59.

8. For additional information, see John M. Ivancevich, J. Timothy McMahon, J. William Streidle, and Andrew D. Szilaggi, Jr., "Goal Setting: The Tenneco Approach to Personnel Development and Management Effectiveness," *Organizational Dynamics* (Winter 1978): 58–80.

9. Sara Kiesler, *Interpersonal Processes in Groups and Organizations* (Arlington Heights, Ill.: AHM, 1978).

10. For additional approaches to managing conflict, see S. P. Robbins, "Conflict Management and Conflict Resolutions Are Not Synonymous Terms," in *The Dynamics of Organizational Theory: Gaining a Macro Perspective*, eds. J. F. Veiga and J. N. Yanouzas (St. Paul: West, 1979), pp. 359–70; Richard B. Robinson, "Conflict Management: Individual Preference and Effectiveness," *Proceedings of the Academy of Management* (1978); Charles R. Milton, *Human Behavior in Organizations: Three Levels of Behavior* (Englewood Cliffs, N.J.: Prentice-Hall, 1981), chap. 14.

11. For research on different methods, see Ivan D. Steiner, *Group Processes and Productivity* (New York: Academic Press, 1972); Ernest Stech and Sharon E. Ratliffe, *Working in Groups* (Skokie, Ill.: National Textbook, 1976).

12. Wendell L. French, Fremont E. Kast, and James E. Rosenzweig, *Understanding Human Behavior in Organizations* (New York: Harper & Row, 1985), p. 241.

13. W. B. Eddy, *The Manager and the Working Group* (New York: Praeger, 1985); Rodney W. Napier and Matti K. Gershenfeld, *Groups: Theory and Experience*, 3d ed. (Boston: Houghton Mifflin, 1985).

14. For in-depth analysis, see P. B. Smith, *Groups Within Organizations* (New York: Harper & Row, 1973); Linda N. Jewell and H. Joseph Reitz, *Group Effectiveness in Organizations* (Glenview, Ill.: Scott, Foresman, 1981).

## CASE INCIDENTS FOR PART 4

### The Boss's Favorite

Martha Collins is the director of finance and accounting for a city in the Midwest. The city manager of the town of thirty thousand appears to be partial toward Cindy Kern, one of the accounting clerks who works for Ms. Collins. The situation has reached the point where the city manager provides special favors for Cindy, such as a special city parking permit. The permit allows her to park in the lot closest to the city office building, although the lot is reserved for the city council and distinguished visitors. The other employees in the finance and accounting section have begun to complain to Ms. Collins about the situation. The employees' unhappiness about the situation is obviously affecting their work.

1. Is it possible that the partial treatment is imagined by the employees?
2. If you were Martha Collins, how would you go about finding out the nature of the relationship between Cindy and the city manager and the extent of the favoritism?
3. What course of action should Martha Collins take to reduce the employee dissatisfaction and restore effective working relations?

### Let Betty Do It

Betty Call recently became the manager of a well-established flower shop. The shop has a large number of steady customers and an excellent reputation in the community.

Betty is highly skilled in flower arrangement and can prepare orders faster than any of the other employees. Since becoming manager, she has prepared most of the orders herself and has insisted on checking everything before it leaves the shop. Betty has become so involved in the preparation and checking of arrangements that she has no time to order supplies or maintain records. Because she believes she has to check the work of twelve employees, Betty is neglecting some of the responsibilities of managing the shop. The other employees are developing the attitude of "let Betty do it."

1. Is Betty functioning as a manager or as a technical specialist?
2. What should Betty do to be a more effective manager?
3. How could Betty help her employees feel more responsible for their work?

### Engineering Improvement Address

A manufacturer of farm equipment conducted a management improvement survey (attitude survey) to determine employee dissatisfactions and areas where management policies and procedures could be improved. After the results were tabulated, the employees in each department elected represent-atives to meet with management and develop specific recommendations for improvement. At the beginning of the meeting in the engineering department, the employees handed the following address to the manager and walked out.

### Engineering Improvement Address

One decade and nine years ago our corporation brought forth on this department, a new system conceived in management and dedicated to the proposition to control all workers under it. Now we are engaged in a great improvement survey testing whether that system, or any system so conceived and so dedicated, can be right for the employees. We are met on another meeting ground of that survey. We have come to discuss a portion of that policy to find a solution so that the department might function in harmony. It is altogether fitting and proper that we should do this. But in a larger sense we cannot communicate, we cannot coordi-nate, we cannot invent and be rewarded under this system. The loyal engineers who struggle here are confused by it far above our poor power to use or under-stand. The corporation will little note nor long remember what we say here, but it can never forget the products that were engineered here. It is for us the unin-formed, rather, to be controlled by this system as those who worked here before us so nobly did. It is rather for us to be here dedicated to the great communication problem remaining before us that from these neglected employees we give in-creased attention to the ideas which they gave to aid the design of the products. That we here highly resolve that these innovations shall not have been given in vain. That this system, under management, shall have a new birth of communica-tion and that recognition of the achievements by the employees for the corporation shall not perish under the system.

1. Why did the employees write the Engineering Improvement Address and give it to management?
2. How strong is the informal organization in the engineering department?
3. What are the most important points that the employees are trying to get across to management?
4. Should disciplinary action be taken against the employees who wrote the address?
5. What should management do in this situation?

## The Open Door

Tom Wood is the owner and president of T. W. Enterprises, which operates six carryout food establishments as its major business. The food store's main product is fried chicken. The six stores are all located within twenty miles of each other in a West Coast city.

Mr. Wood started the business over fifteen years ago and almost all improvements and changes have been initiated and directed by him. He usually refers to the stores as "his stores." Some of the store managers and central office staff have complained to Mr. Wood that improvements need to be made in the stores and some new equipment is needed. Mr. Wood's typical reply is, "When we have the money we will spend it on the most essential items." When asked what he felt were the most essential items he replied, "I will decide that when we have the money."

Over the past three years, the profit percentage of sales and return on investment of T. W. Enterprises has been gradually declining. Mr. Wood attributes the decline in profit to increased competition and rising costs. The six-month financial report of the controller projects a loss for the year unless something is done to increase sales or reduce costs for the next six months.

To obtain ideas on ways to increase profit, Mr. Wood set up a meeting with the six store managers, the controller, and the maintenance manager. Mr. Wood began the meeting by explaining the financial situation the company was in and announcing, "I have always had an open-door policy. I want you to bring me any ideas you have on how to cut costs. You should feel free to come to see me on any problems you have."

During the next month, the store managers were in the central office several times a week, but no one mentioned any ideas for cutting costs or brought up any problems. On several occasions Mr. Wood overheard store managers discussing ways to increase sales and reduce costs with the controller and maintenance manager.

1. Why weren't store managers going to Mr. Wood with ideas and problems?

2. What could Mr. Wood do to increase feedback and make his "open-door" policy work?

3. If you were in Mr. Wood's position in this situation, what course of action would you have taken? (Be specific and explain why.)

4. What guidelines should a manager follow to develop feedback that would identify problems and provide ideas on increasing sales and cutting costs?

# Part 5

# Beliefs and Realities

# Management Beliefs about Human Behavior

_____ *Learning Objectives* _____

After reading this chapter, you should be able to do the following:

1. Describe how assumptions and beliefs about human behavior affect managers' actions
2. Explain the operation of the self-fulfilling prophecy
3. Discuss how the expectations of others affect an individual's behavior
4. Describe how an individual's high expectations for another person can increase that person's performance
5. Identify the Theory X and Theory Y assumptions about behavior
6. Explain how managers' beliefs about behavior affect organizational communication
7. Analyze the impact of management beliefs on overall organizational performance

## Chapter Topics

- Management beliefs about human behavior
- The self-fulfilling prophecy
- Expectations and performance
- Effects of management beliefs
- Theory X and Theory Y
- People are complex and variable

## Preview

Henry Ford is reputed to have stated that "the average employee wants a job that doesn't require hard work . . . most of all he wants a job that doesn't require him to think." Ford's management philosophy, and the attitudes of his employees, were based on his assumptions concerning people. Ford was not alone in his beliefs. Many managers, then and now, believe that people want to be highly paid for little effort. Research shows that employees tend to act the way managers assume they will act. If a manager assumes employees will be lazy and irresponsible, they will tend to behave exactly as expected. Some managers who, on the other hand, treat employees as if they are eager to work and are seeking responsibility find that their employees are neither lazy nor irresponsible. In this chapter, managerial assumptions about behavior and the effects of these assumptions are discussed. Since we like our beliefs to be supported and confirmed, we may behave to make things happen the way we believe they should happen. An individual's successes and failures may be the result of believing that he or she will succeed or fail. People like to prove themselves right. People may even behave in ways that are not in their best interest in order to support their beliefs about behavior.

## SELF-ASSESSMENT ▪▪▪▪▪▪▪▪▪▪▪▪▪▪▪▪▪▪▪▪▪▪▪▪▪▪▪▪▪▪

A powerful determinant of organizational effectiveness is management's beliefs about human behavior. In the following self-assessment, mark the responses that are most nearly correct, based on your experience and knowledge. Each statement or question has a range of possible responses. A scale of 1 to 6 between two words with different meanings allows you to mark either the word that is considered correct or a place between the two words that represents some agreement and some disagreement. Selection of a high number such as 5 or 6 may be either correct or incorrect, just as selection of lower numbers may be correct or incorrect. Some responses may be partly correct and partly incorrect.

Answers based on research by behavioral scientists, with a short explanation of why the response was considered correct, may be found on page 366.

1. Beliefs about what people want and need:

   are generally the   1...2...3...4...5...6   differ between
     same for most                                managers
       managers

2. Beliefs that a person holds often result in:

   actions to support   1...2...3...4...5...6   actions that are
      the beliefs                                counter to the beliefs

3. People tend to act in ways that are consistent with expectations of:

        others   1...2...3...4...5...6   themselves

4. If managers communicate high expectations of employees, employees will:

   tend to expect more   1...2...3...4...5...6   develop resentment
      of themselves                               of added
                                                  responsibility

5. "People dislike work and will avoid it if they can" is a:

      traditional   1...2...3...4...5...6   research-based
   management belief                        finding

6. The belief that work should be broken down into highly specialized elements is a:

      traditional   1...2...3...4...5...6   research-based
   management belief                        finding

7. In the final analysis, people are:

   simple and consistent   1...2...3...4...5...6   complex and
                                                   variable

**8.** A traditional management belief is that people:

must be controlled  $1 \ldots 2 \ldots 3 \ldots 4 \ldots 5 \ldots 6$  control themselves if
allowed to

**9.** Demands of changing work situations require managers to be:

inflexible in actions  $1 \ldots 2 \ldots 3 \ldots 4 \ldots 5 \ldots 6$  flexible

**10.** If an organization is to survive a changing environment, individuals within
the organization must:

be innovative  $1 \ldots 2 \ldots 3 \ldots 4 \ldots 5 \ldots 6$  stick with proven
principles

## MANAGEMENT BELIEFS ABOUT HUMAN BEHAVIOR

Everyone has beliefs about the nature of human behavior. As a result of these
beliefs, people develop ways of interacting with others. Beliefs about behavior
include the attitudes, assumptions, and values we have about why people work
and how to get people to accomplish organizational objectives.

Managers base their actions on what they believe about the behavior of
employees. Based on these beliefs, managers develop strategies to obtain both
personal and organizational objectives, and devise rewards or penalties for
employees.

Our beliefs are learned as we interact with our environment. Beliefs that
have resulted in the satisfaction of needs are reinforced and maintained. Beliefs
learned in organizations are perceived as being consistent, logical, and valid
because of the "evidence of experience." We retain the beliefs that help us to
develop and maintain a satisfying view of the world.

Since people have different experiences in interpersonal relations, their beliefs concerning what people want differ. These belief differences lead to different ways of interacting. If a person believes that people are basically dishonest
and will take advantage of others, his or her communications will be characterized by suspicion and distrust. A person who believes that people are basically
helpful and constructive will relate to people with trust and confidence. Each
person's behavior is derived from a set of beliefs that form a philosophy of
dealing with people.

Figure 13.1 illustrates the ways a manager's beliefs affect the managerial
practices used to achieve productivity. Managerial beliefs about behavior are the
bases for developing principles and concepts of effective management. Management practices and procedures are designed to implement principles and concepts. Employee behavior is affected by management actions that implement
the practices and procedures. The behavior of employees provides the "evidence" that management may use to evaluate the validity of their beliefs.

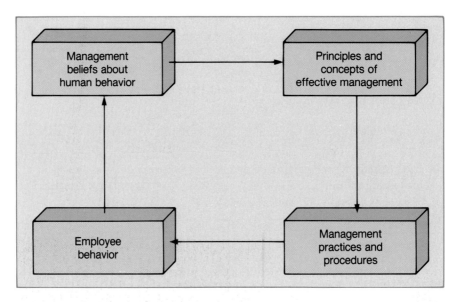

Figure 13.1   The effects of management beliefs.

## THE SELF–FULFILLING PROPHECY

The beliefs a person holds often result in actions that lead to further support for the belief.[1] A student, for example, who believes that he is not smart enough to pass a course does not waste time studying. He fails the course and concludes that his belief was correct. This process of "making" a belief come true is referred to as the **self-fulfilling prophecy**. People are often able to make things happen that they believe will happen; they may fail or succeed primarily because they believe they will fail or succeed.

A person's perceptions play a major role in the self-fulfilling prophecy. If an individual believes that a party is going to be dull, a near certainty is that regardless of what actually happens, the party will be perceived as dull. Perhaps it is; or perhaps the party goer will do everything possible to see that it is. Individuals make prophecies and then ensure that they are fulfilled.

One reason people develop self-fulfilling prophecies is that they obtain satisfaction from "proving" their belief correct. The person who seems to do everything possible to get people to respond negatively may be convinced that other people dislike her. Her behavior encourages people's dislike and confirms the original belief. Supporting a belief may be more satisfying for the individual than being liked.

The operation of the self-fulfilling prophecy takes place in the following four-step sequence:

1. Something is believed to be true.

2. Behavior is based on the belief.

3. Outcomes result from the behavior.

4. Interpretation of the outcomes is perceived to verify the belief.

### Placebo Effect

People also tend to behave in ways that are consistent not only with their own expectations but also with the expectations of others. This is especially true when the expectation comes from an individual who is perceived to be highly competent and authoritative.

In medicine the effect of a patient's expectations has been recognized by physicians for a long time. The patient's trust and belief in the physician can affect the outcome of a treatment. Doctors have been able to use *placebos*, such as sugar pills or a water injection, to relieve symptoms reported by patients. The success of placebos is often cited as an example of the effects of expectations. If a patient expects the pill to reduce the pain, the pain may "go away." This reaction is called the **placebo effect**.

In an experimental study of patients hospitalized with peptic ulcers, 70 percent had "excellent results lasting over a period of one year" when given injections of distilled water and told that it was a new medicine that would cure their ulcers.[2]

Placebos can produce an effect based on the patient's confidence in the physician and the patient's expectations that the treatment will produce desired results. Placebos have been effective in cases involving a variety of illnesses from cancer to the common cold. An example of the physiological effects of placebos to heal tissue is in the treatment of warts. Painting warts with a bright-colored dye and telling patients the wart will be gone by the time the color wears off is as effective as any other wart removal treatment, including surgery.[3]

The reports of the effect of placebos should not lead one to conclude that most people are hypochondriacs or that most illnesses are simply imagined. These studies do provide evidence that the belief in the physician's competence and expectations about results are important factors in healing.

If managers communicate high expectations for individuals, then people will tend to expect more of themselves. Conditions can be created that foster challenging goals and high performance.[4] Most people want to fulfill the expectations of those in positions of authority and responsibility.

## EXPECTATIONS AND PERFORMANCE

The way managers interact with employees is affected by what the managers expect of them. If a manager has high performance expectations, employee performance is likely to be excellent. If the manager's expectations are low, performance is likely to be low. Employee performance tends to increase or decrease to meet management's expectations.[5]

An early observation of the effects of expectations on performance involved training machine operators. In 1890, the U.S. Census Bureau began using Hollerith tabulating machines, which required clerks to punch data on cards.

## Sweeney's Miracle: The Power of Expectations ━━━━━

The case of "Sweeney's miracle" is a dramatic example of expectations influencing performance. James Sweeney was a professor of industrial management and director of the Biomedical Computer Center at Tulane University in the 1960s. Sweeney managed employees whose jobs ranged from maintenance to computer programming. "Sweeney's miracle" involved his expectation that he could train a poorly educated black hospital janitor to be a competent computer operator. He convinced a janitor, George Johnson, to spend his afternoons learning about computers. Because of Sweeney's strong belief, George Johnson's life was profoundly changed.

George was making good progress in learning about computer operations when a university official informed Sweeney that an IQ test had to be passed before operators were allowed in the computer center. George took the test and did not pass. The results were interpreted as an indication that he would not be able to learn computer operations. Sweeney believed otherwise. He had full confidence in his ability to teach and George's ability to learn, and he persuaded the administration to let George continue. Sweeney assured them that George would develop full proficiency as a computer operator. In time, George Johnson became so proficient an operator that he was put in charge of training new employees.[6]

The inventor of the machine considered the work demanding and expected a trained operator could punch about 550 cards a day. After training, the operators produced at the expected rate of 550 cards per day. Some operators began to exceed the expected rate but were discouraged from doing so by their supervisor.

To handle an increased requirement for input data, a new group of two hundred operators were hired. The new group knew nothing about the machine or the expected output rates. After they were trained, the new operators were not provided with an expectation about performance standards. They were encouraged to punch as many cards as they could each day. The new operators were soon producing 1,400 to 2,100 cards a day without being exhausted.

When limiting expectations are removed and the highest possible productivity is encouraged, performance usually improves. Managers should develop high expectations and avoid developing self-fulfilling prophecies for lower than possible performance.

### *Supervisors' Expectations*

Recent studies have repeatedly demonstrated the impact of expectations on performance. An example of the self-fulfilling prophecy occurred when supervisors were told some new employees scored very high on a preemployment exam and that others scored very low.[7]

In fact, what the supervisors were told about employee test scores had no relationship to the actual scores the workers had made on the test. The production records of the employees were evaluated after several months on the job. The analysis indicated that for employees identified as scoring high on the exam, their productivity was significantly higher than the employee average. The productivity of employees identified as scoring low on the exam was lower than average. An analysis of the employee's actual test scores revealed that there was no relationship between individual productivity and the preemployment test score. The results of this study have been interpreted as indicating that a self-fulfilling prophecy resulted from the supervisors' expectations.

A study by Eden and Shani at a military command training center demonstrated the effect of training supervisors' expectations on the performance of trainees.[8] The military trainees were described to their instructors as having either high, regular, or unknown command potential. In fact, trainees were randomly assigned to the three "expectancy classifications." Trainees of whom the training supervisors expected better performance actually did score significantly higher on objective tests of achievement and were evaluated as exhibiting greater motivation. The "high command potential" trainees also scored higher at the end of the course on field demonstrations and reported greater satisfaction with the training. The study provides support for the conclusion that inducing high expectations among supervisors causes them to be both more supportive and more task oriented toward their subordinates, which results in higher subordinate performance.

J. Sterling Livingston reported how district managers' expectations largely determined the performance of insurance agents.[9] A district manager for an insurance company put the highest-producing agents together under the most capable assistant manager in the district. The district manager told this group of "high performers" that they were expected to produce two-thirds of the total sales made in the district the year before. The manager's expectations were realized. The high performers achieved high sales and boosted district performance about 40 percent. The manager's expectations for low-producing agents were also realized. The group composed of low producers actually had a decline in sales level.

The conclusions drawn from this situation were that when people are treated by their managers as super producers, they try to live up to that expectation and do what super producers are expected to do. When people are treated by their managers as low producers, the negative expectation also becomes a self-fulfilling prophecy.

### Developing Expectations in Others

The effect of expectations on behavior does not occur by magic. For expectations to have a positive impact on behavior requires more than wishing or thinking positively. How people are treated by others who are important to them, such as friends, family, co-workers, and managers, is a powerful influence on their behavior. As people interact with these individuals, expectations about their behavior are communicated. People will try to fulfill these expectations, whether they are positive or negative. If people who are important communicate high and realistic performance expectations, individuals will usually set high goals for themselves. If low expectations are communicated, low performance goals may be accepted.

*High Expectations Can Be Developed*    Developing high performance expectations in others requires actions as well as words. The way people are treated can strongly indicate expectations about their behavior. What a person is asked to do and not asked to do indicates expectations about the person's skills and abilities.

The following are actions that can aid in the development of high performance expectations in others:

- Reinforce and support high performance goals when they are expressed by the individual.
- Be positive in your nonverbal communication, including tone of voice, gestures, and eye contact.
- Develop a positive atmosphere in interpersonal relations by indicating you believe the individual can achieve challenging goals.
- Be a supportive resource to help solve problems and achieve goals. Treat the individual as a winner.
- When you are in a position of authority, show high expectations by delegating authority and responsibility. Make challenging assignments.
- Provide information that will be helpful to the individual. Time spent explaining can strongly communicate high expectations.
- Listen with interest when the individual discusses performance and goals. Behavior that shows interest and concern communicates expectations for achievement.

## EFFECTS OF MANAGEMENT BELIEFS

A belief about human behavior may be reinforced as a result of a manager's acting as if it were true. If a manager believes that people dislike work and will avoid it, and people respond as shown in Figure 13.2, a principle of closely controlled employee behavior is adopted. The principle is implemented by designing highly standardized jobs with close supervision. Employees respond to the standardization and close supervision with resentment and a lack of interest. The employees' negative reactions reinforce the manager's belief that people dislike work. When the manager's belief is confirmed, he or she increases the control procedures, which will usually result in increased negative employee behavior.

Each individual's beliefs about management are unique. There can be as many different belief systems as there are people. But beliefs about the nature of

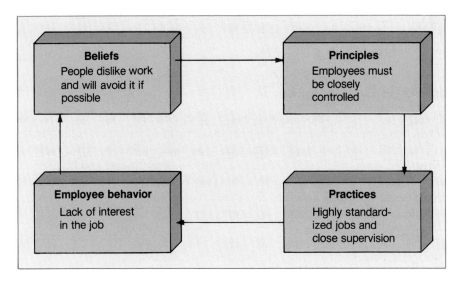

Figure 13.2   Effects of the management belief that "people dislike work."

work behavior tend to conform to general patterns. Manager's beliefs tend to be similar because they have similar backgrounds and experience.

> Regardless of the source of the impression, the manager tends to act more warmly toward those of whom much is expected, reinforcing any sign of professional growth while ignoring or misinterpreting the same behavior by others.[10]

## THEORY X AND THEORY Y

Most discussions of management beliefs and their effects describe two extreme positions. By looking at the two extremes, one can see the range of belief differences that can occur. The potential danger in discussing extremes is that the conclusion may be reached that only two alternatives exist. Keep in mind that the actual beliefs of most managers fall somewhere between the extremes.

The following discussion of two extremes uses the framework developed by Douglas McGregor.[11] He referred to the extremes or boundaries by identifying sets of beliefs as **Theory X** and **Theory Y**. McGregor used the labels $X$ and $Y$ to avoid value-laden terms that could evoke emotional responses.

Behavioral scientists have developed concepts of human behavior that challenge some traditional management concepts. McGregor applied behavioral science findings to develop the concepts of Theory Y. Theory Y has been given many names, including participative management, team management, nonstructured management, and enlightened management. This theory of management, regardless of its specific title, is based on a set of beliefs about human behavior in which people are seen as having positive attitudes toward work.

We will briefly outline both the Theory X and Theory Y beliefs concerning human behavior, describe the principles of management that grow out of these beliefs, and illustrate the effects that changing beliefs about human behavior can have on organizational effectiveness.

## Impact on Organizations

Although the controversies over theories of management and beliefs about human behavior are interesting, the primary concern of managers is the impact of these theories on the operations of their organizations. Management's area of interest and responsibility covers areas within the organization and its environment. Since specific management acts reflect beliefs about human behavior, management principles used in an organization cannot be isolated from the total impact of the organization on employees.

## Assumptions Underlying Management Actions

The actions of management are based on its expectations of results, which are in turn based on beliefs about human behavior. Although individuals vary in their beliefs about others, McGregor formulated what he considered the extremes along a spectrum of potential beliefs. *Theory X* beliefs about human behavior form one end of this spectrum. They include the following:

1. Most people dislike work and will avoid it if they can. Management believes that it must have a system *forcing* workers to perform satisfactorily.

2. Most people lack ambition, dislike responsibility, and prefer to be led. Management believes that it must assume responsibility for workers' performance and behavior.

3. Most people must be controlled and threatened with punishment before they do a good job. Management believes that it must have a system of punishment to successfully alter behavior.

4. Most people are inherently self-centered and are indifferent to organizational goals. Management believes that policies are necessary that attempt to force workers into behavioral molds to meet organizational demands.

5. Most people are gullible, easy to fool, and not very bright. Management believes that the threat of punishment is necessary to produce productive behaviors.

6. Most people are inherently resistant to change. Management believes that individuals will not change their behavior unless forced to do so.

Figure 13.3 illustrates the Theory X view of human behavior.

The other end of the spectrum is occupied by *Theory Y*. It is based on the following assumptions about human behavior:

1. The average person does not inherently dislike work. Work may be a source of satisfaction. Management believes that individuals are productive when the job satisfies their motivation.

**Figure 13.3    A Theory X view of the nature of human behavior.**

2. The average person learns not only to accept but also to seek responsibility. Management believes that individuals can be responsible for their behavior.

3. External control and threats of punishment are not the only means to get people to do an adequate job. Management believes that negative behavior on the part of management usually elicits negative behavior from employees.

4. Commitment to work objectives is a function of the rewards associated with their achievement. Management believes that individuals are committed to work objectives when the completion of those objectives satisfies individual motives.

5. The intellectual ability of the average person is only partially used. The capacity for solving problems is widely distributed. Management believes that individuals are capable of performing their tasks without being led by the hand.

6. People resist being forced to change. Management believes that individuals accept change when the primary pressures for change are self-imposed.

Figure 13.4 illustrates the Theory Y view of human behavior.

## *How Assumptions Affect Management Actions*

Beliefs about human behavior, in themselves, do not bring about managerial action. Management's actions are only derived from the beliefs.

**Figure 13.4    A Theory Y view of the nature of human behavior.**

The assumptions about human behavior that result in *Theory X* actions have led to the following management principles:

1. Work behavior should be controlled by breaking down jobs into specialized elements.
2. There should be established norms of production.
3. Equipment should be designed so that the worker's pace is more or less controlled.
4. Incentive wage payment systems should be used to reward the superior workers and penalize the laggards.
5. Accounting and budgetary controls should be used to make sure that subordinate managers do not deviate from established standards.
6. The amount of information and responsibility given to subordinates should be carefully limited and controlled.
7. The boss can never really trust subordinates.

Under *Theory Y* beliefs, expectations result in emphasizing the following management concepts:

1. Mutual responsibility and shared objectives should be emphasized.
2. There should be a recognition of the interdependence of people in organizations.
3. High standards of performance should be expected. A minimum of external control should be supplemented by self-imposing controls and a high degree of self-direction.

4. Discussion at all levels should be encouraged in order to obtain cooperation.

5. Company objectives and subobjectives should be communicated to all employees.

6. Organizational authority should be widely delegated and organizational structure decentralized. (See Figure 13.5)

## Results of the Application of Management Theories

The consequences of Theory X management have plagued businesses and organizations almost since their beginnings. There are many possible results of the application of *Theory X* management:

1. When rule makers are not available, lower management is afraid to make exceptions, even when the underlying purpose of the rule (cost saving and so on) might be achieved. Thus, lower management avoids making a decision.

   *Example*: A supervisor does not approve overtime, even though it would result in a job being completed at a lower cost, because of a rule that overtime should be used only in "exceptional" situations.

2. Routine action supports the system of rules rather than the underlying management objectives that the system was set up to attain.

   *Example*: Employees always take their coffee break from 10:00 to 10:15 in the morning because of a "rule" on the time for coffee breaks, even though there may be situations in which it would be more productive to take a break when it fits a natural break in completing a job.

Figure 13.5   Effects of the management belief that "people seek responsibility."

3. There can be little sense of achievement, which is one of the key factors in job satisfaction for the subordinates.

    *Example:* Highly standardized jobs and close supervision leave little room for people to use their abilities to the fullest.

4. Management by rules stifles the initiative of subordinates and reduces the possibility of innovations that might increase productivity.

    *Example:* Concentrating on following numerous rules may mean people are unable to make decisions about their job performance or look for ways to increase productivity.

Some of the possible results of application of *Theory Y* are as follows:

1. Lower management focuses on achievement of organizational objectives. Employees are accountable for achieving objectives, and exceptions to rules are made to support increased productivity.

2. Routine actions by employees support management objectives.

3. A sense of achievement, which increases motivation, can be developed by employee involvement in on-the-job decisions.

4. Increased productivity results from initiative and development of innovations.

## Effect of Management Beliefs on Organizational Communication

One of the areas in which beliefs are most clearly reflected is in organizational communication. The communication behaviors of managers are usually a good indication of their beliefs about the nature of human behavior.

*Theory X Approach*    When management holds Theory X beliefs, the information flow is primarily downward. The downward communication focuses on job-related information and announcements of management decisions. Because communication is usually limited to information this is believed absolutely necessary for job performance, the grapevine actively functions to provide information employees are not getting from management. Communication between employees and management is cautious and marked by distrust. Upward communication usually makes heavy use of the grapevine, since formal channels are not receptive to information from lower levels. Often, "spy systems" develop in which employees secretly report information about operations and other employees to managers. Decisions may be based on partial or inaccurate information, because decision making is concentrated at the top of the organization. Upward communication is very limited.

*Theory Y Approach*    The manager who has Theory Y beliefs about behavior will usually develop communication systems where information freely flows up, down, and across the organization. Management encourages upward communication by listening to employees and showing interest in their problems. Employee involvement in decision making increases communication and understanding. Open and honest communication takes place. Since decision making is based on information from all levels of the organization, the accuracy and quality of decisions are improved. The Theory Y orientation makes it possible to develop confidence and trust in organizational communication.

## *Effect of Management Style on Overall Performance*

In conjunction with the concern about increasing effective management of organizations, behavioral scientists have explored the contributions of individuals necessary for an organization to survive and thrive. In general terms, the individuals must exhibit at least three patterns of behavior if an organization is to function effectively in the long run.[12] We can compare how well Theory X and Theory Y styles fulfill these conditions.

1. *Individuals must join and stay within the system or organization.*

   —Under Theory X, the assumption is that individuals will be forced by monetary considerations to join and remain in the organization. However, with competition among organizations for employees, an individual need not join or remain with an organization for purely economic reasons.

   —Under Theory Y, the primary motivation for joining and staying within the organization is the satisfaction of individual needs on the job. The assumption is that people's motivation involves more than monetary rewards.

2. *The individuals in the organization must display dependable behavior in the performance of the roles as defined by the organization. The desired behavior must meet or exceed both quantitative and qualitative objectives of performance.*

   —Although performance is a main concern of Theory X management, it attempts to attain this goal indirectly by concentrating on the rules for performance rather than on the performance itself. Management may attempt to elicit the desired behaviors by using threats of punishment.

   —Theory Y management attempts to construct the work situation so that effective performance depends on employees being able to satisfy individual motives.

3. *The individuals within the organization must exhibit innovative behavior if the organization is to survive a changing environment. This innovative behavior is required under the assumption that no organization's initial structure is perfect or all-inclusive.*

   —Theory X management usually stifles innovative behavior through punishment of behavior not specified by organizational rules.

   —Theory Y management not only recognizes the need for innovative behavior but also attempts to cultivate it at all levels of the organization.

## PEOPLE ARE COMPLEX AND VARIABLE

No one set of beliefs is valid for all people or all situations. Since all people are not alike, there is no one best theory of management. People must be managed as they actually are, not as we would like them to be.

Beliefs about human nature are often overgeneralized. When characteristics of behavior are applied to everyone, the unique character of each individual is ignored. Each individual has a number of needs that motivate behavior at any one time. The importance of individual needs is subject to change depending on the situation. The motivation to perform a job is affected by more than one need, and usually a number of methods are available to the individual for achieving goals.

An individual may respond positively to a number of different managerial approaches. A manager cannot develop one set of management principles that will work with all individuals in all situations. An individual who responds positively to Theory Y management in one situation may respond equally positively to Theory X management in a different situation. At times, employees want management to tell them in no uncertain terms what to do and how to do it.

The nature of an individual's behavior may vary as a result of organizational characteristics and management expectations. The self-fulfilling prophecy effect can result in individuals adapting their behavior to meet the conditions existing in the organization. The characteristics exhibited by employees in adapting to an organization are affected by the type of economic rewards, the methods available to satisfy social needs, and the opportunities for achievement.

Beliefs about human behavior are often not useful because they are oversimplifications and overgeneralizations. Managers should be able to recognize the qualities that make each employee different. Flexibility is essential to meet the demands of different situations and to make use of employees' unique abilities.

## SELF–ASSESSMENT DISCUSSION

**1.** (6) Nearly everyone has beliefs about behavior. Because those beliefs are learned in different environments under different conditions, they vary greatly.

**2.** (1) People will act to support their beliefs. If they believe they cannot perform a given task or activity, they will frequently not try.

**3.** (1, 6) People behave to conform to personal expectations as well as the expectations of others.

**4.** (1) A valuable lesson of human behavior studies is that people tend to live up to expectations of others. Managers who expect high levels of performance and work with employees to achieve realistic goals will have employees who achieve high performance.

**5.** (1) Traditionally, management has believed that people will avoid work if possible and work only for pay. More enlightened management realizes that work satisfies many other needs in addition to economic necessity.

**6.** (1) Since the days of Frederick Taylor in the early part of the century, managers have believed that efficiency can be improved by breaking down jobs into highly specialized tasks. More recently, some managers have realized that overspecialization can result in boring tasks and the smothering of innovation.

**7.** (6) A major fascination that students of human behavior have had for centuries is behavior's complexity and variability. Although all behavior has some similarities and common features, it is, for the most part, different for each individual and affected by many influences in many ways. At this time, no clear explanations can be offered for why people behave as they do.

**8.** (1) A traditional management belief is that people must be controlled. Well-informed modern managers realize that under the right conditions, most people control themselves.

**9.** (6) Without the ability to adapt to change and rapidly respond to situational demands, management fails. Good managers realize that flexibility is required— the willingness to change when change is needed.

**10.** (1) More than ever before, managers must be innovative. Changes in physical, social, economic, political, and technological environments make innovation a keystone of effective management.

## QUICK REVIEW

I. Management Beliefs about Human Nature

   A. People develop ways of interacting with others as a result of their beliefs about human nature.

   B. Managers base their actions on beliefs about the behavior of employees.

   C. Management beliefs determine managerial principles and concepts from which practices and procedures are derived that influence employee behavior. Employee behavior in turn reinforces management beliefs.

II. The Self-Fulfilling Prophecy

   A. The beliefs a person holds often result in actions that lead to further support for the beliefs. People often make things happen that they expect or believe will happen.

   B. Self-fulfilling prophecies are characterized by the following steps:

      1. Something is believed to be true.

      2. Behavior is based on the belief.

      3. Outcomes result from the behavior.

      4. Interpretation of the outcomes is perceived to verify the belief.

   C. People tend to live up or down to the expectations of others. These expectations can have a placebo effect on a person's behavior.

III. Expectations and Performance

   A. Employee performance is strongly influenced by managers' expectations.

   B. When managers have high expectations, employees will also expect more of themselves.

   C. High performance expectations can be communicated by actions as well as by words.

   D. Managers can develop high performance expectations in others by:

      1. Reinforcing and supporting an individual's own expectations.

      2. Being positive in nonverbal communication.

      3. Indicating through positive interpersonal relations that the individual can achieve the goals set.

      4. Acting as a supportive resource.

      5. Delegating authority and responsibility.

      6. Providing information.

      7. Listening to the individual discuss performance and goals.

IV. Effects of Management Beliefs

   A. A manager can reinforce a belief about human nature by acting as if that belief were true.

   B. Negative beliefs about human nature tend to produce highly controlling management policies and procedures.

   C. Beliefs about the nature of work behavior tend to conform to general patterns.

V. Theory X and Theory Y

   A. Theory X beliefs include:

      1. Most people dislike work.

      2. They lack ambition.

      3. They must be controlled.

      4. They are self-centered.

      5. They are not very bright.

      6. They resist change.

   B. Theory Y beliefs include:

      1. The average person does not inherently dislike work.

      2. The average person can learn to seek responsibility.

      3. External controls are not the only means to get people to work.

      4. Commitment to objectives is a function of rewards.

      5. The intelligence of most employees is only partially used.

      6. People resist being forced to change.

   C. Each set of assumptions affects management actions in different ways. Theory X relies on external controls; Theory Y relies on self-control, leadership, and responsibility.

   D. Theory X is punishment oriented; Theory Y is reward oriented.

E. Theory X communication is from the top down and fosters suspicion and mistrust. Theory Y communication is free-flowing among all levels and fosters openness and trust.

F. Individuals must exhibit three patterns of behavior if an organization is to function effectively.

   1. People must join and remain within a system.

   2. They must meet certain standards of behavior and performance in their assigned roles.

   3. They must demonstrate innovative behavior to help the organization adapt to change.

VI. People Are Complex and Variable

A. No one set of beliefs is valid for all people in all situations.

B. Beliefs about human nature are often overgeneralized and oversimplified.

C. Individuals may respond positively to a number of managerial approaches.

D. Flexibility is essential to meet the demands of different situations and to make use of unique abilities of employees.

## KEY TERMS

Self-fulfilling prophecy      Expectations and       Theory X
Placebo effect                  performance           Theory Y

## DISCUSSION QUESTIONS

1. Give an example of how a manager's beliefs about human nature can affect managerial practices.
2. Describe how a self-fulfilling prophecy operates.
3. Give an example of a situation you have observed in which someone has developed a self-fulfilling prophecy.
4. Describe a placebo and give an example of its effects in healing.
5. Give an example of how a manager's expectations for a new employee can help or hinder that employee's productivity.
6. How can managers develop high performance expectations in employees?
7. Describe the Theory X and Theory Y beliefs about human nature.
8. Comment on the statement "A person could rarely develop to his or her fullest potential under Theory X."
9. Why would Theory X beliefs result in management carefully limiting and controlling the amount of information and responsibility given to subordinates?

10. What management actions could help employees develop a sense of achievement that would increase motivation?

11. Discuss the main reasons why beliefs about human behavior are often not useful.

----------------------- **EXERCISE** -----------------------

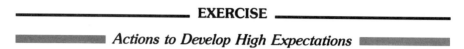 *Actions to Develop High Expectations*

You manage the department of street maintenance for a city of 175,000 people. The city manager has just returned from a management seminar at the state university, which emphasized developing high performance expectations. The seminar presented research findings that demonstrated that high expectations result in high performance and low expectations result in low performance. Since the city revenues are declining, the city manager thinks that the way to maintain adequate city services is to increase employee performance expectations. As a manager, you are to immediately take action to develop high performance expectations in your employees so they will be more productive in doing their jobs.

*Evaluate the following list of actions to develop high expectations.*
Which actions would you take? Which would you take first?

1. Increase the work load of each employee by 15 percent.

2. Increase the competition among employees by posting individual performance levels where everyone can see them.

3. Work with employees individually to set performance goals on their jobs.

4. Have employees identify barriers that prevent them from doing their jobs more effectively and remove the barriers wherever possible.

5. Have a training program for employees dealing with how high expectations lead to high performance.

6. Reinforce and support high performance goals when they are expressed by employees.

7. Express your confidence in employees and let them know you believe they can achieve high performance goals.

8. Show high expectations by delegating authority and making challenging assignments.

9. Ask employees what training would increase their performance ability and see that they get the training.

10. Individually provide employees with specific feedback on the quantity and quality of their performance.

────────────── **TWO POINTS OF VIEW** ──────────────

▰▰▰▰▰▰▰▰▰▰▰   *"Overconsiderate"*   ▰▰▰▰▰▰▰▰▰▰▰

*What would you do if you were the manager?*

You are manager of the facilities planning department of a manufacturing company. Linda Duncan is your most competent planner and can always be counted on to make a maximum effort on any assignment. Linda has an excellent educational background, having received a bachelor's degree in civil engineering and an M.B.A. from a highly respected university. She is always cooperative and a real team player.

Linda is shy, and you believe that she is overly concerned about other people's feelings. Her productivity is affected by her not giving others her work to do if she thinks they have a heavy work load. Her completion of projects depends on work that is done by technical writers, drafters, and typists. Linda sometimes fails to meet deadlines because she did not give the work to others for completion. If her failure to meet deadlines continues, you will not be able to assign her important projects. This could mean that you would not be able to effectively use her training and ability.

Everyone in the department recognizes Linda's competence and productivity, but they also realize they can avoid doing her work because she is never demanding. They also know that Linda will not insist that department standards be met. She never complains about the quality of work done for her. When writing or drafting are not up to standards, she usually tells those doing the work, "Don't bother doing it over—it will be allright." You know that it is not allright when standards are not met, so you must have the work redone. Other employees have told you that Linda seems to lack self-confidence and does not realize her high level of competence.

*What would you do if you were Linda Duncan?*

You graduated in the top 10 percent of your class in civil engineering at a highly respected university and then completed a master's in business administration. You always enjoy working engineering problems, and math was your best subject in school. You have never had any close friends and would rather work alone than depend on others. You have always had difficulty in understanding people and know the other employees don't understand you.

You get your work done without anyone having to pressure you. You don't like to be dependent on the technical writers and drafters to get your projects completed. You don't think the other employees are committed professionals like you are. Your job should not be to "force" them to get your work done and meet the quality standards of the department. The department manager seems to believe that you should be responsible for the work of the writers and drafters, but you think that their performance is management's responsibility.

The department manager has mentioned several times that he is concerned that some of your projects are are not completed by the deadline. Since you always have your part of the work done on time, you believe the late completions are due to management not seeing that the writers and drafters get their part of the project done on time. You are considering proposing to the department manager that you will do your own technical writing and drafting so that your performance will not in any way depend on other employees.

## ENDNOTES

1. G. Salomon, "Self-Fulfilling and Self-Sustaining Prophecies and the Behaviors That Realize Them," *American Psychologist* 36 (1981): 1452–53.

2. Jefferson Fish, *Therapy: A Practical Guide to Social Influence in Psychotherapy* (San Francisco: Jossey-Bass, 1973).

3. Ibid.

4. Robert W. Goddard, "The Pygmalion Effect," *Personnel Journal* (June 1985): 10–15.

5. Dov Eden, "Self-Fulfilling Prophecy as a Management Tool: Harnessing Pygmalion," *Academy of Management Review* (January 1984): 64–73.

6. Cited in Robert Rosenthal and Lenore Jacobsen, *Pygmalion in the Classroom* (New York: Holt, Rinehart & Winston, 1968).

7. C. S. Raben and R. J. Klimoski, "The Effects of the Experimentation Upon Task Performance as Moderated by Levels of Self-Esteem," *Journal of Vocational Behavior* 3 (1973): 475–83.

8. D. Eden and A. B. Shani, "Pygmalion Goes to Boot Camp: Expectancy, Leadership, and Training Performance," *Journal of Applied Psychology* 67 (1982): 194–99.

9. J. Sterling Livingston, "Pygmalion in Management," *Harvard Business Review* (July–August 1969): 81–89.

10. Dennis W. Organ and Thomas Bateman, *Organizational Behavior*, 3d ed. (Plano, Tex.: Business Publications, 1986), p. 180.

11. Douglas McGregor, *The Human Side of Enterprise*, 2d ed. (New York: McGraw-Hill, 1985).

12. Daniel Katz and Robert L. Kahn, *The Social Psychology of Organizations*, rev. ed. (New York: Wiley, 1978).

# Chapter 14

# Sources of Influence: Status, Power, and Politics

_____ *Learning Objectives* _____

After reading this chapter, you should be able to do the following:

1. Understand the ways power and status are developed and used
2. Identify how status and power are linked
3. Discuss the meaning of distributive justice, status congruence, and status compression
4. Understand the differences between power and authority
5. Describe the functions and nature of organizational politics
6. Discuss the expectations of employees regarding the use of influence and authority

# Chapter Topics

- A visit to the world's fair
- Status, power, and politics
- Status—meaning and symbols
- Power
- Politics
- Realities of organizational life
- Expectations, status, and power

# Preview

Throughout history the most admired people, whether real or fictional, have been those who seem to be able to do things others could not. This ability to influence events and other people was seen largely as being either good or evil. Most mythology, legends, and fairy tales depict gods and people who are able to influence others and the events that surround their lives. Heroes were those who could accomplish good and overcome evil. They were the winners, in most cases, while the promoters of evil were usually both villains and losers.

Whether positive or negative, power has been an attractive concept for as long as people have been able to recognize its existence. In addition to power, people have almost universally stratified their societies into levels. Each level has some degree of influence over lower levels. Although democratic societies attempt to erase the lines that divide various classes of people, in reality the levels continue and are easily identifiable. Like it or not, we all live in a socially unequal world, country, and places of work. In his popular text *Humankind*,[1] Peter Farb points out that no society studied by anthropologists, beginning with the most ancient and primitive and ending with current times, has been able to totally avoid some sort of stratification of its members.

Although power is derived from many sources in all organizations, a particularly significant way in which people build power is through politics. Building influence through networking, doing favors, and mutual support agreements is an old and finely tuned art. Those in power positions know how to play the game, and those who aren't usually recognize what is happening but are not considered players. Excellence in performance and knowledge of work are not enough. Those in power know the political climate of their organizations and use it well. Although politics has many negative connotations, it is a reality of organizational life. Understanding how politics work can be the difference between developing or not developing influence.

## SELF–ASSESSMENT

Each statement or question has a range of possible responses. A scale of 1 to 6 between two words with different meanings allows you to mark either the word that is considered correct or a place between the two words that represents some agreement and some disagreement. Selection of a high number such as 5 or 6 may be either correct or incorrect, just as selection of lower numbers may be correct or incorrect. Some responses may be partly correct and partly incorrect.

Answers based on research by behavioral scientists, with a short explanation of why the response was considered correct, may be found on page 392.

1. When we rank people in importance, usually based on how worthwhile we believe they are to society or to a specific group, we are assigning:

   power  1...2...3...4...5...6  status

2. Leadership of a particular group requires which of the following?

   power  1...2...3...4...5...6  status

3. Politics in work organizations is associated with acquiring:

   power  1...2...3...4...5...6  status

4. Authority in work organizations increases which of the following most?

   politics  1...2...3...4...5...6  power

5. In most of the better-run organizations, power is:

   necessary  1...2...3...4...5...6  unnecessary

6. Manipulation of people, events, and circumstances to meet personal needs is the basis for:

   politics  1...2...3...4...5...6  status development

7. Most successful managers, especially in large organizations, understand and use:

   power  1...2...3...4...5...6  politics

8. Employees prefer working for managers who:

   have and use power  1...2...3...4...5...6  avoid power usage

9. In democratic societies and organizations, status and power are:

   neither desirable  1...2...3...4...5...6  both desirable and
   nor present                                present

10. In the United States, as in many other countries, most employees want:

managers who have  1...2...3...4...5...6  managers with neither
symbols of power                                  power nor status
                                                            symbols

## A VISIT TO THE WORLD'S FAIR

When the World's Fair opened in May of 1986 in Vancouver, British Columbia, Princess Diana and Prince Charles of England were highly visible participants. Newspapers gave almost as much space to the royal couple as they did to the well-designed and carefully presented exhibits. Although other important people were also present, none received the attention of Diana and Charles. Compared with other dignitaries, they were the most glamorous, most attractive, and most worthy of attention. They were seen as having both status and power. Not only were they an attraction, but inviting them as the centerpiece of the opening ceremony was an intelligent political action by both the Canadian and British Columbia governments.

In all societies, from the most ancient to the most modern, none have been without some form of ranking members in importance and influence. As human beings, we seem to always admire those who are seen as more influential and more highly ranked in society than ourselves. We also know that some people attempt to increase their rank and influence through manipulation of others, acquiring symbols of power, and associating with higher-ranked people, thus pretending to have influence where little truly exists. To many people, the appearance of rank and influence is as important as their actual possession.

## STATUS, POWER, AND POLITICS

Early in life, most of us realize that some people exert more influence over people and events than do others. Those who are stronger, smarter, more determined, more daring, more attractive, and sometimes more objective judges of behavior are able to get others to do what they want. Although some of the ways an individual influences others may be negative, such as threats of punishment or embarrassment, they are frequently positive. For example, a manager may encourage employees to work toward advancement or show them how to do a specific job easier and better. We measure power by the amount of influence a person has in his or her relationships with other individuals or groups. People who consider themselves powerless are those who believe they have little or no influence. By the same reasoning, people who get their own way most of the time have considerable power.

*Status*    In addition to our perceptions of power, we frequently assign a greater worth or rank to some people than we do to others. Ask who has the higher status in our society, a used car salesperson or a prominent scientist, and nearly everyone will rank the scientist much higher. Although power is acquired and, in some cases, granted to people, status is assigned by individuals to other individuals. In general, **status** *is a method we use to compare one person with another.* We assign special status to people we regard highly or to those we believe deserve special respect or consideration. Those we deem less worthy to society or the group to which they belong are assigned low status. Status is based almost entirely on our perceptions of personal or social worth. It is neither positive nor negative. It is, however, descriptive of a person's rank compared with others.

Power, on the other hand, is often accumulated not through personal characteristics but by persuasion, association with powerful people, manipulation of people and events, and by becoming a part of special in-groups. Techniques used to accumulate and wield power are known as **politics**. Like power itself, politics may be either positive or negative. Politics and power are realities of any modern organization; people need to be accepted into informal communication and influence groups. These in-groups are relatively easy to recognize. They generally comprise people who are seen as either having power or being closely associated with power. To gain their friendship or acceptance, or because of similar interests, others outside these support networks keep members informed of changes, potential key decision outcomes, and organizational gossip. Good organization politicians know whom to ask for information, how to time their actions, and methods of influencing those to whom they report as well as those who report to them.

## STATUS—MEANING AND SYMBOLS

When we believe another person has something more or greater than we do, we are assigning status. Status may be either selective or general. **General status** is the perceived rank of a person when compared with others. **Selective status** refers to a comparison of a single attribute with ours. If someone can consistently win at chess, while we lose, that person has greater status as a chess player. The machinist who is consistently assigned work that requires extreme care, close tolerances, and complete accuracy may not be paid more than other workers in the same classification but will be seen as having greater status. A typist who, because of speed and knowledge, receives requests to do the most important reports is also conferred a higher degree of respect or status by other typists.

Other types of status are determined by the position a person holds in an organization. Presidents have greater status than vice-presidents; secretaries have greater status than file clerks; maintenance mechanics have greater status than custodians.

### *Status Symbols*

To a large extent, status is dependent on the symbols that identify the comparative position of a person with those of others. High status in work organizations is often recognized by the size and furnishings of an office, by parking privileges, by the kind of clothes a person wears, by job title, and by the many other things or conditions we use to compare ourselves with others.

In our society, we expect those who have the greatest authority and responsibility in our organizations to receive the greatest rewards in symbols. The belief that those who do more should have more is called **distributive justice**. In recognition of this principle, seniority is often given some status through longer vacations, selection of job assignments, and personal recognition by upper levels of management. Promotions, presumably based on competence and potential, are usually recognized with higher pay, larger offices, and other symbols.[2] Table 14.1 compares the executive offices at one large company.

Closely related to the principal of distributive justice is the expectation that certain symbols are associated with position. A first-line supervisor promoted to a management department head position may expect to be given a private office, clerical assistance, a telephone, and other symbols associated with promotion. New managers not given the symbols they expect will see themselves as having lower status than other managers at an equal organizational level. Non-management employees also perceive and judge position by the symbols associ-

**Table 14.1**

**Status Indicators in the Executive Offices of Ohio Bell**

| Indicators | President's Office | Vice-presidential Offices |
|---|---|---|
| Room size | Huge | About one-half size of president's office |
| Floor | Parquet wood and oriental rug | Wall-to-wall carpeting |
| Windows | Two window walls with direct view of Lake Erie | One window wall with angled view of Lake Erie |
| Chair | High back to rest neck; padded | Padded and comfortable |
| Desk | Huge, decorative, and luxurious | Smaller, but nice |
| Fixtures | Button to open and close drapes, plus rheostat to control lighting level | Pull rope to open and close drapes, plus switch to turn lights off and on |
| Furniture | Luxurious; many pieces plus liquor cabinet | Nice, fewer pieces; no liquor cabinet |
| Bathroom | Shower; sink with cabinet, large mirror, toilet; decorative wall covering | Sink, toilet; painted walls |
| Entrance | Huge and decorative entry; door at end of hall | Smaller and plainer; door alongside of hall |

*Source:* Don Hellriegel and John W. Slocum, Jr., *Organizational Behavior: Contingency Views* (St. Paul: West, 1976), p. 346.

ated with status. Yet at times, symbols can be inappropriate because they are too lavish for the assignment. A newly promoted manager with a private secretary, carpeted office, and expensive office furniture may have an inflated feeling of status compared with others at similar levels. Symbols associated with status must be appropriate for the position. This is known as **status congruence**. Congruence, as used here, means that the expected symbols and the position must match.

There are many examples of a trend against obvious status symbols. Movement toward **status compression**, the deliberate avoidance of discriminatory status symbols, is strong. At some colleges, professors who are given managerial assignments are seen merely as having a new type of work with no greater status than that of their former classroom work. Many companies have eliminated private offices and personal secretaries except for the top most levels of management. Perhaps most significant is that perceptions of status symbols have changed. As employees become more affluent, they can and do acquire many of the external status symbols that at one time only upper-level management could afford. Luxury automobiles, boats, recreational vehicles, and similar

### Battle of the Badges

At one large West Coast defense plant, what began as a simple means of identifying various employees nearly turned into a full-scale class struggle. The trouble began when employees in the plant were given color-coded ID badges for easy identification.

Blue-bordered badges signified nonmanagement personnel, assigned to specific areas, who required only minimal security clearance.

Green-bordered badges were worn by administrative specialists, technical personnel, first- and second-level managers, and employees such as mail clerks and time keepers who needed to move from one department to another.

Mid- and upper-level administrative assistants and security people wore red badges. Red-badged personnel were listed in a separate section of the company phone book.

Although green-badged employees often earned less money than blue-badged employees, the green badges clearly signified higher status in the organization. Green-badged employees in turn deferred to red badges, although authority levels between the two colors were often similar.

Over a period of time, a clearly defined caste system developed along badge-color lines, and employee relations were marked by friction and resentment. At one point, the dominant union in the company made abolishing the badge colors a contract issue. Recognizing the potential harm that could occur if the situation continued, top management ordered all badge design differences eliminated. Almost immediately, relations among all levels of employees improved.

symbols external to the job are increasingly losing their value as indicators of position.

**Status perception**, however, still remains. One of the more interesting ways status is assigned is by job titles. Since 1925, pollsters have asked thousands of people to identify occupations that have high prestige and those with lower prestige. Remarkably little variation has occurred in perceived status for almost sixty years. Scientists, physicians, engineers, clergy members, and college professors are consistently in the higher-ranked occupational categories. Bartenders, automobile salespeople, taxi drivers, and janitors are among those consistently receiving low-status ranking. Recent information published by both the Gallup Poll and Louis Harris and Associates, two of the best-known survey organizations in the United States, demonstrates the high degree of consistency in the ways occupational status is perceived. Their results vary little from data published during the past five decades. Figure 14.1 shows the relationship between occupation and prestige (status) reported by Louis Harris and Associates and published in the *American Educator*.

Although the data from the Harris poll is not new, it reflects the consistent perception that certain jobs are higher in prestige than others. People who are seen as having greater social worth, or influence on our lives, are awarded higher status than those who are perceived as making few contributions and having little real influence.

## POWER

Like status, power is also part of our everyday language. Some people equate power with control and authority. Closer examination, however, shows that although the terms are closely related, they are significantly different concepts. **Power** *is the degree of influence a person is able to exert in relationships with others*. People with power can get others to accept information or opinion and act in specific ways. Power affects what others do and believe. Power stems from many sources, including personal characteristics, and is used in many different ways. In work organizations, a person's **total power** includes not only personal power but also position power. Unlike control and authority, power is an ability rather than a one-way manipulation of forces or a delegated right.

**Control** involves establishing standards, measuring to determine if those standards are being met, and taking corrective action. Standards may be either formal or informal, but they reflect what is expected in behavior and level of performance. Measurement to determine if standards are being met can be through reports of activities, direct observation, or examination of completed work. Corrective action, if needed, can take a variety of forms from provision of information, repairing or replacing equipment, to disciplinary action in some cases. In driving an automobile, we guide its direction and make adjustments to its speed. These are control activities involving knowing where we want to go and how fast (standards), reading instruments to determine speed (measurement), and taking corrective action (adjusting speed, braking, and guiding). Power is being able to decide standards for others and determine how fast and where they will drive. Control, including self-control, is a power tool but is also a more limited concept. Power may be used to enforce corrective action, but it can also be used to get people to change, engage in specific activities, and support desired points of view.

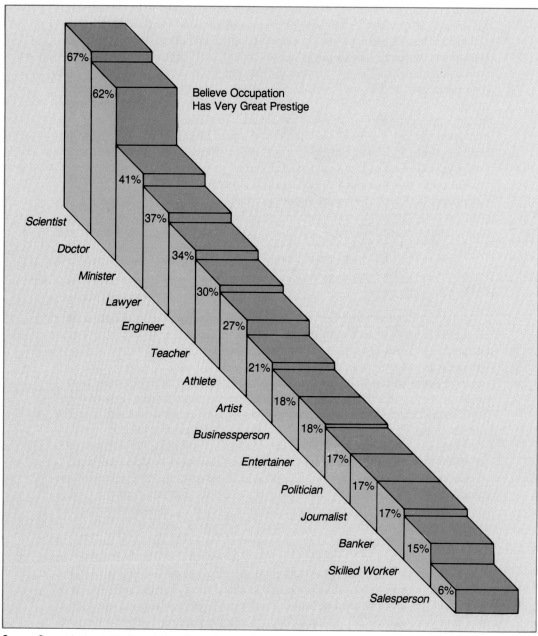

Source: Survey by Louis Harris and Associates, October 8–16, 1977.

Figure 14.1   Prestige: How occupations rate.

**Authority** is the right to decide a specific course of action, implement, approve or disapprove, and change. Like control, authority is a valuable tool, but it is not power. Without the will and ability to act, authority is virtually useless. Although a person may have the right to assign work to employees, recognized power is needed to get them to actually perform the desired tasks. Power is the ability to influence others. Control and authority are two tools associated with power. Regardless of what methods are used to exert power, it is perceived in both negative and positive ways and is nearly always based, even if to a limited extent, on sharing power with others and being influenced as well as influential.

We have only as much power as others will allow us to have. If, as an example, a manager can recommend promotions, discipline, change another person's assignment, or decide whether an employee may continue working, then that manager has a great deal of potential influence, through the use of authority, over others. Whether or not an employee responds depends on the amount of power the manager is perceived as really having.

In some cases, appearing to be powerful is just as important as being powerful. As an experiment, one of the authors of this text demonstrated power to a colleague in an amusing but effective way.

### Sources of Power

In his delightful text *Eupsychian Management*, A. H. Maslow alluded to "baboon power" and "chimpanzee power." [3] Baboons exert power by threats, screams, displays of claws and teeth, and bullying of weaker members of their groups. Chimpanzees, on the other hand, influence members of their groups by showing the way to food supplies, playing with younger group members, and encouraging participation in nearly all activities. Although primate psychologists

---

**Perceived Power** ━━━━━━━━━━━━━━━━━━━━━━━━━━━━

Helen's class was designed for educators who were upgrading their skills in school administration. Students were primarily high school and grade school principals, vice-principals, master teachers, and a few college professors. It was taught in the summer, and everyone including Helen was usually casually dressed. One morning after Helen's class had been in session for approximately twenty minutes, I walked briskly into the room (dressed in a suit and tie) and said to Helen in a curt tone, "I'm sorry, but I must interrupt." Without a smile, I continued, "Will everyone please rise." Every person in the room stood. "Will you now walk outside in an orderly fashion and remain together." My orders were carried out perfectly without question. It wasn't until Helen told her students that they were part of an experiment in perceived power and authority that they realized that I had neither.

may not totally agree with Maslow's analogy, managers often revert to either the baboon or chimpanzee style to influence others in their organization.

Power and dependency are closely linked. Threats, approval, desire to be liked, fear of disapproval or embarrassment, and the need to achieve goals all make us dependent on others to some extent. Dependence means we assign power to others. Many managers, unfortunately, recognize the dependency of nonmanagement employees and use it to strengthen their power. To a large extent, the more we depend on others to decide, plan, and direct our lives, the more power we allow them to have. Personal power is related to the influence we have on others and the degree to which they depend on us.

Classifying all types of power is virtually impossible. A criminal with a knife or a gun has a certain type of negative power. Money is frequently associated with power. Ancient Greeks wrote about the granting or withholding of sexual favors as sources of personal power. Several years ago, J. P. R. French and B. H. Raven developed classifications of power that have become a part of the language of organizational uses of power: [4]

1. **Legitimate power** is derived from a person's position in an organization, job assignment, or recognized leadership functions. It is the kind of power accepted as a normal, justifiable, and necessary component of communication between members of an organization. In many instances, legitimate power is associated with level of authority and is an expected, undisputed part of work relationships.

2. **Coercive power** has its sources in the ability to threaten, punish, or alter another person's self-esteem or job status. Unfortunately, legitimate power is often used coercively when coercion is neither desirable nor necessary. Coercive power can result from perceptions that a peer has damaging or embarrassing information as well as from the more direct threats that come from higher authority. Although it is entirely negative, and its use often breeds counteraction in the form of slower and less effective performance, many managers, for lack of real leadership skills, substitute coercion as their primary tool for direction and control.

3. **Reward power** is somewhat similar to coercive power but emphasizes the ability to approve action, influence promotions, or assign more desirable tasks. B. F. Skinner, in many of his writings dealing with operant conditioning and reinforcement of desirable behavior, points out that reward power is a highly useful tool in promoting change. Employees will repeat desirable actions if they believe that either tangible or intangible rewards will be received as a result of their efforts. They will tend not to repeat actions that result in neither reward nor punishment and will deliberately avoid those that are associated with punishment.

4. **Referent power** is demonstrated when an individual serves as a model for the behavior of others. When employees refer to their manager in quoting work rules or assignments, when they arrive at work at the same time or before the manager does, when they copy the manager's style of work or even dress, then the manager is using referent power. The

manager's attitude, goals, and approach to problems serve as reference points and are adopted by others.

A second type of referent power is based on who we know or associate with, either within the organization or in some cases outside the organization. Employees who know influential people on a personal or social basis may be seen by others as having influence, which may or may not be true. This type of referent power may be developed to strengthen personal security, to obtain higher priorities from service organizations, or to bolster feelings of self-esteem.

5. **Expert power** is derived from knowledge or skill. An employee with specialized statistical knowledge may be courted by those who need his or her assistance in solving problems. Employees who can perform specific tasks faster and more accurately than others are often given special attention.

Managers use all these types of power defined by French and Raven but are not limited to them. Over long periods of time, expert power and referent power seem to be most important. However, expert power is difficult to maintain in many cases, since expertise is a comparative term. An expert is only an expert as long as he or she is seen an knowing more or being able to solve problems and make decisions better than others.[5]

*Psychological Distance*   Other sources of power are somewhat more difficult to recognize but are equally as real as those just reviewed. When an employee is promoted to a managerial position, a psychological distance often develops between the person and his or her former co-workers. **Psychological distance** refers to the recognition that those in positions of authority must have greater influence and a broader organizational perspective than those in positions of less authority.

Psychological distance is a necessary component of any manager's life. Employees expect their managers to be objective, to treat employees equally, to evaluate performance fairly, and to avoid any preferential treatment of other employees. To do all this, managers must remove themselves to some degree from the employee's frame of reference and see situations not only in individual terms but also in terms of the consequences for the organization as a whole.

However, psychological distance extended too far may alienate employees. They may think the manager is aloof, lacks personal sensitivity, or cannot understand their problems. As a result, effective managers have the difficult task of being with their employees yet at the same time remaining apart from them. These managers realize that psychological distance is an essential factor in effective work relations.

Undeniably, power also stems from personal characteristics. Appearance can be a source of power. Other personal qualities, such as conviction, persuasiveness, personal credibility based on past actions, and willingness to accept responsibility, assume authority, and take recognizable risks, are all sources of power. One news reporter said his primary source of power was his "go-to-hell

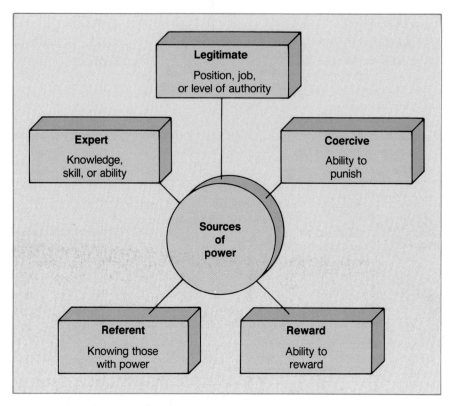

Figure 14.2   Sources of power.

fund." He had systematically saved the equivalent of a year's salary. If he felt threatened or coerced, he could tell his boss to go to hell and not feel he was depriving himself or his family while searching for another job. He reported that the power he felt from having such a fund was reflected in his independent thinking and frequent promotions.

With all its negative connotations, power is a fundamentally necessary component of organizations. Someone must finalize and implement decisions, analyze and correct, set and measure goals, and direct courses of action. Power, when strongly centered in one person or in relatively few people in an organization, ultimately develops dependency relationships. As citizens depend on governmental agencies to solve a variety of problems, so do employees depend on those with recognized power for decisions, information, and support. If power is diffused or spread throughout the organization, then there tends to be less dependency, greater self-reliance, and often less control. Basic organizational patterns, climates, and structures develop from the top-level management view of appropriate power relationships. When no one knows where the power in an organization is located, confusion inevitably results. Although ensuring order and control, power that is too highly centralized can lead to excessive dependency, slow reaction to change, and inefficient use of resources.

## POLITICS

In organizations, the acquisition and use of power can become a kind of political gamesmanship. Employees sometimes can gain a type of referent power by flattering an egotistical manager and by providing special services or favors. In many organizations, politics as well as ability help determine promotions, salary increases, and favorable job assignments. Politics involve not only the way power is developed but also its uses. Recognition of what the boss likes and dislikes is a key to successful political action.

Politics are not only based on creating psychological allies, as is done through flattery, special favors, or alliances with people who represent power, but they have also spawned a variety of political games. Some politics are blatantly malicious. But political gamesmanship can be beneficial as well as destructive. To successfully promote a point of view or influence the outcome of a decision, a manager will often diligently advance his or her point of view to other managers who can either individually or as a group influence the final action. Agreement by two or more people to mutually support the actions of each other is another common and often beneficial political behavior.

*Result of Political Power*   An effective as well as positive political action is the open display of competence, confidence, dedication, and willingness to accept appropriate responsibility. Managers and nonmanagement employees who do their homework, are well prepared for meetings, and who complete significant assignments on schedule or well ahead of time are seen as being more capable. An equally impressive action is the admission of limitations in specialized areas and recognition of the most competent person for the task. Open support of a decision known to be different from one's personal preference, when selectively applied, is still another effective and frequently positive political move.

### Political Games

In a medium-sized city bank in Madison, Wisconsin, a newly hired management trainee carefully noted that the bank manager wore a well-tailored, fur-collared overcoat, hat, and conservative suits and ties. The young trainee spent most of his initial paychecks buying a wardrobe similar to but not as expensive as the top manager's. One day, after he had worn his new clothes for a couple of weeks, he was called into the manager's office for discussions. "Somehow," the manager told the trainee, "you seem to stand out among all the trainees. I'd like you to consider an assignment as my administrative assistant." Today as vice-president of his original bank, with many branches throughout the area, the former management trainee credits his first promotion to the politics of dressing like the boss.

## REALITIES OF ORGANIZATIONAL LIFE

Employees expect their managers to act like managers, to have the symbols of management, and to be able to influence the organization upward, horizontally, and downward. The perceived degree of influence a manager has with other managers strongly influences employee willingness to accept the legitimate positional power of those who direct their activities. By the same token, managers have similar perceptions and expectations of themselves and others.

Status and power are esteemed not only by the status holder but also by those with whom he or she is associated. Most of us enjoy meeting and knowing people of influence. We not only like being associated with power but also value the recognition that often comes with such association. Not all people are status seekers or power grabbers, but many are.

Weak, insecure managers often bolster their power needs by selecting and employing weak, equally insecure employees. These managers see themselves as superior to their employees and relatively more powerful. Successful managers use a different approach. They select and train people for promotion. They believe that a desirable approach is to have employees who want their bosses' jobs. Such managers know that they are judged not only by their own ability but also by the competency of those in their work unit.

Status, power, and politics are all important components of most human interactions, especially at work. The ideal of absolute equality may never be achieved as long as people assign status, recognize power, and use the political

---

### Dirty Tricks in the Corporate Boardroom ━━━━━━

Bill, a manager in a California aerospace company, had suffered the humiliation of having his ideas ridiculed by a colleague, Greg, during a weekly executive meeting. To make matters worse, the joint division chief had witnessed the entire spectacle. Bill carefully thought out a plan of retaliation that would strike at Greg's credibility and prestige.

After the next executive meeting, Bill issued a memorandum outlining specific recommendations to strengthen the company's financial position. Implementation of the plan would be directed by Greg.

Copies of the memo were sent to the division chief and all other members of the executive meeting except one—Greg. His copy was delivered just after he left for the meeting. When the executive session convened, everyone knew about the new plan except the man most responsible for implementing it. Greg protested that he had not seen the memo but was at a loss to explain why everyone else had their copy. The more he tried to prove his innocence, the worse he looked.

Bill had the satisfaction of watching while the division chief criticized Greg's carelessness and lack of organization. He felt sure that next time Greg would think twice before ridiculing someone in front of the executive board.

---

### Political Actions That Can Work ────────────────

All politics involve a certain degree of risk. A simple political action such as building alliances can be a detriment if a manager finds him- or herself identified with the out-group in an organizational realignment. Positive politics involve acquiring power without hurting or degrading others.

1. Willingness to exceed delegated or position authority, if necessary, to accomplish goals that are recognized by higher-level management as desirable. This same tactic can be used in building alliances of peers and lower-level managers.

2. Helping others solve difficult problems, doing favors, and providing information.

3. Building information networks and becoming known to people with greater power.

4. Using direct power sparingly and avoiding creating enemies if possible.

5. Developing alliances with people outside of the organization who have inside organizational contacts, such as key vendors, well-known customers, members of important community organizations, local government officials, and members of key professional associations.

6. Endorsing and supporting causes advocated by upper levels of management.

7. Avoiding conflict and being willing to make concessions and compromises if necessary.

8. Demonstrating loyalty to both those above you in the organization and those who are members of your staff.

9. Seeking counsel from influential organizational sources, especially higher-level managers.

10. Developing trust and confidence. Never betraying confidential information.

11. Displaying enthusiasm for the organization and your job.

12. Learning to use the organization and its policies to accomplish goals.

---

actions of negotiation, compromise, private agreements, and gamesmanship to achieve their personal organizational goals. Political warfare exemplified by power struggles is readily apparent throughout the organization and ultimately affects both individual and group effectiveness. It is easy for the status-power game to become more important than the accomplishment of organizational goals.

Misuse of power is often a major contributor to managerial failure. Employees have little respect for indecisive, fearful managers. They also react negatively to those who are arrogant and overbearing, and who treat employees as inferiors. Effective managers demonstrate strength based on willingness to accept leadership responsibilities that center on supportive relationships. In their organizational roles, supportive managers use their influence both upward and horizontally as well as downward.

## Management Power Styles

**Power styles** that managers use can be viewed in many ways. Some managers use a negative power style defined by David McClelland as **primitive power**. Primitive power is the use of threats, coercion, and force to influence the behavior of others. Because they are able to affect the pay, status, work assignments, and the security of those who report to them, managers who rely on primitive (negative) power may either directly or by implication use threat and coercion as tools in enforcing employee conformity and job performance. Fear of the retribution of such managers may result in cautious, rule-oriented, highly impersonal employee behavior. Such managers may also use selective rewards to achieve similar results. Conformity and obedience are rewarded while other behavior is punished. Primitive power is the traditional "carrot and stick" approach to organizational control.[6]

*Positive Power*    Unlike negative power, positive power is not used as a compensation for weakness or as a demonstration of dominance for the sake of ego satisfaction. Managers who use power positively are concerned with defining goals more clearly, developing involvement and enthusiasm for accomplishing work objectives, and building a supportive relationship between themselves and employees. They tend to be analytical rather than critical, corrective rather than punishing, and see themselves as developers of people.

Although there is no single model of the way managers use power that adequately describes all manager power styles, it is relatively easy in most organizations to observe the relationship between influence and attitudes. High-influence managers with negative or neutral feelings toward employees will tend to use threatening, coercive styles. Low-influence managers with negative attitudes will be suspicious, fearful, withdrawn, and indecisive in the absence of a policy, rule, or written order. High-influence managers with positive attitudes rely on coaching skills, encouragement, delegation, and high but realistic expectations to achieve work goals. Low-influence managers with positive attitudes spend time developing strong friendships, providing personal services, and working toward a "happy climate." They tend to be less concerned about job necessities than being personally liked by their employees. Table 14.2 shows this relationship.

Although the power styles shown in Table 14.2 are based on behavior that may vary a great deal in intensity, managers tend to adopt a primary style. Although conditions may alter their behavior dramatically, they will generally return to the style they have used in the past.

## EXPECTATIONS, STATUS, AND POWER

We have developed many expectations about the nature, benefits, and liabilities of possessing status and power. Status, for example, may be associated with job title, money, or perceptions of social worth to a community. We expect those to whom status is given to use their standing for the benefit of others or for the representation of a set of ideals. Influence is often directly associated with status. Applicants for employment frequently list ministers, teachers, or well-known community leaders as references even though the references may know little about the applicant's past job performance or capabilities.

A strong relationship exists between status and referent power. A reality of organizational life is that employees prefer association with managers who demonstrate the power to effect change, to influence upward and downward in their organizations, and who are skilled in the art of strengthening their position through being able to recognize and use effective politics. The degree of influ-

**Table 14.2**
**Manager Power Styles**

| Degree of Influence | Negative | Positive |
| --- | --- | --- |
| High Influence | Decisive | Decisive |
|  | Blames others | Analytical |
|  | Egocentric | Team oriented |
|  | Critical | Delegates as much as feasible |
|  | Authoritarian | Wants success for others as well as for self |
|  | Reluctant to delegate | Sees self as developer of people |
|  | Motivated by dominance and power | Motivated by personal and team achievement |
| Low Influence | Indecisive | Indecisive |
|  | Rule oriented | Friendly |
|  | Suspicious | People oriented |
|  | Fearful | Supportive |
|  | Critical | Criticizes self |
|  | Does not deviate from rules | Accepts blame |
|  | Motivated by need for survival | Service directed |
|  |  | Motivated by need for approval, friendship, and acceptance |

ence a manager has in the organization will affect the willingness of employees to accept the manager's leadership. The status and power of managers are also important for those who work with them. Recognition is often received as a result of "who you know." Associations with powerful individuals give some people a feeling of power.

Two additional points need to be recognized in viewing power relationships. Over a period of time, the degree of direct influence a person has over another person or group tends to decline. Although this is not always true, a degree of accommodation occurs during association with high-influence people, either in a positive or a negative sense. They begin to seem less fearful, less powerful, and more human. Such changes in the power balance are easily recognized and may strengthen real working relationships.

A second factor is that situations strongly affect the degree of influence a person has or is allowed. In dealing with nonmanagement employees, a manager may be very dominant and have considerable influence. In a staff meeting with other managers of equal or higher rank, the same manager may have no more than equal influence with that of other managers and, in some cases, may have considerably less.

Status, power, and politics are important elements in interpersonal relationships in organizations.[7] People will always recognize power and assign status. Political actions and gamesmanship will probably always be important aspects of achieving personal and organizational goals. Managers must constantly guard against power-status struggles becoming more important than the achievement of organizational objectives.

## SELF–ASSESSMENT DISCUSSION

**1.** (6) Status is assigned to people based on their perceived worth to society or to a specific group.

**2.** (1, 2, 3) Leadership involves influencing others. It is closely associated with power. Leadership positions may also be associated with status, but power is the dominant characteristic of leaders.

**3.** (1) Politics is essentially a set of actions directed toward gaining influence. Political activities are rarely associated with increasing status.

**4.** (4, 5, 6) Authority is nearly always associated with power, although assumed authority can be a political tactic in some cases. If people believe that a person has authority, it is just as effective to the user as real authority.

**5.** (1) Management authorities agree that power is a necessary ingredient in organizations. Someone must exert influence on others. Power, however, can be positive rather than negative. Positive power is directed toward the good of the organization rather than control and manipulation of individuals.

**6.** (1) Manipulation of others and events to achieve personal rather than organizational goals is one way of identifying political behavior. Managers who consistently engage in manipulation of others may use some types of power, but their actions are aimed toward acquiring more power. Acquiring power is the objective of nearly all politics.

**7.** (1, 2, 3, 4, 5, 6) Managers use both power and politics in varying degrees. Effective managers with high levels of positive influence or power rely far less on politics than do managers who are more negative in their approaches. In any case, most managers use both to achieve their goals.

**8.** (1) Employees prefer managers who are able to influence the organization. Managers who exert power both upward and downward are seen as the strongest. Few, if any, employees want a manager who is powerless.

**9.** (6) All societies have both power and status structures. Even in small groups, some people are allowed more influence than others, and some may be seen as having greater overall worth to the group. Although power and status are often embodied in the same individual or individuals, many exceptions exist.

**10.** (1) Unless managers have at least some power symbols (e.g., a private office, reserved parking space, special office furniture), employees tend to believe that managers have little influence. According to the principle of distributive justice, we want people with power and status to *show* they have power and status.

## *QUICK REVIEW*

I. Status, Power, and Politics

    A. Many people react negatively to the realities of status, power, and politics.

    B. Status is related to rank; power, to influence; and politics, to methods used to acquire status and power.

II. Status—Meaning and Symbols

    A. When we believe another person has more or is greater than we are, we assign status to them. Status is position compared with others.

    B. Status may be either selective or general.

    C. Status symbols are the objects, titles, furnishings, and so on surrounding people that determine our perceptions of their position.

    D. Distributive justice is the belief that those who do more should have more.

    E. Status congruence refers to the appropriateness of the symbols for the position.

    F. Status compression is the deliberate avoidance of discriminatory status symbols.

III. Power

    A. The degree of influence exerted is a measure of power.

    B. Power and authority are not the same. Authority is conferred by a task and a higher authority.

    C. "Baboon power" is based on threats. "Chimpanzee power" is based on encouragement and helpfulness.

D. Power has many sources. Some are:
   1. Legitimate power.
   2. Coercive power.
   3. Reward power.
   4. Referent power.
   5. Expert power.
E. Psychological distance is a necessary component of effective manager-employee relations.
F. Power also stems from personal characteristics.
G. Power, when strongly centered, results in dependency.

IV. Politics
A. The acquisition and use of power can become a kind of political gamesmanship.
B. In many organizations, politics as well as ability help people get ahead.
C. Political game playing can be beneficial or malicious, either gaining others' support or destroying their influence.

V. Realities of Organizational Life
A. Employees expect their managers to act like managers.
B. Status and power are esteemed not only by the status holder but also by the person's associates.
C. It is easy for the status-power game to become more important than the accomplishment of organizational goals.
D. Some managers use primitive power based on fear and coercion.
E. Other managers use power to define goals, build morale, and motivate and support workers.
F. It is relatively easy in an organization to observe the relationship between influence and attitudes.

VI. Expectations, Status, and Power
A. We expect status and power to be closely linked.
B. People prefer working for managers who are perceived as having status and influence.
C. Over time, a person's influence, good or bad, tends to decline.
D. The degree of influence a person possesses is strongly affected by the situation.

### KEY TERMS

| | | |
|---|---|---|
| Status | General status | Status congruence |
| Politics | Distributive justice | Status compression |

Status perception      Legitimate power      Psychological distance
Power                  Coercive power        Primitive power
Total power            Reward power          Positive power
Control                Referent power        Power styles
Authority              Expert power

## DISCUSSION QUESTIONS

1. List the names of three people who have both power and status. How did they acquire their present degree of influence and esteem?
2. Why do people expect those in power positions to have symbols of power such as larger offices, greater salaries, and more influence than others?
3. In status surveys certain occupations, such as scientists, physicians, and bankers, consistently rank higher than used car salespeople, bartenders, and undertakers. Explain why this occurs.
4. Explain why physically attractive people seem to have greater influence than physically unattractive people even when both are from the same educational and socioeconomic group.
5. Children of high-status parents tend to get better jobs than children of low-status parents, regardless of levels of education. Why does this occur?

## EXERCISE

### Actions to Improve Your Political Power

You supervise an office that does secretarial work for company executives. You have received a new word processor that is to be assigned to one of the secretaries. You want to assign the word processor so as to improve your own position in the organization regarding status, power, and politics.

*Evaluate the following list of proposed criteria for assigning the word processor to improve your political power.*
Which criteria would you use? Which would be most important?

1. Assign to the secretary who is the fastest typist.

2. Assign to the secretary who has been with the organization for the longest period of time.

3. Assign to the secretary who has the best attendance record.

4. Assign to the secretary who spends the most time talking with the executives.

5. Assign to the secretary who currently has the worst equipment.

6. Assign to the secretary who is the most highly respected by the other secretaries.

7. Assign to the secretary who is seen as being the most cooperative by the executives.

8. Assign to the secretary who would get the greatest increase in productivity by having the new word processor.

9. Assign to the secretary who does work for the highest-ranked executives.

10. Assign to the secretary who has the heaviest work load.

Would you evaluate these criteria for assignment of the new word processor differently if your objective was to maintain cooperative working relations among the secretaries?

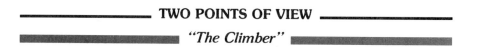

## TWO POINTS OF VIEW

### "The Climber"

*What would you do if you were the department manager?*

You are the manager of the appliance department in a large discount department store. You have been employed in the store for fourteen years, having worked your way up from stocker to salesperson to department manager. You believe that your promotions have been based on your ability and performance. Your department's sales and service have been rated as outstanding by the store manager. During your last annual performance evaluation, the store manager said he thought you were ready for a more important position with more responsibility. You believe that you may be in line for the position of assistant store manager. The current assistant manager will retire in six months, and none of the current managers have as much experience as you do.

The only threat you see to getting the promotion is posed by one of your employees, Gary Holt. Gary is a likable appliance salesperson who continually socializes with the store manager. He is an excellent "politician" who tells the store manager what he wants to hear. Gary arranges to have coffee breaks with the store manager and plays golf with him almost every week. He gives you information from the store manager that you should have received directly from the manager. Gary appears to be the store manager's source of information about the appliance department, and you are seldom asked for any information about your own department. His friendship with the store manager seems to be close. The store manager allows you to let Gary take work time to do personal favors for him, such as picking his children up from school and taking his car to be serviced.

Other employees have told you that if you don't watch out, Gary will steal your promotion to assistant store manager. The employees in the department openly refer to Gary as "Mr. Climber."

*What would you do if you were Gary Holt?*

You are an appliance salesperson for a large discount department store. You graduated from high school eight years ago and have had a number of sales jobs, including selling automobiles, insurance, and tools. This is the most satisfying job you have ever had, and in the eighteen months you have been with the department store, your sales record has been excellent. Each month you have sold more than any of the other salespeople.

You would like to move into a management position and believe that you may have an opportunity with this store. You noticed that the store manager seemed to have few friends and liked to talk with you. As your uncle used to tell you, "It is not what you do but who you know that counts." You have made good friends with the store manager and talk with him every day on your coffee breaks. You try to help the store manager in every way you can, even doing personal favors such as taking his car to be serviced and picking up things from the grocery store. You were sure that you were "in" with the store manager when he started asking you to play golf with him each week.

You know your department manager does an excellent job and deserves the promotion to assistant store manager when the current manager retires in six months. You want the job of department manager and think your friendship with the store manager will get you the job.

The only problem you see developing is that your department manager and the employees in the department clearly resent your associating with the store manager. One of the employees has asked you, "How fast do you plan to politic your way to the top?" You really don't care what the other employees think as long as you can get a management position. You are even considering the possibility of getting the assistant store manager position because you know the store manager thinks he can work with you.

## ENDNOTES

**1.** Peter Farb, *Humankind* (Boston: Houghton Mifflin, 1978).

**2.** David Lawless, *Organizational Behavior* (Englewood Cliffs, N.J.: Prentice-Hall, 1979), p. 386.

**3.** A. H. Maslow, *Eupsychian Management* (Homewood, Ill.: Irwin-Dorsey, 1965).

**4.** John R. P. French, Jr., and Bertram Raven, *The Bases of Social Power*, in *Group Dynamics*, eds. Darwin Cartwright and Alvin Zender (New York: Harper & Row, 1968), p. 259–69.

**5.** Fred Luthans, *Organizational Behavior*, 3d ed. (New York: McGraw-Hill, 1981), p. 393–95.

**6.** David McClelland, "The Two Faces of Power," *Journal of International Affairs* (January 1970): 36.

**7.** For additional material on power and politics see J. Clifton Williams and George Huber, *Organizational Behavior* (Cincinnati, Ohio: South-Western, 1986), Samuel C. Certo, *Management* (Dubuque, Iowa: Brown, 1986), Ricky Griffin, *Management* (Boston: Houghton Mifflin, 1986), p. 437–39, and Robert B. Cialdini, *Influence* (Glenview, Ill.: Scott, Foresman, 1985).

# Chapter 15

# Managerial Effectiveness and Performance Improvement

―――――――― *Learning Objectives* ――――――――

After reading this chapter, you should be able to do the following:

1. Describe the organizational and managerial characteristics that improve performance and productivity
2. Identify the effects and characteristics of an organizational climate that is goal oriented
3. Design a system for goal setting that will improve individual performance and aid in achieving organizational objectives
4. Describe organizational practices that promote innovation and creativity
5. List guidelines for the effective administration of discipline
6. Discuss conditions necessary for developing effective delegation
7. Explain how a supervisor can improve performance and productivity

# Chapter Topics

- Managerial effectiveness and performance improvement
- Goal orientation
- A system for goal setting
- Innovation and creativity
- Constructive discipline
- Delegation of authority and responsibility
- Effective supervision

# Preview

Effective organizational action must, by its very nature, be goal directed. A shoe manufacturing plant must manufacture shoes. An insurance company must sell insurance. Lumber companies must cut and process wood products. Colleges must provide instruction. Successful achievement of organizational objectives is dependent on the effectiveness of managerial ability to define and translate goals into employee action. The entire thrust of modern organizational behavior theory is directed not toward employee satisfaction or happiness but toward achievement of both organizational and personal goals.

Two prerequisites for reaching goals are: (1) managers must be able to define where they want to go, and (2) they must know how to get there. In this chapter, we discuss the necessary ingredients required for defining goals and realizing their achievement.

Productivity depends on management creating an environment that fosters individual performance and team effort. To achieve organizational objectives it is required that people work together in order to reach meaningful goals.

## SELF–ASSESSMENT

Nearly all managers are concerned with ways of improving personal effectiveness as well as employee performance. In the following statements, mark the response that best fits your concept of what will improve managerial effectiveness and employee performance. Each statement or question has a range of possible responses. A scale of 1 to 6 between two words with different meanings allows you to mark either the word that is considered correct or a place between the two words that represents some agreement and some disagreement. Selection of a high number such as 5 or 6 may be either correct or incorrect, just as selection of lower numbers may be correct or incorrect. Some responses may be partly correct and partly incorrect.

Answers based on research by behavioral scientists, with a short explanation of why the response was considered correct, may be found on page 423.

1. The managerial climate that best promotes human effectiveness in organizations is:

goal oriented  1...2...3...4...5...6  cost oriented

2. Levels of employee performance can be raised through the development of:

benefits plans  1...2...3...4...5...6  confidence and self-esteem

3. Effective supervisors treat employees:

as individuals  1...2...3...4...5...6  impersonally

4. Delegation of authority to an employee by a supervisor:

creates resentment  1...2...3...4...5...6  increases interest in job

5. Supervisors are responsible for:

rewarding employees  1...2...3...4...5...6  disciplining employees

6. Leadership styles should be characterized by fairness and:

inflexibility  1...2...3...4...5...6  consistency

7. For delegation to work, it must be:

power oriented  1...2...3...4...5...6  goal oriented

8. Goal setting can encourage achievement through:

individual involvement  1...2...3...4...5...6  fear of failure

**9.** In an authority-oriented work climate, individuals are provided:

positive incentives to  1...2...3...4...5...6  little incentive to
increase effectiveness                                  increase
                                                        effectiveness

**10.** The hot-stove rule states that discipline should be immediate, consistent, impersonal, and:

without warning  1...2...3...4...5...6  with warning

## MANAGERIAL EFFECTIVENESS AND PERFORMANCE IMPROVEMENT

Management has been facing an increasing number of problems in achieving productivity. Many of these problems arise because individuals have left old anchorages, no longer follow old cultural patterns, and have developed greater desires for achievement and self-fulfillment. Most individuals find that they have a greater number of alternatives to choose from, and there are greater possibilities to satisfy needs for achievement, growth, recognition, and responsibility. Many individuals no longer find it desirable to look to authoritative standards as guides. Individuals are seeking meaningful work under conditions where management's power is based on competence and not status in the organizational structure.

There is no shortage of programs to improve productivity. But managers continue to ask, "How do I get employees to achieve organizational goals?" In response to their question, we find articles, books, speeches, and training programs in ever-increasing numbers. Many of the current materials on productivity are collections of gimmicks and procedures designed to produce quick and easy results.

Unfortunately, no easy gimmicks or quick procedures can produce the conditions necessary for long-term individual productivity in organizations. To obtain organizational effectiveness and human productivity, systems must be developed and maintained that will maximize the potential of individuals. Effective management for performance and productivity should have at least the following five characteristics:

1. Goal orientation
2. Innovation and creativity
3. Constructive discipline
4. Delegation of authority and responsibility
5. Effective supervision

## GOAL ORIENTATION

The managerial climate that promotes human effectiveness in an organization has a **goal orientation**. Through goal attainment, individuals satisfy needs for achievement, growth, recognition, and responsibility.[1] When the **organizational climate** lacks goal orientation, individuals tend to seek security and protect themselves from the system. Where there are no specific goals, individuals may function in blind obedience to orders from superiors. Employees may not look for better ways to accomplish objectives but may look only for better ways to satisfy their bosses. In an organization where the boss calls the shots, the individual is provided with little incentive or opportunity to contribute to increased effectiveness of the organization. "Automatic conformity, or obedient jumping through hoops, is little better than a pattern for 'serving time' on the job." [2]

Employees usually characterize such organizations as having arbitrary and unchallenging goals, confusing and restrictive administrative systems (red tape), and interpersonal conflict. These conditions lead to feelings of individual failure and often result in management disapproval and punishment, which in turn produce feelings of guilt, frustration, and apathy. The individual's defenses take the forms of cynicism, hostility, and efforts to obtain need satisfaction from sources unrelated to organizational goals. This behavior further aggravates human relationships, and the unproductive conditions are reinforced (see Figure 15.1).

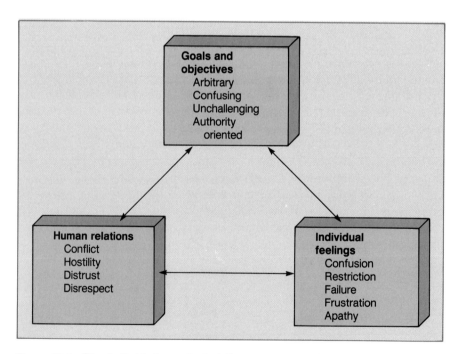

**Figure 15.1**   Climate that lacks goal orientation.

Goal-oriented individuals see job goals as a meaningful part of broader organizational objectives and as a way of achieving personal goals. With goal-oriented management, individuals receive constructive feedback and satisfaction directly from the work itself and the achievement of goals. Knowledge of the job enables the individual to intitiate self-corrective action and to grow with accomplishments.

Goal orientation is supported by management actions that develop meaningful goals, supportive and helpful management systems, and interpersonal respect and trust. These conditions maximize the individual's opportunity to achieve goals and earn approval and reward. The resulting motivation favorably affects the individual's perception of the job and encourages the individual to reach out for greater achievements. Conditions that develop a positive outlook reinforce interpersonal respect and support a process of individual achievement and goal attainment (see Figure 15.2).

## Organizational Goal-Setting Systems

The establishment of goals has often been found to increase the efficiency and effectiveness of individuals, departments, and organizations.[3]

Goal setting, which leads to achievement, has the following characteristics: (1) individuals are involved in the process of setting organizational and specific work goals; (2) individuals are able to relate personal goals to organizational

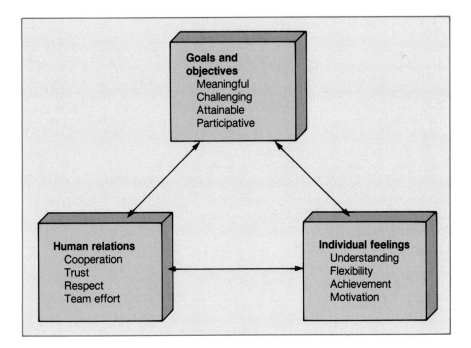

Figure 15.2   Climate that promotes goal orientation.

goals; (3) the organization has supportive and helpful systems for setting and achieving goals; and (4) individuals are able to respond favorably to organizational goals and make a commitment to the organization.

Systematic goal setting can help organizations and individuals within organizations evaluate individual performance and potential. A **goal-setting system** can aid management in measuring the success of other organizational systems and procedures.

An effective goal-setting system should improve on the informal goal setting that occurs naturally in an organization. A formal system can develop a more realistic basis on which individuals can build expectations about their jobs, their organization, and themselves. Formal goal-setting systems can establish a foundation on which a continuous goal-setting process can be built.

If a goal-setting system is to be successful in helping an organization meet its objectives, it must be based on employee involvement and must facilitate the growth and development of individuals.[4] Additionally, a goal-setting system cannot succeed unless the organization is willing to evaluate its programs and systems on the basis of human effectiveness and productivity, rather than on the basis of organizational structure, such as degree of control, proper status differential, and so forth.

*Methods of Implementing Goal Setting*    Two methods are commonly used to implement a goal-setting system. The first method is to start at the top of the organization and then proceed down successive levels. This method has the advantage of emphasizing the relationship of organization-wide objectives to those set at lower levels. It allows people to experience first as subordinates a technique they will later employ as superiors. Implementation from the top down tends to minimize any problems that might arise because of managers employing practices their bosses do not understand or sanction.

A second way to implement the goal-setting system is to install it in one segment of the organization—a branch, plant, or department. This can have the advantage of allowing some learning through experience before the program is extended to other segments of the organization. It also allows for comparisons between units using the system and those not yet involved.

The first step in implementing any managerial system is to decide that it is worth total commitment. A willingness to "give it a try" is not enough. A goal-setting program costs an organization time and effort. If it is to be successful, it requires a continuing commitment by those involved. A commitment to meet together an hour or so a week is not enough. Those involved must construct a goal-setting program that will suit the organization and that they are willing to maintain.[5]

The following description of a goal-setting program is a suggested one. It is not a universal "right way" and should not be considered as such. See Figure 15.3.

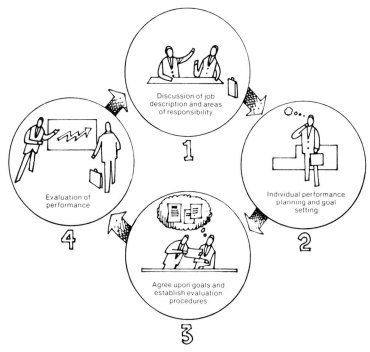

**Figure 15.3    A system of goal setting.**


## A SYSTEM FOR GOAL SETTING


*Position Description*    In the first step, the individual employee discusses his or her job description with the manager, and areas of responsibility are defined. The results the individual is responsible for attaining are specified.


*Individual Goals*    The second step is to obtain agreement of the manager on the duties required of the position. The employee should then prepare a list of goals that represent reasonable performance in each of the areas of responsibility. The employee plans activities so they support the overall goals of the unit and organization.

   In establishing performance goals, the individual must know the goals of the organization and the goals of the particular organizational unit. Every organization imposes some limits on individual activities, and these limits must be communicated to the individual by management. An individual can establish reasonable and obtainable goals only when the overall goals of the organization and the goals of the unit are known.

*Goal Agreement and Evaluation Procedures*   In the third step, the employee and the manager mutually agree on the employee's goals. This step is the most difficult and complicated in the goal-setting procedure. For one thing, the moment the manager asks an ~mployee to raise or lower a goal the individual has set, the goal then be    ,es the manager's, not the employee's.

The manager should act in the role of questioner, adviser, counselor, trainer, developer, and even "warner." The manager should not play the role of God or judge!

The manager and the employee jointly establish the standards, or the checkpoints, to be used by both parties during and at the end of the evaluation period to determine the employee's success in attaining objectives. Examples of such checkpoints are due dates; sales, financial, and cost figures; statistical data; and comparisons.

*Evaluation of Performance*   In the fourth step, the results of a person's performance are evaluated. The individual has either attained goals, exceeded goals, or failed to attain goals. The attainment of or failure to attain a goal is not significant in itself. The most important consideration is, What has the person *accomplished*? A person who establishes extremely high goals and then almost attains them has accomplished more than the person who establishes low goals and then exceeds them. Judgment must be used in evaluating performance. The manager's responsibility is to eliminate undesirable performance and to reward positive achievements appropriately.

Undesirable performance is a warning signal that something must be done. The employee may need additional training or development. Maybe the individual needs additional support resources or new equipment. The individual could be "misplaced" in the current position. After the manager has exhausted all means of help and guidance and the individual continues to show undesirable performance, the manager must take action to transfer the individual to a position in which he or she can achieve positive accomplishments. For the individual's welfare and for the effectiveness of the organization, a person should not be continued in a position in which positive accomplishments cannot be achieved. On the other hand, the manager should appropriately reward individuals who have achieved positive accomplishments.

In these procedures, no mention has been made of personality traits. The psychological causes of an individual's activities are not explored; the individual is not put on a couch and psychoanalyzed. Instead, a person is judged on the basis of *results and accomplishments*. If an individual has serious (not imagined) personality deficiencies, this will inevitably result in undesirable performance. The manager, by eliminating undesirable performance, will probably eliminate the negative impact of personality problems. The task of identifying and solving serious personality problems should be left to the professional.

## Advantages of Goal-Setting Systems

The primary advantages of goal-setting systems are as follows:

- Individuals know in advance the basis for evaluation.
- The manager and employee both understand the responsibilities of the position.
- A goal-setting system should strengthen the manager-employee relationship because it does not require the manager to be an arbitrary judge.
- The system can be self-correcting, helping people set goals that are both challenging and attainable.
- Goal setting helps in identifying training needs.
- The system helps the manager gain a better understanding of employee problems.
- Goal setting treats as a total process a person's ability to identify organizational problems, develop ways of attacking them, translate ideas into action, and carry plans through to results.

## INNOVATION AND CREATIVITY

> The ability to facilitate creativity and innovation is among the most basic of a manager's work responsibilities.[6]

The organization that achieves long-term effectiveness and maximum development must place a premium on **innovation and creativity**. The effective manager realizes that seeking better things to do (effectiveness) is more productive than doing more efficiently the things already being done.

A climate for innovation and creativity cannot be created by gimmicks. Promoting creativity requires challenging objectives and individuals who believe their work is important. In the past, management has often assumed that individuals could be divided into two classes: creative and noncreative. Most individuals in organizations were placed in the noncreative category, and originality was not expected from them. Today, the general agreement is that creative potential is not restricted to a small group but exists to some degree in almost all individuals.

> The capacities of the average human being for creativity, for growth, for collaboration, for productivity (in the full sense of the term) are far greater than we have recognized. . . . [I]t is possible that the next half century will bring the most dramatic social changes in human history.[7]

An organization that has an environment for creativity makes use of creative potential of individuals throughout the organization. The characteristics of the organization reflect the personalities of many employees, at all levels, rather than a few at the top. Creativity and innovation are found in all activities and functions of the organization, including hiring practices, development of objectives, compensation, design of organizational structures, and so on (see Figure 15.4).

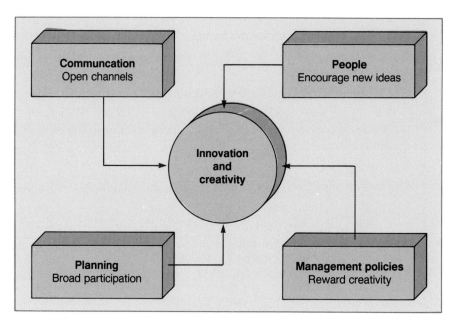

Figure 15.4   Factors contributing to the development of innovation and creativity.

### *Personnel Practices*

To provide an environment for innovation and creativity, the organization should hire a variety of personality types and avoid hiring only people like those already in the organization. Individuals should be hired who have proven their abilities to create and innovate in other organizations. Nonspecialists should be assigned to planning and problem-solving groups. The selection and promotion of individuals should be made only on merit.

### *Communication*

Open channels of communication should be developed and maintained so there is fluid communication.[8] Individuals should be encouraged to communicate with sources outside the organization, such as professional groups. One way to promote open communication is to form "idea" groups that are responsible for obtaining and evaluating suggestions for improving productivity and the achievement of organizational objectives.

### *Planning*

Maximum flexibility should be maintained in long-range planning so that creativity and innovation are not hindered by fixed plans that are difficult to change. The planning process should incorporate an attitude of "give everything a

---

### B. F. Goodrich's Creativity Training

Can you *teach* creativity? The top management at B. F. Goodrich think so. They have developed two courses on creativity—one for supervisors and middle managers, and one for senior management.

The overall objective of the program is to get managers to accept creative thinking as a natural part of daily management rather than an exotic, separate "technology." The two courses each last two and a half days; managers are trained to overcome personal and organizational obstacles to creativity and become more receptive to new or unusual ideas.

The course for middle managers and supervisors concentrates on intra- and interpersonal aspects of creativity. Managers learn how to free their minds to be more creative and open to fresh ideas. They examine how personal relationships can inhibit or encourage creative thinking. Finally, they discuss ways of responding to original ideas and overcoming fears of criticism or ridicule in presenting or receiving new ideas.

The course for senior managers puts greater emphasis on the organizational aspects of creativity and on developing a climate that nurtures and develops creative ideas.

B. F. Goodrich believes that by training management to be more flexible, receptive, and creative, the company can foster creativity throughout the organization without the need to train every employee.[9]

---

chance." There should be broad participation by individuals in all levels in the organization as plans are developed.

### *Management Practices and Policies*

Ideas should be evaluated on their merits and should not be affected by the status of the originator. Top-level management should not develop a close-minded commitment to present policies and procedures. Management must do more than attempt to "follow the leader," whether the leader is another organization or an individual. If an organization is to develop a favorable climate for innovation and creativity, it must have creative managers.

*Supervising for Creativity*   The AC Sparkplug Division of General Motors recognized the importance of management's influence on innovation and creativity and constructed a program entitled "Supervising for Creativity." The program focused on three areas:

1. *The supervisor-employee relationship.* The supervisor should strive to build an atmosphere that encourages new ideas and changes. Supervi-

sors should design positive approaches to stimulate and encourage creativity in each individual. Supervisors should give recognition for all new ideas and commendation when deserved.

2. *Active support of creativity.* The supervisor should actively support the creativity of individuals. Supervisors should maintain effective communications with their own and other departments. A definite or formal procedure should be established for the fair and consistent consideration of all ideas conceived in the department.

3. *The highly creative person.* The supervisor should permit the creative individuals to work in an atmosphere where they can easily try out their ideas. The creative individual should be provided with an environment conducive to study and work. The assignment of work to the creative individual should be done carefully.[10]

In any program to develop innovation and creativity, the managers must understand the creative process and must be creative themselves, not only in technical areas but also in organizational influence and management practices.

> Innovation begins with example. When management acts in an innovative way, and managers at every level show appreciation for good ideas you have a climate that attracts and nourishes creative people, and you will always have innovation.[11]
>
> Harry J. Gary, Chairman, President and CEO, United Technologies

## CONSTRUCTIVE DISCIPLINE

To be effective, discipline should focus on learning and improvement. Poor disciplinary practices can result in resentment and hostility, and cause individuals to develop methods to protect themselves from management. **Constructive discipline** can help to develop a feeling of mutual respect among the individuals in the organization.

### *Objectives of Discipline*

The primary objective of discipline should be to develop effective individual and organizational performance. Discipline is necessary as a form of control only for a small number of individuals. If the organization has a large number of individuals who can be controlled only by disciplinary measures, it should closely examine its selection and retention practices. In some situations, discipline is necessary for the protection of the rights of individuals and the organization.

Constructive discipline should always be results oriented. Discipline should not be used for revenge. When management attempts to get even with employees, the result is usually a decrease in productivity and action by employees to get even with management.

## *Approaches to Discipline*

The most desirable and effective discipline is self-discipline. No organization has sufficient resources to control and police the behavior of all individuals in the organization. Through delegation of responsibility and support from management, individuals can improve their effectiveness through self-discipline. Unless individuals are given responsibility, management should not expect them to behave with a high degree of self-discipline. Where group teamwork exists, management can usually count on group discipline to supplement self-discipline.

Management can avoid many of the problems involved in disciplinary action if rules are seen as reasonable and justified. Individuals will usually observe rules when they understand why they are necessary. Rules should be periodically reviewed; and if they cannot be positively justified, they should be discontinued. The procedures the organization uses for discipline should be developed with broad participation from representatives of the individuals who are subject to discipline. Managers should never forget that discipline problems are usually the result of ineffective management.

## *An Example of Constructive Discipline*

The following case involves the discipline of production workers in a large Douglas fir plywood mill.[12] The management became aware that unsatisfactory work performance and disciplinary matters were being handled in an undesirable manner. The company had developed an informal method for dealing with these situations:

1. The supervisor would either ignore or casually mention initial and minor infringements of rules.

2. Repeated infractions, depending upon the issue involved, usually resulted in discharge, demotion, or suspension of pay.

3. This arrangement had two general consequences. First, there was a general conflict between the management and the union as a result of the union's ability to either lessen the punishment or nullify any effects that it might have by providing a monetary cushion for suspended workers. Second, the discipline system was costly to the company in

    a. the training costs to replace demoted or discharged workers.

    b. the costs of multiple temporary job movements when workers were suspended.

    c. the costs in management time involved in grievance meetings.

4. Usually the procedure produced further incidents, because workers returning from suspension attempted to save face with their fellow workers by repeating previous actions and by producing the feeling among the workers that the union would protect them in almost any grievance situation.

Faced with this situation, the management set out to reexamine the firm's discipline policies and to take remedial action where possible. Management first recognized that discipline problems usually did not occur without warning. The management next considered that the problem might be one of enforcement and that a formal system of written warning slips should be established. They recognized, however, that this system would not, to any great degree, affect the costs mentioned earlier. The managers then reviewed their basic assumptions about human behavior and the effects of punishment. They concluded from their and others' experiences that punishment in itself does not necessarily change behavior.

The conclusion of these managers is supported by recent research of Beyer and Trice.[13] In a field study of the use of discipline on difficult problem employees within a large corporation, the researchers found (1) that mild discipline in the form of informal discussions had a positive effect on performance, and (2) that more severe discipline in the form of written warnings and suspensions was not effective in improving performance.

In the case just discussed, management also concluded that although many motivational factors are involved, the major motivation for satisfactory performance and disciplined behavior is respect for the authority behind the rules (the organization) and respect for oneself. The company therefore decided to adopt the following policy for developing and enforcing disciplined behavior:

1. The company will no longer apply disciplinary demotions, suspensions, or other forms of punishment.

2. When unsatisfactory work performance or lack of discipline occurs, the following steps are followed:

   Step 1: The supervisor will casually remind the worker what is expected of him or her (on the job site).

   Step 2: If another incident arises within four to six weeks, the worker is again casually reminded (on the job) of his or her responsibilities. The supervisor also speaks privately with the worker in an attempt to explain the purpose for the particular rule, to listen for a reasonable excuse, to ascertain whether the incident was unintentional, and to express the hope that the worker can conform to the expected behavior.

   Step 3: If the situation repeats itself within six weeks, step 2 is repeated in the presence of the supervisor's boss. This step is then confirmed with a letter to the worker's home.

   Step 4: If within six weeks of step 3 the incident is again repeated, the worker is called off the job and sent home for the remainder of the day (with pay) and is instructed to decide whether he or she wishes to comply with the expected behavior. The worker is also told that another occurrence within a reasonable time period will result in termination.

3. If another incident does occur within a reasonable amount of time, the worker is immediately terminated.

4. In extreme cases of several incidents in a short period of time, steps 2 and 3 may be skipped. In cases of criminal behavior or in-plant fighting, termination is immediate.

The value of these actions lies in their results. During the first seven months of the plan's operation, two workers were terminated for fighting (before the plan could be announced); three workers progressed through step 4 (two returned to quit, and one had no further incidents); several workers proceeded to step 3 and afterward remained out of trouble; and the conflict between the supervisors and the union was eliminated. As a consequence of these improvements, the company saved both time and money and improved worker productivity in the firm.

### The Hot-Stove Rule

Effective discipline involves learning through experience. What has been referred to as the **hot-stove rule** illustrates four basic concepts of effective discipline.[14] This rule draws the analogy between touching a hot stove and the application of discipline. When an individual touches a hot stove, the discipline (and learning) is immediate, consistent, impersonal, and usually with some warning. The most effective disciplinary process provides advance warning of the consequences of behaviors that are considered undesirable. If these behaviors occur, the consequences are immediate, consistent, and impersonal. When an individual touches a hot stove, there is no question of cause and effect. The burn is the result of a behavior and not because of any characteristics of the individual. The discipline is a result of an act and not directed against the person. The stove is not out to get anyone; everyone who touches it gets burned (see Figure 15.5).

### General Guidelines for Administering Discipline

All managers use some form of disciplinary procedure. When implementing any disciplinary procedures to correct undesirable behavior, the following commonly accepted guides should be considered:

1. The discipline is for the undesirable behavior and not directed against the person.
2. Disciplinary action should take place in private.
3. Discipline should be handled in a constructive manner.
4. Disciplinary action should be the responsibility of the immediate supervisor.
5. Disciplinary action should promptly follow the undesirable behavior.
6. Discipline for similar undesirable behaviors should be consistent.
7. After a disciplinary action, the supervisor should help the employee to perform successfully on the job.

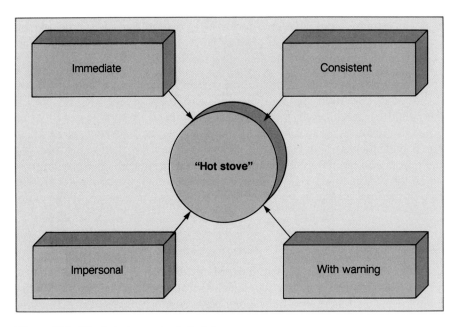

**Figure 15.5**   The hot-stove rule of discipline.

## DELEGATION OF AUTHORITY AND RESPONSIBILITY

Part of any manager's job is to get things done through people. This requires **delegation** of authority and responsibility to achieve organizational objectives. Many managers attempt to perform too much of the job themselves. In doing so, they fail to maximize the use of their own time and the abilities of individuals who work for them.

Delegation makes possible more effective performance because it can place the responsibility for decisions closest to the problems. Individuals most directly involved in an operation are usually the best equipped to solve the problems that occur at their level. Often the tendency is to delegate responsibility one level above the point at which the action is occurring.

Delegation can be motivational when individuals have the authority and responsibility to use their judgment in decision making on their jobs. An effective way to create pride in job performance is to involve individuals in decision making. As a result, individuals become more involved in their jobs and more committed to quality results.

If an organization is to develop individuals capable of advancing in the organization, employees must be given chances to exercise authority and responsibility. An effective way to develop employees is to ensure that they learn to exercise authority and accept responsibility through delegation.  Delegation may not be effective, however, when there is a lack of agreement between superior and subordinate on specific areas of authority and responsibility.[15] The

---

### Advantages of Delegation ════════════════════════

- Manager can't handle everything
- Decisions by people closest to the problems
- Pride in results from one's own judgment
- Feeling of involvement
- Development of employees
- Effective use of individual abilities

---

subordinate may not understand specifically what is necessary to assume authority and responsibility. To delegate effectively, managers must clearly understand their own responsibilities and authority. If they cannot clearly define them, managers will not know what responsibilities or authority can be delegated most effectively. These and other reasons for the failure of delegation are shown in Figure 15.6.

## Goal Orientation

If delegation is to work effectively throughout an organization, there must be a goal orientation. Individuals should understand the relationship of their job to the overall objectives of the organization. When delegation is supported by programs of individual and organizational goal setting, it becomes easier to delegate effectively because individuals understand how their jobs contribute to the overall operation of the organization.[16] Individuals' roles in achieving organizational objectives should be defined by management and employees who must work together to arrive at the results to be achieved. Results should be periodically reviewed, and there should be specific time periods set for accomplishing objectives.

## Delegation Involves Risk Taking

A manager does not always know that subordinates will be able to achieve the desired results. If the manager is unwilling to take risks, he or she usually will not delegate effectively but will attempt to perform too much of the job. When a manager is unwilling to take risks by allowing individuals to make decisions, the chance for individual development and motivation is reduced.

Delegation can become ineffective when individuals perceive the manager as requiring "nothing less than perfection." Under these conditions, individuals will seldom accept responsibility because they will be unable to live up to the manager's expectations. For delegation to be effective, the entire process must occur in a supportive environment where managers seek to help individuals

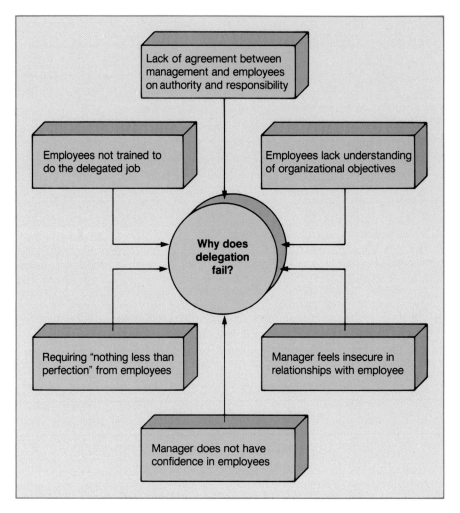

**Figure 15.6**   Why delegation fails.

correct their mistakes rather than punish them when mistakes occur. The process of delegation must be a part of the total learning process for individuals.

### Managers Must Develop Secure Relationships with Employees

When a manager has insecure relationships with individuals, he or she will usually be extremely hesitant to delegate. One reason for insecure relationships is that the manager has no real confidence in the workers. When workers realize that the manager feels this way, they are usually reluctant to accept responsibility. In personal relationships, managers must ensure that individuals understand what is expected of them. To develop an effective understanding with their employees, they must establish a climate of open communication. Individuals should feel free to ask questions and clarify their own positions regarding their authority and responsibility.

For delegation to contribute to maximum motivation, it must provide challenges related to the job.[17] Often, individuals are delegated responsibilities only for the undersirable tasks that the manager does not want to perform. Where delegation works most effectively, individuals are challenged through the delegation of responsibility to make job-related decisions. Workers will be challenged when they are responsible for planning and controlling activities related to their jobs.

## *Focus on Results and Goal Attainment*

Delegation works most effectively when individuals are responsible for results and not for specific steps to be performed. When individuals are responsible for the results in a goal-oriented environment, they will tend to accept responsibility naturally. To encourage this tendency, management must reward those who are effective in achieving results. Management must allow individuals as much latitude as possible in the methods they use to get jobs done. When the focus is on results and goal attainment, there is less need for specific operating procedures, and specific rules can be held to a minimum. When individuals are rewarded for achievement of results, they usually seek out additional responsibility.

*Fix the Problem, Not the Blame*    If delegation is to contribute to the attainment of organizational goals, managers must guard against responding to problems by looking for someone to blame. Problems must be analyzed to determine why they occurred and how management can help individuals avoid encountering the same problem in the future. Management must concentrate on developing effective performance by supporting individual development. This can be done effectively when there is an attitude of helping rather than one of controlling or blaming.

Figure 15.7 shows the various ways in which management can help create a climate for effective delegation.

The delegator's role in an organization requires that the manager develop "the will to manage." A manager with the will to manage gets satisfaction from leading and supporting individuals in the achievement of organizational goals. The manager must enjoy the success of employees.

## EFFECTIVE SUPERVISION

The supervision of employees is a constant challenge. There is always room for improving performance. **Supervision** involves both the utilization of resources and getting work done through the efforts of other people. **Effective supervision** depends on both the individual effort of the supervisor and the productivity that employees achieve. Satisfaction from supervising should be derived from the accomplishments of others.

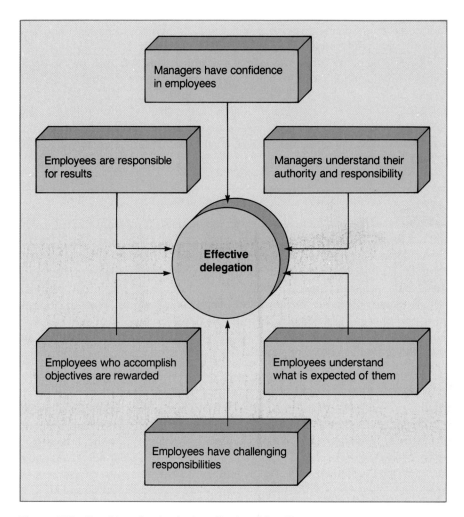

**Figure 15.7**  Conditions for developing effective delegation.

Effective supervision involves much more than giving orders and administering discipline. The supervisor who sees the job as bossing people around finds that people do not respond with their best effort. Most employees expect their supervisor to assume a number of roles, including those of leader, adviser, and consultant. In these roles, the supervisor is responsible for both rewarding and disciplining employees. Providing opportunities for individual need satisfaction through the achievement of organizational objectives is the basis for effective supervision.

The effective supervisor sees the job as an obligation to create a climate of support by being open and receptive to people's ideas. Sharing information and delegating are important in supporting employees.

By relating to your employees in the behavioral style appropriate to each, you can enhance your effectiveness as a supervisor and improve their performance.[18]

Effective supervisors recognize employee needs for responsibility, recognition, and growth. They develop methods that provide opportunities for satisfaction of these needs. Effective supervisors supply information and advice to employees when necessary, but they generally avoid looking over an employee's shoulder. They emphasize personal responsibility and accountability while providing a climate of freedom for work accomplishment.

The role of the supervisor should involve trying to draw out and develop the best of each employee and to direct behavior toward achieving both employee and organizational objectives. To do this the supervisor must earn the respect and cooperative support of employees.

## Supervisor as Leader

The effective leader does not hold the opinion that employees only want "a fair day's pay for a fair day's work." For a few employees this may be true, but many other needs usually exist in a work situation.

The effective supervisor's leadership style usually involves the following:

1. Delegation of as much decision-making authority as the employee can effectively handle
2. Trust in the judgment of employees to try to make the best decision
3. Obtaining input from employees on decisions that will affect them
4. Listening to what employees have to say on issues that concern them

The general pattern of the supervisor's leadership is more important than any one action or behavior. Being consistent in all areas of leadership helps improve productivity.

*Rules*   Employees should know why each rule exists and how rules will be enforced. Rules should be specific and cover only areas over which the organization has legitimate authority. If a supervisor cannot justify a rule to employees, he or she should bring the matter to the attention of the next higher level of management for clarification and interpretation.

*Fairness*   Favoritism should be avoided. However, people are different and may require different treatment in special cases.

When an employee has violated an organizational rule, the following procedure should be used:

1. Approach the individual about it in private.
2. Explain what was wrong and why it was wrong.
3. Allow the individual to explain his or her version. Listen attentively.
4. Do not become emotional.
5. Give the employee an opportunity to suggest solutions.

6. If justified, follow through with the predetermined discipline for such cases.

7. Try to create an atmosphere of learning and improvement rather than one of punishment and judgment.

*Criticism*   Criticizing an employee in private is far better than in front of others. Private criticism allows the person criticized to maintain respect in his or her peer group. Criticism should be stated in matter-of-fact, unemotional tones. It should be presented in relation to job performance rather than personality characteristics. The employee should have an opportunity to explain his or her view of the situation.

*Giving Orders*   Often employees learn more about their jobs if orders are kept to a minimum. Effective supervisors encourage individuals to ask questions. Questions allow the supervisor to display true interest in helping employees do a better job.

Leadership effectiveness, in addition to requiring patience, tolerance, and consistency, is determined by one's skill in developing a personal view of employee behavior. This means that supervisors need to (1) recognize the feelings and attitudes that they bring to a situation, (2) have an accurate evaluation of their own experiences, and (3) develop an ability to understand what others mean by their actions and words.

*Handling Mistakes*   Honest mistakes by individuals must be handled carefully. Snap judgments, criticism, or punishment may achieve a temporary solution, but it won't be long before affected employees will be seeking ways to avoid new responsibilities. In the end, an employee may learn only how to avoid being caught and to push the blame on to others.

However, employee mistakes should not be ignored. When they occur, the supervisor should do the following:

1. Call the mistakes to the employee's attention.

2. Explain the proper action and provide correct information.

3. Find out what the problem was from the employee's point of view.

4. Encourage the employee to learn and improve from mistakes.

5. Avoid embarrassing the employee in front of others.

*Decision Making*   Some supervisors look upon their job as the center of all decision making in their area of authority. The supervisor may think that failing to make each and every decision possible is shirking from management duties. Yet effective supervisors find that letting employees handle work-related decisions whenever possible is often more effective.

---

## Conditions for Participation in Decision Making

When involving employees in decision making, the following conditions should be met:

1. Allow ample time for participation by employees *before* action is required.
2. Participants must have the abilities, knowledge, and experience needed to make job-related decisions.
3. Participants must communicate with each other and with their supervisor.
4. Employees should not feel threatened if they participate or if they decide not to participate.

---

Participation in decision making allows employees to satisfy their needs for achievement, responsibility, and growth. One of the main benefits is to increase individuals' sense of responsibility and self-respect.

### Delegation

Delegation provides individuals the opportunity to achieve, accept responsibility, and earn recognition. Delegation is a way to give individuals broader areas of responsibility than they would otherwise have, including more influence on planning, organizing, and controlling their job activities.

To delegate effectively, a supervisor should do the following:

1. Provide individuals with specific objectives and make certain there is agreement on what is to be accomplished.
2. Help individuals set goals for their jobs—don't set goals for them.
3. As far as possible, allow individuals to develop methods of achieving goals but be available for counseling and support.

Delegation is a way to support the worth and importance of the individual. It frees the supervisor for other work and allows time for planning and coordinating, so the supervisor does not become lost in daily operational details.

### Communication

No single supervisory skill is more important in improving performance and productivity than the ability to communicate. In addition to providing information, supervisors need to be receptive to the complaints and suggestions of employees.

Communication is most effective when it leads to **mutual influence** between supervisor and employees. It should be a two-way street, with ideas, information, and suggestions flowing freely between supervisor and employees. Each should be willing to listen and learn from the other.

The following are suggestions for effective communication:

1. Keep an open mind.
2. Don't enter into a dialogue with the attitude that you are always absolutely right.
3. Do more listening than talking and encourage suggestions.
4. Try to increase face-to-face communication with employees.
5. Be sensitive to the world of the employees. Try to understand the needs of employees.
6. Use direct and simple language. Don't try to impress people with a fancy vocabulary.
7. When listening, be alert to unspoken or unintended meanings in what is said.

A good portion of a supervisor's communication should be in the form of feedback to employees about where they stand and how they are doing. Supervisors should inform employees about changes that will affect them.

Effective communication is based on mutual trust and respect. Employees must believe that they can have the supervisor's attention when it is needed. They must also believe that what is said to their supervisor in confidence will remain in confidence. An effective supervisor never underestimates the value of open lines of communication.

## Positive Reinforcement

All the supervisory behaviors discussed have one thing in common: desired employee behaviors must be reinforced. **Positive reinforcement** is necessary because employees perform in ways that are most satisfying to them. By providing reinforcement, performance can be improved.

A supervisor should be concerned with rewards such as responsibility, recognition, growth, and opportunity for achievement. Some of these can be provided by the supervisor (recognition, responsibility), and some must be "earned" by the employee (growth, achievement).

To use rewards effectively to stimulate better performance, a few essential factors need to be considered:

1. The desired performance level must first be specified and clearly understood.
2. Rewards must be appropriate to the performance and the individual.
3. Rewards should follow as soon as possible after the desired behavior has occurred.

Effective supervision is in itself a positive reinforcement. The more supervisors build employees' positive self-image, the more they will be willing to support efforts to reach organizational objectives.

**Figure 15.8**   Basis of effective supervision.

The factors contributing to effective supervision are summarized in Figure 15.8.

## SELF–ASSESSMENT DISCUSSION

**1.** (1) Goal orientation is a key to effective employee performance, management effectiveness, and organizational success.

**2.** (6) Confidence and self-esteem are keys to performance effectiveness.

**3.** (1) Good supervisors recognize individual differences and treat employees as individuals.

**4.** (6) Delegation of authority to employees is an effective confidence-building technique and creates increased job interest.

**5.** (1, 6) Supervisors are responsible for both rewarding and disciplining employees.

**6.** (6) Leadership is ideally characterized by consistency. Employees want managers with predictable behavior, even if the manager is a strong disciplinarian.

**7.** (6) Effective delegation must be goal oriented.

**8.** (1) When people set goals for themselves in conjunction with their immediate managers, they become more directly and strongly involved in achieving those goals.

**9.** (6) Authority-oriented delegation styles provide little incentive for improved performance. Achievement orientation is far more effective.

**10.** (6) The hot-stove rule states that discipline not only should be immediate, impersonal, and consistent but also should be with warning.

### QUICK REVIEW

I. Managerial Effectiveness and Performance Improvement
   A. Management has been facing an increasing number of problems in attempting to increase performance.
   B. Many individuals no longer find it desirable to look to authoritative standards as guides.
   C. No easy gimmicks can produce conditions for long-term productivity.

II. Goal Orientation
   A. In an authority-oriented climate, individuals are provided with little incentive to increase effectiveness.
   B. Goal-oriented employees see job goals as a meaningful part of organizational objectives and as a means for achieving personal goals.
   C. Goal orientation is supported by a management that depends on meaningful goals and supportive systems.
   D. Goal setting can encourage achievement through:
      1. Individual involvement in goal setting.
      2. Individuals being able to relate personal goals to organizational goals.
      3. Organizations with supportive systems for goal attainment.
   E. Two methods of implementing goal setting systems include:
      1. Starting at the top and then proceeding to other segments of the organization.
      2. Starting with a selected branch, department, or division.

III. A System for Goal Setting
   A. Agreement between employee and supervisor on the individual's job description, responsibilities, and results to be achieved.
   B. Performance planning and setting of individual goals.
   C. Agreement of employee and superior on goals, standards, and checkpoints.
   D. Evaluation of results by both employee and immediate supervisor. Judgment is based on accomplishments.

IV. Innovation and Creativity
   A. Innovation and creativity are necessary for an organization to achieve long-term effectiveness.
   B. An environment for creativity makes use of people's creative potential at all levels and in all activities of the organization.

   C. Factors often contributing to the development of innovation and creativity are channels of communication, encouragement of new ideas, broad participation in planning, and management rewards for creativity.

V. Constructive Discipline

   A. The objective of discipline should be to develop more effective performance.

   B. The most desirable and effective discipline is self-discipline.

   C. Effective discipline involves learning through experience.

   D. Disciplinary action should be directed against the act, done in private, handled constructively, and administered fairly and consistently.

VI. Delegation of Authority and Responsibility

   A. Delegation makes it possible for more effective performance.

   B. Delegation can improve performance when individuals have the authority and responsibility to use their judgments in decision making.

   C. For delegation to work effectively, it must be goal oriented.

   D. Delegation involves managerial risk.

   E. Managers must develop secure relationships with subordinates.

   F. Effective delegation focuses on results and goal attainment.

VII. Effective Supervision

   A. Supervisors are responsible for both rewarding and disciplining employees.

   B. Effective supervisors share information and delegate responsibility.

   C. Leadership style should be characterized by consistency and fairness.

   D. Having employees make work-related decisions whenever possible is most effective.

   E. Effective communication is based on mutual trust and respect.

## KEY TERMS

| | | |
|---|---|---|
| Goal orientation | Constructive discipline | Effective supervision |
| Organizational climate | Hot-stove rule | Mutual influence |
| Goal-setting systems | Delegation | Positive reinforcement |
| Innovation and creativity | Supervision | |

## DISCUSSION QUESTIONS

1. Discuss the characteristics and effects of a goal-oriented organizational climate.

2. Why would an organizational climate in which goals are seen as arbitrary, confusing, unchallenging, and authority oriented develop individual feelings of failure, frustration, and apathy in employees?

3. Under what conditions is goal setting by employees most likely to lead to high levels of achievement?

4. Discuss two methods of implementing a goal-setting system in an organization.

5. What are the advantages of a goal-setting system?

6. What action can management take to develop innovation and creativity in an organization?

7. How can constructive discipline be developed in an organization?

8. Why is it necessary for a manager to develop secure relationships with subordinates for delegation to be effective?

9. Describe the characteristics of a manager you have observed who was an effective delegator.

10. What are the characteristics of an effective supervisor's leadership style?

11. To use rewards effectively, what factors should a supervisor keep in mind?

---

**EXERCISE**

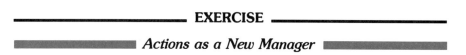

*Actions as a New Manager*

You have just graduated from college and taken your first management position. You have been hired to manage a motel that is part of a large chain of motels. Most of the thirty-seven employees have worked for the motel for more than five years. When you were hired, it was clear that you were to maintain the high levels of customer satisfaction that the motel chain enjoyed. The position of corporate management is that customer satisfaction is a direct result of high performance by employees.

*Evaluate the following list of actions that could be taken by a new manager.* Which actions would you take? Which would you take first?

1. Keep orders to a minimum and encourage employees to ask questions.

2. Establish your position as the manager by criticizing employees in front of others so the criticism will have the greatest possible impact.

3. Work with each employee to set goals for his or her job and establish evaluation procedures.

4. Make sure you understand the policies and procedures of the corporation.

5. Identify and recognize good performance by employees.

6. Meet with employees individually to learn about their jobs and any problems they may be having.

7. Make yourself the center of all decision making by making each and every decision possible.

8. Maintain face-to-face communication with employees by practicing MBWA (Management By Wandering Around).

9. Don't ask employees for any information on how things have been done in the past, because it would weaken your management position.

10. Determine training needed by the employees and see that it is provided.

11. Delegate as much decision-making authority as the employees can effectively handle.

## TWO POINTS OF VIEW

### "The Perfectionist"

*What would you do if you were the manager?*

You are the manager of a machine shop that makes specialized tools and parts for aircraft manufacturers. The employees are highly trained and experienced machinists. You have recently promoted Terry West to be a shop supervisor. Terry has been with the organization for fifteen years, and everyone recognizes him as an outstanding machinist.

After two weeks of Terry West's supervision, the employees working for him requested a meeting with you. They stated that Mr. West was making it impossible for them to get their work done. They characterized him as a nitpicker and perfectionist.

Comments made to you by the machinists included the following: "Terry is rejecting finished parts that meet the specifications because he believes they are not perfect." "The only right way is HIS way." "The supervisor's job has gone to his head." "He wants everything cleaned up twenty times a day—he must think this is a hospital." "Terry may be perfect, but we aren't." "He stands over us like we don't know how to do our job." "If you don't do a job exactly the way he would have done it, then you're wrong." "If he keeps telling me about his high standards, I'm going to get some earplugs."

As you analyze the situation, you conclude that the two most pressing problems are that the machinists may go to your boss with their complaints about Terry West and that the costs in your department are increasing because Terry is rejecting parts that meet specifications.

*What would you do if you were Terry West?*

You have recently been promoted to shop supervisor in the machine shop of a company that makes specialized tools and parts for aircraft manufacturers. You have worked for the organization for fifteen years as a machinist. You were told that you were promoted because you were the best machinist in the shop. You have always had excellent interpersonal relations with the other machinists, and several of them are close friends.

When you accepted the supervisory position, you promised yourself that you would make this the best machine shop in the industry. During your fifteen years as a machinist, you had observed a lot of sloppy work and machinists who had work stations that looked like pigpens. Your first course of action as a supervisor was to personally inspect the parts produced by the machinists and have them reworked if they did not meet the high standards you had set for the shop. Some grumbling took place, but the quality of the work increased to the point where you were very proud of the machinists' performance.

You next focused your attention on the cleanliness of the shop. By inspecting the work stations each morning and afternoon, you were able to achieve a drastic improvement in the appearance of the shop, but the machinists complained even more about the cleanliness standards than they had about the quality requirements. You had thought at the time that complaining about their supervisor was just a way of life for machinists.

Although you are pleased with the progress being made in achieving higher standards of performance, you are becoming concerned about the complaints of the machinists. The secretary for the manager of the machine shop has told you that the machinists had a meeting with the manager to complain about your methods of supervision. She told you that they had requested "in no uncertain terms" that the manager shape you up, "or there will be big trouble."

## *ENDNOTES*

1. E. A. Locke and G. P. Latham, *Goal Setting: A Motivational Technique That Works!* (Englewood Cliffs, N.J.: Prentice-Hall, 1984).
2. M. Scott Myers, "Conditions for Manager Motivation," *Harvard Business Review* (January–February 1966): 66.
3. Don Hellriegel, John W. Slocum, and Richard W. Woodman, *Organizational Behavior*, 4th ed. (St. Paul: West, 1986), p. 441.
4. Miriam Erez, P. Christopher Earley, and Charles L. Hulin, "The Impact of Participation on Goal Acceptance and Performance: A Two-Step Model," *Academy of Management Journal* (March 1985): 50–66.
5. James C. Naylor and Daniel R. Ilgen, "Goal Setting: A Theoretical Analysis of a Motivational Technology," *Research in Organizational Behavior* 6 (1984): 95–140.
6. John R. Schermerhorn, Jr., *Management for Productivity*, 2d ed. (New York: Wiley, 1986), p. 504.
7. Douglas M. McGregor, *The Professional Manager* (New York: McGraw-Hill, 1967), p. 244.
8. Richard L. Daft and Richard M. Steers, *Organizations: A Micro/Macro Approach* (Glenview, Ill.: Scott, Foresman, 1986), p. 573.
9. From *Management Review* (March 1980): 29–30.
10. Walter J. Friess, "A Case History on Creativity in Industry," in *Creativity: An Examination of the Creative Process*, ed. Paul Smith (New York: Hastings House, 1959), p. 192.
11. From a speech by Harry J. Gary, quoted in *Business Week*, 27 July 1981, p. 89.
12. John Huberman, "Discipline Without Punishment," *Harvard Business Review* (July–August 1964): 62–68; John Huberman, "Discipline Without Punishment Lives," *Harvard Business Review* (July–August 1975): 6–8.
13. Janice M. Beyer and Harrison M. Trice, "A Field Study of the Use and Perceived Effects of Discipline in Controlling Work Performance," *Academy of Management Journal* (December 1984): 743–64.

**14.** George Strauss and Leondard R. Sayles, *Personnel: The Human Problems of Management*, 3d ed. (Englewood Cliffs, N.J.: Prentice-Hall, 1972), pp. 267–68.

**15.** Herbert M. Engel, "Understanding Effective Delegation," *Modern Office Technology*, (July 1984): 82–88.

**16.** Samuel C. Certo, *Principles of Modern Management*, 3d ed. (Dubuque, Iowa: Brown, 1986), p. 210.

**17.** Don Canuth, "Key Factors in Positive Delegation," *Supervisory Management* (July 1984): 6–11.

**18.** Anthony Alessandra and Jim Cathcart, "To Supervise Effectively: Know Your Employees' Behavioral Style," *Supervisory Management* (September 1985): 37–40.

---

### CASE INCIDENTS FOR PART 5

---

###  The President's Method of Improving Management 

William Davis is president of Davis Finance and Credit Corporation. He is committed to continuing management education and frequently attends management development seminars at universities in the area.

The most recent seminars that Mr. Davis attended were on philosophies of management. The seminars emphasized the work of Douglas McGregor and his Theory X and Theory Y concepts. The material presented in the seminars convinced Mr. Davis that his company would be more effective if Theory Y management was practiced by all his managers.

To implement Theory Y, he bought copies of McGregor's *The Human Side of Enterprise* and sent a copy to each manager in the company with the following memo:

> To:   All Managers/Davis Finance and Credit Corporation
> From:   William Davis, President
> Subject:   Management Practices

I have recently become convinced that we must begin practicing Theory Y management. Accompanying this memo is a copy of *The Human Side of Enterprise*, which explains how to practice Theory Y management. I expect each of you to read this book over the weekend and begin implementing the management practices next week.

Note that we are committed to Theory Y. You should realize that managers who do not implement Theory Y practices will find it difficult to remain with this organization.

1. Are the president's actions consistent with the assumptions and practices associated with Theory Y?

2. What reactions do you think the managers will have to President Davis's memo?

3. What other courses of action could the president take to implement Theory Y?

### The Overtime Decision

In a natural gas company, an order was issued by the president prohibiting supervisors from authorizing overtime under any conditions. A repairman was working on one of the company's gas pipelines that had developed a leak and had to be shut down. While the line was being repaired, gas had to be supplied by rerouting it through another distribution system, which increased the company's cost.

About an hour before quitting time, the repairman realized that the job could not be finished during regular working hours. He asked the supervisor whether he should work overtime to finish the repair. He estimated that it would require two hours. The supervisor telephoned the maintenance manager, since he did not want to make a decision on an exception to the overtime order. The maintenance manager did not want to make a decision either, so he telephoned the construction manager, who told him to use his own discretion. The "decision" was transmitted down the line to the supervisor, who was told to use his discretion.

1. What are the reasons for and against the supervisor approving the overtime?

2. What decision do you think the supervisor made and why?

3. What was the president's objective in prohibiting superviors from authorizing overtime?

4. What assumptions do you think the president had about employees and human behavior?

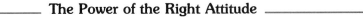

## The Power of the Right Attitude

"Your approach to customers should be as customer service specialists rather than salespeople," said Grace Mitchell to her five district managers. As marketing manager for Topcop Electronic Office Systems Company, Grace had been largely responsible for much of the company's recent growth in a highly competitive market. "All of our salespeople not only must look and act like professionals, but they must see themselves as experts in helping customers solve office problems with Topcop equipment. They've got to learn to analyze problems and fit the right equipment to the right job. If the problem can be solved without new equipment, fine. In the long run, we'll have the customer's trust."

As the meeting ended, Leron Wilson, who headed the large southwestern district, remarked to Diane Stone, eastern district manager, "Grace knows her stuff. If we could get all our salespeople to have the same attitude she has, we'd have it made." "I agree," returned Diane. "She's one of the few people that I've worked for that I really admire. She looks at long-range results before the immediate bottom line."

1. What kinds of power did Grace use to get the support of her management staff?

2. If salespeople emphasized products instead of service, what action would you predict Grace would take?

3. How can Grace get her staff to reflect the same attitude she has?

## The Secretary

Mr. David Owens is the new regional marketing manager for Scientific Products, Inc. He is thirty-six years old, and top-level management considers him among the most effective sales managers in the company. He is often consulted by the vice-president for marketing on major marketing decisions, and the rumor is that he is being groomed for a vice-presidential position.

On assuming this new managerial position, Mr. Owens found that he had an effective sales force composed of highly motivated and extremely competent salespeople. His major problem in the regional office appeared to center on the secretary, Judy Campbell. The salespeople began making frequent comments about the problems they were having with the secretary. He heard statements such as: "I hate to come in the regional office because I get insulting remarks from the secretary." "I have never seen a secretary who complained so much about her work." "You should do something about the secretary—she thinks she runs the company." "The secretary challenges every statement I make. I am getting damn tired of it." "There is too much back talk from the secretary."

Mr. Owens tried to respond neutrally to the comments from the salespeople and to evaluate the work of the secretary objectively. Judy had been in the position for four years and had come well recommended from her previous job. But Mr. Owens began to notice other problems related to her performance. There was little resemblance between the letters and sales memos he dictated and what was typed. When he pointed this out to the secretary, she usually commented that she had captured the intent and tried to write the correspondence in the most effective way.

He had difficulty finding material that should have been in the office files. On several occasions when he had asked Judy to locate materials, she began going through the papers on his desk to look for the information.

Judy was also responsible for supervising four clerk typists who worked in the office. At times they appeared to not have work assigned or were working on items of low priority when higher priority work was not being done.

Mr. Owens reached the conclusion that the secretary was trying to do a good job as she saw it, but that she defined the job differently from the way he or the salespeople did. After thinking the situation over, Mr. Owens decided that he would attempt to correct matters by pointing out to Judy areas where he thought her behavior should be changed. He pursued this strategy for two weeks. He let Judy know when she made statements that irritated the salespeople and when work was not being performed as he thought it should be. The result of this strategy was that he received prolonged arguments from Judy as to why the salespeople were wrong and why work wasn't getting done.

1. If you were Mr. Owens, what specific course of action would you take to correct the situation?

2. What communication would you have with Judy Campbell regarding the content of the communication and the method of communication?

3. What guidelines should a manager follow in attempting to change or discipline the behavior of an employee like Judy?

# Part 6

# *Values and Responsibilities*

# Change: Stimulation, Guidance, and Control

_____ *Learning Objectives* _____

Many factors affect people in organizations. After reading this chapter, you should be able to do the following:

1. List some major changes in society during the past twenty years
2. Describe major characteristics of change
3. Explain ways innovation and creativity are tied to planned change
4. Utilize techniques of change introduction
5. Identify major change trends
6. Understand change as an inevitable part of both individuals and organizations

# Chapter Topics

- Change: invasion of the future
- Characteristics of change
- Types of change
- Managing change
- Organizational change techniques
- Innovation and creativity
- Problems and promises

# Preview

As the twentieth century draws to a close, many historians will note that it has incurred more changes than any—and perhaps all—of the previous centuries. At the beginning of the century, the automobile was a crude novelty, seen by many as a short-lived fad that would never replace the horse. For some, airplanes held much lower esteem. No practical use could be foreseen for their future. Electricity, which had limited applications, was viewed as a force unavailable to most people. The majority of rural homes, as well as many homes in metropolitan areas, had neither running water nor indoor toilets. Space travel, satellite communication, television, freeway systems, modern medical techniques, and large-scale international travel and commerce were either unimaginable or the subject of speculation. Computer technology, lasers, microchips, and the host of technical advances that are part of today's language were beyond belief.

One way to grasp some of the changes that affect our lives is to scan through any public library. Most books and magazines reflect changes in our society, the political organization of the world, and the diversity of humanity. In each of its monthly issues, *Scientific American* magazine has two feature sections dealing with change. *Science and the Citizen* is concerned with recent scientific advances. Its brief articles focus on changes that either affect or will affect people now and in the future. Another section deals with science news of one hundred years ago and fifty years ago. Both highlight that we live in a world that is changing in many ways.

In 1971 one of the few remaining truly primitive tribes was discovered in the Philippine Islands. Called the gentle Tasaday, they have been extensively studied by anthropologists. Shortly after their introduction to the modern world, a well-meaning but unthinking member of a scientific party left metal knives and axes to replace the stone tools traditionally used by the Tasaday. As a result, their lives have been forever changed. Food gathering has become much easier, but unfortunately, destruction of their surrounding environment has been widely evident. A simple technical introduction has made a once primitive society not so primitive. Every change causes other changes. In the near future, the Tasaday might be neither primitive nor gentle. They are likely to become indistinguishable from the rest of us.

## SELF-ASSESSMENT

Change is an inevitability of existence. In work situations as well as in other aspects of life, the control and direction of change is a major concern. Complete the following statements as you view change and its effects. Each statement or question has a range of possible responses. A scale of 1 to 6 between two words with different meanings allows you to mark either the word that is considered correct or a place between the two words that represents some agreement and some disagreement. Selection of a high number such as 5 or 6 may be either correct or incorrect, just as selection of lower numbers may be correct or incorrect. Some responses may be partly correct and partly incorrect.

Answers based on research by behavioral scientists, with a short explanation of why the response was considered correct, may be found on page 461.

**1.** When faced with the possibility of doing things differently, people usually:

resist change  1...2...3...4...5...6  seek change

**2.** In real-life organizational settings, most changes are:

relatively minor and  1...2...3...4...5...6  major
routine                                              management and
                                                     employee
                                                     problems

**3.** Change for change's sake has been found to be:

desirable and meaningful  1...2...3...4...5...6  neither desirable
                                                 nor meaningful

**4.** Most deliberate change centers on:

specific areas  1...2...3...4...5...6  broad, general
                                       areas

**5.** Managers have learned that planned change:

offers tangible benefits  1...2...3...4...5...6  has proven to
                                                 lack any real
                                                 organizational
                                                 benefits

**6.** Management of change begins:

with the recognition that  1...2...3...4...5...6  when change
change is needed                                 occurs that has
                                                 not been planned
                                                 or expected

**7.** A key to encouraging innovation and creativity is:

a quick and appropriate  1...2...3...4...5...6  a deliberately
            response                                  slow response
                                                               after careful and
                                                               exhaustive
                                                               evaluation

**8.** Direction of change defines the way present conditions:

affect the rate  1...2...3...4...5...6  alter future
    of change                         events

**9.** A technique for minimizing resistance to change is to introduce change:

all at once to lessen  1...2...3...4...5...6  a little at a time
    long-range effects

**10.** Introduction of new technology into the work place is nearly always viewed by employees as:

a welcome relief from  1...2...3...4...5...6  a threat
    routine, boring jobs

## CHANGE: INVASION OF THE FUTURE

A common question that well-meaning adults ask children is, "What are you going to be when you grow up?" The question is, by its nature, virtually unanswerable. Although there are some jobs whose titles remain relatively unchanged, most of today's jobs did not exist when the people performing them were children. Even in those jobs that have the same title, the actual work, in most cases, has been significantly altered. We live in a world where robotics, computers with the potential for artificial intelligence, biotechnology that allows us to direct evolution, automated offices, and a flood of new approaches to improving the quality of work life are everyday events. How easily we forget that every accepted technological development brings changes in required job skills that are difficult to predict. We know only that everything changes—an undeniable fact of our existence.

*Everything Changes*    Change affects every part of our lives but is most easily recognized in the work place.

One of the first major newspapers to convert to modern computerized type setting, automatic presses, and automated insert additions was the *Miami Herald*. Modernization eliminated numerous traditional skills such as linotype and stereotype operators. It also created new jobs in computer programming, key data entry, and computerized equipment maintenance. To make the changes, management at the Miami newspaper developed innovative approaches that have served as models for other newspapers. Displaced employees were retrained for new jobs, older employees were given advanced retirement benefits, and all employees were indoctrinated into changes resulting from the newer technologies of producing daily news. Through careful planning, management had successfully managed a major change that directly affected each of its employees.

In a real sense, management of organizations is the management of change. Familiar clichés such as "It's the same old thing," "Nothing has really changed," and "You're the same as you always were" are simply not true. Change is constantly occurring in all people and in all things. Rather than let change occur as a natural consequence of the passage of time, knowledgeable managers work toward creating conditions that help control and direct events to ensure the growth and ultimate survival of their organizations. Failure to recognize change can be disastrous not only to a specific business but also to an entire industry.

Since 1970, Japan has rapidly gained an increasingly large share of the world automobile market for a number of reasons. According to James E. Harbour, one of the automobile industry's top consultants, U.S. automakers have failed to recognize changes in public tastes, including appreciation for both quality and economy.[1] Unions have failed to recognize the impact of both wages and work practices on operating costs.

Although recent union concessions and a spirit of employee-management concern that is new to the industry may help, the road to recovery will be difficult. A major reason for the Japanese cost advantage is productivity as well as wages. An average Japanese car is assembled in fourteen worker hours, compared with thirty-three hours for the average U.S. car. Greater use of robotics, improved production techniques, and the efficient use of labor all contribute to the lower rate. Although U.S. managers know the old techniques no longer work, change will be expensive, time-consuming, and painful. A great many of the needed approaches to improvement are under way at General Motors, Chrysler, Ford, and American Motors.

The invasion of the future is seen most dramatically in the rise of information-related activities. Estimates are that in 1982, almost 55 percent of the work force was engaged in the business of "generating, producing, handling, storing, transmitting, or regurgitating knowledge and information," according to Joseph F. Coates, one of the country's leading research specialists on the future.[2] Dr. Coates also points out that new occupations in the fields of energy, materials, and genetics will alter the qualifications required of the work force at a steadily increasing pace.

In 1980, the largest population age group was 20–24 years, with both the 15–19 and 25–29 age groups only slightly smaller. By the year 2000, the 35–39 age group will be the largest, with the 40–44 and 45–49 age groups close behind. One interpretation of such data is that the major work force is steadily becoming older. As a result, society in the year 2000 will reflect the values, attitudes, and beliefs of a group older than those of the mid-1980s. Work organizations will primarily comprise employees who will be, on the whole, the oldest work force in average age ever seen in the United States.

Rapid growth in new technologies, coupled with changing lifestyles, age groups, economic and political forces, as well as the way society views itself, all create a clouded view of the future.

## CHARACTERISTICS OF CHANGE

Change has a number of special characteristics that most people recognize from personal experience. For a variety of reasons, primarily habit or routine, these qualities or special features of change are frequently ignored. At least three are of vital importance to all people in work organizations and especially to managers. The first of these is **rate of change**, or the speed with which change takes place. Another significant aspect is the *direction* of change. A third characteristic involves the *diffusion* of change far beyond its point of origin.

### *Rate of Change*

During the lifetimes of most living adults, more technological and social change has occurred than in the entire previous history of humanity. A considerable body of evidence indicates that changes may continue at an even greater pace than in the past. Change, however, does not occur at the same rate for all things or sets of conditions. With the development of the small electronic calculator and its ultimate reduction in price, the slide rule—in 1974 still the primary calculating tool of students and professionals in engineering and science—has become virtually obsolete. On the other hand, the common graphite-tipped wooden pencil has changed very little since 1658, except for the addition of the eraser in the early 1700s. More subtle changes in our society have also taken place at different rates and in more complex ways.

Nearly all organizations are affected by rate change. Rapid change affecting a large segment of an organization can create a great deal more difficulty than step-by-step, carefully controlled rates of change. In addition to rates of change, managers are faced with the more unpredictable direction of change.

### *Direction of Change*

**Direction of change** is the term used to define the way present conditions will alter future events.

Beginning in the early 1930s and extending through the mid-1950s, many people believed that the small airplane—or at least some type of personal flying vehicle—would become a commonly accepted part of nearly everyone's lives. High school students were encouraged to take courses in aviation technology; books and newspaper articles hailed the coming of the air age. Aviation did change rapidly, with a tremendous impact on public transportation, but not in the predicted direction. Private aircraft as a percentage of total transportation has changed very little, while commercial air transportation has grown into an essential industry.

Direction of change as well as rate of change can cause significant problems for organizations. Some change in direction is reasonably predictable. During the past ten years, there has been a steady acceleration of unionization of federal, state, county, and municipal employees. We can predict that this change from nonaffiliated to unionized public employees will continue for some time. Other directions of change are not as easy to forecast. When the laser system of producing amplified pure light was announced in 1960, few people imagined the many directions of change it would bring. Lasers are used to treat certain eye disorders, to serve as part of some computer memory systems, to drill precise holes in steel, and to determine the exact location of a football when there is doubt about whether a first down has been made. These represent only a small number of the activities laser technology has changed. Figure 16.1 shows the varying rates and direction of change in three other areas.

In work organizations, managers are constantly concerned with the direction of the marketplace. Will the public buy more synthetic clothing than natural fiber clothing this year? What will be the requirements of new governmental regulations? Will unions ask for more benefits or shorter hours? What new technological shifts will affect the organization? Will environmental concerns outweigh production demands? All these questions demonstrate a concern for the direction of change. The need to accurately predict the course of change is as vital as forecasting how rapidly it will occur.

## Diffusion of Change

One change frequently causes other changes. The term *diffusion* means "to spread out." In most cases, change is diffused over a wider area than anticipated.

**Diffusion of change** is frequently called the "domino effect" (see Figure 16.2). An amusing television or state presentation (and a frequent pastime of some children) involves setting up hundreds of dominoes so that when the first one is pushed over, it sets up a chain reaction that runs until they all eventually

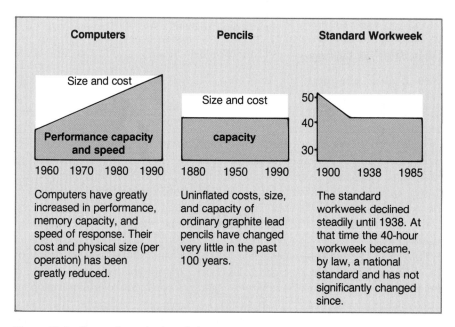

**Figure 16.1**   Comparison of rates of change.

Figure 16.2   **The domino effect.**

tumble. If dominoes are arranged in complex patterns, we can witness their fall in several different directions.

In work organizations, we frequently see diffusion. A change of weather in California that results in smaller tomato crops may in turn cause price increases in catsup and tomato paste sold in New York, layoffs at food processing plants, loss of sales by suppliers to food processors, local decreases in business activities because of lower plant payrolls, increased numbers of people receiving unemployment compensation, and either increased taxes or a rising federal debt to offset the added costs.

> At the Cordoban Chemical Company, employees accrue seniority both in their jobs and in the plant. In the event of a reduction in the work force due to lack of work, senior employees may displace employees with less seniority in lower job classifications for which the senior employees qualify. In a recent layoff due to automation of test equipment, highly skilled test technicians "bumped" process inspectors who in turn bumped processors. Affected processors displaced loaders and packers with still less seniority. The loaders and packers, in some cases, bumped custodians who displaced, in a few instances, cafeteria dishwashers. A layoff in the test area resulted in a dishwasher hunting for a new job!

Managers must constantly recognize the diffusion of change throughout an organization. A change in procurement procedures may result in changes in several other departments, such as accounting, receiving, inspection, and materi-

---

### Change and the Ripple Effect ━━━━━━━━━━━━━━━━━━

For nearly fifty years, the General Electric manufacturing plant in Ontario, California, had been one of the primary producers of electric irons in the country. Then in the spring of 1982, economic conditions forced General Electric to close the plant. The action had an immediate impact on the 850 employees laid off; and over the following days and weeks, that impact rippled outward, affecting an ever-widening circle of workers and businesses.

First hit were the service shops and establishments in Ontario. Since the 850 General Electric workers no longer had money to spend, the town's economy began to slow down. As a result, 1,200 workers in grocery stores, banks, barber shops, and many other establishments were also laid off. Next to feel the pinch were parts manufacturers and suppliers who could no longer sell their products to the GE plant. They were soon letting some of their workers go as well.

Yet the story in parts of Mexico and Indonesia was quite different. After closing its Ontario plant, General Electric opened new facilities in these two countries to manufacture plastic rather than metal household products.

One change—and rapid, multidirectional, diffuse effects.[3]

---

al control. It is virtually impossible to change any part of an organization or the way it operates without affecting, to some degree, all of its other parts.

### Coming Together

Rate of change, direction of change, and diffusion are all important concepts and usually affect organizations at the same time.

Although the General Electric case seems extreme, it is an all-too-common example of the widespread effects of only a moderate change. A dockworkers' strike in New Orleans may affect wheat prices in Montana if the strike prevents shipping to overseas markets. A simple change in the interpretation of tax laws may affect millions of taxpayers.

Change may occur slowly, rapidly, or at any rate. It may be helpful or harmful—or more likely, helpful to some and harmful to others. Either way, it cannot be stopped, only managed or altered.

### TYPES OF CHANGE

In addition to the characteristics of change (rate, direction, and diffusion), many types of change affect organizations. All require careful management attention. Each type of change can occur at different rates, can travel in many directions, and can diffuse throughout not only an organization but also a whole society.

Although we cannot list all of the types of changes that organizations are concerned with, we can classify some important types of change into three major categories. *Technological changes* that involve new equipment, materials, or facilities are the easiest to identify. A second type of change more difficult for management to deal with includes the shifts in attitudes, values, and beliefs, known as *social change*. The third category we call *internal change*. It includes the changes that affect day-to-day work activities and which are directly under management's control. Changes in job assignments, organizational structure, personnel practices, procedures, equipment, and facilities (apart from technological shifts) are grouped in the third category. These three types of change are shown in Figure 16.3.

Managers aware of change forces must plan effective ways of introducing new concepts, ideas, and courses of action. Changes within the work force also influence managerial change strategies.

### Technological Change

Whenever we find a new or better method for doing things, it frequently involves what has become known as **technological change**. In some areas of work, technological change is far more noticeable than other kinds of change. Computer-terminal cash registers and the widespread use of registers with electronic price-reading devices have changed the entire retail industry. Inventory data, departmental efficiency, clerical errors, and market planning data are available to management on an immediate request basis. Banks have moved to install more electronic tellers, electronic records management, and electronic transfer of funds. New skills are required and old ones no longer needed. Computerized production control and automated manufacturing using so-called smart machines have changed the meaning of mass production. Medical centers

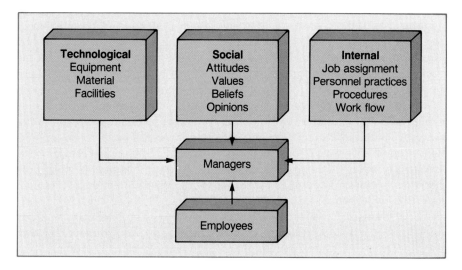

**Figure 16.3** Organizational change forces.

throughout the world rely to a large extent on automatic analyses of examination data to help in diagnosing patients' illnesses. Although machines are, in many cases, performing repetitive operations considered boring to most employees, technology is also reducing the challenge of other jobs.

Introduction of new technology into the work place is nearly always seen as a threat by the employees affected. Although some job displacement can occur, introduction of technological change is most often accompanied by a shift in employee assignments and skills rather than absolute reductions in the work force. Mechanization has drastically reduced the number of people in certain industries, such as agriculture, but increased production has created more jobs in food processing, distribution, sales, and allied service industries.

> In a desperate move, an owner of a small plant that processed local fruit into jelly and jam asked for a management consultant's help in reducing costs. A major expense item was the handling of bulk sugar shipped by rail in hundred-pound sacks to a nearby warehouse and then by truck to the plant, where the sacks were stored and emptied as needed into cooking vessels. The consultant suggested installation of a tank to hold liquid sugar that could be automatically metered during the cooking process. The entire sugar handling problem, along with its workers, was eliminated. Improved efficiency, however, ultimately resulted in expansion of the plant and an increase of additional personnel in other activities such as marketing, purchasing, shipping, and distribution.

In a world whose population will double during the next twenty-five years, with a corresponding doubling of needs (and doubling of impoverished as well as affluent people), survival will depend on increased efficiency not only in work methods but also in technology. Choosing appropriate technology, training employees, and promoting acceptance of new job requirements will continue to be major challenges to managers of work organizations.

## Social Change

Managers have little chance of controlling the **social change** that influences their organizations. Social change occurs when a large segment of the general population adopts a different set of values. Major social changes can be the result of economic shifts, threats of war, alteration in personal values, resource shortages, or any number of factors that directly or indirectly change or threaten individual and group lifestyles. In its direct effect on management, social change is most evident in attitudes toward authority, increasing demands for work that is personally rewarding, introduction of women into the work force, enforcement of equal economic opportunity, legislative requirements, and the compression of pay differentials between skill levels. Astute managers carefully note changes in social climate and adjust to their requirements rather than resist their almost overwhelming force.

Social change also affects employees in clearly discernible ways. Younger employees often exhibit different value systems than older employees, which results in mutual misunderstanding and, frequently, open dissension. Many younger employees do not show what older workers believe is proper respect. The younger employees also have expectations that differ from those of their

---

### The Computer Age Gap

As New York computer executive Charles Lecht laments, "If you were born before 1965, you're going to be out of it." Lecht is referring to the explosion in micro- and minicomputer use that has hit the 1980s. Even now, conventional typewriters, file cabinet storage, and familiar office procedures are rapidly disappearing as companies convert to the "electronic office." Small computers are becoming more powerful, memory units more compact, and printers more sophisticated. Soon every field of work and knowledge will find ways to employ these versatile machines.

Surprisingly, children adapt to computer usage much faster and with more imagination than their parents. Steven Jobs, cofounder of Apple Computer, Inc., observes, "Those kids [today's grade schoolers] know more about the new software than I do." Steven was only thirty-one in 1986—hardly an old-timer.

Perhaps the change is best reflected by the ten-year-old who stated, "When I grow up, it's going to be the Computer Age. It won't affect parents. They're out of the Computer Age. They had their own age."[4]

---

work organizations and their unions. They willingly revolt against the traditional values of both in demanding faster promotion, less control, and greater personal freedom. Managers report that the "new employee" is less frightened of authority and less subservient than more traditional employees. Younger employees' potential may prove to be a primary asset to management in the long run. They are forcing managers to reexamine their own beliefs and methods of dealing with employees. Bradford Boyd, in his excellent *Management Minded Supervision*, points out that, ultimately, work is controlled by employees, not managers.[5] Whether work is accomplished is the choice of the employee, not the manager. Increasingly, employees realize this.

In the widely read book *Work in America*, published by the Department of Health and Human Services, a study by researchers from the University of Michigan emphasizes a long-term social change recognized by management theorists for many years. In rating job characteristics such as security, safety, pay, adequate help and assistance, seeing the results of one's work, and other similar items, interesting work was chosen as the most important job consideration by more of the 1,053 employees sampled than any other factor rated. Although the need is not new, many workers increasingly seek interesting work that is relevant to their lives. A major challenge facing management now and in the future is the necessity as well as the desirability for providing work that allows personal psychological growth opportunities as well as pay.

Evidence indicates that Americans adjust rapidly to social change. Prior to 1964, many colleges and universities, particularly is southern states, had no blacks participating in sports programs. By 1974, an all-white student body or athletic program was considered an oddity. Before 1972, women assigned to field engineering positions by utility companies were virtually nonexistent. Today, in contrast, women are in nearly all utility company classifications, including the previously male-dominated field engineering positions. The same changes, noticeable at first but now so common that they are unnoticed, are true for nearly all fields and levels of work. Problems do arise, however, from sometimes unexpected sources. When women patrol officers began working as partners with male officers, one city police chief reported that, although he had few problems with the new officers, the wives of male employees were constantly checking and accusing his department of encouraging "home wrecking." After a few months, complaints subsided and women patrol officers were fully accepted by both fellow workers and the community at large.

***Wage Compression***    Although it is essentially an economic problem, wage compression also marks a major social change. Truck drivers often earn more than dock managers; school custodians may be paid nearly as much as school principals and considerably more than beginning teachers; workers in a warehouse often earn as much and frequently more money than the office manager for the facility. Differences between money paid for necessary work requiring little skill and work requiring long periods of specialized training have steadily been compressed. Trained personnel are often resentful, and management may believe it is paying too much for too little. On the other hand, workers performing the low-skilled tasks resent what they perceive are the unfair attitudes of skilled employees. The disappearance of financial elitism in the work force has in many cases become a reality.

Management's success in dealing with social change hinges on sensitivity to rapidly changing values, recognition of forces that bring such changes, and flexibility in adjusting policy and organizational style, rather than resistance to such changes. Effective communication, planned participation, improved job design, and careful implementation of policies are all necessary.

## Internal Change

Within all work organizations, changes are constantly taking place. Those based on management decisions and unrelated to technology or social change are called **internal changes**. Many changes are relatively routine and cause few management problems. Others are far more difficult and require careful attention. The impact of change is determined by how much it disturbs what employees perceive as a balanced, nonthreatening situation. Change in job assignment in some organizations, where people are usually assigned one particular set of tasks, can be threatening and cause a great deal of unrest. In organizations that regularly rotate employees through a variety of assignments, job shifts may seem perfectly normal and routine.

Changes in organization structure, such as combining departments or creating new functions, are frequently difficult for both managers and nonmanagement employees. Changes imply a shift in power—someone new will be in

---

## Communicating a Change ━━━━━━━━━━━━━━━━━━━━

Long before it was generally recognized by other employees, the project manager of a large chemical producer's "Environmental Equipment Development" program learned that new approaches by a competitive firm would eventually cause his project, the equipment manufacture, to be abandoned. Subsequent discussions with higher-level management confirmed that all people associated with environmental equipment development would have to be terminated if they couldn't be placed in other segments of the organization. To meet current obligations, the project manager was told he would have to keep his work force of twenty-three specialists working at close to peak efficiency for sixty days and then lay them off in a period of two weeks.

The project manager knew that his department would learn of the impending reduction in force. As he saw it, his alternatives were: (1) try to hide the real impact of the layoff until work on hand was nearly complete, (2) tell selected personnel that they would be affected, (3) let his section managers break the news as the rumors became widely known, or (4) call all of his department to a meeting and explain what he foresaw for the forthcoming period. He chose to follow the last alternative and openly explained the situation. He also let workers know that he was working with the personnel department to help relocate as many people as possible and was personally contacting other firms who might need the special skills possessed by his employees. Contrary to his worst expectations and those of his immediate superior, morale actually increased and work was accomplished on time. One of his section heads explained, "We knew it was coming, but somehow hearing it from you made it seem not quite as bad and not your fault."

---

charge. As long as organizational changes in structure are nonthreatening to those affected, there is little resistance. A perceived loss of status or position of influence can be disrupting to those affected.

No change in an organization other than complete closure affects employees and management as traumatically as a major reduction in work force.

Although openness and honesty are not always cure-alls, they are effective starting places in planning organizational change of any kind.

As we observed earlier, one could not list all of the kinds of changes that occur as a result of managerial action within an organization. The degree of success a manager has in implementing changes is dependent on careful assessment of how employees will react to the change and to the ultimate goals planned. Effective managers of change use a variety of techniques to assure smooth transitions from old to newer and more effective ways of accomplishing work.

## MANAGING CHANGE

In a real sense, managers accomplish work not only through the efforts of others but also through planning, organizing, implementing, and controlling change. They must recognize the human processes involved in change and know how to use a variety of techniques in introducing it. Management of change begins with the recognition that change is needed. Asking the right questions is a good place to start planning for change. What needs to be done to accomplish work easier or more efficiently? Why are we doing this the way we are? How can we improve what we're doing? Planned changes begin not only with identifying needed change but also with the recognition that people are going to be affected. Success or failure may depend on their reactions.

### *Reactions to Change*

Nearly sixty years ago, William Isaac Thomas, a sociologist well known at the time, identified what he believed to be the four basic personality forces, or "wishes," of people:

1. The wish for new experiences
2. The wish for security
3. The wish for recognition
4. The wish for response

Although modern behavioral science has long since abandoned Thomas's view of personal needs, his viewpoint is useful in looking at reactions to change.

Many people, as Thomas predicted, do seem to seek new experiences. Studies of limited-scope, repetitive jobs, such as stacking boxes all day long, counting forms, filing reports, checking bottles for cracks and dirt, sorting grocery coupons, or any other "dull" jobs, consistently show high rates of turnover, absenteeism, or other symptoms of dissatisfaction. In such cases, employees usually seek and welcome change. When change is not initiated by management, employees will frequently create their own by disrupting work, staging an accident, or in some cases, developing a resentment toward management. A growing body of evidence indicates that employees who are provided a variety of activities with minimum successive repetition of the same task show a greater degree of job satisfaction. This observed need for new experiences can be a valuable clue to managers responsible for designing jobs.

However, according to Thomas's theory, when change is perceived as a potential or possible threat, it is frequently resisted. With the exception of those who constantly seek risks as a way of obtaining recognition, self-esteem, or self-fulfillment, most people are somewhat dubious of change that can be a threat to their status, influence, pay, or job.

In planning for change, then, managers are faced with two seemingly conflicting types of human behavior: the need for change and the **change resistance,** both acting simultaneously.

Some resistance to change may be based on a logical analysis of its probable effects. If a change is seen as making work more difficult or less efficient,

---

### Making the Move Smooth ━━━━━━━━━━━━━━━━━━

When it became obvious that it had outgrown its present facilities, management of the Gulf-Western Telephone Company decided to move to a new, more modern, and larger facility. When the announcement was made, virtually every manager was deluged with complaints. "The new facility is too far away." "Parking is no good at the new place." "The new building is in a strange neighborhood." The complaints went on and on.

To help ease the disruption caused by the impending move, employees were taken in groups by their immediate supervisor and his or her department manager on a guided tour of the new facility. All employees were shown exactly where their desk or work station would be located, where they would park, the new cafeteria, and given a tour of neighboring shopping centers. Prior to the move, a map of the new facility provided to each employee showed their new office and even desk location by number. Complaints were dramatically reduced. When the actual move was made, there was little turnover in personnel or loss of efficiency.

---

resistance will frequently be apparent. A great deal of resistance to change, however, is emotional and is the result of fear of failure, loss of security, or lack of understanding of possible benefits. Over a period of time, managers have developed ways of alleviating both types of resistance, as shown in Figure 16.4.

1. Encouraging participation in planning and implementing change by the people directly affected is a useful method of minimizing resistance. A north-central railway company placed a large piece of plywood on the wall of the employee lunchroom with a simple sign asking "How should the shop be remodeled?" After some hesitation, small models of carefully labeled machines and equipment began appearing on the board. At the end of a two-month period, the shop superintendent announced that a study had been made of the employees' shop layout and that it had been accepted by management. The new shop is still a source of pride to the employees who helped in its planning.

   Participation in developing procedures, improving work methods, and setting goals has also been effective. In introducing change through participation, however, management must carefully avoid any suggestion of manipulation, condescending attitudes, unfounded criticism of employee efforts, and failure to explain lack of management action. Once destroyed by improper or inept handling of decisions based on employee participation, management credibility is usually lost forever.

2. Change in many cases can be introduced in small increments. Gradual, step-by-step changes allow adjustment over an extended period of time. An example of this technique is the introduction of metric measurement

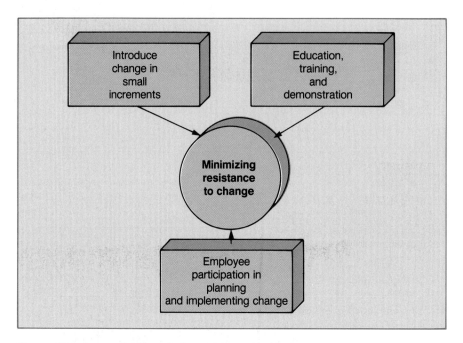

**Figure 16.4**   Approaches to reducing resistance to change.

in the United States. In work organizations, new equipment or methods are frequently added in gradual steps.

3. If properly administered, education and training that demonstrate the personal as well as organizational benefits of the planned change can often alter resistance to change. Care must be taken to explain both disadvantages as well as overriding advantages when education for change is undertaken.

Although many techniques of introducing change are available, a cardinal rule in all is to carefully plan, expect some resistance, and realize that most people will adapt to positive change with positive attitudes. Unless definite benefits can be seen by the people most affected, however, change introduction can be a bumpy road.

## Three Types of Change, Three Types of Results

During the past few years, a number of major changes have affected the core values and way of life for many people. In work organizations, these changes are especially significant. The following are three important changes that will probably continue for some time into the future:

1. *The changed status of women in organizations.* With little doubt, a highly significant social change of the twentieth century has

been the changing status of women in organizations, especially in the United States. As late as the end of the 1960s, women in the work place were most often thought of as "cake winners." By the end of the 1970s, most women in organizations were major contributors to family income, sole supporters of themselves and frequently their children, and in many cases, major wage earners for family units. In the 1980s, women have increasingly become part of higher levels of management and have earned parity with men in most professions. As time progresses, women and men will have little or no status difference in organizations. Although political offices are still dominated by men and most chief executive officers of major Fortune 500 companies are men, such will probably not be the case by the year 2000.

2. *Internationalization of industries.* Business schools of major universities are increasingly urging their students to become involved in international business studies. Companies have operated on an international basis for many years, and extensive evidence indicates that many industries are becoming international. With the advent of a joint General Motors–Toyota corporation in Fremont, California, a true international industry came into existence. In the construction industry, skilled professionals, equipment operators, and craftspeople from developed Asian and European countries find themselves working alongside Canadian, Australian, and U.S. counterparts on projects that represent a joining together of several international construction companies. As both transportation and communication on a worldwide basis continue to improve, internationalization of entire industries will become more feasible and economically sensible.

3. *Office automation.* Large-scale computerization of manufacturing has had mixed results. Some organizations have learned that the best approach is to introduce computerized technology in small steps rather than in large doses. Both the Ford Motor Company and General Motors Corporation have been trying to develop plants of the future, and both have discovered that automation may not be a total cure-all. James Harbor, one of America's best-known automobile industry consultants, has said that automation so far has turned out to be more show than substance. This trouble in manufacturing, however, has not been true of office automation. Word processing, records maintenance, computerized accounting, a wide range of data-based information systems, and new multiuser computer communication systems have changed most offices forever and will continue to do so. Almost every type of organization has been able to successfully organize its office operations. A consequence has been a continuing series of profound changes in office operations, required skills and knowledge, and organizational formats.

## ORGANIZATIONAL CHANGE TECHNIQUES

Although most deliberate change centers on a specific problem area, altering the basic way an entire organization functions is sometimes desirable. Nearly all such changes come from the recognition that interpersonal relations, attitudes, or fundamental ways of managing and operating need improvement.

Some popular change techniques include management by objectives, organizational development, survey feedback, behavior modification, transactional analysis, and contingency approaches. Frequently, two or more methods are used simultaneously. A brief description of these approaches to change will show how they differ.

### *Management by Objectives*

Approximately twenty years ago, Dr. Peter Drucker, a highly respected management writer, consultant, and university professor, stated that the only way management performance can be objectively evaluated is by results. If a manager commits him- or herself to achieving specific, clearly defined, measurable objectives within a definite time period, then performance can be measured according to what was or was not achieved. Drucker's philosophy, although not a new or revolutionary concept, served as a basis for the development of what is now popularly called **management by objectives (MBO)**. In its simplest terms, MBO is a systematic approach to setting organizational goals and determining how well they have been attained.

Although most careful management planning includes some elements of the MBO process, the system has some unique features:

1. MBO ideally involves everyone in an organization. Each person defines in clear, unambiguous terms what he or she intends to achieve in a given period of time, how he or she will achieve the intended goals, and when each of the separate goals will be attained. These personal objectives are then discussed with the person's immediate supervisor or manager. A consensus between manager and subordinate is reached regarding the measurability and appropriateness of individual goals. The consensus discussion also takes into account whether the goals truly represent the scope of the employee's assigned area of responsibility. After the goals and plan of action are agreed to by both the manager and the subordinate, a goal review timetable is also set.

2. Periodically, as determined by the review timetable, progress toward goal achievement is discussed in additional manager and employee interviews. During such discussions, the employee reports to the manager on progress and problems in reaching the previously set goals. One of the MBO's strongest points is its value in shifting responsibility for the attainment of job objectives from the manager to the employee.

3. For employees in managerial positions, the process is similar. Each manager defines goals, timetables, and plans of action, which are discussed with and refined in meetings with the next higher level of management. As in the case of nonmanagement employees, periodic reviews are also arranged. Managerial goals include not only personal goals but also departmental or divisional goals. At the highest executive levels in the organization, top management sets overall objectives for the total organization as well as personal goals. Top-management goals are frequently reviewed by special committees or boards. Since goals are discussed fully at each level in the organization, they are mutually supportive. By "mutually supportive," we mean that the employee's goals support those of his or her department and manager. Each manager's goals support those of higher-level management as well as the overall organizational objectives. Conference sessions that include other managers are used to coordinate departmental and divisional goals. Such goals are also submitted to top management for review.

*MBO Requires Training*   For an MBO system to work effectively, it must become the guiding philosophy of an organization. Some organizations have tried MBO and discontinued its use. A primary difficulty is that MBO can, if not carefully planned and directed, become a massive paperwork system of elaborate records and reports. It is also dependent on the careful training about its use throughout the organization and the enthusiastic backing of top management. Some managers believe that MBO puts a great deal of pressure on individuals to set and meet goals, and that the danger of too many "easy" objectives is always possible. Perhaps its greatest strength, however, is its concentration on results rather than subjective evaluation of performance.

To better understand MBO in action, let us examine Table 16.1, the Personal Objectives Plan of Sherry Gunderson, an accounting technician who works for Howell Office Supply Company.

The actions marked with a double asterisk (**) are special problem-solving activities. On the date Sherry and her immediate manager have previously agreed upon, they will meet to again review objectives and progress toward their accomplishment. In circumstances beyond Sherry's control, such as a change in procedures or actions by another department, objectives may be altered and completion dates changed. This type of MBO procedure allows Sherry, as well as her manager, to evaluate job performance against actual accomplishments. Although Sherry's goals are short-range, objectives that take longer periods of time may be used equally well.

Although, as mentioned earlier, MBO requires considerable effort and a great deal of coordination to work properly, its advantages are usually greater than the problems it creates. Organizational change is brought about through the systematic encouragement of careful planning, the commitment to both individual and organizational goals, and the evaluation of performance against tangible achievements. Because of its focus on individual responsibility in accomplishing work, MBO can be one of management's strongest motivational

**Table 16.1**

Personal Objectives Plan of Sherry Gunderson

| Job Objectives | Objective Action | Completion Date |
|---|---|---|
| Classifying procurement documents | Decrease classification errors to less than 2% from present 3% | June 1 |
| Verification of document completeness | O.K.—No action required | |
| Posting procurement actions | Have all posting complete within 24 hours of issue | June 1 |
| Completing procurement document daily report | Develop simpler report format for management review** | Aug. 15 |
| Maintaining procurement document files | O.K.—No action required | |
| Providing accounting procurement data to data processing | Develop summary data form for easier interpretation | Aug. 15 |
| Collecting procurement data for market analysis | Submit data to marketing department no later than 10 A.M. daily | Immediately |

tools, especially in types of job assignments where employees control their own work pace. Where productivity is determined largely by machine or conveyor speed and in highly routine activities, the system is likely to have less value.

MBO fails when the system is used as a threat or when the setting of objectives becomes so routine they are meaningless. MBO also fails when the system of recording and evaluating objectives is so burdensome and complex that both management and employees rebel. The steps in MBO are summarized in Figure 16.5.

## *Organizational Development*

**Organizational development**, usually known simply as **OD,** is a popular term that describes many long-range approaches to changing the basic ways an organization operates. It can incorporate a wide variety of training and personal development of systems for improvement. Although a precise definition of OD is difficult, certain characteristics are common to many OD programs:

Organizations that have OD programs frequently use outside consultants who have the necessary expertise, objectivity, and analytical ability to evaluate organizational operations. The consultant is recognized as being outside the normal political forces of the organization and can effectively act as a primary force or agent of change. As time passes, OD will most likely become a more clearly defined method of organizational analysis and change with increasing influence on management thinking.

## Characteristics of OD Programs

1. OD is concerned with the effectiveness of the total organization rather than concentrated retraining of managers or installation of management development programs.

2. OD is planned. A specific set of actions is designed to improve the climate, health, and effectiveness of an organization.

3. OD is not a specific technique but is instead a systematic approach to redirect the energies of people in organizations to more effective behavior.

4. OD tries to help answer the fundamental management questions, Where are we now? Where do we want to be? and How do we get there?

### *Survey Feedback*

As a method for changing behavior in organizations, the **survey feedback** system has had considerable success. Developed by the Survey Research Center at the University of Michigan, the survey feedback system includes a question-

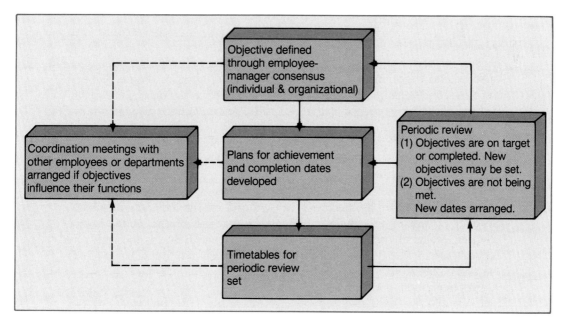

**Figure 16.5**   MBO in action.

naire used to gather information about an organization. The data is then given to the managers of the organization with interpretations usually provided by an outside consultant. After discussion of the survey information in meetings between managers and their subordinates, employees are encouraged to participate in planning corrective actions for problems revealed by the questionnaire. Areas covered by the questionnaires include a wide range of organizational functions. As in the use of many other change techniques, a consultant may be involved in helping to develop and interpret data. The consultant also assists managers, beginning with the top and working through each level, in their meetings with their subordinates and in the planning of actions to correct problems that have been defined. If not carefully used, survey feedback methods have the inherent weakness of creating defensive behavior on the part of many managers and polarizing differing points of view.

## Behavior Modification

Growing largely out of the work of the well-known psychologist B. F. Skinner, **behavior modification** as an organizational change method is relatively new. From a theoretical point of view, it is relatively easy to understand, but it is sometimes difficult to implement.

Over thirty years ago, Skinner and other behaviorists developed well-documented studies of the effectiveness of respondent conditioning and the principle of reinforcement. **Respondent conditioning** involves rewarding desired behavior and not rewarding undesirable behavior. If we want to train a dog to respond to a whistle, we can whistle and show the dog a reward such as a dog biscuit. When the animal approaches out of curiosity or comes to get its reward (i.e., the biscuit), we also give it a friendly pat and say "Good dog!" or some other appropriate and friendly phrase. After a few trials, the dog will come when we whistle whether we have a biscuit or not. It will respond to the reward of expected praise or affection rather than food. As long as it can expect a reward of some kind, the animal will continue to come to us when we whistle. The dog has been conditioned. Its behavior has been modified to our desires. Its continued response is strengthened by the expectancy of a reward for correct performance.

During his early studies, Skinner found that animals, if properly rewarded, can be trained to do a variety of fairly complex tasks. Repeated rewards are called **positive reinforcements**. Skinner found that for effective reinforcement, a carefully planned schedule must be followed. Constant rewards, too closely spaced, are not as effective as those timed to meet the animal's need. A plate full of corn left in a pigeon's training box is not as effective as the reward of a few grains of corn for pecking the correct lever. Rewards must also be properly timed. The most effective rewards are those that immediately follow the desired behavior.

Skinner also found that positive rewards, such as praise or food, are generally more effective than negative reinforcement, such as punishment. When neither rewards nor punishment is present—a condition of no reinforcement—**extinction** occurs. Extinction refers to the loss of a behavior. A tape recording of our whistle, with no pat, praise, or biscuit, will soon result in our dog's ignoring whistles altogether. Further studies by Skinner and others demonstrated that respondent conditioning also works with people. Human behavior can be shaped or modified by rewards and punishments using techniques similar to those used with animals.

Behavior modification, as respondent conditioning is popularly called, has some intriguing possibilities for management application. One of the best documented examples of the potential of behavior modification in industry is its application at the Emery Air Freight Company in Los Angeles.[6] At Emery Air Freight, supervisors were carefully and thoroughly trained to praise work correctly performed by employees, such as keeping records of activities, improving delivery times, or responding to telephone requests for information. In one department, employees were required to package goods for shipment by air. The size and shape of packages used was critical. Skinner had each employee record the size and type of box used on a checklist sheet each time an item was packaged. The checklist gave the employee immediate reinforcement that his or her performance was correct. At carefully planned interviews, supervisors reviewed the checklists and made favorable comments about the employee's accuracy to further reinforce the desired behavior. A 90 percent reduction of packaging errors was attained almost immediately after the system was installed. Similar types of reinforcement procedures (i.e., checklists for immediate feedback, coupled with praise) were designed for other types of activities. The results were beyond the expectations of Emery's management. Several hundred thousand dollars in actual savings were realized the first year of the program. Over two million dollars were saved during its first three years.

Successful reinforcement in work situations is dependent, then, on two factors: (1) immediate feedback in the form of clearly identifiable evidence of correct behavior and (2) the expectancy of rewards (or in some cases, the avoidance of punishment). As we noted earlier, behavior modification techniques are not new, but their application in work organizations has been limited because of lack of trained specialists to sell and develop behavior modification programs. The terms *respondent conditioning* and *behavior modification* also create images of manipulation, brainwashing, and "big brotherism" to some people. It is likely that skilled consultants will eventually create a less frightening terminology, and behavior modification will become a more widely applied organizational change force than it is today.

Behavior modification has been widely used in special education programs and correctional institutions, although its full potential in work organizations is yet to be realized. Unlike many other change techniques, behavior modification concentrates on specific operational problem areas rather than the total organization.

### Quality of Work Life

Many of the techniques used to encourage and direct change in organizations are proven, valid, and workable approaches to moving organizations in desired directions. Unfortunately, gullible managers often listen to consultants who are both ignorant and incorrect in their methods. Many managers also fall into the trap of accepting untested popular psychology theories that are potentially harmful. Because they are busy and often seeking expert help, they may become victims of incompetent advisers.

A move that shows definite promise and, to a large extent, avoids the pitfalls of false prophets is known as **quality of work life**, or **QWL**. QWL is not based on a definite theory, technique, or system, but is primarily concerned with building a climate of mutual respect between management and employees. Although not new in its approaches, QWL is a worldwide movement that seems to be finding its greatest resistance in the United States where many managers see it as another way of pampering already spoiled employees.

Although no specific system has been clearly defined, the QWL movement seems to have certain underlying principles that encourage shared responsibility, increased individual responsibility and authority, and a greater consultative relationship between managers and employees. Status differences are diminished, and the concept of shared partnership is encouraged not only between managers and employees but also between employees and employees as well as among managers of various departments. Companies such as Westinghouse, Kodak, AT&T, General Motors, Martin Marietta, General Foods, Weyerhauser, and others have found that less concern with control and increased attention to positive work relationships, job design, and shared decision making pay off.

Table 16.2 outlines some of the key ingredients of the QWL movement.

---

**Table 16.2**
**General Quality of Work Life Principles**

---

1. Jobs are designed to optimize job depth. When feasible, employees are given control over essential task decisions and are responsible for their achievement.

2. Whenever possible, ''natural work teams'' are formed where each member is an essential ingredient of a productive effort. At Volvo in Sweden, employees work as a team of ten to twelve people to assemble an entire automobile rather than individually installing a single component on an assembly line. Other companies have adopted similar methods.

3. Management teams work as problem-solving and goal development groups to achieve more functional organizational formats and improved work flow. Organization functions are considered more important than individual departments.

4. Decisions affecting employees, their work, new products, procedures, or policy changes are discussed with employees. Decisions are not implemented until total employee input has been received. Decisions are evaluated against both employee and management recommendations. Management avoids the ''we know everything'' type of control, which is frequently counterproductive.

5. Most important, a climate of partnership between managers and employees is encouraged rather than the all-too-frequent adversarial relationships.

6. Managers become resource people, evaluators of performance, and developers of people rather than controllers of people.

Perhaps most seriously, the QWL movement challenges traditional authority and accountability relationships, as well as traditional adversarial union-management relationships. It is difficult for both employees and managers, long accustomed to task-oriented authoritarian values, to change to an essentially people-oriented, task-achievement type of thinking. Undoubtedly, some employees may find working for managers who accept total responsibility, make all essential decisions, and are highly directive but benevolent easier to work for than those who encourage personal responsibility, team effort, and decisions by employees. The extent to which the QWL movement becomes an accepted reality rather than a lip-service philosophy remains to be seen through the 1980s and 1990s. At best, it promises that cooperation between management and employees can yield better products and services at lower costs with greater personal satisfaction. At worst, it can be another popular notion that neither management nor employees can accept.

## NEW TRENDS IN MANAGEMENT

During the early part of the 1980s, Japanese management was looked on as a model that U.S. managers should emulate. Although quality circles and increased employee involvement in plant decision making have had some impact, interest in Japanese styles seems to have waned. Managers appear to prefer to work out their own solutions than to copy those of others. Both Mazda and Honda get more production for far less investment in facilities, equipment, and labor in their United States operations than do any of the home-based American companies. Even though evidence suggests that Japanese managers are able to run large-scale organizations in the United States as effectively as they do in Japan, most U.S. managers have been unable or unwilling to fully benefit from their techniques, with the possible exception of high-tech industries.[7]

In his 1986 text, *Management in the Third Wave*, Alan Raymond points out that some organizations in the United States have managed to change into what he calls "organic organizations."[8] These organizations have at least four common characteristics:

1. Innovation and creativity are highly prized values. Their development is encouraged and sought after.
2. Bureaucratic practices are avoided. Practices are simple, clearly communicated, and effective.
3. Organic organizations see their employees as members rather than as employees. Managers genuinely want and expect employees to contribute more than skills. Employees are expected to believe that the organization is theirs and that its success or failure is dependent on the employees' actions and decisions.
4. Flexibility and responsiveness to change is also a common element of third-wave organizations, which consciously seek to meet the demands of the future.

The quality of work life movement and the **third-wave organic management** envisioned by Alan Raymond have a great deal in common. Both stress people involvement in the work place and human relations built on mutual trust, confidence, and performance expectations. William Ouchi, author of *Theory Z*, voiced a similar theme.[9] Ouchi, in his work with the Hewlett-Packard Corporation and other high-tech industries, noted that innovation, care for people, and concern for the overall health of the organization are important considerations in developing a management posture that will be effective through the few remaining years of this century.

Change, as Edgar Huse pointed out, is best accomplished when many people are involved and top-down change notions are abandoned.[10] Years ago Kurt Lewin observed that the process of deliberate, planned change may be viewed as a three-step process:

1. *Unfreezing.* When old ideas and ways of doing things are clearly no longer effective or adequate, people are more receptive to change; in some instances, they may actively seek change.

2. *Changing.* As new concepts, ideas, values, and organizational structure are introduced, people adopt them to replace concepts created by the unfreezing process.

3. *Refreezing.* After new concepts, ideas, and values are used for a period of time, they become part of people's lives in the same way in which old beliefs, values, and attitudes were. If, after being tested, the new behavior is inadequate, the whole change process begins again.

We are all travelers in time. Our travels are always into the future. Each of us must make our own map of the best paths to take.

## INNOVATION AND CREATIVITY

Planned change offers several tangible benefits. Improved processes, increased employee satisfaction and effectiveness, and better understanding of personal roles are just a few that are readily recognized. Additional benefits can also occur when employees at all levels are encouraged to develop new approaches or an entirely new process to accomplish their work. Managers who consistently fail to make use of the creative intelligence of their employees not only are discouraging the use of a valuable human asset but also are preventing their organizations from reaching full potential.

Although a number of organizations give lip service to the encouragement and development of new ideas, workable programs are, unfortunately, rare. Because they fail to listen or respond, or because they see concepts developed by subordinates as personal threats, some managers, either directly or indirectly, discourage innovation and creativity.

Suggestion plans that offer monetary rewards for cost-saving or work improvement concepts are widely used to encourage innovative or creative ideas. Some suggestion plans work fairly well; others become so bogged down in evaluation proceedings that a year or longer can pass before an employee's ideas are either accepted or rejected. In a few organizations, employees' suggestions are responded to promptly with a preliminary reward or an explanation of why the suggestion cannot be used. Those given preliminary acceptance are evaluated further. Finally, a percentage of the suggestion's cost savings or an explanation of why it cannot be used is given to the employee.

In small manufacturing organizations, plans that encourage cost-saving ideas and benefit the entire work force are relatively common. Ideas that are incorporated into regular work activities result in added pay for everyone in the organization.

From time to time, managers will ask employees to submit ideas for improvement. Only when such requests are sincere and not manipulative tricks to give employees a false sense of participation are they successful. Employees' ideas for improvement or new ways of performing must be responded to as promptly as possible with an explanation of why they can or cannot be used. Failure to do so eventually results in a lack of new concepts and limited performance improvement.

## PROBLEMS AND PROMISES

Change is an inevitable fact of existence. In its many forms, it affects people in organizations constantly. Managers of organizations are also managers of change. Recognizing that change is taking place and determining its probable direction and speed and the extent of its diffusion are vital management functions. Only by learning to observe, understand, predict, plan, implement, control, and evaluate change can a manager be truly effective. When problems are recognized and traditional or habitual solutions fail, change is necessary. Change for change's sake, however, is neither desirable nor meaningful.

Although deliberate, well-planned change is frequently desirable in nearly every aspect of organizational life, our thinking and psychological makeup often prevent us from realizing that change is needed. We feel comfortable with the familiar and seldom feel the need to seek new or better ways of getting things done. The feeling of doing things right can also be one of our worst enemies, particularly in the world of work.

## SELF–ASSESSMENT DISCUSSION

**1.** (1, 6) People both seek and resist change at the same time. Many people would like change, but when faced with the actual prospects of real change in their lives, especially if its consequences are uncertain or unknown, they will frequently resist.

**2.** (1) Most changes in organizations are relatively minor and routine. They are handled without any significant disturbance to the normal work flow or habitual patterns of employees.

**3.** (6) Deliberate change just for the sake of change is neither desirable nor meaningful. Needed change that is carefully planned and implemented frequently has lasting benefits.

**4.** (1) Although some types of change may affect an entire organization, most change is centered on a specific area or activity.

**5.** (1) Most planned change that is based on sound analysis and demonstrated need is beneficial.

**6.** (1) Management of change begins when the need for change is recognized.

**7.** (1) A quick and appropriate response to innovative and creative ideas is necessary to encourage employees to develop new approaches to their jobs and the work of their organization.

**8.** (6) Change direction is a measure of the way present events will affect future events. When the price of gasoline dropped in 1986, the United States actually experienced a decline in the general cost of living for several months.

**9.** (6) Change that is introduced in small increments is better assimilated and accepted than massive, all-at-once changes.

**10.** (6) Introduction of new technology is nearly always perceived as a threat to employees. Requirements for new skills, the possibility of being displaced by technology, and lack of confidence in the technology's ability to improve work life all contribute to the fear of technological change.


## QUICK REVIEW

I. Change: Invasion of the Future
   A. Change affects every part of our lives.
   B. Jobs and organizations are changing more rapidly than ever before.

II. Characteristics of Change
   A. Rate of change is the speed with which change takes place.
   B. Direction of change defines the way present conditions alter future events.
   C. Diffusion of change is the way one change frequently causes other changes.
   D. Rate, direction, and diffusion of change usually affect management at the same time.

III. Types of Change
   A. Technological changes involving new equipment, material, or facilities are the easiest changes to identify.
   B. Social change occurs when a large segment of the population adopts a different set of values.
   C. Internal changes are those changes based on management decisions rather than on technology or social change.

IV. Managing Change

    A. Management of change begins with the recognition that change is needed.

    B. When change is perceived as a threat, it is resisted.

    C. Although some resistance to change is logical, much is emotional.

    D. Management can minimize resistance to change by:

        1. Introducing change in small increments.

        2. Educating and training employees and demonstrating the new equipment or procedures.

        3. Enabling employees to help plan and implement the change.

V. Organizational Change Techniques

    A. Management by objectives (MBO) concentrates on results that can be objectively evaluated. Ideally, MBO involves everyone in the organization.

    B. Managers and employees set well-defined goals, review progress toward those goals, and evaluate their achievement.

    C. Organizational development (OD) uses many techniques in changing the basic ways an organization operates. It is concerned with change in the total organization.

    D. Survey feedback is a system of initiating change based on questionnaire and discussion data.

    E. Behavior modification creates change by rewarding and reinforcing the desired behavior.

    F. Quality of work life (QWL) is a major organizational change movement primarily concerned with building a climate of mutual respect between management and employees.

    G. New trends in management have evolved in the past few years.

VI. Innovation and Creativity

    A. Managers who fail to use their employees' creative intelligence are frequently failing their organizations.

    B. Some managers discourage innovation and creativity.

    C. A key to encouraging innovation and creativity is a quick, appropriate response.

VII. Problems and Promises

    A. Change affects people in organizations constantly. Management must try to forecast and manage change.

    B. Deliberate, well-planned change is desirable, but often our old habits prevent us from realizing that changes are needed.

## KEY TERMS

Rate of change
Direction of change
Diffusion of change
Technological change
Social change
Internal change
Change resistance

Management by
 objectives
Organizational
 development
Survey feedback
Behavior modification

Respondent conditioning
Reinforcements
Extinction
Third-wave organic
 management
Quality of work life

## DISCUSSION QUESTIONS

1. Some people seem frightened when faced with technological change, even though the change may be beneficial. Why does this occur?

2. Authorities have stated that the United States has changed from a producing to a buying nation and will never regain its position as the world's most innovative and productive country. Is this statement correct? Explain your response.

3. Psychologists have learned that adult attitudes are difficult but possible to change. What is a good technique for changing negative attitudes to more positive ones in work organizations?

4. Why haven't Japanese management techniques become more popular in this country?

5. Best-run organizations try to avoid being bureaucratic. What does being bureaucratic mean?

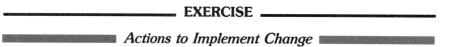

## EXERCISE

### Actions to Implement Change

You are the manager of the branch office of a large bank. The twenty-seven employees who work in the branch office handle the complete range of banking transactions for customers. The bank is installing a new computer system that will require some changes in the procedures for processing customer transactions. To implement the new procedures, you will have to change some job assignments, and the employees will have to use new methods of recording transactions. The success of the new computer system will depend on effective implementation by the current employees.

*Evaluate the following list of actions to implement the changes.*
Which actions would you take? Which would you take first?

1. Explain to employees how the new system will affect them and the performance of their jobs.

2. Have representatives of the company train the employees in the use of the new system.

3.  Let the employees vote on how to implement the procedures necessary to implement the new system.

4.  Promote feedback from employees by encouraging questions about the new system and how they will be affected.

5.  Don't tell anyone about the new procedures until the system has been installed and the new procedures must be used.

6.  Communicate "the complete story" about the new system, including advantages, disadvantages, and potential problems.

7.  Provide employees with information about how the system has worked in other banks where it has been implemented.

8.  Where possible, adapt implementation of the new system to fit the needs and preferences of the current employees.

9.  Severely discipline anyone who strongly objects to the new system as an example of what will happen to anyone who opposes the new system.

10. Have sessions with employees to set goals for effective implementation of the new system.

---

**TWO POINTS OF VIEW**

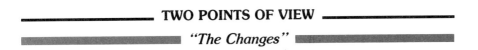

*"The Changes"*

*What would you do if you were the supervisor?*

You are a recent college graduate who has been hired to supervise the computer data processing functions of a savings and loan company. To provide the necessary processing services in the most efficient manner, you believe that changing some of the operational procedures is necessary. You have also proposed the purchase of a new computer to keep up with the "state of the art" in computer data processing. You are convinced that all the changes you have proposed are absolutely necessary if the savings and loan is to be competitive with the continuing deregulation of financial institutions.

Frank Armstrong has worked in the data processing section longer than any other employee and is the senior programmer. He has worked his way up by learning programming on his own, and does not have a college degree. Frank has stubbornly resisted any changes you propose and will institute new procedures only after repeated direct orders. Frank tells other employees that he knows the system better than anyone else. Another employee told you he heard Frank say that "no young college punk can possibly know what is going on unless he has worked in the field for at least five years." When you try to discuss changes with Frank, he argues that what is working should not be changed.

Frank appears to be gaining the support of the other employees in his opposition to the proposed changes. You realize that you cannot effectively implement new procedures or install a new computer without the cooperation and support of the employees.

*What would you do if you were Frank Armstrong?*

You are the senior programmer for a savings and loan. You have worked for the company for fifteen years and are highly respected for your knowledge of computers. You programmed most of the current system and are familiar with its every detail. You like working for the savings and loan and enjoy the type of work you are doing. Some of the employees had encouraged you to apply for the supervisor's job when it came open, but you have absolutely no desire to ever have a management position. You want to program and operate computer systems. A supervisor's job appears to you to be a "bucket of worms" because you must deal with people who are difficult.

The new supervisor of the computer data processing function is a nice enough young man, but he lacks experience. He seems to want to change things so they will be more like the systems he learned about in college. Because of his lack of experience, he has proposed changes that are expensive and will cause customer dissatisfaction. The current computer can effectively handle the projected processing load for the next five years, but the new supervisor wants "state of the art." His new computer would be fun to work with and a super status symbol, but the company would be spending money unnecessarily. Your philosophy has always been "If it works, don't fix it."

With deregulation of financial institutions, it is extremely important for the savings and loan to minimize costs to compete effectively. If you cannot convince your new supervisor that the proposed changes are not in the best interest of the company, you are considering going to the president, who is a longtime friend.

### ENDNOTES

1. Andrew C. Brown, "The Man Who Warns Detroit 'This Is War,' " *Fortune*, 8 February 1982, p. 38.
2. Joseph F. Coates, "The Changing Nature of Work," *VocEd.* (January/February 1982): 27–29.
3. Based on CBS program "60 Minutes," 7 March 1982.
4. Based on Fredric Golden "Here Come the Microkids," *Time*, 3 May 1982, pp. 50–56.
5. Bradford Boyd, *Management Minded Supervision*, 4th ed. (New York: McGraw-Hill, 1980).
6. CPM Films, "Behavior Modification," 1975, narrated by B. F. Skinner and Emery Air Freight Company officials.
7. *Wall Street Journal*, 13 May 1986.
8. H. Alan Raymond, *Management in the Third Wave* (Glenview, Ill.: Scott, Foresman, 1986).
9. William Ouchi, *Theory Z* (New York: Ballentine Books, 1980).
10. Edgar Huse, *Management* (St. Paul: West, 1981).

# Unions: Organizations Within Organizations

———————— *Learning Objectives* ————————

After reading this chapter, you should be able to do the following:

1. Understand the underlying motivations for people forming and joining unions
2. Acquire a knowledge of basic collective bargaining terminology
3. Define the importance of representation, due process, and jurisdiction to the union-management relationship
4. Relate some of the early historical events of unionism to current union-management relations
5. Learn major collective bargaining issues
6. Describe differences between unions in the United States and those in other countries
7. Understand the decline of unionism in the United States

# Chapter Topics

- Why people form unions
- Unilateral and bilateral relations
- Language of labor relations
- Issues in collective bargaining
- Individuals and unions
- Special problems in union-management relations
- Personal security and representation
- Grievance procedures
- Into the future
- A short look backward

# Preview

In retrospect, the 1980s have not been good years for unionism in the United States. Declines in overall membership that started in the early 1970s have continued. Proposed union-sponsored legislation has failed at both the federal and state levels. Many companies have taken increasingly stronger tactics against traditional union actions that have usually been effective. It is too early, however, to count unionism out as a powerful force in many organizations. Twenty million people with a common identity—that of being union members—constitutes the single largest group in the United States exclusive of major political parties.

Causes of the decline in union influence are many and complex. Traditional manufacturing industries, especially steel and automobiles, which have been a major mainstay of large unions, have declined in number of employees. Both mining and construction, also traditionally unionized industries, have increasingly become nonunionized. A mixture of public perceptions, changing employment patterns, more capable management, somewhat dated political stances of some union leaders, as well as highly publicized corrupt leadership in some unions, have all had an impact on union growth and effectiveness.

Regardless of their difficulties, union leaders are promising a strong comeback as a major part of organizational life in the United States. Although proving their statements either correct or incorrect may take several years, unions are still an important component of organizational life and will probably remain so for the foreseeable future.

## SELF-ASSESSMENT ▰▰▰▰▰▰▰▰▰▰▰▰▰▰▰▰▰▰

Many people do not fully understand union-management relations—even those who deal with unions in the work place. To examine your own knowledge and perceptions, mark the following items with the answer that best fits your beliefs. Each statement or question has a range of possible responses. A scale of 1 to 6 between two words with different meanings allows you to mark either the word that is considered correct or a place between the two words that represents some agreement and some disagreement. Selection of a high number such as 5 or 6 may be either correct or incorrect, just as selection of lower numbers may be correct or incorrect. Some responses may be partly correct and partly incorrect.

Answers based on research by behavioral scientists, with a short explanation of why the response was considered correct, may be found on page 482.

1. People join together to form unions primarily to:

    obtain more money   1...2...3...4...5...6   influence management
       and benefits

2. History has shown that most unions are:

       pro-management   1...2...3...4...5...6   anti-management

3. Which type of management style is most likely to be successful in dealing with unionized employees?

       participative-   1...2...3...4...5...6   authoritarian
         democratic

4. In enforcing civil rights laws, the U.S. Supreme Court has:

       made seniority   1...2...3...4...5...6   upheld the legality of
     protection of union                           traditional seniority
             members                               rules of labor contracts
       unenforceable

5. Over the past ten years, unionism has gained primarily in:

      high-technology   1...2...3...4...5...6   government and
           industries                             service industries

6. In well-managed unionized organizations with effective unions, employees may express:

         dual loyalty   1...2...3...4...5...6   single loyalty to their
                                                  union

7. Due process is not an exclusive union-management concern. It is basically a guarantee of:

a fair hearing  1...2...3...4...5...6  the right to
individually negotiate

8. A primary purpose of unionism is to establish:

unilateral personnel  1...2...3...4...5...6  bilateral personnel
rules                                                    rules

9. Approximately what percentage of the total work force in the United States belongs to unions?

10...20...30...40...50...60

10. Which of the following countries has the lowest percentage of its work force belonging to unions?

Japan...United States...Belgium...England...Holland...Sweden

## WHY PEOPLE FORM UNIONS

**Unions** have been in existence for at least one hundred years before the United States developed from the thirteen original colonies. Cordwainers (shoemakers), printers, and tailors formed isolated unions to improve work hours and increase pay. Early unions were all made up of employees in skilled trades. They did, however, have several characteristics still true of union organizations today. Perhaps most important, they were made up of employees who believed that collectively they could deal with management more effectively than they could as individuals. They had as their primary goals better wages, hours, and conditions of work. Like their modern counterparts, the early unions wanted guarantees from management that agreements would be honored.

The United States work force numbers about 110 million people, some of whom are unemployed but still eligible for work. Of these, slightly more than 20 million belong to labor unions. Simple arithmetic reveals that for each person in the work force who is a union member, five employees are not. Although they are clearly a minority of all workers, unions exert a powerful influence on the national economy, on the way organizations are run, and on local, regional, and national politics. Whether admired or detested, unions are a reality of life that affects everyone. Table 17.1 lists the largest unions in the United States today.

In some instances, the only way employees believe they can influence management is through the collective power of unionism. By joining together, they are able to obtain concessions from management that would be much more difficult to achieve as individuals. At the core of all union activities is the concept that unified groups of employees have greater influence than individuals in dealing with management.

**Table 17.1**

**The Twenty-Three Largest Unions in the United States, 1981**

| Employee Group | Membership |
| --- | --- |
| Teamsters | 2,000,000 |
| Automobile workers | 1,800,000 |
| Steel workers | 1,400,000 |
| Electrical workers (IBEW) | 1,000,000 |
| Machinists | 943,280 |
| Carpenters | 820,000 |
| Retail clerks | 650,876 |
| Laborers | 650,000 |
| State, county, and municipal | 648,160 |
| Service employees | 648,000 |
| American Federation of Teachers | 550,000 |
| Meat cutters | 525,000 |
| Communication workers | 498,743 |
| Hotel and restaurant | 451,989 |
| Operating engineers | 421,395 |
| Ladies' garment workers | 340,936 |
| Clothing workers | 510,000 |
| Paper workers | 324,000 |
| Government (AFGE) workers | 300,000 |
| Musicians | 300,000 |
| Mine workers | 250,000 |
| Painters | 192,700 |
| Electrical workers (IUE) | 165,000 |

*Source: World Almanac* (New York: Newspaper Enterprise Association 1981), pp. 135–36.

*Note:* More recent figures are essentially the same, although some unions may have lost 10 to 15 percent of 1981 membership.

## UNILATERAL AND BILATERAL RELATIONS

Traditionally, at least as many people believe, an adversarial relationship has existed between management and employees. In most companies, managers make the rules and employees follow them. This one-sided rule making is known as a **unilateral relationship**. As long as employees think the rules are consistent, fair, and applied with judgment and some degree of flexibility, they generally accept them. Effective managers will usually make an effort to avoid dissension between themselves and employees. A stable work force is an essential asset in most organizations.

Realistically, however, differences between managers and employees are almost inevitable. Managers are concerned with organizational goals such as productivity, quality, costs, schedules, implementation of plans, determination of new goals, and effectiveness of the work force. Employees frequently value personal needs such as pay, benefits, fair treatment, proper work assignments,

---

### Support Your Local "Operating Engineers"? ━━━━━━━

Red Bluff, California, city police learned that law enforcement officers in other parts of the state were receiving their uniforms and "safety equipment" (guns, bullets, and the like) free from their cities or counties. In Red Bluff, police had to buy their own equipment and uniforms.

The obvious inequity became a major point of dissatisfaction. When the officers petitioned the Red Bluff City Council for a change in policy, they were repeatedly turned down. The police believed their only recourse was to form a union.

To obtain help in their organizing efforts, they contacted a number of unions for advice and assistance. After some hesitation, they decided against forming their own local and instead joined the Union of Operating Engineers, whose membership was primarily heavy equipment operators. Nevertheless, as "operating engineers," the police were able to negotiate a written contract with the city that provided an allowance for purchasing uniforms and safety equipment.[1]

---

opportunity to develop and advance, and personal security. Although the two points of view are not necessarily opposed to each other, they can easily serve as a basis for major differences in the ways organizational priorities are viewed. Employees who think that management is not interested in employee needs and values show their resentment. Management also resents any problems caused by the work force in productivity, quality, excessive costs, or schedules. When each side views the other as violating its own needs and organizational expectations, conflicts arise that are difficult to heal.

To gain some influence over management rule making, protect threatened security, increase financial benefits, ensure fairness, and control their job destiny to some degree, employees will form unions to deal as a group with management. When managers and employees jointly arrive at a set of personnel rules affecting wage, hours, and conditions of work, the rules are written and signed by both parties. Joint rule making by management and employees establishes **bilateral relations**.

In those organizations with bilateral relations, neither side may change the rules without the consent, through negotiation, of the other. **Negotiation** is the process that organized employee groups use to reach agreements. Anytime people talk with each other and mutually agree on a course of action satisfactory to both, some negotiation takes place. An important principle called ***quid pro quo*** forms the basis for negotiation. *Quid pro quo* literally means "something for something." Each of the negotiating parties, in this case management and organized employees, gives and receives through the negotiation process.

To gain an in-depth understanding of collective bargaining relationships, a great deal of study and experience is usually necessary. Some key terms associated with union-management relations are helpful in grasping the basics of this complex subject.

## LANGUAGE OF LABOR RELATIONS

Over a period of many years, managers and union employees have developed a set of terms to describe their relationship and the rules that are negotiated. Although we are not concerned with the entire vocabulary of labor relations, some terms are essential:

An *appropriate unit* is defined as employees with common interests and/or similar jobs who join together in a unit. All technicians, for example, may be an appropriate unit, while all clerical personnel in the same company may be another appropriate unit. Once a union is formed, the appropriate unit name is usually dropped and it is known only as the unit or bargaining unit.

*Bargaining and negotiating* are essentially the same process of give and take to reach agreement. The terms are used interchangeably. **Collective bargaining** is a somewhat broader term that includes all of the relationships between management and unionized employees.

A *contract or agreement* is the written result of negotiations. In its basic form, it is a set of personnel rules that both employees and managers must follow. A **contract**, sometimes called an agreement, is a legal document and binds both parties to its contents.

A *federation* is an association of affiliated locals and internationals. The single federation in existence today is the AFL–CIO (American Federation of Labor–Congress of Industrial Organizations). Its primary purpose is to influence national politics and national policy related to work, employment, and other social goals.

A *grievance* is a written employee complaint. It is processed by a steward or employee representative through a negotiated step-by-step grievance procedure.

An *international* is a group of similar locals that have joined together to exert political influence at a local level, determine common policy, and provide a service organization for member locals. The International Association of Machinists and Aerospace Workers; United Automobile Workers; Teamsters, Warehousemen, and Chauffers; United Steel Workers; and Ladies' Garment Workers Union are all examples of internationals.

A *local* is the basic organizational unit of union members. It is like a troop in scouting organizations or a chapter in a social or philanthropic organization.

*Management rights* define management's personnel rights, such as the right to hire, terminate, lay off, promote, transfer, assign work, discipline, train, and so on.

*Recognition.* Under current law, management must recognize a union formed by more than 50 percent of the employees, usually by election process, as the sole bargaining agent for employees. The union is the representative of all employees in the appropriate unit whether those employees have become union members or abstained from union membership.

*Representation* means that on all personnel matters, including pay, benefits, discipline, promotion within union classifications, seniority, overtime, transfers, discharge and any other personnel matter, employees will be represented by the union. A *steward* or employee representative speaks for the union on behalf of the employee and is charged with protecting the employee and ensuring that management does not violate negotiated rules.

A *shop* is the place where union members work. A shop may be an insurance company, hospital, factory, school, department store, farm, or any other place of work.

*Unions* are, in the simplest terms, groups of employees recognized by management as legitimate partners in the rule-making process.

A *bargaining unit* is a term frequently used to define the union at a particular location.

*Union security.* Rules that are negotiated, preserve the union, and ensure its perpetuation and maintenance are known as union security. Such rules include *checkoff*, which makes union dues automatically deductible from an employee's check and defines the type of shop as either an *open shop* with voluntary union membership, an *agency shop* where all employees pay an amount equivalent to dues regardless of membership in a union, or a *union shop* where membership is automatic after thirty days of employment, and other related union clauses.

## ISSUES IN COLLECTIVE BARGAINING

There are many issues in collective bargaining. Most contracts will include at least twenty to thirty articles, each dealing with a separate issue or set of issues. In addition to those dealing with work rules (schedules, amount of work, break times, smoking regulations, and so on), pay for time worked, pay for time not worked (vacations, holidays, breaks, personal time off), seniority, grievance procedures, benefits, and overtime distribution, numerous other issues are important to employees.

A difficult issue to address is employees' desire to work in a system that meets their needs for fairness, equity, opportunity, and responsive management. As robots replace many traditional manufacturing jobs and electronics changes the nature of the office, employee relations in both unionized and nonunionized environments become crucial.[2] Douglas Fraser, past president of the United Automobile Workers International Union, has been, like many other progressive union officials, a leader in defining the future course of union-management relations. He views the future as one that must include greater job security, improved productivity based on technological advances, greater worker participation in corporate decision making, and rededication to quality. Many managers are restating Fraser's views in their own words. Significantly, there is some indication that union-management relations are cautiously moving toward a more cooperative stance. In a widely syndicated newspaper article, Fraser summed up what he believes the survival of America may depend on, at least in part:

> The key to the future depends greatly on whether there can be a broader move toward shared responsibility between unions and corporations—a shared responsibility that involves greater decision-making power and job security for workers.
>
> Those of us who want to see more economic and social justice in America must be willing to take risks and try new approaches. . . . As we attempt to develop

more progressive labor-management relations, we won't forget that those who insist on making cooperation impossible make confrontation inevitable.[3]

## INDIVIDUALS AND UNIONS

Individual union members are sometimes torn between loyalty to their union and its goals and the realization that survival of their organizations is directly tied to their own personal survival. Although they may successfully develop a *dual loyalty* to both their union and their work place, at times these two organizations may have divergent goals.

Managers, especially first-line supervisors who work directly with the labor force, also face problems in dealing with union employees. Their ability to direct the work force, discipline, schedule and assign work, promote, give performance evaluations, establish general rules of conduct, and make decisions regarding job content (what an employee can and cannot do) is often limited by the labor contract.

There are two prevalent views of administration of union-management contracts. One view is that the contract is a legal document and must be followed to the letter. In some work places, "do it by the contract" is a standard phrase. Another view holds that the contract is a set of guidelines for both management and employees and that the spirit of the agreement is as important as its literal language. Under this view, some flexibility in interpreting provisions is allowed by both management and employee representatives, especially when special circumstances are involved. Management and union representatives attempt to use the contract as a positive tool for improving relations rather than as a means of policing each other's actions.

## SPECIAL PROBLEMS IN UNION–MANAGEMENT RELATIONS

**Seniority** is a time-honored principle in union-management relations and is frequently found in modified form as part of the general policies of nonunion organizations. In its simplest form, seniority is usually defined as the length of service a person has with a company in a specific job classification. Its primary purpose is to assure employees that in the event of reductions in the work force, those with greatest seniority will be laid off last. The principle of seniority can also cover benefits such as promotional opportunities, job assignments, shift preference, work location, amount of vacation, retirement benefits, choice of vacation schedules, and opportunity to transfer. Employees with greater length of service have several advantages over newer employees.

However, seniority can cause problems in organizations with affirmative action plans designed to increase opportunities for women and minorities in jobs from which they were previously excluded. Seniority systems can frustrate the aims of these plans by protecting long-term seniority employees, frequently white males, to a greater degree than workers employed as part of an affirmative action effort. In the event of a reduction in force due to economic recession, loss of contracts, or other reasons, less senior employees are laid off first.

Employees hired under affirmative action programs are likely to be among the less senior and are most vulnerable to layoffs.

In a famous court case in 1977 (*International Brotherhood of Teamsters* v. *United States*, 431 U.S. 324), a ruling was made that if a seniority system was established without the purpose of discriminating, the seniority provisions of such contracts were not an unlawful employment practice, even if the system has some discriminatory consequences.[4] In effect, the Supreme Court said that traditional seniority systems based on a simple length of service provision were satisfactory provided other personnel practices were not discriminatory.

Several attempts have been made to find alternative seniority systems, but few have actually been put into practice. One approach is the establishment of dual seniority. *Dual seniority* is the establishment of two seniority lists. On one list, employees with an excess of a predetermined number of years—for example, five—would be listed by job classification in order of seniority. On another list, employees who were part of a program designed to meet affirmative action goals with less than five years' experience would be listed in order of length of service. If a reduction in force occurred, the same percentage of workers from each list would be affected. When a work force reduction of 5 percent occurred, 5 percent of the employees from each list would be laid off. A substantial number of employees hired as part of equal economic opportunity goals would retain their jobs. Even this system has drawbacks. Unions usually insist that recalls from layoffs be by order of seniority. In such cases, the most senior employees from the "regular" employee list would be recalled first.

A related problem is associated with the rule of reasonable accommodation. *Reasonable accommodation* means that organizations will try to arrange special schedules or conditions of work regardless of union rules if the situation requires it. A person who will not work Saturdays or evenings because of religious prohibitions may be provided a special assignment to accommodate his or her beliefs. Inevitably, such treatment is seen by other employees as discriminatory and preferential. Management is frequently caught in the dilemma of trying to decide between the need to comply with the principle of reasonable accommodation and the equal need of maintaining both the spirit and letter of a written union contract.

A critical issue that management faces, especially supervisors of employees who perform the organization's day-to-day activities, is treatment of employees after a strike. Strikes are costly, difficult experiences for both employees and managers. Resentment on both sides can build during the strike period. Effective managers know that rebuilding normal, friendly relationships after a strike has been settled is much wiser than attempting to make employees feel guilty for their actions.

## PERSONAL SECURITY AND REPRESENTATION

In addition to its bargaining for pay, benefits, favorable work rules, and a system of formalized employee-management relations, unions also ensure employee security in several ways. We have already mentioned seniority provisions that protect employees and afford workers numerous other benefits based on their length of service. Two other important protections are also offered by union-management agreements: jurisdiction and grievance procedures.

**Jurisdiction** is, in its simplest form, the protection of a worker's job through union membership in a given craft. For example, electricians, carpenters, machinists, clerks, and automobile assemblers usually belong to different unions. Because different types of work are associated with a particular union, only that union's members are allowed to perform the work. For instance, only members of the electrician's union can repair electrical switches; carpenters, and only carpenters, may install doors; clerks, and only clerks, may file. Members of a union may perform only that work covered in the job descriptions of its members.

Not only is there union jurisdiction, but also members of the same union may be protected equally as well by their job descriptions. Storekeepers in a factory take inventory and report shortages in items. They also issue parts and material and maintain appropriate records. Production control specialists who need to know the availability of materials and supplies in order to plan production runs may not count or record supplies. To do so would be a violation of the storekeepers' job rights. Jurisdiction and rights conveyed by job descriptions assure employees a degree of job protection. Management's flexibility in assigning work is restricted to specific specialized job descriptions. The familiar "and other duties as assigned" job description phrase is usually not valid in union-management relations.

Perhaps the most important protection offered through union membership, other than seniority, is the right to due process. Unlike seniority, due process applies to all employees regardless of length of service. **Due process** is the guaranteed right to a fair hearing in the event of an action against an employee by management or the belief that management has acted improperly in its treatment of an employee. To ensure that due process is properly administered, nearly all labor-management agreements contain a grievance procedure.

---

### How to "Keep on Truckin' "

The job of truck driver got a new twist at one United Grocers store in Houston, Texas. Normally, produce orders are filled by warehouse workers who stack the needed items on forklift carriers, drive them to the loading stations, and load the produce into waiting trucks.

However, local Teamster Union drivers were able to negotiate a contract forbidding anyone other than a Teamster member to set foot in the trucks. At the present time, groceries are left stacked on the docks at the truck's rear entrance. The truck driver hand loads the boxes, drives to the destination, and then unloads the produce. The process is time-consuming and costly but ensures that only Teamster drivers are allowed to do "truck work."

## GRIEVANCE PROCEDURES

**Grievances** are formal written complaints requiring management action. Most people complain about something at work at one time or another. When the complaint becomes serious enough to discuss with management, it may become a grievance.

Some grievances are based on facts. A wrong has been done or believed to have been done. In most cases, there is also a more subtle reason. An employee who is dissatisfied but unable to correct the dissatisfaction may look for a grievance cause to vent his or her anger.

> Susan Snell normally would dump dirty ashtrays in the wastebasket, pick up scattered paper, and generally clean her boss's office. The custodian had filed a grievance demanding six hours of back pay at overtime rates for compensation resulting from Susan's conference room clean-up activities. She had a right to clean around her regular work place (her desk) but not the adjoining conference room. After going through the regular grievance procedure, the custodian was paid and Susan was instructed to no longer clean the conference room. It was later learned that the custodian had on occasion flirted with Susan and had been consistently rebuffed. He told a friend that he would find a way to show her where she really stood.

Experienced managers can sense dissatisfaction and frequently prevent grievances by counseling, changing work assignments, or simply sharing information. A key to grievance prevention is the development of a climate of trust and confidence that minimizes the need for formalized complaints.

Although there is not a uniform set of procedures used by all organizations to settle grievances, Table 17.2 outlines features found in many contracts.

---

**Table 17.2**
**Typical Grievance Procedure**

|         | Union Actions | Management Actions |
|---------|---------------|--------------------|
| Step 1. | Employee submits grievance to management. | Management either settles or rejects grievance. |
| Step 2. | If not settled at first step, employee and steward submit grievance to next level of management. | Higher management settles or rejects grievance if not settled at first step. |
| Step 3. | Chief steward submits grievance to top management representatives, usually a labor relations specialist, for a formal hearing. In some cases, a grievance committee of union and management members constitutes third step. | Top management, usually represented by a labor relations specialist, hears grievance and settles or rejects if not settled at second step. In case of committee, committee settles or rejects. |
| Step 4. | Both sides jointly submit grievance and facts to an arbitrator (independent third party) for settlement. Arbitrator's decisions are binding on both parties. | |

---

In reviewing Table 17.2, keep in mind that there is a definite time period between each step in the grievance procedure and that arbitration is used only if management and the union cannot agree on an interpretation of contract provisions or if the union disagrees with management actions toward an employee. **Arbitration** involves using a third party, usually a member of the American Arbitration Association, to settle the grievances. Since arbitration is expensive, involves an outsider, and means the final decision is uncertain, both unions and management usually strive for settlement before going to arbitration. Arbitration costs are normally shared equally by management and the union representing the employee.

**Grievance procedures** are the primary tool in union-management relations. They are the regulators of actions by both sides and form a basis for rule clarification as well as redress of management actions toward employees. The number and types of grievances are frequently a barometer of the health of union-management relations.

---

### As the Wheel Turns

After a relatively long era of labor peace, the mid-1980s witnessed labor beginning to reassert itself as a significant force in management's decisions affecting employees. In 1986, a strike by the Communications Workers Union affected over 150,000 of its employees and many other telephone workers not part of the AT&T system. Although wages was an issue to some extent, guaranteed security was the key to strike settlement. Security, job quality, and work rules are becoming increasingly important in the settlement of negotiations. With the approach of the 1990s, union strategy and methods of dealing with management are likely to change. Long strikes are less threatening than they were in the past, and management, backed by favorable Supreme Court decisions, has used a variety of methods to offset union efforts to apply pressure for increased economic benefits and favorable work rules.

During the 1930s, unionism in the United States experienced its most favorable political support. To a large extent, the support continued through the 1960s and mid-1970s. Since then, a decline has occurred in both numbers of unions and their political influence. In the immediate work place, however, many supervisors feel frustrated and, to some extent, intimidated by union rules and lack of flexibility in dealing with personnel issues. From an objective point of view, interpersonal relations with employees, disciplinary actions, and other personnel-related matters are not necessarily blocked or hampered by the presence of a union contract. Union-management agreements or contracts are rules that both sides must follow. Managers at every level, who look at the agreement as a rule book for them as well as for employees, usually have the least difficulty in dealing with day-to-day personnel problems.

## INTO THE FUTURE

Evidence already indicates that new work methods will increase the number of jobs where employees will be machine supervisors, programmers, and directors rather than assemblers, office clerks, inspectors, or manual technicians.[5] Many of today's jobs will no longer exist or will be significantly reduced in number by 1990, and by the year 2000 an entirely new cycle of jobs will emerge. These trends are reflected in an overall decline in union membership, as shown in Figure 17.1. Unions draw most of their strength from older industries.

New jobs mean new skills, different demands, and, most important, new relationships between management and employees. Highly probable is that traditional, authoritarian management approaches will continue to decline and that status and power differences between managers and employees will be far less evident than in the past.[6] We predict that out of this, new relationships between management and unions will also emerge.

## A SHORT LOOK BACKWARD

We have deliberately avoided the legal and historical framework of union-management relations, as well as other important issues, in an attempt to illustrate a few factors that affect on-the-job human relations in a work environment. Unions are organizations with both formal and informal structures in much the same way as management. Well-organized unions with capable lead-

*Source:*   World Almanac Book of Facts, 1986 (New York: Newspaper Enterprise
            Association) and Information Please Almanac (Boston: Houghton, Mifflin, 1986).

Figure 17.1   Union membership as a percentage of the total labor force.

ership are much more successful in achieving bargaining goals and influencing management policy than are those unions whose leadership is concerned primarily with personal gain. By the same token, management that is thoughtful and goal directed, with high expectations for itself and its employees, is also more likely to relate well with its workers as employees *and* as union members. Unfortunately, management and union bottom-line thinking, which concentrates on short-range goals, immediate rewards, and a win-lose philosophy, all too often blocks real progress.

## SELF–ASSESSMENT DISCUSSION

1. (1, 2, 3, 4, 5, 6) A great deal of the motivation for unionization centers on improvement of pay and benefits. In the long run, influencing management in its decisions regarding employees is equally important. In many cases, there are multiple reasons for employees to form and support unions.

2. (2, 3, 4, 5) Often, unions are neutral toward management. In some instances, unions will be supportive of management efforts to keep a plant open or to improve organizational health, while in other cases they will strongly object to management actions and decisions.

3. (1, 2, 3, 4, 5, 6) Appropriate management style is dependent on many factors, including the situation, the type of employees, and the manager's most comfortable way of behaving. No one style is best, regardless of the presence or absence of a union.

4. (6) In recent rulings, as well as in the past, the Supreme Court has upheld seniority provisions in labor agreements, provided those agreements were not designed to discriminate against classes of employees protected by the Civil Rights Act.

5. (6) Few high-technology industries have been unionized. In recent years, unions have made their greatest gains in organizing government and service employees.

6. (1, 2) If management and union officials are perceived as fair, honest, and competent, employees will be loyal to both management and the union. If either side is perceived as being dishonest or incompetent, loyalty may shift.

7. (1) Due process is concerned with the right to a fair and impartial hearing. In work organizations, it is primarily focused on assuring fairness in the handling of grievances and disciplinary matters.

8. (6) A primary union objective is to establish bilateral relations with management. In this case, the term *bilateral* refers to wages, effort, and other conditions of work being established by both management and employees.

9. (20) Most authorities agree that current union strength is approximately 19 percent of the total work force. Accurate union membership is difficult to obtain because of the large number of locals and the reluctance of unions to divulge membership figures.

10. (United States) Compared with most developed countries, union membership is lowest in the United States. Our tradition of individualism and distrust of

collective action in most forms seems to have discouraged union development in this country.

## QUICK REVIEW

I. Why People Form Unions

   A. Unions have been in existence for at least one hundred years before the American Revolution.

   B. Unions make up about 20 percent of the total work force.

   C. Collective bargaining stems from the desire to influence management.

II. Unilateral and Bilateral Relations

   A. One-sided rule making is unilateral.

   B. Managers and employees who agree on rules that both have made are governed by bilateral relations.

   C. *Quid pro quo* means give and take, or "You scratch my back, and I'll scratch yours."

III. Language of Labor Relations

   A. Language of industrial relations includes terms unique to collective bargaining.

   B. The language includes both terms in the contract and terms associated with negotiations and collective bargaining.

IV. Issues in Collective Bargaining

   A. Most labor-management contracts include twenty to thirty contract clauses, each dealing with a different issue.

   B. Issues include pay, benefits, schedules, seniority, grievance procedures, arbitration, and many related issues.

V. Individuals and Unions

   A. Employees may be faced with dual loyalties, both to management and to the union.

   B. Contracts may be used either as a means of improving employee relations or as a weapon by management or unions.

VI. Special Problems in Union-Management Relations

   A. Seniority is a major principle in union-management relations, protecting workers on the basis of their length of service.

   B. Seniority can cause problems in companies that have established affirmative action programs.

VII. Personal Security and Representation

   A. In addition to numerous other benefits, unions offer two important protections to workers: jurisdiction and grievance procedures.

B. Jurisdiction is the protection of a worker's job through union membership in a given craft.

C. Workers are also given the right to due process in which they are guaranteed a fair hearing.

VIII. Grievance Procedures

A. Grievances are formal written complaints requiring management actions.

B. Although there is no uniform set of procedures, most contracts spell out specific grievance steps.

C. If union and management cannot settle an issue, it may be referred to arbitration and settled by a neutral third party.

IX. Into the Future

A. New methods of work and new types of jobs will require a new relationship between labor and management.

B. Status and power differences between workers and managers are likely to be much less evident than in the past.

## KEY TERMS

| | | |
|---|---|---|
| Union | Collective bargaining | Due process |
| Unilateral relationship | Contract | Grievance |
| Bilateral relations | Seniority | Arbitration |
| Negotiation | Jurisdiction | Grievance procedure |
| Quid pro quo | | |

## DISCUSSION QUESTIONS

1. Union leaders have publicly stated that by the mid-1990s, unions will have regained their former strength and influence. Do you agree? Explain.
2. What groups do you think will show the greatest increase in unionism in the next ten years? Why?
3. Job security has become an important union goal in recent years. Why has this occurred?
4. Few high-technology companies are unionized, including those that have been in operation for many years. Why has this occurred?
5. Unionism is strongest in the northeastern, north-central, and West Coast sections of the United States. Why are unions largely concentrated in these areas?

## EXERCISE

### Actions to Prevent Unionization

You have been hired as a consultant for a hospital. You are to determine courses of action the hospital's management should take to prevent the employees from forming a union. The nurses and maintenance employees have been having meetings to discuss the formation of a union. Over 50 percent of the nurses and over 80 percent of the maintenance employees have attended meetings to discuss organizing. The hospital's management wants to take immediate action to prevent unionization.

*Evaluate the following list of actions to prevent unionization.*
Which actions would you take? Which would you take first?

1. Set up grievance committees composed of members elected by the employees. The committees would make recommendations to management on all employee grievances submitted to them.

2. Analyze the pay and benefits at other hospitals in the area. Where your pay or benefits are less than the area averages, immediately increase them.

3. Provide a training program for all supervisors in communication and human relations.

4. Conduct a survey of all employees to determine the nature of complaints and specific problems they believe could be solved by unionization.

5. Establish a department of employee communication to keep employees informed by publishing a newsletter and having employee meetings.

6. Form small groups of employees who do similar work to meet weekly, and provide input on decisions that would affect them.

7. Delegate more authority and responsibility to employees for problem solving and decision making.

8. Have a social get-together twice a month so managers can get to know employees better.

9. Determine the employees who are most actively promoting the organization of a union and fire them.

10. Don't make any changes in working conditions without getting input from employees.

---

## TWO POINTS OF VIEW

### *"Control"*

*What would you do if you were the manager?*

You have recently been promoted to quality control manager in a manufacturing firm. Your boss informs you that he is receiving complaints that your inspectors are sending items back to production as "defective" that meet specifications. You are instructed to immediately improve the work done by the inspectors, because the production employees are filing grievances about work being returned to them that has nothing wrong with it.

You learn from the former quality control manager that before leaving, he had traced most of the inspection errors to Tom Davidson, one of five final inspectors. Since you want to check things out for yourself and be fair to all the inspectors, you assign another inspector to check the work of all five final inspectors. As soon as they heard of your procedure to check their work, all but Tom came to you and protested. They said their work had always been accurate and everyone knew that the last manager had traced the problem to Tom.

The inspectors said that if you put this procedure into practice, they would go over your head to the manufacturing manager with their complaint. They also said that if this was a power play to show how much control you have, you would force them into a position where they would have to organize to protect their rights. You know they have been contacted by a union that is trying to organize the plant.

*What would you do if you were an inspector?*

You are a final inspector for a manufacturing firm. The quality control manager who has been your boss for the past eight years has recently retired. His replacement is a young man who has been with the company for two years as a materials inspector. Your new boss seems to be insecure as a manager and is trying to prove he is in charge.

All the final inspectors know that there has been a problem of items that meet standards being rejected and sent back to production. This makes the production employees angry because they get criticized by management when items are returned. The previous quality control manager had traced the problem to Tom Davidson, one of the final inspectors. Tom is new on the job and was poorly trained.

Your new boss has assigned another inspector to check the work of all the final inspectors. He says he is doing this because he does not know the source of the problem of work being returned that has nothing wrong with it. You believe he knows the problem is being caused by Tom, but he wants to prove he is in control. Along with the other final inspectors, you have objected to this procedure of reinspecting your work. If your new boss is not going to deal with the actual problem but instead pull a power play, the inspectors may have to have more bargaining power. You think it may be time for the inspectors to seriously consider unionizing. Since a union representative has recently contacted the inspectors, it would be easy to pursue formation of a bargaining unit.

You are considering going over the quality control manager's head to tell the manufacturing manager that if the power play is not stopped, the inspectors are going to start organization meetings to form a union.

### ENDNOTES

1. Based on interview with member of Red Bluff, California, Police Department, November 1981.
2. Reported on "60 Minutes," 14 March 1982, CBS Television Network.
3. Douglas A. Fraser, "Justice Means Taking Risks and New Approaches," *Los Angeles Times*, 14 March 1982.

**4.** E. Edward Herman and Alfred Kuhn, *Collective Bargaining and Labor Relations* (Englewood Cliffs, N.J.: Prentice-Hall, 1982), pp. 124–26.

**5.** *1986 Information Please Almanac* (Boston: Houghton Mifflin, 1986), p. 54.

**6.** John R. Schermerhorn, Jr., *Management for Productivity* (New York: Wiley, 1986), p. 535.

# Social and Ethical Values and Responsibilities

_____ *Learning Objectives* _____

After reading this chapter, you should be able to do the following:

1. Understand the importance of social responsibility and ethics in current organizational life
2. Describe the ways companies are dealing with on-the-job issues of discrimination, substance abuse, and emotionally troubled employees
3. Explain the meaning of ethics and ethical dilemmas
4. Identify major social, legal, and ethical problems in organizations
5. Describe trends in social responsibility and ethical considerations on the job
6. Understand some of the difficulties related to ethical and social decisions in the work place
7. Develop insight into some of the special problems of ethics and social responsibility

# *Chapter Topics*

- Beyond profits, products, and services
- Social change at work
- Protectors of society
- Troubled employees, alcoholism, and drug abuse
- Right or wrong—the ethical dilemma
- Value ranking and ethical decisions
- General concepts and ideals
- Sex in the office—a special issue

# *Preview*

In early 1986, the U.S. Supreme Court made a historic ruling that the Civil Rights Act of 1964—specifically, the Title VII (equal employment opportunity) provisions—apply to all races regardless of past discrimination. Determining the impact of the Court's decision will take years, but it calls attention to the nation's ongoing concern with fairness and equity. Discrimination because of national origin, ethnicity, sex, age, race, or physical condition has long been a target of social activists—and still is. We are a nation with a vast guilt complex because of the seemingly unfair treatment of some groups of people based on emotional prejudices.

Equality of opportunity, however, is just one aspect of social and ethical responsibility. What is honest and dishonest becomes increasingly unclear as society becomes more complex. Is it illegal for employees to copy a word-processing computer program for home use, even though the program was bought by the employer and licensed for use by only the employer? What if the employee uses the program primarily for work-related report preparation and only occasionally for private use? Is it okay to copy a personal letter on the office copier? These are the types of questions that involve ethical decisions. Some are minor, and some are based on principles that are meant to never be violated.

Social and ethical responsibilities are difficult to define and even more difficult to police and enforce—an individual, organizational, and societal problem.

## SELF-ASSESSMENT ▬▬▬▬▬▬▬▬▬▬▬▬▬▬▬▬▬▬▬▬

This self-assessment is somewhat different from others in the text. Its questions and statements are intended to help you assess your own personal social and ethical position. Each statement or question has a range of possible responses. A scale of 1 to 6 between two words with different meanings allows you to mark either the word that is considered correct or a place between the two words that represents some agreement and some disagreement. Selection of a high number such as 5 or 6 may be either correct or incorrect, just as selection of lower numbers may be correct or incorrect. Some responses may be partly correct and partly incorrect.

Answers based on research by behavioral scientists, with a short explanation of why the response was considered correct, may be found on page 514.

1. The statement has been made that the most discriminated against person in the United States is the white male between the ages of twenty-four and twenty-seven.

    agree  1...2...3...4...5...6  disagree

2. If a person accidentally learns of a new invention a company has not yet publicly announced, it is ethical to buy stock in the concern before the price rises, as it is sure to do after the announcement.

    agree  1...2...3...4...5...6  disagree

3. In most states, sex between consenting adults is legal. Is an affair between a manager and his or her administrative assistant ethical?

    agree  1...2...3...4...5...6  disagree

4. Marion is black and qualified for a promotion. All other qualified employees are white, and some are equally as qualified. There are no black employees in the open position.

    Marion should receive  1...2...3...4...5...6  Marion should
      special consideration                      compete on the
                                                 same basis as all
                                                 other employees

5. Tom Henley is an expert at market analysis and market trend predictions. Recently he has shown indications of being a chronic alcoholic.

    he should be fired  1...2...3...4...5...6  an attempt should
                                               be made to
                                               rehabilitate him

6. The work force must be reduced by three people. Maria Juarez is a recent employee but the only Hispanic in her department.

Maria should not be   1...2...3...4...5...6   Maria should be
considered for layoff                                considered on the
                                                     same basis as other
                                                     employees

7. When it comes to morals, what is right for one person may be wrong for another.

agree   1...2...3...4...5...6   disagree

8. Food and drug laws ban certain products from being sold in the United States. When companies sell these products to other countries, the practice is:

legal   1...2...3...4...5...6   unethical

9. Morality and ethics are determined largely by:

societal values   1...2...3...4...5...6   religious teachings

10. The most dramatic social movement in the United States is probably the changed status of:

black people   1...2...3...4...5...6   women, regardless
                                       of race

## BEYOND PROFITS, PRODUCTS, AND SERVICES

For just a moment, stop and think about these basic questions: Where do the wood, metal, glass, and plastic of the buildings we use come from? Where do we get our clothes? Our food? Automobiles? Television sets? Furniture? Electricity? To a large extent, the answers are the same. Many, if not nearly all, of the things we use, enjoy, and need in life are supplied by organizations. Organizations influence not only the lives of those who make up their work force but also society as a whole.

Perhaps more so than in other countries, Americans have recognized organizational influences that go beyond profits, products, and services. Through the actions of a combination of dedicated pressure groups such as the National Association for the Advancement of Colored People (NAACP), Ralph Nader's Consumer Advocates, the National Organization of Women, environmental protection groups such as the Sierra Club, and many other associations and unions, people have become more aware of the social responsibilities of work organizations. Responding to public demands, federal, state, municipal, and local governmental agencies have enacted legislation that forces managers of organizations to be increasingly responsible for not only their own organizations but also the concerns of society as a whole.

## A Real Cover-Up

According to Parliament Speaker Hojatoleslam Akbar Hashemi-Rafsanjani of Iran, women's hearts and brains are smaller than men's. He also asserts that there is "no such thing as equality between women and men." Not only are women not equal, according to the Speaker, but Western countries that have given more liberty to women are in a mess. Rafsanjani says that physically weaker women are being forced to strictly obey the "order of the veil" for their own good.

Regulations of the veil require that women, "for their own good," cover themselves from head to foot, leaving only the face and hands exposed. Those who violate these regulations, including foreign visitors and non-Moslems, are subject to penalty of the law. Penalties are usually two to three months in a reform camp, where instructions on proper dress are given daily by a clergyman. Stockings that are too thin or a single lock of hair that is exposed can lead to arrest and the reform camp.

Prior to the present government, most women in Tehran wore Western dress and were moving toward more equal status with men. Times change.[1]

Although many top managers for many years have recognized the social impact of their organizations and have actively sponsored programs designed to improve the well-being of society as a whole, the concept of the social responsibility of management is relatively new. Management's primary social responsibilities fall into four major areas:

### *Areas of Social Responsibility*

1. Promotion of equality of opportunity
2. Protection of the environment and conservation of resources
3. Concern for the health and safety of employees both on and off the job
4. Promotion of ethical standards in their actions and those of their employees

In addition, management is expected to participate actively in community projects and to promote services and legislation that will benefit everyone. These and other related social pressures not only have created tremendous burdens but also have caused a reassessment of management attitudes and traditional management rights.

### *Social Responsibility*

During most of its history, the United States was economically poorer than it is today. Subsistence, survival, and profits were more important goals for both organizations and individuals than they are now. As time passed and the country grew in economic strength, a phenomenon occurred that has had tremendous historical impact. A great middle class developed as the dominant segment of the country's population. The lines between the haves and have-nots became far less clear than before. No longer was there a clear division between rich and poor. In addition to survival needs, other societal goals for work organizations became increasingly important.

At first, the new awareness of the social responsibilities of work organizations was highlighted by laws regulating monopolistic practices and restraint of trade. In addition, the responsibility for on-the-job safety shifted from the employee to the employer. A further emphasis was placed on regulating the relations of organizations with shareholders of its stock. Today, as individual income increases, new social objectives for work organizations are being directed, in some cases voluntarily and in others by legal mandate, toward the development and enforcement of equal work opportunities, environmental and pollution control, and consumer protection.

The old goals of profit, growth, and survival are no longer enough. Work organizations must be socially responsible. Although deplored by many managers, social responsibility is an increasingly important part of managerial and organizational life. In simple terms, **social responsibility** is the acceptance by management of the reality that organizations must act in the public interest in their pursuit of profit and provision of goods and services. Public interest involves that which the public, not management, defines as of greatest importance. Social goals of equal opportunity, preservation of the physical environment, and concern for the users of products and services provided by organizations are all within the public interest, as shown in Figure 18.1. When these are at least partially achieved, new goals will doubtless become apparent.

Realistically, social responsibility as seen by the general public is frequently in conflict with organizational goals. The question always remains, Whose interest is public interest?

### Equal Opportunity

"When I first started in this business," remarked the personnel manager of a large multiproduct manufacturing company, "if a manager wanted all redheads over five feet eight inches tall, that's what we'd recruit and hire." "We had," the personnel manager continued, "a battery of tests each employee was required to take. If their scores weren't right, they wouldn't be hired. Promotions were based pretty much on who the manager liked. Our only women supervisors were in jobs that required running departments such as clerical pools and records keeping departments that were traditionally all women. In our factory, all supervisors were men, even in departments that were predominantly made up of women."

"Now it's different," the manager smiled. "We no longer have all black custodians, all white female clerks, and all white male supervisors. Everyone has an equal chance. Strangely, most of us don't care what sex or color gets a particular job. It's whether they can perform or not that counts."

Within organizations (and outside them as well), few issues have caused as much controversy as the legal and social mandate to provide equal opportunity.

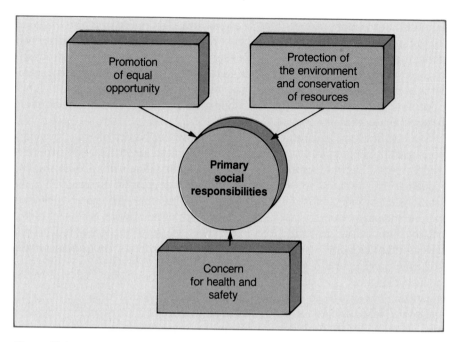

**Figure 18.1**   Management's primary social responsibilities.

Although it is an honored moral value of our society, **equal opportunity** has been much abused. Equality is lost when people are either given or not given consideration for employment, training, or promotion because of their race, color, sex, age, size, national origin, physical handicap, religion, or any of the other non-job-related ways we classify people. Rewards are often given for how well people are liked rather than how well they perform. Self-reliance goes undeveloped when whole classes of people are dependent on public assistance because of lack of job opportunities.

With certain notable exceptions, the most opportune jobs, especially with status and power, have been dominated by white males. Managers, and unions by virtue of their own value systems, have developed and perpetuated a tradition that for most of our history has suppressed the opportunities of many to achieve qualifications for the more highly skilled and highly paid jobs.

## SOCIAL CHANGE AT WORK

Few people will openly admit their own prejudices. Statements such as "Some of my best friends are [black, Hispanic, Jewish, Moslem, Polish]," however, are a certain indication of bias. For many years, social psychologists have studied the values associated with esteem or feelings of self-worth that develop in both groups and individuals. If another person by virtue of race, religion, color, national origin, lifestyle, accent, socioeconomic background, skill level, or any of a number of other characteristics is seen as being "different," that difference is often interpreted as inferiority. Visible differences, such as color and sex, as well as invisible differences, such as religion and national origin, are important. Although mistrust, suspicion, and **prejudice** have been pronounced and still are between identifiable groups, changes in our social values are reducing some of the traditional preconceptions that people have about each other.

Social value change is often slower than it seems. Prior to 1750, women in the colonial United States were, for the most part, treated equally to men in all respects. As a result of the influence of European customs during the latter 1700s, women were relegated to a different set of roles. They became housewives, childbearers, objects of admiration, and property of their husbands or fathers. They had little or no real influence. Not until 1920 did women attain the constitutional right to vote. During World War II, women entered fields of employment traditionally held by men. But by 1950, they had been "demoted," for the most part, back to "women's jobs" as grade school teachers, nurses, garment industry workers, small parts assembly workers, textile mill workers, clerical workers, retail salesclerks, and switchboard operators. Even in these assignments, opportunities for promotion were minimal. During the late 1960s and early 1970s, long-smoldering resentments surfaced. With help from a series of legal mandates and highly vocal organizations, women moved into male-dominated fields that offered greater opportunity.

For blacks, Hispanics, and other minorities, the pattern has been much the same. Through carefully planned and ably led organizations such as the National Association for the Advancement of Colored People, the Urban League, and the Southern Christian Leadership Conference, blacks have been able to weaken many traditional barriers and influence the passage of laws that guarantee their basic constitutional rights. Other minority groups have experienced similar gains through similar organizations.

A primary concept of the equal opportunity movement is the commitment to "job-related" selection devices (interviews, tests, and evaluations). "Job-related" means, in essence, that an employer must not ask preemployment questions or establish occupational requirements unless they can be proven to relate directly to the job for which the employee or applicant is being considered. As a result of a series of legal rulings, including the often-reported *Griggs* v. *Duke Power Company* case that first challenged the necessity of a high school diploma and the passing of an intelligence test as requirements for employment, many organizations no longer require paper-and-pencil tests in their preemployment screening. They are too difficult to prove related to the job.

The transition to equal opportunity has not been easy. To overcome past discrimination, organizations have voluntarily (or involuntarily, under court order), openly given preferential treatment to protected classes—women and minorities—even though the law specifically prohibits preferential treatment. Results have not always been satisfactory:

1.  Open preferential treatment has, at times, created deep-seated resentments within both the existing work force and the community.

2.  Some women and minorities have taken personal advantage of civil rights laws by claiming discrimination when it has been doubtful that any unfair treatment existed.

3. Managers have often used women and minorities as showpieces in work areas that were formerly all white or all male in order to demonstrate equal employment. In the early 1970s, a common practice was to have a black or other minority group member in the front office—a person who was highly visible evidence that the organization was complying with equal opportunity requirements.

4. Job adjustment for people with a heritage of being denied equal employment opportunities for hundreds of years has been, in some cases, difficult. Attitudes of fellow workers, imagined injustices, and lack of confidence based on fear of failure have all contributed to major management-employee relation problems.

Sensitive managers have, in many cases, been able to effectively minimize the adjustment and attitudinal difficulties exhibited by both the existing work force and the new, nontraditional employee. The key to their success has been attending to both real and imagined injustices with careful, corrective efforts. Employees who know that they were hired because they are needed and that they are expected to perform and be rewarded or disciplined like other employees adjust more readily and make greater progress. An equally important factor affecting successful adjustment is the careful training of all levels of management to recognize potential personnel problems and to deal with them openly, impartially, and promptly.

Unfortunately, some managers and employees seem blind to the reality of a changing work force. Their personal bias based on deep cultural traditions has impeded true achievement of equal opportunity. As a country, we have exercised our ability to discriminate against people all too well.

## The Legal Framework of Social Policy

Since U.S. citizens share equally under the law the responsibilities and the protection of government, Congress, in 1964, reinforced the concept of equality and fairness by extending it into the work place.

Few laws have affected the responsibilities of organizations as dramatically as the federal **Civil Rights Act of 1964** and its subsequent amendments in 1972. Under Title VII of the act, any employer or union of fifteen or more people is prohibited from discriminating against any person because of race, religion, color, national origin, or sex. Although many responsible organizations had voluntarily instituted nondiscrimination programs long before 1964, systematic exclusion of many U.S. citizens from the work force continued. Reinforced by state fair employment practice laws, investigative rulings of the federal Equal Employment Opportunity Commission, and court interpretations of equal opportunity laws, management has been forced to build work forces that are representative of the community as a whole. In effect, the Civil Rights Act has made work organizations primary agents of social change, a role often perplexing and sometimes in conflict with other organizational purposes.

*Civil Rights Act*   A major concern in many organizations has been the development of the concept of "protected classes." Although the Civil Rights Act specifically prohibits preferential treatment, administrators of the law have held that because of past inequities, setting specific hiring, training, and promotional goals may be necessary to build a more representative work force. Programs to implement this concept are called **affirmative action** programs. Under this interpretation of the Civil Rights Act, women, blacks, Hispanics, American Indians, and Asians have become protected classes. As protected classes, they may, under certain conditions, be given preferential treatment in employment and promotion. If an employer has no protected classes in a specific job classification, special recruitment to find qualified women or minorities may be undertaken. In many cases, the traditional "rule of three," in which the highest three test scorers are given preference in employment or promotion, is altered to provide opportunities for people who have previously been excluded from certain jobs. Those who scored lower than the top three have equal consideration with top scorers under the altered rules. Refusal by a work organization or union to take affirmative action in building a work force that represents the community at large can have severe consequences.

When the employment service of a medium-sized Louisiana city found that few black applicants were qualifying for police and fire department openings, an intensive investigation was launched. Three major factors were found that contributed to the problem:

1. Some well-qualified black applicants were fearful of public reaction from other blacks and from white conservatives if the applicants became part of the police force.

2. Tests used for applicant selection were found in some instances to be culturally biased.

3. Many black people were suspicious of the motives of a city that had for almost two centuries denied them equal opportunity.

A special public employee selection board was established to recruit black applicants. To avoid possible legal entanglements with the "rule of three" provisions of the city's personnel regulations, oral interviews were weighed much more heavily than written tests in the selection procedure. After three months of concentrated effort, the selection board had developed eligibility lists of applicants that included a fair representation of the city's ethnic distribution. Special indoctrination and training sessions were developed for those selected to fill existing openings and for the previously all-white male work force as well. In the six years that the program has been in effect, only minor public outcry has occurred over the procedures. The integration of the work force went far more smoothly than predicted. Recently, when one of the original black fire fighters was promoted to the position of department chief, it was accepted as a routine, normal event. Before 1970, the event would have been unthinkable to many people in the city.

## Special Problems

Regardless of philosophical implications, the reality of affirmative action will be a part of employment and personnel activities for the foreseeable future. For both employees and managers, several special problems exist. From a management point of view, the doctrine of fairness is the most difficult. What the various laws affecting social policy state, and what courts have ruled, are of particular concern. Applications, interviews, and tests may ask only job-related questions. Most personnel specialists know that it is virtually impossible to construct any selection device that can be proven perfectly job related. The law states that an employer may not give preferential treatment to any employee, yet preferential treatment to protected classes is regularly assigned by the courts. Employers must know not only the law but also the way courts interpret the law's intent. A few of the major laws affecting personnel, not including the Fair Labor Standards Act and those that affect union-management collective bargaining relationships, are shown in Table 18.1.

From an individual employee's point of view, problems are often more complex than those encountered by management. Three true incidents exemplify some of the many different problems (the names of the companies and individuals have been changed):

Sandra Holmquist was the first woman in Telo-Comm Electronics' all-male market planning department. Although she was hired, admittedly, to break the sex barrier, her qualifications were excellent. Sandra's college training included both marketing and electronic technology. At twenty-seven, she was attractive and hardworking but apprehensive about being accepted by the other employees. On several occasions, she was on the verge of quitting Telo-Comm because of both covert and open sexual approaches by her fellow workers. She was also told, not only by her fellow employees but also by women in other departments, that she had the job only because of her sex. When her immediate supervisor was moved to a higher-level job, Sandra was recommended for promotion to manager of technical market planning. Three days after assuming her new duties, a complaint was filed with the state Fair Employment Practices Commission alleging preferential treatment because of sex by Telo-Comm management. The Fair Employment Commission investigation concluded that Sandra was indeed qualified for her new assignment and that Telo-Comm had not violated the provisions of the Fair Employment Practices Act. Sandra has subsequently received additional promotions but still has nagging doubts concerning her full acceptance by other managers as well as employees.

Joe Mitsubi, a correctional institute parole officer, was told by his immediate supervisor that he would probably not be promoted, although his qualifications were outstanding. The Department of Correction's policy was to match supervisory parole officers ethnically with the majority of parolees. Since there were almost no prisoners with Japanese ancestry at Joe's assigned institution, there was no way for him to be "ethnically matched." He subsequently transferred to another agency within the state government that needed a qualified management trainee.

Steve Morgan, who has a Ph. D. in anthropology, was told "confidentially" by several university deans of social science that they would like him on their staff, but their next hires were going to have to be either women or minorities. The U.S. Department of Health and Human Services was threatening withdrawal of funds for

**Table 18.1**
## Major Personnel-Related Laws

| | |
|---|---|
| Equal Pay Act, 1963 | Prohibits paying women less than men doing equal or similar work. |
| Civil Rights Act, 1964 (amended 1972) | Title VII requires equal treatment, regardless of race, color, religion, sex, or national origins, in all personnel actions. Applies to all employers or unions except for certain specific exemptions such as native Americans and bona fide religious orders. |
| Fair Employment Practices Act | State-level equal opportunity acts. |
| Age Discrimination Act, 1967 (amended 1980) | Prohibits discrimination based on age for persons between forty and seventy years of age. |
| Occupational Safety and Health Act, 1970 | Mandates minimum safety and hygiene standards. |
| Workers' compensation laws | Enacted by all states; ensure employees of losses due to job-related injuries or illnesses. |

failure to hire minorities. Steve finally went to work for a friend in the construction business as a public relations manager.

Although it benefits many, the force of affirmative action has also created problems and sometimes unpredictable injustices.

### Problems in Attitudes

Few people will openly admit their own prejudices, and most of us at least profess a belief in equality and fairness. In spite of the force of law and the gradual reduction of racial, sexual, and national background barriers to job opportunities, the concept of preferential treatment to balance the ethnic and sexual composition of the work force has created deep resentment that is expressed in many forms.

*Women and minorities have most often been the recipients of criticism, not because of what they themselves have done or not done, but because they are frequently perceived as receiving preferential treatment.*

Although management may stringently try to balance a largely white male work force by giving minorities and women "nontraditional jobs," its actions may be interpreted as deliberately excluding eligible white males. Increasingly, young qualified males are protesting what they believe are discriminatory practices. Supreme Court rulings on discrimination against white males point out that preferential treatment of women and minorities is illegal; yet ethnically balanced and sexually representative work forces must be achieved.

Gradually, however, the stories of the Joes, Sandras, and Steves are disappearing. There is greater acceptance of women into previously male-dominated fields and acceptance of minorities in jobs from which they were previously excluded. Unfortunately, the problems of prejudice and individual adjustment are still with us. Important questions remain: "Are they there primarily because they are female or minorities, or because of their qualifications?" Conversely, "Am I here primarily because I am female or a minority, or because of my qualifications?"

## PROTECTORS OF SOCIETY

Although equal opportunity, to some extent, may continue to be a major issue for the foreseeable future, it is not the only social issue management faces. Concern for the use of resources, protection of the environment, safety and quality of products, as well as consumer reaction, are all part of management's expanding areas of responsibility. Managers are increasingly realizing that their actions and therefore their responsibilities extend far beyond their place of work.

> In Azusa, California, a process was developed to convert spoiled and unmarketable fruit into an excellent supplement to cattle fodder. Shortly after the conversion plant using the process went into operation, the surrounding area was enveloped in an overpowering stench similar to that of spoiled fruit. A local citizen's group sought and obtained a court injunction prohibiting the plant from further operation until controls for the odor could be installed.

Over the past twenty years, public concern for our environment has developed into a strong **environmental protection** movement. Various public and government groups have put increasing pressure on companies to control or eliminate pollutants.

However, a major deterrent to voluntary assumption of responsibility for environmental protection has been the frequently prohibitive costs. Although covers on its processing tanks and filters on external ventilators can help control odor at the Azusa cattle fodder supplement plant, it may be far more difficult and expensive for a chemical manufacturer to dispose of waste products.

Management decisions can have a significant impact on environmental problems, but the issue is complex. Although work organizations are frequently blamed, a great deal of pollution is the result of consumer demand for convenience products. We don't want to give up our automobiles, canned drinks, no-return bottles, prepackaged food, double-wrapped gum and candy, or especially, jobs in companies that belch smoke and dump sewage into rivers. Pollution exists for many reasons. The question here, however, is, How can management take a leadership role in protecting the environment? In all probability, pollution of our air, water, and land will continue; but if it is not controlled, neither organizations nor society will survive.

### On-the-Job Environmental Protection

Managers, as contributors to the shaping of society, may do a variety of things to encourage protection of the environment. Many companies have developed programs designed to encourage employees to ride in car pools, thus saving gasoline, reducing pollution, and alleviating congestion of highways. Some organizations have experimented with providing vans to selected people willing to pick up a number of other employees so all can ride in one vehicle.

Sponsorship of clean-up campaigns that encourage both employees and their children to become aware of pollution is another effective way of developing concern for environmental issues and the importance of individual action. Most significant, however, are the contributions management makes by setting in-house examples of waste control and cleanliness and demonstrating concern for its impact on the community.

Management can, and in many cases voluntarily does, act to control its organization's pollution problems. Organizations must, however, in addition to management action and example, conform to increasing legal requirements.

### Management, Environment, and the Law

During the 1950s and 1960s, a growing awareness of damage being done to our environment began to stir the consciences of many people. Comedians joked endlessly about smog in Los Angeles. When people in nearly every large city in the United States finally realized that Los Angeles was not alone in its air pollution problems, the jokes were no longer funny.

In 1962, Rachel Carson's beautiful and touching *The Silent Spring* served as a catalyst to encourage public action on environmental issues. Her book focused on the damage being done by the most widely used pesticide throughout the world, DDT. Once hailed as a means of saving humanity from hordes of insect infestations, which in many cases it did, DDT was found to be killing not only insects but fish and birds as well. Eventually, largely through public pressure, DDT was removed from use as a general insecticide.

Managers whose organizations created pollutants of any kind came under legal and public scrutiny. In one instance, a public outcry was raised when industrial pollution was found to be making Lake Erie incapable of supporting life. Companies that had traditionally disposed of industrial waste in streams that fed not only Lake Erie but also other bodies of water were forced, by law, to take stringent pollution control measures. Public concern for our physical environment grew steadily.

Many laws designed to protect the environment have been enacted by federal, state, and local governments over a number of years. A problem for management is determining which agencies have jurisdiction. In 1977, the Dow Chemical Company withdrew plans for building a giant chemical-processing facility in northern California largely because of difficulties in determining environmental protection measures and securing related permits. Over one hundred

---

### Shelling Out for Environmental Protection ━━━━━━━━━

At times the government seems to work against, not for, the environment. The Blue Diamond brand almond-processing plant came up with an ingenious plan for turning discarded almond shells into energy to help run the facility. The concept was the brainchild of a joint effort between Imotek Corporation and the Almond Growers Association. It was to be the only large-scale biomass energy production unit of its kind.

But government experts vetoed the original design for controlling unwanted ash and odor by-products and instead specified a system that Imotek engineers thought would not work. After only a short time in operation, the plant began emitting a penetrating odor and spewing a fine brown ash into the air. The ash coated nearby neighborhood shrubbery and homes. Almost overnight, citizen pickets sprang up, protesting the plant's pollution.

Imotek engineers went to work on the problem. Within three months, they had modified the system back to their original design. This time it worked—without the help of government experts "protecting" the environment.[2]

---

different government agencies were involved in water, air, and solid waste pollution controls.

To unify administration of environmental protection laws at the federal level, the **Environmental Protection Agency** was established in 1970 to coordinate government action in the areas of air, water, solid waste, toxic chemicals, pesticides, and radiation pollution control. Some of the agency's actions, especially in establishment of motor pollution control standards of automobiles and sewage treatment standards, have drawn sharp criticism. Managers of some organizations frequently cite environmental protection rulings as primary contributors to inflation and loss of productive capability.

From a practical point of view, companies are often faced with difficult, conflicting demands and ever-increasing paperwork requirements from the hundreds of agencies with which they deal. Consumers demand less expensive, better-quality products and services, yet those same consumers also blame management for failing to be concerned with the environment in which all of us live. Managers must plan operations that produce products, services, taxes, and jobs and at the same time meet society's demands for less pollution, better use of scarce resources, and greater corporate social responsibility.

Despite all the uncertainties, we do know this: *Only society in the future can determine the true long-range effectiveness of today's social policies in work organizations.*

Not all environmental control efforts have the happy ending of the Imotek story located above. Kaiser Steel Company's Fontana Plant began closing its facility in the spring of 1982. After many years as the West Coast's largest steel producer, the company cited two major reasons for the plant shutdown. Unreasonable union demands were originally thought to be the primary difficulty. After union employees moderated their requests, it was then noted that Kaiser had spent over $30 million in a failed attempt to meet federal environmental control standards. Further expenditures would be financially prohibitive and still could not guarantee that federal standards would be met.

## TROUBLED EMPLOYEES, ALCOHOLISM, AND DRUG ABUSE

Nearly every organization is faced with problems related to employees who are chemically dependent or suffer relatively severe long-term emotional difficulties. Although no easy answers are available, most organizations recognize that trying to rehabilitate valuable, trained employees with such problems is frequently less costly than replacing them.

At Bechtel Corporation, a large international construction and engineering corporation, estimates are that it costs $10,000 to replace a problem employee. TRW and Caterpillar both report similar figures, exclusive of training time.[3]

Of all employee problems, **alcoholism** has been most prevalent and most studied. The National Council on Alcoholism estimates that problem drinking costs American corporations between $13 and $20 billion annually. Absenteeism, accidents, and sick leave usage by problem drinkers may be sixteen times higher than the rate for average employees. Although these statistics are formidable, reliable studies indicate that rehabilitation programs have been successful in 50 to 75 percent of the cases.

Many different approaches have been developed to handle alcoholic employees, with supervisory counseling and referral to outside agencies by far the most common. Threats of dismissal or demotion only encourage an employee to conceal the problem. Open, nonthreatening discussion seems to be a necessary first step toward achieving employee cooperation. Most organizations utilize competent outside agencies for actual rehabilitation. A close follow-up is usually made of employees completing treatment; and if a relapse occurs, another rehabilitation attempt may be tried. However, in some cases suspension and termination may be necessary. In most instances, large corporations report that an attempt is nearly always made to "save" the employee before termination.

Caterpillar Corporation reported that of 990 employees referred for treatment since their program began, 414 were completely rehabilitated. A follow-up study indicated a 50 percent decline in lost hours, a 31 percent decline in accidents on the job, and 75 percent fewer disciplinary actions for treated employees.

Drug and emotional problems are more difficult to recognize and treat than alcoholism. Although no accurate statistics are available, the number of drug-related employee problems is increasing. At the present time, there are few policies other than termination for blatant use of illicit drugs such as marijuana, cocaine, and heroin, since in most cases, use of these substances is considered

---

### Big Costs, Worse Habits ━━━━━━━━━━━━━━━━━━━━━━━━

**Chemical abuse** costs companies about $70 billion annually in lost productivity and health benefits. This does not include the cost of operation of CDR (chemical dependency rehabilitation) programs or EAP (employee assistance programs) currently used by about 35 percent of all Fortune 500 companies. An increasing number—approximately 45 percent in 1986—of Fortune 500 companies and many smaller ones are screening applicants for drug use.

Fifty train accidents and several airplane accidents from 1975 to 1986 have been directly linked to drug-or alcohol-impaired employees. Also estimated is that two-thirds of employees entering the work force between the ages of eighteen and twenty-five have used drugs; of these, many continue to use them during working hours.

Some analysts believe that recent declines in U.S. productivity can be traced, at least in part, to drug usage. The problem is a large, complex, and especially difficult one, not only for work organizations but also for society in general.[4]

---

illegal under current law. The difficulty in determining when an employee is addicted rather than an occasional user compounds the problem. Companies with some success in rehabilitation of alcoholics may need to take the same tactics in handling some types of drug users.

Emotional problems are usually recognized by noticeable changes in behavior, such as increased irritability, withdrawal from social contact, excessive tiredness, fits of temper, forgetfulness, or unusual physical symptoms. Most emotional symptoms will pass in a relatively short period of time. When they persist, however, a generally unwise approach is for supervisors to assume the role of counselors or attempt to talk employees out of their troubles. Like alcoholics, chronically disturbed employees should be referred, usually through appropriate medical or personnel services, to agencies that can provide expert counseling. Some corporations have developed widely publicized employee assistance programs or hotlines for troubled employees to use in seeking help. Unlike alcoholics, emotionally troubled employees will usually willingly seek and accept help rather than hide their problems.

## RIGHT OR WRONG—THE ETHICAL DILEMMA

From 1973 to 1980, when gasoline prices were soaring, oil companies came under sharp attack for disregarding public interests and deliberately profiteering at the expense of national inflation. Even now, with the current oil glut, these companies have never fully recovered from this criticism. Many people still view them as giant manipulators of government policy and the controllers of other segments of the economy.

---

### A Hotline That Works ━━━━━━━━━━━━━━━━━━━━━━━━━━━━━

Control Data's dial-for-help program has been so successful that the company is now selling the plan to other organizations.

The program is administered by Control Data's Life Care Institute and provides a variety of telephone and face-to-face counseling. Workers can call into the twenty-four-hour hotline to get help with any type of personal problem, whether or not it is job related. The hotline staff has dealt with everything from alcoholism to alimony. Over seven years, 30,000 of the company's 48,000 employees have used the hotline.

At the present time, thirty-seven organizations, including the National Basketball Association, are buying the Control Data program for their own employees.[5]

---

Oil companies are not the only ones who suffer from a declining public image. Almost daily, news items reveal instances of corporate kickbacks, bribery, cover-ups, deceptive advertising, and unfair treatment of employees. A substantial portion of society believes that business corporations, especially the large, highly visible ones, are interested only in profits and totally disregard the well-being of society. Government agencies also suffer the same tarnished image. The General Services Administration has been accused of paying as much as thirty-two dollars to have a key duplicated (usually no more than three dollars at a local hardware store), issuing contract payments for work never performed, and continuing to accept kickbacks and bribes. Department of Agriculture grain inspectors, Federal Department of Transportation highway inspectors, and a host of other government officials have been accused of illegal and unethical practices that go uninvestigated and unpunished.

Social responsibility and ethics in organizations are part of the same general concerns. Although social responsibility is directed toward issues related to the effect of an organization's actions on society in general, ethics deals with the somewhat clouded issues of what is right and wrong.

### *What Is Ethics?*

**Ethics** concerns matters of right and wrong and of good and bad. The original Greek word meant "character." The Romans had a corresponding word meaning "customs." We learn from ancient wisdom that character is judged by the customs of the particular group of people we are working or living with.

Ethics and morals are first learned from our parents and are "relearned" as we grow older as part of the development of our total system of attitudes and values. Our values—and thus our concepts of right and wrong—are strongly influenced by the values of our parents and by our environment. A person raised in a midwestern farming community has different values from one raised in an eastern inner city. One whose father was a banker has different values from one whose father was a railroad engineer. Without making judgments about them, these differences must be recognized.

Values also differ because of cultural heritage. To take a minor and funny example, compare western and eastern United States traditions on wearing hats. The westerner believes that it is right to wear his beloved broad-brimmed hat in the house, even at mealtime. An easterner would never think of wearing a hat in the house, and wearing a hat at the table would be a great wrong.

This example makes the point that "right" or "wrong" is established by what are called **reference groups**, as well as by our early training. A major problem in the study of organizational ethics is that there are so many different reference groups, such as union members and CPAs, in our American society. The people we deal with in supervision and management come from many different kinds of reference groups. They have different values; they have different expectations. Dealing with the various value systems of employees poses numerous problems for managers at all levels and makes business and organizational ethics something few people want to talk about.

## *Approaches to Individual Ethical Decisions*

If you read summaries of what is written about ethics, you find that ideas of the "right thing to do" fall into four classes: See Figure 18.2.

1. *A rigid set of rules.* In all ages, from the beginning of written history to the present, many people have said that the only right and safe thing to do is to follow a rigid set of rules that apply in all circumstances. Easily

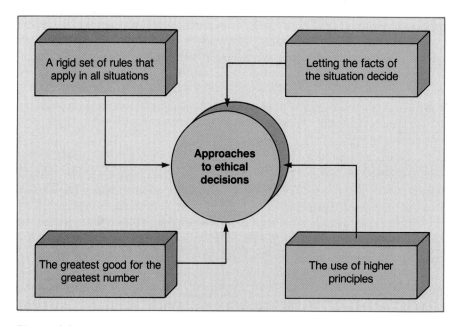

Figure 18.2   Approaches to individual ethical decisions.

demonstrated is that this is a dangerous approach to follow, especially in business. Here is an example from civil society: It is universally accepted that to lie is wrong. If, however, you were a visitor in a totalitarian country and saw a well-known freedom fighter pass you on the street, a person you knew had been in jail, would you tell anyone, especially the police? Your answer would probably be no. You know that many people will lie to save the life of someone they consider worthwhile. The principle of absolute rules does not work as a rule of ethics.

2. *The greatest good for the greatest number.* The greatest good for the greatest number is a rule of life that has been advocated for many years. Any viewer of television will see that many public figures adopt this principle. But any viewer of television will also see that many good people reject this principle. The minority does have rights—the greatest good for the greatest number could mean slavery, oppression, or death for a certain number of people. This is intolerable in American society.

3. *Situation ethics.* A currently popular approach is to determine the rightness or wrongness of each individual decision by the facts of the situation. The "best" judgment of the decision maker results from the nature of the existing situation. In the extreme of this approach, each situation is decided independently of personal past experience or the past experience of others. This approach can be dangerous and unworkable because we cannot act today without being influenced by what we did yesterday. An individual should not decide and act independently of what others think and what others have previously done. Although the situation *is* an important factor in any decision, the situation cannot dictate the rightness and the wrongness by itself. Workable principles must be applied. One of the early writers on **situation ethics** in the 1960s, Joseph Fletcher, appealed to people to make the situation a factor, but not the only factor.[6] He tried to move people toward the approach described in the next paragraph.

4. *Use of higher principles.* Most values that our parents taught us or those which we have learned in our lifetimes can be ranked into a system. Some values rank higher to us than others. Each person's ranking is different. The most consistent and satisfactory system of ethics for humanity today is the commitment to a rank of values and the use of the highest values in making ethical decisions. It is to this fourth principle that the remainder of the chapter is devoted.

### Why Managers Face Ethical Dilemmas

Managers often face **ethical dilemmas** simply because they deal with a broad range of human behaviors and with many groups and cultures. They must deal with individuals who adhere to codes of conduct differing from their own. This poses a complex set of conditions. Few philosophers attempt to gauge the "rightness or wrongness" of managerial decisions. If philosophical underpinnings do not exist, we can, as managers and concerned individuals, adopt an operational approach and take actions, make decisions, and resolve differences. A simplistic approach based upon mindlessly following "tried and true" advice often leads to unsatisfactory results.

*Case I:* The technical director of a paper company was called in by the vice-president of operations and was told: "Go to the state technical meeting next week and be sure to take the plant trip. The company you'll tour has a new process they have been keeping under wraps. We could use it—find out how they do it!" When the technical director arrived at the plant, the tour host told all concerned that the new process was a trade secret and requested guests to stay close to their guides. The visitors were not to see any part of the plant involved in the new process. Ignoring strong group tradition against violation of courtesies extended guests, the technical director "lost his way" and found the control room of the new process. He was discovered there by an executive of the competing company as he was frantically copying operating data. He never got another job.

*Case II:* The development projects manager of a major aerospace component company was not impressed when a young test engineer came to him with a problem. The young man had gone over his project engineer's head to complain that the concept and design for a new aircraft braking system were faulty and that performance tests were rigged to conceal the defect. Even though the project engineer in question was notorious for his inability to accept criticism, the superior manager followed company tradition and refused to investigate the project engineer's brake program. He told the complainer to forget about his worries; the project engineer could handle the matter. The company went ahead with rigged tests and test data. When the customer put the faulty brakes on a test aircraft, they heated to the point that they fused on landing, almost wrecking the aircraft and endangering the pilot. At that point, the test engineer and an associate resigned their jobs and told their stories to the authorities and the press. As a result, the company lost the contract and suffered a lot of bad publicity.[7]

The two cases just cited had unfortunate consequences because the decision makers blindly followed "rules" instead of analyzing the total situation and applying useful general concepts after such analysis. In Case I, the unfortunate technical director was afraid he would lose his job if he did not follow orders, but failed to recognize that the group tradition against violating the "guest rule" was so strong as to make him a virtual outcast if he did. In Case II, the superior manager made the mistake of not knowing his own subordinate and not knowing enough details of the task to properly evaluate the justifiable complaint of the junior employee. The lower status of the junior employee was interpreted as not only lower status but also lower credibility.

## VALUE RANKING AND ETHICAL DECISIONS

Honorable business decisions rest on the decision maker's strong sense of personal worth. Along with the forces in the individual, forces in the task, forces in the other people involved, forces in the environment, expectations of the group, and general concepts and ideals in the community all bear on an ethical decision. The relationships of these factors are shown in Figure 18.3.

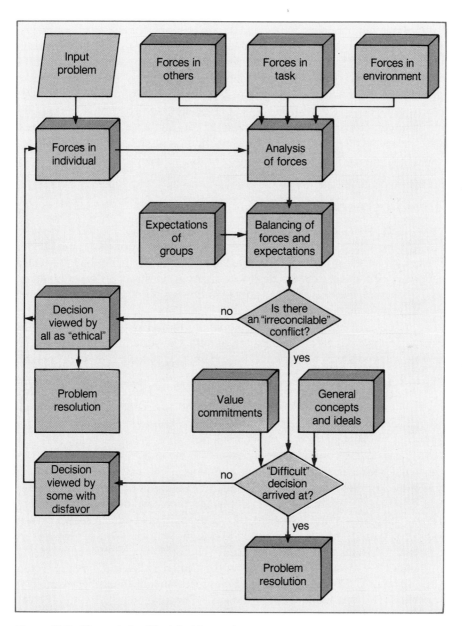

Figure 18.3   Elements in ethical decision cycle.

## Forces in the Individual

We have already stated that one of the primary forces in any person is the set of experiences from early childhood. These forces are so important that many people believe that an individual would have no value system at all unless he or she had experienced strong inputs from parents and other closely associated adults. We know today that people who react in an "instinctive" manner are those who have not examined the values gained in their own childhood. An effective member of society must build on the best of what is learned in the first six years to develop his or her own value system. Another major set of forces in the individual is the experience in adolescence and early adulthood. The judgments of peers and superiors about actions have a major effect on our ideas of right and wrong. Finally, as we progress in early adulthood into positions of responsibility, the reactions from bosses, associates, and subordinates even further modify our idea of right and wrong and produce forces in us as individuals. These forces are often in conflict. This is the human situation. Every decision we make produces a reaction that produces a force within us.

## Forces in Others

Every situation we face is different. This is especially true of the forces in other people in the situation. These people may be our bosses, our associates, or our subordinates. They may be exactly the same people by name, but they have changed since the last time we dealt with them. A construction superintendent may be asked to work his crew an extra four hours after completing the normal eight-hour shift. He may say yes or no. A moral or an ethical situation is involved. It is well known that tired people are more likely to make mistakes. Construction is a dangerous occupation at best. The superintendent must wonder if the lives of any of his crew will be endangered by having to work an extra four hours.

If they have just come back from a restful weekend and have been working well, safely, and harmoniously, he may feel "right" in accepting the responsibility for the additional work. It will be an advantage to his firm, it will be an extra pay for his workers, and presumably it will not affect their well-being.

Suppose, to the contrary, this is the fourth day in a row that overtime has been requested. If the superintendent's employees have worked twelve hours each of the last three days, they are likely to be tired, out of sorts, and prone to make mistakes. They are the same people, but they have become predisposed to errors, they could hurt themselves, they could kill somebody. In such a case, it would be "wrong" for the superintendent to accept the requirement for an additional four-hour shift no matter how badly the company needed it.

Many of the most important firms in the United States, such as the Exxon Corporation or DuPont, give great weight to forces in individuals before making a decision. The top management of Exxon Corporation, for example, gives major consideration to the personal situation (ages of children, health conditions, lifestyle, and so on) of second-level managers before reassigning them to positions of greater or different responsibility in the company. In a *Fortune* magazine interview, the former chairman of what is now Exxon Corporation stated that in making such a determination, the company wanted to be sure that the best interests of the company and the best interests of the individual were served.

### Forces in the Task

To give an example of the forces in the task, let us look at coal mining, a hazardous occupation. Miners and managers alike realize the dangers involved. Many miners and supervisors die every year in industry accidents. The economy of the United States, however, requires continual mining of large amounts of coal. An ethical and responsible mining manager will not, because of hazards, avoid the assignment of managing a coal mine. The manager's principal obligation is to see that mining is carried out under optimum precautions to protect the lives of the miners as well as increase efficiency.

### Forces in the Environment

Business today operates in a confusing social and legal environment. Although an ideal, the letter of the law is often so confusing and, in the judgment of many, occasionally so wrong that open defiance of it is sometimes considered an ethical action. Change through the judicial process may be hoped for. Also clear is that mere adherence to the letter of the law does not make a person honorable or ethical. Most of us know of many scoundrels who have never broken the law as written but have violated its intent. Widely believed in the United States today is that it is more important for business to adhere to the spirit than to the letter of the law. Many well-intended laws have such serious defects that an unethical person can deprive fellow citizens of their just rights without violating the letter of the law. The managers in Case II had certainly violated the spirit of the law but suffered no punishment for it.

### Expectations of Others

We have already commented that the firm is made up of many groups of people among its managers, employees, customers, and stockholders. We have further noted that the values and expectations of these various groups are extraordinarily different. The modern firm exists in many different communities. The local plant or operation is one community; a large firm spread over the entire country is another community.

Many citizens of the city in which an organization is located have group expectations that differ from those of the firm's employees. The people that work for the firm have ties to the town, with its different expectations. Furthermore, they have ties to churches, fraternal associations, family groups, and ethnic groups. Each of these has valuations different from those of the firm, as well as valuations different from each other. Moreover, the employees may be members of labor unions and one political party or another. Additional conflicts may arise because of the different values of these unions and parties.

A common expectation within the labor force in a given firm may be something like "Never rat on the boss, even though you think he or she is doing the wrong thing." Common expectations among professional and technical groups might include "Sure it would be a good idea to have the plant open for technical personnel from competitive companies, as long as they realize they are our guests and stay away from designated Company Confidential areas." The technical director in Case I became unemployable because of his violation of this group expectation. Common expectations of unions are that seniority will be honored above all else in the maintenance of employment. A common expectation of citizen groups is that the firm will "be a good neighbor" in encouraging its employees to take an active role in civic affairs and in complying voluntarily with environmental protection regulations. A common expectation of church-related groups is that the company will never deceive the public in its advertising or in public relations communications. All these differing expectations are not necessarily conflicting, but in some situations they may be.

## GENERAL CONCEPTS AND IDEALS

When we were small children, we were all exposed to absolute concepts such as "Always tell the truth." Another colloquial absolute is "If you can't do the time, don't do the crime." Still another is "There's no such thing as a free lunch!"

We have already commented that these absolutes are of use to us and are necessary in building the value commitments by which we may live. For example, we all know and honor the imperative "Thou shalt not steal," but is it wrong for the employees of a supermarket wrecked in a tornado to remove canned food from the ruins to distribute to starving survivors of the natural disaster?

In the past year or so, the issue of bribery has received much publicity. We know nothing can be accomplished in certain countries abroad unless officials, minor or major, are persuaded with money to do their duty. If you are moving your household goods into a foreign country, is it wrong to pay a surcharge of 10 percent on top of all the legally imposed fees to see that the goods are delivered in time for you and your family to do the most effective job possible for your company?

Real conflicts occur in deciding the right thing to do in a given situation from a personal point of view. A twentieth-century theologian and philosopher, Paul Tillich, once remarked, "Every event in our lives takes place in two worlds; the world of concrete realities and the world of ideal sentiments." We must balance the demands of both worlds.

Earlier, we spoke of the underlying theme of this chapter, that there are greater goods (or "rights") and lesser goods (or "wrongs"). One of the greater goods is that we should not kill or harm other human beings. Yet we all know that there are times when violating this great good may be possible and necessary for us. In protecting our own life or the lives of those near and dear to us, it is right and proper for us to take human life. This is virtually a universal moral code in the United States. Widely accepted, although less universally so, is that it is right to take a human life in the defense of our country. We must judge, in each instance, which is the greater good. But we must have our own firmly established systems of values and priorities if we are to make such judgments and live with the consequences.

## The Operational Approach to Ethical Dilemmas in Practice

The following case describes an incident that took place only a few years ago. In this case, the decision maker, an airline pilot, followed the entire procedure illustrated in Figure 18.3. A later discussion with him about the incident resulted in the writing of this chapter and the paper that preceded it.[8] See if you can determine what the decision maker was thinking and how he balanced the forces in developing a desirable and ethically correct decision.

*Case III:* As has been well documented, passenger pilots of major airlines are truly operational managers. Their minor decisions, if incorrect, may cause opportunity losses of thousands of dollars. A major pilot error may cost tens of millions of dollars as well as hundreds of lives. Pilot-managers must have the ability to rapidly assess the many facets of a complex situation and arrive at an operational decision. In this case, the captain arrived for preflight check in a drunken state. The ground operational staff discreetly ignored his condition, but when the first officer arrived a few moments later, things were different. Drawing the older man aside, the first officer asked in a low but firm tone, "Captain will you turn yourself in, or shall I have to?" The captain proceeded immediately to the chief pilot's office and voluntarily grounded himself. Drying out took six months, but he has returned to flying for several years now without touching a drop. The two men have flown together often since the incident and are on good terms with each other. The younger pilot's only repercussions came from some other senior pilots who didn't like his violation of the axiom "Never blow the whistle on your boss!"

Case III had a desirable outcome for all concerned. It did not result from applying a rigid, if valid, rule—in this case, "Drunken pilots must not fly!" Rather, it resulted from the first officer's rapid operational assessment followed by a decision to force the captain to ground himself. The younger pilot had to assess the forces acting in four elements of the situation: (1) in himself, (2) in the other individual, (3) in the task, and (4) in the environment. He then had to determine their interactions and the ethical (or traditional) impact on each force and apply his value concepts in making a viable decision.

The first officer had three choices: (1) to ignore the captain's condition and trust to luck and his own skill as a pilot to carry the flight through, (2) to go to the chief pilot, or (3) to persuade the captain to do so himself. A number of first officers have covered for a drunken captain by getting the captain to agree to let them handle the takeoff and any landings before the captain sobered up. The first officer, in this case, recognized that the captain was an alcoholic. Covering for him would not have helped him in the long run. Passengers, furthermore, have the right to expect *two* competent, alert pilots up front. Going directly to the chief pilot was a last resort, because it would bypass the vital step in recovery from alcoholism in which individuals recognize for themselves that substance abuse may ruin them. Clearly, it was in the best interests of the airline, the public, the two individuals—and of the task of accomplishing a transcontinental flight—for the captain to ground himself. The copilot expected repercussions for violating "tradition," but he thought he could adapt to pressure. It would have been a worse violation of traditional authority for *him* to have gone to the chief pilot.

## SEX IN THE OFFICE—A SPECIAL ISSUE

A troublesome issue involving both ethical values and principles of social responsibility is the use of power to gain sexual favors. Sex in the office has two sides. On one hand, it involves the use of threat or promise of promotion by a manager, usually a male, to obtain sexual compliance from an employee at a lower level. In 1980, the Equal Employment Opportunity Commission (EEOC) issued sex discrimination guidelines covering sexual harassment on the job. **Sexual harassment** includes behavior such as sexual advances, requests for sexual favors, or other verbal or physical conduct of a sexual nature directed toward an employee or applicant for work. Three general conditions generally define sexual harassment:

1. Submission to or toleration of such conduct is an explicit or implicit term or condition of employment, appointment, promotion, or performance evaluation.
2. Submission to or rejection of such conduct is used as a basis for personnel decisions of any type.
3. The conduct has the purpose or effect of interfering with the employee's work performance or creating an intimidating, hostile, offensive, or otherwise adverse working environment.

The other side of the problem concerns sexual conduct based on the **willing consent** of both parties. Public knowledge of the matter may be embarrassing to an organization because of unfavorable publicity and the impact on the organization's public image. A secretary who becomes pregnant and names her boss as the father, a male employee who claims his female boss propositioned him after they were discovered sharing a hotel room, and accusations against companies by suspicious husbands or wives are only a few of hundreds of types of sexual conduct at work based on mutual consent.

Many people doubt the wisdom of corporate executives engaging in highly visible relationships that direct unfavorable attention to the organizations for which they work. Most employers would prefer to keep private affairs private. Like many other facets of organizational life, the proper course of action to take when conflicts between individual privacy and corporate image occurs is not clear.

## SELF–ASSESSMENT DISCUSSION

1. (6) Although some people will undoubtedly cite cases of discrimination against young, capable white males, they have the highest employment rate in

the United States. In many cases, both white and black women have better opportunities than young black males.

2. (6) According to the Securities Exchange Commission rules, using information unavailable to others, such as pending mergers, new products, and similar data, for personal gain before its availability to the public is not only unethical but also illegal.

3. (6) Even though some behavior is legal under existing law, it may be considered unethical or immoral by any group of people. Most organizations discourage affairs between employees on the basis that they nearly always lead to a breakdown in personal and work relations. This is especially true in cases where one employee reports to another.

4. (3, 4) Under existing law, race, color, national origin, or sex may be used as a job qualification to meet affirmative action goals of a balanced work force. This does not mean that an employer must take a less-qualified person. In Marion's case, the employer must compare her qualifications with those of others. If she qualifies, both her status as a woman and as a black person may be used as additional qualifications. Recent challenges to this interpretation of equal opportunity may change current interpretation of the law.

5. (2, 3, 4, 5) Many organizations have concluded that substance abuse, whether alcohol or illicit drugs, is so pervasive in our society that firing people for substance abuse is no longer feasible. Large organizations have developed rehabilitation programs, and smaller ones are encouraging talented but dependent employees to seek help. In some cases, however, employees resist changing destructive alcohol and drug use and ultimately must be terminated.

6. (1, 2, 3, 4, 5, 6) According to the U.S. Supreme Court, traditional seniority systems are perfectly legal. Also legal is attempting to meet affirmative action goals by maintaining a work force representative of the population of the area in which the organization operates. Union rules, company policy, and past practice will all affect Maria's continued employment with the company.

7. (1) Morals are based on personal or religious values. What may be perfectly moral for one person can be blatantly immoral for another. Abortion, nudity, and cohabitation by unmarried partners are just a few examples.

8. (6) With little doubt, the practice is legal but unethical.

9. (3, 4, 5) Moral values are primarily based on religious teachings, while ethics are based on societal values, regardless of religious teachings.

10. (6) Historians and sociologists of the next century will probably cite the changed status of women in Western society and particularly in the United States as one of the most dramatic and profound social movements experienced by any society. Although the civil rights movement of the 1960s, led by outstanding black men and women, began a major shift in the way all groups were treated, especially in educational and job opportunities, changes in the status of women in the work force and in society in general cut across all lines of color and ethnicity.

## QUICK REVIEW

I. Beyond Profits, Products, and Services
  A. Social responsibility falls primarily into three areas of concern:
    1. Promotion of equal opportunity.
    2. Protection of environment and conservation of resources.
    3. Concern for health and safety both on and off the job.

II. Social Change at Work
  A. Social value change is slower than technological change.
  B. The results of affirmative action programs have been mixed, at times achieving the goal of equal opportunity, at times resulting in further discrimination.

III. Protectors of Society
  A. Pollution is a troublesome by-product of our affluent economy.
  B. Most companies resist complying with costly environmental protection measures.
  C. Concern for the use of resources, protection of the environment, safety and quality of products, and consumer protection are all part of management's expanding areas of social responsibility.
  D. Management must answer the question, How much profit must be sacrificed for social goals?
  E. Many organizations deal with troubled employees, alcoholism, and drug abuse.

IV. Right or Wrong—The Ethical Dilemma
  A. Ethical systems can be grouped into four categories:
    1. Applying a rigid set of rules in all situations.
    2. Determining the greatest good for the greatest number.
    3. Basing one's ethical decisions on the circumstances of a particular situation.
    4. Using higher ethical principles as the basis for operational approaches to ethics.
  B. The many diverse groups and cultures with which management deals often present managers with ethical dilemmas and values conflicts.
  C. A simplistic approach to ethics generally leads to unsatisfactory results.

V. Value Ranking and Ethical Decisions
  A. Honorable business decisions rest on the decision maker's strong sense of personal worth.
  B. Several forces must be considered in an operational approach to ethics:
    1. Forces in the individual.

2. Forces in others.

3. Forces in the task.

4. Forces in the environment.

5. Expectations of others.

VI. General Concepts and Ideals

A. Absolute concepts are useful to us in building our values commitments.

B. Conflicts occur when absolute concepts and ideals clash with real-world situations.

C. We must have a firm system of values and priorities to make judgments and weigh consequences.

VII. Sex in the Office—A Special Issue

A. Sexual harassment includes sexual advances, requests for sexual favors, or other sexual conduct that interferes with a person's work or intimidates a person on the job.

B. Public knowledge of sexual conduct between consenting employees can also create problems for the firm and damage its public image.

## KEY TERMS

| | | |
|---|---|---|
| Social responsibility | Environmental Protection | Ethical dilemmas |
| Equal opportunity | Agency | Situation ethics |
| Prejudice | Alcoholism | Value ranking |
| Civil Rights Act of 1964 | Chemical abuse | Sexual harassment |
| Affirmative action | Ethics | Willing consent |
| Environmental protection | Reference groups | |

## DISCUSSION QUESTIONS

1. What do you consider the most pressing social responsibility issue facing organizations during the next ten-year period? Explain.

2. Are organizational ethics improving or declining? On what do you base your choice?

3. Should the U.S. government take a stronger position in assuring equal opportunities for all people? Should those laws apply to both legal and illegal aliens? Explain.

4. How stringently should environmental safety concerns be enforced? Do you think environmental issues are a real concern for most people?

5. Should all job applicants be required to take tests to determine if they are users of illegal drugs? Why or why not?

─────────────────── **EXERCISE** ───────────────────

*Actions to Resolve an Ethical Dilemma*

You are a regional manager for a company that owns convenience stores. One of the male store managers in your region has been accused of sexual harassment by a female clerk. Your investigation produces clear evidence that the employee was sexually harassed by the store manager. You also find evidence that the store manager has requested sexual favors from other employees in return for a high performance evaluation. When you report the situation to your boss, he instructs you to "get the employee to drop the complaint and protect the store manager." Your boss made it clear that he does not want any bad publicity.

*Evaluate the following list of possible actions to resolve an ethical dilemma. Which actions would you take? Which would you take first?*

1. Offer the clerk money to drop the accusations against the store manager.

2. Transfer the clerk to another store and give her a raise.

3. Obtain a lawyer to advise you on your personal legal position if you follow your boss's instructions.

4. Immediately start looking for another job.

5. Take the information from your investigation to the company president without telling your boss.

6. Try to negotiate with your boss so the rights of the employee will be protected and the store manager will be disciplined.

7. Tell the employee to drop the accusation because she can't win, and assure her it will never happen again.

8. Send the information from your investigation to the local newspaper so they can see that justice is done.

9. Do nothing unless the clerk takes legal action that involves you.

10. Tell the clerk of your boss's instructions and advise her that she can take her accusations to the Equal Employment Opportunity Commission.

─────────────────── **TWO POINTS OF VIEW** ───────────────────

*"Who's Cheating?"*

*What would you do if you were the supervisor?*

You are the supervisor of the plastic molding machine section in a manufacturing company that makes sporting goods. The machine operators are paid on an incentive system, which provides a bonus for output in excess of standards set by industrial engineers. The operators are continually tampering with the counters on their plastic molding machines, turning them forward to indicate more units than were actually produced. You have been aware of the tampering for over six months. At first you ignored the problem because the increases averaged less than 5 percent over actual production.

In the last month, the increases reached over 20 percent and your boss instructed you to "stop the cheating on the molding machines and punish the cheaters." You secretly installed counters in your office that measured the actual production of each machine. The operators had no knowledge of your system to check on them. You kept track of the daily production of each operator for two weeks and compared it with the counters on the machines. You made up the payroll from your secret counter records of production. When you gave out the paychecks, you told the operators, "We have measured the actual output on the machines, and that is what you get paid for. You cheaters are lucky I don't fire all of you. The next one of you I catch cheating on the production count will be laid off without pay for a week."

When they asked you how you knew anyone was cheating on the count, you replied, "None of your business. You are paid for production. I'm paid to make sure you don't get paid for more than you actually produce."

The next day the operators went to your boss and said they were not going back to work until you apologized for calling them "cheaters." Your boss then called you in, and you confronted the operators with the information about the secret counters. The operators admitted that they had turned the counters forward, but they insisted that it was not cheating. They said, "We only turned the counters forward when we could not get production because the machine was down through no fault of ours." They also contended that your secret counters were a form of invasion of privacy and unethical spying on them.

*What would you do if you were a machine operator?*

You operate a plastic molding machine for a company that manufactures sporting goods. You are paid a bonus for production that exceeds the standards set by industrial engineering. All the operators can easily exceed the standards and get the bonus pay if the machines are kept in good working order. Recently the machines have been down much of the time because the company has not done preventive maintenance or replaced worn-out parts. From your point of view, management's failure to repair the machines is cheating you out of pay that you deserve.

To get the pay you deserved, you turned the production counters on your machine forward to indicate the production you would have achieved if you weren't forced to stop for repairs. All the operators agreed that they were not going to let management cheat them out of pay that they could have earned.

When your supervisor handed out the checks, he said that he had measured actual output and that was all anyone was going to get paid for. He also threatened to fire anyone who turned the counters forward and accused all the operators of being cheaters. To put it mildly, his accusations and threats made you and the other operators boiling mad. After all, the company was cheating the operators out of pay.

The next day, you and the other operators went to your supervisor's boss and demanded that he apologize. The supervisor was called in, and he told the operators of his secret counters, which you and the others consider unethical spying and an invasion of privacy. If your supervisor wants a war, the operators can sure give him one. You might just find it difficult to cooperate with him or may even go as far as to sue him.

### ENDNOTES

1. James R. Glenn, Jr., *Ethics in Decision Making* (Wiley, 1986).
2. Based on interview with Sue Sharp, executive assistant, California Almond Growers Association, 19 February 1982.
3. Adapted from Nick Correale, "Alcoholism," unpublished paper, California State University, Sacramento, California, May 1982.
4. Compiled by Bob Shallit, *McClatchy Newspapers*, June 1986.
5. Adapted from *Forbes*, 22 June 1981.
6. Joseph F. Fletcher, *Situation Ethics, the New Morality* (Philadelphia: Westminster Press, 1966).
7. Kermit Vandiver, "Why Should My Conscience Bother Me?" in *Organization and People*, ed. J. B. Ritchie and Paul Thompson (St. Paul: West, 1976).
8. E. F. Thode and D. L. Costley, "A Contingency Approach to Managerial Ethics," *Proceedings, Southwest Division, Academy of Management, 18th Annual Meeting*, San Antonio, March 1976.

# Personal Development and Career Success

## _____ *Learning Objectives* _____

This final chapter deals with some important life decisions. Readers may find it helpful to learn to do the following:

1. Understand that career personal success is both a societal and individual set of values
2. Develop a comprehension that others are concerned with our personal development
3. Appreciate that interests, abilities, and expertise change during a normal lifetime
4. Recognize that organizational life, like all other aspects of living, is subject to many pressures and many changes
5. Develop an appreciation that all career development is ultimate self-development
6. Appreciate the value of periodic assessment of interests, values, and need for psychological growth
7. Accept the realities of life with both its promises and its pitfalls

# Chapter Topics

- Personal success and career development
- Success and personal development
- Organizational career development plans
- Career development and the individual
- Keys to success
- A managerial perspective

# Preview

Societies view success in many ways. A prizefighter may measure it in numbers of opponents knocked unconscious; a banker in amount of other people's money invested for the bank's benefit; a farmer in the number of bushels of corn per acre; a physician in numbers of patients healed; a pilot in numbers of hours flown; an individual in goals attained. The list is endless.

Two difficult questions people ask themselves are, What do I *like* to do? and What *can* I do? Neither is easy to answer. Frequently, what individuals may like is not what they can do. Realistic self-development centers on identifying personal strengths, possibilities of development, and weaknesses that are not likely to be overcome. A person may like, as an example, the idea of being a great musician. Without the finger dexterity, tonal acuity, and ability to rapidly comprehend musical sequences, what that person likes will and can never be what he or she is able to do.

Truly successful people are those that have identified both what they like to do and what they realistically can do. They understand their realistic limitations and know that they have strengths that have not yet been developed. Success for them—and perhaps for all of us—lies in doing not only what we like to do but also what we can do best.

Although all people have realistic limitations, the possibilities for self-development and career success are still great and almost endlessly varied. A great danger exists, however, in unrealistic self-limitation and lack of effort to set and achieve meaningful personal goals.

## SELF–ASSESSMENT ▰▰▰▰▰▰▰▰▰▰▰▰▰▰▰

This self-assessment is like that in Chapter 18. It is designed to assist you in evaluating where you are, where you want to be, and ways of attaining your life goals. Each statement or question has a range of possible responses. A scale of 1 to 6 between two words with different meanings allows you to mark either the word that is considered correct or a place between the two words that represents some agreement and some disagreement. Selection of a high number such as 5 or 6 may be either correct or incorrect, just as selection of lower numbers may be correct or incorrect. Some responses may be partly correct and partly incorrect.

Answers based on research by behavioral scientists, with a short explanation of why the response was considered correct, may be found on page 541.

**1.** Lifelong learning is something that is:

highly desirable  1...2...3...4...5...6  out of style and unneeded

**2.** Which of the following factors is most important?

job security  1...2...3...4...5...6  interesting work

**3.** What do you enjoy most?

leisure time  1...2...3...4...5...6  interesting and challenging work

**4.** In accepting employment, which is most important?

an opportunity to learn and achieve  1...2...3...4...5...6  starting pay

**5.** During early stages of a person's career, which is most important?

geographic location  1...2...3...4...5...6  career development opportunities

**6.** Which of the following are most significant to job success?

management that is helpful  1...2...3...4...5...6  personal initiative

**7.** In a work situation that offers little opportunity for advancement or change to a different assignment but pays well, a person should:

seek other opportunities  1...2...3...4...5...6  stick to a sure thing

**8.** The longer a person stays in a specific type of work:

the easier it is to    1...2...3...4...5...6 the more difficult it is
           change                                          to change

**9.** When dealing with the politics of organizational life, a person should realize that:

job politics are not    1...2...3...4...5...6 job politics can be
    as important as                                      important to career
       hard work                                         development

**10.** Most job difficulties arise because of:

personality factors    1...2...3...4...5...6 incompetence


## PERSONAL SUCCESS AND CAREER DEVELOPMENT

A few years ago, Liam Hudson, a Scottish professor in Edinburgh, observed that some students did best in tasks that required following rules, utilizing systematic approaches to problem solving, and careful detail.[1] Such students seemed to be more comfortable with subjects such as conventional mathematics, accounting, physics, and analytical studies, which require logical, step-by-step reasoning. Hudson identified such students as **convergent thinkers**.

Other students Hudson observed were more imaginative, less organized and less precise, and seemed to rely more on their feelings than on logic. These students, called **divergent thinkers**, tended to be people oriented, better at creative tasks than convergent thinkers, more imaginative, and better able to deal with ambiguity. But they were also less orderly and precise than their counterparts.

Hudson postulated that if his observations were correct, a number of predictions could be made. Divergents assigned to convergent tasks would not be successful. Convergents assigned to divergent tasks would at best be dissatisfied. Although there is not a great deal of research to support Hudson's hypothesis, David Kolb at the Massachusetts Institute of Technology has extended Hudson's original studies and has developed a strong body of evidence that people have different preferred learning styles.[2] Their styles of learning, to some extent, determine their job preferences.

Our point in mentioning the Hudson/Kolb theories is that success in life and career may be at least partially dependent on choosing types of work that match our styles of thinking and learning. We are just beginning to understand some of the factors that lead to job success. A number of personality elements, ranging from our inherited physiology to our environments, learning, cultural values, early childhood development, family structure, and other life experiences, are likely to affect the choices we make and our concepts of success and failure.

> **More Workers Refusing Promotions** ━━━━━━━━━━━━━
>
> Heywood Klien, staff reporter for the *Wall Street Journal*, reports that a number of managers are doing what was once unthinkable—refusing a promotion. He points out that resisting a promotion can brand an employee as disloyal or lacking ambition, but some managers see it as a way of managing their own careers. In some cases, managers turn down promotions into dead-end jobs so they can later accept jobs that offer brighter future prospects. Others, however, want to avoid a difficult future boss or simply want to enjoy life more.[3]

## SUCCESS AND PERSONAL DEVELOPMENT

Some people view success in terms of personal achievement, money, approval by others, power and influence, and competence. Others may equate success with self-determination, freedom of choice, and independence from organizational constraints. Although no universal definition exists, our society seems to look at success in terms of progressive achievement, organizational advancement, stability, and movement into higher socioeconomic brackets.

Becoming increasingly clear, however, is that success defined by general societal values and success defined by individuals may be different. One midlevel executive with a major south-central gas transmission corporation recently turned down a substantial promotion for several reasons.[4] "First," he stated, "I don't want to move, because I like my job. It has more variety and freedom than the new job could offer. In addition, this is where my children have their roots and where most of my friends live. The extra money and prestige isn't worth destroying my present lifestyle." Although some people are able to successfully reject an offer of promotion, for others it is more difficult. **Career development** usually means continually acquiring increased knowledge, skill and competency, and as a result being promoted to successively higher levels in an organization. Employees, managers, and organizations share the career development process.

## ORGANIZATIONAL CAREER DEVELOPMENT PLANS

As part of their long-range personnel planning, some companies such as Sears, Carborundum, Xerox, IBM, and a number of federal government agencies have utilized career management techniques. These include encouraging employee education and self-development, maintaining updated personnel information, providing specialized training, and carefully appraising performance to help employees identify strengths and areas needing improvement. Some also identify a progressive sequence of assignments for employees who demonstrate the desire and ability to work at increasingly more responsible tasks.[5]

Formal career development programs are still, unfortunately, the exception rather than the rule. In all probability, most managers realize the value of assisting employees in development of their capabilities. A. L. Camp, a former director of manufacturing for Aerojet-General Corporation and subsequently the vice-president and president of Cleveland Tool Company in Cleveland, Ohio, once stated that he believed a manager's single most important task was to be a "developer of people." [6] Camp's basic philosophy hinged on encouraging all levels of personnel who demonstrated the desire and ability (1) to accept more responsibility, (2) to constantly set high but achievable goals, (3) to assess their own performance, and (4) to become less dependent on higher levels of management for key job decisions. Camp views management's roles in career development as coaching, providing performance assessment and feedback, and setting a climate for acceptance of personal responsibility.

Although individual managers, especially those at upper organizational levels, are helpful in establishing a climate for career development, formal programs should be established. Such career development efforts must also be supported by organizational policy and top management commitment. Many organizations are beginning to realize the importance of **human resource planning (HRP)**. HRP involves the careful analysis of available personnel resource needs for the future, technology changes, market projections, and other related factors to determine potential organizational needs. It seeks to make the optimum utilization of existing people as well as projected new hires. A part of well-founded HRP efforts is the identification of training needs and advancement potential for individual employees. As computer programs in personnel become more sophisticated, career management can be more thoroughly integrated into overall human resource plans.

Although organizations have a major responsibility in providing career development programs, opportunities, and data for employees, individual desire and energy ultimately, make career development efforts work.

## CAREER DEVELOPMENT AND THE INDIVIDUAL

Thirty years ago, Abraham Maslow noted that some people are able to define their roles in life more easily than others.[7] They identify what they *like* to do and what they *can* do. Once they have found a satisfying successful activity, they work at perfecting their skills. These **self-actualized** people are those who are able to fulfill their needs for competence, achievement and "doing what they should do."

Not all of us, unfortunately, are able to easily identify career paths that will self-actualize us for long periods of time. However, identification of career goals is a necessary first step. Although many people find careers largely by accident and coincidence, many others may find they are constantly seeking a type of work for which they feel suited.

Several approaches are useful. Many colleges and universities offer career counseling and testing services. Users of the career programs can more easily define their personal aptitudes, limitations, interest patterns, and potential marketable skills. Larger cities have private career counseling services, which may be expensive but can also be helpful. In some instances, state and federal employment services will offer some degree of career advising.

Once a career choice has been made, one must develop a personal career development plan. Randall Schuler notes that a successful personal career management plan should result in a realistic awareness of skills, abilities, weaknesses, needs, values, career opportunities, and a sense of self-esteem and self-worth.[8] The following are some possible steps that can be taken:

1. List the activities you like and dislike.
2. Evaluate skill levels needed for activities liked.
3. Obtain training and proficiency in a preferred activity.
4. Carefully survey potential job markets.
5. Apply for jobs that look challenging, even if it means relocating geographically.
6. Work hard.
7. Learn organizational politics.
8. If you change jobs, leave on friendly terms by your own choice.

Years ago, some newspaper reporters were famous for developing a "go to hell" fund, which was the equivalent of a year's salary put aside in a separate bank account. If they thought they weren't achieving what they wanted at their work place, or believed they were incompatible with the boss, they could tell the job, and in some cases the boss, to "go to hell." They were financially secure at least for a year while they hunted for other work. Although we do not advocate everyone having a go-to-hell fund, a reality of life is that for many reasons, some jobs just do not work out the way we had hoped. People who are able to maintain contacts with other organizations, develop professional friendships, and make new contacts through membership in associations frequently find moving to another job easier.

### *Personal Values and Career Development*

New employees often need to understand several key realities of work life. These include that most organizations require greater conformity than many new employees like; that some managers are both power and control oriented; that bright people are frequently assigned to dull jobs; and that economic necessity can often override other personal considerations.

Few people in today's economic, technological, and socially complex world work at a single occupation, at one place, with the same skills more than a short period of their lives. As organizations change, both jobs and people change. It seems to make sense that personal career values must include the realities of organizational life and change. By **personal values** we mean those things that

---

### Flexibility and Personal Control

In his highly interesting text *Management in the Third Wave*, H. Alan Raymond states that to be successful in the environment of the next twenty-five years, we must learn to assess our personal assets and weak points.[9] Once we have defined what is needed to be where we want to be, we must strengthen our assets without excessive effort. It's a good rule, according to Raymond, to maintain personal flexibility. To be able to change when change is necessary is one of the keys to personal success. To accomplish this, he states that we should never buy when we can rent; never have things we cannot use often; maximize our access to useful information; and maximize our ability to work by using the latest computerized resources, personal alliances, and continuous education. He also adds that we should know our hard assets (money and property) and be prepared at any time to shift them to more profitable use.

Whether or not a person agrees with Raymond, his concepts are provocative. In a world of increasing technological, social, and economic change, success or failure may depend on the need for personal flexibility. It is, in essence, willingness to recognize that our physical, social, and psychological environment is never the same from one time period to the next.

---

an individual believes are personally important, such as interesting work, a sense of responsibility and contribution, some self-determination and independence, and good interpersonal relations with other members of the organization, both management and nonmanagement. Expectations must be realistic; but if they are totally at odds with organizational style, seeking other work is frequently better than remaining locked into an unsatisfactory and often stressful pattern of work.

Although many younger employees are competent, trained, energetic, and want to please, these characteristics alone are not enough to ensure success. Younger employees must also realize that every organization has its own political style. People either become part of a network of in-groups or find themselves excluded from these informal support networks. An isolated individual is more vulnerable and may become a victim of the **bleeding shark syndrome**. When a shark bleeds, it is often attacked by other sharks. Likewise, people in organizations who, knowingly or unknowingly, offend a member or members of a support network in-group may be constantly attacked rather than helped by others in the network.

### *Time and Careers*

In his book *You Can't Go Home Again*, Thomas Wolfe portrays the futility of trying to go back in time, to be as we once were, and to expect the world to remain the same. As people grow older, not only do their careers develop but also their life directions change. Daniel Levinson and a group of colleagues developed what has become widely recognized as the *Levinson model of career change*.[10] About every seven to ten years, our lives undergo major and sometimes traumatic changes. Some of these life stages are depicted in Table 19.1.

There are many models of career change patterns other than the one popularized by Levinson. All have a common element: as people mature, their career interests and directions change. Although changes are not universal in that no two people are affected precisely the same way, most people seem to have reasonably consistent patterns of development and change.

---

**Table 19.1**

**Levinson's Model of Career Change**

| Age | Major Change Event |
|---|---|
| 16–22 | *Pulling up roots.* Individuals assert independence and self-confidence. Some who prolong parental ties become underachievers. |
| 22–29 | *Entering adulthood.* Lifestyle and career are selected; jobs are established, and first encounters with career success, failure; realization of competencies occur. |
| 29–32 | *Change.* During this period, the career matures and many individuals seek change through a series of job relocations, geographic moves, and redirection of lifestyle. At this point, they solidify their personal values and life direction. |
| 32–39 | *Career advancement.* During this period, the job often becomes the dominant feature of a person's life. Organization skills are frequently at their peak, and it is the period during which many make their most significant career moves. It is, unfortunately, frequently a period of family stress, and social readjustment in that career and organization become more important than social contacts. |
| 39–43 | *A midlife crisis.* This event may occur for some people during this period. Individuals may look back on their achievements with resentment, sadness, or, in some cases, pride. A growing number of people attempt to make radical career and lifestyle changes during the midlife crisis. Not everyone views this period as a crisis. For some, it is a period of increased renewal of goals and achievement. |
| 43–50 | *Openness and self-development.* Many people recognize this as a period of settling down. For many, careers have peaked, competencies and confidence have been developed, and there is a renewed interest in activities outside of work. |
| 50 and over | *Maintenance and reflection.* After the age of 50 until retirement, many employees continue the pattern developed earlier but with increasing awareness that significant changes in lifestyle are unlikely and that promotions will come slowly, if at all. For some, it can be a period of high productivity and renewed interests in a diversity of activities. For others, it may become a period of "working for Friday" so weekends can be enjoyed more than day-to-day job routines. |

### *Allness and Resistance to Change*

A difficult individual career problem, originally identified by William C. Haney, is the development of an attitude of **allness**.[11] Allness occurs when individuals begin to believe that they know all about a particular subject or occupation, and as a result become unwilling either to accept change or to examine alternative ways of doing things. Individuals who say, "This is the way I've always done it and always will," are expressing allness. Their minds are made up; they don't wish to consider new facts.

Allness is all too common in many management people who have been at the same or similar organizational levels for many years. In their view of the world, things and people are unchanged and unchanging. New problems are solved in old ways. Attitudes, values, and beliefs remain frozen. Often only traumatic personal experiences can break the all-wall and let established managers be shaken loose from the secure but ineffective allness behavior.

Nonmanagement employees, especially those with well-established patterns of behavior, may also exhibit the same type of allness that characterizes some managers. They resist change, criticize new methods, complain about different approaches, and refuse to consider the potential benefits of new work methods and new technologies, or the impact of evolving societal values.

When organizations are dominated by allness, they often follow policies that can ultimately lead to bankruptcy and massive loss of jobs. Management has historically suffered from the shortsightedness of allness. Ford Motor Company, headed by Henry Ford III, fired Lee Iacocca largely because of Iacocca's desire for change. Iacocca went on to become the most recognized automotive manufacturing and marketing leader at Chrysler Corporation; he successfully led the movement toward revitalization of the U.S. automobile industry. Many people wondered why Ford continued to slide downward as Chrysler edged upward as a leader in the automotive field. Allness stops not only careers but companies as well.

### *Self-fulfilling Prophecy*

Some ancient philosopher is credited with saying, "We are what we think we are." Many researchers and psychologists have written that self-image is a vital determinant of success.

Their research indicates two important and closely related concepts. People who think they will succeed have a greater chance of success than those who think they will fail. Similarly, people who others think will succeed have a greater chance of success than those others think will fail. Athletic coaches who believe their teams are winners are more likely to be successful than those who believe their teams are failures. By the same reasoning, the coach who thinks, "My teams are the best," has an edge on those who are doubtful of their team's ability.

In organizations, individual managers who are winner oriented have winning-oriented employees. They are the group most likely to be high achievers and may be the ones to excel and earn recognition as the best. Few, if any,

---

### Esprit de Corps

Tucson, Arizona, has what is probably the country's best garbage collection corps. Led by an enthusiastic ex-"ecology technician," the ultramodern refuse collection system is well disciplined and technically superior, and recognized as the best large-city unit of its kind. Tucson's mayor, city council, and managers of the sanitation workers' staff as well as nonmanagement employees all know that their success stems largely from the fact that they *believe* they're the best and others take pride in their achievements. [12]

---

careers are built on timidity, lack of confidence, and fear of failure. Winners are people who believe they are winners.

### *Career Development Assistance*

Many organizations have developed approaches to help employees in their career development. In Illinois, the State Department of Personnel uses its Performance Appraisal System (Figure 19.1) as a basis for career development. California's State Department of Finance has inaugurated a self-assessment approach that may be applicable in many other states to help employees assess their personal strengths and weaknesses as potential managers (Figure 19.2).

Unfortunately, many employees do not take advantage of personal development opportunities when they are offered. Active encouragement by managers is necessary. In many instances, as shown in Figures 19.1 and 19.2, personal development is tied directly to the employee's formal performance evaluation in order to emphasize both the need and advantages of additional training and experience.

### KEYS TO SUCCESS

Two dominant factors seem evident in much of the literature related to career development. Perhaps the most important is the necessity for continual assessment of personal skills, knowledge, attitudes, effective interpersonal relations, and the degree to which personal goals are being met. Awareness of personal limitations and strengths and development of strategies to offset weakness as well as accentuate strengths is an important ingredient of career management. See Figure 19.3

In addition to self-assessment, a realistic view of organizational life is equally necessary. A common error made by some inexperienced entrants into career programs is the belief that they can change an organization's style or that if conditions are unsatisfactory, they will soon improve. New workers must recognize that if opportunities are limited, if the political climate is distasteful, or if a low level of trust and confidence exists within the organization, it may be time to

State of Illinois
**DEPARTMENT OF PERSONNEL**
Springfield, Illinois

**INDIVIDUAL DEVELOPMENT AND PERFORMANCE SYSTEM**

| 1. EMPLOYEE'S NAME - LAST, FIRST, MIDDLE | 2. DEPARTMENT, BOARD OR COMMISSION | 3. DIVISION OR INSTITUTION |
|---|---|---|
| 4. EMPLOYEE'S SOCIAL SECURITY NUMBER | 5. EMPLOYEE'S PAYROLL TITLE | 6. TIME IN CURRENT TITLE _____ YEARS _____ MONTHS |
| 7. PERIOD OF REPORT  FROM        TO | 8. TYPE OF REPORT ☐FIRST PROBATIONARY ☐FINAL PROBATIONARY ☐ANNUAL ☐SALARY INCREASE  ☐LAYOFF ☐DISCHARGE ☐OTHER (SPECIFY)_____ | |

**GENERAL INFORMATION**

An objective centered performance evaluation system provides for the collaborative review of employee performance and for the establishment of appropriate work and developmental objectives.

The form itself is a neutral instrument. The value of the system will be determined by the amount of effort individuals are willing to devote to the objective setting and evaluation processes. This evaluation system requires continuous communication between the employee and the supervisor.

The system is an attempt to make the process of evaluation more rational. It helps the employee and supervisor understand more fully what is involved in doing their jobs as well as clarifying the relationship of their work to the work of others around them. This approach helps reduce the problem of misunderstanding by requiring that the employee and supervisor meet and jointly agree to a set of objectives, in order of importance, for the employee's job. The individual gets direct feedback on how he is progressing through the use of the quarterly review sessions. The organization benefits by being better able to plan and coordinate its functions for more effective and economical delivery of services.

The objectives of the organization and the objectives of the individual should be integrated as closely as possible. Those employees who see their own objectives being accomplished, while at the same time achieving the objectives of the organization, are more interested, more motivated and, therefore, more effective in performing their jobs.

The establishment of employee objectives is a five-step process which may be illustrated as follows:

| 1 EMPLOYEE'S ROLE Discuss areas of re-responsibility relating to objectives and self-development needs. | 2 Prepare list of objectives for discussion with supervisor. Discuss and agree on work objectives for this period. | 3 Prepare plans of action to meet objectives for approval of supervisor. Perform the job to be done. | 4 Review progress and discuss any problems with supervisor. | 5 Make self-evaluation and evaluate results for annual appraisal. Prepare list of objectives for next period. |
|---|---|---|---|---|
| INFORMATION TO BE SHARED Organization objectives; major job responsibilities; self-development needs | OBJECTIVE SETTING | PLANS OF ACTION FOR JOB TO BE DONE | QUARTERLY PROGRESS REVIEW | EVALUATE PERFORMANCE ANNUALLY. RESET OBJECTIVES. |
| 1 SUPERVISOR'S ROLE Communicate and discuss appropriate objectives. | 2 Prepare a list of objectives with employee. Discuss and agree on work objectives for this period. | 3 Approve plans of action for achieving work objectives and review with higher management. | 4 Review progress. Make adjustments as required. Provide coaching and assistance. | 5 Evaluate performance and results for annual appraisal. Prepare list of objectives for next period. |

Each employee will be counseled by his supervisor and a copy of this form filed in the individual's personnel folder not less than once every twelve (12) months. Results of quarterly progress review sessions need be recorded only on copies retained by the employee and the supervisor.

A minimum of three (3) copies of this form will be required--one for the supervisor, one for the employee, and one for the personnel files. Additional copies may be required if needed. If employee position is at a level (unskilled, etc.) that does not lend itself to objective setting, indicate by inserting "N/A" (Not Applicable) wherever necessary.

DP-201R (2-74)                                                                                              Page 1 of 4

**Figure 19.1**   Illinois Individual Development and Performance System: Performance Appraisal Form.

**PART I. APPRAISAL OF OBJECTIVES.**

Supervisor is to list and evaluate all objectives for which the employee was held accountable during the last reporting period. Mark the appropriate column for each objective.

| | Objectives | | |
|---|---|---|---|
| | EXCEEDED | MET | NOT MET |
| | | | |

**PART II. GENERAL APPRAISAL OF EMPLOYEE PERFORMANCE**

Complete items 1 through 8 for all employees and items 9 and 10 when applicable. Differences between ratings by employee and by supervisor must be discussed.

| | TO BE COMPLETED BY EMPLOYEE | | | TO BE COMPLETED BY SUPERVISOR | | | |
|---|---|---|---|---|---|---|---|
| | EXCEEDS EXPECTATIONS | MEETS EXPECTATIONS | NEEDS IMPROVEMENT | EXCEEDS EXPECTATIONS | MEETS EXPECTATIONS | NEEDS IMPROVEMENT | INSUFFICIENT OPPORTUNITY TO OBSERVE |
| 1. JOB KNOWLEDGE: Consider overall knowledge of duties and responsibilities as required for current job or position | ☐ | ☐ | ☐ | ☐ | ☐ | ☐ | ☐ |
| 2. PRODUCTIVITY: Evaluate amount of work generated and completed successfully as compared to amount of work expected for this job or position | ☐ | ☐ | ☐ | ☐ | ☐ | ☐ | ☐ |
| 3. QUALITY: Rate correctness, completeness, accuracy and economy of work - overall quality | ☐ | ☐ | ☐ | ☐ | ☐ | ☐ | ☐ |
| 4. INITIATIVE: Self motivation - consider amount of direction required - seeks improved methods and techniques - consistence in trying to do better. | ☐ | ☐ | ☐ | ☐ | ☐ | ☐ | ☐ |
| 5. USE OF TIME: Uses available time wisely - is punctual reporting to work - absenteeism - accomplishes required work on or ahead of schedule | ☐ | ☐ | ☐ | ☐ | ☐ | ☐ | ☐ |
| 6. PLANNING: Sets realistic objectives - anticipates and prepares for future requirements - establishes logical priorities | ☐ | ☐ | ☐ | ☐ | ☐ | ☐ | ☐ |
| 7. FOLLOW-UP: Maintains control of workloads - allocates resources economically - insures that assignments are completed accurately and timely | ☐ | ☐ | ☐ | ☐ | ☐ | ☐ | ☐ |
| 8. HUMAN RELATIONS: Establishes and maintains cordial work climate - promotes harmony and enthusiasm - displays sincere interest in assisting other employees | ☐ | ☐ | ☐ | ☐ | ☐ | ☐ | ☐ |
| 9. LEADERSHIP: Sets high standards - provides good managerial example - encourages subordinates to perform efficiently - communicates effectively | ☐ | ☐ | ☐ | ☐ | ☐ | ☐ | ☐ |
| 10. SUBORDINATE DEVELOPMENT: Helps subordinates plan career development - grooms potential replacements - gives guidance and counsel | ☐ | ☐ | ☐ | ☐ | ☐ | ☐ | ☐ |

**Figure 19.1** Illinois Individual Development and Performance System: Performance Appraisal Form *(cont.)*.

EMPLOYEE'S NAME · LAST, FIRST, MIDDLE

**PART III.   REMARKS BY SUPERVISOR.**

Comment on employee's outstanding achievements.  When "not met" is checked in Part I or "needs improvement" is checked in Part II describe the reasons for this rating, and what remedial steps were taken.

**PART IV.   EMPLOYEE OBJECTIVES FOR NEXT REPORTING PERIOD.**

To be established by the employee with input, advice, and agreement of the supervisor.  Objectives should be set for each major area of job responsibility, ranked in priority order, and be as measurable as possible.  Personal development objectives may be included.

Page 3 of 4

**Figure 19.1    Illinois Individual Development and Performance System:
Performance Appraisal Form** (cont.).

**PART V. EMPLOYEE'S COMMENTS.**

Employee may comment on all or any part of the information contained in this document, including the evaluation process. If the employee does not concur with the evaluation, check the appropriate box and explain reasons for disagreement.

**PART VI. SIGNATURES.**

EMPLOYEE'S SIGNATURE                         PAYROLL TITLE                         DATE

☐ I DO NOT CONCUR   (USE PART V FOR COMMENTS)

SUPERVISOR'S SIGNATURE                       PAYROLL TITLE                         DATE

☐ I HAVE PERSONALLY DISCUSSED THE CONTENTS OF THIS DOCUMENT WITH THE EMPLOYEE AND WE HAVE AGREED TO THE OBJECTIVES SET.

NEXT HIGHER LEVEL SUPERVISOR SIGNATURE (REVIEW)      PAYROLL TITLE                 DATE

AGENCY HEAD SIGNATURE (REVIEW)               PAYROLL TITLE                         DATE

**PART VII. QUARTERLY PROGRESS REVIEW.**   (This can be initiated by either the employee or the supervisor.)

The employee and supervisor are to meet quarterly to review progress toward previously agreed upon objectives. If the original objectives need to be adjusted, use the space below to document the change. The employee and supervisor should date and initial the document at the time of each review.

1st quarter
Date _____
Initials:
Emp. _____
Sup. _____

2nd quarter
Date _____
Initials:
Emp. _____
Sup. _____

3rd quarter
Date _____
Initials:
Emp. _____
Sup. _____

(DO NOT WRITE BENEATH THIS LINE)

For use only if third party consultation is required.

Page 4 of 4

**Figure 19.1**   Illinois Individual Development and Performance System: Performance Appraisal Form *(cont.).*

STATE OF CALIFORNIA

## INDIVIDUAL DEVELOPMENT PLAN
FOR FUTURE JOB PERFORMANCE OF PERMANENT EMPLOYEES

STD. 637  (10/78)

| EMPLOYEE'S NAME   *(LAST, FIRST, MIDDLE INITIAL)* | DATE OF THIS PERFORMANCE DISCUSSION | |
|---|---|---|
| CIVIL SERVICE TITLE | POSITION NUMBER | DATE OF LAST PERFORMANCE DISCUSSION |
| STATE DEPARTMENT | SUBDIVISION OF DEPARTMENT | EMPLOYEE'S HEADQUARTERS |

| PERFORMANCE OBJECTIVES -- Goals for further improvements in job performance during the next year in order to meet or exceed standards for the employee's present job or to develop employee skills. | PLANS FOR ACHIEVING OBJECTIVES -- Specific methods by which the employee can work toward accomplishing his or her performance objectives (in-service training courses, college courses, rotation, special work assignments for training purposes, etc.). |
|---|---|
| | |

*I HAVE PARTICIPATED IN A DISCUSSION OF OVER-ALL JOB PERFORMANCE*

| SIGNATURE OF EMPLOYEE | DATE | SIGNATURE OF SUPERVISOR | DATE |
|---|---|---|---|
| ▶ | | ▶ | |

*(Over)*

**Figure 19.2**   California Department of Finance Career Development Form.

**PERFORMANCE APPRAISAL SUMMARY**
OF PAST JOB PERFORMANCE OF PERMANENT EMPLOYEES
STD. 637 (2/78) — REVERSE

| PERFORMANCE FACTORS | I | M | E* | COMMENTS* |
|---|---|---|---|---|
| **1.** **QUALITY OF WORK:** Consider the extent to which completed work is accurate, neat, well-organized, thorough, and effective. | | | | |
| **2.** **QUANTITY OF WORK:** Consider the extent to which the amount of work produced compares to quantity standards for the job. | | | | |
| **3.** **WORK HABITS:** Consider the employee's effectiveness in organizing and using work tools and time, in caring for equipment and materials, in following good practices of vehicle and personal safety, etc. | | | | |
| **4.** **RELATIONSHIPS WITH PEOPLE:** Consider the extent to which the employee recognizes the needs and desires of other people, treats others with respect and courtesy, inspires their respect and confidence, etc. | | | | |
| **5.** **TAKING ACTION INDEPENDENTLY:** Consider the extent to which the employee shows initiative in making work improvements, identifying and correcting errors, initiating work activities, etc. | | | | |
| **6.** **MEETING WORK COMMITMENTS:** Consider the extent to which employee completes work assignments, meets deadlines, follows established policies and procedures, etc. | | | | |
| **7.** **ANALYZING SITUATIONS AND MATERIALS:** Consider the extent to which the employee applies consistently good judgment in analyzing work situations and materials, and in drawing sound conclusions. | | | | |
| **8.** **SUPERVISING THE WORK OF OTHERS:** Consider the employee's effectiveness in planning and controlling work activities, motivating and developing subordinates, improving work methods and results, encouraging and supporting employee suggestions for work improvements, applying policies, selecting and developing subordinates in accordance with State Personnel Board and departmental affirmative action policies. | | | | |
| **9.** **PERSONNEL MANAGEMENT PRACTICES:** Consider the extent to which the employee understands and applies good personnel management practices including affirmative action and upward mobility. Does the employee contribute effectively to the implementation of State Personnel Board and departmental equal employment opportunity policies and to the attainment of affirmative action goals? | | | | |

GENERAL COMMENTS OR COMMENTS ON OTHER FACTORS

*The supervisor may make "Comments" only, or may use rating categories only, or may use either or both methods of appraisal on any performance factor, as he or she prefers. The rating categories are:
     I - Improvement needed for performance to meet expected standards.
     M- Performance fully meets expected standards.
     E- Performance consistently exceeds expected standards.

**Figure 19.2    California Department of Finance Career Development Form** *(cont.)*.

**EMPLOYEE CHECK LIST**
**FOR**
**APPRAISAL AND DEVELOPMENT INTERVIEW**

On_____we will have an "A. & D." discussion.

During our appraisal and development discussion we will talk over your present job—what your duties and responsibilities are and how well you are fulfilling them—and also plan constructively for your future job development.

Attached is a copy of the form we will complete. You may use this form as a work sheet to prepare for our discussion.

This check list can help you plan for our meeting. The following questions will give you some idea of the things we might talk about during our discussion.

## PRESENT JOB

1. Are all of my duties and responsibilities clear?

2. Do I, and my supervisor, have a common understanding of what I am supposed to do, and how well I am supposed to do it?

3. Is there anything about my present job that I do not like? Can anything be done to change this?

4. How well am I doing my job? What, specifically, do I do best? What, specifically, do I not do so well?

5. If I were filling out my appraisal form, what comments would I make, and what check marks would I make? (Perhaps you should write these down.)

## FUTURE JOB DEVELOPMENT

1. What are my long-term job goals and objectives? My specific short-term goals?

2. What, specifically, could I do in my present job, or in my present civil service classification, that should help me obtain these goals?

3. What specific things can I do to take advantage of the strong points I listed under 4 above, and to build up the things which were not so strong?

4. What job assignments that might be available would help make me more useful to the Department?

5. What training do I need to do my present job better?

6. What outside study or education do I need to prepare myself for my next job?

**DAS-PM 011 (8/74)**

**Figure 19.3   Personal Development Check List.**

leave. Voluntarily changing jobs is, in some cases, preferable to continuing in a situation in which career opportunities are limited and personal needs unsatisfied. We are not advocating impulsive job-hopping, but rather periodic evaluations of whether the present job and organization are meeting your personal and career needs or have the potential for meeting those needs in the future.

## A MANAGERIAL PERSPECTIVE

Arthur Elliott Carlisle has written of an interview conducted with an oil refinery manager named McGregor.[13] McGregor is an extraordinarily successful manager who has an unusual management style. He insists that those employees who report directly to him solve their own operating problems. As chief executive of the refinery, McGregor refuses to make decisions his lower-level managers are hired to make. Once a week, McGregor holds a meeting with his immediate staff and asks them to review the decisions they've made and the number of employees they have helped. McGregor insists that employees get help from others with whom they work, not the general manager.

Each of his submanagers has learned McGregor's technique of refusing to solve problems he was not hired to solve. The submanagers insist that supervisors solve their own work problems. Supervisors transmit the same type of downward decision making to their employees. In McGregor's plant, every employee and manager is reponsible for identifying and finding solutions to work problems within their sphere of operations and expertise. It is more than participation. Active involvement, not only in routine assignments but also in decisions directly affecting productivity, quality, costs, schedules, facilities usage, and a variety of other factors, is a job requirement. Decisions are reviewed after they are implemented. Mistakes are discussed openly and seldom made more than once. Promotions are based, at least in part, on the quality of decisions.

McGregor recognized that a supply of qualified subordinates had to be developed for the future and that time was a scarce commodity. He designed and implemented a managerial system "that had as its hallmark self-development for his employees, and efficient operation for his employer, and time for himself to actively consider the impact of future developments on his unit." [14] McGregor had built a successful management system by insisting people take responsibility for their own jobs.

Although not every manager is a McGregor and many companies require different approaches than oil refineries, development of employees can have many benefits. McGregor's employees were the ones most avidly recruited for promotional positions by the company's other refineries. His plant is known as the most well run and efficient. McGregor also has more time to pursue his favorite recreational activity—playing golf.

Perhaps the most important lesson to be learned from the McGregor story is that the development of people means, in the final analysis, providing the methodology for encouraging and even insisting on self-development.

## SELF–ASSESSMENT DISCUSSION

1. (1) For enjoyment of a fuller life as well as personal and career development, lifelong learning is necessary.

2. (4, 5, 6) People who are highly successful usually believe that doing interesting and challenging work is more important than security. Taking risks for the opportunity to achieve is common among people who consider themselves and are considered by others as successful.

3. (5, 6) Most people enjoy leisure and getting away from their day-to-day work. Those who have interesting and challenging jobs usually tire of leisure quickly and look forward to returning to work.

4. (1, 4) For those entering a career field or changing fields, the opportunity to learn and achieve is more important than starting pay. Pay and opportunity will increase as experience is gained. For experienced professionals, achievement and starting pay may be decisive factors along with other considerations such as the organization, geographic location, management style, and similar job characteristics.

5. (6) Moving from one geographic location to another is often necessary to assure adequate career development. Opportunities are not always found in a single area.

6. (6) Personal initiative, competence, and commitment are the most important factors in achievement of personal development and career success.

7. (1, 6) For those who have not fully developed career paths, movement to another job, organization, or geographic location may be the best way to get a stalled career back on path. Others have found work they like, that pays adequately, and offers satisfying assignments even though promotional opportunities may be limited. In such cases, change is neither desirable nor necessary.

8. (6) The longer a person stays in a specific place of work, type of job, or location, the more difficult change becomes. Individuals become identified with their jobs. Potential employers tend to react unenthusiastically to people who seek change after many years with an organization in a single type of work.

9. (6) Effort, competence, good working relationships, and support of organizational goals are important job considerations. For those seeking advancement, an understanding of organizational politics is essential. Usually, those who are perceived as members of the "in" group are the ones promoted.

10. (1) Personality factors are far more likely to create job difficulties than outright incompetence. Most people learn to do their jobs, but clashes or difficulties in working with others are primary causes of job failure.

## *QUICK REVIEW*

I. Personal Success and Career Development

    A. Career choices may be linked to the way people think.

      B. Convergent thinkers tend to be precise, controlled, and well organized.

      C. Divergent thinkers tend to be people oriented, imaginative, creative, intuitive, and not well organized.

  II. Success and Personal Development

      A. Success as viewed by society and as viewed by individuals may be different.

      B. Career development usually means continually acquiring increased knowledge, skill, and competency.

  III. Organizational Career Development Plans

      A. Formal career development programs are the exception rather than the rule.

      B. Human resource planning seeks to determine the most effective use of individuals and the potential employment needs of the organization.

      C. Individual effort ultimately makes career development work.

  IV. Career Development and the Individual

      A. Self-actualized people are able to define and fill career needs.

      B. A successful career management program involves a realistic awareness of skills, abilities, weaknesses, needs, and a sense of self-worth.

      C. Personal career values must acknowledge the realities of organizational life. Competency, training, energy, and the desire to please do not necessarily guarantee career success.

      D. Levinson believes we go through a major change in our career development about every seven to ten years.

      E. Allness is the belief by a person that he or she "knows it all" and no longer needs to consider new ideas.

      F. The self-fulfilling prophecy states that "we are what we think we are."

      G. Many organizations have developed career identification and planning assistance to help employees advance and grow.

  V. Keys to Success

      A. Continual assessment of skills, knowledge, attitudes, and interpersonal relations is necessary to successful career development.

      B. A realistic view of organizational life and the willingness to change are necessary career development ingredients.

      C. All career development is ultimately self-development.

  VI. A Managerial Perspective

      A. In some companies, all employees and managers are responsible for identifying and solving their own work problems.

      B. Such programs demonstrate that developing people means providing the means for and insisting on self-development.

## KEY TERMS

| | | |
|---|---|---|
| Personal success | Human resource | Bleeding sharks |
| Convergent thinkers |   planning | Career change |
| Divergent thinkers | Self-actualized person | Allness |
| Career development | Personal values | Self-fulfilling prophecy |

## DISCUSSION QUESTIONS

1. Why are personal and career development ultimately considered self-development?
2. Explain the importance of learning to recognize major life changes.
3. Why is continuous education important to lifelong success?
4. H. Alan Raymond states that it is important to understand where you are in relationship to where you want to be. What does this mean?
5. How can an individual best prepare for changes that may occur in the future?

——————————————— **EXERCISE** ———————————————

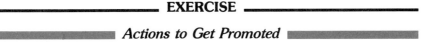

*Actions to Get Promoted*

You are an assistant department manager in a large retail clothing store. You have been in your current position for four years and have received excellent performance evaluations. You enjoy the clothing business and would like to stay with your present employer. You believe that unless you get a promotion soon, your career is dead-ended. Since the store manager has not even mentioned the possibility of promotion, you need to take actions on your own.

*Evaluate the following list of actions to increase your chance for promotion.* Which actions would you take? Which would you take first?

1. Request a transfer to another department to broaden your experience.

2. Take classes at the local college to increase your educational background.

3. Make a realistic evaluation of your strengths and weaknesses.

4. Get the employees who work for you to tell the store manager you should be promoted.

5. Directly inform the store manager that either you get promoted, or you are going to look for another job.

6. Make suggestions to the store manager on how to increase sales and reduce costs in your department.

7. Have customers write the store manager when they compliment you on the quality of service you provided.

8. Do personal favors for the store manager whenever you can.

9. Put in extra hours without pay and make sure that the store manager knows that you are working the extra hours.

10. Read retail marketing magazines and send summaries of the articles that apply to the clothing business to the store manager.

11. Tell the store manager you would be willing to change departments in order to get a promotion.

---

## TWO POINTS OF VIEW

### *"A Development Effort"*

*What would you do if you were the manager?*

You are the manager of the finance department for a city government. You realize that Ron Seely, a new accountant, needs a broad range of experience to develop into a productive member of the team. You decide to help Ron by making him your assistant and assigning him special projects to complete on his own that will broaden his experience. When Ron seemed reluctant to accept the assignment as your assistant, you thought it was just the young man's lack of self-confidence.

But as you gave more projects to Ron, he was able to accomplish less of his own work in budget analysis. When he expressed his concern to you about not being able to complete his work on budget analysis, you told him the other employees would be able to get it done. Ron's performance on the special assignment is outstanding, and you believe he is making rapid progress in developing the necessary breadth of abilities. You want Ron to develop into a first-rate professional employee and know that he has a lot to learn.

With the reduction in city revenues and cuts in federal funding, your department is under pressure to make city services more cost effective. You have encouraged your employees to develop methods for cutting costs, and you have increased everyone's work load. Even with the increased work loads, the city manager has informed you that you will have to lay off one professional employee. To gain input to help decide which employee will be laid off, you ask each professional employee to evaluate the others in terms of the most and least valuable individuals. After collecting their evaluations, you found that each employee had named Ron Seely as the least valuable professional employee. It was evident that from the other employees' point of view, your development effort had not been effective.

*What would you do if you were Ron Seely?*

You are the newest accountant in the finance department of a city government. Your job as a budget analyst is your first professional job since graduating from college with a degree in accounting. You know you have a lot to learn about the accounting systems used by the city government. Soon after you began the job, the manager of the finance department asked you to work as his assistant and do special projects that he would assign you. Knowing how much you had to learn about city budget analysis, you tried to discourage him from assigning you as his assistant. You thought there was no way you could learn budget analysis if you had to do special projects. The department manager insisted that you become his assistant, so you have devoted all your efforts to the special projects he assigns. Most of these projects have nothing to do with your job of budget analysis, and they are time-consuming.

You believe you must make a maximum effort on the special projects. Since you are assigned a new special project as soon as you get one completed, you are not able to do your job of budget analysis. The other employees must do the work you should be doing. They are not at all happy with the extra work load and have told you they don't appreciate your "special position" as assistant to the manager.

As a result of reductions in city revenues, the city manager has instructed the finance department to lay off one professional employee. The department manager obtained input from all the professional employees as to whom they thought was the least valuable. As you expected, you were the employee named least valuable by all the other professional employees. If the department manager makes the layoff decision based on the employee input, you will be the one to go. Since you have been doing the special projects assigned by the manager, you don't think it would be fair for you to be laid off. You know the other employees did not like having to do your work, but that was not your doing.

## ENDNOTES

1. Liam Hudson, *Contrary Imaginations* (Middlesex, England: Penguin Books, 1966).
2. David A. Kolb, et al., *Organizational Psychology: An Experiential Approach*, 3d ed. (Englewood Cliffs, N.J.: Prentice-Hall, 1981).
3. Heywood Klien, *Wall Street Journal*, 18 May 1981.
4. Personal interview with Harry A. Todd, Sr., July 1981.
5. Randall S. Schuler, *Personnel and Human Resource Management*, 3d ed. (St. Paul: West, 1986).
6. Interview with A. J. Camp, 1978.
7. Abraham Maslow, *Motivation and Personality*, 2d ed. (New York: Harper & Row, 1970).
8. Schuler, *Personnel*.
9. H. Alan Raymond, *Management in the Third Wave* (Glenview, Ill.: Scott, Foresman, 1986).
10. Daniel K. Levinson et al., *The Seasons of a Man's Life* (New York: Knopf, 1978).
11. William V. Haney, *Communication and Interpersonal Relations: Text and Cases*, 4th ed. (Homewood, Ill.: Irwin, 1979).
12. Extracted from "20/20," ABC Television Productions, New York, 14 May 1982.
13. Arthur Elliott Carlisle, *Organizational Dynamics* 5 (Summer 1976): 50–62. Full text quoted in William F. Glueck, Lawrence R. Jauch, and Sally A. Coltrin, *The Managerial Experience* (Hinsdale, Ill.: Dryden Press, 1980).
14. Ibid.

## CASE INCIDENTS FOR PART 6

### The Suggestion for Change

Lou Blake is the supervisor of a production line manufacturing camp trailers. Part of the manufacturing process includes the installation of a water supply system that is currently constructed of copper tubing. After a great deal of investigation and testing, Nancy Park determined that the copper tubing could be replaced by a new type of plastic tubing that would cost less than one-third as much as copper tubing and would be much easier to install. Nancy's tests indicated that the plastic tubing would hold up better than the copper with much less chance of the connections leaking. Nancy suggested this change to Lou, who then sold the idea to top management. Lou never told them that it was Nancy's suggestion. Lou received all the credit for the improved product and, as a result, received a cash bonus for the suggestion and a salary increase.

1. What effect will Lou Blake's action have on the willingness of other employees to make suggestions that will improve the product or cut costs?
2. What action should Nancy Park take to receive credit for her suggestion?
3. How should Lou Blake have handled the suggestion from Nancy Park?

### What's Fair Is Fair

John Crago stated briefly but firmly, "We will give a flat seventy cents per hour shift differential. Every person who works on the second shift will receive an added seventy cents per hour plus a paid lunch period." Marie Higgins retorted, "We want a 10 percent hourly increase, not a flat seventy cents per hour." "Since our base rate is seven dollars on the average," argued John, "seventy cents per hour *is* 10 percent." "Not for everyone," countered Marie.

1. Why did Marie want a flat percentage instead of a seventy cents per hour increase?
2. Is 10 percent for shift differential too much or too little? Support your point.
3. How would this shift differential affect morale?

### A Private War at the Public Works

At forty years of age, Chris Minanaro was an aggressive, intelligent, and unusually attractive executive. She was the only woman to hold the position of public works director for the city of Three Rivers. All of the Public Works Agency's major service department managers were men. Two of the managers, Les Watkins and Walt Hinkle, were openly resentful of Chris's promotion to director. Each had applied for the director position at the time Chris was promoted. Both had stated their suspicions that Chris's relationship with the city manager was more than a working one.

"Besides being the city manager's playmate, the fact that she's Filipino and female tells me she knows all of the city supervisors on a more than personal basis," stated Les Watkins in a meeting with other managers.

"That's right," echoed Walt Hinkle. "Sex will get you where brains won't."

Two days later, Chris asked Les and Walt into her office for a private meeting. "I understand you two think I was promoted because of my sex, not what I know," she began. "For fifteen years, I've worked my way up in the city because I wanted to succeed. I've earned everything I've got. How would you feel if I asked you two, 'How'd you like a promotion? Come up to my place tonight and do what I tell you and you'll get one.' How would you like that?" As Chris talked, she became coldly angry. "If I hear one more rumor or innuendo about me that is started by either of you, you're going to be out on the street. You may even have to answer to me in court. I hope that's clear."

The next morning, Chris was notified by Alan Braden, personnel director for Three Rivers, that a formal charge of sexual harassment had been filed against her by Watkins and Hinkle. "Chris, I know you didn't, but both swear that you stated, 'How'd you like a promotion? Come up to my place tonight and do what I tell you and you'll get one," Alan reported.

Chris thought back over her conversation with Watkins and Hinkle. "Alan," she replied, "the whole thing is taken out of context. What do I do now?"

"I'm afraid it's going to be rough," Alan responded slowly. "They've already released their side of the story to two reporters with the *Three Rivers News*."

1. What possible errors did Chris make?

2. What ethical and social responsibility factors are involved in the case?

3. Does Chris have a defense for herself? What can she do?

―――――――――― **When Are Trade Secrets Fair Game?** ――――――――――

Quicktype memory typewriters were successfully being marketed to schools, government offices, and some private businesses. As a comparatively small typewriter producer, it was constantly struggling to gain a larger share of the vast electronic typewriter market.

Shortly after Brad Ferris was hired as design engineer, he met with Beverly Langely, Quicktype's manager of research and development. "Just before I left Telecom Electronics," Brad began, "I was working on an interface between electronic typewriters and small computers. It's a simplified system that would make it possible to attach a Quicktype machine to any standard micro- or minicomputer so the typewriter could be used as either a printer or an input terminal. What do you think?''

"How far along is the design?'' asked Beverly.

"Far enough to start prototype production,'' replied Brad enthusiastically. "It could give us a jump on the whole field of interface devices.''

"You're right, and it sounds great,'' said Beverly, "but there may be some serious problems—at least ethically.''

1. What are Beverly's ethical concerns?

2. Should Quicktype produce Brad's interface?

3. Identify a similar ethical dilemma. How can it be resolved?

# Appendix

# Organizational Evaluation Questionnaire

I. *Working Conditions*

  A. *Physical Conditions*

    Do the employees have adequate space to do their jobs?

    Do the employees have adequate tools and equipment to do their jobs?

    Are adequate safety precautions taken to protect the employees on their jobs?

    Are the environmental factors (light, air, and so on) comfortable for employees?

    Are there adequate provisions for non-job-related facilities (parking lots, rest rooms, and so on)?

  B. *Orientation*

    Do the employees have adequate information to effectively perform their jobs?

    Do the employees fully understand work rules?

    Are the employees kept informed of changes in the organization?

  C. *Job Security*

    Are the employees assured of a job as long as they perform effectively?

    If layoffs occur, are they done fairly and consistently?

    Do the employees understand the procedures for layoffs?

  D. *Pressure to Produce*

    Is there unreasonable pressure for better performance?

Do the employees have to find meaningless work to do in order to look busy to their superiors?

II. *Work Groups*

A. *Cooperation*

Do the employees work together as a team?

Do the employees help each other in their jobs?

Do the people in the organization get along well together?

B. *Training*

Do the employees need more training to do their jobs well?

C. *Job Performance*

Do the employees encourage each other to improve their job performance in output of *quantity?*

Do the employees encourage each other to improve the *quality* of their job performance?

III. *Social Groups*

What are the social groups within the organization?

What functions do the social groups perform for the employees?

What functions do the social groups perform for the organization?

IV. *Status*

What are the status symbols within the organization?

What are the functional status indicators?

What are the dysfunctional status indicators?

V. *Economic Rewards*

A. *Pay*

Are the employees paid fairly compared with similar organizations?

Are the employees paid fairly compared with others in the organization?

Do the methods of pay accomplish their goals?

What is the basis for pay increases?

Do the employees accept pay increases as fair and adequate?

B. *Benefits*

Does the organization assist employees in preparing for their retirement?

Does the organization assist employees in their insurance programs?

Does the organization have a good sick-leave program?

Does the organization assist employees in the cost of educational activities?

VI. *Management Policies and Administration*

   A. *Communication of Information*

      Do all individuals in the organization understand the organization's objectives and policies?

      Are there areas where policies do not exist or are not understood?

      Are the employees given information concerning the organization's financial situation?

      Are the employees always informed of important changes before they occur?

   B. *Fairness of Policies and Administration*

      Are policies and rules applied equally to all employees?

      Are there employees who receive unjust discipline?

      Does the organization have unnecessary rules?

   C. *Advancements and Promotions*

      Are advancements and promotions based on merit?

      Are the employees who receive advancements and promotions the most deserving in the organization?

      Are qualified employees allowed to transfer to better jobs within the organization?

      What are an employee's chances for advancement in the organization?

      Are the employees confident that they will receive advancements and promotions when they are capable of handling the job?

VII. *Satisfaction with the Nature of Work*

   A. *Freedom*

      Are the employees free to use their own ideas while performing their jobs?

      Are the employees allowed to set their own pace on the job?

   B. *Growth*

      Are the employees able to learn new skills on their present job?

      Are the employees able to further their educations while with the organization?

   C. *Responsibility*

      Are the employees responsible for decisions related to their jobs?

      Are the employees responsible for planning and organizing their jobs?

   D. *Achievement*

      Are the employees able to use their abilities on their jobs?

      Do the employees gain personal satisfaction from doing their jobs?

E. *Influence*

Are the employees able to influence the manner in which their jobs are performed?

Are the employees' recommendations used in decisions concerning their jobs?

F. *Interest*

Do the employees find their work interesting?

Does time pass slowly for employees?

VIII. *Supervision*

A. *Communication*

Do the supervisors let employees know where they stand?

Do the supervisors like to obtain employees' ideas for improving their jobs?

Are the supervisors easy for employees to talk with?

Are the employees free to make constructive criticisms of their supervisors?

Do the supervisors give clear and understandable instructions?

Do the supervisors give employees all the information they need to do their jobs well?

B. *Trust*

Do the supervisors live up to the promises they make to employees?

Do the supervisors give honest answers to employees' questions?

Are the supervisors fair in their dealings with employees?

C. *Job Competence*

Are the supervisors effective organizers?

Are the supervisors able to evaluate the employees' work?

Are the supervisors effective planners?

Are the supervisors well trained in human relations?

Do the supervisors possess the technical qualifications to do their jobs well?

D. *Consideration*

Are the supervisors considerate of the employees' needs and interests?

Do the supervisors genuinely look out for the interests of the people in their areas?

E. *Delegation of Responsibility*

Do the supervisors allow employees to make decisions on their jobs?

Do the supervisors like employees to make decisions without checking with them first?

Do the supervisors expect outstanding job performance from employees?

F. *Recognition*

Do the supervisors attempt to gain recognition for employees who deserve it?

Do supervisors reward those who perform their jobs well?

G. *Supervisor-Employee Relationship*

Do the supervisors bring out the best in the people in their areas?

Would the employees prefer to have different supervisors?

# Glossary

**achievement motivation:** The need to get things accomplished. Usually the need to be part of an organization that excels or the need to gain personal goals.

**achievement-oriented leadership:** Leadership that is goal directed rather than based on personal power or survival needs.

**adaptation:** The tendency to, over a period of time, become accustomed to repeated events, sensations, styles, or rules. For example, a person may become adapted to background noise at work and learn to ignore it.

**adaptation level:** The degree to which a person is able to adjust to his or her environment. Some situations allow rapid adaptation, while others are more difficult.

**affiliation motive:** The need to associate with others, to receive approval, acceptance, friendship, or love.

**aggression:** Usually attack behavior; expressions of hostility, or in some cases, intense determination to achieve a particular goal.

**agreement:** In labor-management relations, a contract governing wages, hours, and conditions of work legally binding on all parties. Labor contracts govern all personnel matters between union employees and management.

**allness:** The belief by a person that he or she knows all about a subject, thing, job, event, or person. Unwillingness to accept new or different information or concepts.

**approach-approach conflict:** Internal conflict or stress that occurs when a person is required to choose between alternatives that are equally desirable.

**approach-avoidance conflict:** Internal conflict or stress that occurs when a person has a strong desire to act, change, or choose but is fearful of the consequences, or the consequences are uncertain.

**arbitration:** In labor-management relations, a procedure using a neutral third party to resolve grievances that management and labor are unable to solve. Costs of arbitration are usually split evenly between management and the union.

**artifacts:** Adornment worn or displayed that tells something about a person, such as jewelry, clothing, or office decor.

**association theory:** Sometimes known as behaviorism. The belief that specific behavior is associated with specific types of events or stimuli.

**authority:** The right to act, decide, choose, give orders, or institute change. Most authority comes from organizational position and is delegated downward. However, the consent of the governed is authority derived from the people and granted to leaders.

**avoidance-avoidance conflict:** Internal conflict or stress that occurs when a person is experiencing or faced with undesirable conditions and any alternative seems equally undesirable. "Out of the frying pan, into the fire."

**behavior:** Any act by a person either overt (visible) or covert (hidden). All behavior is a response to some internal or external stimulus.

**behavior modification:** A technique for shaping or directing behavior by rewarding correct behavior and ignoring or, in some cases, punishing incorrect behavior.

**behavioral theory:** See *association theory*.

**bilateral relations:** Personnel rule making by both managers and employees, usually associated with labor agreements between union and managers.

**bleeding sharks:** People in trouble at work who are attacked rather than helped by others.

**bureaucracy:** A system or organization with highly structured divisions of labor, specialization of work, rules, regulations, reporting systems, and controls.

**career change:** Change in type of work, organization, level of management, or geographical location as a result of new technology, promotion, change in interests, reduction in force, termination, development of new competencies, or change in lifestyle.

**career development:** All of the actions necessary to enhance career goals, such as training, specialized experience, gaining expertise and skills, and learning to be self-directed.

**career management:** A systematic, planned approach to career development.

**change:** Any alteration of events, people, circumstances, or situations. Differences that are a function of time.

**change diffusion:** The ripple effect of change. Every change has a tendency to cause or direct other changes. This process is known as diffusion.

**change direction:** Change may be either upward (as in prices), downward (as in loss of sales), or in several directions at once (computers cost less but do more).

**change rate:** The speed at which change occurs; technical change generally occurs rapidly, while social change generally occurs slowly.

**change recognition:** A developed ability to foresee significant change and plan to use it to best advantage. Change recognition allows planning for the future with a higher degree of certainty.

**change resistance:** The tendency to reject change that is externally imposed or over which a person has no influence. Resistance to doing or thinking differently.

**chronemics:** Use of timing as a nonverbal communication. Being late or early to meetings is an example.

**civil rights:** Right of every person regardless of race, color, religion, national origin, or sex to fundamental opportunities, liberties, and responsibilities guaranteed by the constitution.

**climate:** See *organizational climate.*

**closure:** The tendency to perceive things in whole and continuous patterns. First noted by Gestalt psychologists.

**coercive power:** Power that comes from threat, ability to punish, disapprove, withhold promotion or pay, or to demote, terminate, or assign punitive tasks.

**cognitive theories:** Personality and learning theories that state people choose their reactions to both internal and external stimuli based on interpretations of the stimuli and the expected consequences of their responses.

**communication:** The act of understanding and being understood. Sending, receiving, decoding, and interpreting messages.

**communication channels:** Any of the verbal and nonverbal sources of communication.

**communication links:** The number of people or steps between the originator of a message and its receiver. Each link weakens the probability of message accuracy.

**conformity:** Following rules precisely. Obeying group norms or slavishly copying the actions, dress, or speech of others.

**constructive discipline:** Disciplinary action designed to train or correct rather than punish.

**convergent thinking:** Thinking and actions that are precise, well ordered, dependent on rules and regulations, with close adherence to detail. Low tolerance of ambiguity.

**coordination:** Actions taken to inform and assist to ensure that people are working in an organized, planned, smoothly flowing work pattern.

**creativity:**   Generation of new ways of acting, new explanations, unique methods of solving problems, or any activity that utilizes a previously unknown or unused approach to a human activity.

**credibility:**   The degree of confidence, trust, honesty, truthfulness, knowledge, and/or skill assigned to an individual or group.

**decoding:**   Interpretation of either verbal or nonverbal messages.

**defense mechanisms:**   Any behavior adopted to protect a person's symbolic self, self-image, or ego.

**delegation:**   Assigning tasks and the authority to complete those tasks.

**destructive competition:**   Competition based on the concept of winning at all costs regardless of consequences to others.

**direct communication:**   Face-to-face communication or voice-to-voice communication. Any communication directly between two people.

**directive leadership:**   Leadership style based on giving orders, directing activities of others, or setting goals for others to achieve.

**divergent thinking:**   Thinking and learning that is more dependent on feelings, intuition, and creativity than that of convergent thinking. Less dependent on rules, precision, detail; comfortable with ambiguity.

**due process:**   The right to a fair hearing, to present both sides of a story, to face an accuser, to be treated without one-sided, arbitrary action.

**effectiveness:**   Getting things accomplished correctly, on time, within costs.

**efficiency:**   Getting things accomplished correctly in minimum time, minimum costs, with optimum utilization of resources.

**emotion:**   Psycho-physical reaction to situation or other people. Feelings that result in physical changes such as increased heartbeat, sweating, eye dilation, tenseness, and so on, and/or feelings such as joy, fear, disgust, desire, and so on.

**empathy:**   Understanding another person from that person's point of view. Understanding feelings and ideas from another's frame of reference.

**encoding:**   Converting ideas, perceptions, and feelings into symbols, such as words on pictures, that may be used in message transmission.

**environmental protection:**   Any action taken to preserve or improve air, water, land usage, or other natural aspects of the world.

**equal opportunity:**   Nondiscrimination in job opportunity because of race, color, religion, natural origin, sex, or in some cases, age and physical handicap.

**esteem needs:**   Needs for approval, recognition, status, feelings of self-worth, ego satisfaction.

**ethical dilemmas:**   Conflicts between ethical values, each of which may seem positive or acceptable. Usually based on a conflict of needs. (If bribery of an official in a foreign country is accepted in that country in order to obtain business, should an organization engage in bribery?)

**ethics:** Personal values of correct and incorrect behavior, honesty. Societal values of honesty, truthfulness, fairness, and equity.

**expectancy theory:** The theory that behavior is directed by the value of a potential outcome and the anticipated consequence of the action.

**expectation:** Anticipation of the outcome or consequences of an event or set of circumstances.

**expert power:** Power that is derived from special knowledge, skills, ability to solve problems or provide needed information.

**extinction:** Disappearance of behavior because of the lack of reinforcement.

**feedback:** Literally, the response to a signal or communication. In organizations, the reaction to a decision or communication. In communication, the reaction and response from one communicator to another.

**Fiedler's contingency approach:** Fiedler's theory that as conditions change, so should management styles. The style of management is contingent on conditions present. In times of high stress, authoritarian styles may be appropriate. As conditions improve, a move toward participative styles is necessary. In very good conditions, additional "tight ship" methods may be needed.

**flexibility:** The condition or ability to change as conditions and environments change.

**formal:** For official use. Usually refers to policies, procedures, signed memoranda.

**formal status:** Status because of job title, level of responsibility, or degree of authority.

**frame of reference:** Personal perception or viewpoint based on one's experience, cultural values, attitudes, beliefs and values.

**frustration:** Reaction to a blocked need, unresolved conflict, unsolved problem, or incomplete or unstarted effort.

**goal:** A desired outcome of a planned series of actions.

**goal-directed behavior:** Actions centered on specific goals.

**goal orientation:** Behavior that is consistently directed toward well-defined goals.

**goal-setting systems:** Formal written procedures for defining and implementing goal-directed behavior.

**great person theory:** The theory that leaders are born, not made.

**grievance:** A written formal complaint from an employee to a supervisor.

**grievance procedure:** A systematic series of steps for resolving grievances.

**group:** More than two people gathered together with coordinated efforts to achieve common goals.

**group dynamics:** The ever-changing relationships among group members. Interaction among group members.

**group pressure:**   Unwritten, informal pressures by group members to force individual members to conform to group norms.

**hot-stove rule:**   A system that calls for immediate corrective action, or in some cases punishment, when a rule infraction occurs.

**human potential:**   The belief that all people can achieve more, do more, and develop their full capabilities.

**inference:**   Jumping to conclusions. Development of a belief about an event, person, or circumstance without full knowledge of factual data.

**innovation:**   Utilization of existing resources in new and different ways. Developing unique solutions or approaches to problems. See *creativity*.

**institutional power motivation:**   The use of personal power to achieve goals of the organization or institution rather than the use of power for personal self-serving reasons.

**interaction theory:**   Recognition that no event occurs by itself. People constantly give and receive from their environment, other people, and activities.

**internal change:**   Change that occurs within an organization. May involve people, technology, organizational format, climate, product or service orientation, and types of work.

**jargon:**   Language associated with a particular job or type of work that has little or no meaning to those not associated with the work. The word *scupper*, for example, has little meaning to people outside the building trades.

**job enrichment:**   A technique popularized by Frederick Herzberg for improving performance by providing greater employee control and responsibility for all aspects of assigned tasks.

**job overload:**   Increasing the number of tasks, amount of work, or level of responsibility beyond an employee's ability to perform.

**kinesics:**   Body language including posture, body movements, facial expressions, pointing behavior, eye blinks, and any other physical movements.

**language and meanings:**   Meanings are in people, not in words or language. Language is a symbolic encoding and expression of concepts, feelings, information, sensations, and perceptual interpretation. It is not reality.

**leader-member relations:**   In Fiedler's leadership theory, leaders must have effective relations with group members to be successful. Power position and task orientation are also leadership factors, according to Fiedler.

**leadership:**   The act of obtaining voluntary compliance from others. Influencing others because they want to be influenced or because they believe and support the leader's perceived power.

**legitimate power:**   Power derived from a job title, position in organization, status symbols, or in some societies, age.

**levels of abstraction:**   In communication theory, generalizations based on incomplete information. The first level is based on contract or observation.

Each subsequent verbal or pictorial representation of the event is an additional abstraction level.

**line organization:**   Organizational components and its members directly involved in producing the end product or service of the organization.

**management by objectives:**   A management system based on achievement of well-defined, attainable, time-limited, quantitative goals and objectives at every level and by every person in an organization.

**managerial grid:**   A system developed by Robert Blake and Jane Mouton for measuring management style based on both concern for people and concern for task accomplishment.

**message isolation:**   In situations in which multiple messages are being given, the necessity for selecting only those with significant meaning.

**morals:**   Basic values of right and wrong, good and bad. Usually cultural or religious in origin, as opposed to ethics, which are societal in origin.

**motivation:**   Internal causes of behavior. Drives, needs, and desires that precede and cause activities.

**multiple channels:**   In communication theory, the concept that understanding is enhanced by communicating through as many sensory modes as possible, including speech, touch, vision, and odor.

**natural work units:**   Tasks that are related to each other by skill, knowledge, or required expertise.

**need satisfaction:**   The theory that all behavior is designed to satisfy a need or a set of needs.

**needs hierarchy:**   Maslow's theory that lower-order needs must be at least partially satisfied before higher-level needs become operational. Physiological and safety needs, for example, must usually be satisfied before social and psychological needs are important to an individual.

**negotiation:**   The process of give and take between management and unions (or any other parties) in reaching agreement based on compromise.

**nonverbal communication:**   Communication based on media other than spoken words or written material. Includes paralanguage, proxemics, kinesics, pictorial representation, chronemics, and so on.

**norms:**   Expected (normal) behavior of a group.

**nothing jobs:**   Jobs that have little interest or value to workers other than the pay received for their performance.

**objectives:**   Those goals an individual or group decides must be accomplished. Good objectives are specific, measurable, assigned to individuals or groups and are time limited (scheduled).

**organizational centrism:**   A belief that a particular unit of an organization is more important to the success of the entire organization than are other units.

**organizational climate:**  The feeling, tone, spirit, or degree of voluntary cooperation found in organizations.

**organizational structure:**  Division of work as well as levels of responsibility and authority in work organizations.

**paralanguage:**  Use of voice tone, inflection, timber, amplitude, and emphasis to give meaning to spoken phrases.

**participation:**  Involvement by all members of organizations in key decision process. Sharing of power between managers and employees.

**path-goal theory:**  The theory that leaders must clarify goals and show followers how goals must be reached.

**perception:**  Interpretation of sensory awareness. The act of interpreting what is seen, heard, smelled, tasted, felt, or sensed in other ways such as anticipation based on past events.

**perceptual processes:**  The awareness and interpretation of both external and internal stimuli. Involves awareness, organization, and interpretation of data in whole and continuous patterns.

**performance evaluation:**  The assessment of a person's performance in achieving job objectives.

**performance feedback:**  Providing performance evaluation both formal and informal.

**permissive leadership:**  Leadership that allows both individual and group contributions and decisions independent of leader's desires. A form of nonleadership.

**personal development:**  Individual improvement of skills, knowledge, expertise, and long-range perspectives.

**physiological needs:**  Needs for biological survival such as food, air, water, warmth, sleep, elimination, and so on.

**placebo effect:**  Change based solely on belief, incorrect information, attitudes, or values rather than on fact.

**politics:**  Behavior deliberately aimed at gaining or increasing power, agreement, or support.

**positive reinforcement:**  Feedback and rewards for correct or desired behavior.

**power:**  The degree of influence an individual has over another individual or group.

**power motivation:**  Motivation based on the need to control, direct, shape, and alter. May be negative or positive.

**prejudice:**  Bias toward another, usually based on race, color, religion, national origin, sex, or physical disability. An attitude rather than a fact.

**primitive power:**  Self-serving, negative use of power.

**proxemics:**  Use of space, distance, and arrangement to communicate deep-seated personality factors.

**psychological contract:**   Mutual expectations of employees and managers that are unspoken but real. Managers expect productivity, quality, attendance, pride, honesty, and so on. Employees expect fair treatment, proper assignments, help when needed, participation, and so on. As long as expectations are met, the contract is in force.

**psychological distance:**   Recognition of role differences between managers and nonmanagers creates both status and power differences. The distance is necessary, but can, if too wide, lead to distrust and suspicion.

**psychological needs:**   Needs for recognition, esteem, worthwhileness, status, and responsibility—ego satisfaction needs.

**psychological noise:**   Distortion of communication caused by emotion, inferences, values, beliefs, perception of situation, or previous experiences.

**quality of work life:**   An organizational philosophy that concentrates on development of a work climate that views both managers and employees as responsible for success or failure of the enterprise. It holds that strong supportive relationships between employees and managers are necessary for optimization of goal achievement.

*quid pro quo:*   Something for something. You scratch my back, I'll scratch yours. Do me a favor; I'll do one for you.

**referent power:**   Power that comes when people refer to a person, use that person as a model, or adopt his/her beliefs, philosophy, or attitudes.

**reinforcement:**   Reward or punishment immediately following an action or behavior that tends to shape future behavior. Rewarded behavior is usually repeated; punished behavior is usually avoided.

**responsibility:**   The obligation to perform, act, carry out job assignments, meet work expectations, act on perceived needs, or take a position on a set of principles.

**reward power:**   Power derived from giving both tangible rewards such as money and promotion or intangible rewards such as approval and recognition.

**role:**   Behavior that is shaped by the situation, expectations of others, learned experiences, and observations of others.

**role ambiguity:**   Uncertainty of appropriate behavior in a situation or psychological-social setting.

**role conflict:**   When requirements are added to a role that were not anticipated or desired. A work group leader may understand both employee and management points of view and why they differ. Conflict occurs when the leader must take either management's view or that of the employee's.

**role expectation:**   The expectation of behavior of others or self in a particular psychological-social setting.

**safety needs:**   Needs for protection, security, certainty, absence of risk.

**selective awareness:**   In perception theory, the observation that we are aware of only some things in our environment and totally unaware of others.

**selective exposure:**   In perception theory, the observation that we are exposed to only a relatively few of the factors present in our environment.

**self-actualization:**   Self-fulfillment. Defining and doing those things that are personally satisfying. Maslow's highest need.

**self-fulfilling prophecy:**   Reality that is shaped by beliefs. Making things come out the way we believe they'll come out.

**seniority:**   Length of service in a job, department, or organization.

**sensory stimulation:**   Stimulation through the senses and emotions.

**sexual harassment:**   Any act, proposal, or suggestion of compliance in sexual conduct as a condition of work or promotion. Any sexual proposal or suggestion that interferes with the performance of work.

**situation ethics:**   Appropriate behavior in terms of fairness, honesty, and correctness determined by situation.

**situational leadership:**   Leadership style and skills determined by situation rather than by personal characteristics.

**social change:**   Changes in attitudes, values, beliefs, and lifestyles by a majority of a given population.

**sociobiology:**   The belief that there are genetic predispositions to much of human behavior. Behavior is both limited and enhanced by genetic factors.

**staff:**   That part of an organization whose members are engaged in support, advisory, planning, legal, or other functions not directly associated with the end product or service of the organization. In some cases, the word *staff* is used to denote employees of the organization or a special group of employees.

**status:**   The perceived rank of a person when compared with others. Perceived social worth of an individual in a particular society, group, or organization.

**status awareness:**   Sensitivity to status differences in organizations, social group, and society in general.

**status compression:**   The tendency for status differences to become less far apart over a period of time or as social values change.

**status perception:**   Assigning status based on the way a person is seen rather than knowledge of position, power, wealth, or other status characteristics.

**status symbols:**   Symbols associated with position, power, wealth, educational level, socioeconomic condition, or other status designators. Symbols include dress, office size and furniture, location, type of automobile, and so on.

**stereotyping:**   Assigning behavioral characteristics to people because of race, national origin, heritage, job title, organizations, geographic origins, and so on.

**steward:**   An elected union employee representative who represents both the employee and the union in grievance resolution or other conflicts with management. Stewards are usually employees who function as representatives on an as-needed basis.

**stress:**   A tension reaction to threat, fear of failure, attainment of goals, compressed schedules, poor interpersonal relations, or any of a variety of other anxiety- or emotion-inducing job factors.

**stress carriers:**   People who are crisis oriented and induce stress in themselves and others as a usual behavior pattern. Can also apply to situations typically stress inducing.

**stress management:**   The act of controlling and directing stress as an energizing rather than as a destructive force. Also, the act of creating working environments without undue or destructive stress.

**supportive climate:**   A work climate that emphasizes voluntary cooperative, mutual assistance, analysis rather than criticism, and providing help and information when needed.

**survey feedback:**   An organizational development technique that utilizes survey data that is summarized and given to the survey respondents, who in turn interpret the data and suggest actions.

**symbolic value:**   Worth and desirability based on symbols rather than reality. Desk size, office location, job title, office equipment, type of automobile, and so on, all have greater symbolic value than real value.

**symbols and reality:**   The concept that symbols are not reality. Words (symbols) are not the things they describe. Maps (symbols) are not the territories they depict. Pictures (symbols) are not the objects drawn or photographed.

**task structure:**   Activities directed toward accomplishing a task, set of tasks, or series of objectives. According to Fiedler and others, a necessary component of effective managerial leadership.

**technological change:**   Change in organization, jobs, and society because of introduction of new technologies. Introduction of automobiles, telephones, and computers are examples of technological changes affecting society at large.

**Theory X:**   Douglas McGregor's label for traditional management assumptions that people do not like work, shun responsibility, are not normally creative, and must be controlled.

**Theory Y:**   Douglas McGregor's label for management assumptions that work is as natural to people as play and that under the right conditions, people enjoy work, seek responsibility, are normally creative, and are self-controlled.

**Theory Z:**   William Ouchi's label for management and employee assumptions that organizational success is dependent on managers and employees working in partnership, each sharing responsibility for the organization's achievements or failures.

**traits and abilities:**   Early studies of leadership attempted to identify specific characteristics (traits) and skills (abilities) common to all leaders. Such studies have yielded little useful results.

**union:**   An organized group of employees who collectively bargain with management to reach bilateral agreements on issues of wages, hours, and conditions of work.

**valence:**   In expectancy theory, the attractiveness or desirability of a particular goal or incentive. The strength of a behavior is directly related to the valence of the goal or incentive.

**value:**   Anything that has personal worth or meaning. Values are based largely on religious, moral, and societal precepts learned at an early age and modified throughout a person's life.

**value ranking:**   Deciding which values are most important in a person's life. If telling a lie will prevent another person from being hurt, is it more important to be truthful or to prevent hurt? The response depends on a person's value ranking.

**withdrawal:**   A psychological retreat from conflicting, boring, or threatening situations. Fantasy (daydreaming), falling asleep, physically leaving, and suicide are all withdrawal behaviors.

**work redesign:**   A technique of rearranging, changing, adding to, or deleting specific tasks to make a job more challenging, more interesting, and affected employees more productive.

# Name Index

# Subject Index